Understanding Mark's Gospel

"Keown brings alive both Mark's Gospel and its first-century world in *Understanding Mark's Gospel*. His easy-to-read, engaging style draws the reader into each passage of Mark's narrative, producing a well-rounded, thorough introduction to Mark's Gospel. Throughout, Keown explains how the events in Mark should shape the lives of Christians today, creating an informative, thought-provoking, and practical book."

—**Julia van den Brink**, Laidlaw College

"Keown has put together a detailed yet wonderfully approachable study on the Gospel of Mark, offering his readers insight and inspiration in equal measure. Assessable and challenging, this is a fantastic companion for the working preacher, pastor, and congregation member alike. I can't recommend it highly enough."

—**Andrew Gardener**, The Vine Church, Hong Kong

"I often suggest to students who want to study the New Testament in more depth that they start with Mark's Gospel. Keown's new book *Understanding Mark's Gospel* is a great way to be guided to that greater depth of understanding and that richer level of insight. This easy-to-read book will open up Mark's Gospel in fresh and exciting ways, both for new readers of Mark's Gospel and for those who have read the gospel many times. *Understanding Mark's Gospel* will also assist its readers in reaching the goal that Mark the evangelist had in mind when he wrote his gospel—that we as readers might encounter Jesus and grow in faith in him."

—**Paul Trebilco**, University of Otago, New Zealand

"This is an excellent guide to the Second Gospel. Keown writes in simple and accessible English—but covers all the key issues and is engaged with the latest scholarship, so that he offers an impressive breadth of learning. The great strength of his approach is setting out clearly all the options for contentious issues and giving supporting reasons for each before offering his own view. This will be a useful guide to all students of this dynamic gospel."

—**Ian Paul**, Fuller Theological Seminary

"Dr. Mark Keown was my thesis supervisor at Laidlaw College, New Zealand, and I am delighted to endorse *Understanding Mark's Gospel*, the first publication of our Tyrannus Textbook series."

—**Paul Cheng**, Tyrannus Online Seminary

"Those who have known of Mark Keown for a while and read some of his earlier books will be eagerly anticipating this one. While it is written in the same easily readable style, it should not be mistaken for a superficial book. It is the fruit of many years of working with Mark's Gospel both in the classroom and in the pulpit. Readers will not only find valuable insights into this, the first gospel to be written, but also food for their souls and challenges for their way of life."

—**Philip Church**, Laidlaw College

Understanding Mark's Gospel

―――― Tyrannus Textbook Series ――――

Mark J. Keown

WIPF & STOCK · Eugene, Oregon

UNDERSTANDING MARK'S GOSPEL
Tyrannus Textbook Series

Copyright © 2021 Mark J. Keown. All rights reserved. Except for brief quotations in critical publications or reviews, no part of this book may be reproduced in any manner without prior written permission from the publisher. Write: Permissions, Wipf and Stock Publishers, 199 W. 8th Ave., Suite 3, Eugene, OR 97401.

Wipf & Stock
An Imprint of Wipf and Stock Publishers
199 W. 8th Ave., Suite 3
Eugene, OR 97401

www.wipfandstock.com

PAPERBACK ISBN: 978-1-7252-8551-4
HARDCOVER ISBN: 978-1-7252-8552-1
EBOOK ISBN: 978-1-7252-8553-8

Unless otherwise noted, Scripture quotations are from The ESV® Bible (The Holy Bible, English Standard Version®), copyright © 2001 by Crossway, a publishing ministry of Good News Publishers. Used by permission. All rights reserved.

12/10/21

Contents

List of Illustrations | x

Acknowledgments | xi

Abbreviations | xiii

Introduction | xv

Lesson One: An Introduction to Mark's Gospel | 1

    The Synoptic Gospels and Their Relationship 1

    Authorship 6

    Who Was John Mark? 8

    Date 9

    Provenance 10

    Setting 11

    Audience 12

    Textual Issues 12

    Context 14

    Arrangement and Structure 17

    Other Key Features 18

    Questions 32

Lesson Two: John's Ministry, Jesus's Anointing, Disciples Called, Power and Controversy (1:1—2:17) | 33

    The Title (1:1) 33

    The Ministry of John the Baptist (1:1–8) 34

    Jesus's Baptism and Anointing (1:9–11) 36

    The Temptation (1:12–13) 37

The Kingdom of God and the Required Response (1:14–15)   39

The Ministry of Jesus (1:16—8:26)   42

Questions   57

Lesson Three: More Controversy, Power Encounters, and Parables (2:18—4:34) | 59

Fasting (2:18–20)   59

The Parables of the Wineskin and Cloth (2:21–22)   60

Jesus Is Lord of the Sabbath (2:23–27)   63

Jesus Heals on the Sabbath (3:1–6)   64

The Healing of Crowds (3:7–12)   66

The Appointing of the Twelve (3:13–19)   67

Is He Mad or Demonized? (3:20–34)   70

The Parable of the Sower, Soil, and Seeds (4:1–20)   73

The Parable of the Lamp (4:21–23)   79

The Parable of the Measure (4:24–25)   80

The Parable of the Growing Seed (4:26–29)   81

The Parable of the Mustard Seed (4:30–32)   83

Parables Summary (4:33–34)   84

Questions   84

Lesson Four: More Miracles, the Sending of the Twelve, and John's Death (4:35—6:29) | 86

The Calming of the Storm (4:35–41)   86

The Exorcism and Sending of the Demoniac (5:1–20)   89

The Raising of Jairus's Daughter and Healing of the Bleeding Woman (5:21–43)   94

A Prophet without Honor (6:1–6a)   101

The Sending of the Twelve (6:6b–13)   104

The Identity of Jesus and the Death of John the Baptist (6:14–29)   107

Questions   111

Lesson Five: Two Feedings, More Miracles, and More Controversies (6:30—8:13) | 112

    The Feeding of the Five Thousand (6:30–44)   112

    Jesus Walks on the Sea of Galilee (6:45–52)   116

    Jesus Heals Many (6:53–56)   119

    Clashes over Purity (7:1–23)   120

    The Healing of the Syrophenician Woman's Daughter (7:24–30)   128

    The Healing of a Deaf and Mute Man (7:31–32)   130

    The Feeding of the Four Thousand (8:1–9)   132

    Jesus Refuses to Give a Sign (8:10–13)   134

    Questions   137

Lesson Six: Jesus Warns, Peter's Confession, and Jesus's Discipleship Training Program Begins (8:14—9:32) | 138

    Warnings Against the Pharisees and Herodians (8:14–21)   138

    The Healing of a Blind Man (8:22–26)   140

    Peter's Confession (8:27–30)   142

    The First Passion Prediction (8:31–33)   145

    Take Up Your Cross and Follow Me! (8:34–9:1)   148

    The Transfiguration (9:2–13)   152

    The Exorcism of a Boy with an Evil Spirit (9:14–29)   157

    The Second Passion Prediction (9:30–32)   161

    Questions   162

Lesson Seven: Jesus's Discipleship Training Program Continues (9:33—10:16) | 163

    Greatness Is Found in Service (9:33–35)   163

    The Importance of Children (9:36–37)   165

    A Permissive Attitude (9:38–41)   166

    Avoid Sinning and Causing Others to Sin (9:42–48)   170

    Be Salty (9:49–50)   174

    Divorce, Marriage, and Adultery (10:1–12)   176

    The Blessing of the Children (10:13–16)   181

    Questions   184

Lesson Eight: Discipleship Training Continues, and Jesus Enters Jerusalem (10:17—11:11) | 185

    The Rich Young Man (10:17-31)   185

    The Third Passion Prediction (10:32-34)   193

    Christian Leadership Is Service (10:35-45)   194

    The Healing of Blind Bartimaeus (10:46-52)   202

    The Entry to Jerusalem (11:1-11)   206

    Questions   209

Lesson Nine: Jesus Curses a Tree and Clears the Temple, and Controversies Intensify (11:12—12:40) | 210

    The Cursing of the Fig Tree (11:12-14)   210

    The Clearing of the Temple (11:15-19)   211

    The Withered Fig Tree and the Importance of Faith and Prayer (11:20-25)   215

    Jesus's Authority is Challenged (11:27-33)   217

    The Parable of the Tenants (12:1-12)   220

    Paying Taxes to Caesar (12:13-17)   223

    Marriage at the Resurrection (12:18-27)   224

    The Great Commandments (12:28-34)   227

    Jesus Is *Adonai* (12:35-37)   231

    Beware the Teachers of the Law (12:38-40)   233

    Questions   236

Lesson Ten: The Widow, the Olivet Discourse, and the Lead-Up to Jesus's Death Begins (12:41—14:42) | 237

    The Widow's Offering (12:41-44)   237

    The Destruction of the Temple and Signs of the End of the Age (13:1-13)   238

    The Tribulation and the Return of Christ (13:14-37)   243

    Anointing at Bethany (14:1-9)   248

    Judas Betrays Jesus (14:10-11)   252

    The Last Supper (14:12-25)   253

Jesus Predicts Peter's Denial (14:26–31)   257

Anguish in Gethsemane (14:32–42)   259

Questions   262

Lesson Eleven: Jesus's Arrest, Trial, Crucifixion, Burial, and Resurrection (14:43—16:8, 20) | 263

Betrayal and Arrest (14:43–52)   263

Before the Sanhedrin (14:53–65)   265

Peter Denies Jesus (14:66–72)   270

Before Pilate (15:1–15)   271

Mocked and Beaten by the Soldiers (15:16–20)   274

Crucified (15:21–32)   275

The Death of Jesus (15:33–41)   279

Jesus Is Buried by Joseph of Arimathea (15:42–47)   282

Jesus Is Risen (16:1–8)   285

Jesus Appears and Commissions the Disciples (16:9-20, disputed)   287

Questions   288

How Then Are We to Live?   288

Final Questions   290

Bibliography | 291

Subject Index | 297

Author Index | 349

Scripture Index | 353

Illustrations

Figure 1: The Griesbach or Augustinian Hypothesis | 3

Figure 2: The Four-Source Hypothesis | 4

Figure 3: The Farrar or Farrar-Goulder Hypothesis | 4

Figure 4: The Wilke Hypothesis | 5

Figure 5: Jesus's Ministry in Galilee | 15

Figure 6: Jesus's Ministry in Palestine | 16

Figure 7: Herod's Temple | 212

Acknowledgments

THANKS TO MY BELOVED friend Professor Dr Paul Cheng for his invitation and support in writing this material. It is an honor and a privilege to partner with you in this. I also extend my thanks to the whole team at Tyrannus Online Seminary in Kuala Lumpur. I thank Laidlaw College for employing me so I can do such writing. I love nothing more than exploring the Scriptures, and to be given the opportunity to do this and write about God and his Word professionally is a great privilege. My undying love goes to my beloved wife Emma. Of course, my greatest thanks go to God—Father, Son, and Spirit—for all you have done, are doing, and will do. Although I will have to wait until eternity to thank them in person, I also express gratitude to the apostle Peter whose message is contained in Mark's Gospel, his scribe and interpreter John Mark of Jerusalem, and all those who helped in its writing back in those days. I honor them for their service, and all who lost their lives in the horrific period in which Mark was written.

Abbreviations

ABD	*Anchor Bible Dictionary*
ANE	Ancient Near East
AV	Authorized Version
BDG	Arndt, William F., and F. Wilbur Gingrich. *A Greek-English Lexicon of the New Testament and Other Early Christian Literature: A Translation and Adaption of the Fourth Revised and Augmented Edition of Walter Bauer's Griechisch-Deutsches Worterbuch zu den Schriften des Neuen Testaments und der ubrigen urchristlichen Literatur.* 2nd ed., revised and augmented by F. Wilbur Gingrich and Frederick W. Danker from Walter Bauer's 5th ed., 1958. Chicago: University of Chicago Press, 1979.
BDAG	Danker, Frederick William, ed. *A Greek-English Lexicon of the New Testament and Other Early Christian Literature.* 6th ed., based on Walter Bauer's *Griechisch-Deutsches Wörterbuch zu den Schriften des Neuen Testaments,* edited by Kurt Aland and Barbara Aland, with Viktor Reichman, and on previous English editions by W. F. Arndt, F. W. Gingrich, and F. W. Danker. Chicago: University of Chicago Press, 2000.
COQG	Christian Origins and the Question of God
DBL Greek	*Dictionary of Biblical Languages with Semantic Domains: Greek (New Testament)*
DJG	*Dictionary of Jesus and the Gospels.*
DJG2	*Dictionary of Jesus and the Gospels,* 2nd ed.
DNTB	*Dictionary of New Testament Background*
EBD	*Eerdmans Bible Dictionary*

EDB	*Eerdmans Dictionary of the Bible*
EDNT	*Exegetical Dictionary of the New Testament*
ESV	English Standard Version
HIBD	*Holman Illustrated Bible Dictionary*
ISBE	*International Standard Bible Encyclopedia*
KJV	King James Version
LBD	*Lexham Bible Dictionary*
LSJ	Liddell, Henry George, Robert Scott, Henry Stuart Jones, and Roderick McKenzie. *Greek-English Lexicon with a Revised Supplement*. 9th ed. Oxford: Clarendon, 1996.
NAC	New American Commentary
NBD	*New Bible Dictionary*
NIDNTTE	New International Dictionary of New Testament Theology and Exegesis
NIGTC	New International Greek Testament Commentary
NIVAC	NIV Application Commentary
parr.	parallels
PDBS	*Pocket Dictionary of Biblical Studies*
PDSNTG	*Pocket Dictionary for the Study of New Testament Greek*
PNTC	Pillar New Testament Commentary
P. Oxy	Oxyrhynchus Papyri
Q	*Quelle*
SBT	Studies in Biblical Theology
SIG	*Sylloge Inscriptionum Graecarum*
SNTSMS	Society for New Testament Studies Monograph Series
Str-B	Strack, H.L., and P. Billerbeck. *Kommentar zum Neuen Testament aus Talmud und Midrasch*. 6 vols. Munich: 1922–61.
UBSHS	United Bible Societies Handbook Series
WBC	Word Biblical Commentary

Introduction

THIS IS THE FIRST textbook written for the Tyrannus Online Seminary in Malaysia but published to be used elsewhere by those who want to learn more of God's word. It is designed to be understandable, opening up deeper ways of engaging with the Bible. It involves eleven chapters in which students can read the passages and then consider the expository comments made about the text. Each lesson and chapter ends with questions that can be discussed by readers. There are also videos that accompany the book which can be accessed on the Tyrannus website. The whole purpose of this is to deepen faith and lead people to live more passionately and rightly for God.

The author of this volume is Mark J. Keown, who is honored to be given the opportunity to contribute. Mark is senior New Testament lecturer and biblical academic lead at Laidlaw College based at the Henderson campus in New Zealand. Prior to this, he published a number of works, including commentaries on Philippians, a two-volume discussion of Mark's Gospel, *Jesus in a World of Colliding Empires*, and a *Taster to the New Testament*. If you like what you read here about Mark's Gospel, you might consider reading his other more detailed book on Mark, which highlights Jesus against the backdrop of the kingdoms of the world at the time.

We do hope you enjoy this work and that it brings glory to God.

Lesson One: An Introduction to Mark's Gospel

MARK'S GOSPEL IS A fabulous, fast-moving account of the life of Jesus Christ, the Son of God.[1] Mark begins with John's prophetic ministry, Jesus's baptism, and then Jesus's story until his resurrection. The key theme is the kingdom of God, with Jesus as the king who establishes God's reign. The name Jesus is the Greek version of Joshua. The disciples who were called by Jesus believed that he was a new Joshua, who would lead the Twelve to overthrow the Romans and deliver the land. However, Jesus was a reframed Joshua, with a vastly different plan.

Mark describes Jesus's entry into the land, his utterly shocking demise, and his resurrection. In 1:1—8:29, Jesus is revealed as the Messiah, the Christ, God's anointed. After the confession by Peter, Jesus revealed that he is not a military messiah to smite the Romans, as expected; instead, he is a Servant King. The disciples are taught how to live as his disciples. They struggle to understand Jesus. They are devastated when he dies. They are hiding or fearful and bewildered when he rises. We are left at the end (16:8) with questions: What has happened? Who is this man? Mark himself clearly knows: he is the Messiah, the Son of God. He writes in the hope that his Roman readers and we who read Mark's Gospel today will come to the same conclusion.

The Synoptic Gospels and Their Relationship

Before considering Mark's Gospel, we must understand the relationship of the Gospels to each other. The word gospel is derived from the *euangelion*, which means "good news." In the early to mid-second century, the four Gospels as we have them were grouped as a unit. Three of the Gospels are

---

1. A number of witnesses do not include "Son of God" but it is most likely original. See Keown, *Jesus in a World*, 1:142.

called Synoptic Gospels. Synoptic comes from two Greek words, *syn* (with) and *opsis* (seeing), producing the idea "seeing together." The Gospels can be viewed together in a synopsis and compared; hence, their designation. They have much common material. Scholars consider why.

Several possible ways of explaining the relationship can be rejected. First, some have suggested there is no relationship at all and that they were written independently. This is very unlikely. For example, if we consider the blessings of the children in Matt 19:13–15, Mark 10:13–16, and Luke 18:15–18, we see that there are "twenty-eight common Greek words out of the thirty-seven in Mark, the thirty-eight in Matthew, and the thirty-nine in Luke."[2] It is clear from this and many other examples, similarities in the framing material in the Gospels, and similar OT quotations that, in some way, the different Synoptic writers used material found in the other Gospels. So how do we explain the similarities? Which Gospel writer used the material from other Gospels?

There is a range of possibilities that are usually ruled out today. Some consider that there was an original now-lost well established and circulated oral Gospel (*Urevangelium*) that was used by the three writers. Another idea is that there was an earlier Aramaic Gospel that was used by the writers. These ideas and a range of others are not taken seriously today.[3]

A minority of scholars consider that Matthew's Gospel was written first, Luke used Matthew, and Mark used both Matthew and Luke. This theory is sometimes called the Griesbach hypothesis, named after an eighteenth-century writer who argued for it. Others call it the Augustinian hypothesis, as Augustine held to it in the fourth to fifth century. This diagram shows how it works:[4]

---

2. See further Keown, *Discovering the New Testament*, 1:111. See for other examples Stein, "Synoptic Problem," 784. For a more detailed and updated analysis, see Baum, "Synoptic Problem."

3. See further Keown, *Discovering the New Testament*, 1:112–14. On the three-source hypothesis and the Papias hypothesis, see Keown, *Discovering the New Testament*, 1:119–21.

4. For the diagram and further, see Keown, *Discovering the New Testament*, 1:115.

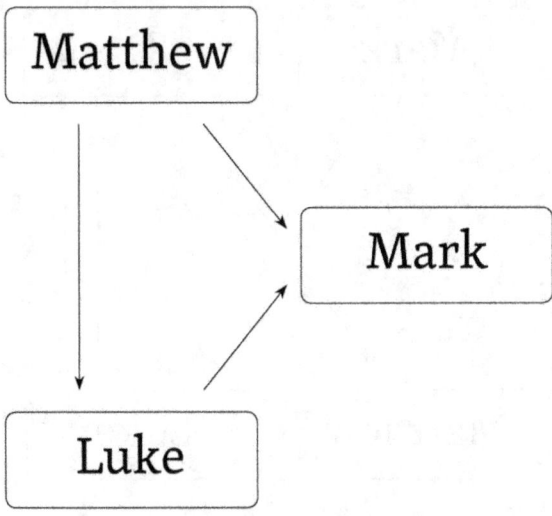

Figure 1: The Griesbach or Augustinian Hypothesis

Since the nineteenth century, New Testament scholars have increasingly supported the view that Mark's Gospel was written first and that Matthew and Luke both used Mark as a source for their Gospels. There is also a lot of material found in both Matthew and Luke (but not Mark). A good example is the account of the Roman soldier (Matt 8:5–13; Luke 7:1–10). The ethical material in Matt 5—7 and Luke 6 may also be derived from a common source.

The majority of scholars believe Matthew and Luke had access to another document that is now lost, nicknamed Q, short for *Quelle*, the German for "source." This remains the majority view, although there is considerable debate over whether Q is a written source or a blend of written and oral tradition. It is also agreed that Matthew and Luke had access to other material of their own. An example in Matthew is the sheep and goats judgment scene (Matt 25:31–46). In Luke, a good example is the parable of the rich man and Lazarus (Luke 16:19–31). Matthew and Luke then used Mark, Q material, and their own material. Scholars label Matthew's unique material M and Luke's material L. Scholars then call this the four-source hypothesis. Here is how it looks in diagrammatic form:[5]

---

5. For the diagram and further detail, see Keown, *Discovering the New Testament*, 1:115–17.

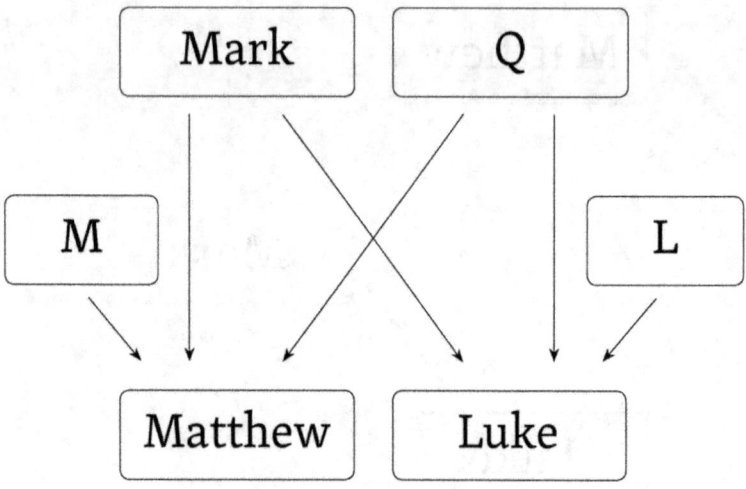

Figure 2: The Four-Source Hypothesis

Others remain skeptical concerning the existence of Q, and so two other possibilities, in particular, are posited. First, some consider that Matthew used Mark and that Luke then used both Mark and Luke, dispensing with the need for Q. This is sometimes called the Farrer-Goulder hypothesis, named after two of its significant proponents. It looks like this:

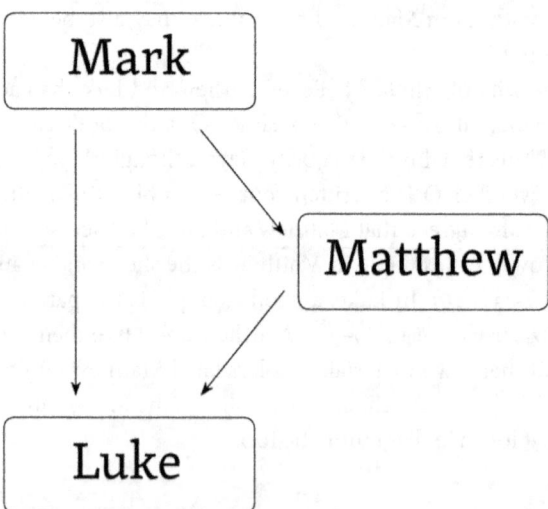

Figure 3: The Farrar or Farrar-Goulder Hypothesis

The final view of note that originates from the nineteenth century is the Wilke hypothesis (after its originator), which reverses the order of the Farrer-Goulder hypothesis. This perspective considers that Mark wrote first, "Luke used Mark, and Matthew relied on both Mark and Luke."[6]

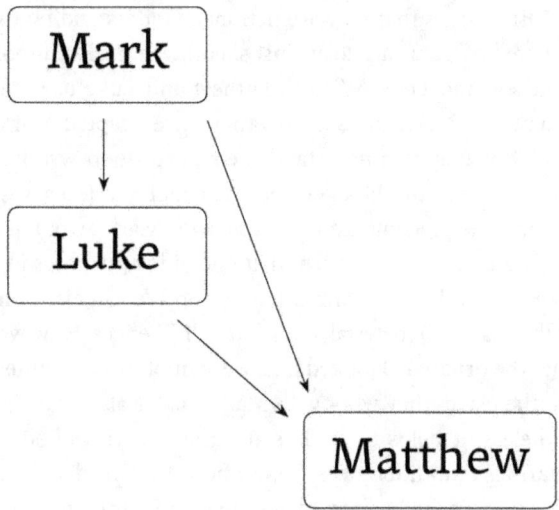

Figure 4: The Wilke Hypothesis

Conclusion

The vast majority of scholars accept that Mark was written first. It is surmised that rather than shorten an acknowledged sacred text like Mark's Gospel, an early Christian writer would be more likely to add to it. There are many points of verbal agreement and order between Matthew, Luke, and Mark. Mark's Greek is less polished than Matthew and Luke's. The different Greek suggests that it is more likely that the two others tidied up Mark's Greek, rather than that Mark replaced their more polished work with his less elegant Greek. Hence, it is very likely that Matthew and Luke both used Mark's material. Then, Matthew also used Luke, or Luke also used Matthew, or there was another document or documents on which they drew—Q. Luke mentions in Luke 1:1 that many had written about Jesus when he wrote, raising the possibility of such a document or documents. In addition, some of the passages in Matthew and Luke are very similar, as is the order of their material, suggesting a common source. The order is also similar. Hence, while both the

---

6. Keown, *Discovering the New Testament*, 1:118–19 (also the diagram).

Wilke and Farrar-Goulder views are possible, it is more likely that the four-source hypothesis is the best option.

This discussion raises the question of whether it matters much. At one level, it does not, as each Gospel must be interpreted as it is and in its own right. However, the matter is important historically as we seek to defend the Gospels against charges that they are fictional. Understanding the way they were constructed helps us argue against skeptics. It is also important when we read Matthew and Luke. Where Matthew and Luke use Mark, we can compare them with Mark and see how they have adapted Mark's material. Such comparisons help us understand their purpose in writing it. For example, Luke often adds to Mark's Gospel the detail that Jesus was praying as an event occurred (e.g., compare Luke 3:21 with Mark 1:10; Luke 6:12 with Mark 3:13). These additions confirm that one of his purposes in the Gospel was to call readers to lives of committed prayer. We can also compare Matthew and Luke's use of Q material and see the differences. However, as we are not sure what the original Q looked like, we cannot discern quite as much as we can from the places they work with Mark's material.

Nevertheless, it helps us understand their writings better as we examine similarities and differences. So, we need to consider the question of how the Gospels came to be formed and make up our own minds. We then interpret the Gospels with this in mind.

Authorship

Tradition holds that the writer of the second Gospel is John Mark of Jerusalem. While many scholars have questioned this assumption,[7] there are sound reasons to accept that this is correct. We will now consider the main arguments for accepting this view.

Papias (ca. AD 60–130) was the bishop of Hierapolis in Asia Minor (Turkey). Irenaeus (ca. 120–203) states that Papias heard John teach, and this indicates that he was well connected with the early Christian community.[8] Papias records that Mark was "the interpreter of Peter" and that he "wrote down *accurately* whatever he remembered of the things said and done by the Lord, but *not however in order*." He adds that Mark made no mistakes in recording

---

7. See Keown, *Discovering the New Testament*, 1:134–36. Arguments against the author being John Mark include questions over Papias's reliability, the original anonymity of the Gospel, the commonness of Mark as a name at the time, and questions of geography that suggest to some it was written by someone who was not a native of Galilee, Samaria, or Judea. Hence, other authors are proposed, including a different Mark. However, the early church evidence for John Mark is impressive (below).

8. Irenaeus, *Haer.* 3.39.1.

Peter's material.[9] Papias's testimony indicates from a trustworthy early church source that Mark's Gospel represents the essence of Peter's teaching on Jesus in Mark's words. The only Mark in the Bible is John Mark, and so it is fair to think that he is the author.

Other arguments support that Mark is the author and that he was linked to Peter. Later Christian writers, without exception, confirm that Mark wrote the second Gospel in the NT.[10] The superscription "according to Mark" (*KATA MARKAN*) was added in the early second century and also supports that Mark is the author.[11] First Peter 5:13 confirms a very close relationship between Peter and Mark ("my son") and places Mark in Rome (Babylon) at the time of Peter's death. Paul's letters also substantiate that Mark was in Rome in the 60s (Col 4:10; Phlm 24). Besides, his Greek style is "simple and unsophisticated."[12] Mark also has many translated Semitisms (Hebrew and Aramaic), which would align with someone who is a first-century, Greek-speaking Jew from Jerusalem.[13] He regularly references Aramaic and Hebrew and gives the Greek translation. Martin Hengel writes: "I do not know any other work in Greek which has so many Aramaic or Hebrew words and formulae in so narrow a space as does the second gospel."[14] As discussed in the previous section, Matthew and Luke both used Mark's Gospel as a basis for their accounts of Jesus. Their doing so suggests that they recognized the importance and historicity of Mark and supports that it had Peter as its source.

Overall, it seems that Mark's Gospel was written around Peter's death by crucifixion by Nero sometime around AD 64–65.[15] Mark wrote down in Greek the essence of the gospel Peter shared. As such, Mark is based on the testimony of Peter, who walked with Jesus from his baptism until his resurrection. Support for the idea that Peter is behind the Gospel also comes from Richard Bauckham, who persuasively argues that there are

9. Eusebius, *Hist. eccl.* 3.39.15.

10. See Irenaeus, *Haer.* 3.1.2 (AD 180); Tertullian, *Marc.* 4.5 (ca. 200); Clement of Alexandria, *Hypotyposes* (ca. 200), according to Eusebius (*Hist. eccl.* 6.14.5–7); Origen, *Comm. Matt.* (early third century), according to Eusebius (*Hist. eccl.* 6.15.5) and probably the Muratorian Canon (ca. 170–200). Justin Martyr, in the mid-first century, mentions the "reminiscences of Peter" in conjunction with a Markan quote (*Dial.* 106). Guelich, *Mark 1–8:26*, rightly states: "We really do not have any basis for this distinction in the Church tradition."

11. Hengel, *Studies in Gospel of Mark*, 74–81.

12. Hurtado, *Mark*, 11.

13. On Semitisms in the NT, see Bowden, "New Testament Semitisms"; Black, "New Testament Semitisms"; Hengel, "Literary, Theological and Historical Problems," 246.

14. Hengel, "Literary, Theological and Historical Problems," 246.

15. Stoops, "Peter and Paul."

indications in the Gospel that Peter is the primary source for the Gospel.[16] For example, Peter is named first and last of the apostles (1:16; 16:7), indicating he is probably Mark's primary source.[17] Peter is also very prominent in the Gospel, and at points, Mark writes that Peter "remembered" events, suggesting his hand in the Gospel (e.g., 11:21; 14:72). Some have also noted that the pattern of Mark's Gospel follows reasonably closely the arrangements of Peter's preaching in Acts (the *Kerygma*).[18]

So, it seems decisive that the second Gospel is the work of John Mark from around the time of Peter's death in the mid-60s AD. The primary source for his Gospel was Peter.

Who Was John Mark?

John Mark may be mentioned in the Gospel. Some scholars consider that the young man who flees naked at Jesus's arrest is a reference to the author of the Gospel (14:51–52). If so, it would make Mark an eyewitness to the final portion of Jesus's life. Furthermore, if Mark is in the garden during Jesus's arrest, his home may have been the place where the Last Supper was experienced and where the Spirit came upon the church at Pentecost. However, such things are not certain.[19]

The name Mark is mentioned eight times in the NT, and all likely refer to the same person. These tell us that he was also called John (Acts 12:12, 25; 15:37). Hence, John in Acts 13:5 and 13 is the same person, so he is also named John Mark. He was Barnabas's cousin (Col 4:10).[20] His mother was called Mary and was possibly a sister or sister-in-law of one of Barnabas's parents; she lived in her own home in Jerusalem (Acts 12:12). This likely means that Mark's father was deceased. His home was a meeting place for the Jerusalem church (Acts 12:12). His mother was very hospitable, hosting Barnabas and Saul when they brought a monetary collection from Syrian Antioch to help the poor during famines in the forties during the reign of Claudius (Acts 11:27–30). When Paul and Barnabas returned to Antioch, they took John Mark along with them (Acts 12:25).

John Mark then became an early church missionary. He went with Paul and Barnabas on their first Antiochian missionary journey as their

---

16. Bauckham, *Jesus and the Eyewitnesses*, 155–81.
17. Bauckham, *Jesus and the Eyewitnesses*, 165–72.
18. See Dodd, "Framework of Gospel Narrative."

19. See, e.g., Brooks, *Mark*, 238: "The view that the reference is an autobiographical one pointing to John Mark may be the most probable, but it is still nothing more than a possibility."

20. LSJ, 137, notes that the term means "first cousin" or, more generally, "cousin."

assistant (Acts 13:5).[21] However, for some reason, John Mark returned to Jerusalem, deserting Paul and Barnabas (Acts 13:13). When they returned and prepared for their next mission, Paul and Barnabas had a severe dispute over him. Paul refused to take him on the next journey, clearly upset over his departure on the previous trip. Barnabas wanted to take him. Barnabas's support may suggest that the reason Mark had returned was a family reason, such as his mother dying.[22]

When the time came for the second Antiochian missionary journey, Barnabas wanted to take Mark with them again. However, Paul did not agree because of Mark's earlier desertion. Barnabas supported Mark, there was "a sharp disagreement" between the two mission leaders, and they split up the mission (Acts 15:36–41). Barnabas and Mark went to Cyprus to evangelize and strengthen believers. Paul took a new assistant, Silas, and went to visit the churches planted on the first Antiochian missionary journey.

We know nothing of Mark again until the early 60s, where he is mentioned again as one of Paul's coworkers in Col 4:10 and Phlm 24. In a letter written around the time of Paul's death (at the same time as Peter's), Paul describes him as "very useful to me for ministry" (2 Tim 4:11). We can see then that Paul and Mark were at some point reconciled and worked together for the gospel. As noted previously, Peter also mentions Mark from Rome in 1 Pet 5:13, describing him as his "son." As such, Mark was a significant missionary in the early church, closely connected with Paul, Peter, and Barnabas. He was well-positioned to write the Gospel. His role in mission also means that his Gospel is not just a plain presentation of Jesus. It is a summary of the gospel by one of the great early missionaries and a co-worker of Paul, Peter, and Barnabas. It is the first written Gospel and so Christianity's first "missional tract." It became the basis for Matthew and Luke, and so we can see that John Mark is one of the most influential people in the history of the church and world.

Date

The earliest that Mark could have been written is the date of Jesus's resurrection, which occurred in AD 30 or 33, depending on one's chronology of Jesus's life.[23] The latest it could have been written is in the mid-second

---

21. The Greek term *hyperetēs* means "one who functions as a helper, freq[uently] in a subordinate capacity, helper, assistant" (BDAG, 1035).

22. Hence, his relative Barnabas would support this if it was a family member who had died. Paul may have been less sympathetic because of the exigencies of the gospel.

23. For a comparison of the arguments over whether Jesus died in AD 30 or AD 33, see Hoehner, "Chronology" (who argues for AD 33 for Jesus's death), and Donfried, "Chronology: New Testament," 1:1010–22 (who argues for AD 30 for Jesus's death). I

century when Mark begins to be quoted outside of the NT in the writings of later Christians.

There are three main ideas on the date of Mark's Gospel. The first is those who propose it was written in the 40s. If so, the "abomination that causes desolation" in 13:14 refers to Caligula attempting to set up his image in the Jerusalem temple.[24] Some argue that Peter left Jerusalem after escaping imprisonment and went to Rome in AD 42 to establish the church there.[25] However, few today accept this view.

The second is the 50s. There is evidence that Peter went to Corinth before AD 55, the latest date for 1 Corinthians (1 Cor 1:12; 9:5). Some consider he also went to Rome. Such a visit is supported by the fourth-century historian Eusebius, who states that Peter went to Rome during the reign of Claudius (AD 41–54).[26] However, a trip to Rome is challenged by the lack of any mention of Peter in Paul's letter to the Romans written ca. 56–58.

A third option is the 70s and 80s. However, such a late date is unlikely due to the strong early church tradition associating Mark's Gospel with Peter's death, which occurred in the mid-60s. Further, if Luke-Acts is written in the 60s (as suggested by the end of Acts), Luke's use of Acts indicates a date in the 60s rather than the following decades.

The fourth, traditional, and best option is a time around Peter's death (AD 64–65). Aside from the early traditions that accept this date, further support comes from the emphasis on discipleship and suffering in the Gospel. Finally, the way the fall of Jerusalem is described in Mark 13 suggests that it was written before the city's destruction in AD 70.

Provenance

Mark was likely written in Italy and probably in Rome. A range of early church traditions support this, including the Anti-Marcionite Prologue to Mark,[27] Irenaeus,[28] and Clement of Alexandria (AD 150–ca. 215).[29] Also supporting Rome are the Latinisms in the text. These are Greek words that are derived from Latin terms. Examples include centurion (Lat. *centurio*,

---

prefer the latter but recognize that we are uncertain.

24. Torrey, *Four Gospels*, 261–62.
25. Wenham, "Did Peter Go to Rome."
26. Eusebius, *Hist. eccl.* 2.14.6.
27. On the Anti-Marcionite Prologues, see McDonald, "Anti-Marcionite (Gospel) Prologues." These are short prefixes added to the Gospels of Mark, Luke, and John challenging Marcion's rejection. Some date them in the fourth century. However, he notes that De Bruyne and others agree on AD 160–180.
28. Irenaeus, *Adv. Haer.* 3.1.2
29. Eusebius, *Hist. eccl.* 6.14.6–7.

15:39, 44, 45), legion (Lat. *Legio*, 5:9, 15), and denarius (Lat. *denarius*, 6:37; 12:15; 14:5).[30] The writer has also translated Hebrew and Aramaic words (Semitisms) into Greek, suggesting that it is written among gentiles. Another interesting possibility linking Mark with Rome is the mention of a certain Rufus in Rom 16:13. The earlier references to Mark in Rome with Peter (1 Pet 5:13) and Paul (Col 4:10; Phlm 24) suggest Rome is the most likely place. References to taking up one's cross could also link the Gospel to Peter's death; he was crucified upside down.[31]

Setting

If it is right to place Mark's Gospel in Rome in the mid-60s, the setting is vital for understanding the Gospel. Before the 60s, Christianity was seen as a sect of Judaism. In the 60s, it began to be recognized as something distinct from Judaism and came to the attention of the Roman rulers. Persecution began to increase. Then, after the great fire of Rome, Nero persecuted Christians severely, blaming them for the fire (AD 64). Some Christians were dressed in animal skins and torn apart by wild animals. Others were crucified and even set ablaze at night to light his garden.[32] After this, Peter and Paul were killed by Nero. Mark was no doubt written not only to lay down the story of Jesus and record Peter's account of Jesus but to encourage Christians suffering persecution.[33] Lurking behind the Gospel then is Nero, who, in the 60s, became a complete tyrant. Mark uses language used of the emperor, such as Son of God, and presents Jesus as a completely different type of ruler. He is establishing God's reign not as a new Joshua, a Davidic-type warrior-messiah, Alexander the Great, or Caesar, but as a Servant Messiah. Rather than take the world with violent military force, he comes as a Servant of God to establish God's peace through service and crucifixion. The Romans loved Augustus Caesar, the first of the Roman Emperors, for establishing the *Pax Romana* (peace of Rome). Jesus is God's chosen Son who comes to establish the peace of God through using his power to heal and deliver people from sin, dying as a ransom for the world, and rising again as Messiah and Son of God. Mark's Gospel calls people to take up their crosses and follow him in the path of humility and service, spreading the good news that the kingdom of God is here: repent and believe the good news.

30. Others include poll tax (*census*, 12:14), peck measure (*modius*, 4:21), governor's official residence (*praetorium*, 15:16), a Roman coin (*quadrans*, 12:42), quart measure, pitcher (*sextarius*, 7:4), executioner (*speculator*, 6:27), and to flog (*flagellum*, 15:15).

31. For other possibilities for the place of writing, see Keown, *Discovering the New Testament*, 1:139–40. These include Egypt, Syrian Antioch, or Galilee.

32. Tacitus, *Ann.* 15.44.

33. Eusebius, *Hist. eccl.* 2.25.5–8. See further Garland, *Mark*, 28–31.

Audience

Christianity probably began in Rome through pilgrims attending Pentecost who established the church when they returned from Jerusalem. The church was initially Jewish in ethos. In AD 49, Claudius kicked all the Jews out of Rome because of tensions over Chrestus, who is likely Christ.[34] Aquila and Priscilla were two of those expelled (Acts 18:2). The expulsion shows that the Christian community had grown and had met stiff resistance from Jews. The exile left the Roman church as a small gentile community. In AD 49, the Jerusalem Council also met and decided that circumcision and law observance were not required (Acts 15). On his second Antiochian mission, it is likely Paul sent the letter from the Council to Rome. The small Roman gentile Christian community was then able to preach the gospel of grace and faith to others, and the church grew. New leaders emerged. When the Jewish Christians returned, there appear to have been tensions between the returning Jews and gentiles. Romans was likely in part written to resolve the tensions between Jews and gentiles in the church (especially Rom 14—15). Philippians 3:1–11 and Hebrews (ca. AD 62–63) suggest this continued up until the time Mark was written.

The church at the time of Mark seems to have been mainly gentile and under pressure from the Roman rulers and the Jewish community. It was written only a few years before the Jewish-Roman war (AD 66–70). Jewish nationalism was on the rise. Peter and Paul were about to be killed by Rome. Mark's Gospel was more than likely written to encourage the mainly gentile Christians facing persecution from all sides and the horror of the death of its great leaders. It encourages readers to endure the suffering Christians should expect and to live by the pattern laid down by Jesus the crucified Messiah, taking up their crosses and following him as faithful disciples.

As Mark was writing down Peter's Gospel, he also likely had his eye on Christians across the whole Roman Empire. As Edwards says, "These data indicate that Mark wrote for Greek readers whose primary frame of reference was the Roman Empire, whose native tongue was evidently Latin, and for whom the land and Jewish ethos of Jesus were unfamiliar."[35]

Textual Issues

As we read Mark's Gospel in versions other than the KJV or NKJV, we notice that there are missing verses. These deletions are because the KJV and NKJV are based on the Textus Receptus, which is now recognized by

---

34. Suetonius, *Claud.* 25.4.
35. Edwards, *Gospel According to Mark*, 10.

most textual scholars as an inferior text. Some of the verses included in the KJV and NKJV were probably not original to the text. These jumped verses are put into footnotes. They include 7:16; 9:44, 46; 11:26; and 15:28. The most significant of these ommissions is the longer ending of Mark. This passage is found in all versions of the Bible, usually with indications that it is not original (16:9-20). There are three possible endings to Mark's Gospel found in the texts.

First, there is a shorter longer ending found in a few seventh to ninth century uncial[36] Greek manuscripts and some old Latin and other versions.

> And all that had been commanded them they told briefly to those around Peter. And afterward Jesus himself sent out through them, from east to west, the sacred and imperishable proclamation of eternal salvation.

This ending is clearly a later addition added by some to give Mark a more satisfying ending.

The second ending is the usual longer ending found in Mark 16:9-20. This ending is found in the Textus Receptus,[37] the majority text,[38] a range of other texts, the *Diatessaron*,[39] and the early church writers, Irenaeus and Jerome. There are several versions of this.[40] Most contemporary Bibles aside

---

36. Writing in uncial is a formal style of handwriting with large rounded letters (capitals), each separated from the next, found in Latin and Greek codices. As a classification of NT manuscripts, *uncials* is not used to refer to all NT manuscripts written in uncial characters (about 650), but only to continuous-text manuscripts so written on parchment (about 270). It comes from the Latin *uncia*, "twelfth" (our word *inch* is derived from it), apparently a reference to the size of the letter compared to cursive script. Uncial manuscripts are designated in the critical apparatus by capital letters (e.g., ℵ, A, B, Ψ) or numbers preceded by 0 (e.g., 0170). See further DeMoss, *PDSNTG*, 126.

37. This refers to the texts used for Luther's original German Bible, the early Tyndale translation, and the KJV (or Authorized Version, AV). However, most textual critics believe that there are earlier, more accurate texts.

38. The majority text does not actually exist but is created by comparing all known manuscripts forming a text with the readings that are most common across all known texts. When it was formulated in the fourth century, it was based on a wide range of texts with many errors that had crept in by this time.

39. On the Diatessaron, see Hixon, "Diatessaron." Named from the Greek *dia tessarōn*, "through four," the work is a harmony of the four Gospels traced to Trajan in AD 172. Only a single manuscript fragment exists (0212). Beginning with John 1:1-5 and Luke 1:1-4, and ending with John 21:25, it deletes John 7:53—8:11 but includes elements of the long ending of Mark. It is faithful to the Gospels, but was rejected when Tatian was considered a heretic.

40. One Greek manuscript, Codex Washingtonianus (032) (also Washington Manuscript), includes the following after v. 14: "And they excused themselves, saying, 'This age of lawlessness and unbelief is under Satan, who does not allow the truth and power of God to prevail over the unclean things of the spirits [*or*, does not allow what lies under the unclean spirits to understand the truth and power of God]. Therefore reveal

from the KJV and NKJV include these words in italics or accompanied by a note stating that the passage is an interpolation.[41]

Most textual critics today consider this ending inauthentic. First, it is missing from the two significant uncials, Codex Sinaiticus (ℵ) and Codex Vaticanus (B). Both Jerome and Eusebius, writing in the fourth century, state that the verses are not original. Third, the material is not consistent with the Greek of Mark's Gospel and appears to be a summary based on Luke's writings, with hints of John's Gospel.[42] Hence, some second-century writers added the summary to give Mark's Gospel a more satisfactory ending.

As such, Mark's Gospel appears to end at Mark 16:8. This ending appears a little strange, especially as it ends with the Greek *gar*, "for." Some contend that the original ending on the scroll was lost. Alternatively, Mark was interrupted and never completed the Gospel, perhaps because of Nero's persecution. However, the most likely view is that 16:8 is indeed the end of Mark. It ends with the women in fear and bewilderment concerning what has happened to Jesus and what they should. The ending could be a literary device to draw the reader into the same questions: Who is Jesus? What should I do? If this is true, then arguably, this is a quite brilliant way to end the Gospel and hints at Mark's purpose. He states that Jesus is the Messiah and Son of God and narrates his life. He challenges readers to consider: Who is this man? What should I do? Mark hopes that readers will recognize that he is the Son of God, place their faith in him, and go and tell the world.

Context

Jesus ministered throughout the nation, especially in Galilee, including a time of ministry to the north of the nation in what we now call Lebanon. The maps below summarize Jesus's movements and focus.[43]

---

your righteousness now'—thus they spoke to Christ. And Christ replied to them, 'The term of years of Satan's power has been fulfilled, but other terrible things draw near. And for those who have sinned I was handed over to death, that they may return to the truth and sin no more, in order that they may inherit the spiritual and incorruptible glory of righteousness that is in heaven'" (from Metzger, *Textual Commentary*, 103).

41. An interpolation refers to a portion of the text that is not original to the biblical book but, during the process of copying, was intentionally or unintentionally inserted into the text (see DeMoss, *PDSNTG*, 74).

42. We can see evidence of Luke 8:2; 24:13–32, 46–49, 50–53; John 20:11–18; Acts 1:9–11; 2:1–4; 3:1–10; 28:1–6.

43. See Keown, *Discovering the New Testament*, 1:1:150.

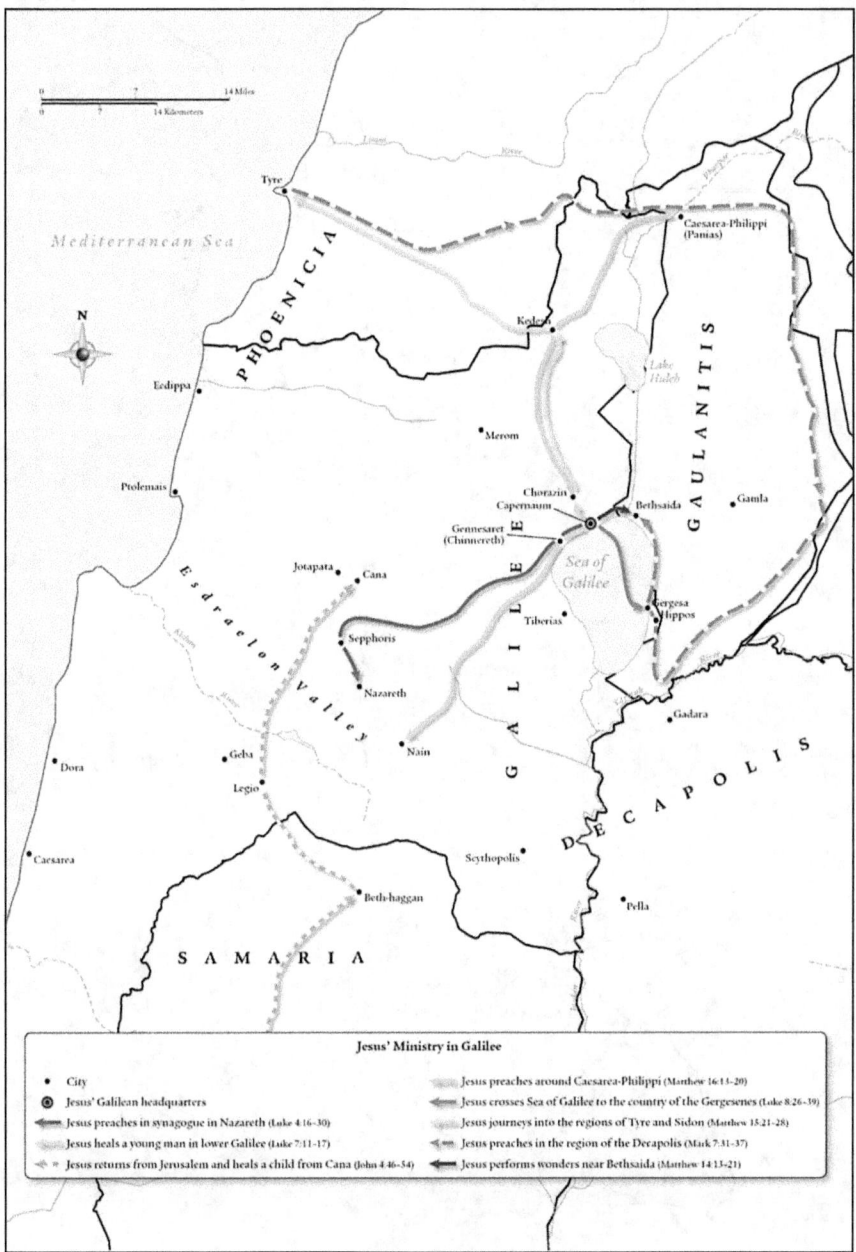

Figure 5: Jesus's Ministry in Galilee

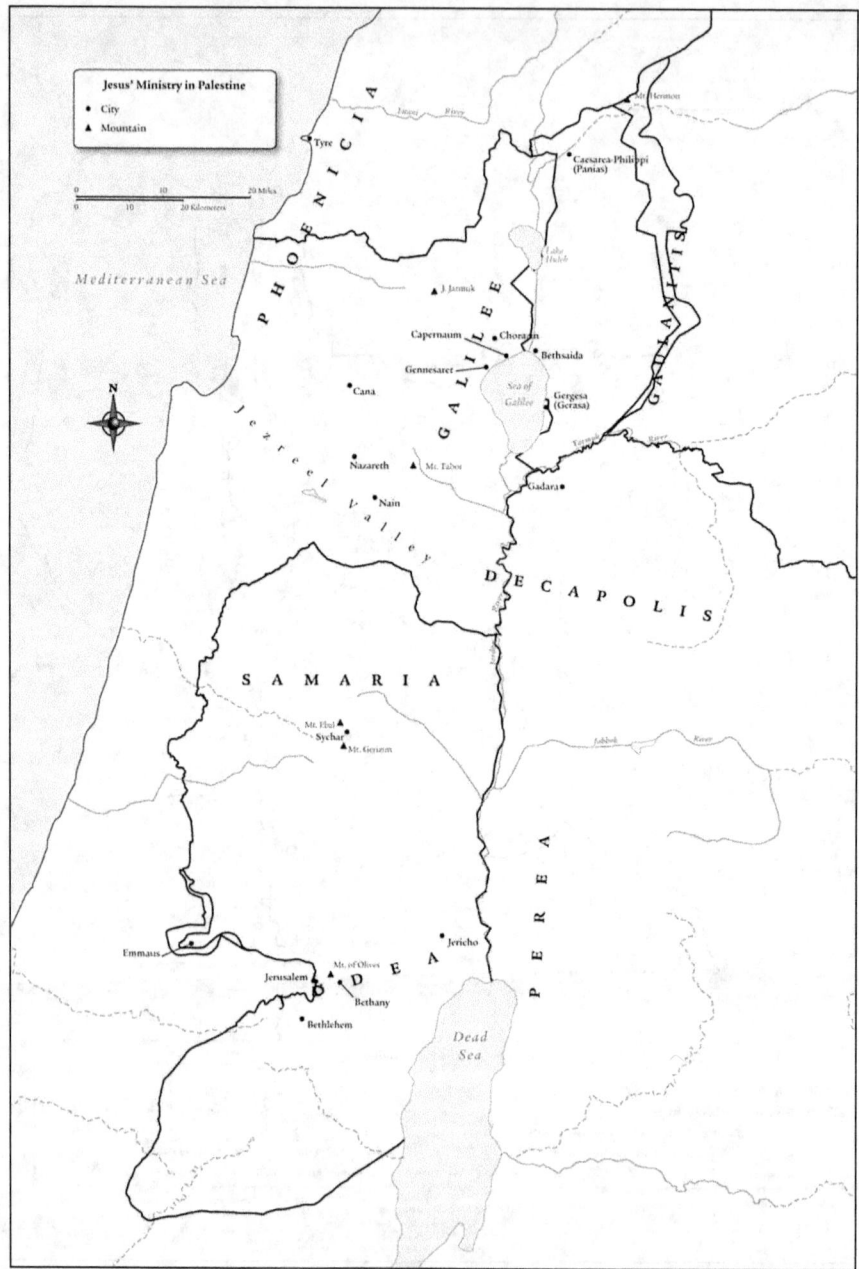

Figure 6: Jesus's Ministry in Palestine

Arrangement and Structure

Mark's Gospel can be broken up into two main sections:

Part One: The Revelation of Jesus as the Messiah and Son of God (1:1—8:29)

Part Two: The Revelation of Jesus as a Servant Messiah (8:30—16:8)

Part One, in which Jesus is revealed as the Messiah, culminates in Peter's confession of that very thing. We can break it down further:

1. The Title (1:1): "The beginning of the Gospel of Jesus the Christ and the Son of God."

2. The Ministry of John the Baptist (1:1-8): As with Samuel and David, the prophet John precedes the Davidic King.

3. Jesus's Baptism and Anointing (1:9-11): In a further parallel with Samuel and David, the prophet John then anoints this King (1 Sam 16:12-13).

4. The Temptation (1:12-13): The Messiah wins his first battle.

5. The Kingdom of God and the Required Response (1:14-15): The proposition of the Gospel

6. The Ministry of Jesus (1:16—8:26): Calling disciples of the kingdom (a renewed Israel), power ministry of healing and deliverance, proclamation, personal encounters, clashes with Jewish leaders

The center of Mark is the confession in 8:27-29, where at Caesarea Philippi, a city named after the royal figures Caesar and Philip the Herod (named after Philip the father of Alexander the Great), the real King is revealed: Jesus, Israel's Messiah.

Part Two focuses on what kind of messiah, with Jesus teaching and demonstrating to his disciples what it means to be a disciple of the kingdom. He does this by example as he uses his power for the marginalized and powerless. Jesus also instructs the disciples through verbal teaching. Finally, Jesus demonstrates what his kingdom is all about through his death. Through crucifixion, Jesus gives his life as a ransom for many (10:45). Through his shed blood, he inaugurates the new covenant (14:24). Jesus dies; all appears lost; yet, his tomb is empty. An angel announces his resurrection. The women are left bewildered and afraid. As we read, it is up to us to consider for ourselves who Jesus is.

A more detailed structure will be given below before we begin to consider the Gospel itself in each section.

Other Key Features

Jesus and His Identity

The original Gospel was anonymous, probably intentionally so that the message is Jesus and not the writer Mark or his source Peter. The point of the Gospel is to present Jesus as the Messiah, the Son of God, who came to establish God's reign, and to invite people to respond with repentance and faith (1:1, 14–15). There is no infancy narrative, so Mark is purely interested in Jesus's ministry up until his resurrection. He demonstrates his messiahship with acts of power to help those in need and reveals his true identity to his disciples, who hear and heed the call of the kingdom. We are left to decide for ourselves who this man is (4:41).

There is a double layer to Mark's Gospel. Mark knows who Jesus is. He is Messiah (seven times; see 1:1; 8:29; 14:61). He is the true Son of God (eight times), who even calls God "Abba Father" (14:36). He is Daniel and Enoch's Son of Man (fourteen times; Dan 7:13–14; 1 Enoch 37—71). He is the Lord (five times). He is God incarnate who forgives (2:5–11), rules the Sabbath (2:28), calms a storm (4:35–41), raises the dead (5:29–43), walks on water (5:45–52), provides food for Israel in the wilderness (6:30–44; 8:1–10), and is transfigured in blazing glory on the Mount of Transfiguration (9:2–8). He is the teacher, who brings God's word with astonishing authority;[44] the wisdom of God (cf. Prov 8:22–31; 1 Cor 1:30). The prophets from Moses to John the Baptist brought God's promises for the future. Now, God's people are to "listen to him" (9:7). Jesus is God's voice to the world.

Set in the context of Rome, he is presented as a contrast to the Caesars. They ruled the world, having supposedly brought it peace. The Caesars were seen as an incarnation of the gods and were called Lord and Son of God. To this world, Mark declares that Jesus is its actual ruler.

In a Jewish setting, Mark declares Jesus the fulfillment of Israel's dreams of the expected one who will bring God's redemption. They hoped for liberation from gentile rule. Jesus came to do something grander: liberation from sin for all people, including Israel. He recalls and transcends the conqueror Joshua; David the great king on whom the Messiah would be patterned; and Moses, Israel's provider, lawgiver, and leader.

---

44. Mark 1:22; 4:38; 5:35; 9:17, 38; 10:17, 20; 12:14, 19, 32; 13:1; 14:14.

Furthermore, Jesus's real enemy is not Caesar or even the Jewish leaders with whom he clashed regularly, but Satan, who has the world trapped in sin. He defeats Satan in the wilderness to begin his mission (1:12–13). He drives out demons.[45] He is accused of working as Satan's emissary; yet, he performs miracles by the power of God (3:22–27). He preaches the word that Satan seeks to steal from human hearts and minds, showing that there is a war going on for every person's soul (4:15). He sent his disciples to engage in that same war, not with worldly weapons (cf. 2 Cor 10:3), but with the power of God to deliver people from sin and Satan (6:7, 13). They must beware of Satan corrupting their understanding of the gospel and mission, or they too will fall (8:33).

As noted, in the first half of the Gospel, Jesus's identity as Messiah is revealed. In the second half, he shows them what kind of Messiah he is: a Servant Messiah. The disciples are directly instructed to walk in the same pattern, with cross hung over their backs as they relentlessly serve those in need and proclaim the good news of the gospel of the kingdom.

Diverse Responses to Jesus

Through Mark, we get a range of responses that challenge us to respond correctly to him but also to be prepared for a range of reactions from people as we preach the good news. Some know who Jesus is, including John the Baptist (1:7–8);[46] demons who reluctantly recognize him, unable to resist his divine power (1:23–24; 3:11; 9:20); and Bartimaeus (10:46–52).

Then there are the disciples who are drawn to Jesus and follow him with immediacy (1:16–20; 2:13–17); hang in with him, impressed by his power; but struggle to comprehend who he is. At times they are utterly terrified (4:35–41) or do not understand him (6:50–52), causing Jesus to ask, "Do you still not understand?" (8:21). Ultimately, they do understand him as Messiah (8:29). However, after this, as Jesus begins to predict his death, they are again bemused and confused (8:31–33; 9:32; 10:32). When he dies, they do not come to claim his body and bury him but desert him, with only the women watching from a distance (15:40).

Unsurprisingly, for a Gospel that has its source in Peter, Peter dominates. He is mentioned first and last (1:16; 16:7), the first-named respondent

---

45. See Mark 1:27, 32, 34, 39; 3:11, 15; 5:13–18; 7:26–30; 9:38.

46. Mark does not include the Q material (Matthew and Luke) concerning John sending disciples to question Jesus about his identity. These passages suggest that even John questioned who Jesus was, perhaps because he was confused by his non-militaristic approach (cf. Matt 11:2–6; Luke 7:18–23).

to Jesus's summons (1:16–20; 3:16). With John and Jacob (James),[47] he forms Jesus's inner circle (5:37; 13:3; 14:33). He recognizes Jesus as Messiah (8:29) but is then rebuked for challenging Jesus (8:32–33). He is the mouthpiece for the disciples (8:29; 10:28; 11:21). He courageously claims he will never deny Jesus but fails dismally (14:29, 31, 54, 66–72). He does stay with Jesus in Gethsemane, only to fall asleep in weakness (14:37). Ultimately, in Mark's Gospel, he deserts Jesus. The existence of Mark's Gospel and the widely acknowledged link between Mark and Peter indicates that the story of Peter's restoration recorded in John 21 was known to Mark's Roman readers. We see, then, in the life of Peter, a parallel to the story of many believers who are drawn to Jesus, stumble along in their lives as disciples, yet become leaders among God's people.

Some are impressed with him but do not recognize him as Messiah. Some, like Herod Antipas, believe him to be John the Baptist raised from the dead (6:14; 8:28). Others see him as Elijah restored (6:15; 8:28; cf. 2 Kgs 2; Mal 4:5–6), or a prophet (6:15). Such diverse perspectives prepare us for a world in which people have all sorts of views of Jesus. Some are quite impressed by him but are not yet disciples. They are "near to the kingdom of God" (12:34). They enter when they recognize that he is the Messiah and Son of God and yield to his rule.

Some entirely reject Jesus, such as the demons mentioned earlier. They acknowledge Jesus as God's Son but continue to seek to destroy him and his work. Then there is Judas, who tragically accepts the call to follow, only to reject and betray him.[48] He symbolizes the story of many who step out on the journey of faith, only to fall away and deny Jesus. Many in Nazareth reject Jesus, failing to understand how the boy they saw grow up in Joseph's home can be Messiah. Because of their unbelief, Jesus could do only a few miracles there (6:1–6). They are like those who who cling to their church traditions and fail to see God raising new leaders to bring renewal in their midst.

The Jewish leaders oppose Jesus from the beginning when Jesus claims the power to forgive sins (2:6). Clashes go on and intensify.[49] They seek to

---

47. The Greek *Iakōbos* transliterates the Hebrew for Jacob; hence, I prefer to use *Jacob* for the second son of Zebedee (also bracketed with James) and others with the same name in the NT. The name *James* developed from the Latin *Jacobus* with the *b*-sound over time shifting to an *m* and so became *Jacomus* in Latin Bibles. When the English Bibles were first produced, based on both Greek and Latin texts, *James* was preferred. See Fruchtenbaum, *Messianic Jewish Epistles*, 207.

48. Mark does not include Judas's remorse, so what happens to Judas is not explained (cf. Matt 27:3–5; Acts 1:15–19).

49. See Mark 2:16; 3:22; 7:1–23; 9:14; 11:27; 12:14, 19, 28.

kill him.⁵⁰ They conspire with Judas and the Romans to kill Jesus and succeed (14—15). Jesus did not quite fit their expectations of a messiah who would reveal himself to them, adhere to their interpretations of Israel's law, call them to his side, and take back the nation from the Romans.

Throughout the Gospel, there are those who are drawn to Jesus but never fully grasp who he is. Then there are the crowds⁵¹ or the masses.⁵² They are amazed by Jesus's teaching (1:22, 27) and power (1:32-33; 5:20, 42). He is so popular that he remains in the wilderness rather than towns (1:45). Many see him as a prophet (6:15; 8:28). When he enters Jerusalem, an excitement that he is Messiah is exploding (11:1-11; cf. Zech 9:9; Ps 118:25-26). They love his teaching in his final week (12:37). However, when he is arrested and tried, they reject him, preferring Barabbas (15:6-15) and abuse him at his crucifixion (15:21-31). The Gospel ends with this note of rejection from the people of Israel echoing in the air.

Mark's Gospel gives every possible response to Jesus. The readers are challenged to discern who Jesus is for themselves and decide for themselves. The hope of Mark the writer is that we yield entirely to Jesus as Messiah and Son of God and work with him for the extension of his kingdom.

The Messianic Secret

A well-discussed feature of Mark is the so-called messianic secret. This descriptor is used to describe those places where Jesus commands others, whether demons or people, to be silent over his identity.⁵³ Additionally, at times, Jesus teaches his disciples rather than the crowds.⁵⁴ He instructs his disciples not to tell others about his messiahship (8:29-30) and his transfiguration (9:2-8).

In 1901, William Wrede argued that this shows Jesus did not see himself as the Messiah, and his followers created this after his resurrection. However, this is unlikely, as Jesus quite clearly acknowledges his messiahship (8:29-31; 14:62). There appear to be three reasons for his secrecy. First, knowledge of his identity would excite messianic expectations that

---

50. See Mark 8:31; 10:33; 11:18; 14:1, 43, 53; 15:1, 31.

51. "The crowds" (*oklos*), see Mark 2:4, 13; 3:9, 20, 32; 4:1, 36; 5:21, 24, 27, 30, 31; 6:34, 45; 7:14, 17, 33; 8:1, 2, 6, 34; 9:14, 15, 17, 25; 10:1, 46; 11:18, 32; 12:12, 37, 41. Cf. Mark 14:43; 15:8, 11, 15.

52. "The many" (*hoi polloi*), see Mark 1:34; 2:2; 3:7, 8; 4:1; 5:21, 24; 6:31, 34; 8:1; 9:14; 11:8; 12:37.

53. E.g., Mark 1:25, 34, 43-44; 3:12; 5:43; 8:26, 30.

54. See Mark 4:13, 34; 7:17; 9:28-29, 30-31; 10:10-11; 13:3.

could see people rise in revolt (John 6:15; Acts 5:36; 21:38). Jesus would then be seen as one of many who tried to rise up in a revolution in the period leading to the Jewish-Roman war in AD 66–70.[55] Second, the discovery of his messianic status could thwart his mission as people were excited with hopes of the overthrow of the gentiles. This concern is somewhat realized when Jesus's warning is disregarded, and he must adapt his mission as a result (1:45). Third, Jesus wanted to emphasize the importance of the cross and self-giving in his mission.[56]

Jesus's Ministry

Large parts of Mark up to his arrest describe his ministry. Recognizing the elements of his mission is critical for us, who, as the body of Christ, will continue his mission. Elsewhere, I have noted these core aspects of his ministry:[57]

- Calling disciples and appointing and sending apostles[58]
- Teaching and preaching, especially in parables (4:1–20) and ethical teaching scattered through the material[59]
- Healing and deliverance (ten healings/deliverances/resurrections and three summaries), praying (1:35–37)
- Feeding the poor (two accounts)
- Miracles over nature (two accounts)
- Encounters with individuals (e.g., the Syrophoenician woman, the rich ruler) and groups (e.g., children)
- Friendship with sinners, lepers, children, and others who are marginalized

---

55. See Witte, "Messianic Secret," who notes similar uprisings recorded in Josephus, *Ant.* 20:97, 167; *War* 2:54, 261.

56. Witte, "Messianic Secret," who tells readers that some explain it because Jesus wanted to avoid politically explosive self-designations before the completion of his mission at his second coming. However, that is not likely, as Jesus was quite comfortable using Son of Man, which is also a politically charged term (especially 1 En. 37–71).

57. Keown, *Discovering the New Testament*, 1:164–65.

58. Mark 1:16–20; 2:13–14; 3:16–19.

59. Mark 1:21–28, 38–39; 4:1–34. See Keown, *Discovering the New Testament*, 1:165–66, who notes a whole range of ethical teaching, e.g., cross-bearing (8:34–38); humility (9:33–35), childlikeness (10:13–16), renouncing sin (9:47–50), divorce (10:1–12), wealth (10:17–31), servant leadership (10:35–45), paying taxes (12:13–17), love for God and other people (12:28–34), and radical generosity (12:41–44).

- Challenging Jewish leaders[60]
- Clashing with the powers of darkness (1:12–13; 3:20–30; 8:33) and the casting out of demons

Fulfillment of Hope

After the title, the blended prophetic quote in 1:2–3 speaks of John as the long-awaited Elijah announcing Jesus as the fulfillment of Israel's hopes (cf. Isa 40:3; Mal 3:1; Exod 23:20).[61] In John, the silence of the prophets was coming to an end (1 Macc 9:27; cf. 4:46; 14:41). The death of Jesus is interpreted as the blood of a new covenant, recalling Exod 24:8 (14:24). Jesus is the fulfillment of the OT hopes concerning the Messiah and one that is crucified,[62] the Son of Man,[63] the prophet (9:7, cf. Deut 18:15), the Servant of Isaiah.[64] In Jesus, all the hopes of Israel were coming to fruition. However, his intent was not the liberation of Israel from foreign rule, but the deliverance of the whole world from sin and its devastating consequences.

---

60. Mark 2:6-12, 18—3:6; 3:22–30; 7:1–21; 8:11–13; 11:27—12:38.

61. See also Mark 9:11; cf. Mal 4:5.

62. See Mark 1:11; 9:7; cf. Pss 2:7; 12:10–11; 15:24, 29, 34; 22:1, 7, 18; 118:22–23, 25-26; Mark 11:9–10.

63. See Mark 12:36; 13:26; 14:62; cf. Ps 110:1; Dan 7:13.

64. See Mark 1:11; cf. Isa 14:60–61; 15:4–5; 42:1; 53:6–7. Other possible OT connections include 2 Kgs 1:8; Zech 13:4 in Mark 1:6; Gen 22:2 in Mark 1:11; Ps 103:3; Isa 43:25 in Mark 2:7; Deut 23:25 in Mark 2:23; 1 Sam 21:1–6 in Mark 2:25–28; Isa 6:9–10 in Mark 4:12; Joel 3:13 in Mark 4:29; 1 Kgs 17:18 in Mark 5:7; Lev 18:16 in Mark 6:18; Esth 5:3, 6; 7:2 in Mark 6:23; 2 Chron 18:16; Jdt 11:19 in Mark 6:34; Isa 29:13 in Mark 7:6–7; Exod 20:12, 17; Lev 20:9; Deut 5:16 in Mark 7:10; Isa 35:5–6 in Mark 7:37; Jer 5:2; Ezek 12:2 in Mark 8:18; Mal 4:5–6 in Mark 9:11–12; Deut 24:1, 3 in Mark 10:4; Gen 1:27; 2:24; 5:3 in Mark 10:6–8; Exod 20:12–16; Deut 5:16–20; 24:14 in Mark 10:19; Gen 18:14; Job 42:2; Zech 8:6 in Mark 10:27; Isa 56:7; Jer 7:11 in Mark 11:17; Isa 5:1–2 in Mark 12:1; Gen 38:8; Deut 25:5 in Mark 12:19; Exod 3:2, 6, 15, 16 in Mark 12:26; Lev 19:18; Deut 6:4–5; Josh 22:5; 1 Sam 15:22 in Mark 12:29–31, 33; Isa 45:21 in Mark 12:32; Hos 6:6 in Mark 12:33; 2 Kgs 12:9 in Mark 12:41; Isa 13:10; 34:4, Ezek 32:7–8; Joel 2:10, 31; 3:15 in Mark 13:24–25; Deut 4:35; Isa 45:21 in Mark 12:32; 1 Kgs 22:17; 2 Chron 15:6; Isa 19:12 in Mark 13:8; Mic 7:6 in Mark 13:12; Dan 9:27; 1 Macc 1:54 in Mark 13:14; Dan 12:1 in Mark 13:19; Isa 13:10; 34:4; Ezek 32:7–8; Joel 2:10, 31; 3:15 in Mark 13:24–25; Zech 2:6, 10 in Mark 13:27; Deut 15:11 in Mark 14:7; Exod 12:6, 15 in Mark 14:12; Ps 41:9 in Mark 14:18; Zech 13:7 in Mark 14:27; Lev 24:16; 27:17 in Mark 14:65; Ps 69:21 in Mark 15:23, 36; and Amos 8:9 in Mark 15:33. See Jackson, *New Testament Use of the Old Testament*.

The Kingdom of God

As in the other Synoptics, the kingdom of God is the dominant theme of the Gospel. The kingdom has come near in Jesus, so people are summoned to repent and believe the good news (1:14–15). The Herods and Caesar rule in the political sphere, but Jesus is bringing God's kingdom into the midst of the world's empires in a new way. Jesus is King—Israel's Messiah, the Son of God, the Son of Man, to whom has been given all dominion. The spiritual reign of Satan is now being plundered. The parables of Mark focus on the kingdom. The kingdom has come through God's word; it is planted in the carnage of a fallen world, and it is now in an unstoppable hidden invasion of the world that is underway (4:26–34). The miracles function as signs of the kingdom, showing that God has come to heal, set free, save, and restore his world.

In the passion narrative, Jesus is condemned by the combined forces of Israel and Roman leadership. He dies on the cross designed for a revolutionary, Barabbas, whose name means "son of God" (15:7, 11, 15). When Pilate asks the Jewish leaders what he should do with "the king of the Jews," they demand his death (15:12). He is mocked viciously as a king, clothed in purple, crowned with thorns, and ridiculed (15:17–20). He is crucified, dying a criminal's or slave's death under a mocking sign, "the king of the Jews"—a colossal irony, for this declares to the world his kingship (15:26). On the cross, he is mocked again, challenged to come down (15:31–32). Nevertheless, he is declared to be the Son of God by a Roman soldier (15:39).

These things all come to pass because the kingdom of God is unlike any kingdom before or since. There are no armies and violent revolution. This kingdom is about love, service, humility, healing, and restoration. The kingdom Jesus inaugurated will be extended by its subjects serving the world and sharing the gospel with grace. It will culminate with Jesus's return in glory, coming on the clouds of heaven. For this day, we wait.

Discipleship

Mark's Gospel has a strong emphasis on discipleship. A disciple is a *mathētēs*, a student or apprentice. A master-student relationship is part of the Jewish tradition, seen, for example, in the relationships of Moses and Joshua (Exod 24:13)[65] and Elijah and Elisha (1 Kgs 19:16).[66] Rabbis had

---

65. "Then Moses set out with Joshua *his aide*, and Moses went up on the mountain of God." The Hebrew *sharath* here has the notion of service or minister.

66. "Also, anoint Jehu son of Nimshi king over Israel, and anoint Elisha son of

disciples, as did John (2:18). In Judaism, however, the apprentice sought out a teacher and asked to be a disciple. In Mark, Jesus takes the initiative (1:16–20; 2:13; 10:21).

The heart of discipleship is found in Jesus's appeals to "come after (*deute*) me" (1:17) or "follow (*akaloutheō*) me" (2:14; 8:34; 10:21, 28). A great example is Bartimaeus, who followed Jesus on the way. Jesus gave him the freedom to do what he wanted, yet he chose to follow Jesus and become a disciple (10:52).

The ideal of discipleship is seen in the four fishermen leaving everything to follow Jesus (1:16–20), as does the tax collector Levi (Matthew) (2:13–16) and the healed demoniac (5:1–20). Contrastingly, the refusal of the rich ruler to sell his possessions, give to the poor, and follow Jesus, represents a preference for the world over the kingdom (10:17–22).

Jesus shockingly summons the disciples to prioritize their group over their family commitments.[67] The call to discipleship is a call to take up crosses and suffer for the cause of the kingdom (8:34–36). Faith or complete trust and dependence is the right response for the disciple, as is repentance and repudiation of sin (1:15; 9:42–50). Faith makes people whole or saved (*sōzō*) (4:40). The prayer of the true disciple is, "I do believe; help me to overcome my unbelief!" (9:24).[68] All are to have faith and confidence in prayer (11:22–24, cf. 9:29). Still, even Jesus, on one occasion, did not have his prayers answered as he wanted (14:32–42).

Other aspects of true discipleship are evangelism, healing, and deliverance (1:17; 6:7–13; 8:38; 13:10); care for the poor and needy (6:37); ethical purity (7:21–23); service of others (9:35; 10:43–45); marital fidelity (10:1–12); love of children (10:13–16); and making our wealth available to the work of the kingdom (10:17–31). At its heart is an emulation of our Lord Jesus: denying ourselves, taking up our crosses, following Jesus, and putting the kingdom ahead of everything in our lives (8:34–37).

Action Orientation

One of the remarkable aspects of Mark is its "action orientation." Mark's concern is not a precise chronology, but the fantastic teaching and actions of Jesus and discipleship. His account moves along rapidly, with few indicators of time and vague links. Interspersed throughout the accounts is the

---

Shaphat from Abel Meholah *to succeed you* as prophet."

67. See Mark 3:31–34, cf. 1:16–20; 2:13–17; 10:19, 29–31.
68. We should all pray this regularly.

adverb "immediately" (*euthys*) (forty-two times).⁶⁹ Mark also joins many sentences with *kai*, giving the sense of "and . . . and . . . and."⁷⁰ Indeed, one is almost breathless as one reads it in the original Greek. Mark uses such devices to picture Jesus always on the move, performing miracles, debating opponents, and teaching his followers. He employs "and it happened" (*kai egeneto*) nine times, giving little idea when.⁷¹ Some examples are Jesus entering Galilee and preaching, with no specific temporal indicators (1:14). Then he is beside the sea (1:16; 2:13; 3:7–12), a leper approaches him (1:40), he returns to Capernaum "after some days" (2:1), he ascends a mountain (3:13), he returns home (3:20; 6:1), he meets scribes from Jerusalem (3:22), and his family visits him (3:21, 31). Mark 1:21–34 occurs on one Sabbath and 1:35–39 on the next day, springboarding an undetailed period of preaching in Galilean synagogues.⁷²

There are dramatic features like "heaven being *torn* open" (1:10, italics added). Events important to Matthew and Luke are condensed, e.g., the temptation (1:12–13; cf. Matt 4:1–11; Luke 4:1–13) and his ethical teaching (2:13; cf. Matt 5—7; Luke 6:19–49). Mark's Jesus is a missionary man on the move, looking for the next opportunity to minister to the lost (1:38–40).

Markan Sandwich

Mark is very cleverly written. It is full of irony and other literary features. One of the most interesting of these is the so-called Markan sandwich. Edwards writes: "Each sandwich unit consists of an A¹-B-A² sequence (a chiasm),⁷³ with the B-component functioning as the theological key to the flanking halves."⁷⁴ Below are some sandwich units agreed upon by schol-

---

69. *Euthys* is especially found in the account of Jesus's ministry (Mark 1: twelve times; Mark 2: two times; Mark 3: once; Mark 4: four times; Mark 5: four times; Mark 6: five times; Mark 7: once; Mark 8: once; Mark 9: three times).

70. For example, Mark 1:33, 34, 35, 36, 37, 38, 39, 40, 41, 42, 43, 44, all begin with *kai*, "and."

71. Mark 1:9; 2:23; 4:4, 39; 9:7 (twice), 26.

72. See further Keown, *Discovering the New Testament*, 1:167–69.

73. A chiasm is based on the Greek letter *chi*, which is shaped like an X and which is a rhetorical device whereby parallel lines of a text correspond in an X pattern (see Pazia and Petrotta, *PDBS*, 24–25). This verse is a neat little example:
A¹ "Take heart"
B¹ "I am"
A² "Do not be afraid."

74. Edwards, *Mark*, 11.

ars. The central B sections are highlighted, as this is where the theological focus is found. The sandwich units include at least these listed below:[75]

Mark 3:20–35

A¹ Criticism by Jesus's family (3:20–21)

B *Criticism by Jewish leaders (3:22–30)*

A² Criticism by Jesus's family (3:31–35)

Mark 5:21–43

A¹ Jairus's daughter (5:21–24a)

B *Healing of the hemorrhaging woman because of faith (5:25–34)*

A² Jairus's daughter (5:35–43)

Mark 6:16b–31

A¹ Sending out the Twelve (6:6b–13)

B *Death of John the Baptist, ending the era of the prophets (6:14–29)*

A² Sending out the Twelve (6:30–31)

Mark 11:12–25

A¹ Cursing of the fig tree (11:12–14)

B *Clearing of the temple (11:15–19)*

A² Cursing of the fig tree (11:20–25)

Mark 14:1–11

A¹ Plot to kill Jesus (14:1–2)

B *Jesus anointed for burial at Bethany (14:3–9)*

A² Plot to kill Jesus (14:10–11)

---

75. Other possibilities (which I think are a bit forced) include Mark 2:1–12 [healing of paralytic, part 1—Jesus's authority to forgive sin (2:5b–10a)—healing of paralytic, part 2; Mark 3:1–6 [Sabbath healing—purpose of Sabbath—Sabbath healing]; 7:1–23 [washing hands—Corban—washing hands]; 9:36—10:16 [blessing children—divorce—blessing children]; and Mark 13:5–23 [false Christs—Jerusalem/temple destruction—false Christs].

Mark 14:53-72

A¹ Peter's denial (14:53-54)

B *Jesus's trial and condemnation (14:55-65)*

A² Peter's denial (14:66-72)

Mark 15:40—16:1

A¹ Women (15:40-41)

B *Burial of Jesus (15:42-46)*

A² Women (15:47—16:1)

These chiastic structures show the creativity of Mark as a writer and alert us to interpretative aspects of his narrative.

Irony

A feature of Mark's Gospel is the use of irony, often seen in unexpected things. One aspect of this is that while Jesus is rejected consistently by the Jewish elite, the wrong people are commended for faith, such as the Syrophoenician gentile woman (7:29) and the bleeding woman (5:34). Another example is Bartimaeus, who perceives Jesus's identity, while even the disciples do not fully recognize Jesus (10:35-52).

There are other aspects of irony. The first evangelist sent is not one of the Twelve, but the demoniac of Mark 5:1-20. When Peter confesses Jesus as the Messiah, Jesus immediately rebukes him, creating an almost comical rebuke and counter-rebuke situation seen in the use of the same verb *timaō* three times (8:30-33). One of the greatest ironies is that the only person to perceive Jesus to be the Son of God at his death is not a Jewish leader or disciple, but a gentile centurion (15:39). Another irony is that Joseph of Arimathea condemns Jesus, yet then buries him (14:55; 15:42-47).

Jesus's Death

Mark's Gospel has been described as "a passion narrative with an extended introduction."[76] This description is not entirely accurate, because the first

---

76. Kähler, *So-Called Historical Jesus*, 80n11. He described all the Gospels in this way. However, he was very skeptical about the Gospels, seeing them as a construct of the early church.

thirteen chapters are of critical importance to understanding Jesus and his mission. However, the death of Jesus is indeed the climax to Mark's story. The Gospel begins with Jesus being well-received (1:22, 28, 45). Soon his outrageous claims, such as his power to forgive and claim lordship over the Sabbath, will incite the wrath of the Jewish leaders (2:5–7, 16, 23; 3:6). He is accused of being demonized (3:22). He is challenged concerning food purity laws (7:1–16) and divorce (10:1–12). Jesus knows his ministry will end in death instigated by the Jewish leaders (8:31–32; 9:31; 10:33–34: see also 9:9). Jesus knows that he has come to serve and give his life as a ransom for many (10:45).

The Jerusalem leaders become more vehement to see him killed after his clearing the temple (11:18). This fury intensifies as Jesus engages them in public debate (11:27—12:34). The parable of the tenants again predicts his death at the hands of the Jewish leadership, exacerbating their endeavors to end his life (12:1–12, especially 6–8).

The passion of Christ is spread over two chapters describing treachery (14:1), anointing for burial (14:1–9), and betrayal by one of his own (14:10–11, 18–20, 43–45). At his final meal with his followers, Jesus speaks of his body broken like bread and his blood poured out like wine as the ratification of the covenant (14:24). Another reference to his death is Zech 13:7, where Jesus is the struck shepherd and his sheep (the disciples) are scattered. He predicts Peter's forthcoming denial, which tragically comes to pass (14:27–31, 66–72). His threefold prayer in the garden of Gethsemane again shows that Jesus was painfully aware of his fate (14:36). Jesus is a victim of great violence (14:43, 47, 65; 15:16–20). Nonetheless, he demonstrates what is now the heart of Christian ethics in his absolute refusal to use his power to liberate himself (14:48–50). Through it all, the worst of human depravity is seen in injustice (14:53–59), political machinations (14:60–64; 15:1–15), mockery from Romans, the other crucified men, the people and Jewish leaders (15:16–20, 27–31), horrific crucifixion, and painful death (15:24–37). All humanity is implicated as both Jews and gentiles conspire against him, sentence him, and kill him. The release of Barabbas, "son of God" and revolutionary, and Jesus's crucifixion in his place symbolize Jesus's death for sinners throughout time (15:1–15).

In all this, Jesus fulfills Israel's story. Jesus is now the Passover Lamb who takes away the sins of the world (14:12–26; cf. 1 Cor 5:8; John 1:29). A new and more glorious Passover has occurred, liberating the lost sheep of God from bondage to Egypt (sin). The Day of Atonement is superseded by the death of Jesus. The rending of the curtain to the inner sanctum of the temple gives all humankind access to the throne room of God via the blood of Jesus (15:38; Lev 16). Jesus's death fulfills the hopes of the dying and resurrected

Servant of God in Isaiah 53, as well as the crucified and vindicated Davidic king of Psalm 22. Mark does not develop a propositional theology of the death of Christ. It is Paul and the writer of Hebrews who do this. However, Mark's narrative summons us to think deeply about every aspect of Jesus's death, to see the profound way in which it fulfills Israel's story and brings the redemption for which Israel yearned and which the world needs.

Jesus's Resurrection

While there are no resurrection appearances in Mark, Mark's account ends with resurrection, as do the other Gospels. There is a stone rolled away, an empty tomb, and the words of the young man (an angel) stating that Jesus is risen and will meet them in Galilee (16:1–5). There are also anticipations of the resurrection.[77] We are left in 16:8 with the words "for they were afraid." As noted earlier, this is a brilliantly abrupt ending, leaving the reader wanting more and asking questions like "What happened next? Did the women tell them?" And more profoundly, "What am I to make of this story and man?" The answer is in the Gospel. Mark's Gospel exists because the women did go and tell the men. We do not know from Mark's Gospel alone whether they went to Galilee, but we can surmise that Peter was told, as Mark has written down his story. He wants us to "repent and believe the good news" (1:15). It is up to us to decide what to do with it.

Ongoing Mission

Toward the end of Matthew, Luke, and John, and at the beginning of Acts, Jesus sends his disciples to take the gospel to the world so that people can repent, believe, experience God's forgiveness, and be his disciples.[78] As discussed, the original scroll of Mark ended at 16:8 and so does not have such a commission. Does this mean Mark's Gospel lacks a missional dimension? Not at all. Mark begins with the mission of John the Baptist, and then Jesus, full of the Spirit, begins his mission (1:2–15). The Twelve are then sent out without material provision, and they preached the kingdom, cast out demons, and healed the sick (6:7–13).

When they return, Jesus feeds the five thousand. Embedded in this narrative is the imperative clause "you give them something to eat" (6:37), a challenge to the people of God to respond to those they encounter in

---

77. See Mark 8:31; 9:1, 31; 10:34; 14:27–28.
78. Matt 28:18–20; Luke 24:46–49; John 20:21; Acts 1:8.

material need with radical generosity (cf. 10:21; 12:41–44). The parable of the sower is not just about Jesus's mission but also prepares the disciples for the differing responses they will receive as they preach the word (4:1–20). The parable of the lamp speaks of believers bringing the secrets of the kingdom into the light (4:21–22). The seed parable talks of the gospel growing by God's power in secret (4:27). The mustard seed parable speaks of the kingdom growing to be the dominant ideology of the world, presupposing the spread of the gospel (4:30–32).

Those who wish to be disciples are not to be ashamed of Jesus or his words, even if they end up taking up crosses for his sake (8:38). In 13:10, Jesus tells the disciples that "the gospel must first be preached *to all nations*" before the consummation of this age (13:10; italics added). This cosmic mission is mentioned again in 14:9. Here, Jesus declares that the account of the woman anointing his feet will be told, "wherever the gospel is preached *throughout the world*" (14:9; italics added). Then, at the consummation of this age, when Jesus returns, he will send angels to collect God's chosen people from "the four winds, from the ends of the earth to the ends of the heavens" (13:27).

By the time of Mark's writing, the mission had spread into what we call North Africa, Lebanon, Syria, Turkey, Greece, and Rome. As argued elsewhere, Mark knew that there were masses of people to the north into Europe; the northeast into Russia; east as far as China; and south, deeper into Africa. He knew there was much work to do before Jesus returned.[79] The Gospel is written to ensure that the message that Peter and the other disciples preached in these regions would be that it be taken to the whole world. This mission is our ongoing task.

The Fall of Jerusalem and the Return of Jesus

Some think that Mark believed that Jesus was about to return. However, this is flawed. As noted earlier, like all first-century Jews, Mark knew the world was much larger than the few regions the gospel had penetrated and was aware that the gospel must be preached to all living people. The second problem is those who read Mark 13 as being merely about the fall of Jerusalem.[80] A better reading recognizes that the chapter is double-layered, predicting both the fall of Jerusalem (see especially 13:2–4, 30) and the return of Christ (13:10, 13, 24–27)—indeed, the first event prefigures the second.[81] We must take care

---

79. Keown, "Imminent Parousia," 242–63.
80. For example, Wright, *Jesus and the Victory of God*, 339–67.
81. See Keown, *Discovering*, 178–79.

not to create a rigid timetable concerning the end of the age. Instead, we are to continue to serve (13:34) and to consider the times and be prepared (13:28–30, 35–37), ready for when these things come to pass (13:32–34).

Questions

- How do we best account for the relationship between the Synoptic Gospels?
- What sort of person do you think John Mark was?
- How do you think the situation in Rome in the 60s could have affected the way Mark shaped his story of Jesus?
- Do you think Mark 16:8 represents the original end of Mark's Gospel? If not, why do the earliest copies end there? If so, why does Mark end the Gospel like this?
- What is the value of the longer ending of Mark's Gospel?
- What is the kingdom of God?
- Why did Jesus keep his identity a secret?
- Who is Jesus for you?

Lesson Two: John's Ministry, Jesus's Anointing, Disciples Called, Power and Controversy (1:1—2:17)

The Title (1:1)

THE FIRST SECTION OF Mark deals with John the Baptist and the preliminaries to his ministry, beginning in 1:14. It begins with the title *KATA MARKON*, which means "according to Mark." As we have discussed in the introduction to Mark, this was added sometime in the second century AD. It also indicates that those who added it believed Mark wrote this gospel. The Gospel, then, is his version of the story of Christ.

The real subject matter of Mark is found in 1:1 in the phrase "the Gospel of Jesus Christ (the Son of God)."[1] This clause is the real internal title of his work. Thus, the book is a presentation of the good news, the *euangelion*. This word is formed from *eu* (good) and *angelion* (message). The content is Jesus, the Messiah, the Son of God.

Mark then, as the first written full Gospel, represents the development of the good news from an oral presentation to a written record. The term *euangelion* picks up the idea in Isaiah of the hope of the glorious victory of God for those in Babylon.[2] Hence, it is a message of deliverance, salvation, and victory over the enemies of God. It has a political edge. In the Roman world, *euangelion* speaks of good news, especially regarding the emperor, e.g., a victor or the birth of a son. Hence, the word would have appealed to Mark's Roman readers; it is the story of the victory of God through Caesar Jesus.

---

1. Some manuscripts include "Son of God," others do not. I think it should be included; see the discussion in Guelich, *Mark 1—8:26*, 6. Metzger, *Textual Commentary*, 62 gives it a {C} rating, indicating it is possibly authentic.

2. Isa 40:9; 41:27; 52:7; 61:1.

Jesus is the Greek for Joshua and hence connotes interest in Jesus as a new Joshua come to drive out the Romans (cf. the Canaanites). *Christ* is the Greek *Christos*, "anointed one," translating *mā·šîᵃḥ*. The term is a technical one pointing to the Jewish hopes of a Davidic king who would come and establish God's reign for all eternity. Most associated this with violent revolution (see especially Pss. Sol. 17).

"The Son of God" in the minds of first-century Jews was effectively synonymous with Christ, referring to the king (see especially Ps 2). However, as Mark's Gospel plays out, we see that Mark is not merely talking about Jesus as the king, the royal son of God; he is God the Son!

The Ministry of John the Baptist (1:1–8)

The Gospel does not begin with an infancy narrative and genealogy as do Matthew and Luke (Matt 1—2; Luke 1—3). Neither does it begin with a preamble on Jesus as the divine *Logos* as in John (John 1:1–18). Instead, after the declaratory title, it begins with the ministry of John the Baptist. Beginning with an account of John the Baptist points to his tremendous importance as a prophetic forerunner to Christ for the early Christians. He is important because he marks the transition from prophet to Messiah. He is the last prophet of the pre-Christ era. His role is to declare and anoint the king. We see this in the Davidic tradition as Samuel anoints Saul and David (1 Sam 9:1–27; 16:1–13), Nathan anoints Solomon (2 Kgs 1:28–53), Elisha anoints Jehu (2 Kgs 9:1–13), and so on. Jesus is legitimized as a Davidic Messiah by the prophet of God.

John's ministry is seen in the early church as a fulfillment of OT expectations that one would come before the Messiah to prepare the way for his coming (1:2 cf. Mal 3:1; Isa 40:3). His ministry was preparatory, calling people to repent and confess their sins. This summons anticipates new Christians doing the same as they come to Christ. Their forgiveness is symbolized by baptism, which washes away their sin (1:4–6).[3] He is also a preacher declaring this baptism. His proclamation anticipates Jesus, who also will preach the word (1:14–15). Later, apostles and disciples would

---

3. See Dockery, "Baptism," who writes: "The practice of baptism is widespread. Examples include the Hindu rituals in the Ganges River, the purification ritual in the Babylonian cult of Enki, and the Egyptian practices of purifying new-born children and the symbolic revivification rites performed on the dead. *Baptizō* and related terms were used to define ritual practices in early Cretan religion, Thracian religion, Eleusinian mystery religions and in several gnostic groups and cults." See also Guelich, *Mark 1—8:26*, 17.

preach the word to the world. We are charged to continue preaching Christ, calling people to repent of their sins, believe, and be baptized.

John, then, is the first direct preacher of Jesus. John's impact is enormous even if Mark is hyperbolic when he speaks of "the whole Judean countryside and all the people of Jerusalem" (1:5).[4] People were desperate for liberation from foreign oppression, and when John came, they no doubt hoped God was about to act to free them. Little did they know that the coming Messiah would not free them from foreign oppression, but would die to free them from sin. The focus of John and then Jesus on Israel reminds us that salvation comes first to the Jew and then to the nations: salvation comes from the Jews (John 4:22; Rom 1:16).

John was a radical in the tradition of the prophets like Elijah and Elisha, wearing camel's hair and a leather belt and eating locusts and honey (1:7, see 2 Kgs 1:8).[5] We learn more of him from Luke, who tells us that John stands in the Nazarene tradition (Luke 1:15; cf. Num 6:3). Later on, Jesus refers to him as Elijah, widely expected to precede the Messiah. This hope is fulfilled in John the Baptist (9:12; cf. Mal 4:5). In John, Elijah rejects that he is Elijah (John 1:21, 25). However, the question was directed at Jewish hopes that Elijah would come as Israel's liberator, like the Messiah in other prophetic traditions. This John rejects. However, he is Malachi's Elijah figure.

His message points forward, focused on Christ, the "stronger one."[6] Later in Mark, Satan is implied to be "the strong man," but Jesus is stronger and binds him (3:26–27). Jesus comes after John. He is superior, and he will baptize people with the Spirit (1:7; cf. Ezek 36:25–27).[7] These OT connections show that Mark's Gospel is a continuation of God's big story begun at creation and culminating in the new heavens and earth. Christ's coming is *the* moment of God's intervention and salvation.

---

4. Guelich, Mark 1—8:26, 19.

5. 2 Kgs 1:8: "They replied, 'He was a man with a garment of hair and with a leather belt around his waist.' The king said, 'That was Elijah the Tishbite.'"

6. Scholars debate who this means: 1) God; 2) the Messiah; 3) the Son of Man; 4) the eschatological prophet; 5) an unknown eschatological figure. Most opt for 1 to 3; I prefer 2 (1:1) with "Son of God." See for discussion Guelich, Mark 1—8:26, 21-22.

7. Rabbinic teaching forbade Hebrew students from untying the master's sandals, cf. Guelich, Mark 1—8:26, 22.

Jesus's Baptism and Anointing (1:9–11)

Jesus comes south from Galilee to be baptized in the Jordan by John the Baptist (1:9), where he receives the Spirit and hears the audible voice of God saying, "This is my son, whom I love, with him I am well pleased" (1:10–11). John is God's appointed prophet anointing God's appointed King. Indeed, the Hebrew mā·šîᵃḥ and Greek *Christos* mean "anointed one." When prophets like Samuel, Nathan, and Elisha anointed the Davidic king, they anointed them with oil. In this instance, Jesus is anointed with the Spirit. He is the final eternal Davidic King.

As such, this represents a kind of commissioning by God. The tearing of the heavens speaks of the reopening of the way between God and humankind. When Adam and Eve fell, there was a barrier placed between God and people, symbolized by them being shut out from the garden and an angel blocking them from entry (Gen 3:24). Now, that heaven is opened, and the Spirit falls. This moment is the beginning of the last days. Later, the temple's curtain will tear as Jesus dies, and the way to God for humankind will be opened (15:38).

We thus see God intervening in the present with his power, filling the heart of his Messiah and Son. This anointing was expected in the prophets (cf. Isa 11:1; 61:1; Luke 4:18–20). Theologically, this is a coronation, the voice of God declaring Jesus his beloved and pleasure, recalling Ps 2:7. It further reminds us of Abraham taking his beloved son Isaac for sacrifice (Gen 22:2). Not only is Jesus the anointed Davidic King and God's Son, but he is also the anointed Servant of Isa 42:1: "Behold my servant, whom I uphold, my chosen, in whom my soul delights."

The baptism, then, anticipates Mark's presentation of Jesus as the Messiah King (1:1—8:29). In addition, it points to his identity as the Messiah Servant (8:30—16:8). The Spirit falling "like a dove" and the subsequent manifestations of the Spirit, such as Pentecost (Acts 2:1–4), point to what happens when the Spirit comes. The Spirit's impact is often unexpected and supernatural. The image of the Spirit coming as a bird also takes us back to creation, where the Spirit hovered over the waters as God created the world (Gen 1:1–2). Here, the Spirit comes to Jesus in the waters and anoints him. Thus, we see the beginning of the new creation, where God will save those people who repent and believe the good news and ultimately, after Christ's second coming, will recreate the heavens and earth (Rev 21—22). This scene also points to the humility of Christ, who submits to baptism at the hands of his cousin.

It also reminds us all that baptism is an essential part of the Christian life. Paul's theology makes it clear that when we believe, we are baptized and anointed with the Spirit, who seals us for eternal life (2 Cor 1:21–22; Eph 1:14). The Spirit is a deposit guaranteeing our salvation. The Spirit imparts gifts and transforms us to be more and more like Jesus.[8] The Spirit is God in us, enabling us to serve him as we work out the gift of salvation we have received (Phil 2:12–13). He is the Paraclete of God, our advocate, helper, comforter, and counselor.[9]

It is essential to consider the voice of God speaking over Jesus at his baptism. This moment occurred before he entered his ministry, yet he is *already* God's beloved with whom God is well pleased. This delight is how he views those who yield to his reign. When we come to him in repentance and faith, we are his beloved, and he is pleased with us. This love is experienced before we have done anything other than yield to him. So this moment speaks of our identity and status in him. From this knowledge, we are spurred on to serve him, not to gain his love, but to reciprocate his love for us. We need to note the connection here to the transfiguration, where again Jesus is declared God's beloved Son, and we must listen to him. These two great moments—Jesus's baptism and transfiguration—are critical for our understanding of who he is and who we are.

The Temptation (1:12–13)

Remarkably, the first thing the Spirit "immediately" (*euthys*) does is drive Jesus out into the desert to combat Satan for forty days. The Greek for "drive out" is *ekballō*, which is a term used often in Mark of Jesus driving out demons,[10] the tearing out of an eye (9:47), Jesus driving sellers from the temple (11:15), and the son being thrown from the vineyard (12:8). There is a strong sense of compulsion here. Often Israel's king would go into battle after anointing to demonstrate his power. So, Saul defeats the Ammonites (1 Sam 11), and David defeats Goliath (1 Sam 17). Here, the ultimate enemy of humankind and God, Satan, "the adversary," is Jesus's enemy. Jesus defeats him, anticipating his final defeat through the cross and return of Christ, where Satan is thrown into the lake of fire (Matt 25:41; Rev 20:10).

The thrusting of Jesus into temptation indicates that the leading of the Spirit does not always take us into prosperity and material blessing. It is vital to grasp this. Prosperity teaching suggests a limited view of God's purposes. Jesus is hungry; but, what we see is that God is with him through his angels, ministering to him. He is also with the wild animals, showing Jesus's power

---

8. See Rom 8:1–17; 12:4–8; 1 Cor 12—14; Eph 4:11.
9. See John 14:16, 26; 15:26; 16:7.
10. See Mark 1:34, 39; 3:15, 22, 23; 6:13; 7:26; 9:18, 28, 38.

over the creation, his deep love of animals, and their peace with him, their creator. This passage also points to the ultimate fulfillment of Israel's hopes for the messianic age, when there will be peace between humankind and wild animals (e.g., Isa 11:6–8; 65:25). Jesus is the new Adam in his garden, at peace with animals that could tear him apart.

This passage speaks to us. We will face times of tempting and testing. Still, we should remember God's promise through Paul:

> No temptation has overtaken you that is not common to man. God is faithful, and he will not let you be tempted beyond your ability, but with the temptation he will also provide the way of escape, that you may be able to endure it (1 Cor 10:13).

Jesus was tempted in every way but was without sin (Heb 4:15). By the Spirit, who was in Jesus and is now in us, we have the power to overcome temptation, and we must seek to do so. We need to remember Jesus's words to Peter: "Watch and pray that you may not enter into temptation. The spirit indeed is willing, but the flesh is weak" (14:38). We must resist sin (9:42–50).

To achieve his purposes, as with Jesus here, God will sometimes allow us to be led into combat and suffering. The ensuing struggles will strengthen us and prepare us for more challenges ahead. It is only in the eschaton that we will know God's full blessing of being free from such suffering, testing, and temptation (Rev 21:1–4).

We are comforted that Jesus had two things to help him in his suffering. First, angels (*diakoneō*) served him (1:12–13). In Heb 1:14, angels are "ministering spirits sent to serve those who will inherit salvation." We see this here. Second, Jesus had the Spirit with him, strengthening and enabling him.

The forty-day experience parallels the wilderness experience of Israel, who spent forty years in the wilderness, where God was with them in fire and cloud and provided the manna (Exod 16:35). Sadly, that generation of Israel failed the test and did not inherit the land. Jesus, however, triumphs. Hence, Jesus is the new Israel, who succeeds where the old Israel fails. The experience also recalls the forty days Moses spent on Mount Sinai receiving the Ten Commandments (Exod 24:18). Jesus then is the new Moses bringing God's revelation. Later, on the Mount of Transfiguration, God would declare "listen to him": Jesus is now the authoritative mouthpiece of God to the world rather than Moses. Here we see Jesus fulfilling the history of Israel in his being the Servant Messiah (cf. Elijah in 1 Kgs 19:4–8). To know more about the temptation, we need to read Matthew and Luke's accounts that fill out the story (Matt 4:1–11; Luke 4:1–13).

The Kingdom of God and the Required Response (1:14–15)

We now begin looking at the section that runs from 1:14 to the confession of Christ's messiahship in 8:29. In this section, Jesus reveals himself as the Davidic Messiah King and Son of God to his disciples through the miracles and teaching. The whole section is about the failure of the disciples to grasp that Jesus is the Messiah until the confession at Caesarea Philippi. We also see the varying responses of others. The Jewish leaders are dismayed by Jesus, rejecting him and wanting him dead. The crowds come hungry for signs and wonders, but do not fully grasp who he is. For them, he is a prophet. Jesus's ministry is directed at bringing the kingdom of God, restoring the world in the direction of God's great dream and project. He is looking for those who will be drawn to him and fully grasp that he is the Messiah. He does not want that widely known, or people may revolt against Rome (which is repugnant to Jesus). We see the disciples struggling to understand him and Jesus patiently continuing to show them that he is the Messiah, even if he is deeply frustrated at times. We see his immense power and hear his message. What Mark the Evangelist wants is for us to recognize that Jesus is God's Son and believe in him.

We now turn to the first part of this section. This account is the launch of the first part of Mark that culminates in the revelation that he is the Messiah and Son of God. The first period of Jesus's ministry is in Galilee (1:14—3:6).

Mark 1:14-15 signals the beginning of Jesus's ministry to Israel and the world. John is put in prison by Herod, suggesting the end of the era of promise declared by Israel's prophets and the launch of the fulfillment of the hopes of Israel and the world. As such, Jesus begins, and "the time is fulfilled." We hear the central theme of the Gospel of Mark clearly stated: the kingdom of God. It is at hand, meaning that it is breaking in through the person of the King, the Messiah, the Son of God. We see the essence of Jesus's ministry: "preaching the good news of God." We see here what is required: repent and believe. Right now, we should pause and check our hearts: have we repented, turned our minds away from sin to God? Do we truly believe? If there are things in our life from which to turn away, now is the time. Specifically, there are three elements here:

The Time Is Fulfilled

The Greek *kairos* here has the sense of the appointed time. The OT has that sense of longing, as Israel, under oppression from foreign rule since the Babylonian exile in 587 BC, has longed for God to move in history to bring liberation. Mark is powerfully saying, "It is happening now!" The Greek word for "fulfilled" (*peplērōtai*) is placed first in the sentence, giving it prominence. It is in the perfect tense of *plēroō*, speaking of something established but ongoing. Hence, it is not yet complete and will not be until the gospel is preached to all nations (13:10). Still, the hopes and promises of God are being fulfilled in the coming of the Messiah. As many know, New Zealanders love rugby. In 1987, we won our first Rugby World Cup. Then, World Cups came and went, and New Zealand could not win. Then, in 2011, the New Zealand All Blacks again won. There was great rejoicing. What is happening in Jesus is way more significant and more important than sport. So, we should always rejoice (cf. Phil 4:4; 1 Thess 5:16).

The Kingdom of God Is Near

The proximity of the kingdom could indicate that it is about to happen. If so, this could mean it is about to come when Jesus rises from the dead and the Spirit is poured out at Pentecost. It would then have the same sense as 9:2, where Jesus speaks of the kingdom of God coming in power, which many scholars think refers to the resurrection. Here, it probably means that the reign of God has come close in the person of the King Jesus—the Messiah and Son of God. The King has entered human history in Galilee. He is announcing himself as King (see Luke 4:18–19; cf. Isa 61:1).

The OT expectation of the coming of the anointed one from the line of King David is now being fulfilled in Jesus (e.g., Isa 9:6–7). The hope of Daniel for one like a Son of Man is coming to pass (Dan 7:13). We call this an inaugurated eschatology whereby the reign or kingdom of God has begun in the presence of Jesus. This kingdom will extend as the good news of the kingdom is preached and it penetrates the world (4:26–29). It will grow to be the largest of all ideologies in the world (4:30–32). This kingdom will be consummated when Jesus returns, evil is destroyed, and Jesus is enthroned over an entire creation at peace with God. Then, the whole world will be God's kingdom, free from enemies. Still, the kingdom is now near in Jesus. We live two thousand years later, and the good news has spread all over the world, including New Zealand, Malaysia, and almost everywhere. So, the kingdom declared in 1:15 is well on its way to filling the world.

Repent and Believe the Good News

Mark's Jesus now declares the expected response to the message he preaches. He tells readers what will enable people (including them) to enter the kingdom. We are not automatically in the kingdom of God. We must hear its message and yield our allegiance to the King of the kingdom, Jesus Christ, the Son of God and Messiah. Mark's Jesus tells us how. There are two imperatives or commands here.

Repent

The first imperative is the verb *metanoeō* that goes with the noun *metanoia* (repentance). The Greek word compounds *meta* (change) with *noia* (mind).[11] As such, it means to change one's mind. In Jewish thought, this is more than a mental shift; this is a redirection of the course of one's whole life. We turn from all ideas of evil and sin to doing good as God our King directs us.

Believe the Good News

The second component is to believe (*pisteuō*). It has the meaning "believe to the extent of complete trust."[12] We can use a whole range of other ideas to fill this out: believe the content of the gospel, trust in our Triune God, yield to his reign, pledge allegiance, accept what God says. Essentially, it means believing in the God of the Bible and living by his commands. The content of belief is the good news or the gospel. We believe the whole story of God and our place in it as children of God who have been forgiven of our sins because Jesus died for us, rose again, and is our Lord. As Mark writes, his Gospel is the first written account of Jesus. Hence, it means believing in his Gospel, without picking and choosing the bits we prefer. The *euangelion* term was used in the Greco-Roman world of the good news of the Roman Empire. Well, Mark is declaring the good news of God's reign. God's kingdom is the only real empire that trumps all empires. As noted on 1:1, *euangelion* language is used by Isaiah as he declares the "good news" that Israel is coming out of exile in Babylon and returning home.[13] Now, God is delivering all humankind from its exile

---

11. BDAG, 640–41.
12. *DBL Greek* 4409, #2.
13. See Isa 40:9; 41:27; 52:7; 60:6; 61:1, see also Nah 1:15.

from an intimate relationship with God due to sin. They are being called into his kingdom through Jesus, the King of kings. As a proclamation of the good news, Mark's Gospel is lovely, for "how lovely are the feet of him who brings good news" (Isa 52:7). Hence, readers must join Jesus, Peter, and Mark in sharing the gospel, so that people have the opportunity to repent and believe its message. If we are not telling people the good news, they will never enter God's glorious reign.

The emphasis on proclamation illustrates that Jesus's ministry was one of preaching the good news, or what we call today, evangelism. It is no accident that the ministry of Jesus begins with preaching here and in the other Gospels. Preaching the good news then is the center of the ministry of the church as it fulfills the ministry of the body of Christ. The purpose of preaching is salvation, spiritual healing, and the restoration of the original relationship God intended for all people that was shattered at the fall. It is shalom or wholeness.

The Ministry of Jesus (1:16—8:26)

The Call of the Fishermen (1:16–20)

After his initial declaration of the coming of the kingdom, King Jesus begins to extend God's reign. A kingdom needs subjects, and these fishermen are the first of the renewed people of God on earth. Instantly, we see that Jesus's ministry is not of one man saving the world; his is a team ministry. With a team, he will redeem a world. He calls four fishermen to be his disciples. Notably, Jesus did not go to Jerusalem and summon to himself the hotshot Jewish priests who, like Paul, were rapidly advancing in Judaism (Gal 1:14). He did not call the high priest, the Herodians, the ruling council of seventy-one (the Sanhedrin), the Sadducees, the Pharisees, the leaders of the Qumran community, or Israel's best warriors. Instead, he called humble fishermen. He did not call gentiles either; he called Jews. His team began with the people of Israel. He did not initially call women, probably due to the patriarchal context.

Nevertheless, as time goes on, gentiles like Luke, who wrote the third Gospel, will be called (Col 4:11, 14). Later, women will travel with him.[14] Luke's Gospel will end with women charged to preach the good news of the resurrection to the men in Jesus's team.

The call is radical and absolute. "Come after me." Do not muck around. Leave everything. Leave your jobs. Leave your families—although we see

---

14. Mark 15:40–41; 47; 16:1–8; Luke 8:1–3.

that later, Peter's wife travels with him, showing that they did not leave their immediate kin (1 Cor 9:5, cf. 1 Tim 5:8). Peter and Andrew "immediately" (*euthys*) leave their nets. Jacob (James) and John "immediately" leave their father, Zebedee. We must remember here that first-century Israel was patriarchal; the family followed the religious devotion of the *paterfamilias* (oldest male). Amazingly, these men defy their culture and unhesitantly follow. In a culture that valued community, family, and honoring one's father and mother above almost anything, this is an astonishing response that would have brought shame both to themselves and their families.

However, the call to the kingdom is the priority; we are to "seek first the kingdom and his righteousness" (Matt 6:33). We are to be prepared to give up everything. Later, the rich young man will be called to do the same thing but will not have the courage (10:18–22). In contrast, the four former fishermen exemplify the ideal response to the kingdom. We see here the importance of the kingdom of God. It is more important than our own lives, our families, our work, and everything.

We see here an important theme in Mark: total and radical allegiance to the new King, which is the prototypical response of a person to the kingdom. This also indicates a transfer from the hegemony of Israel and the absolute rule of the Roman Empire to subjection to God's rule expressed in Jesus, Messiah and Son of God.

They are told that Jesus will make them fishers of people. We have seen that preaching is central to Jesus's ministry. Here, he promises them that he will train them to do the same. When they heard Jesus say this, they likely thought they would be killing the Romans and liberating the nation, because fishing was used as a metaphor for war.[15] On the contrary, Jesus is not talking about physical war; he is calling them to evangelism. They will no longer fish for sea creatures but will seek to win people to Christ. Evangelism then is like fishing; we go out, throw out lines and nets, bait people, and win them to the kingdom.

We see there that the ministry of the kingdom is not just evangelism but also training people, making them disciples. Put another way, evangelists are missionaries who share Christ, and, when people repent and believe, train them to be disciples. Such a process is how the church goes on and grows: we become disciples, we lead others to Christ, they become disciples, and they

---

15. See Kgs 19:28 (Isa 37:29); Job 41:1 (cf. 2 Chron 33:11); Jer 16:16 (cf. Ezek 47:10); Ezek 12:13 (cf. Ezek 17:20; 19:8); 29:4–5; 32:2–3; Hab 1:14–17 (cf. 1QpHab 5:12–16; 1QpHab 5:2). See too Qumran texts 1QHa 13:7–8; 4Q429 Frag. 1 1:2–3; and CD-A 5:15–18. See also other Jewish texts (1 En. 56:1; Jos. Asen. 21:21; Mart. Ascen. Isa. 3.5; Philo, *Mos.* 2:250; T. Dan. 2.4; and T. Ab. [A] 8.10).

do the same. We are to multiply ourselves. Evangelism and discipleship are the heart of the ministry of the church.

We can note here also that Jesus is shifting the disciples away from following the law and teachers of the law here. They are to follow him. That is Christianity 101. Notably, the first name of a disciple mentioned in the Gospel is Simon (Peter). He will also be last named (16:7). His naming in this way likely indicates he is the primary source of Mark's material. The double naming of Zebedee may indicate he was part of the Christian community as well. Jacob (James), John, and Peter will form Jesus's inner circle or executive circle (e.g., 5:37; 9:2; 14:33). Jesus calls us all to various leadership roles as he determines.

We also need to be careful not to over-literalize this and apply it in fullness to all Christians. All Christians are called to leave their past lives of sin behind them. However, not all are called to leave behind their vocations. Many are to remain "fishing for real fish." Nevertheless, where someone remains in a vocation in society beyond the church, he or she will also fish for people and bring God's transformation to that part of the world.

Jesus Teaches with Authority (1:21–28)

Jesus then enters Capernaum. The town is his home base in Mark's Gospel; perhaps he lived in the home of Peter or in a house he himself built. He visits the synagogue on the Sabbath, and he begins to teach (1:21). Not only does Jesus preach, but he teaches, although the difference is not that clear as we study the two words in the NT. In both ways, he articulates God's message to all people.

We see here the continuity between the institutions of Judaism and Christianity. Jesus would have attended synagogue all his life (in Nazareth). As an adult male, he would have had the freedom to teach in the synagogue. When he spoke, he would have read from the OT scrolls kept safely in the Torah or holy ark, the Aron Kodesh. They were handed to him, and he sat down to teach as Jewish teachers did. We see this pattern in Luke 4:16–21. The theme of his teaching was set in 1:14–15 as the kingdom of God. Luke 4:18–19 shows Jesus citing an adapted OT passage (Isa 61:1–2)[16] and seeing himself as the one foreseen in the passage. It is likely that his teaching here is similar.

The authority of his teaching causes people great astonishment. He does not teach like the scribes. The scribes (*grammateus*) had roles like copying documents; teaching the Torah and other traditions; working in

---

16. He leaves off reference to God's vengeance and inserts a portion of Isa 58:6.

the temple, royal courts, or administrations; advising political figures; doing ancient science; being people of wisdom, elders, judges; sitting on the Sanhedrin; or writing documents for important leaders. Some were Pharisees, Sadducees, priests, or Levites.[17] Such rabbinic teachers tended to cite other rabbis, justifying everything they said with the authority of others. We see this in the Mishnah, which records Pharisaic teaching after the fall of Jerusalem. For example, in *m. Git.* 1:1B, "Rabban Gamaliel says, 'Also: He who delivers [a writ of divorce] from Reqem or from Heger [must make a similar declaration].'" They did not teach with directness but always quoted others. Jesus taught directly with personal authority. Empowered by the Spirit (Luke 4:14), he taught straight from the heart of God. As noted above, he also placed himself in the center of God's purposes. We can also note that Mark emphasizes Jesus's teaching ministry.[18]

Jesus also casts out demons. In the synagogue, there was a man with an unclean spirit, another name for a demon or evil spirit. Ritual purity was essential to the Jews, and such a being made a person unclean and saw him or her marginalized. Westerners tend to write these off as ancient explanations of mental illness. However, for Mark, Jesus, and the other NT writers, they were real, and Jesus had the power to deal with them. Ancient Jews saw them as fallen angels, and this is likely what they were (cf. Rev 12:7). If they were angels, this may presuppose some prior heavenly conflict, which ancient Jews saw referenced in Gen 6:1–4, Isa 14:12–20, and Ezek 28:1–19. There is an apocalyptic aspect to Mark, a battle between good and evil, and Jesus represents goodness. Thes fallen angels are beings of corruption. They can inhabit and destroy a life, as in this case.

The demon speaks through the man, showing that demons have the power to take control of a mind and vocal cords and speak through them. Notably, after John the Baptist, we have the first being to recognize Jesus's divine identity in Mark. In recognizing him, demons show their awareness of his mission. However, they do not believe in him in the sense of 1:15. Instead, this demon believes in him but shudders (Jas 2:19). He recognizes Jesus's power to destroy him. He also calls Jesus "the Holy One of God." Earlier, from the lips of John the Baptist, Jesus is "the stronger one" (1:7). Here, he is purity, holiness, and otherness incarnate. His strength contrasts vividly with the demon, who is "unclean"; Jesus is "clean." He is from God, of God, and is God. He has God's power coursing through his body.

17. Peter Tan-Gatue, "Scribe."

18. There are frequent references to Jesus's teaching and address as teacher (cf. rabbi); see Mark 1:21, 22, 27; 2:13; 4:1-2, 38; 5:38; 6:2, 6, 34; 8:31; 9:17, 31, 38; 10:17, 20, 35; 11:18; 12:14, 19, 35, 38; 13:1; 14:1, 14, 49.

Jesus's complete authority over the demonic world is demonstrated a second time (the first being in his temptation). He rebukes him, commanding his silence. We see here the messianic secret for the first time; Jesus does not want to incite a rebellion if people get wind of who he is.

There are three classifications of such commands for silence. First, Jesus commands silence from demons (1:26; 3:11; 5:6; 9:20). Notably, Jesus does not silence demons where his identity is not an issue (cf. 5:1–20; 7:24–30; 9:14–29). Second, Jesus commands silences from his disciples where his identity is concerned (8:30; 9:9). In 9:9, Jesus limits them speaking of the transfiguration until after his death and resurrection. This silencing indicates that his full identity—messiahship—will be fully only grasped after his death and resurrection. Third, Jesus commands silence from others, but these commands are broken (1:40–45; 5:21–43; 7:31–37). Here, the demons are silent, but not those who attend worship at the synagogue (see below).

Jesus commands the demon to leave, again showing his complete authority. The demon convulses the man and then leaves with a loud cry. We see the power of the demon but the superior power of Jesus. The kingdom is breaking in, and evil is being driven back. This inbreaking will continue as the church spreads throughout the world.

The crowds are stunned. They are amazed at his ministry. They debate among themselves what this is. They are blown away by his new authoritative teaching. Then the word of what happens begins to spread. Jesus's fame expands through Galilee. Despite Jesus wanting to limit people's awareness of his potential, which would lead perhaps to revolution, people cannot stop talking about Jesus. This spontaneous spread of the news about Jesus is evangelism as it should and could be if we allow the excitement of being Jesus's people and of the wonders of the kingdom to grip our hearts. Jesus's fame would spread even faster. Ultimately, it will spread to all nations (13:10). Our job is to keep extending it, gossiping the gospel to the world.

The healings and deliverances or exorcisms of Jesus give insight into the kingdom of God; they point to the future kingdom as a place free of disease, suffering, and evil in any form. These healings and deliverances anticipate the fullness of the kingdom to come, when there will no shred of uncleanness and evil in the restored world. The devil and his angels will be destroyed (Rev 20:10). All evil will be shut out of the city; "nothing unclean will ever enter it, nor anyone who does what is detestable or false (Rev 21:27; cf. 21:4, 8). This hope is the dream of the new heavens and earth found in the OT, and it is coming to pass in Galilee of all places (cf. Isa 65—66).

Healings in Capernaum (1:29–34)

Jesus goes to the home of Simon and Andrew and is told that Peter's mother-in-law has a fever. He takes her by the hand and raises her from her sickbed, healed. It is unclear whether the healing is due to Jesus's power transmitted by touch, or whether he healed her with a prior word or even silently, then raised her. What stands out is that there is no magical incantation or spell; he heals with absolute power and authority. Jesus is now not only the herald of the kingdom (1:14–15), teacher of the Jews, and deliverer from demons (1:21–28), but he is a healer sent from God. His power is being unleashed on planet Earth, bringing God's restoration.

After the woman's healing, she waits upon the team of Jesus, Peter, Andrew, Jacob (James), and John. Her doing so fits with the cultural expectations of a woman in the home returning to her defined role as a mother and homemaker in a patriarchal society. We can see that the miracles of Jesus not only bring physical restoration, but they bring wholeness in terms of vocation and involvement in the community of God's people. Jesus's healings are more than merely the restoration of an individual. They restore communities as transformed individuals are welcomed into wider society. The contribute to the transformation of the world.

This healing says nothing about women having to be limited to housekeeping for all of eternity. What is important is that the woman is healed and able to go back to serving others, the heart of Christian discipleship. She is thus an exemplary disciple who follows after the pattern of the Son of Man, who came not to be served but to serve others (10:45). Greatness comes through service, and she uses her freedom to demonstrate eminence (9:35; 10:43).

Incidentally, this incident shows that Peter was married and makes the Roman Catholic concern for celibate singleness for popes and priests exceedingly strange, especially as they see Peter as the first pope. Another small issue raised here is Peter's supposed origin in Bethsaida (cf. John 1:44). This seeming contradiction can be resolved as he may have moved to Capernaum since his marriage, or perhaps he had more than one home as a fisherman.[19]

What happens in vv. 32–34 implies that again, as after the synagogue exorcism, his fame spread. That evening, many people from the town brought the sick and demon-possessed to Jesus for healing and exorcism, no doubt attracted by Jesus's power to heal. This passage is a typical healing summary in which Mark summarizes the ministry of Jesus; who knows how many people were healed and set free that day? The summary reinforces that one of the critical reasons for Jesus's attraction was his healing power. Such an appeal is

---

19. Guelich, *Mark 1—8:26*, 62.

unsurprising in an age where there was no public medical service as we have today. While there was some level of medical help available for the wealthy, the vast majority of people relied on natural healing, magic, folk remedies, and prayer. Here, we see the poor people of Capernaum coming in the hope of healing. In a world that was even harsher than the most impoverished third-world areas of our times, life expectancy was in the late thirties. Hence, news of a healer would be huge.

In most healing encounters in the Gospels, Jesus is approached for healing; it is unusual for Jesus to initiate healing or go looking for the sick. "Brought" here is in the imperfect tense, indicating a long continuous period of drawing people. The mention of "all" and the "whole town" are hyperbolic, but indicate that a good number came for help. It was not just the sick who come, but those troubled by demons. We can also note that Jesus healed "many" but not specifically "all" who came, indicating perhaps that some were not healed. Alternatively, it may be taken that "all" simply indicates the "many" who were healed. These people represent not only the sick and demonized but the poor, those who were troubled by being marginalized in Israel's society. Hence Jesus's ministry is a ministry not only of healing but one of caring for the poor. Later, Mark will reinforce Jesus's passion for the poor (10:21; 12:42; 14:7), an aspect of his ministry that Luke picks up more explicitly.

Here again, Jesus demands that the demons conceal his identity "because they knew him," i.e., they recognized who he was. Again, the forces of evil recognize Jesus. This silencing is the second instance of the "messianic secret," with Jesus concealing his identity.

We see here the importance of healing as an aspect of Christian ministry. As we encounter non-believers through our lives, when they are in need, we should offer prayer. God works as we lay hands on and pray for those in need. We should also have prayer available in every church setting. Sometimes people are not healed or delivered of demons when we pray for them; as Christians, we should also care for them through health services. Wherever we are, we bring God's healing and deliverance through prayer and good works.

Jesus Prays (1:35)

It is implied in v. 36 that this occurs when Jesus is alone, as Simon and others go hunting for him. Jesus goes in the very early hours of the morning, showing his commitment to prayer. The verb is imperfect, speaking of a period of prayer. He goes in the dark into the natural world to be alone, and he prays.

We see this happen again in 6:46 as he goes up a mountain to pray alone, after which he walks on water to the disciples. The power of prayer is emphasized in 9:29, where the disciples could not deliver a demon, and Jesus had to do so. It is reemphasized in 11:24, where Jesus assures his disciples that if they have sufficient faith, whatever they ask for is granted. They are told, too, to ensure that they forgive others as they come to prayer, to be assured of God's forgiveness (11:25). However, while they are to pray, they are not to do so with pretentious long prayers to impress others (12:40). Just in case we start to think that we can have anything we ever want through prayer, Jesus himself prays in the garden of Gethsemane, only for God to refuse his request for deliverance from the cross (14:32–38). Sometimes God has other plans. Nevertheless, disciples are to be prayerful for God's strength to ensure that they can withstand temptation (14:38). We see here the importance of prayer, something Luke will emphasize even more in his Gospel and Acts.

Jesus's Mission of Preaching (1:36–39)

Simon and others are surprised to find that Jesus is gone, and they go hunting for or pursuing him. When they find him, Simon tells Jesus that everyone is searching for him. After the earlier large healing meeting, they probably wanted him to continue to minister among them. Effectively, they wanted him to become their pastor. Jesus, however, needs to take the gospel of the kingdom and herald its arrival to the whole nation, beginning in Galilee. He refuses to remain in one place, but is an itinerant, moving on from place to place, preaching the good news of the kingdom and calling people to repent and believe the good news. Thus, Jesus is progressively moving out to restore all of God's people and the world, beginning in Israel. He also casts out demons again, showing that preaching and deliverance are closely aligned in the ministry of Jesus. We see here the essence of the mission of the kingdom of God: we are to take the gospel to the world and bring God's deliverance to those in bondage to Satan. The salvation of the world began with Jesus in Galilee and Judea. It continued with the first Christians. As God's church today, we too must not be isolated from the world. We must continue to take this gospel to all nations (cf. 13:10).

Jesus Heals a Man with Leprosy (1:40–45)

Here we have a second healing encounter after the healings at Peter's house. This time, Jesus heals a man with leprosy. Leprosy in the Scriptures is not necessarily the same as today's Hansen's disease but referred to a range of skin conditions. Ancients were very concerned about contagious diseases, so they had strict rules concerning how to treat people who may have been contagious (see Lev 13—14). This man was no doubt marginalized from mainstream society and desperate for healing.

He approaches Jesus and begs him on his knees to heal him. This speaks of his desperation and respect for Jesus and his capabilities (1:40). So then, this encounter is not a casual moment in which Jesus goes around healing every sick person; he responds to this particular man's desire for healing. The man knows about Jesus's power to heal if he so desires; hence his statement "if you are willing, you can make me clean." His words show his faith. We can bring our sicknesses to God in such a way, and it is up to God to decide what is best for us. What God decides is always best!

His appeal is not for healing but cleansing, as leprosy was seen as uncleanness (Lev 13—14).[20] His desire is for healing and then being seen as clean by the wider community, enabling his restoration to Israel's society. With lepers' marginalization, perceived uncleanness, and contagiousness, the healing is not merely physical; it is social. We should note too that those who were sick were also seen as sinners. Their sickness was understood to be a result of someone's individual and personal sin.[21]

Jesus restores him at every level here. One of the outstanding features of Jesus's ministry is now found: his compassion. The Greek does not read "filled with compassion" but only "with compassion." However, the word is placed first after *kai* (and) and so it has prominence. Consequently, "filled with compassion"[22] is the correct translation. The word *splanchnizomai* is not merely a mouthful; it is a beautiful word. It means the viscera, the gut. When used figuratively as here, *splanchnizomai* has the sense of Jesus being moved in the depths of his being, in his inner parts, for this man. Such heartfelt compassion is the love of God in Christ for those in need. He sees the crowds of disadvantaged people and loves them with deep compassion.[23] Such affection describes how Jesus views the sick and demonized. Wonderfully, this is how

---

20. Guelich, *Mark 1—8:26*, 73, notes that the term "leper" comes from *lepein*, meaning "to scale or peel off." Lepers were considered ceremonially unclean (Lev 13—14), were prevented from entering Jerusalem, and were marginalized because they were seen as contagious. Leprosy was interpreted often as divine punishment for sin, one of the worst evils to afflict a person, and was considered a living death. To be healed was equivalent to being resurrected from death (see 2 Kgs 5:7; Str-B 4:745).

21. Jesus challenges this theology in 2:1–12 and in other places, including the healing of the blind man in John 9 and Luke 13:1–5.

22. Some manuscripts prefer "being angered," and so Guelich, *Mark 1—8:26*, 73, takes it this way. However, Metzger, *Textual Commentary*, 65, gives good reasons to take it as "compassion."

23. See Mark 6:34; 8:2; see also Matt 9:36; 14:14; 15:32; Luke 7:13.

he sees us, whatever our condition. The term is also applied to the Samaritan, who cares for the man injured by the road (Luke 10:33).

Similarly, the father shows such compassion for the lost son (Luke 15:20). We should show such compassion to unbelievers, sinners, and those in need. This benevolence should move us to serve others.

Jesus then touches him. His touching a leper is a remarkable act from a holy man in a Jewish context. A religious leader would avoid touching the man due to potential contamination. If a Jew touched something unclean, he or she became unclean. Jesus, however, has no such fear, as he knows that his power to cleanse is more potent than any uncleanness in the man. Hence, Christians need not be terrified of being contaminated when among sinners. The power that is in us is greater than that which is in the world (1 John 4:4). We should be unafraid to act compassionately, to reach out to help those who are sick and the seemingly "untouchable."

We see Jesus's immense healing power as he heals with a word and touch so that leprosy instantly leaves the man. This healing potency is a release of the same power by which God spoke creation into being. It is the power of God to heal as he wills.

Then Jesus commands him very sharply not to tell anyone. Instead, he is to go and show the priest he is healed and cleansed as per Jewish legal requirements. This direction takes us into the elaborate requirements for those healed of a leprous condition according to Lev 14.[24] Jesus commanding this man to make the necessary offerings shows that Jesus did not come to abrogate the law but fulfill it. Before his death resolved the problem of human sin, where there could be the response of repentance and faith, it was still required that God's people follow Levitical law. However, once

---

24. In this passage, a priest decides whether the leprous problem is gone, and he is to take two live clean birds, cedarwood, scarlet yarn, and hyssop. He then kills one of the birds in an earthenware vessel over fresh water; takes the living bird, cedarwood, scarlet yarn, and hyssop; and dips them with the living bird in the blood of the dead bird. Then the liquid is sprinkled seven times on the cleansed person. The living bird is then released. The healed person then washes his or her clothes, shaves his or her hair, and bathes in water. The healed person can come into the camp but remains outside the tent for seven days. Then the person shaves off all bodily hair, washes his or her clothes, bathes in water, and then is clean. Then, on the eighth day, the healed person takes two unblemished male lambs, one unblemished year-old lamb, and a grain offering with oil. Then, he or she is stood before the door of the tabernacle, and the priest offers one of the lambs as a guilt and wave offering. Blood from the guilt offering is put on the right ear lobe, right thumb, and right big toe. The priest then puts oil on his own left hand and sprinkles it seven times. What remains is put on the right ear lobe, right thumb, right big toe, and on the healed person's head. The priest then offers the sin offering for atonement for the cleansed person, then a burnt offering, and a grain offering. If the leprous person is poor, other provisions are made.

Jesus died for our sins, this was no longer required. Nonetheless, while he ministered, Jesus fulfilled the law. In so doing, he became an unblemished sacrifice who deals with our sins and those of the whole world.

Despite the man being commanded to go to the priest, instead, he goes out and preaches the word. He simply could not stop himself telling the world, despite being told not to. In actual fact, his healing filled him with a passionate desire to share the message of his healing. We see in his desire to share his testimony how evangelism works best as the gospel spills out of us, as we realize what God has done for us. At one level, this man disobeys Jesus, and this is not great. Nevertheless, at another level, he is a role model of the Christian who is so overwhelmed by the compassionate healing power of God that he cannot help himself. He disobeys the law but does something more significant: he tells others about Jesus!

The consequence is that Jesus cannot enter towns and villages. Instead, he ministers in the wilderness areas around the towns. Anyone who has traveled through Israel and Palestine knows that there are vast swaths of such land. People came to him from every direction, yearning for deliverance and healing.

Jesus Forgives and Heals a Paralytic (2:1–12)

Jesus returns to Capernaum.[25] "After some days" is typically vague Markan chronology. The last time Jesus was there, he had exorcised a demon from the man in the synagogue, healed Peter's mother-in-law, healed and delivered many others who had been brought to him, and evaded them when they wanted him to remain and be their healer and teacher (1:21–34). Since then, he had taught and done miracles throughout Galilee, including healing the leprous man. It is no surprise that a considerable crowd gathered, confirming that his healing ministry was a massive drawing card.

He speaks (*laleō*) the word (*logos*). The verb is the usual term for speaking, but here has the sense of preach. The content was likely the kingdom (1:14–15). His teaching may have included some of the ethical teachings recorded in the Sermon on the Mount and Plain (Matt 5—7; Luke 6:20–49). He may also have preached some of the parables found in Mark 4. Whatever he said, preaching is again shown to be central to his ministry.

---

25. Although some people see here an example of a Markan sandwich, this seems unlikely.

    A¹   Healing of paralytic, part 1 (2:1–5a)
    B   *Jesus's authority to forgive sin (2:5b–10a)*
    A²   Healing of paralytic, part 2 (2:10b–12)

There is a huge crowd present (*ochlos*). Such crowds are a characteristic feature of Mark's Gospel, with the term used thirty-eight times, speaking of Jesus's stunning attraction. The crowds are being challenged to consider who Jesus is and what his presence means. Crowds of people in the future will read Mark's Gospel and are equally challenged to believe.

While he is speaking, four men bring a paralyzed man. They are desperate, as seen by their determination to get in. They climb up onto the roof, likely by a ladder, carrying the man on his bed or pallet. The roof was likely made of mud or other organic materials.[26] No doubt, this interrupted Jesus's message. However, some interruptions are welcome! They lowered the man down. Jesus seeing their faith was probably due to their determination to reach him for healing (cf. 5:25–34).

Rather than healing the man, as is usual, surprisingly, Jesus states his forgiveness.[27] Why Jesus did this is a little unclear. It no doubt has something to do with the view that was common in those days that if someone was sick, this was God's punishment for their sins. He may also have wanted to take the opportunity to declare his power and authority to forgive sins.

In v. 6, we meet those characters referenced in 1:22 as teachers who lack authority compared to Jesus. As noted, they had a range of roles within Israel's politics and religion (which were intertwined). Some were members of the Pharisees, Sadducees, priests, or Levites (see further 1:22). While they were mentioned in 1:22, here they come to challenge Jesus. Perhaps they had heard of the synagogue members responding so positively to Jesus's teaching as compared to theirs.

The clash of Jesus and the scribes is the first controversy narrative in Mark. Hearing him pronounce forgiveness, the scribes question Jesus in their hearts, critiquing him silently. They consider him a blasphemer because, for a zealous Jew, only God can forgive sins (e.g., Exod 34:6–7; Isa 43:25; 44:22). For these observers, Jesus is crossing the line from human authority to that of God. For them, this is heinous. They do not realize that while Jesus is fully man, yet for Mark, he is also fully God. Jesus pronounces forgiveness at other points in his ministry (Luke 7:48).

In v. 8, we see Jesus's prescience, his capacity to see into the hearts of people. Mark is full of moments of his prophetic insight.[28] His prophetic

---

26. Ebeling, "Roof," writes: "Roofs were built upon lintels and beams made of wood or stone; wooden poles were placed across these supports and then covered with mud and other organic materials."

27. Some see this as a divine passive whereby Jesus merely assures him that he is forgiven by God. The reaction of the authorities suggests that Jesus himself took the prerogative to heal him.

28. See Mark 2:8; 5:39; 8:31; 9:1, 31; 10:33–34, 39–40; 11:2–3, 14; 12:8, 43–44;

insight is the second indicator of Jesus's divinity in the passage. We see this most clearly in John 2:24, where John writes: "He knew all people." Full of courage, he challenges their questioning.

He then gives them a riddle, asking if it is easier to pronounce the forgiveness of the paralyzed man or his healing. This puzzle is the first parable in Mark. The Greek *parabolē* means "throwing alongside" and so has the sense of comparison. Parables then are riddles, sayings, and longer stories that compare one thing with another. Jesus is famous for using them to compare the kingdom and its life to everyday examples. He draws on his culture, using simple and familiar ideas to convey aspects of God's work. Parables can be longer complex stories like the parable of the sower (4:1–20) or the parable of the tenants (12:1–11). They can also be shorter, as in this case, where he uses a riddle. One of the characteristics of parables is their power to call us to imagine and challenge us to respond. They demonstrate the power of stories in preaching. We should use stories and sayings as we preach, following Jesus's example.

It is debated what answer Jesus has in mind. Some would say forgiveness is harder, as only God can forgive. Hence, to heal proves he can forgive.[29] Others contend the healing is harder because it demands evidence at that moment, whereas forgiveness cannot be proven until we face God.[30] However, Jesus's question in context is more creative than some either/or answer. As noted above, many in the ancient Jewish context considered that sickness was evidence of personal sinfulness. Hence, if God had forgiven him, he would be healed. Conversely, if he were healed, it would prove God's forgiveness.

Jesus does not wait for an answer. He heals the man to demonstrate that he has authority on earth to forgive sins. His healing proves he is forgiven. Jesus thus challenges the direct link between sickness and personal sin. All sickness is a result of the fall of humankind, but personal sickness is not necessarily due to personal sin. It could be; but more often than not, it is not. Other passages make a similar point, including Luke 13:1–5 and John 9:1–5. By healing the man, Jesus demonstrates his authority.

We see Jesus introduce a new name for himself, the Son of Man. This title is Jesus's favorite way of describing himself. Unlike "Messiah," which was a dangerous political term, the term was ambiguous for hearers familiar with Israel's Scriptures. It could mean he is a human, a son of Adam (e.g.,

---

13:2–37; 14:18–21, 26–31, 36.

29. France, *Gospel of Mark*, 127. He sees this as an "easier to greater" or a fortiori argument. See also Brooks, *Mark*, 259.

30. Guelich, *Mark 1—8:26*, 88.

Num 23:19; Job 16:21; Ps 8:4). It could indicate he is a prophet; the descriptor is used this way many times of Ezekiel (e.g., Ezek 2:6, 8; 3:25, see also Dan 8:17). Finally, it could be the transcendent figure of Dan 7:13 to whom has been given all authority over the world. It is also found across 1 En. 37—71 of an agent of God who brings redemption and judgment.

Without a doubt, here Jesus is invoking Daniel's Son of Man (and perhaps 1 En.). Interestingly, in Ps 80:17, the Son of Man is also the Messiah, and this connection could also be being made here. In 1 En 37—71, he is the Elect One, the Son of Man, and the Messiah all wrapped up in one. Jesus assumes the title because it fits with the messianic secret; people would not easily decode it. However, the disciples and we, as later readers, can see what Jesus has in mind. For whatever reason Jesus employs Son of Man, he has the authority on earth to forgive sins. Later on, he will die and provide the means for bringing the forgiveness of sins—his death for our sins.

In v. 11, Jesus demonstrates he is indeed the Son of Man of Daniel and heals the man, proving his forgiveness for those who understand sickness as being a consequence of personal sin. The crowds are again amazed as he takes up his bed or pallet and leaves. They cry out, "We never saw anything like this!" We see the central theme of Mark: Who is Jesus? Who can do all this stuff? The answer: Jesus, God's Son, the Messiah, and the source of our forgiveness. As we will now see, this clash with the scribes is the first of a series of controversy encounters that will culminate in the Jewish leaders seeking to destroy Jesus (3:6).

Jesus Calls Levi and Dines with Sinners (2:13–17)

Here we have a second call narrative in Mark after the call of the fishermen (1:16–20). We also have a second controversy moment, this time not over blasphemy but eating protocols. Jesus is beside the Sea of Galilee ("the sea"), and he teaches the whole crowd, indicating those who were at the previous healing and forgiveness in Capernaum. This context could be the setting for the Sermon on the Mount in Matt 5—7. Here, despite the brevity of the description, we again the importance of teaching in Jesus's mission.

As Jesus is walking along the shore, just as he had spotted the fishermen and called them, he sees Levi collecting taxes at his tax booth. Such people (also called publicans)[31] were usually locals contracted by the Roman government to collect tolls and taxes; we might call them the IRD (Internal Revenue Department) in New Zealand. On the main roadways, they took

---

31. From the Latin *publicanus*, referring to public contractors who collected taxes.

taxes off travelers carrying goods and items for trade. Guelich suggests Levi was one who took "indirect taxes" such as sales taxes, customs taxes, transport taxes, and tolls, rather than "direct taxes" such as poll and land taxes.[32] Some, like Zacchaeus, had authority over areas and teams and so were called "chief" tax collectors (Luke 19:2–10). They made their money by demanding additional payments above the Roman expectation. They were hated not only as traitors to the nation but as greedy and corrupt thieves.[33]

Levi is a son of Alphaeus, as is the other Jacob (James, 3:18),[34] whom many scholars accept to be Matthew. This connection is based on Matt 10:3, where he is named as Matthew the "toll collector" (see also Matt 9:9). Matthew then is perhaps his renewed name in Christ, similar to Cephas being renamed Peter. The father could be the same Alphaeus who is the father of Jacob (James) or a different person. Another set of brothers amongst the disciples would be unsurprising in light of Peter and Andrew, Jacob (James) and John. We cannot know for sure.

Levi is sitting taking taxes. Jesus calls him, "Follow me."[35] To follow Jesus is a summons to be a disciple. Jesus calling him is very interesting. On the one hand, Jesus is summoning Levi away from his hated profession, and this could be seen as liberating him from Roman oppression.

On the other hand, summoning such a person as Levi to join him could potentially cause Jesus to be criticized by zealous Jews who despised the tax collectors and wanted Roman oppression to end. Levi's response is an ideal of discipleship. There is no mention of him taking the money on the table; he simply gets up and follows Jesus.

Then, in v. 15, Jesus is reclining at Levi's home, and many other tax collectors and sinners are with them at the table. We are told by Mark that many such people followed Jesus. Here we see Jesus, the friend of sinners. Just as it was controversial for a holy Jew to touch a leper, Jesus would be criticized for allowing himself to eat with the unclean, something strictly forbidden. Despite this, Jesus is unconcerned about contamination; instead, he is concerned that he sit with people who respond to the kingdom of God. Like the formerly paralyzed man in the previous passage, they have had their sins forgiven and are not unclean. Jesus's friends are not the elite, but any sinful people who want to hang out with him.

---

32. Guelich, *Mark 1—8:26*, 100.
33. See further Miller, "Tax Collector."
34. See also Matt 10:3; Luke 6:15; Acts 1:13.
35. The Greek *akalouthei moi* is different from *deute opisō mou* in 1:17, but the intent is the same.

Again, there are scribes present. These may be the same people we met in the previous passage, people who were critical of Jesus's forgiving the man. Now, they are described as scribes of the Pharisees, indicating that they are from that group (something mentioned above). The Pharisees were significant Jewish leaders who were very concerned about obeying Jewish law. They believed in the OT Scriptures and had created a whole range of oral laws to ensure that they were kept. They were very concerned about ritual purity, including not eating with sinners. They were also passionate about fasting and keeping the Sabbath, so later they clash with Jesus over these things (2:18–20; 2:20—3:6; 7:1–23).

This time they do not question inwardly but openly challenge Jesus's disciples, asking them why Jesus eats with such people. It is, however, Jesus who responds with a saying that captures the heart of his mission: those who are healthy or strong do not need a doctor; Jesus has come to call sinners, not the righteous. There is an irony here, of course. For Jesus, all are sinners, so he is talking about those who think they are healthy, i.e., the self-righteous. Jesus is looking for those who recognize their need for forgiveness. Like a doctor who heals the sick, he heals them of their sin and its consequences. Jesus, then, can be likened to a great physician.

We see another of the great features of Jesus's mission: his friendship with sinners. We must take note of this and ensure that we are not a church that separates itself from the world into holy huddles. While we should gather together for worship, edification, and fellowship, we must go into the world and be the friends of the sinners in our world. Some of the sinners will be Levi-type people who turn from their sin and become believers. I was one of those people many years ago. Now I follow Jesus. Jesus is looking for sinners who will respond and find healing. We are to be their friends.

Questions

- In what way does 1:1 explain the purposes and contents of Mark?
- What is the role of John the Baptist?
- What is the center of Jesus's message, and what should our response be?
- What is the kingdom of God?
- Recall your own conversion experience, baptism, experience of the Spirit, and testing by Satan: how does reading of Jesus's beginnings help us make sense of our call and life?

- Why does Jesus call people like fishermen and tax collectors?
- Why did Jesus teach with such authority?
- Does Jesus heal today?
- Consider Jesus's withdrawing to pray: what does that tell us about the importance of prayer?
- What does Mark 1:36–39 tell us about our priorities as the church?
- What is the role of faith in healing?
- Which is harder?—"Your sins are forgiven" or to heal someone?
- What does Jesus's friendship with tax collectors and sinners tell us about mission?
- What else stands out for you in this chapter?
- What stands out to you as encouragement for you to continue to live out your faith?

Lesson Three: More Controversy, Power Encounters, and Parables (2:18—4:34)

Fasting (2:18–20)

WE NOW HAVE A third controversy or conflict narrative. This time, Jesus is challenged concerning why his disciples do not fast (unlike the disciples of John the Baptist and the Pharisees) (2:18). We see here that the Pharisees had disciples, as did John the Baptist. The idea of having disciples then is not a Christian innovation, but part of the Jewish tradition. One can trace it back to Moses and Joshua or Elijah and Elisha, as well as to some of the other OT prophets. We can see such relationships in the Greek world among philosophers, religious leaders, and in the various mystery cults and other religions. Jesus also calls disciples to him. However, usually in Israel, a disciple approached a teacher, asking to be a disciple and following that person and his principles. In rabbinic tradition, a "learner" or "student" (*tlmyd*) joined a rabbi, seeing him as "my great one," "teacher," or "master." We see Jesus approached on occasion, such as a scribe who approached Jesus wanting to be his disciple (Matt 8:19).[1] In such instances, Jesus challenged these people to follow him without hesitation, showing that he expected complete obedience and devotion. Otherwise, Jesus took the initiative as with the fishermen, Levi, and, we can presume, the other disciples.

Significantly, both John's disciples and those of the Pharisees were at this time fasting. Fasting was important in Judaism at times of mourning (1 Sam 31:3; 2 Sam 1:12) or repentance (Matt 6:16), with prayer as an act of submission to God. The three principal fasts were the Day of Atonement, the New Year, and a national fast for previous calamities. Some Pharisees fasted twice a week.[2] It could be that this occurred on one of these occa-

---

1. See also Luke 9:57, 61, and the rich young ruler in Mark 10:17–22.
2. Guelich, *Mark 1—8:26*, 109.

sions, such as the Day of Atonement. If this is so, then it would be very unusual to see disciples of a holy leader who were not participating in a fast as were the others.

Whatever the situation, it is Jesus who answers the query from the disciples of the other religious leaders. He tells them a short parable. The sons of the bridal chamber represent the friends of the bridegroom, whom we might see as the best man and others on the groom's side of a bridal party. Jesus asks whether they would fast while they are celebrating the wedding with the bridegroom. The answer is clearly no![3] They will enjoy the party. Who fasts during the wedding feast of a friend? As long a time as they have the bridegroom with them, they are not able to fast. However, Jesus tells them that the day will come when the bridegroom is taken away, and then they will fast. The bridegroom being removed is the first prediction of Jesus's future death. He is the bridegroom, and the church is the bride of Christ. When he is taken away by death, he will be mourned, and in despair, his disciples will fast. We see here one of the foundations of the idea of the church as the bride of Christ and Jesus as our bridegroom (cf. Rev 18:23; 21:2, see also Eph 5:22–33).

This command could mislead Christians to reject the practice of fasting. The parable of the Pharisee and the tax collector could also support this (Luke 18:12). However, such a conclusion is not necessary. Jesus fasted during his temptation (Matt 4:2). He gave instructions on fasting without making a public show (Matt 6:16–18). Anna in Luke 2:37 fasts night and day at the temple. Paul, Barnabas, and other Antiochian Christians fast, then God speaks, sending Paul and Barnabas into mission (Acts 13:2–3). Christians appointed elders with prayer and fasting (Acts 14:23). As such, fasting remains a crucial Christian practice that, along with prayer, brings us closer to God. We must not make a show of such practices, for such things do not make us superior Christians, even if they do aid our spiritual lives.

The Parables of the Wineskin and Cloth (2:21–22)

There is no conjunction linking this to the previous pericope; hence, this could be a new section. Alternatively, it could continue from the previous. Either way, Mark has placed this parable here in a section on Jesus's clashing with Judaism, indicating that it is to be interpreted with his conflict with Judaism in mind. Both speak of the new and the old. The new is

---

3. This is implied by the Greek question that begins with *mē*, indicating that it expects the answer no. See Louw and Nida, *Greek-English Lexicon*, 1:666 (69.15).

the kingdom of God breaking in through Jesus, the Messiah and God's Son. The old is Judaism into which the kingdom is coming. There are two parables here essentially making the same point: the new work of God will not be received into Judaism without collateral damage. Both parables are from the world of everyday life.

The first is the parable of the new and old cloth (2:21). This story comes from the world of sewing, where mainly women made clothes and other items for life.[4] The parable of the camel through a needle's eye (10:25) also comes from this kind of background. Here, Jesus draws on his knowledge of sewing cloth, stating that no one would stitch new cloth onto old, or the new would shrink, and the new cloth would come away. The point Jesus is making is clear: the incoming kingdom and Judaism, as it was at the time, are incompatible. In context, the Jewish leaders are clashing with Jesus, and this is to be expected.

The second parable of the wineskins comes from the world of winemaking. Wine was a critical agricultural product, alongside grain and oil.[5] It was also helpful in a world where water was sometimes undrinkable. Israel and Palestine are ideal environments for producing grapes and wine. Isaiah's Song of the Vineyard shows that Jesus was not the first to use a parable based on wine (Isa 5:1–7). Grapes were trodden, pressed, and fermented. Wine in the OT is linked to joyfulness[6] and relief for one's suffering,[7] although drunkenness was frowned upon.[8] The presence of wine also signified God's blessing.[9]

Wine features in Jesus's ministry, especially his turning water into wine (John 2:1–11), the Last and Lord's Supper (14:23–24),[10] and the eschatological feast (14:25).[11] The wineskin was a "vessel made of animal skins and used

---

4. Irvin, "Sew," notes that during the early Bronze Age (2000–1500 BC), the needle was developed. We are uncertain when sewing to make garments became general practice. Representations on the Nineveh gate may show Judeans wearing sewn garments (end of seventh century BC). There are other texts that indicate the sewing of cloth (Ezek 13:18; Job 14:17; 16:15). In Eccl 3:7, there is a time to tear and sew. John 19:23 speaks of Jesus's seamless robe which would have taken over four hundred hours to produce.

5. I am indebted in this paragraph to Kelly, "Wine."

6. See Judg 9:13; Isa 24:11; Zech 10:7; Ps 104:15; Eccl 9:7; 10:19.

7. Prov 31:6; Matt 27:34, 48; Mark 15:23, 36; Luke 10:34; 23:36; John 19:29; 1 Tim 5:23.

8. Prov 20:1; 23:21; Gal 5:21; Eph 5:18; 1 Pet 4:3.

9. See Gen 27:28; Deut 7:13; 11:14; 32:14; 33:28; Hos 2:8; Hag 2:19; Ps 104:14–15; Prov 3:9–10; Eccl 9:7–9.

10. See also Matt 26:27–28; Luke 22:20; 1 Cor 11:25.

11. See also Matt 26:29; Luke 22:20, 28–30; 1 Cor 11:26.

for holding wine, strong drink, water, and other liquids (e.g., Josh 9:4–13; Job 38:37; Ps 119:83; Matt 9:17)."[12] Jesus's point is again clear: the kingdom of God and Jesus represent new wine. Judaism is now old, outdated, and weak. The incoming kingdom and King will not be able to be contained in Judaism. They will break through into the wider world and shatter Judaism and its customs. While Judaism has gone on since Jesus, it was forever changed; and from a Christian point of view, God's work in the world continues in the kingdom of God and not Judaism-aside-from-Jesus.

Overall then, the two parables illustrate what is happening as Jesus ministers. He is being challenged by Israel's leaders. Their conflict will intensify in the next passages and culminate in them conspiring to have Jesus killed. Put simply, the old structures of Judaism cannot contain the new movement of God in the kingdom. Unless there is a shift toward the freedom of the kingdom, there will be a rupture in the old religious patterns of Israel.

Some consider that the water to wine miracle has a double meaning (John 2:1–12). Not only does Jesus demonstrate authority in turning water into wine, but in so doing, he illustrates the coming of a new era. The story is followed in John by Jesus declaring that he is the fulfillment and replacement of the temple of Judaism, seen at his resurrection.

In the broader scheme of things, the parable of the wineskins speaks to us in the present. God is always doing something new. When new movements of God come along, usually the older, more established churches find it hard to accept. Examples include the Reformation, the rise of Pentecostalism, and the subsequent charismatic renewal. It can be as simple as a church having an influx of young people passionate about the gospel. Such things can cause churches that are old wineskins to rupture. The new wine is being poured into old wineskins, and they break. Patches of new cloth are being sewn onto the old cloth, and it breaks away. It is a truism that stands the test of time that old religious patterns cannot contain new movements, something seen in mainline denominations that resist attempts of leaders to renew them. We who are older Christians must ensure that our wineskins and cloth remain elastic to accommodate God's movements of renewal when they come. Our hearts must not become hard and calloused. Our church practices must be, to a degree, elastic. Otherwise, our churches and denominations will die.

---

12. Barry et al., eds., "Wineskin."

Jesus Is Lord of the Sabbath (2:23–27)

We come to a fourth controversy story. This time, it happens on the Sabbath while Jesus. Jesus and his disciples are walking through the grain fields and are eating the heads of corn. They are challenged by some Pharisees as they do so (2:23–24). Their query shows that now Jesus and his disciples are being followed, even on the Sabbath. We see the deep suspicion those of the old cloth and wineskin had toward Jesus, the new wine of God.

In fact, what Jesus and the disciples are doing is acceptable in the Torah. While it was unlawful to use a sickle to harvest a neighbor's field, it was permitted for the hungry to eat from the heads of the corn (Deut 23:25). For the Pharisees, who had a raft of oral laws to ensure the laws of the OT we kept, Jesus and his disciples are lawbreakers. For the Pharisees, the Sabbath could be broken only for life-threatening situations. Among the Essenes at Qumran, it was forbidden to help an animal giving birth or one that had been trapped in a cistern or pit.[13] The Pharisees and rabbis had a list of thirty-nine things that could not be done to break the Sabbath.[14] As Guelich says, "Only life-threatening situations or dire personal needs could supersede the sabbath law (*Mek. Exod.* 31:12)."[15]

Jesus responds by citing an example from the OT where David and his friends entered the tabernacle at Nob and ate five loaves of the bread that was to be eaten only by priests (1 Sam 21:1–6). Jesus here draws on the sacred Scriptures to try to show the Pharisees the error of their interpretation. This passage, along with Deut 23:25, should have convinced them that Jesus and his disciples were not breaking the law.

Jesus then declares to the Pharisees that the Sabbath was made for the good of humankind rather than the converse. That is, the day of rest, worship, and recreation is so that people can be restored. Indeed, it finds its roots in the creation account and the Ten Commandments (Gen 2:2–3; Exod 20:8–11). As such, its purpose is not to bind people up in legalistic concerns not to abrogate the law, but to enable people to be restored. Here, Jesus and his disciples are hungry. They eat from the grain. Eating food is restorative. Hence, whatever the laws of the Pharisees say, what he and his team did was a good thing.

In v. 27, Jesus makes another statement that violates the line between humankind and God: he declares himself the Lord of Sabbath. Such a claim was as sacrilegious as forgiving people of their sins. There is only one God of

---

13. See CD 11.13–14, cf. Matt 12:11; Luke 13:15; 14:5.
14. See *m. Šabb.* 7:2, see also m. *Beṣah* 5:2.
15. Guelich, *Mark 1—8:26*, 121.

the Sabbath in Israel's tradition: God, Yahweh. For example, the Sabbath in Exod 20:10 is "to the Lord your God"; God commands its observance (Deut 5:12). In so doing, Jesus is declaring his deity, for the Sabbath was created at creation on the day of God's rest (Gen 2:1–4). By declaring himself Lord over the Sabbath, Jesus is claiming the place of God, and this is blasphemous. Little wonder that the leaders desire to destroy him (3:6).

This passage is illustrative of how God's people, zealous to preserve correct doctrine and traditions, can place law over love. The Sabbath must be governed by what is restorative for people, ruled by love and not the minutiae of the law. It is not to be a law that enslaves people. So, should Christians observe the Sabbath? The Sabbath for Jews was Friday sundown until Saturday sundown. Christians were comfortable to stop worshiping on the Sabbath, preferring to meet on Sunday, the "Lord's day" (Acts 20:7; 1 Cor 16:2; Rev 1:10). They became committed to this day as if it were the Sabbath. This devotion is because the idea of a Sabbath rest is central to the creation account (Gen 2:2–3). Hence, we can surmise that one day dedicated to God, rest, and recreation is good for us. However, this must not become a legalistic imposition as it was for Jews. We are under grace, not law. So, it is right for Christians to uphold the principle of the Sabbath—to take a day a week to rest, worship, and restore. However, this does not have to be any given day. Some have to work on a Sunday to provide for their needs. That is OK. They should take another day as their Sabbath. Furthermore, we must not fall into the trap of legalizing the Sabbath regulations, or we lose sight of the grace of the gospel.

Jesus Heals on the Sabbath (3:1–6)

Here we have the fifth controversy story in succession. On this occasion, it is a Sabbath and a healing narrative. The synagogue in mind appears to be Capernaum, although this is uncertain. It is the Sabbath. In any synagogue, this is the busiest day of the week, as people come to worship. Jesus is there as a faithful Jewish man. There is also a man there who is disabled, having a withered or paralyzed hand.

There are also opponents present, watching him closely. We learn in v. 6 that they are Pharisees and Herodians. Seeing as this is Galilee, the Herodians are likely from the court of the son of Herod the Great, Herod Antipas, who from 4 BC to AD 39 was tetrarch of Galilee. As such, we now have the Jewish leadership beginning to collude together against the threat of Jesus. The man with the withered hand may have been put there to set Jesus up, provoking him to heal.

Jesus is unafraid of his critics and stands the man up in the congregation.[16] Placing the man in the center could indicate that Jesus was deliberately provoking his opponents; at the least, he was challenging their authority and interpretation directly. He then asks his accusers whether it is lawful (legal) to do good/to save or to do evil/to kill[17] on the Sabbath (3:3–4). The law permitted helping a person if his or her life was in danger. An example is the Mishnah text, *m. Yoma* 8:6: "Any case in which there is a possibility that life is in danger thrusts aside the sabbath law."[18] However, this man's life is not under threat; hence, Jesus will become a lawbreaker in their eyes if he heals the man.

His accusers do not answer, and we see real emotion from Jesus as he scans the room. The term translated "angry" is *orgē*, a term used of God's wrath expressed in eternal judgment (e.g., Rom 1:18; 2:5, 8; 1 Thess 1:10; Rev 19:15). This anger is the righteous wrath of God expressed through his Son against those who would refuse the healing of a disabled man because of their pedantic legalism. Quite rightly, Jesus is furious with them.

Jesus's response is further explained as "grief" (*syllypeō*), which has the sense "'to feel hurt or grief with someone or at the same time."[19] This anger and grief are due to the hardness of their hearts. The Greek for hardness is *pōrōsis*, which has the sense "of complete lack of understanding, dullness, insensibility, obstinacy."[20] It can be troubling to see Jesus's anger here. However, the biblical narrative is clear that there is a time for righteous anger.

A great example is the clearing of the temple, where Jesus drives out traders and lenders, overthrows tables and chairs, and cries out against the abuse of the temple (11:15–19). His anger at times shows us that while God and his Son are love, this love at times expresses itself in anger at injustice and the abuse of God's purposes. What is impressive here is that Jesus does not direct his wrath at them and act in judgment as he had the power to do. Instead, he acts with healing grace, giving these critics more opportunity to respond with repentance and faith. Similarly, presently, in Christ, by the Spirit, God is delaying his wrath against unrighteousness. He is patient, and we should count his patience as more opportunity to do God's work so that people can come to repentance (2 Pet 3:9, 15). Jesus's profound grief at the

---

16. Guelich, *Mark 1—8:26*, 134, states that "those attending a synagogue sat on stone benches around the walls or squatted on mats on the floor."

17. We have here examples of antithetical parallelism, where you have two parallel statements that are antithetical to one another. This is common in the Hebrew Old Testament.

18. See also *m. Šabb.* 6.3; 12.1; 18.3; 19.2.

19. BDAG, 956.

20. BDAG, 900.

hardness of their hearts is that which God feels toward fallen humankind (cf. Gen 6:1–4). Our hardness hurts God.

The healing displays the immense power of Jesus to heal. Before the eyes of everyone present, his hand is restored. What should then have happened is that all people in the synagogue, including the Pharisees and Herodians, had fallen on their knees worshiping God and recognizing in Jesus God's power. Instead, they plot to destroy him. The term for destroy is *apollymi*, a term used through the NT of eternal destruction (1:24; 8:35). There is an irony here, for in their desire to destroy Jesus, they are sealing their eternal *apollymi*.

Jesus had hinted at his death earlier when he spoke of the bridegroom being taken away. Here, we see the explicit evidence of the Jewish leaders wanting him dead. They will ultimately succeed.

The Healing of Crowds (3:7–12)

Mark 3:7–35 includes further ministry in Galilee. Mark 3:7–12 is a healing summary, the second after 1:33–34. In v. 7, Jesus withdraws from Capernaum and the threats of the leaders to a place beside the sea. For Jesus, it is not yet his time, so avoidance of his future killers makes sense. This location could have been east of Capernaum and perhaps Bethsaida. It may have been south toward the Church of the Beatitudes, Tabgha, or Magdala. While the Pharisees do not like what Jesus has done, the crowds, who adore him, follow him. There is no indication that they are yet disciples; they seek signs (see 1 Cor 1:22). His fame in Capernaum and its environs is stunning.

Jesus's attempts to withdraw are futile because of his popularity. We are again reminded of why Jesus kept his messiahship secret; if he allowed news of his messiahship to spread, there could be a scene like John 6:14–15. In this passage, the crowd becomes aware that Jesus is the long-awaited prophet like Moses (Deut 18:15–18).[21] They attempt to seize Jesus and crown him, no doubt wanting him to set them free from Rome.

What is interesting is the origin of these people. The people come from the area he is in, Galilee, and from Judea, which was the southern part of the tripartite Israel of the time. While some come from Jerusalem, others come from Idumea (southeast of Judea), and others from the Transjordan or Perea. Some even come from Tyre and Sidon to the northwest of Galilee. Significantly, none come from Samaria, which lay between Galilee and Judea, or the Decapolis to the northwest.[22] This diverse crowd, however,

---

21. See also Acts 3:22–23.
22. Guelich, *Mark 1—8:26*, 146, observes that the Decapolis and Samaria are

indicates that Jesus's ministry is expanding. While many who came were no doubt Jews from these areas, we cannot rule out many being gentiles. If so, this anticipates the future gentile mission.

Not only is there a large crowd, but they are crushing him as they reach forward, longing to touch him to experience God's healing. One can here imagine a scene from a third-world country at a religious gathering where people reach out, hungry for God. We need to remember that 90 percent of Israel was living at subsistence level or below at the time, and access to medical facilities was nigh on nonexistent. They were poor. They died young. A healing evangelist would be a glorious gift from God. Hence, it is no surprise to see them seek to touch him to experience his healing power (cf. 5:27–28). We get an idea of the earthly Jesus: he simply radiated the power of God. Wow! We should be as hungry for Jesus as they were.

Hence, it is no surprise to see the people reaching for Jesus. Many were successful, for Jesus healed many and drove out demons. Jesus sensed that things were getting dangerous and asked his disciples to prepare a boat. While the text does not specify it, this was probably to give him a place to stand to teach the crowds as in 4:2. It also enabled them to control the crowd. Whether he taught or not, we cannot be sure, but he indeed healed some and drove out demons from others. His exorcisms and healings again illustrate the enormity of his ministry to the sick and marginalized (3:9–11). Such restorative acts are essential to bringing God's shalom, the peace of the kingdom. Jesus's ministry was holistic. While evangelism is critical and lies at the center of our mission, we are also to care for the poor and bring God's healing and deliverance. The kingdom of God is about the restoration of the *whole person*.

We see again that the demons recognize who Jesus is. Their response is to fall before him and shout out that Jesus is the Son of God. Their veneration shows that Satan and his demons know full well who Jesus is. We can contrast this with the Jewish leaders who cannot grasp it, blinded by Satan and his hordes. We see here also Jesus's complete authority and power over demons and their recognition of him. He commands them not to tell who he is, another example of the "messianic secret" (3:12).

The Appointing of the Twelve (3:13–19)

We are unsure what mountain Jesus ascends (see the note on the translation), but he does so. He calls to himself those he wants and appoints them as twelve apostles. The appointment from a larger group indicates that there

---

notably absent.

were many disciples (cf. 2:15). However, Jesus chooses from the group his leaders. Similarly, in the church, God singles out those he wants for his leaders. We are to respect his right and authority to do so and honor those he chooses. However, we are not to worship them and put them on a pedestal as if they are super Christians. They are people like us.

The term "apostle" (*apostolos*) was a sparsely used political term that had the sense of an ambassador or emissary. Hence, an apostle is perhaps best understood as an ambassador of the kingdom commissioned to take the good news to the world and establish colonies (churches) across the world.

Apostles are given three functions. First, they are to be with Jesus. Being called to be with him speaks of a close relationship with Jesus as the foundation of all Christian leadership.[23] In Jesus's time, this would have meant traveling with him and learning from him through his teaching and observing his example. For us today as leaders, it means reading the word avidly and having an active prayer life in which we relate to him. Second, they are sent to preach the good news of the kingdom. Those set apart for Christian leadership will always have a ministry of preaching and teaching. Hence, they must be committed disciples, learners, lifelong students, continually adding to their knowledge of God's word and work and passing it on to others. Third, they are given authority to cast out demons. Exorcism is an essential aspect of leadership; we are to lay hands on those in need and pray for their deliverance.

Significantly, Jesus appoints twelve. Twelve recalls the tribes of Israel and suggests Jesus is constituting a new people of God. He is Joshua, they are the Twelve; with them, he will now take the kingdom through the land. His work in the land is not a military invasion to drive out the Romans, although the disciples probably expected this until after his death. It is a spiritual invasion where the kingdom is preached, people are liberated from sin and its consequences, and the liberated ones become people of the kingdom within the world of colliding empires in which they dwell.

The Twelve included the fishermen we had met earlier by the Sea of Galilee. We learn here that Jesus gave the name Peter to Simon. The renaming is recorded in Matt 16:18, Peter meaning "rock." We get a sense of the strength of character into which this man will grow as he becomes the leading figure in the early church. We are also told that the sons of Zebedee, John and Jacob (James), were named by Jesus *Boanerges*, meaning "sons of thunder." The epithet could refer to their powerful preaching or, as is more likely, their thunderous personalities. We see their fervor when they

---

23. One thinks here of John's theology of abiding in Christ (e.g., John 15:4, 6–7; 1 John 1:24; 2:27–28; 4:13).

ask Jesus for the supreme seats of power on either side of him (10:35–37). It is reflected again when John attempts to shut down a person driving out demons in Jesus's name (9:32). A third instance is when they seek to call down fire from heaven to destroy a Samaritan town (Luke 9:54).

Matthew the tax collector is likely the Levi called earlier in Mark 2. Jacob (James) is designated a son of Alphaeus to distinguish him from Jacob (James), the brother of John. He may also be Levi/Matthew's brother (see earlier on 2:14). Simon is designated a Zealot. The Zealots peaked in the AD 60s, and some question whether this is read back on Simon. However, there were many messianic movements before and after Jesus leading up to the war with Rome. Furthermore, Mark writes as the Zealot movement is coming to a head. As such, the label Zealot likely speaks of his revolutionary tendencies.

Judas may be from Kerioth but may also be a revolutionary from the deadly group of assassins known as the Sicarii.[24] They were renowned for sneaking up to people in a crowd, knifing them, and moving on. Having a tax-collector among a group of zealous potential revolutionaries was a potentially explosive mix. As discussed on 2:13–17, tax-collectors were seen as traitors to Rome. What we see is that Jesus is bringing humankind together and breaking down longheld hatred by the power of love. Having such diverse people on the same team speaks of the reconciling power of the gospel of the kingdom. We learn the names of other apostles, including Philip, Bartholomew, Thomas (who will doubt Jesus's resurrection in John 20:24–29), and Thaddeus. The passage ends on a somber note, again portending Jesus's doom: "who betrayed him."

It is noted that these are all men and so precludes women from ministering. However, this is obviously false thinking as these men are all Jews as well, and this is not read as precluding gentile leadership in God's church. All it tells us is that Jesus's first group of chosen and called leaders were Jewish men. He saw that as the best way to start his mission to redeem the world. It also makes sense as twelve are representative of the twelve tribes of Israel, the sons of Jacob, a renewed Israel constituted around Christ.[25]

Another point to note from this passage is that serving as a Christian as a minister or missionary should start with the call of Christ rather than selfish ambition, personal appointment, or even ordination. Ordination that recognizes the call of Christ on a person's life is legitimate, but ordination that presumes to stand in place of Christ to call a person to ministry is

---

24. See further Wenkel, "Sicarii," *LBD*.

25. Guelich, *Mark 1—8:26*, 158, correctly observes that this is not a replacement of Israel, but the fulfillment of the restoration of all God's people.

not. "They came to him" indicates that they accepted the call. Responding in this way is what we are to do if we are called by Jesus to his service. God's people in every place desperately need God-called leaders. Swaths of humans have yet to hear the gospel. We need to be open to his call, and when he summons, we come to him.

Is He Mad or Demonized? (3:20–34)

This passage is another example of the Markan sandwich, with two encounters matched together, one encounter broken in two, each part framing the other encounter.

> A¹ Criticism by Jesus's family (3:20–21)
>
> B Criticism by Jewish leaders (3:22–30)
>
> A² Criticism by Jesus's family (3:31–35)

This particular narrative is framed by Jesus's encounter with his family. In between, there is his clash with scribes who accuse him of being an emissary of Satan.

In this passage, Jesus comes under critique from his family and, more vigorously, from another group of Jewish leaders. Jesus goes to an unspecified house in an uncertain location,[26] a typically vague setting in Mark's fast-moving narrative. There is, as usual, a large crowd gathered, so large that he and his disciples have no time to eat.

Their lack of time for self-care shows them prioritizing ministry to the crowds over their personal needs. Such sacrifice is an example of the self-denial Jesus would challenge disciples to emulate in 8:34. Similarly, we should be dedicated to our ministry. However, we must not push this too far and burn out through overwork and lack of self-care. The long haul of ministry calls for hard, sacrificial service, but caring for one's own needs is still very important if we are to stand the test of time.

Jesus's family approaches him, no doubt concerned for his health as he has been working hard, preaching, teaching, healing, and delivering from demons. The Greek is strong here; they want to seize him (*krateō*).[27] The forceful language shows real concern. Some are even saying that he is

---

26. This could be his home in Capernaum, Nazareth, or, as I have taken it, an unspecified location.

27. BDAG, 564.

behaving like a madman; the Greek *existēmi* sometimes meaning "to be out of one's normal state of mind," "to lose one's mind, be out of one's senses."[28]

This episode illustrates the experience of many who have followed Christ: incomprehension among family members. They see us as "out of our minds." I experienced this at my conversion, being marginalized and ridiculed by my family. Such maltreatment is one of the costs of the gospel; indeed, Jesus knew his coming would divide families (Luke 12:51–53). However, the good news is what comes toward the end of this section: when we come to Christ, we come into a new family, the family of God, and God cares for us, as should our brothers and sisters in Christ.

This episode is another controversy account and is known as the Beelzebub controversy. It is linked with the previous, probably because it reveals different reactions to Jesus.

The story then shifts from Jesus's family to the arrival of scribes from Jerusalem. We have then the third encounter with these Jewish leaders (2:6, 16). These are from Jerusalem, rather than what seems to have been locals in 2:6 and 2:16. Their arrival from the capital suggests that the news about Jesus had spread to Jerusalem, where the religious leaders of the nation were based. Their interpretation of Jesus's powerful ministry is that he is demonized, driving out demons because he is possessed by Beelzebul. The name most likely originates from Baal-Zebub, a god of Ekron (2 Kgs 1:2) and a name meaning "lord of the flies."[29] Essentially, it is another name for Satan,[30] seen in the phrase "the ruler of the demons" and "how can Satan" in vv. 22–23.

Jesus's response is not direct; instead, he uses a series of rhetorical questions and short, pithy parables. He asks, "How can Satan cast out Satan?" The implied answer is, he would not do this, for that would be stupid and self-defeating. In v. 24, Jesus states a truism demonstrated repeatedly in history: a kingdom will fall if it is divided against itself in war. Israel knows this to be true, since after the death of Solomon, the kingdom became two, Israel in the north and Judah in the south. Ultimately, both fell into exile at the hands of the Assyrians and Babylonians.

Similarly, a house divided against itself is not sustainable (v. 25). The division of families is also well-known in Israel's history, such as the rivalry between the brothers Aristobulus II and Hyrcanus that ended Israel's independence when Rome invaded in 63 BC. Similarly, this point is illustrated by the division of the realm of Herod the Great after his death.[31] Verse 26

---

28. BDAG, 350.
29. Silva, *NIDNTTE*, 1:505.
30. See Matt 10:25; 12:24, 27; Luke 11:15, 18, 19.
31. Stein, *Mark*, 183.

restates v. 24, all to make the point that if Satan turns on his own, he will be divided, and doing so will bring about his demise.

Verse 27 shifts the focus. Mark's Jesus cites a situation where someone wants to steal the possessions of a wealthy and powerful person. To do so would require capturing the owner and binding him up, allowing the thief to have the run of the house to plunder it. Here, this speaks of Jesus's deliverance ministry whereby he has entered Israel and the world, delivering people from their sin, taking captive the strong man Satan, plundering his work of holding captive humankind, and so liberating us. Jesus's words are a subtle critique of the religious leaders of Israel, with Jesus turning their critique on them. Under their watch, people are under Satan's thumb, and Jesus is liberating people from him. His challenge to Satan calls to mind the temptation first, then the subsequent liberation of people from demons. However, it is more than just deliverance. Every good act that brings transformation to others and shifts the world from evil to good is a further plundering of Satan's realm.[32] Consequently, as we go out and engage the world, pray, minister to the needs of others, share the gospel, and do works of love, we are extending the kingdom. Just as salt flavors food and light overcomes darkness, so Satan is plundered as believers do good work (cf. Matt 5:13–16).

Verses 28–30 should be understood in the context of the scribes accusing Jesus of ministering by the power of Satan. The section is introduced with real solemnity: "I tell you the truth." Jesus tells them that all sins can be forgiven except the sin against the Holy Spirit. Such a sin has eternal consequences and for it there is no forgiveness (see also Matt 12:31; Luke 12:10; Gos. Thom. 44). Just what does Jesus mean here? In context, the answer is found in the clause "he has an evil spirit" in v. 30. The sin in view appears to be Jewish leaders attributing the work of the Holy Spirit to Satan. The sin in mind can be read generally as "the individual's culpable rejection of or refusal to recognize God's redemptive activity."[33] However, it may be more specific, where one ascribes the work of God to the hand of Satan. As Guelich puts it, "In other words, to attribute the work of the Spirit through Jesus to demonic forces is the ultimate calumny for which there is no forgiveness."[34]

If so, we need to listen very carefully to this warning and be very cautious about criticizing the work of other Christians and attributing it to Satan. An example of this might be cessationists who claim that the spiritual gifts are purely limited to the time of the apostles. Hence, where

---

32. Guelich, *Mark 1—8:26*, 177, wants to limit it to merely exorcisms; but the exorcisms are signs of the coming of the kingdom, whereby Satan and evil are defeated and, in the world to come, there will be no evil. I find no reason to agree with him.

33. Guelich, *Mark 1—8:26*, 180.

34. Guelich, *Mark 1—8:26*, 180.

someone appears to demonstrate such gifts, it is easy to attribute this to Satan. However, this may be the sin against the Spirit. Similarly, some Christians flippantly speak against ministries or spiritual encounters they find disagreeable such as the charismatic renewal or the so-called Toronto Blessing. Although we as God's people must always be discerning concerning such things, we must not go as far as attributing what might be the work of the Spirit to Satan. We are better to wait and watch closely to see the fruit of such things. In time, it will come to light.

The final section returns to Jesus's family. Waiting outside, they summon him to them. Jesus does not respond, calling those with him to look around at each other. Those who do God's will are his family. Jesus here is prioritizing the people of God over his family. Jesus's words should not be read as a summons to neglect our families. Instead, Jesus reminds disciples that their priority as God's people is our Christian family into which we were called at conversion.

In a first-century Jewish context, this is a radical statement. Aside from God, one's family was the most significant thing in life. Shame was brought on the family when one prioritized others over them. However, this is the call of the kingdom. We see this at other points in Jesus's mission. An example is the two men who came to Jesus with a desire to follow him but wanted first to go home, one to bury his father and the other to say goodbye. Jesus tells them to follow him immediately. To be disciples of Jesus, they must make the kingdom their priority (Luke 9:57–62).

Similarly, Jesus even goes as far as telling his disciples to hate their own families if they wish to follow him (Luke 14:26). Such a statement is not to be taken literally but points to us putting God's work ahead of our immediate families. Jesus's words need to be balanced with 1 Tim 5:8, where a Christian who fails to provide for his or her own family is worse than an unbeliever. Overall, Jesus is teaching us that our primary family is God's people, and while we are never to neglect caring for our own family, God's people take priority.

The Parable of the Sower, Soil, and Seeds (4:1–20)

Although this chapter is linked to the previous in the original language with the Greek *kai*, "and," in reality, it is a separate chapter with a collection of parables arranged by Mark. Parables were a huge part of Jesus's ministry. They are stories based on real first-century Jewish life, with a second layer of meaning concerning the kingdom of God. They are powerful in that they summon us to interpret them and respond as we understand the story and find ourselves in them. While parables are found prior to Jesus in such instances as Nathan's critique of David's sin against Uriah with Bathsheba (2 Kgs 12), Jesus was unique in that he made parables the central plank of his preaching ministry alongside ethical maxims. No doubt Mark 4 and its parallel chapters in Matt 13 and Luke 8 represent a gathering together of stories Jesus preached regularly across the nation. The central theme is undoubtedly the kingdom of God. They not only challenge us to interpret them and yield to the King who teaches us through them, but they encourage us to use stories as we preach. These stories are timeless. They are accessible to children, stick in the mind, and continue to speak powerfully to us as we grow old. Nothing beats a good story, especially one that teaches us about the kingdom of God.

As in 3:9, Jesus teaches from a boat on the Sea of Galilee. On the previous occasion, he healed and delivered demons. Here, he teaches. Again, the crowd is massive. Parables were mentioned in 3:23 when Jesus responded to the criticism of the scribes. Now, we get introduced to more of Jesus's fantastic little stories.

A parable is given in 4:1–9 and then explained in 4:13–20. The parable begins in v. 3 with "listen." Notably, it finishes with another appeal to listen (an inclusio): "Let anyone with ears to hear, listen." Jesus's words here may be intentionally humorous, as wheat also has ears, and Jesus's appeal may play on the idea. In this parable, Jesus is summoning his hearers, and Mark is inviting his readers to consider what Jesus is saying. In Hebrew thought, to listen is to obey. To not obey is not to hear. Indeed, each day, Jews recited the Shema, named after its first word, meaning "hear and heed" (Deut 6:4–5). Such an appeal reminds us of Jas 1:22, where Jacob (James) urges his readers to "be doers of the word, and not hearers only, deceiving yourselves."

The appeal to listen is followed by "look," translated "behold." With this appeal, we are called to imagine with our mind's eye the picture Jesus will paint for us with his words. For ancient Israelites, this would not have been difficult, for likely they saw people sowing in the fields routinely. Indeed, it is possible that as Jesus was preaching, he pointed to some who were sowing crops nearby, so this may have been an actual moment where he was teaching them from real life. For us, it is a little more difficult at one level. However, all we need to know is that in the ancient world, sowing preceded plowing, unlike in contemporary practice. The path then would have been a track around the field that was not plowed. This was the first phase. A sower sows the seed, then there are four scenarios, each of which imagines a situation in the evangelistic process.

First, in v. 4, some seed falls on the side of the path where there was no soil, and birds came and ate the seed. Jesus in vv. 14–15 explains its meaning. The sower sows the word, raising the question of who the sower is. At the moment, it is Jesus, bringing the word to Israel. However, Jesus is not the only one proclaiming the word. He sends the apostles to do this (3:14; 6:7–13). Then, in 13:10, the gospel will be preached to the whole world (see also 14:9). As Mark writes in the 60s, the word would have been preached across regions around the Mediterranean by Peter and others. Mark was then preaching the word through his Gospel. All this was on behalf of Jesus by his Spirit. Hence, the sower is Jesus on behalf of God, through all manner of Christians who share their faith. We are also to be faithful to the Great Commission God has given his church. Hence, this parable speaks to all who share God's word on behalf of Jesus.

It tells us that there will be different responses. Jesus tells the disciples in vv. 14–15 that when the word is shared with some people, sometimes it appears to be received, but just as a bird swoops in and eats a seed on the ground, Satan steals it away from their minds. Such seed stealing calls to mind 2 Cor 4:4–6. Paul writes that "the god of this world," Satan, "has blinded the minds of the unbelievers, to keep them from seeing the light of the gospel of the glory of Christ."

Who are such people? In the first setting of Jesus's ministry, it is the Jewish leaders who hear Jesus. When they listen, rather than repent and believe, they want to kill him. Another example is the rich ruler, who walks away sad when he hears Jesus's summons (10:18–22). In Mark's setting in Rome, it is the Jewish leaders who reject the gospel and the Roman rulers who persecute Christians. Around this time, Nero imprisons Paul, Peter, and others;[35] unleashes death on Rome's Christians after the Great Fire of Rome;[36] and then has Peter and Paul killed. For us, as we preach, it is the many who hear the word, but it bounces off them.

We all know such people, and we should not be surprised. Such rejection has a Satanic dimension. We must pray for those people, that they will hear the word, be protected from Satan's deceit, have softer and open hearts, and come to faith.

Incidentally, these are the sorts of people mentioned in v. 12, where Isa 6:9–10 is cited. They are those who see Jesus in action and hear his message but cannot comprehend that he is the Messiah and Son of God. They are like those at the time of Isaiah (eighth century BC) who heard Isaiah preach but

---

35. For example, Aristarchus (Col 4:10) and Epaphras (Phlm 23), who were both in Rome in prison with Paul.

36. Tacitus, *Ann.* 15.44.

never turned from their sins. Ultimately, they were destroyed by exile as a result. They are those in Mark's setting in Rome who were reacting against the Christian faith and persecuting Christians. It is those in our contexts who react against the faith.

The passage tells us that while the purpose of the word of God is always salvation, the result (*hina*) of the word of God coming to many is hardened hearts and reaction. There is always hope for such people, that they will turn at the end, as many do. So, we should expect that when we share Christ, some will simply not get it and even actively oppose us. Still, rejection should not put us off sharing the gospel as we take up our crosses for Jesus's sake.

Second, in vv. 5–6 and vv. 16–17, are those who hear the word of God, receive it enthusiastically and joyfully, and last a short time as Christians. However, like plants in shallow soil, when challenges to their new faith come, they fall away (*skandalizō*, v. 17). Jesus lists tribulation and persecution, as these were common reasons at the time for people falling away.

In Jesus's setting, this might have included the likes of Judas, who joined the disciples but then turned on Jesus and became his betrayer. It included Peter and the other disciples who Jesus predicted would fall away (14:27, using the same Greek word, *skandalizō*). Despite Peter's protestations (14:29), they abandoned Jesus after he was arrested and denied him. The good news is that Jesus was prepared to take them back! So, there is hope if we deny Jesus.

In Mark's setting, it would have included any who were giving up the faith because of Nero's persecution. It might also have included Demas. From Rome, Paul sends greetings to the Colossians and Philemon from Demas in Col 4:14 and Phlm 24. However, in his final letter, he says of him that he has deserted him because of his love for the world (2 Tim 4:10). He may have fallen away. Those to whom Hebrews is written, who are falling away to Judaism, could have been in this group. Any people who were seduced by Judaizers or other false teachers would have been in that group (e.g., the recipients of Galatians; readers of 2 Peter and Jude; those warned in 2 Cor 10—13; Phil 3; 1 Tim 1:3–7; 2 Tim 3:1–9).

In today's setting, it is those who come to Christ but drop away. In fact, in the Western world, in the last fifty years, there have been millions like this. It is a contemporary tragedy. However, this should not be a surprise to us; this is expected, even if it is tragic. We must pray for them and reach out to these lost sheep because, as in the case of Peter's restoration, there is always hope. This passage does show that it is possible to fall away. We should, then, expect some with whom we share Christ to make a commitment and when the going gets tough, fall away. This is a sad reality of mission. We do all we can to ensure this does not happen, but happen it will. Again, this should not stop us from sharing our faith.

The third group are those mentioned in v. 7 and explained in vv. 18–19. They hear the word and become Christians and begin to grow. However, their faith does not produce fruit. It is a little unclear what fruit constitutes in the parable. It could be the fruit of converts. It could be the fruit of lives where people yield to the challenge to deny themselves and take up their crosses. Such people become more Christlike. It could be the fruit of serving Jesus. In all likelihood, we should not be too concerned to narrow this down. It is likely all of the above: the fruit of lives that do good, emulate Christ, serve God, and share faith so that others can hear the word.

Here some people come to Christ but have a choked faith that does not produce much. They are mostly unchanged by their encounter with Christ. They may go to church and do all the right things, but their lives, from a Christian point of view, produce nothing. They then are those who go through the motions and are nominal. They are more concerned about the cares of their lives, such as business, money-making, or having a great life. While they participate in church, they are more concerned about money than the kingdom. They are materialistic believers.

In Jesus's time, Judas was a bit like this, as he was a thief (Matt 27:3; John 13:29), although he fits better in the previous group. Demas may have fallen into this category (see the previous paragraph). In Mark's world, those in 1 Tim 6 who love money may also have been among such people. In our world, churches are full of such people. They have become Christians and may attend church. However, they are more concerned about their wealth and acquiring more. They produce little for God. Sadly, we should be unsurprised to see this. As with the earlier categories, we do all we can to ensure people are fruitful Christians and not nominal pseudo-Christians whose faith is crushed. Still, when we see this, it should not stop us from proclaiming the gospel. Such things are to be expected.

One of the puzzles of this passage is whether these people are still Christians or not. Jesus is not clear. The answer should not detain us; that is up to God. What we must do is not allow ourselves to become like this. We must challenge others to assess themselves to see if they are in the faith, producing the fruit in which God delights (2 Cor 13:5).

The final group is those who hear the word, come to faith, and give their lives over to serving our King and his kingdom. They produce a great crop. The yield of thirty, sixty, and one hundred times is seen by some scholars as astonishing, as it is estimated that the average yield was a 7.5 to 10 percent increase. However, others question this, arguing that this is above average but not extraordinary.[37] It is probably right to see a hint of overabundance here, illustrating the miraculous power of the word to propagate itself. Such a plentiful harvest is seen at times in Luke-Acts, where Luke gives this parable and then mentions the power of the word to spread (e.g., Acts 6:7; 12:24; 13:49; 19:10, 20).

So, some hear the word and produce huge harvests of converts, good works, and service to God's church, mission, and the needs of the world. The supreme example of this is Jesus himself. He is the seed of God who died and became the mustard tree that is the largest in the garden of the world. Then there are the great apostles, Peter and Paul, not to mention the others. There are also many other great disciples of whom we read in the NT: women like Mary Magdalene, Priscilla, Lydia, Nympha, Junia, Phoebe, Euodia, Syntyche, and others who did great things for Jesus;[38] and men like the other apostles, Stephen, Philip, Timothy, Silas, Titus, Apollos, and more.[39] There are also Luke and Mark, who wrote Gospels.

In our world, these are the many Christians who faithfully serve God. Some seem insignificant, yet they are God's joy for their quiet, relentless service; churches are full of such people. Some are luminaries like the late great Billy Graham, John Stott, William and Catherine Booth, and the like. We should aspire to be part of this fourth group. The hope of such converts is why we share our faith. We want to see God take sinners formerly useless, like Onesimus (whose name means "useful"), save them through his word, and turn them into workers useful to God's purposes (Col 4:9; Phlm 22). My own experience is just that. God took me, a university dropout, and turned me into a NT scholar. We must watch that the thorns of the world do not grow up and choke us, making us unproductive. No! We go to our graves, serving him with all we have got! Amen.

We need to say a little more about vv. 11–12. As noted above, it is a citation of Isaiah. It can be read in a harsh way, where we take the *hina* that launches v. 12 as a purpose clause. Taken this way, Jesus preached intentionally in parables with the purpose that (*hina*) Israel would reject him. If this is the correct reading, then Jesus did not want people outside the kingdom to become believers. His desire would then be to ensure that they rejected him and killed him.

---

37. See Guelich, *Mark 1—8:26*, 195.

38. Mary Magdalene (John 20:1–18), Priscilla (Acts 18:2, 18–26; 1 Cor 16:19; 2 Tim 4:10), Lydia (Acts 16), Nympha (Col 4:14), Junia (Rom 16:7), Phoebe (Rom 16:1–2), Euodia, and Syntyche (Phil 4:2–3).

39. Stephen (Acts 6—7), Philip (Acts 8; 21), Timothy (all over Paul's letters and Heb 13:23; 1—2 Tim), Silas or Silvanus (Acts 15—17; 1 Thess 1:1; 2 Thess 1:1; 1 Pet 5:14), Titus (2 Cor 2:13; 7—8; Gal 2; Titus), Apollos (Acts 18), and more.

However, a better reading is to take the *hina* that launches v. 12 as signaling a result clause. Jesus wants all people to hear his preaching, repent, believe the good news, and enter God's reign for eternal life. He came to seek and save the lost, not to condemn them (Luke 19:10; John 3:16–17). However, as in the time of Isaiah, when Israel rejected the prophet's message, Jesus knew that many would not see and hear and believe. It is a result clause. Some will believe as they hear the parables and his teaching. The mystery of the kingdom of God is given to them. Others will not. Jesus's rejection did lead to his death—not because Jesus preached to ensure that they would kill him (even if he knew this would come to pass), but *because* they rejected him. It is their fault, and so God's wrath on them is just. This latter view is a much better way to understand this passage.

The final thing to note is the importance of evangelism. This parable should encourage us to go and share our faith. Some will reject it outright while others will receive it, only to fall away. Some will appear to believe but produce no fruit. Some will become full-blown fruitful Christians. We can quickly become discouraged when there are more who reject the gospel than accept it. However, Paul warned us that there are times of preaching that are "in season" and others that are "out of season." That is, there will be times when many will become mature Christians from our evangelism, and at other times, many will not.

In all times, we are to hear Paul's words urging Timothy to keep proclaiming the word and doing the work of an evangelist (2 Tim 4:2). Whatever the harvest conditions, we are summoned to plant the word, water it, and allow God to make it grow (1 Cor 3:6). We are called to be faithful, and God brings the harvest. We must not give up evangelizing because it is hard. We keep believing, we continue loving, and we persevere in sharing the gospel with gentleness, respect, and words full of grace, seasoned with salt (1 Pet 3:15–16; Col 4:5–6).

The Parable of the Lamp (4:21–23)

Verse 21 is clear and continues the theme of mission, but not merely verbal proclamation, the shining of light (cf. Matt 5:16). Jesus asks two questions. The first begins with *mēti*, and so expects the answer no. His point is that a lamp that is brought out for use, presumably when it is getting dark. It is not put under a basket. The basket here is a *modios*, which was a measure of grain, about 8.7 liters (cf. Judg 7:16). In this case, it refers to the container in which the grain was held.[40] Nor is it put under a *klinē*, or couch.

---

40. Balz and Schneider, "μόδιος."

Instead, the light is to be brought out to maximum effect; otherwise, the light is blocked. The lamp probably here refers overall to the kingdom of God and its message. It is like a lamp that is on a stand and through which all will be revealed. It also has an individual application. So, the believer is not to hide his or her light under a container or couch to block out the light. Believers are to be the light of the world (cf. Matt 5:16) and let their light shine before others. Similarly, they are to shines as lights of the world amid a crooked and depraved generation (Phil 2:15). That this is the case is supported by what follows in 4:24–25.

Verse 22 is difficult to translate in Greek; however, following v. 21, its meaning is clear. What is not hidden is to be revealed and to be brought into the light. This verse reinforces the meaning of the previous verse. The kingdom was hidden. Now it is not hidden; it is to be spread abroad like a light.

In verse 23, Jesus challenges hearers to truly hear what he is saying and not only listen but obey. They are to recognize the kingdom and its light. They are to respond with repentance and faith. They are to transmit the light to the world.

The Parable of the Measure (4:24–25)

The first part of the verse is a warning to be concerned about what we listen to and to whom we listen. The implication is that readers should listen to Jesus and obey him (see v. 23). He is the King, sent from God, and his word is to be listened to above all voices (9:7).

We have another principle of the kingdom from the perspective of living in the world. The parable is premised on reciprocity, a common first-century perspective, seen throughout the NT and in many cultures. That is, the more we give on behalf of the kingdom, the more we will receive from God. It sort of says, "You cannot outgive God," a familiar maxim which we often hear. In terms of the kingdom and what has preceded, those who have the secrets of the kingdom will discover more as they listen carefully and heed Jesus's teaching. Those who do not have this understanding because they do not listen will find that what they do have will be taken away. This final aspect is a warning of eternal punishment. So then, this parable is a great encouragement to take what we have been given and put it to work for God, whether it be our finances, our giftings, our time, or our very lives.

Jesus's teaching here raises the question of whether this promotes prosperity teaching, which advocates that if we give to God, we will experience material prosperity in this world. This passage does support the reciprocity principle in terms of God: God rewards those who give to him. However, it says nothing about *when* we receive God's blessings of prosperity. Other NT texts tell us that we receive these in the eschaton, what Jesus calls "treasure in heaven" (10:21).[41]

Prosperity teaching involves an over-realized eschatology by which God's blessings are experienced in the present, while the wider NT suggests that most of us will experience this in eternity. It also lacks a theology of redemption through suffering in a fallen world. Indeed, if we receive in the present, this money is not for our pleasure and prosperity. It is to be used for God's work, such as building the church, extending God's mission, and bringing social justice. Nor does this passage support making the reciprocal giving of God our motivation for serving him. If we do this, we are motivated by personal gain and not by wanting to please God, build the church, and extend his mission. Prosperity teaching inadvertently distorts the essential principle of Christian giving. We do not give because God will reward us; we give because he already has blessed. We give without strings attached, unconditionally. So we should not seek to inspire people to give because God will give back. Encouraging this is dangerous and encourages wrongly motivated giving. Instead, we teach them that while God does give back, we give to please God and not to receive back. We also remind them that their reward is kept in heaven for them, and whatever wealth they have in the present is to be used for God's glory. We give out of gratitude to a God who gives more.

The Parable of the Growing Seed (4:26–29)

The growing seed parable is one of Jesus's stories using the formula "the kingdom of God is like," which is especially common in Matthew (see also 4:30).[42] As with the parable of the sower, Jesus uses the agrarian metaphor of the seed. He likens the kingdom of God to a farmer who plants seeds (4:26).[43] This time, the farmer is God acting through Jesus. The person in mind is any farmer who, year after year, begins the harvest process by scattering seeds on

---

41. See also Matt 13:44; 19:21; Luke 12:33; 18:22.

42. Matt 13:24, 31, 33, 43, 44, 45, 47, 52; 18:23; 20:1; 22:2; 25:1; Luke 13:18.

43. Guelich, *Mark 1—8:26*, 240, suggests that the seed is the focus of the parable and not the farmer. Yet, both are important. The farmer represents first God through Christ, and then his disciples planting the seed of the kingdom as they engage in mission (which is, in fact, Christ).

the ground. Then, he sleeps and rises night and day.[44] The seed sprouts and grows up, although the farmer does not know how it grows.

The thinking here represents a first-century pre-scientific world where we cannot explain the growth of a seed. Now, to an extent, we understand the process of germination whereby the seed grows roots and sprouts. We know that a seed is dormant until it is woken by water. A plant needs three things to grow: light, food, and water. Light provides the energy for photosynthesis, whereby light energy is converted into food. The seed also draws water by sending out roots that deliver water to the growing plant. As such, it can grow.[45]

Still, while we now have more idea of the processes involved in plant growth, we do not understand why it occurs and how to generate it from nothing. As Christians, we know that God has put in place this process. Even today, we know that a plant grows by itself, i.e., it is packed with the necessary ingredients for its growth; all it needs is water and light.

The Greek "by itself" is *automatos*, from which we get the English automatic. It speaks of the internal power of the seed. The process of growth is given in simple terms, first the stalk, then the head, then the full grain in the head ready for harvest. The kingdom then is like this. It has been planted in the seed of Christ and his message through his ministry. The kingdom is now growing through the attraction of new converts who are also growing in the same way. These new converts also plant seeds, and more believers spring to life. Ultimately, the harvest of the kingdom of God will be complete. God will then bring in the harvest. The farmer's incomprehension could reflect the incredulity of the world, recognizing but not understanding this growth.

Like the mustard seed parable that follows, this story is prophetic and, to this day, is being fulfilled in the world. The seed of the kingdom and God's word is moving across the world as an unstoppable force. It has spread through almost every nation. Sure, in some places, it hits obstacles, and there are fewer Christians and more apathetic ones. Nevertheless, when we look around the world, the gospel continues to grow and penetrate as more and more people are converted. As such, history is proving this parable true! This fulfillment confirms that Jesus was also a prophet, or better, the Prophet (Deut 18:15–18).

Such a prophetic realization can be used apologetically to challenge unbelievers concerning the truth of the Christian message. The parable

---

44. Guelich, *Mark 1—8:26*, 240, notes that "the reversal of sleeping and rising, night and day, reflects the oriental understanding of a 'day' beginning at sundown."

45. "How Do Seeds Sprout?"

speaks of the imperceptible and unstoppable growth of the kingdom. Such teaching is a source of great comfort to those of us who live in Western settings where the gospel's influence is seemingly weakening. While the influence of the kingdom appears to be waning, we must remind ourselves that God's seed is unstoppable. Indeed, the seeds of a new burst of growth are presently being seen in places like New Zealand as God brings into our country passionate believers from other nations. This immigration is bringing alive the church in cities like Auckland.

God always finds a way for his gospel to extend, for it is an unstoppable force like the organic growth of seeds. As Paul says, "The word of God cannot be chained" (2 Tim 2:9, my translation). Similarly, Jesus says, "I will build my church, and the gates of Hades will not overcome it" (Matt 16:18). The Spirit of God and the power of the gospel will continue to bring the harvest this parable prophesies. Then, God will bring in his harvest. In the meantime, we continue to sow the seed of the word of God.

The Parable of the Mustard Seed (4:30–32)

Jesus again compares the kingdom of God to everyday agrarian life. The parable tells the disciples that the kingdom begins as the smallest of all garden seeds in their context, the mustard seed. Indeed, the mustard seed was often mentioned in Jewish folklore as the smallest seed.[46] As in the previous parable, the kingdom grows and becomes the largest of all garden plants superseding the others. The seed is either Jesus's ministry of the word or the kingdom he is planting. The difference is minimal.

The parable calls to mind Ezek 17:22–24:

> Thus says the Lord GOD: "I myself will take a sprig from the lofty top of the cedar and will set it out. I will break off from the topmost of its young twigs a tender one, and I myself will plant it on a high and lofty mountain. On the mountain height of Israel will I plant it, that it may bear branches and produce fruit and become a noble cedar. And under it will dwell every kind of bird; in the shade of its branches birds of every sort will nest. And all the trees of the field shall know that I am the LORD; I bring low the high tree, and make high the low tree, dry up the green tree, and make the dry tree flourish. I am the Lord; I have spoken, and I will do it."[47]

---

46. Guelich, *Mark 1—8:26*, 249.
47. See also Dan 4:11–12, 20–21.

The parable speaks of the future, immense size of the kingdom. The birds represent the nations. The story then pictures the people of these nations settling in the kingdom's branches.[48] At a time when the kingdom included Jesus and his disciples, this was an astonishing parable. It heralded a day when the kingdom will be the largest of all kingdoms, rulers, religions, ideologies, and authorities.

Stunningly, this has occurred, as we see in our day. Through people sent by God's Son to plant the seed of Jesus and the word, in the years after Jesus, the kingdom extended throughout Europe. Once more of the world was discovered, it filled the Americas, Oceania, and Australasia. It is now penetrating more deeply into Asia and even into the Middle East. This kingdom is indeed the most significant ideology and religion in the world. It began as a tiny seed of an idea found in the person of Jesus. Now, it has spread to be a massive tree in the garden that is God's world. As with the previous parable, we have a fulfilled prophecy, with Christianity now unquestionably the world's leading religion.[49]

Interestingly, we have a connection to Eden here. In this tree, God is rebuilding what was shattered by the fall. The story of the kingdom will culminate in the vision of the new heavens and earth in Revelation 21–22. Heaven and earth will merge. There will be a city and in its center, the garden of God, where the nations find healing and their people, eternal life.

Parables Summary (4:33–34)

Here, we have a pithy statement summarizing the extent of Jesus's teaching. Mark explains that he used parables publicly to the extent of the people's capacity to listen. Nonetheless, in private, he explained everything to his disciples. These words form a frame with 4:10–13, whereby Jesus taught in parables to the crowds but taught directly to his disciples.

Questions

- Should Christians fast? Why? Why not? Share your experiences.
- What does the parable of the wineskins teach us about renewing the church today?

---

48. Alternatively, the birds are enemies of God (cf. vultures), who nest in the shade of the kingdom without fully becoming a part of the tree.

49. See Hackett and McClendon, "Christians Remain World's Largest Religious Group."

- Should Christians keep the Sabbath? If so, in what way?
- Should we see healings and exorcisms today? In the same way? Why? Why not?
- Why did Jesus choose twelve apostles and why those kinds of men, e.g., fishermen, tax collectors, and zealous nationalists?
- Is a Christian's first priority the natural family or the people of God?
- What is the sin against the Spirit in 3:29?
- What is the central message of the parable of the sower?
- What is the central message of the parable of the lamp?
- What is the central message of the parable of the measure?
- What is the central message of the parable of the growing seed?
- What is the central message of the parable of the mustard seed?
- Why did Jesus teach in parables?
- How do we understand Mark 4:11–12?

Lesson Four: More Miracles, the Sending of the Twelve, and John's Death (4:35—6:29)

The Calming of the Storm (4:35–41)

AFTER THE PARABLE COLLECTION, Mark returns to the narrative of Jesus's ministry. This account will culminate in the confession of Jesus's messiahship in 8:29. This section happens within Galilee as Jesus itinerates through the region, crisscrossing the lake, and ministering.

Toward the evening of the day of teaching in parables, Jesus summons his disciples away from the crowds to cross the Sea of Galilee. They do so in boats. Such movement could mean that they crossed over to the Transjordan region or merely moved along the coast.

As they are traveling, there is a great storm. The term *lailaps* indicates a tempest, whirlwind, windstorm, or hurricane.[1] This event recalls Jonah 1:4: "And Yahweh hurled a great wind upon the sea."[2] The link to Jonah does not mean that this is a judgment on the disciples and Jesus as it did with Jonah. Still, both involve rough weather at sea and the danger of death.

The adjective "great" is *megas*, so we could translate this as a "megastorm." The storm was so powerful that the boats were beginning to fill up with water, which would have ultimately meant sinking. Such a storm is no surprise, for as any visitor to Galilee knows, "the Lake of Galilee was—and still is—infamous for sudden squalls. Surrounded by mountains at most points, the lake swirls violently when a strong wind enters."[3] Due to Mount Arbel (181 m tall) and other sharp cliffs on the western shore, strong winds often blow up and funnel onto the lake. They hit the Golan hills on the

---

1. BDAG, 581.
2. See also Job 38:1; Wis 5:23; Sir 48:10. See Stein, *Mark*, 242.
3. Brooks, *Mark*, 87.

eastern side and cause the winds to ricochet and blow back onto the lake, creating powerful storms and large waves.[4]

Amazingly, while all this is happening, Jesus is fast asleep in the boat on a cushion. Now that is the peace of God! Cushions were customary furnishings on boats used for reclining, sitting, or rowing.[5] Again, this calls to mind Jonah, who was asleep while chaos reigned in the boat that was about to sink (Jonah 1:5). The links to Jonah and others indicate that Jesus is the new Jonah.[6]

The disciples are the very converse of Jesus asleep at peace. No doubt full of fear, they awaken him, questioning whether he cares that they might drown. They address him as teacher (*didaskalos*). He is not yet Messiah and Son of God to them, despite the demons crying this out as he drives them out. Their understanding is still developing.

The term for perishing is *apollymi*, used in the NT of eternal destruction, but here of being destroyed or killed on the sea. Their cry is that of the desperate who do not understand God and his Son. They question whether he cares for his people. Of course, he cares immensely for them. He cares for all his creatures, even an individual sparrow. God knows the number of hairs on their heads (Luke 12:6–7). As such, they need not fear. As 1 Pet 5:7 says, "Cast all your anxiety on him because he cares for you" (NIV).

Jesus then demonstrates to his disciples that he does indeed care. He gets up. He rebukes the wind with two Greek words with very similar meaning. "Be quiet" is *siōpaō*, used in Mark of people being silent, including Jesus at his trial (14:61; see also 3:4; 9:34; 10:48). The second is *phimoō*, which has the sense of "muzzling" an animal (1 Cor 9:9; 1 Tim 5:18). Jesus used it earlier in silencing the demon that he then drove out in his first Markan miracle (1:25).

The response of the sea and the wind is instant. The wind ceases, and both the wind and the sea become extremely calm. The term for "greatly" or "absolutely" here is *megas* again; hence, the mega-storm becomes a mega-calm.

On one level, this demonstrates that Jesus cares deeply for his people. His concern and power are a source of great comfort to us when we are facing the storms that life in a fallen world brings. More fundamentally, it illustrates Jesus's power over the natural elements and speaks of his divinity. For the ancients, the sea represented disorder and chaos. Creation took the chaotic primordial sea and brought forth order from chaos (Gen 1:1–2). A flood brought uncreation. The waters receding saw a recreation. The sea was

---

4. Winstead, "Galilee, Sea of."
5. Bromiley, "Cushion," in *ISBE*, 1:840.
6. Matt 12:39–41; 16:4; Luke 11:29–32.

also a place of God's enemies, such as the sea serpent, Leviathan, or dragon (Job 41:4). The sea itself became a metaphor for Israel's enemies.[7]

The Exodus was the great event of liberation, where the sea was a force of destruction of Israel's enemies. Recalling the Exodus, Joshua split the Jordan so that Israel could cross over into the land for the conquest (Josh 3). He also made the sun stand still to win a battle (Josh 10:13).

Here, we see that the new Joshua's absolute power to calm the sea with mere words speaks of his divine power to free his people from threat through control of the natural order. For Mark and his source Peter, this is another indication of his divinity. For the disciples at this point, they are not so sure who Jesus is.

Jesus then challenges his disciples with two questions. The first questions their courage: "Why are you so spineless (*deilos*)?" *Deilos* means cowardly (Rev 21:8). It is used in Deut 20:8 and Judg 7:3 of those afraid to go to war (see also 1 Macc 3:56). His second question digs deeper into their understanding of his identity: "Do you not yet have faith?" They have not yet fully understood just whom they are dealing with in Jesus. He is the Messiah and God the Son.

We also see here the link between fear and faith. True faith is fearless, i.e., trusts in God despite and amid terrible circumstances. It appears here that the presence of faith is evidence of a lack of faith. However, fear itself is not the issue. Fear is a natural response to life-threatening situations, but when we are afraid, we should trust God. So, this story is really urging us to trust God even in the most dangerous life-threatening situations. Jesus is always with us, even if he is seemingly asleep on a cushion. If we trust him, we will get through anything. We can do so because he is God the Son, who has complete control over the creation.

The disciples' response is not to lock onto who Jesus is and confess his messiahship; this will come later. Instead, their response is greater fear. The Greek is creative, using a verb and closely related (cognate) noun to convey the idea of real fear: "They feared with great fear." Again, *megas* is used, used earlier of the mega-wind, and then the mega-calm. After Jesus had done "the impossible," they became mega-afraid. *Phobos* language has a semantic range that includes awe to abject terror. Here, there seems to be a blend of both. They are both terrified of and full of awe at Jesus's power and authority.

Their perplexity is seen in the final question in which they discuss Jesus's identity. They ask, "Who, then, is this being that even the wind and the sea obeys him?" When one has grown up in the Jewish story, the answer

---

7. E.g., Isa 30:7; Ps 87:4; Ezek 29:3–5, 32:2–8; Jer 51:34.

would seem to be self-evident; Jesus is Immanuel, God with us (Matt 1:23). However, to them at this stage, Jesus is just a man, someone John baptized. While he is powerful, he is not using his force to deliver Israel. As such, they can see his power but are not yet sure of his identity.

This verse articulates the central theme of Mark's Gospel: Who is Jesus? The Gospel ends with the women in much the same state at the empty tomb: full of bewilderment and fear. Mark writes proclaiming the good news of Jesus and allowing the message to call us to recognize he is the Christ and God the Son. Readers are challenged to read the Gospel and make up their minds. Mark and Peter, whose gospel Mark shares, want us not merely to ask, "Who is this?" Through their writing, God is calling us to open our eyes, perceive his identity as God the Son incarnate in the man Jesus, and then fall to our knees and worship him.

The Exorcism and Sending of the Demoniac (5:1–20)

We come to another fantastic story of deliverance, building more and more a picture of Jesus with full sovereign power over nature and the forces of evil. The area Jesus enters is uncertain, as here we have one of the most significant textual challenges of the NT. The options in the ancient Greek sources are three: Gerasenes, Gadarenes, or Gergesenes. We have the same problem in Matt 8:28 and Luke 8:26.

While the region of Gerasenes could be original in Mark based on the texts, this is unlikely as the city of Gerasa was around fifty km (thirty mi) from the lake, and the region did not extend to it. Gadara was closer, only ten km (six mi) from the lake, and its territory extended to the water. However, there are no hills or caves in the area that make sense of the story. An alternative, proposed by Origen in the early to mid-third century, is Gergesenes. However, his reasoning was faulty, as no town called Gergesa has been found.

The best option is a town by the name of Gerasenes, a small village that is today called Kersa, which is possibly a derivative of Gerasa. Here, there are steep hills and cave-tombs a km or so to the south. Indeed, if one visits the area on the northeast edge of the sea, Kersa makes perfect sense. Moreover, Decapolis was only a couple of km away (v. 20).[8]

Wherever he is, Jesus steps ashore from the boat into what was almost certainly a gentile region. The presence of a demon-possessed man in

---

8. See further the discussion in Brooks, *Mark*, 89–90.

the tombs is not surprising, especially with people unable to restrain him and him prone to loud outbursts and self-mutilation (5:1–5). The response of the demoniac demonstrates that demons are devoted to the death and destruction of people.

This man is comfortable in the tombs, a place of terror to first-century people, a place where demons lived. It also shows that this man was rejected by the community, living in a place of uncleanness with the dead. The demon leads the individual to self-mutilation and superhuman strength. Guelich notes that this man shows the four characteristics of insanity in Judaism: 1) running about at night (5:5); 2) spending the night in a cemetery (5:3); 3) tearing one's garments; 4) destroying what one has been given.[9] However, his insanity is demon-induced. Self-mutilation in the Scriptures is also linked with pagan worship. A good example is Elijah and the priests of Baal, who cut themselves to invoke their god (1 Kgs 18:28).

This man is fiercely strong and so calls to mind the "strong man" in Jesus's earlier encounter with the Pharisees (3:27). In his debate with them, Jesus stated that the strong man must first be bound. Jesus will enact this here. The passage also reminds us of Mark's description of Jesus as "the stronger one" (1:8). Here, Jesus will demonstrate this not merely by restraining the man but by liberating him from possession by a whole legion of demons. Following the calming of the storm, we have yet another indication of Jesus's immense power as Messiah and God the Son.

Verse 8 tells us that when Jesus comes to him, Jesus demands that the demon leave the man. The imperfect *elegen* (from *legō*) suggests that Jesus had not yet succeeded, implying resistance from the demon horde in the man. These evil spirits are the sorts of demons that are very resistant, and deliverance requires prayer (cf. 9:29).

As in other instances, the demon recognizes Jesus (v. 7; cf. 1:24; 3:11). He asks Jesus what he will do with him. He names him Jesus, Son of the Most High God. This name for God emphasizes Jesus's complete supremacy over any other claimants to the name God. "Most High God" has its origins with Melchizedek King of Salem (Jerusalem) (Gen 14:18–22; Heb 7:1). It is found throughout the OT and NT, referring to God.

Interestingly, the demonized slave girl in Philippi uses it of Paul and Silas, who were preaching the way of salvation and are slaves of the Most-High God (Acts 16:17). The twofold use suggests the term is used by the demonic forces of hell.[10] Nevertheless, while the hordes of hell know who Jesus is, aside

---

9. Guelich, *Mark 1—8:26*, 278.

10. Num 24:16; Deut 32:8; Pss 46:4; 50:14; 57:2; 73:11; 78:35, 56; 107:11; Dan 3:26; 4:2; 5:18, 21; Luke 1:32, 35; 8:28.

from the odd exception, the Jewish leaders will never know, and the disciples are slowly learning. Then again, merely knowing who Jesus is will not save them, for they must also submit fully to his lordship.

In response, the man pleads with Jesus not to torment him (v. 7). His appeal likely refers to the torment of eternal destruction reserved for the demons and their master (Matt 25:41; Rev 20:9). He seeks to invoke a vow on Jesus (*okrizō*) to this effect. Some see this as an attempt to curse Jesus; however, this is unlikely. The vow he makes is in the name of God, a most solemn oath, even from a demon.[11] We are not to make such oaths and demands using God's name (Matt 5:33–37).

The response is not instant. Jesus asks the demon its name (v. 9). The demon speaking through the man responds, "Legion."[12] While this is not necessarily literal, as that would involve as many as six thousand demons, it indicates many demons.[13] In that there are two thousand pigs present, there could be that many, although even that is dubious.

The name "legion" is from the Latin and invokes thoughts of the Roman military. We see here that the new Joshua has not come to destroy the Roman legions with the forces of God, something Jesus could do at any point were he so to choose Matt 26:53). Instead, he has come to declare war on the demonic legions that inhabit, corrupt, and destroy humankind. He has also come to deal with the problem that allows the demons to do this—our sin.

This passage resonates with Eph 6:10–18, where Paul carefully explains that our war is not with people and their institutions. The war is spiritual, with Christians battling demonic forces that lie behind human institutions, inhabit them, and work through them to enslave and destroy us. This man represents Jesus driving Satan and his angels back.

Through the man, the demon begs Jesus not to send the demons outside the region and asks to be sent into the herd of pigs nearby. The desire to remain in the region could relate to the idea of demons attached to particular regions as territorial spirits.[14] The pigs confirm that the setting is a gentile context, as mishnaic law strictly prohibited Jews from raising pigs (*m. B. Qam.* 7:7). It is also an area of tombs into which Jesus as a Jew should not go, for it

---

11. The Greek *ton Theon* is not an address of Jesus as God. This would require the vocative (address) of *Theos*. It is the basis of the sought-after promise. Furthermore, he has just named Jesus "Son of the Most High God" and clearly in context, he is God's Son, not God.

12. Guelich, *Mark 1—8:26*, 281, notes that "legion" was a Latin loan word designating a Roman unit or brigade which at the time was fixed at six thousand.

13. Brooks, *Mark*, 90.

14. Hooker, *Gospel*, 143.

was unclean (mind you, that sort of thing did not stop Jesus elsewhere). The large herd indicates that the pigs were for food and commercial purposes.[15]

Interestingly, Jesus agrees to the request. His affirmative response shows that the demons recognize his authority and that he is comfortable with the demons remaining in the area. Furthermore, Jesus seems to be okay with sending them into pigs. Hence, he does so, and they enter the two thousand pigs that then plunge down the slope and over the cliff and drown (vv. 9–13). The demons' response and that of the pigs demonstrate Jesus's total power over the demons and the natural world. The death of the pigs again shows the destructive power of the demonic, who seek death and destruction.

Why would Jesus agree to do this? A range of explanations is given. Some find it offensive, particularly in light of Christian morality and ecological sensitivities. It is seen by others as a folktale and untrue. To protect Jesus from critique, some believe it was the man who caused the pigs to go off the cliff as he ran around madly. Again, to preserve Jesus's integrity, some rightly recognize that it is not Jesus who causes the pigs to die, but the demons. Still, Jesus sent the demons into the pigs. Some simply cannot see a reason.

One possible answer relates to our understanding of demonology in the first century. In that time, it was understood that evil spirits did not want to be free to wander, but sought a body to inhabit. Hence, entering the pigs was better than being in one person.

However, a better reading of the story views it from the perspective of the value of human life and that person's well-being. The reaction of the townsfolk shows their false values. When they see the man well (5:15), they should be delighted to see the man healed. However, all that concerns them is the economic loss of the pigs. For Jesus, while all animals are of value, a person's well-being is far more important than that of pigs.

Similarly, a person is of much more value than any money lost. The locals place animal life and material gain above the good of the man. The event drives to the heart of the gospel, the restoration of people's relationship with God and their wholeness. By sending the demons into the pigs, Jesus exposes the people's values. They then seek for Jesus to leave the region rather than yield to him as King and invite him into their city to minister among them (cf. John 4:40).

This story is an example of where people put their business interests and economic well-being before those of the kingdom of God. An economic concern is understandable at one level, as two thousand pigs would represent a great deal of money. Nevertheless, the value of one human life restored is

---

15. Guelich, *Mark 1—8:26*, 281.

of far greater worth. Due to their distorted economic concerns, these people prefer to allow the forces of darkness to terrorize this man and region. They should have rejoiced that he was set free. They should have responded by honoring Jesus and bringing their sick for healing.

Jesus's decision to send the demons into the pigs does not mean that Jesus has no concern for animals. However, in this case, he is prepared to use animals to help people realize that there is nothing more valuable than a person and his or her wholeness. One of the dangers of the current ecological movement is that we begin to value animals above humans. Certainly, we should work hard for a sustainable future and reduce the ecological destruction of the planet, but not at the expense of human need. Elsewhere, even one sparrow is valuable to Jesus and his Father (Matt 10:29; Luke 12:6). Earlier in Mark's Gospel, Jesus was with the wild beasts (1:13). Jesus loves all animals, but he loves us more, for we are created in his image to join his family if we but believe.

In vv. 18–20, Jesus begins to leave. The man begs Jesus to go with him. Stunningly and unusually, Jesus forbids him from joining his group of disciples. Elsewhere, the likes of Bartimaeus are welcomed to join Jesus (10:46–52), if they are prepared to pay the cost (10:17–22; Luke 9:57–60). Jesus's refusal could be because the man is a gentile, and while the message of Jesus is for the world, it must first begin in Israel. After his resurrection, gentiles will be attached to Jesus and be welcomed into Christ's inner circle. Such a conclusion fits with the messianic secret. Jesus silences Jews and demons within Israel who recognize him. He does not silence the demons or this man, probably because the man is outside of the nation and will minister among gentiles. Hence, there is no chance of a revolution if he does so.

However, Jesus does not rebuke the man for asking to join him. Moreover, importantly, he assigns a ministry to him. He sends him home to tell his people of the Lord's mercy and healing. We see here that Jesus calls, welcomes, summons, sends, and commissions us at his leisure and pleasure. He has his reasons, and we are simply to obey.

The man's response is obedience, and it represents the ideal of discipleship. He does what Jesus commands. He testifies to what God has done in his life throughout the Decapolis, a ten-city region in southern Syria and northeastern Palestine, which at the time was part of Syria.[16] This passage gives us insight into what is required of disciples. Ministry for God is not self-selected but assigned by Christ. We should also take note of the contrast

---

16. See Ciampa, "Decapolis." Pliny the Elder, *Nat.* 5.74, gives the earliest list of the ten cities: Damascus, Philadelphia, Rapana, Scythopolis, Gadara, Hippo [=Hippos], Dion, Pella, Galasa [= Gerasa], and Cantha. However, this may refer to a geographical area rather than to the specific cities.

between the people of the town and the exorcized man. The locals reject Jesus; the man wants to join Jesus and obeys him. Those wanting to be disciples are to emulate the man's response.

On reflection, this is a striking moment. This man is almost certainly a gentile. He is not one of the disciples. He was formerly a deeply wounded and demonized man and so a terrible candidate for ministry. He would probably have been seen as a hopeless case. However, he is the first person sent to do evangelism in Mark's Gospel,[17] even though he is ill-equipped. We see here another fantastic example of how God takes the downtrodden and turns them into ministers of his gospel.

All in all, we have here another extraordinary example of healing in the Synoptics. This event is not merely a physical and spiritual deliverance, but the restoration of community. The shalom of the kingdom is breaking in through Jesus. The heinously demonized man is restored. As he is returned to his family, the community itself experiences God's healing.

The Raising of Jairus's Daughter and Healing of the Bleeding Woman (5:21–43)

What a story! We have two miracles jammed into one, using the Markan sandwich, with the importance of faith highlighted in the healing that lies at the center of the chiasm:

Mark 5:21–43

A^1 Jairus's daughter (5:21–24a)

B Healing of the hemorrhaging woman because of faith (5:25–34)

A^2 Jairus's daughter (5:35–43)

Both involve the number twelve—a woman held in bondage for twelve years and a twelve-year-old child. The bleeding woman has suffered for as long as the child has been alive. We see in this passage Jesus's compassion for females who are suffering, as he addresses them affectionately, heals them, and raises them from the dead. The power of God is liberating men like the demoniac, and women and children like these people.

Hot on the heels of Jesus calming the storm and driving out a legion of demons from the demoniac, it is clear that Mark is summoning us as

---

17. In 3:14, Jesus chooses the Twelve and empowers them so that "he might send them out to preach." He does not actually send them until 6:7–13.

readers to see the immense power of Jesus and to recognize his identity as God's Son.

As in other situations in Mark, in this account, two stories are blended into one (e.g., 3:20–35; 11:12–23). There is a healing and then the resurrection of a girl from the dead. Both again demonstrate Jesus's immense power. Jesus can drive out a legion of demons, heal a woman who merely touches him, and raise the dead. Who is this man? Mark's answer: Jesus, Christ, Son of God—or better, God the Son!

In v. 21, Jesus returns from the region of the Gerasenes to the more familiar area of his ministry, probably in Capernaum. Again, a great crowd gathers. His ministry in this time was like a magnet to people in need; he always drew a crowd. We are not told what Jesus is doing; probably, he is teaching and healing.

He is approached by a ruler of the synagogue, an *archisynogōgos*. The "'president of the synagogue' (*archisynagōgos*) was an elected position of esteem in the Jewish community. This leader had responsibilities for arranging the synagogue services and overseeing the building concerns."[18] We know the name of the man, Jairus, which has the meaning "he enlightens." After Jesus's earlier clashes with Jewish leaders, his approach has a note of doom. However, this man's intent is not malicious; he genuinely wants Jesus's help. We see here that while the Jewish leadership almost universally reject Jesus and conspire to have him killed, some from the leadership are drawn to him. These include Jairus, Nicodemus (John 3:1–9; 7:50; 19:39), and Joseph of Arimathea (15:43). Later, Paul would become Jesus's follower, as would other priests and Pharisees (Acts 6:7; 15:5). The naming of Jairus likely means he became a Christian, joined the movement, and was a source for Mark's Gospel.

His genuineness is seen in him falling at Jesus's feet, an act of homage. He approaches Jesus and asks him earnestly (many times) to heal his daughter by Jesus laying his hands upon her. He is clearly aware of the healing power of Jesus. If this is Capernaum, he was likely there when Jesus performed his first Markan miracle, driving out a demon and teaching with authority in the synagogue (1:21–28). He would have been witness to Jesus's forgiveness and healing of the disabled man (2:1–12) and the healing of the man with a withered hand on the Sabbath (3:1–6). He may also have been aware of Jesus's healing meeting at Peter's home (1:29–34). News of Jesus's other work around the region would also have come to him (3:7–12).

His twelve-year-old daughter was near death with an unspecified problem (5:22–24). Such a situation should not surprise us, as life expectancy

---

18. Guelich, *Mark 1—8:26*, 295.

was only around forty, and children often died of a multiplicity of diseases with which we can quickly deal today.

This man is important because he is a Jewish leader who had witnessed Jesus's power and did not then demand a sign. He recognizes God in Jesus. He thus is breaking ranks from his fellow Jewish leaders, who want Jesus dead. His approach shows that there will always be some from the powerful who come to Jesus. He also demonstrates great faith in Christ, having heard of Jesus's healing power. Jesus's response illustrates his grace, as he immediately goes with the man. Jesus was prepared to respond to anyone who approached him with genuine need. We can contrast this man to the rich young ruler to whom Jesus also responds but who goes away sad. We also see a contrast with Jesus's refusal to let the delivered man come with him in the previous passage. This man is a Jew, and Jesus will go to his house and heal for him. Again, a large crowd follows him. In v. 25, the narrative shifts to the second part of the healing encounter, to the bleeding woman. It will return to Jairus and his daughter in v. 35.

The power of Jesus to draw crowds is seen again as he is mobbed en route to the synagogue ruler's home. The verb *synthlibō* is found only here in vv. 24 and 31 and compounds *syn* (with) and *thlibō*, which has the sense of pressing or crushing.[19] One can imagine the crowded Middle Eastern street with animated crowds crushing the man imbued with power.

The woman is not named, unlike Jairus, indicating she is not the source of the story. Her bleeding is most likely menstrual. If so, she would have been unclean and marginalized from the community. In Lev 12:1–8, a woman after childbirth must be purified for forty days, eighty for a girl. She is also unclean during her menstruation. She is forbidden from anything holy and thus from the sanctuary. After purification, she must offer the appropriate sacrifice before she is then "clean from her flow of her blood." In Lev 15:19–30, a woman with a bloody discharge during menstruation is unclean, as is anything that comes into contact with her for seven days. However, if she has a discharge of blood at other times, for "all the days of the discharge she shall continue in uncleanness" (v. 25). Furthermore, every bed, seat, or anything she touches is unclean, requiring the person who comes into contact to bathe and wash his or her clothes. After the flow stops, she must make the appropriate sacrifices.

These legal requirements indicate that the woman should not be out in public in contact with others. Hence, she is unclean and making others unclean by doing as she does. So then, what this woman does is bold and

---

19. A related noun, *thlipsis*, speaks of persecution, i.e., being pressed down or crushed. See Silva, *NIDNTTE*, 2:461.

socially dangerous as not only is she a woman, but in her uncleanness, she would defile Jesus, the holy man.[20] She will also make Jesus unclean if she touches him or his cloak, meaning he should then bathe and wash his clothes. As such, what happens after her healing is even more astonishing: the seemingly unclean Jesus resurrects the dead girl! He should have gone to bathe and wash his clothes rather than go to the house of the dead child. Of course, touching the dead will also make him unclean. Hence, we get a sense of Jesus's total disregard and concern for such things as clean and unclean laws (see also 7:1–23). Of course, he was not unclean, as evidenced by God's power to heal in him.

The woman is also poor, having used up all her financial resources seeking help from physicians. This encounter calls to mind the story of Tobit, who spent money on doctors in the hope of healing his eyes that had been blinded by sparrow's droppings. Tobit writes, "I went to the physicians to be healed, but the more they treated me with ointments the more my vision was obscured by the white films, until I became completely blind" (Tob 2:10).[21]

As such, this encounter is another example of Jesus being moved to care for the poor. We will see this again when the disciples are told, "You give them something to eat" (6:37) and when the rich ruler is sent to sell his possessions and give to the poor, which he is not prepared to do (10:21). While Luke's Gospel emphasizes this dimension of Jesus's ministry, it is already present in Mark.

This woman had also been sick for twelve years, which counterbalances the twelve years of life for the girl. One female is released from twelve years of bondage; the other is released from death at age twelve.

The woman may have been unclean, but she had spiritual insight, unlike the so-called clean religious leaders (Jairus, a recent exception). She rightly perceived that all she needed to do was touch Jesus's cloak, and she would be healed. Later, whole crowds in Gennesaret would come reaching to touch him and experience his healing (6:53–56).

Some see here evidence of a belief in magic, but it can equally be seen as a recognition of the power of Christ. What this indicates is how power

---

20. Guelich, *Mark 1—8:26*, 296.

21. See Kee, "Medicine and Healing," 4:660, who avers that the few references to doctors in the OT see them as unreliable (Gen 50:1-14; 2 Chron 16:12; Job 13:4; Jer 8:22—9:6; 46:11; 51:8). However, there is also evidence in Judaism of seeing physicians as God's agents (see especially the Greek-influenced second-century Wisdom of Sirach, 37, 38, and Josephus, *War* 2:136; *Ant.* 8:44-45). In the NT, Jesus notes positively that "those who are well have no need of a physician, but those who are sick," implying that he understands the need for doctors (Matt 9:12; Mark 2:17; Luke 5:31). There are also negative statements such as this (Mark 5:46; Luke 8:43).

emanated from Jesus's being, even his clothing. Her touch causes Jesus's power to flow from him to the woman. It is notable that the flow of power healing her is immediate (*euthys*, v. 29), again showing the propinquity of Christ's power, another classic Markan theme. Interestingly, the phrase "flow of her blood" (*hē pēgē tou haimatos autēs*) is almost identical to the Greek of the LXX of Lev 12:7 (*tēs pēgēs tou haimatos autēs*). This Levitical allusion confirms the nature of her problem but also her healing, ritual purity, and social reintegration. The Jewish fear was that her uncleanness would flow to Jesus. The converse is the case. His power flows to her, activated by her faith and need.

Despite there being tens or even hundreds of people touching him, Jesus immediately (*euthys*) feels the power go out from him from this one woman's touch. His doing so indicates that although the flow of his power is involuntary, Jesus was aware of his power and his ability to use it. As we see later, it is the woman's faith that the Spirit in Jesus sensed, and this draws his power from him.

We see other points in the NT narrative where the power of God can be transmitted through cloth (Acts 19:12). The implication of Acts 5:15 is that Peter's shadow could bring healing. Even more importantly, in 6:13, the apostles heal with the use of anointing oil. Hence, Protestants overreach when they repudiate Catholic understandings of the use of oil and holy water in healing, even perhaps healing through statues. While some of the theology undergirding this is flawed, there is no reason that God cannot do such things. Indeed, if he can use oil, he can heal in any manner he chooses.

Feeling his power, Jesus stops, looks around, and asks who touched him. Not surprisingly, the disciples ridicule this as they see the vast crowd and the implausibility of finding the perpetrator. Jesus stopping in this way causes the woman to come forward and identify herself. She does so with fear and trembling, indicating her genuine terror, but also her immense courage (real courage is seen where there is genuine fear). Perhaps knowing that she has violated the ritual purity of Jesus and the many in the crowd she had touched, she falls before him. Her response may be due to a combination of fear and a desire to worship her healer.

Jesus responds compassionately, calling her daughter (*thygateia*).[22] Naming her thus can be read as Jesus calling her *his* daughter. More likely, she is being identified as a daughter of Abraham and God, a part of the

---

22. Note too in the next section the reference to "your daughter," speaking of Jesus's warm attitude to this woman. Just as Jairus loved his daughter and was concerned for her healing, so is Jesus concerned for Jairus's child, who is suffering, and he releases her from her bondage.

covenant community. Despite her discharge and uncleanness, she is still part of God's family.

Jesus tells her that her faith has made her well or saved her. His pronouncement speaks of her inner heart attitude that Jesus perceived and that drew his power out. This inward faith was demonstrated in her confidence that he could heal her by touch. The Greek here is *sōzō*, in the perfect tense, indicating that her healing continues into the present. The use of *sōzō*, "save," is double-layered, speaking not only of her healing but her salvation to come (cf. 1:15). She is also healed socially, now able to reintegrate into Israel's religious life (after making the appropriate sacrifices). Hence, her healing is not only physical but spiritual and social. The blessing "go in peace" was a typical Semitic farewell[23] invoking the fullness of God's *shalom*, i.e., complete restoration.

In v. 35, the scene shifts to the second frame in the Markan sandwich, to Jairus and his sick daughter. Some people come from Jairus's home and inform Jairus that his daughter is dead, that he should leave Jesus alone. We can see that they consider Jesus the teacher, showing that they do not yet perceive his real identity as Messiah and Son of God. We do not learn of Jairus's reaction, whether he is frustrated at Jesus or the woman at delaying Jesus's getting to his home to save his desperately ill daughter. Perhaps seeing the healing of the woman gave Jairus great hope. This hope is now dashed.

However, Jesus overhears them speaking and speaks to Jairus, telling him not to be afraid. The command *mē phobou*, "do not be afraid," was said by God to Abram in Gen 15:1. Isaiah told Israel not to be afraid of the Assyrians (Isa 10:24) and that God would deliver them from Babylon (Isa 41:13; 43:1). God spoke to Daniel with the same words in a vision that changed his very appearance (Dan 10:12, 19). An angel also spoke these words to Zechariah, as did Gabriel to Mary (Luke 1:13, 30). God twice said these words to Paul (Acts 18:9; 27:24) and the ascended Jesus once to John (Rev 1:17). In other Gospels, Jesus also said these words to Simon Peter (Luke 5:10), the disciples (Luke 12:32), and Israel (John 12:15). These words directly address Jairus's undoubted terror. "Do not be afraid" is a word from God to us in every situation.

Jesus then adds, "Just believe." Again, this transcends the context and speaks to us in any situation. It also recalls the juxtaposition of the themes of fear and faith in the calming of the storm (4:40). The antidote to fear is faith or trust. For us, whatever we face, this should speak as a word from God: "Do not fear, only believe."

---

23. Guelich, *Mark 1—8:26*, 299.

Jesus does not wait any longer but takes his inner circle of Peter, Jacob (James), and John with him. Again, we see Jesus's freedom as Lord to choose his leaders and assign them appropriate roles. Peter, Jacob (James), and John are often called Jesus's inner circle or executive leaders. They are set apart for significant leadership roles in the church to come. Jesus takes them with him, as he does on the Mount of Transfiguration and in Gethsemane (9:2; 14:33).

They come to the house that has now become a typical Middle Eastern mourning context with loud wailing and emotional lament. Those mourning may have included professional mourners[24] or, as is more likely, Jairus's family in the depth of despair.[25] Years ago, I watched my twenty-three-year-old sister die and saw the deep lament and pain of my family, especially my parents. There is nothing as hard as losing a child and family member, especially one so young.

Jesus addresses the mourners, telling them that the girl is just sleeping. His words raise the possibility that she was not dead but in a deep coma. However, the context makes this very unlikely, unless we assume that the people were stupid. Ancients knew a dead body as well as we and arguably more, for with people dying young and often, they saw death all the time. That she is dead is confirmed by the report in v. 35 and the mourning in v. 38. What Jesus means is that her death is not yet permanent; he can awaken her to live (although, ultimately, she, like all people, will die).

Their response is to laugh at him. The Greek *katageleō* has the sense of "to ridicule" someone.[26] Jesus then sends them outside and takes the child's parents and his inner group into the room where she lies. He then takes her by the hand, violating matters of ritual purity through making contact with a corpse.[27] The words of healing are the transliteration of Aramaic, the language Jesus would have primarily spoken. Others transliterations recorded in Mark include *Corban* ("given to God," 7:11), *ephphatha* ("be opened," 7:34), *Abba* ("Father," 14:36), and *Eloi Eloi lema sabachthani* ("My God, my God, why have you forsaken me?," 15:34). In Matthew, we also have *mammon* ("money," Matt 6:24) and *raka* ("fool," Matt 5:22). Here, Jesus says *Talitha koum*, "Little girl, get up," healing her with touch and word.

As with the woman with the issue of blood, the girl is raised and healed instantly (*euthys*). We see the immense power of Jesus, even over

---

24. Hooker, *Mark*, 150.

25. Guelich, *Mark 1—8:26*, 301, notes that "even the poorer families had mourners that usually included two flute players, a woman to lead in antiphonal singing or chanting accompanied by hand clapping and percussion instruments."

26. BDAG, 515.

27. Guelich, *Mark 1—8:26*, 301.

death—another indicator of his divine power. Such displays of his might do not necessarily prove that he is God or God the Son. Elijah and Elisha similarly raised children from the dead (1 Kgs 17:17–24; 2 Kgs 4:32–37). However, the way he did it should have alerted those present to Jesus's identity. For Mark, he is the Messiah and the Son of God, and the right response is to fall at his feet, as did Jairus and the healed woman.

Nothing specific is said about Jairus's faith, and all indicators are that the family was filled with the converse, unbelief. Hence, we cannot immediately say that it was Jairus's faith that caused the healing. It was definitely not the faith of the girl or the family. As such, we see the mystery of faith and healing in this passage. Sometimes, we can see that faith is a reason for healing. At other times, Jesus simply takes the initiative and heals. His response is his prerogative; yet not our will, but his be done.

In v. 43, we see the messianic secret again as the girl, her parents, and Peter, Jacob (James), and John are told to be silent about this. News of the resurrection of the girl after Jesus's walking on water, driving out a legion of demons, and publicly healing the bleeding woman could explode a revolution. Such a revolt is not Jesus's desire. Instead, he is seeking a "relovution," whereby, by the love of God, the world is transformed. Notably, the parents are urged to provide for the girl's needs. She may be healed, but she needs food to continue to live. They are charged with fulfilling their responsibility.

A Prophet without Honor (6:1–6a)

With his disciples, Jesus now shifts location from Capernaum and the area beside the Sea of Galilee to Nazareth, some forty-five km west (1:9, 24). He likely visited his family, who were no doubt relieved to see him after having tried unsuccessfully to intervene in "his madness" earlier (3:21, 31). As was his custom as a faithful Jew living under the Torah, Jesus goes to the synagogue on a Sabbath. There, he teaches. The event may be the same as that which Luke recounts in Luke 4:16–30; however, there are significant differences. First, unlike here, there are no miracles recorded in Luke. Second, there is no reference in Mark to the content of his sermon. Third, and more importantly, there is no attempt to kill Jesus in Mark's account. As such, this is probably a different visit.

As in Luke's account, the initial response by many is astonishment (cf. Luke 4:22). Then they raise questions concerning him. They query the origin of his power to do the miracles he does and then his wisdom. They then ask how it can be that the boy they watched grow up among them with his mother, brothers, and sisters, who worked among them as a carpenter, could have such power.

Mention of his family has some intriguing features. First, Joseph is not mentioned, which may indicate he is dead. Jesus is the carpenter, and so his stepdad may have died before his baptism and ministry. Second, we learn the names of his brothers. They are all named after significant figures in Israel's story. Jesus is likely named after Joshua son of Nun or the high priest after the exile (Hag 1:1; Zech 3:1). Jacob (James) is named after the grandson of Abraham, who was renamed Israel. Joses is another form of Joseph, recalling the son of Jacob who governed Egypt. Judas is named after Judah. Finally, Simeon was another of the sons of Jacob. We can see that they were a genuinely Hebrew family. Perhaps one might say that Jesus was a "Hebrew of Hebrews," as was Paul (Phil 3:5). Third, Jesus had sisters, although we know little of them. Fourth, all these children surely rule out the Roman Catholic idea of Mary's perpetual virginity. Finally, Jesus was a craftsman.[28]

Any positive views of Jesus are overshadowed by these questions that stopped people from seeing that Jesus was a prophet, let alone the Messiah and Son of God. Instead, they become offended at him. The term *skandalizomai* has the sense of being a stumbling block or causing them offense (causing a scandal).

Jesus's response is to quote an old proverb: "Only in his hometown, among his relatives, and in his own house is a prophet without honor." This maxim is a saying recorded in some form in all four Gospels and the Gospel of Thomas (v. 4).[29] It is also found in some form in external sources such as the Oxyrhynchus Papyrus and Plutarch.[30] The rejection of the prophets is found as a recurring theme in the Scriptures.[31]

This saying rings true into the present age. People today often struggle to accept that Jane or Johnny, who grew up among them, has grown up and is capable of God's work. Sadly, often a person making his or her way in ministry has to move on to another context to find admiration. We see this in theological studies, where locals often show little real appreciation for the

---

28. The Greek *tektōn* was used for manual workers of stone, metal, and wood. Justin Martyr (*Dial.* 88) in the mid-second century notes that Jesus made plows, yokes, and other farm instruments. See further Silva, *NIDNTTE*, 4:467–70.

29. See Matt 13:57; Luke 4:24; John 4:44; Gos. Thom. 31.

30. P. Oxy. 1.6 AND *Exil.* 604D. Plutarch writes: "You would find that the most sensible and wisest people are little cared for in their own hometowns" (Campbell, "Why Did You Abandon Me?," 102).

31. Stein, *Mark*, 283, notes 2 Chron 24:19; 36:16; Neh 9:26–30; Jer 35:15; Ezek 2:5; Dan 9:6, 10; Hos 9:7; Matt 5:12; 23:29–31, 34–35; Luke 6:23; 11:47–51; 13:33–34; Rom 11:3; 1 Thess 2:15; Heb 11:32–38; and Rev 11:1–10; 16:6; 18:24.

great achievements of scholars, whereas these scholars are held in esteem elsewhere. Such rejection just seems to be the way it is; we cannot see past their backgrounds.

In v. 5, Mark states that Jesus could do no miracles in Nazareth. However, while this sounds absolute, this is then qualified, that he could do a few of them. Matthew's version softens 6:5, shifting the language from "could not" to "did not," seeing this less as Jesus's inability and more as his unpreparedness to do miracles. Either way, Jesus's power to do miracles appears to have been somewhat limited.

Verse 6 tells us why. Jesus is amazed at the unbelief of his people. Mark is hinting that it was a lack of faith that led to this inability or unpreparedness to do miracles in Nazareth. As such, this again points to the Markan link between faith and healing. Again, we face the question concerning the relationship between faith and miracles. Not every miracle in Mark involves a statement of faith, nor do the majority of miracles mention faith.[32] Some do, including the disabled man (2:1–12), the bleeding woman and Jairus (although Jairus's faith is not mentioned, he is urged to believe, 5:21–43), the Syrophoenician woman (7:24–30), the demonized boy (9:14–29), and Bartimaeus (9:46–52). It is common to read into the miracles that lack a direct reference to faith the assumption that faith was determinative in Jesus acting as he did. However, this is not sound exegesis and is dangerous.

What we have in Mark is data that tell us that faith is a determinative factor in many instances where Jesus heals. However, there are other times that Jesus acts without any reference to faith. This inconsistency shows that faith is one factor and not the only issue. Furthermore, we make the mistake of jumping to our context and assuming we should and could have the same fantastic success as Jesus, if only we had enough faith. Such a view is presumptuous, for God's purposes are more complex than this.

Even Jesus did not have all his prayers answered in the affirmative, as shown in the garden of Gethsemane (14:32–50). There, Jesus prayed thrice for deliverance from the cross while showing his complete trust on God, his Father. God essentially said, "No, I have other plans, namely, to save a world through your death." Hence, we cannot jump into a hyper-faith theology that expects God to act if we have enough faith. Instead, we place our trust in God and believe in him for his healing. Then we accept his decision and believe in him just as much, whatever he does.

Here, however, the lack of faith appears to have caused Jesus to do fewer miracles. Could this be one of the reasons that atheistic contexts do not

---

32. See Mark 1:21–34, 40–45; 3:1–6, 7–12; 4:35–41; 5:1–20; 6:30–44, 45–52, 53–56; 7:31–37; 8:1–10; 8:22–26.

see as many miracles as we hope? Is it because we place our trust in science and medicine more than God that we see few miracles? Does our unbelief have the effect of blunting the power of God to work in our context? These are difficult questions to answer, certainly, but perhaps it is so.

The Sending of the Twelve (6:6b–13)

The section from Mark 6:6 to 31 is another of Mark's framing sandwiches. In it, the death of John lies at the center. It is central because John marks the last of the prophets, the end of the OT prophetic period. The frames concern the twelve apostles. Hence, we see the end of one era and the beginning of another. We see here the transition from the prophetic to the apostolic age.

Mark 6:16b–31

A^1 Sending out the Twelve (6:6b–13)

B *Death of John the Baptist, ending the era of the prophets (6:14-29)*

A^2 Sending out the Twelve (6:30-31)

After his pretty unsuccessful attempt to evangelize his own family, Jesus leaves Nazareth. The Greek suggests he went in a circuit around the villages teaching and ministering.[33] This period of ministry likely focused on Galilee, although it may have included Judea (cf. Matt 9:35). He then summons to himself the twelve apostles he had appointed for the task of mission in 3:13-19. Their authority over unclean spirits recalls 3:15. The term for summoned (*proskaleō*) carries the technical sense of the setting apart of these twelve for a specific ministry. We know that Jesus's group of disciples included more than just the Twelve; hence, we see again Jesus's freedom to appoint those he wishes to lead his mission.

They are sent out. The Greek is the verb associated with *apostolos*, *apostellō*, from which the term mission comes (*missio*, the Latin meaning "to send"). They are sent out in pairs ("two by two"). Sending in pairs is common across the early Christian tradition.[34] The need for at least two may also be due to Jewish legal tradition requiring two to three witnesses.[35]

---

33. The Greek of *periagō* is imperfect past tense, indicating a period of teaching. Guelich, *Mark 1—8:26*, 315, notes that teaching here should not be taken too narrowly and includes preaching and healing/deliverance ministry. The term *kyklō* suggests going around teaching on a circuit.

34. See Matt 10:2-4; Luke 10:1 (of the seventy-two); Acts 13:1-3; 15:39-40.

35. See Deut 17:6; 19:15, cf. Matt 18:16; John 8:17; 2 Cor 13:1; 1 Tim 5:19.

Otherwise, it is due to travel conditions, safety, and mutual support.[36] They have the authority to preach, heal, and expel demons (6:7, 12–13). The granting of authority over evil spirits indicates Jesus's complete authority and ability to grant that authority to his followers at will. Being sent involves first being called.

Using a forceful Greek word for "command" (*parangellō*),[37] Jesus instructs them. His appeal reads like a military commander instructing soldiers. Alternatively, it can be paralleled to a sports coach instilling the game plan into his or her team. The instructions appear to relate only to this mission rather than universally. This mission then is a training exercise. They are to put into practice what they have observed in Jesus. It is also preparation for the evangelization of the world.

The instructions are to take the barest of essentials and trust in God's provision for their mission. They can take sandals for traveling on the harsh roads of ancient Galilee and Judea. They can take a tunic (*chitōn*), a shirt worn next to the skin by both men and women.[38] However, they are not to take a spare *chitōn*. They are to take no food provisions (literally, "no bread"), no money on their belt (*zōnē*), and no traveler's bag or knapsack (*pēra*).

The *pēra* was used by Cynics, who begged as they traveled. Some have tried to argue that Jesus was a Cynic, an anti-establishment philosopher. However, neither he nor his disciples were anything like this. They did not beg, nor were they anti-establishment. They were dependent on God and those God provided to assist them. They did not *directly* oppose the status quo, but challenged the leader to be faithful to God's call, and preached the kingdom of God and repentance.

As noted, this was a training exercise and does not mean that modern mission should replicate their financial limitations. Indeed, Paul urged the very opposite: self-supporting mission through one's vocation (e.g., 1 Cor 9:1–15). With that said, modern churches, seminaries, evangelistic organizations, and mission agencies would do well to give people a taste of such a training exercise. They should also ensure that they do not cross the line from dependence on God to begging.

As far as accommodation was concerned, they were instructed to stay where they were welcomed until leaving the setting. Where the apostles were not welcomed, they were to shake off the dust from their feet as a

---

36. Guelich, *Mark 1—8:26*, 321.

37. BDAG, 769, notes it means "to make an announcement about something that must be done, give orders, command, instruct, direct of all kinds of persons in authority, worldly rulers, Jesus, the apostles."

38. BDAG, 1085.

testimony against those who rejected them. Doing this was a sign of symbolic judgment against those who spurned them. It symbolically implied that they renounced the very soil on which the town stood. Some Jewish sources indicate that Jews leaving gentile territory would act in such a way (*m. Toh.* 4:5). Paul and Barnabas did this very thing when leaving Pisidian Antioch (Acts 13:51).

In vv. 12–13, Mark summarizes their mission. They went and preached that people should repent, turning from their sins to God. They cast out demons and, using anointing oil, healed many who were sick. We see the power of God in Christ being gifted to others. Aside from the exorcised demoniac in 5:19–20, this represents the genesis of the mission of the church. Jesus authorizes and empowers people to continue the mission; we are those people. The use of oil is not surprising as oil was seen as having a therapeutic healing effect (Isa 1:6; Luke 10:34) and was used in the early church for healing (cf. Jas 5:14–15). We can continue to use anointed oil today.

Jesus was not a one-man-band. At the center of his mission strategy was the equipping of others for mission. His initial purpose was to train the Twelve. If the right reading in Luke 10:1 is the seventy-two, then these twelve each trained teams of six to join them. In Acts, the whole church of one hundred twenty receives the Spirit and is empowered to be Christ's witnesses throughout the world (Acts 1:8; 2:1–4).

Another seven were appointed in Acts 6:1–8. Two of them, Stephen and Philip, became great evangelists of the church. Others joined them as the Spirit enabled. Now, there are bodies of God's people all over the world, and mission is their business. These missionaries include those traveling across cultures proclaiming the gospel. They include people in their local contexts. Wherever they are and wherever they go, they share Christ in their attitudes, lives, words, and deeds: at work or school, with families and friends, in social clubs, and as they go from place to place. The term mission is not merely to be used to describe those going overseas to share Christ, but all of us. Mission begins at home.

We are not to be individuals in mission. Our job is to work with others. We are also to replicate ourselves as leaders by making disciples who mature and themselves become disciple makers (Matt 28:18–20). We should not be threatened when God raises talented people to serve alongside us. Indeed, we should pray for the Lord of the harvest to raise such people up (Matt 9:38). When they emerge, we should delight in them, nurture them, and teach them also to train others. In this way, the church will never stagnate but will grow as God raises others and brings more and more people into his kingdom.

We see here the nature of our mission. Our mission is to join God in the restoration of whole communities. At the mission's center is preaching, deliverance, healing, and the restoration of those we meet along the way. Those of us appointed by God to follow in the footsteps of the Twelve must accept the call and go and do likewise. In so doing, the kingdom penetrates society, and it is renewed by those being transformed in Christ.

The Identity of Jesus and the Death of John the Baptist (6:14–29)

The passage begins with something coming to Herod's hearing, although we are not sure what has come. It certainly includes Jesus's name. He may have come to hear about Jesus through Herodians, who had observed Jesus heal the man with a withered hand in the synagogue (3:1–6). The missional activities of Jesus's apostles ministering throughout Galilee may also be in view.

The Herod here is Herod Antipas, tetrarch of Galilee at the time. He was born in 20 BC, son to Herod the Great and to Malthace, his Samaritan mother. At age sixteen, he was appointed tetrarch of Galilee and Perea in 4 BC and ruled to AD 39. He was then banished to Gaul (France) because of Herodias's ambition for Herod Antipas to gain the kingdom from Caligula, the then Roman Emperor. Herod's opponents plotted against him, making known that he had massive stashes of weapons.[39] In reality, Herod was not king; that office was held by Tiberius Caesar Augustus. He was one of those puppet or client kings put in place by the Romans to govern the region and thus serves as an excellent example of those who ruled in the ancient world.[40] Sadly, some contemporary leaders look more like him than Jesus.

Mark takes this opportunity to inform readers of the different ideas floating around concerning the identity of Jesus, which, in many ways, is the key theme of the Gospel of Mark. The list is more or less repeated when Peter confesses Jesus's messiahship (8:28).

The first possibility circulating was that Jesus was a resurrected John the Baptist with his power to do miracles. Such a view of Jesus suggests at least three things. First, John was dead, which will then be narrated. Second, some at the time believed in the possibility of resurrection. Such a hope makes sense because many in Israel hoped for the resurrection from the

---

39. Josephus, *Ant.* 18:245–56.
40. Guelich, *Mark 1—8:26*, 329.

dead (e.g., Dan 12:1–3). Third, the idea of Jesus being John raised could hint that John performed miracles, although we have no record of this.

A second idea concerning Jesus was that he was Elijah. Such an interpretation of Jesus is not surprising as Elijah had not died. Instead, he had been translated to heaven in a whirlwind while in a chariot (2 Kgs 2:1, 11). Unsurprisingly, this led to the hope that he would return. Elijah was also a miracle worker as was Jesus, even if Jesus's miracles outstrip anything in the OT.

There were expectations in Judaism that Elijah would return, preceding the Messiah, based primarily on Malachi.[41] Such hope is seen in 9:11, as the disciples ask Jesus: "Why do the scribes say that first Elijah must come?" Jesus then states, "Elijah does come first to restore all things" (9:12). He explains that John the Baptist is the fulfillment of this hope (9:13), while Jesus himself is the Messiah.

We see this expectancy on the cross as Jesus cites Ps 22:1. His words are misinterpreted as a call to Elijah (15:35–36). John's Gospel also references this hope as the Baptist is asked whether he is Elijah, which he denies (John 1:21, 25). Later in Mark, on the Mount of Transfiguration, Elijah appears in person with Jesus. His doing so rules out that Jesus is Elijah (9:4–5). Luke also develops the idea of John as Elijah in his Gospel (Luke 1:17; see also 4:25–26). As such, it is not surprising that many saw Jesus as Elijah announcing the coming of the Messiah. The disciples themselves may have contemplated this possibility.

The third view was that Jesus was "a prophet like one of the prophets," suggesting that he was another God-sent herald like Jeremiah (Matt 16:14). This perspective is also unsurprising, as Jesus itinerated, preached the kingdom of God, and did miracles (even if to a degree never before seen).

For Mark, all these views are inadequate. Jesus is the Christ, the Son of God (1:1). Demons know this. The tension is building to the point where Peter confesses it. Sadly, the general populace cannot see it. A small number will, but most never come to this realization. In v. 16, we are told that Herod holds the first view, considering Jesus a resurrected John. This verse creates a bridge to the account of Herod's killing of John.

The story of John's death is pretty straightforward, even if it is horrific—a classic example of ancient politics and imperial behavior. Herod imprisoned John because Herod's wife Herodias, previously married to his brother Philip, did not like John's preaching that condemned her and Herod's marriage as unlawful. However, from fear and uncertainty about John, Herod was unwilling to have him killed. At Herod's birthday feast, Herodias's daughter's dancing caused Herod, no doubt aroused by her dancing, to make the insane

---

41. See Mal 3:1; 4:5, see also Sir 48:1–14; 4Q558 = 4QVision.

offer of up to half his kingdom. Rather than make the most of this ridiculous offer of wealth and power, she asked for John's head on a platter. Reluctantly, this was granted, and John was beheaded. He was then buried by his disciples. This account has a range of spinoffs for Mark's narrative and our understanding of Jesus that need to be drawn out, even if briefly.

First, it is a shockingly sad story, for John was a prophet of God sent to prepare the way for God's Messiah and Son. His death in such a manner is horrific.

Second, we see the difference in morals between this typical worldly royal figure and Jesus. As will be discussed further on 10:1–12, the Caesars were famous for their sexual dalliances. The Herods were no different. Their idea of marriage is not in any sense Christian or faithful to Jewish law.

Herod Antipas's first wife was the daughter of the ruler of Arabia (Nabatea), Aretas IV Philopatris (ca. 9 BC–AD 40). On a trip to Rome, Herod fell in love with his brother's wife, Herodias. She then divorced his brother Philip, and they married. Her divorce and remarriage led to a war between Herod and Aretas. According to Josephus, Herod lost the war because he had killed John.[42]

John the Baptist's critique was based on Lev 18:16: "You shall not uncover the nakedness of your brother's wife; it is your brother's nakedness." Similarly, in Lev 20:22: "If a man takes his brother's wife, it is impurity. He has uncovered his brother's nakedness; they shall be childless." Later in Mark, Jesus will repudiate adultery and sexual immorality as evil (7:22–23). He will also summon the disciples to be faithful in marriage (10:1–12). We see here the clash of the world's view of sexuality and marriage and that of the kingdom. In societies full of sexual immorality, believers must hold to this ethic with love and grace.

Third, we see John functioning as a true OT prophet calling the King to account. This pattern is seen with Samuel and Saul, Nathan and David, Elijah and Ahab, and many other times in the OT.[43] In doing this, John showed immense courage challenging Herod and Herodias.

Fourth, we see the weakness of Herod, who, while considering John a righteous and holy man and being intrigued by him, was easily swayed by his own desires. No doubt, he had drunk too much by the time Herodias danced. Undoubtedly, her dance was erotic, and Herod was moved by his sexual desire. As so often in such situations, the consequences were appalling. In one moment, a life can be shattered with such weakness. God's people must be determined and resist such temptation.

---

42. Josephus, *Ant.* 18:109–16, 136; Dicken, "Herod Antipas."
43. 1 Sam 15; 2 Sam 12; 1 Kgs 18.

Fifth, we should note Mark's genius in placing this story before the feeding of the five thousand. Placing it before the five thousand enables us to see the vivid difference between the imperial patterns of the ancient world and the kingdom of God. Herod's party is self-centered; it is his birthday. Herod invites the leading military commanders and figures of Galilee to the feast. Waiters provide for their every need. The meal is lavish and opulent, with dancing and sensuality. During the meal, Herod makes the ridiculous offer of half his kingdom. Then, a prominent enemy of the state is assassinated. Revoltingly, his head is brought into the center of the party on a dish.

Contrast this with what follows. There is no celebration of Jesus's birthday in the Gospels. In fact, while we celebrate Christmas on 25 December (for some 6 January), we have no exact idea of his date of birth. Aside from Matthew and Luke recording his birth, it was of little interest to Jesus or the Gospel writers.

At the five thousand, Jesus's "military commanders" are present, having returned from their first mission. As we will see, they are not waited on hand and foot by servants. Despite Jesus withdrawing with them to rest, crowds gather. Rather than send them away so he can celebrate with his leaders, he ministers to them. There is no invitation to the elite; anyone who desires to be there is present—the poor, disabled, broken—sheep without a shepherd. Indeed, the elite of Galilee, including Herod, are welcome to join the party. However, they do not, because their so-called king, Herod, is partying with them up the road.

Rather than use the crowds to wait on him and his team, Jesus has compassion for them. He teaches them the word of God. Rather than having a party, he feeds the crowd. Unlike the gluttony up the road, the food is simple, but it is ample. There is no erotic dancing. The "military commanders" are not served; instead, they are summoned to wait on the crowds. The leaders are the servants. The leftovers are sufficient for their needs, which will be satisfied after they have completed their service.

Here we see the clash of the patterns of the kingdoms of the world and Jesus. Mark is inviting us to see the power of what Jesus is doing and learn what we are to do as a result. While the rich get richer and gather together in their elite, celebrity culture, ignoring the plight of the needy, the true King of the world ministers where the pain is. Despite great tiredness, he and his disciples serve those in need. Such sacrifice is the kingdom of God in action.

Sixth, this is one of the NT accounts that shows the historicity of the NT. The figures in the account of the death of John can be cross-referenced to Roman history. The event caused a war. Josephus also records that Herod had

John put in prison and beheaded at Machaerus, which was a fortress to the east of the Dead Sea.[44] We can trust the historicity of the NT.

Finally, the story ends with John's disciples going to get his body and placing it in a tomb. Later, Jesus will also die. Sadly, no one from his family or the Twelve will come to get his body. It takes one of the Sanhedrin to realize who Jesus is, come and get him, and bury him in his tomb. Aside from the women and Joseph, Jesus was abandoned.

Questions

- What do we learn about Jesus and our Christian life from the calming of the storm?
- What is your answer to the question of 4:41?
- Why did Jesus tell the demoniac to share the message of what happened to him after silencing the others healed by him?
- What does the healing of the bleeding woman tell us about Jesus and our mission?
- What does the raising of Jairus's daughter tell us about Jesus and his power? What does it tell us about some in Judaism's leadership?
- Why did Jesus tell the apostles not to take any provisions for the mission journey in Mark 6?
- What does the banquet in which John the Baptist was killed tell us about the context and empires at the time?

---

44. Josephus, *Ant.* 18:116–19; Guelich, *Mark 1:1—8:26*, 330.

Lesson Five: Two Feedings, More Miracles, and More Controversies (6:30—8:13)

The Feeding of the Five Thousand (6:30–44)

As noted above, the mission of the Twelve frames the death of John. This is another example of Mark piecing together and linking stories, such as Jairus and the bleeding woman in Mark 5 and the fig tree and temple cleansing in Mark 11. The Twelve return and report what has happened in their mission.

Jesus's response is to encourage them to go and find a private place to have some rest. From v. 45, we know that for Mark, this is on the other side of the lake from Bethsaida. The location could then be anywhere along the shores away from the city, as "on the other side" is very imprecise (cf. Luke 9:10). Jesus does this because they were so busy with people coming and going that they did not have time to eat—this on top of having just returned from a busy mission trip. Their seeking rest speaks of the importance of having a break for recreation, worship, prayer, recovery, and sustenance after a period of intense ministry. Self-care is an essential aspect of having a long and fruitful ministry. Too many Christian leaders are burning out. We must take care of ourselves. We must also take care of our families and ensure they are not destroyed by our busyness.

However, the attempt is unsuccessful because they are seen slipping away in the boats, and crowds follow them and even go ahead of them on the shore, meeting them when they land. Again, we see the amazing impact of the ministry of Jesus and now his apostles.

As they arrive at the place, they are hoping to have a rest. However, the crowd that had tracked them in their boats along the shore is there waiting. Despite their need for rest and recuperation, when they saw the crowds, we are told that Jesus had compassion on them. The Greek term for compassion is again *splanchnizomai*, a term used of Jesus's attitude in 1:41, literally meaning the "bowels" and so speaking of Jesus being deeply moved in his inner being at their plight. This term speaks of Jesus's motivation for mission. As we consider the hapless state of humankind in today's chaotic world, we should be motivated in the same way.

The reason is that they are "like sheep without a shepherd." This illustration is another agrarian image in a world where shepherds carefully tended sheep, even knowing them by name. For Israel, God is shepherd, most wonderfully in Ps 23: "The Lord is my shepherd" (Ps 23:1).[1] The people of God are then sheep, not meaning that they are dumb (although they can be), but that they are a flock under God's care. Israel's leaders are also understood as shepherds, including the king (2 Sam 5:2; 2 Chron 11:2), especially David (Ps 78:71); judges (2 Sam 7:7; 1 Chron 17:6); Cyrus (Isa 44:28); prophets (Jer 17:16; Zech 11:4, 7); and general leaders (Jer 22:22). The image of sheep without a shepherd had a rich history in Israel at times when they were leaderless.[2]

Of particular note is Ezek 34, where the prophet castigates the failure of Israel's leaders to care for the flock, and so they are scattered with no shepherd. As a result, they will be destroyed. The Lord himself will be shepherd, searching for the lost sheep and bringing them home to care for them. Ezekiel then predicts that a Davidic shepherd will be raised to feed them (Ezek 34:23).[3] Jesus is the fulfillment of this hope (Matt 2:6). In John, he is the good shepherd (John 10; see also Heb 13:20). For Matthew and Luke, he seeks the lost sheep (Matt 18:10–14; Luke 15:7). His final act will be to divide the flock into sheep and goats in judgment (Matt 25:32). In eternity, Jesus will be our eternal shepherd (Rev 7:17). Christian leaders are charged with shepherding God's flock (e.g., 1 Pet 5:2). Indeed, the Greek for "pastor" is shepherd (*poimēn*, e.g., Eph 4:11).

Later in Mark, Jesus will cite Zech 13:7 of his death and the scattering of the disciples (14:27). Here, the great Davidic shepherd sees God's people, leaderless and harassed, and is filled with compassion and moved to act (v. 34). His first action is not to feed them with food, but to feed them spiritually. He teaches them. We see here Jesus, God's Davidic shepherd, feeding his sheep with the word of God, the most important of foods for God's people. As he says elsewhere, "A person does not live by bread alone, but by every word that comes from the mouth of God" (Matt 4:3, my translation).

1. See also Gen 48:15; Ps 28:9; Isa 40:11; Jer 31:10.
2. Num 27:17; 1 Kgs 22:17; 2 Chron 18:16; Zech 10:2; 11:4–17.
3. See also Ezek 37:24; Mic 5:4, 6.

As the end of the day is drawing near, the disciples, probably with genuine concern for the crowds, want to send them away to get food. However, the Davidic shepherd has other ideas. He gives them a simple command: "You give them something to eat," in which "you give" is placed first and has emphasis. This statement represents an important moment. Up to this point, the ministry of the disciples was spiritual: preaching the word, casting out demons, and healing. Jesus here introduces another dimension: when they are ministering and come upon people in need of feeding, they are to feed them. This statement adds social justice to the ministry of the church. We are to feed the flock of God with spiritual food, the word of God. Where there is impoverishment, we are to feed them physical food as well—social justice as a component of our mission.

Another angle here is the importance of Christian hospitality. The Gospels include many references to eating. In the ancient world and many cultures today, hospitality is critical for forming strong communities. Here, Jesus and the disciples host a meal. It is simple yet filling. Needs are met. At the heart of a community's life is eating together. Christians welcome the other into their homes and dine with them. Evangelism flows naturally in such environments. Indeed, it is probably around the meal table in homes dotted all over the biblical world that Christianity spread most. Westerners tend to be very individualistic and like to retire into their homes, shut the door, and do their own thing. We see here something different, hospitality and dining together.

The disciples estimate that it would cost two hundred denarii to feed the crowds. A denarius was a laborer's pay for a day. In New Zealand, two hundred eight-hour days' wages would be around $28,000 (about 74,400 RM). That is a substantial sum and would require a great deal of food. Their question of whether to go and buy that much food is likely laced with disbelief. Indeed, it is unlikely they had that much money, although the question could indicate they do. There may even be mockery in the question.

Jesus does not rebuke them for any failure but asks what resources they do have: five loaves and two fish. Jesus then performs the miracle. He orders the disciples to group the people. The Greek is most intriguing; they are to recline *symposia symposia* (banquet by banquet). The grass is green, perhaps suggesting that this is spring near Passover (March to June).[4] In v. 40, we have another delightful Greek phrase to describe the groups that reclined: *prasiai prasiai*. The term means "garden plot," and so we have the crowd reclining

---

4. Brooks, *Mark*, 109.

"garden plot, garden plot."[5] We then have them in garden party groups. Like flower gardens on the lawn, they adorn the grass.

The image of a garden invokes ideas of Eden and creation. People can eat freely from any tree. Jesus is enacting a new creation. The garden party also anticipates the future of the church. Groups of fifty to a hundred or more will soon be dotted all over the world, eating together and welcoming strangers. Later, Jesus would warn the disciples of the scribes and their penchant for sitting in the best seats in the synagogue and at banquets. Here, there are no best seats—or better, all seats are best; they all eat together in groups. Notably, the disciples are not even seated; they are waiting on the crowds.

The groups were about fifty to one hundred people each. The action of Jesus taking the five loaves and the two fish, looking up to heaven, blessing them, and breaking the bread invokes ideas of the sacraments, even if this itself is not sacramental (14:22) The miracle occurs after this sometime in the passing of the food from Jesus to the disciples and as they distribute it. Speculating further on the details is utterly futile; Mark simply assumes it has happened, and we are left uncertain how and exactly when.

Among the disciples are the mighty apostles, tired and hungry, having just got back from their first mission, the ones serving. Their effort in waiting on others reminds us of the call of the Christian leader: doing mighty works of ministry, yet donning an apron and serving, even when exhausted.

Verse 44 tells us that everyone ate and was satisfied. The term *chortazō* invokes ideas of people full and well-fed. This great feast anticipates the great banquet and wedding feast, where all God's people will dine with him at the eschatological banquet when Jesus returns (Matt 22:1–14; Luke 14:16–24, cf. Isa 25:6–8).

"They" in v. 43 suggests it is the apostles who pick up the leftovers. Food is not to be wasted. There are twelve full baskets left over. The number is significant because it means one for each of the apostles and any with them. They can now get the rest and recuperation Jesus wanted them to have (v. 31). Serving Christ will include interruptions to help the poor and inviting people to eat with us in our homes. God will supply all our needs according to his riches in Christ Jesus (Phil 4:19). We will sometimes have to wait to rest. However, rest we then must do, to be renewed for further ministry. Verse 44 is stunning, telling us there were five thousand men present. The Greek is the plural of *anēr*, "man," and so this does not include

---

5. BDAG, 860, has "garden plot, garden bed" and there is no reason to translate the two uses differently.

women and children. There could then have been anything from five thousand to twenty thousand people in attendance.

This whole scene invokes the provision of manna in the wilderness (Exod 16). Jesus here is Yahweh present and active, feeding the crowds in the wilderness. Prophets fed others in need. Elisha fed one hundred men with twenty loaves of barley and fresh ears of grain (cf. 1 Kgs 18:4, 13). Some food was not eaten, as in Jesus's miracles. Hence, those who experienced this would know Jesus was empowered with God, but unable to be sure whether he was God incarnate or a mighty prophet. Most assume the latter; we know he is the former. Soon Peter will declare this.

There is so much to draw from this miracle. We must ensure that we get away from ministry and rest. God provides. Sometimes we will be interrupted. When we are, we care for those in need. Jesus is full of compassion and the great shepherd. The people of the world who are sheep without a shepherd need him, if only they knew. Christians are to feed the world spiritually and physically. A little bit can go a long way. Our ways are not the ways of Herod and the world. God can turn five loaves and two fish into a meal for thousands. In Christ, God is creating a new people. We should always give thanks for our meals. Christian leaders and men can and should wait on tables. Jesus is God! Wow, what a lesson!

Jesus Walks on the Sea of Galilee (6:45–52)

Jesus forces or compels the disciples to get into the boat and go to the other side. Luke places this event near Bethsaida, while Mark sees this as on the other side of the lake (cf. Luke 9:10). We can try to harmonize this to remove the difficulty or accept that the Gospels are eyewitness testimony rather than perfectly polished modern history. If we accept this, then all that is different is the location. We are not sure where it happened.

Again, there is immediacy in the account (*euthys*). We see Jesus seeking solitude for prayer. He needs his space to with God his Father; so do we (cf. 1:35). Here then, is another reminder of the importance of our prayer life in having a faithful and fruitful ministry.

Jesus sees them struggling on the water, which might have been preternatural insight, or he could have seen them from the hill. The Sea of Galilee is around twenty-four km (fifteen mi) long and ten km (six mi) wide,[6] and as it was dark, some kind of spiritual insight must be in view. As noted in the account of Jesus calming the storm, strong winds were caused as winds came funneling in from the west because of Mount Arbel

---

6. Winstead, "Galilee, Sea of."

and the cliffs, crashed into the Golan Heights, and then bounced back onto the lake. The disciples had struck such a wind and were struggling to make headway. The boat in question could be like the so-called "Jesus boat" or "Galilee boat," which is 8.2 by 2.3m (27 by 7.5 ft).[7] For a sailing vessel, a headwind is always tricky.

Jesus then sets out after them, not in a boat as one would expect, but walking on the lake. Walking on the waters calls to mind Job 9:8, where God tramples the waves of the sea. Such an event shows that Jesus is something unprecedented; human beings do not usually walk on the sea.

By the fourth watch of the night, he has reached them. Primarily for military purposes, the Romans divided the night into four periods of three hours each. The first was *opse*, "the evening, late," which is the first watch (6–9 p.m.) (11:11, 19; 13:35). Second, *mesonyktion*, literally meaning "the middle of the night" (9 p.m.–12 a.m.).[8] The third watch is *alektorophōnia* meaning "at the crowing (*phōnē*) of the rooster (*alektōr*)" (12–3 a.m.) (13:35). Finally, the fourth is *prōi*, meaning "at dawn" (3–6 a.m.) (13:35, cf. 1:35). This event happened during the fourth watch and so in the early morning toward dawn.[9]

The term for "passes by" is *parerchomai*. It is used of God's angel passing over Israel's firstborn (Exod 12:23) and of crossing through the Red Sea (Josh 4:23; 6:8). It is also employed to describe Israel passing through the Jordan River into the promised land (Num 32:21, 27). Jesus coming on the water and passing by (same Greek word) also connotes thoughts of theophanies where God appears and passes by Moses and Elijah.[10] As such, Jesus here is demonstrating his divine power.

According to Mark, he intended to pass by the disciples. However, they saw him and predictably believed him to be a *phantasm*, a spirit, an apparition, or a ghost.[11] They cry out (*anakrazō*), the same term used of the demonized man in 1:23. Again we see the fear of the disciples.

There have been many attempts to find an explanation for Jesus walking on the sea (literally, "upon [*epi*] the sea"). Two of the main approaches are to see Jesus walking on submerged stones or mud flats exposed by the wind,[12] or rendering *epi* as "by" instead of "upon."[13] Another sugges-

---

7. Hilgert, "Ships; Boats," 4:484.
8. See Mark 13:35; Luke 11:5; Acts 16:25; 20:7.
9. Bratcher and Nida, *Handbook*, 422.
10. See Exod 33:19, 22; 34:6, cf. 1 Kgs 19:11.
11. BDAG, 1049.
12. See Derrett, "Why and How Jesus Walked."
13. See Jeremias, *Proclamation of Jesus*, 87.

tion is that he walked on ice on the sea.[14] However, *epi* plus genitive more commonly means "upon," and the whole story pivots on the disciples' thinking that Jesus was a ghost and terror. Rationalistic explanations miss this point; if indeed he had been walking on rocks, flats, or ice, or merely walking beside the sea, then there would have been no fear or thoughts of him being a specter.

Jesus responds with words of consolation: "Take heart, I am, do not be afraid." The first term is *tharseō*, a courage term that will be used by people encouraging Bartimaeus that Jesus is calling him (10:49). It summons the disciples to "be courageous."[15] The final clause, *mē phobeisthe*, is synonymous with *mē phobou*, used by Jesus to Jairus (5:36). It also effectively parallels *tharseō* in the first part of the statement, so we have here a chiasm.

The center of the chiasm is *egō eimi*. Most translations opt for "it is I," to translate *egō eimi*. However, the words are the Greek translation for the name of Yahweh.[16] The phrase is used frequently in John's Gospel in his "I am" sayings.[17] The chiastic structure and Jesus walking on the sea suggests that Jesus is assuming the name of God in the OT and so claiming divinity. This should not surprise readers, as Jesus has already said as much by forgiving sin (2:5), claiming lordship over the Sabbath (2:28), calming a storm (4:35–41), feeding the five thousand, and performing innumerable other miracles. Later, Jesus will use the same formula in his response to the high priest, which causes the high priest to condemn him (14:62). As here, it is likely Jesus used the divine name. Jesus is not merely the Son of God; he is God the Son.

Again, we see Mark's antithesis between fear and faith; the disciples respond in fear rather than faith. Rather than passing by, Jesus joins them in the boat, and instantly the wind abates. Jesus does not even command the wind; it just subsides. We see here Jesus's complete supremacy over the natural order, seen earlier in the calming of the storm. He is God the Son.

Quite naturally, the disciples are utterly and exceedingly amazed (v. 51). Such things do not happen! Their response may seem appropriate. For Mark, however, it is inadequate. He gives a reason why: they did not understand the bread and their hearts were hardened.

Contemporary readers tend to interpret this as understanding that the heart is the seat of emotions in contrast to the mind as the seat of rationality. On the contrary, the heart has the Hebrew sense of mind, i.e.,

---

14. Fairhurst, "Jesus Walked on Ice."
15. BDAG, 444.
16. Cf. Exod 3:14; Isa 41:4; 43:10–11; 45:22.
17. See John 4:26; 6:20 (walking on water); 6:35, 41; 8:12; 9:9; 10:11, 14; 11:25; 14:6; 15:1; 18:5, 6.

their minds were blinded to the reality of who Jesus was. That is, they did not understand; they just could not grasp who Jesus was. At this point, they had had the seed of the word implanted, but Satan was stealing it away (see 4:1–20; 2 Cor 4:4).

What Mark means is that they should have clued into who Jesus was at the feeding of the five thousand. They had seen him do all the things noted above, and then with five loaves and two fish he had fed a crowd of five thousand to twenty thousand people. They should have seen that he was God the Son, the Messiah, Daniel's Son of Man, the Prophet, all rolled up in one. He is the One. Alternatively, as argued in *Jesus in a World of Colliding Empires*, he is Theo, "the Expected One."[18]

The miracles of Jesus are effectively visual parables calling for interpretation and understanding. As signs of the kingdom, they must be interpreted theologically and discerned spiritually. The disciples were unable to understand the miracle and its implications. Their failure to this point and later understanding of Jesus's messiahship shows the way they progressively came to understand Jesus's identity. Such is our experience today; we come to know Christ and fully understand him more and more as we journey with him. We live as if God is saying, "Keep journeying, pilgrim. Come deeper. There is more!"

Jesus Heals Many (6:53–56)

This passage is a healing summary, the third thus far in Mark (1:32–34; 3:7–12). During these meetings, Jesus healed many of illnesses and delivered from demons. Hence, the miracles we have of Jesus are like a highlights reel. Gennesaret was also known as Ginosar, a town in the area of Naphtali between Capernaum and Magdala. It lay on the western shore of the Sea of Galilee. In the OT, it was called Kinnereth (Deut 3:17; Josh 11:2; 19:35). The term could refer to a fertile plain around 200 m (656 ft) above sea level and over 400 m (1312 ft) above the Sea of Galilee. The area spread to the west, north of Magdala (which is 212 m below sea level).[19] Jesus and the disciples may have landed there because they were blown off course by the wind.[20]

We see another example here of the rapid movement in Mark's Gospel with Jesus on the move, crisscrossing the lake. His fame is abundantly clear as

---

18. Keown, *Jesus in a World*, 1:76.

19. See the descriptions in Josephus, *Ant.* 3:515–18; Strabo, *Geog.* 16.2.16. An important road, the *Via Maris*, passed through Gennesaret, linking Megiddo to Hazor, Syria, and Mesopotamia. See Long, "Gennesaret."

20. Long, "Gennesaret."

he moves through the area, pausing in the towns, villages, and countryside, and people come running with the sick for healing. Their running to him shows their desperation. They were aware of his power to heal through his clothes, perhaps due to the healing of the bleeding woman in Mark 5. We can note that "*all* who touched it were healed" (italics added). We see his absolute power over sickness. Again, Jesus is God the Son, and Mark wants us to know it. The unleashing of such power may not be just to heal the sick but to get the blind and hard-hearted disciples to perceive who he is.

Clashes over Purity (7:21–23)

Here we have the resumption of controversy, which has been absent from the narrative since Mark 3. Pharisees and teachers of the law again come down from Jerusalem (cf. 3:22), perhaps attracted by the spread of interest in Jesus. News had reached them in the capital.

They "gathered around Jesus," suggesting that they were examining his ministry and challenging it. They observe that his disciples are violating Jewish eating customs[21] and are eating with unclean "unwashed" hands (7:2).[22] Eating with unclean hands was a feature of the theology of the Pharisees and Essenes. Verse 3 is an explanatory note for Mark's gentile readers, explaining Jewish customs. The Pharisees do not eat anything without washing their hands, including washing after returning from the marketplace and washing their eating and cooking utensils.

In v. 5, they directly ask Jesus why they do not "walk (*peripateō*)" in the traditions of the elders. These traditions were an extensive set of rules that were developed by pious Jews to ensure that the Torah was not violated. We ran into a similar problem in 2:23—3:6 concerning the Sabbath. Cleanness was part of the obsession with holiness in Israel's traditions. It was critical to keep oneself pure before a holy God. Uncleanness could be transmitted through other people (the sick, dead, unholy, sinful, and the gentiles) and things like unclean food.

In v. 6, Jesus does not give any explanation but directly and provocatively challenges them through the words of Isa 29:13. Initially, they were probably cited in Hebrew, but Mark draws on the LXX. In its original setting, the saying comes from Isaiah's song predicting the savage destruction

---

21. Guelich, *Mark 1—8:26*, 364, notes that this is covered "by the sixth division of the Mishnah (*Tohorot*) with twelve tractates, the eleventh of which is on 'hands' (*Yadaim*)."

22. One example is *m. Yad.* 1–2, which describes the water, the amount (one and a half eggshells), and the means necessary to wash one's hands ritually.

of Jerusalem by Babylon. The passage foresees Jerusalem besieged and then destroyed. God will come as the Lord of hosts "with thunder and with earthquake and great noise, with whirlwind and tempest, and the flame of a devouring fire." The nations will attack the city. The warning is utterly brutal, with the people's eyes blinded to what is coming. They are not able to read the words of the vision.

Verse 13 of Isa 29 is a word spoken directly from God. While the people honor God with their lips, their hearts are far from him. They have been taught to fear God, but they have no genuine awe of him in their hearts. Then Isaiah brings a message of hope that God will do wonderful things, including the deaf hearing and blind seeing and people finding refreshed joy in the Lord (Isa 29:18–19). He foresees the day when Jacob is no longer ashamed (Isa 29:22).

Here in Mark, Jesus (Messiah and Prophet) draws on Isaiah's words spoken to the people of Jerusalem before the exile to the current generation of Israel's leaders. He is the new Isaiah. They are like Israel's spiritually deaf, blind, and ignorant leaders who rejected Isaiah. They cling to the old wineskin of their traditions and cannot see what God is doing. There is more than a hint of warning that just as Babylon destroyed Israel over six hundred years before, this could happen again. This devastation will be more directly predicted in Mark 13, and Rome will besiege Israel and destroy Jerusalem and the temple in AD 70. However, the restoration dreamed of in the latter part of Isa 29 is coming to pass through Jesus, who heals the blind and deaf. While Israel will be destroyed, this healing will spread to the nations.

The Isaianic quote points out the hypocrisy of the leaders of Israel. They honor God with their lips. However, they are a million miles from God in their thoughts and beings ("hearts"). They worship God in vain or to no end (*martēn*).[23] Their teachings come from human origin and not from the heart of God. They are beset with the prevalent religious problem, hypocrisy. Their duplicity should cause us to consider whether our words and actions are aligned; they must be, if we are genuinely God's people.

The latter part of the verse is applied in v. 8: "teachings that are commandments of people." This critique refers to the tendency of the Pharisees to create oral law to support the core biblical injunctions. These traditions were a fence around the law (*m. 'Abot* 3.14). These laws, including Sabbath and ritual purity regulations, were declared to be of inferior status to the "weightier matters of the law." The important things include the two greatest commandments and others seen as central in Jesus's teaching (12:29–31, cf. Matt 23:23).

---

23. BDAG, 621.

Verses 9–13 present an example of how the Jews violated the essence of God's law in favor of constructed traditions. Jesus cites two crucial texts from Mosaic law. The first is the fifth of the Ten Commandments. Each Israelite was commanded to honor his or her parents (Exod 20:12; Deut 5:16). The second gives the consequences for failing to do so; that person is to be put to death (Exod 21:17; Lev 20:9).

Both of the laws confirm the fundamental point that children should honor their parents. Furthermore, they should care for them in their old age. Emphasizing the care of elderly people is appropriate for those of us in social contexts where the elderly are often left to fend for themselves and confined to retirement villages, rest homes, and hospitals. Other cultures care for their elderly through family structures, as was the case in ancient Israel and the Greco-Roman world. This passage endorses this.

Jesus here implies that the Jewish leaders who fiercely hold to the traditions of their fathers are violating the Torah. As such, they deserve to die. Of course, at no point does Jesus endorse the death penalty. Instead, in Christ, God is delaying the destruction of the ungodly to give people time to repent (2 Pet 3:9, 15). Nevertheless, the warning is still crystal clear. Their destruction will come to them if they continue to do this, destruction first through Rome and ultimately (if there is no repentance) to eternity.

Jesus then exposes a specific way in which they violate the law through the use of the Corban tradition. The term "Corban" comes from the Hebrew or Aramaic *qorbān*, which is transliterated into Greek as *korban*. It is translated by Mark as *dōron*, "gift" here (see also Matt 15:5). The term was invoked by Jews to declare that something is dedicated to God. However, they could still use what was declared Corban for themselves. The Jewish leaders were using this as a way to void their required commitment to care for their aging parents. There is a range of rabbinic passages that support this. Josephus mentions the practice.[24] Now the essence of the law is love, whether for God or others.

Hence, Jesus singles out this particular bit of Pharisaic sophistry to show how the letter of Jewish tradition could sometimes be hostile to the spirit of the law, in this case, the fifth commandment. The Jewish leaders had found a way out of the need to care for the mother and father by declaring that any gift is devoted to God. As such, it no longer needs to be given to the parents. In so doing, they nullified the word of God by a tradition.

The final clause of v. 13 suggests that Jesus had a list of other things that he could have used in this way. Earlier, he had exposed them concerning

---

24. DeHoog, "Corban."

the Sabbath. Later, in his last days in Jerusalem, he will debate them on a range of other matters.

In vv. 14–15, Jesus returns to the matter of ritual purity and uses the occasion to teach the crowd, including the Jewish leaders. He challenges the whole basis of Israel's concern for unclean food and hands. It is not what goes *into* people through eating and drinking that makes them unclean; it is what comes *out* of their hearts that is unclean. Real purity and impurity come from the heart, through the mouth, and not from what is eaten (see also *Gosp. Thom*, 14).

Interestingly, it took the early church a long time to completely grasp that eating food does not render a person unclean. In Acts 10:14–16, Peter required a vision from God to convince him that he could eat unclean food. This vision opened the way for him to enter the home of Cornelius and lead his family to Christ (Acts 10:17–33).

The clash between Paul and Peter in Syrian Antioch was on this very thing. When Jews concerned for ritual purity in eating came to Antioch, Peter withdrew from eating with gentiles for fear of the Jews, influencing Barnabas and other Jews. Paul's rebuke was due to seeing that if not addressed, the church would forever be divided between Jews and gentiles. (Gal 2:11–14).

In some passages, Paul draws a distinction between "strong" Christians who understand that food should not be rejected because it is unclean and "weak" Christians who find this difficult to accept.[25] However, the strong are to consider the weak as they decide whether to eat or not. The Jerusalem Council in Acts 15 speaks of putting aside these things.

Mark 7:17–23 takes place in a home after Jesus's teaching. Jesus explains that what we eat goes into our stomachs and is expelled into the toilet. It does not make us unclean in a ritual sense. What makes us unclean or gives evidence of our inward uncleanness is not what goes in, but what comes out of our hearts.

Verse 21–23 is a chiastic structure:

A^1 For inside from the heart of a person come forth evil designs

B A list of such evil designs and things

A^2 All these evil things come from within and defile a person

A^1 and A^2 both state that it is the heart that produces evil and defiles. Such things are "evil designs" and "evil things." The heart is the source of corruption. Evil flows from sinful hearts. The things then listed are evil, and

---

25. See Rom 14:1—15:3; 1 Cor 8:1–13.

disciples must resist them. Jesus lists twelve sins. We must thoroughly understand each one of them, as we who are God's beloved children must live to please him—not to earn his favor, for we already have it—but to please our God out of gratitude for all he has done and will do for us.

Sexual Immorality

The Greek *porneia* means all manner of sexual relationships outside of monogamous and heterosexual marriage.[26] These things include same-sex and non-consensual sexual activity, incest, and anything other than a monogamous, consensual, heterosexual marriage.

Theft

The term here is *klopē*, meaning "theft, stealing."[27] *Klopē* would include the taking of the property of another person, whether a paper clip or a million dollars. Christians are scrupulously honest where other people's possessions are in view. The term could potentially challenge the Pharisees and teachers of the law as they were manipulating the law to steal from their parents.

Murder

The term is *phonos* and speaks of murder and killing. The associated verb *phoneuō* is used in the Ten Commandments, and so this endorses this law. Christians are divided on the pacifist view that a Christian can never kill or endorse it, or that a Christian can kill as a last resort (e.g., a Christian policeman). Jesus never killed while on earth but did warn of the eternal destruction of those who defy God. What we can know for sure is that we should not murder, and if killing is necessary, it is an absolute last resort. This term would also rule out abortion and actively committing euthanasia.

---

26. Those who try to water it down to this or that sin and exclude some sins like homosexuality do so in the face of insurmountable evidence that in the NT, *porneia* is a term for all sexual activity outside of a monogamous heterosexual marriage where there is consent. See BDG, 693, who rightly state it refers to "every kind of unlawful sexual intercourse."

27. BDAG, 550.

Adultery

Again, we have a term that recalls the seventh of the ten commandments, "do not commit adultery" (Exod 20:14). There, the verb *moicheuō* is used; here *moicheia* is employed. Both passages reject any sexual relationship between a married person and someone other than the spouse.

The rejection of *porneia* and *moicheia* raises the question of how Mark's Jesus views a second marriage. In Mark, the answer is no, when a person divorces and remarries (10:1–12). A remarriage is adulterous. In the wider NT, there are more permissive passages. In Matthew's rendering of Mark 10, remarriage is permitted where there is *porneia*, "sexual immorality" (Matt 19:9). Paul, in 1 Cor 7:12–16, possibly permits remarriage where an unbelieving spouse divorces a believer. These passages suggest that while God's ideal is faithful marriage, the early church felt that there are occasions where a second marriage may be seen as legitimate.

Christians also must remember that we live under grace and not law. Hence, these are not laws that must be upheld to be saved. Instead, they are virtues for which we strive, doing our very best. God's grace will still cover a multitude of sins. However, we must not rely on this, or we cheapen God's grace and make it meaningless. Overall, single Christians should seek to be celibate and sexually pure. Married Christians should be committed to being faithful and loving husbands and wives. Divorce is a last resort but sometimes a necessary outcome.

Greed

The term is *pleonaxia*, which speaks of "the state of desiring to have more than one's due, *greediness, insatiableness, avarice, covetousness.*"[28] *Pleonaxia* can refer to a desire for money, sex, power, alcohol, or drugs; indeed, a desire for anything that becomes insatiable. Greed is one of the greatest sins of our world, as consumerism drives our economies. We are encouraged toward greed continually as we are enticed through advertising to feel a need to acquire and consume more. We are to resist this and live contented and simple lives, being greedy to use our resources for the needs of others, not for self.

---

28. BDAG, 824, italics in original.

Malice

The term *ponēros* can be a general term for evil as it is in v. 23. Here, it likely speaks of malice towards others.

Deceit

Dolos means "taking advantage through craft and underhanded methods, deceit, cunning, trickery."[29] These are tactics of the devil. Such deception is found among Christians who seek to manipulate situations toward their perspective. Paul reviles such tactics; they are not of God (2 Cor 4:1–3; 1 Thess 2:3–6). Christians are to be open and honest, transparent, and authentic people.

Debauchery

The term *aselgeia* means a "lack of self-constraint which involves one in conduct that violates all bounds of what is socially acceptable, *self-abandonment*."[30] It includes sexual immorality, greed, debauchery, licentiousness, drunkenness, and drug abuse, and would involve all aspects of our culture that mirror the profligate Greco-Roman culture. The ancient Romans were famous for their debauchery. Our world is not much different and is arguably getting worse. Christians are to resist and reject such living.

Envy

The phrase *ophthalmos ponēros* (literally, "the evil eye") was used of those who looked at someone with malice and cursed another person with the intent that they experience harm. It is hard to find one word for this as it can distort its meaning. The phrase also has different meanings in some cultures. At its root is malice, derived from envy. Some translations use "envy" (ESV, NIV, LEB, NRSV) or "evil" (NET).[31] However, better options might be malice, hatred, nastiness, meanness, resentment, or malevolence. Christians are not to harbor hatred towards others. This is repugnant.

---

29. BDAG, 256.
30. BDAG, 141, italics in original.
31. Bratcher and Nida, *Handbook*, 235.

Slander

The term is *blasphēmia*, which can refer to blaspheming God or to slandering other people.[32] Possibly both are in mind. Christians do not break the third commandment and misuse God's name or slander him. Nor are we to speak of others slanderously. We praise and worship God. We do not malign others.

Arrogance

The Greek here is *hyperēphania*, which has the meaning "a state of undue sense of one's importance bordering on insolence, arrogance, haughtiness, pride."[33] It is thus a person with an inflated ego, full of one's own importance, who thinks he or she is better than others. Pride is a subtle sin because we can often be arrogant and not know it. That is, we can seem nice on the outside, but we are always trying to manipulate things to our view because we think our perspective is superior. Such a vice is particularly dangerous for those who are gifted, whether by looks, intelligence, or physical attributes. Due to their confidence in their great attributes, such people can unwittingly put others down and fall prey to arrogance. We must search our hearts and remove all vestiges of self-importance.

Foolishness

This last term translates *aphrosynē*, which conveys a "state of lack of prudence or good judgment, foolishness, lack of sense, moral and intellectual."[34] We are to seek God's wisdom.

Jesus concludes by declaring these things "evil." They start in the heart—the passions and mind. Such things are evidence of our corruption. They come from the pit of hell. We must resist these things and not lead others into them (see later on 9:42–50).

---

32. The term has the sense of "reviling, denigration, disrespect, and slander" (BDAG, 178).

33. BDAG, 1033.

34. BDAG, 159.

The Healing of the Syrophoenician Woman's Daughter (7:24–30)

Here we have another healing encounter. It is intriguing for several reasons, not the least, the interaction between Jesus and the woman. Jesus is in Tyre. Tyre was a town formed over two thousand years before Christ on the Phoenician coast, about thirty-five km (twenty-two mi) south of Sidon and around fifty km (thirty mi) northwest of Capernaum. Tyre was once a city with an island that Alexander joined to the mainland of Phoenicia, creating a peninsular. It was very prosperous around one thousand years before Christ and was a key ally of David and Solomon. Alexander conquered the city, and it came under Seleucid control in 198 BC, falling to Rome in 64 BC. It was a Roman province with some autonomy.[35] People from Tyre and Sidon had earlier come to Jesus for healing (3:8). Today, this area is in Lebanon, to the north of Israel and Palestine.

What is interesting for us is that Tyre is gentile territory. We have here one of the rare times that Jesus encounters a gentile (although there may have been many encounters during the healing summary events). It sits alongside his encounter with the Roman centurion as a crucial passage concerning Jesus's attitude to gentiles while on earth (Matt 8:5–13; Luke 7:1–10).

Verse 24b–c is fascinating. Jesus enters a house shrouded in secrecy. He does not want anyone to know he is there. His desire for secrecy may again be the messianic secret (if this is a Jewish home). Alternatively, it could mean it is the home of a gentile. Another possibility is that he simply wanted to rest or instruct his disciples privately. Jesus, however, was recognized, perhaps by people who had come to him earlier (3:8).

Immediately (*euthys*), a woman came to him, presumably in the home, and fell at his feet, a sign of homage and submission. She is described as a Greek, the term *Hellēnis* here used as a synonym for a gentile. More specifically, she is a Syrophoenician, "an inhabitant of Syrophoenicia, a district which was so called because Phoenicia belonged to the province of Syria."[36] In early church tradition, she is known as Justa, and her daughter was Bernice.[37]

What follows is intriguing. The woman asks Jesus to exorcise a demon from her daughter, who is not present with her (v. 30). Jesus's reply sounds very reluctant and harsh. However, when unpacked, it is not necessarily so.

---

35. Ferry, "Tyre."
36. BDAG, 977.
37. *Clementine Homilies*, 2.19; 3.73; Plummer, *Gospel*, 188.

He is hesitant, stating in roundabout words that the children (of Israel) must be filled first. His reluctance could hint at what Matthew makes explicit: his mission must first be to God's historic people Israel (Matt 10:6; 15:26; cf. Rom 1:16). The gentile mission will come later.

Jesus states that it would not be right to throw the children's bread to the dogs. "Bread" here seems to be spiritual (Matt 4:4), referring to Jesus's ministry of proclamation of the word, healing, and other acts of restoration. The "table" speaks perhaps of the eschatological banquet and the breaking in of the hospitality of God (cf. Luke 14:15–24). The great banquet has begun, and the children of Israel are being invited. This woman is trying to gatecrash the party, one might say.

"Dogs" can be taken negatively, as dogs were generally despised, and Jews used the language to describe gentiles. However, the Greek for dogs is *kynarion*, "little dog" and perhaps puppy. Jesus is also the creator of all animals and even hung out with them in 1:13 during his temptation. So, it is hard to know if Jesus said this with a glint in his eye, thinking positively of her while wanting to minister to Jews first.

In v. 28, the woman answers with great ingenuity. She calls Jesus "Lord," which could simply mean "master, esteemed one" or have a more christological meaning, whereby she perceived him to be more than a mere person or prophet. She draws on the prevailing situation of little dogs running around and eating scraps off the table, a common enough thing in the ancient world and many contemporary situations as well. She is also identifying herself as part of the household in which the food is being eaten. She seeks to join the great eschatological feast. She acknowledges that the Israelites are God's children. She just wants to eat the scraps of the ministry of the King.

She draws to mind the great gentile women who feature in Jesus's genealogy: Rahab the Canaanite and Ruth the Moabitess. This situation calls to mind the passages in Matthew and Luke where people will come from the east and west and dine at the table of God with Abraham, Isaac, and Jacob (Matt 8:9–13; Luke 13:28–30). This woman is determined to be there. She is allowed in, and Jesus heals her daughter, feeding this hungry "puppy of God."

The encounter causes Jesus to respond affirmatively, telling her that her word has convinced him to deliver the demon from the daughter. So, while there is some reluctance on Jesus's part, he responds to the "barking" of this "puppy," and heals the daughter. The woman returns home and finds the girl on the bed, freed of the demon.

This passage and the earlier legion encounter (5:1–20) show that the gospel is breaking out of its Jewish setting into the gentile world. Such moments anticipate what will come in the future when the disciples preach the gospel to the nations (13:10). Mark is written from Rome in the 60s, and by this time, many "little dogs" were eating the scraps falling from God's dining table. Indeed, this continues to happen throughout the world. At a similar time in the 60s, Paul uses similar language, telling the Philippians to "watch out for the dogs!" (Phil 3:2, my translation). He means those who are forcing gentile converts to Judaize, coming under Jewish law, to be justified by faith. His language and this event anticipate the rejection of Jesus by Israel, as "dogs" from the world worship him.

We also see here the power of Jesus to heal across space and distance with a word. This capacity reinforces him as a man of supreme, divine power. Other such healings include the Roman centurion's servant (Matt 8:5–13; Luke 7:1–10) and the royal official's son (John 4:46–54).

The Healing of a Deaf and Mute Man (7:31–32)

Sidon is north of Tyre, so Jesus's return to Galilee is by a circuitous route. It involves him moving north from Tyre through Sidon and then southeast across the Leontes River past Caesarea Philippi and onto the east of the Jordan, so approaching the Sea of Galilee from its east in the Decapolis area.[38] What is more important than understanding the exact movement of Jesus and his group here[39] is that he lands in gentile territory, continuing his ministry there. In the Decapolis, a man is brought to him who is deaf and has a severe speech issue. These people may know of Jesus because of the testimony of the former demoniac throughout the Decapolis (5:1–20). The people are unnamed ("they"). The man's speech impediment is likely due to his deafness. The man could be a gentile, but we cannot be sure.

The healing is unusual for a range of reasons. First, Jesus takes the man away on his own or in private to heal him. It is unclear why Jesus would do this except to suggest that in each setting, Jesus, guided by the Spirit of God, was led to do things in particular ways. If this is so, we must be very attuned to the Spirit as we minister to people for their healing. We do not necessarily do the same thing every time.

The second remarkable aspect is how Jesus heals the man. To this point, Jesus has healed people with a word and or touch. Here, he goes through a more complicated ritual. He puts his fingers in the man's ears and then spits. It was believed in Greco-Roman and Jewish thought that spittle had a

---

38. Metzger, *Textual Commentary*, 82.

39. Scholars note the great difficulty of discerning what Mark is saying here. The geographical sequence is very difficult, as it does not work as described. See Guelich, *Mark 1—8:26*, 393, for some options.

therapeutic function. Later, in 8:22–26, as well as in John 9:1–7, spittle plays a role in healing blindness.[40] In this instance, we cannot be sure where he spat and whether he touched the man's tongue with the spit or his hand. What is likely is that he used the saliva in some way; otherwise, why mention it?

He then looks up to heaven and groans. One can understand why he looked up to heaven: he looked to his Father and his power. His groan is another fascinating aspect of the healing. The Greek *stenazō* can mean a sigh.[41] It could be a groan of frustration, sadness, anger, or a signal of his power ready to be released.[42] The term is used to describe the groans of believers suffering as they yearn for God's redemption (Rom 8:23; 2 Cor 5:2, 4). In Heb 13:17, it is used of obediently yielding to Christian leaders without moaning. In Jas 5:9, believers are not to grumble against one another. We simply cannot be sure why Jesus groans or sighs here.

Jesus then speaks the Aramaic word *Ephphatha*. Here we have the third time Jesus uses Aramaic in Mark, and the second time in healing (5:41; 7:11).[43] It is translated by Mark for a Roman audience: "Be opened." It is thus a voice of command to the tongue.

As so often in Jesus's ministry, the healing is immediate, with the man instantly able to hear and speak (7:33–34). As in other situations, Jesus commands secrecy. His appeal for silence is unusual, because Jesus is in the Decapolis and not in Galilee or Judea, and so revolutionary tendencies are not likely. It seems that as in Tyre, at times, Jesus simply does not want the word spread about him.

As in 1:45, the recipients are not deterred from preaching about what has happened. The response is astonishment: "And they were astonished beyond measure" (v. 37). The statement "he has done everything well" perhaps echoes the creation narrative in Gen 1:31.

This passage represents a messianic fulfillment of the OT hope of the messianic era: "He makes the deaf to hear and the mute to speak" (cf. Isa 29:18; 35:5–6). As with all Jesus's miracles, it also points forward to the eschaton, where all such maladies will be healed. It speaks into the present, encouraging us that where we find people with sickness, we should lay hands on them, for God can do amazing things. It warns us that healing can be a complicated thing and not merely a matter of saying a word.

---

40. Guelich, *Mark 1—8:26*, 394, who notes Pliny, *Nat. Hist.* 28.4.7; Tacitus, *Hist.* 6.18; Suetonius, *Vesp.* 7 and Str-B, 2:15–17.

41. BDAG, 942.

42. BDAG, 942.

43. See also Mark 14:36; 15:34; Matt 5:22; 6:24.

Whether a person is healed or not by prayer, we are to care for the disabled, a core aspect of our mission.

The Feeding of the Four Thousand (8:1–9)

We now have a second time in which Jesus feeds a giant crowd, a miracle of provision (6:30–44). Again, bread is involved. So, just as God provided manna in the wilderness for Israel, Jesus here supplies bread (cf. John 6:25–59). He is thus God's presence on earth, providing for his people. We can recall that Jesus was disappointed with the disciples for not understanding his identity, based on the feeding of the five thousand (6:52). This miracle then serves to give them another opportunity to perceive who he is. Jesus's central purpose is to get them to the point where they know he is God's Messiah and the Son of God. This moment is fast approaching, and the second miracle will help in this.

The miracle appears to happen in the area of the Decapolis, so many gentiles were likely present (7:31). As throughout Mark, there is another large crowd gathered. They are hungry, having been with Jesus for three days. Their need points to their poverty, which is not surprising, as most in the nation were living below the baseline. In the former feeding, the disciples took the initiative. Here, Jesus does. The reticence of the disciples indicates a failure on their part.

After summoning them, Jesus tells the disciples he has compassion on the crowd. He is deeply moved in his inner being for the plight of the poor (*splanchnizomai*). The verb is prominently placed first in the sentence to highlight it. Again, we are challenged to see the masses of the poor across the world and be moved to action.

Jesus also expresses concern that due to their impoverished state, they will collapse if they were to leave now and take the long journey to their homes in the Middle Eastern heat. The fact that some have come from afar reinforces the idea that there were gentiles in the crowd.

In v. 4, the disciples enter the scene. After Jesus had instructed the disciples "you give them something to eat" in the five thousand narrative (6:37), one would expect them now to take the initiative. However, the disciples demonstrate their lack of understanding by asking how it would be possible to feed this many people in the desert. Despite all that Jesus has done, they still do not realize his identity and capability.

There is no rebuke by Jesus, showing his immense patience with the disciples despite the frustration we know he has with them (6:52). His forbearance is a lesson to all of us who lead others in the name of Jesus. We must be patient. People can take a long time to get it. Instead, as he had asked earlier (6:38), Jesus asks how many loaves they have. This time they have seven. Seven could have some symbolic force, perhaps speaking of sufficiency or completion. However, this is not developed and is uncertain.

Unlike the earlier feeding where it appeared to be spring (6:38), there is no indication of the time of year. Jesus simply directs the crowd to sit on the ground. Uncommonly for an ancient meal setting, as at the feeding of the five thousand, there are no "best seats";[44] all are on the same level, including the disciples (cf. 12:39). If anyone should be in the best seat, it is Jesus, and he is the host who serves the crowds. As with the five loaves earlier, he takes the seven loaves. Whereas earlier, Jesus blessed the meal (6:41), here he gives thanks. While no object of the thanks is given, undoubtedly, it is God. He breaks the bread into pieces, anticipating his own body broken for the disciples later (14:22). While the miracle occurs somewhere in the giving of the bread to his disciples and its distribution to the crowds, it is again fruitless to speculate more on how or when it occurred.

There is a second distribution of a few fish. The Greek is *ichthydion*, the diminutive of *ichthys*, and so means "small fish." The smallness of the fish intensifies the drama of the miracle. He blesses (*eulogeō*) the fish. Earlier, he had given thanks (*eucharisteō*). The ideas are probably much the same, involving thanking God and blessing the food to their bodies. These are distributed. Hence, we have two consecutive miracles: the multiplication of both the fish and the bread. Jesus is the host and waiter. We see here Jesus, the humble Servant King.

As in 6:42, in v. 8, the people are satisfied (*chortazō*). This time rather than twelve baskets of leftovers, here there are seven. It is difficult to see anything symbolic in the seven, although it may indicate the fullness of provision. This time, Mark uses *anthrōpos* rather than *anēr*, indicating that the number of men, women, and children together is four thousand.

The power of the story is found in the second feeding miracle and its placement. The feeding of the five thousand did not have the desired effect of opening the hearts and minds of the disciples to who Jesus was. Since then, Jesus has walked on water, healed masses of people even through his clothes, and healed a Syrophoenician woman's child and a deaf man in gentile territory. Now Jesus feeds a crowd again. The miracle is designed not only to demonstrate his power to Israel and the world and invite them into the kingdom, but to get the disciples who will carry on his mission to understand who Jesus is. The passage shows that they are still blind. They do not take the initiative to feed the crowd. They question how it can be

---

44. Compare Matt 23:6; Mark 12:39; Luke 14:7–11; 20:46.

done. As Guelich notes, every appearance of the disciples in the narrative to this point speaks of their incomprehension in regards to Jesus's identity.[45] However, the narrative is moving to the point where they do.

This passage reinforces the earlier account of the feeding of the five thousand and speaks of the importance to Christian mission of feeding the poor, of hospitality, and of trust in God to provide and multiply what we have got as we do these things. It reminds us of God providing manna in the past. It points to the future eschatological banquet where there will be no more poverty, and God's people will live with him, experiencing the fullness of his provision. Come, Lord Jesus, come (1 Cor 16:22)!

Jesus Refuses to Give a Sign (8:10–13)

Having left the Decapolis, Jesus travels across the lake by boat to Dalmanutha. The region was found on the northwestern shore of the Sea of Galilee. We have here the only reference to this place in ancient literature. In 1970, the level of the lake was low, enabling ancient anchorages to be viewed. Those found included Capernaum, Magdala, and another north of Magdala and west of Capernaum, which may have been Dalmanutha. If this is correct, it was a small anchorage, perhaps in the Magdala region. Another possibility is that the Aramaic word originally meant "enclosure, anchorage," and it was initially "the anchorage of the district of Magdala" which came to be known as "Dalmanutha of the district of Magdala."[46] What we can be confident of is that it was an area west of the sea.

Again, Pharisees challenge Jesus, the first since the unclean and clean debate in 7:1–23. This time we are not told from where they originated. The Greek *syzēteō* can have the more neutral meaning "discuss" or, as here, "dispute, debate, or argue."[47] Hence, they seek him (*zēteō*) to take him on. We sense here the rising tension between Jesus and the Jewish leaders.

The Jewish leaders want a sign from heaven. Their demand is likely for evidence that God has sent Jesus. Such a challenge recalls Moses returning from Midian and performing signs to prove his credentials to Israel's leaders as their savior. Signs of authentication included his staff becoming a snake, his hand becoming leprous, and the water of the Nile turning to blood (Exod 4). At one level, this is a reasonable request, as any good leader wants to ensure someone who rises to prominence like Jesus is not a theological renegade. At another level, it is ludicrous. Jesus has just fed four thousand

---

45. Guelich, *Mark 1—8:26*, 404.
46. Strange, "Dalmanutha."
47. BDAG, 954.

people in the wilderness. Earlier, he had performed innumerable miracles, calmed a storm, walked on water, and fed five thousand men and others. These were mostly performed in synagogues or other public settings. The Pharisees and other Jewish leaders had never been forbidden from traveling with Jesus. They could have joined him and observed him and seen all this. They could have gone and inquired as to the veracity of the claims circulating from the likes of Jairus, the synagogue ruler, and others. As such, their request is inexcusable. What more could Jesus do?

One of the hallmarks of Jesus is that he never used his power for his own ends, whether to improve his situation or to prove to others that he was from God. A good case in point is the temptation, where he refused to turn stones to bread despite being hungry (Matt 4:3–4; Luke 4:3–4). Another example is his arrest, trial, and crucifixion, where he could have saved himself at any point but did not.

So, when the Pharisees come looking for some compelling evidence of his power, he refuses them. A "sign from heaven" suggests either an apocalyptic cosmic display of power or perhaps a sign from God (who dwells in heaven). Jesus is not in the business of using his power to prove his identity. He uses his power to restore others. He is compelled by compassion, and his power as God the Son is only for others in need. Even the earlier calming of the storm and walking on water can be seen in this light. In each situation, he saved the disciples struggling in the harsh Galilean weather. The turning of water to wine in John 2 was also a stunning miracle, but its primary motivation was to ensure the host was not shamed if the wine ran out. When he raised the widow of Nain's son (Luke 7:11–17), he did this as much for the widow as the deceased boy; she would have been destitute without him.

The final clause of v. 11 states that they were "tempting him." The term *peirazō* was used in 1:13 of Satan testing or tempting Jesus. It is used in 10:2 and 12:15 again of his being tested. Here, either translation can work, "test" or tempt," although the latter is closer to Mark's intent here. They are testing him and his credentials. However, at a more fundamental level, they are emissaries of Satan seeking to tempt Jesus to use his power to get their support. We see here the subtlety of power. There is always the easy way and the hard way. Christian leaders must be vigilant to ensure they are not using their power illegitimately to get done what they desire, i.e., for their own ends. We work in God's way for his agenda and the genuine needs of others. As such, Jesus will not be drawn; he sees through their duplicity.

Hence, they are testing him by tempting him to use his power for his glory. They are demanding that Jesus is authenticated by God so that they may join him. In a sense, the Pharisees are doing a sensible thing. They believe that the Messiah is coming at some point. Before forming an alliance with him, they want to be sure he is the Messiah. Their expectations are military, expecting a Messiah who was spiritually imbued with power to draw together God's people and to drive the Romans out of the country. Jesus is the Greek for Joshua. Jesus's behavior is provocative. He has power; he may be the Messiah. Hence, they want him, like Moses, to prove himself, and then they will join him against Rome. They have no real idea of what Jesus is doing. Mind you, at this stage, even the disciples did not fully understand Jesus, although they were beginning to recognize his identity as Messiah.

Jesus responds with a great sigh. We saw Jesus sigh earlier in 7:34. However, it was not entirely clear why. Here his reason is apparent: he is frustrated to the depths of his very being (his spirit). Who can blame him? He has just fed four thousand, and the Pharisees want yet more miraculous evidence of his identity. "Their condemnation is deserved" (Rom 3:8).

Jesus's irritation is confirmed in his words: "Why does this generation ask for a sign?" Why indeed, what with all he had done. Paul confirms the Jewish obsession with vindicating signs in 1 Cor 1:22: "For Jews demand signs." Jesus answers with a conditional "if . . . then" sentence without the "then" clause (the apodosis). Notably, this kind of conditional sentence expects an emphatic *no* answer. So, will a sign be given to this generation? Absolutely not! His refusal to give them a sign is probably because he knows that no sign would suffice for these unbelievers. He also knows that his extraordinary ministry should be sufficient for observers and that he will never use his power for anything other than human need, certainly not to impress people.

So, he outright refuses the sign. However, in parallel passages, the sign of Jonah (the resurrection) is given as the sign (Matt 12:39; 16:4; Luke 11:29–30). This marker refers to his death and resurrection. However, even that will still not be enough for most Jews after he rises from the dead (cf. Luke 16:31). In v. 13, in true Markan style, Jesus again moves on across the lake.

Today, people (including some Christians), can sometimes be like these Pharisees. They think that there must be miracles to prove God to the world. However, this misunderstands how God is winning people to him. The signs the world needs are creation, life itself, the marvelous goodness of the world, love, Jesus Christ in history, the church, and his power to renew our lives. Some people out there are not satisfied. They demand more. They simply cannot see what is obvious: there is a God. Jesus is his Son. We should repent and believe.

Conversely, some Christians think God should do miracles to prove himself. We can get frustrated with God, asking, "Why don't you do more?" Such an attitude fails to acknowledge that God has done enough. More miracles will not fix the problem, because miracles can be explained away. We should pray for healing and other miracles where there is a genuine need. God may respond with a fantastic miracle. We must not demand them of God as if he needs to do them. There is enough evidence for people if they only have eyes to see.

Questions

- What is different from Jesus's feeding of the five thousand and four thousand and Herod's birthday party? What does this tell us about the kingdom?
- Who are the people of the kingdom?
- What does "you give them something to eat" say to us today (6:37)?
- What does Jesus walking on water tell us about his identity?
- Read carefully the list in 7:21–23. What does each item say to us about the way we are to live and how the church is to respond to a world full of sin?
- What do the two healings and feedings in gentile territory tell us about Jesus's mission?
- What does Jesus eating with the crowds in gentile territory tell us about relations across race, culture, and ethnicity in the kingdom of God?
- Why does Jesus refuse to give any signs to the Jewish leaders?

Lesson Six: Jesus Warns, Peter's Confession, and Jesus's Discipleship Training Program Begins (8:14—9:32)

Warnings Against the Pharisees and Herodians (8:14–21)

ON THE TRIP FROM Dalmanutha, the disciples realize they have only one loaf of bread with them. Their forgetfulness is not the point of the story and should not delay us, aside from showing that forgetfulness is a universal human condition.

With this in mind, Jesus uses the metaphor of leaven (or yeast) and bread to warn them (v. 15). In the biblical world, leaven or yeast "was just a piece of fermented dough kept from a previous baking."[1] It was either added to the water in the kneading trough, to which flour was added, or put directly into the dough for kneading (cf. Matt 13:33). Leavened bread rose; unleavened bread did not. Annually, during the Feast of Unleavened Bread, and in all grain offerings, all yeast was removed.[2] Leaven is used figuratively in the NT of something that enhances or corrupts. In Matt 13:33, the kingdom is likened to the leavening of bread, causing the world to rise (so to speak). Elsewhere, Paul cites the saying "a little leaven leavens the whole batch of dough," when warning of the dangers of sin corrupting the church (1 Cor 5:6; Gal 5:9).

As with Paul in the references above, here Jesus alludes to the false teaching and ideas of the Pharisees and Herod Antipas. This critique could focus on the more specific issue of their demand for a sign but was likely broader, encompassing all the false ideas that caused them to reject Jesus and the kingdom.

---

1. Barry et al., eds., "Leaven."
2. E.g., Exod 12:15, 19; 13:7; 23:18; Lev 2:11.

Verse 16 could indicate that the disciples misunderstood Jesus, thinking that in some way, he was referring to their failure to bring bread. Alternatively, they are so distracted by the problem of not having enough bread that they simply do not hear Jesus. They should not have given a second thought to their failure to bring enough bread, because twice Jesus has fed enormous crowds with a paucity of bread. So, they had within their group the power to survive, as God would provide for their needs (Matt 6:24–34; Luke 12:22–34; Phil 4:19).

The seven questions[3] that follow focus on the feeding miracles. Jesus begins asking them why they are talking about their lack of bread. He follows it up by asking whether they still do not perceive and understand. He asks whether their hearts are hardened, with the implication that they are (remembering that the heart includes the mind).

The fourth question in v. 18 draws on Jer 5:21 and recalls Mark 4:12, which cites Isa 6:9–10. In Jer 5, the prophet rebukes Jerusalem for her failure to repent and portends her destruction. In Jer 5:15, a nation will come and bring destruction—Babylon. Then in Jer 5:18, there is a shift to hope as God promises not to end Israel. They will continue in another nation. He is told to proclaim to Israel, who have become a "foolish and senseless people, who have eyes, but see not, who have ears, but hear not." In v. 23, he bemoans their "stubborn and rebellious heart." Sadly, for them, their iniquities have turned against them (v. 25). He goes on to rebuke the leadership of Israel for their failure. Jesus here likens the disciples to Israel at the time of Jeremiah. They have eyes and ears but cannot see and hear. They are blind and deaf spiritually.

The fifth question leads to the sixth and is paralleled by the seventh. "Do you not remember" leads into the final question, "Do you not yet understand?" Between these two framing questions, Jesus asks concerning the number of baskets left over after the two feedings. The disciples rightly recall twelve and seven.

The implication is that with Jesus's overwhelming power to provide for their needs, the disciples need not worry about bread. They have more than enough with the one loaf for the thirteen of them (and more, if there are others there, too). After all, Jesus can feed up to twenty thousand with five loaves and two fish. Furthermore, as they are worried about providing

---

3. 1) Why are you discussing that you have no bread? 2) Do you not yet comprehend nor understand? 3) Have your hearts been hardened? 4) Have you eyes but never see and ears but never hear? 5) And do you not remember? 6) When I broke five loaves of bread for the five thousand, how many full baskets did you pick up? 7) Do you not understand?

for their material needs, they are not tuned into the spiritual danger of the ideas of the Pharisees and Herod.

The Jewish leaders' demand for a sign, as noted in the previous section, shows that they are corrupted with false ideas of power. They want a warrior Messiah to drive out the Romans and bring in God's reign, subjugating the world to God. They want Jesus to authenticate himself so that they use him as a pawn in their political machinations. He refuses to play such games. His power is for the poor and needy and sinners who need salvation. They also consider Jesus as at best a prophet, and Herod sees him as John the Baptist resurrected. They are obsessed with religious rituals like Sabbath and fasting. They are blind to Jesus.

Put another way, Jesus is saying to them:

> Unlike the Jewish leaders, disciples, read the signs! What more do you need? Why are you worried about bread when the bread of life is before you? Do not be like the Pharisees, who do not read them and continually demand more!

Jesus is warning that the Pharisees' yeast of unbelief, hard-heartedness, and signs demanding (spiritual greed; always wanting more and never being satisfied) will corrupt their faith, unless they can come to realize who Jesus really is.

The central theme here is seeing, perceiving, and understanding, i.e., recognizing Jesus for who he is. What follows continues this thread as a blind man is healed. This double-barrelled healing will mirror the effect of the two feedings on the disciples.

The Healing of a Blind Man (8:22–26)

This passage is important structurally. In it, Jesus heals a blind man. This healing follows from Jesus challenging the spiritual blindness and deafness of the disciples. In the passage, the man is healed with a two-step process. This twofold healing is likely intentional for a range of potential reasons. It mirrors the two feedings and their effect on the disciples' spiritual sightedness or lack thereof. The first feeding left them without understanding (6:52). The second feeding was followed by a warning against spiritual blindness like that of the Jewish leaders. In what follows, the disciples will finally confess his messiahship. Their blindness concerning Jesus's identity is over. However, they still do not understand what kind of Messiah he is.

This healing also parallels the last miracle Jesus performs in Mark before Jerusalem, the healing of blind Bartimaeus (10:46–52). The restoration of Bartimaeus's sight precedes Jesus's entry to Jerusalem and the events leading to and culminating in his death. He will then rise. The disciples' blindness concerning the servant nature of his messiahship will finally be removed entirely (except for Judas). They will know that Jesus is the Servant Messiah, who is their Savior and their life example.

Hence, this double healing represents the culmination of the first phase of their growing spiritual sightedness: they see Jesus is Messiah, even if they have not yet a full spiritual understanding of him. We see here the creative way that Mark has woven the stories of Jesus together so that there are hidden messages and links everywhere. Mark is a treasure trove of such things.

Jesus comes to Bethsaida, his second visit to the city (6:45). However, last time, he did not spend any time there. Instead, he went up a mountain to pray and then walked across the lake. Now, he enters the town. Bethsaida means "house of fishing," which is a clue to its economic importance. Initially, it is the home of Andrew, Peter, and Philip (John 1:44). In other Gospels, Jesus condemns the town (Matt 11:21; Luke 10:13).

At the time of Christ, Bethsaida was under the tetrarchy of Philip (4 BC–AD 34), one of Herod the Great's sons and a brother of Antipas. Philip renamed it "Julias" after Augustus Caesar's daughter Julia.[4]

The site is disputed. One possibility is Et-Tell. However, this is 2.5 km north of the present shoreline of the Sea of Galilee. The other is El-Araj, which is closer to the shore. There is much excavation at Et-Tell, and it may be the original site, with the water from the lake reaching it in earlier times.[5] There is evidence of fishing in the so-called "House of the Fisherman."[6]

Wherever it was then, some people bring a blind man to Jesus to heal him (8:22). For some reason, Jesus takes him outside of the village. Later he tells the man not to go into it. Refusing him entry could be because of something in the city that was offensive to Jesus (see the critique of the town above). Otherwise, we have another case of the messianic secret; he does not want a revolution if people perceive who he is.

Jesus again uses spit to heal, as he had with the deaf and mute man (see also 7:33). This time he appears to spit in the man's eyes and lay hands on them. Jesus does this once, with the man's vision restored partially. He then

---

4. See Josephus, *Ant.* 18:26, 106; *War* 2:167; 4:398.

5. Udd and Winstead, "Bethsaida," note that three reasons are given for Bethsaida being one and a half km inland: 1) tectonic activity; 2) flash floods causing increased sediment; or 3) ancient water levels being higher (however, other harbors from the NT era are at approximately the same level).

6. See further Udd and Winstead, "Bethsaida."

lays hands on him a second time, and the man is fully restored. Jesus then sends him home, prohibiting him from going into the village (Bethsaida).

This double healing is unique in the Gospels, as all other healings are immediate. Hence, there must be a reason. Likely, the progressive healing of the man corresponds to the gradual spiritual awakening of the disciples who, to this point, have failed to fully perceive Jesus's identity despite successive signs and especially the provision miracles. In the following pericope, as this man was physically healed, they gain spiritual sightedness. They finally recognize who Jesus is. It is only after the healing of Bartimaeus that Jesus will be fully revealed not just as the Messiah, but the *Servant* King. It will take his death and resurrection for them to move from seeing Jesus like a vague tree outline to the full clarity of who he is.

Peter's Confession (8:27–30)

This moment is the first real climax of Mark's Gospel to this point. Mark is careful to state the location: they were among the villages around Caesarea Philippi. The town is about forty km (30 mi) north of the Sea of Galilee, where most of Jesus's mission was spent. It lay at the foot of Mount Hermon, the highest mountain in the Israel region. The city was itself 350 m (1148 ft) above sea level. It was a strategic northern location.[7]

In the time of Alexander the Great, a shrine was dedicated to the god Pan, the Greek god of forests, deserted places, flocks, and shepherds. It came to be known as Panium.[8] The district of Panias was given to Herod the Great by Augustus Caesar (20 BC). A temple was built for Augustus by Herod, and it was called Paneas and Panium.[9] The area was given to Herod's son Philip after his death.[10] Philip extended the town and renamed it Caesarea Philippi after Tiberius Caesar and himself (2 BC). He had his residence there, and it was the capital of his region.[11]

As such, the city was politically significant. It represented the alliance of the two kings who tower over the genesis of the Christian movement: the Caesars and the Herods. Caesar represented Rome, which then ruled the world. Herod represented Israel's military and monarchical aspirations.

---

7. Caesarea Philippi is not to be confused with Caesarea Maritima on the west coast of the Great Sea northwest of Jerusalem. It was named in honor of the Emperor Caesar and expanded by Herod Philip.

8. Polybius, *Hist.* 16.18.

9. E.g, Josephus, *Ant.* 15:360–61.

10. Josephus, *Ant.* 17:189.

11. See Algie, "Caesarea Philippi."

There is more than a hint that Jesus chose this place to have his messiahship revealed because of its name. The kingdom of God is established through Jesus, the Messiah in a Roman and Herodian context. While Caesar and Herod have power, Jesus is King over all.

There is no mention of ministry, adding to the impression that Jesus takes the disciples there as he senses they are coming to realize his identity. As they are traveling (on the way), in v. 27, Jesus asks them how he is viewed by the people. Evans makes the point that Jesus here uses rabbinic question-answer mode.[12] The three options mentioned at the time of the killing of John in 6:14–16 are given: 1) John the Baptist revived (this was Herod Antipas's view); 2) Elijah, knowing that there were Jewish expectations of his return (see further on 6:14–29); or 3) one of the prophets of old, suggesting a prophet like Isaiah, Jeremiah, or others in Israel's tradition.[13]

Jesus then asks for their perspective. To this point, Peter has some degree of primacy among the disciples, named first as an apostle (3:16) and one of Jesus's inner circle.[14] His only words to this point in Mark's account are from 1:36: "Everyone is looking for you." Now we hear his second statement: "You are the Christ." Peter breaks rank from other Jews. Jesus is not John resurrected, Elijah, or merely a prophet; instead, he is the long-awaited Messiah of God who has come as God's agent for the deliverance of his people. Such a statement suggests the OT hope has come to fruition in Christ.[15] This statement is the moment to which Part One of the Gospel had been headed.

---

12. Evans, *Mark 8:27—16:20*, 13.

13. Some, like France, *Gospel of Mark*, 328, take this to refer to Jesus as one of *the* prophets resurrected; however, I think it is more likely that Mark means he is one "like" the prophets of old.

14. E.g., Mark 5:37, see also 9:2; 13:3; 14:33.

15. See 2 Sam 7:14; Isa 9:1–7; 11:1–9; 16:5; 22:22; Jer 23:5; 29:16; Jer 33:15; Ezek 34:23–24; 34:24–28; Amos 9:11; Zech 12:7. Evans, *Mark 8:27—16*, 15, states that 4Q521 (= 4QMess Apoc) 2 and 4 ii 1 anticipate a time when "heaven and earth will obey his [God's] Messiah." This text goes on to tell of *proclaiming the gospel to the poor, of healing, and even of resurrection of the dead* (lines 8–12). This is a close parallel to Jesus's teaching in Matt 11:5 and Luke 7:22. Other references in the scrolls refer to a *a military Messiah* who will defeat Israel's enemies. In CD 19:10–11, the enemies of the renewed covenant "will be delivered up to the sword at the coming of the anointed (Messiah) of Aaron and of Israel" (cf. CD 20:1; 1QS 9:11). 4Q252 (= 4QpGena) 1.3–4 speaks of *"the coming of the anointed one of righteousness, the branch of David."* According to other texts, this branch of David (cf. Jer 23:5; 31:15; Zech 3:8; 6:12) will *engage Israel's enemies in battle*, possibly *slaying the Roman emperor* himself (e.g., 4Q285 [= 4QMg] 5 1:1–6). This portrait is consistent with the expectations of the author of the Psalms of Solomon, who in ch. 17–18 longs for a Davidic Messiah who will *drive Gentiles out of Israel and purify the land.*

As discussed on 1:1, *Christos* translates *mā-šîᵃḥ* ("anointed one"), a technical term for the long-awaited Davidic king through whom God would establish his reign for all eternity. It was commonly expected he would bring Israel freedom from foreign rule and usher in the eschaton (see further on 1:1).

Peter is the first person to comprehend Jesus's identity fully. He has moved from the spiritual blindness that frustrated Jesus immensely to perceiving who he is, even if dimly, as if a moving tree. From this climax to the first half of the Gospel, Jesus will teach them what it means. It has nothing to do with violent revolution but with the establishment of God's reign through the death and resurrection of the King. The lifestyle of the kingdom is not a glorious overpowering of the world, but humble service, holy living, care for those at the margins, love, and sharing the gospel in cruciform attitudes, deeds, and words.

Still, they have yet to learn this. Jesus has completed the first stage of his purposes: his disciples now know that he is the anointed King of Israel and indeed the world; the Messiah of God, the Christ, the King of the world come to earth. One might say that this is the first conversion in the NT, the first person to be a *Christ*ian. Peter and the others have a lot to learn from here. Peter has, so to speak, "come to Christ."

The passage ends with Jesus forbidding them to tell others. It is important to note that Jesus does not deny Peter's statement. Later, before the high priest, he will affirm it (14:62). Instead, he warns them to keep it quiet. The Greek translated "solemnly warn" is *epitimaō*, previously used by Jesus in Mark of rebuking a demon (1:25), censuring the wind (4:39), and telling demons not to give away his identity (3:12). The latter sense is found here: he firmly commands them not to give away his identity. We have the central example of the messianic secret (noting that Jesus has just been recognized as the Messiah by a person for the first time). Revelation by the disciples of his messianic status could create a revolution among the general populace.[16]

The command, though, would have surprised the disciples, who would have wanted to tell the world. They would do that later. Jesus now has to teach them about what kind of Messiah he is, and once they fully understand that he has died for the sins of the world and risen, they will tell others. There is a fascinating interplay of the term *epitimaō* in this passage. Jesus orders them sharply to be silent (8:30). He then speaks of his death. Astonishingly, in that Peter had just stated he is the King of Israel, the apostle rebukes Jesus (8:32). Jesus then rebukes Peter, speaking to Satan (8:33). Later he will again

---

16. Evans, *Mark 8:27—16:20*, 15.

rebuke demons (9:25; 10:48). Later, the disciples will rebuke children who want to come to Jesus, only to be reprimanded (10:13). There is a great deal of rebuking going on in Mark's Gospel.

The First Passion Prediction (8:31–33)

Now that the disciples know that Jesus is the Messiah, Jesus instantly begins to teach them what kind of Messiah he is.

> **Discipleship Instruction One:** *Jesus is the Messiah and Son of Man, who must die and rise from the dead.*

Again, the Messiah is the same person as the Son of Man. While he is a transcendent ruler of the world, he must suffer, be rejected by the Jewish leaders, be killed, and rise again after three days. The word must (*dei*) is a divine imperative; it must happen because God has deemed it must happen.[17] No detail is given concerning his killing. However, in the next section, Jesus will urge all potential believers to "take up your cross and follow me." This injunction indicates Jesus knew he would be crucified; however, he does not clearly state this at this point. He leaves that as an implied idea.

As discussed briefly on 2:10, where the term is first used, Son of Man is Jesus's favorite self-designation. The term has an inherent ambiguity, perhaps referring to a son of Adam, a person (e.g., Ps 8:4), a prophet like Ezekiel (e.g., Ezek 2:6), or the transcendent figure of Dan 7:13. In the vision of Daniel, after the four beasts representing four kingdoms, "there came one like a son of man, and he came to the Ancient of Days and was presented before him." In Ps 80:17, the Son of Man is connected with the Messiah.

This figure is given absolute rule over the world forever. This idea is further developed in 1 En. 37—71, dating from the first century BC, and was undoubtedly known by many at the time of Christ.[18] In this document, the Son of Man, the Elect One, and Messiah, is a gloriously transcendent pre-existent figure like the *Logos* of John 1:1–2. He was concealed from the beginning. He will stand gloriously over all God's worshiping people. To him belongs all righteousness and judgment to remove evil, including all empires that defy God. He will sit on a glorious throne over all rulers. His people will dine with

---

17. This Greek word *dei* ("it is necessary") carries the sense of divine imperative, i.e., in the purposes of God, it is utterly essential for this to occur.

18. See Charlesworth, *Apocalyptic Literature*, 1:6–7, who dates the Book of Similitudes ca. 164–05 BC. It is also found in 4 Ezra, but this postdates the NT and so should not be utilized in such a discussion as this.

him forever and ever.[19] So, in the Book of Similitudes, Jesus is the Elect One, the Son of Man, and the Messiah, all wrapped up in one.

As such, here, Jesus assumes this identity that speaks of an eschatological figure who will come with great glory, destroy evil, and reign over all nations forever. What Jesus does with the figure is unprecedented. This Son of Man will suffer severely, be rejected by Israel's leaders, and be killed, to rise three days afterward. Some scholars, like Evans, argue that there are glimpses of his suffering in the conflict in Dan 7:15–28 (especially vv. 21–22, 25). However, it is not the Son of Man who suffers there; it is his people. Some try to alleviate this by seeing the Son of Man as a corporate figure. However, this is unnecessary.

What Jesus is doing here is taking the well-known transcendent figure the Son of Man and fusing it with the hope of a suffering Servant found in Isaiah 52:13—53:12 and of a suffering Davidic king in Ps 22. Indeed, in Jesus's incarnation, all of Israel's eschatological hopes come together within the shape of Isaiah's suffering Servant. This intertwining of expectations is an innovation in Israel, with there being no real notion of a suffering Messiah or Son of Man. No one before the time of Jesus identified the Servant figure in the four so-called Servant Songs in Isaiah[20] with the Messiah or Son of Man. Nor did people recognize that Ps 22 pointed to the Messiah being crucified and rising to vindication; a quick read sees the uncanny resemblance. When Jesus cited Ps 22:1 on the cross, these links could and should have been made.

Jesus then fuses the notions of Lord, Son of God, Son of Man, Christ, and the prophet (to name a few), with the suffering Servant and Messiah. The mode of the Son of Man's glorious triumph is the path of the Servant to the cross, to the grave, and only then to the glory of the Son of Man seen in Dan 7:13–14 and 1 Enoch.

In this passion prediction, three groups will conspire in his death. The elders were groups of seven lay men who exercised some civic and religious leadership, most often at a synagogue level. These members of the lay nobility constituted "the third and least influential" group within in the Sanhedrin (after the Sadducees and Pharisees).[21] The chief priests were the group of priests from the Sanhedrin, centered in Jerusalem, with ultimate

---

19. See 1 En. 46:3, 4; 62:5, 7–9, 14.

20. See Barry, "Servant Songs," who states that the songs are found in Isa 42:1–4 (with Isa 42:5–9); Isa 49:1–6 (with Isa 49:7–12); Isa 50:4–9 (with Isa 50:10–11); Isa 52:13—53:12; and possibly Isa 61:1–3. Notes of suffering are found in Isa 42:4; 49:4; 50:6–7; and especially Isa 52:13—53:12 that picture the Servant dying for the nation's sins, being buried, and rising to intercede for sinners.

21. Osborne, "Elder," 202.

administrative oversight of the temple.²² The scribes were mentioned earlier on 2:6 as religious figures working in religious and political life, including some Pharisees, Sadducees, priests, and Levites.²³ Later, this prediction will be fulfilled as the Sanhedrin and other Jewish leaders work together to bring Jesus down. Mention of his being killed points forward to the cross. His resurrection looks toward the empty tomb. "After three days" is reckoned inclusively, and so Jesus died on a Friday (the first day) and was raised on the next Sunday (the third day).

In v. 32, Jesus says this publicly or openly (*parrēsia*). With such bold and public speech, the disciples should have been well prepared for Jesus's death, considering that this is the first of three such clear-cut statements. However, they have no idea what he is talking about because messiahs do not die; they kill others in their conquests. The idea of the leaders rejecting Jesus, leading to his death, likely surprised them as well; they assumed that the leaders would ultimately get behind Jesus. They perhaps thought it was some kind of parable.

Peter's response is to take Jesus aside and rebuke him. The Greek is again *epitimaō*, the term Jesus used as he warns the disciples to be silent concerning his identity. Peter's motivation is unclear. Likely, he is telling Jesus not to speak as if he is going to die. There is great irony here. Peter has just confessed that Jesus is the Messiah, meaning that he is Israel's King and ruler of the world. Surprisingly, he has the temerity to order Jesus around. We see that Peter is still an immature leader who has not quite come to terms with Jesus and himself concerning Jesus. Jesus is Lord. We do not command him; he commands us. Peter's attitude warns us as leaders not to overstep the boundaries of authority but to respect those God has placed in authority over us.

Then Jesus turns, sees the disciples, and counter-rebukes Peter with the same Greek term *epitimaō*. His words are fascinating as he directs his statement at Satan. The Hebrew term *śā·ṭān* means "adversary." Jesus may be using it in this sense, saying to Peter, "Get behind me adversary." He may be directly calling Peter Satan, assuming he is possessed by the devil. However, considering that Peter has just confessed Jesus's messiahship, this seems unlikely. Most probably, Jesus is speaking directly to Satan, who stands behind the patterns of power the world assumes. That is, Satan has influenced humanity so that they cannot conceive of the establishment of peace through peaceful means, love, and service. To be honest, many today are stuck in this same deception.

---

22. Hurst and Green, "Priest, Priesthood," 636.
23. Tan-Gatue, "Scribe."

The world at the time was full of colliding empires, nations, and tribes. Men ruled with armies, intrigue, wealth, women, and the imposition of power and favor. Peter has such a worldview. He assumes Jesus as Messiah will gather Israel's people behind him, destroy the Romans, and ultimately take over the world. He is wrong. Jesus's way is more profound and involves a world voluntarily submitting to his rule as they see the deep wisdom of a crucified Servant King and the power of humility, service, and love to change the world. He is not calling Peter Satan; he is rebuking the fallen angel who is corrupting the world. Peter and Satan do not understand the ways of God, which was always to win the world through a crucified Messiah.

This passion prediction is the beginning of their instruction concerning what kind of Messiah he is: a Servant Messiah. It also will involve him teaching them what it means to be a subject of the King, a disciple. They must walk in line with the pattern he will lay down.

Take Up Your Cross and Follow Me! (8:34—9:1)

After Jesus rebukes Satan, he calls the crowd along with his disciples. It is essential to recognize this because it confirms that what follows is not just for those who are already disciples, but for anyone present listening. The crowd could potentially have included Jewish leaders, gentiles, as yet unconverted Jews, and others. It also instructs the disciples who are following what they must be prepared to do. As contemporary readers who have heard the call of God, this is what is required of us. We must be crystal clear on what follows. In the call, the second lesson is given.

> **Discipleship Instruction Two:** *Anyone who wants to be a disciple of Jesus must recognize that Jesus's death is the example they are to follow, and so they must be prepared to be a humble servant who suffers as he did.*

The essence of discipleship is not just that Jesus is a suffering Messiah, but that those who follow him must imitate him, following the pattern he laid down in his life and death: humility, service, sacrifice, and suffering to the point of death, in whatever way that comes. Three statements apply to all potential followers. Two rhetorical questions are then posed. Then, there is another statement. The final statement is a prediction.

The first statement tells anyone who wants to be a follower of Christ what he or she must be prepared to do. It is important to note first that a Christian here is defined as being a follower of Christ. A "Christ-follower" is arguably an excellent definition to use when asked what we believe: "I am a follower of Christ." Alternatively, "I am a follower." Again, "I am a follower of the way." We see the importance of following or coming after Jesus in the call of the first disciples (1:17; 2:14) and the rich young Jewish man (10:21).

To follow Jesus, one must first deny oneself. This self-denial means to place the needs of others ahead of our own. Denying oneself is somewhat controversial in some contexts where self-denial is seen as a bad thing. However, while this can lead to poor self-care, this is Jesus's summons to us. The needs of others and the interests of Jesus and the kingdom of God are more important than our own. It is the path of service and humility, considering the interests of others as more important than our interests.

The statement that they must take up his or her cross anticipates Jesus being crucified. If they had had ears to hear him, they would have realized this, for it was the Romans who crucified in this period and place. What the saying means is that to take up one's cross is to be prepared to walk in the footsteps of a crucified Messiah,[24] relentlessly serving others, denying oneself, all the way to death. It involves a preparedness to suffer and die for our faith.

Severe suffering and death is a real issue in many countries where Christians are threatened with physical persecution and death. In others, they are maligned and mocked. Whatever we face, to take up our crosses is to be prepared to endure it for the sake of Christ and the gospel. Later, Jesus will carry his cross. Then Simon will carry it. Jesus will die crucified. At the time of Mark, Peter and Paul were facing death or had just died. Many had recently been killed in the Neronian persecution after the fire. Earlier, Stephen was stoned (Acts 7:54–60); Jacob (James) was beheaded (Acts 12:1–2); and Peter, Paul, Silas, and others were imprisoned. Antipas will lose his life in Asia (Rev 2:13). Since then, millions have been persecuted and have died. Today, Christians continue to be persecuted and die. A follower of Jesus knows rejection and maltreatment go with the call of God. Nonetheless, because of what Christ has done for us and what he has for us in the future, by the power of the Spirit, we are prepared to endure suffering for his name's sake. Furthermore, where we do not die for our faith, we are called to spend our lives until our final breath for Christ. Such dedication is the challenge of discipleship.

Then there is a severe warning. The person not prepared to lose her or his life in this way will lose it.[25] The Greek here is referring to eternal

---

24. Evans, *Mark 8:27—16:20*, 25, notes that "in rabbinic parlance a disciple is urged to take up the yoke of Torah or the yoke of the commandments (e.g., *m. 'Abot* 3:5; *m. Ber.* 2:2)."

25. Evans, *Mark 8:27—16:20*, 25, informs us that the reference to saving and losing one's life is paralleled in a later rabbinic writing: "Everyone who preserves one thing

destruction. Denying Jesus, we may have a great life on earth, but we will reap judgment. Conversely, if we are prepared to deny ourselves, take up our cross, and spend our lives in his service, we will save our lives in an eternal sense. We will receive the gift of eternal life announced when Jesus comes to judge his world.

In the first of the rhetorical questions, Jesus asks, what does it profit someone if one gets the whole world and lose one's life? Well, for a short period, one enjoys the wealth of the world. Then, one is destroyed for eternity. Living this way is short-term gain for eternal loss. Next, he asks what can be exchanged for a person's life. The implied answer is nothing is worth that. As Evans puts it, "No sane person would knowingly exchange his life for any amount of wealth."[26] A person may end up with the riches of the world, but then that person dies and cannot take the wealth with him or her. Instead, the person reaps eternal destruction.

Such a person is the rich man in Luke 16:19–31. The rich ruler in 10:17–22 is a case in point. He has "the world." He refuses to give it up when challenged. He goes away sad. Later, he may have done what Jesus asked. Otherwise, he is lost for all eternity. This question speaks of the infinite value of a person's life. It is worth giving up everything for eternal life (cf. Matt 13:44–46). This passage is also ironic. Those who give their lives for Christ and the gospel, as children of Abraham and God, inherit the world (cf. Rom 4:13; 8:17). To follow Christ to death is ultimately to gain the world.

In v. 38, Jesus challenges his hearers never to be ashamed of Christ or his words. If so, when Jesus comes again, ablaze with glory, with his mighty angels, he will be ashamed of us. The converse is also true. If we are bold to share our faith and never deny Jesus, he will never be ashamed of us but will grant us the glories of eternal life. We are to emulate Paul, who cries out, "I am not ashamed of the gospel" (Rom 1:16) and "Do not be ashamed of the testimony about our Lord" (2 Tim 1:6). We are to emulate Paul's example in Phil 1:20 where, as he prepares to face Nero, he is exceedingly hopeful "that I will not be at all ashamed, but that with full courage now as always Christ will be honored in my body, whether by life or by death."

Here, we also see Jesus's view of his people at the time: they are idolatrous, betraying God for false gods and ideas. Israel is sinful, full of vice and corruption. They are full of self-righteousness. They think God has sent Joshua-Messiah to destroy the sinful gentiles. However, they are no better than

---

from the Torah preserves his life, and everyone who loses one thing from the Torah will lose his life" ('Abot R. Nat. B §35).

26. Evans, *Mark 8:27—16:20*, 26. He notes Menander, who writes in *Syr. Men.* 843: "Nothing is more valuable than [one's] life."

the gentiles. They must heed the call to deny themselves, take up their crosses, and follow him, unashamed at his words, or they will be lost forever.

We have an excellent description of the return of Christ here: "in the glory of his Father with the holy angels." This depiction resonates with 2 Thess 1:7, where "the Lord Jesus is revealed from heaven with his mighty angels." Many Israelites believed in a future Messiah and still do but at the eschaton. Jesus, the Messiah, stepped into the center of time unexpectedly. However, he will come again as Israel expects, and they will look on the one they pierced with mourning (Zech 12:10; John 19:37; Rev 1:7).

The final words of Jesus in this speech declare that some of those standing with him on that day will not taste death until the kingdom comes powerfully. The meaning of this disputed. Some see the coming of the kingdom as Christ's *parousia* mentioned in 8:38. However, for a range of reasons, this is unlikely.

First, with the expectation that the NT writers like Mark, Matthew, Luke, and Paul believed that the gospel must be declared to all nations before Christ's return, this is implausible. At the time of the writing of Mark, the gospel had barely begun to penetrate the then known world. The writers knew of Africa; east to China; north into Europe, Britain, and Scandinavia; northwest into Russia; and west to Spain. They had barely begun the job.[27]

Second, these words in 9:2 are immediately followed by the transfiguration. Many scholars consider that rather than the parousia, it is this event to which Jesus is pointing when speaking of the kingdom coming in power. Alternatively, Jesus is pointing both to the transfiguration and his resurrection (below).

Third, Jesus's words point to the coming of the kingdom in its fullness in the resurrection and Pentecost. This third view is most likely. The hearers are being told that they will not experience death before the kingdom of God comes with power, God raising Jesus from the dead, and pouring his Spirit out on his people. The transfiguration also prefigures this event, so Jesus's words may refer to both events, albeit acknowledging that the resurrection and Pentecost are primarily in view.

A final word needs to be said concerning this passage. For disciples who have no understanding that Jesus is to be a crucified Messiah and that his mission is non-militaristic, this would sound like a war speech. Mention of crucifixion would lead them to expect imminent war with the Romans, who commonly crucified threats. The ideas in the speech are what are expected of soldiers about to engage in battle: deny oneself, be prepared to be crucified, follow Jesus into the battle, give their lives for the cause and kingdom, and

---

27. Keown, "Imminent Parousia," 242–63.

stand up boldly for Jesus. Taken this way, 9:1 would have been a great encouragement: while people always die in battle, some of the disciples will not die in this war and will see Joshua's great victory. However, we know looking back as Mark and Peter want us to, that Jesus has no intention to fight the Romans. The war he is fighting is a spiritual one, plundering the dominion of Satan and setting people free from sin and its consequences. The path to this victory is the cross. The patterns of the conflict are humility, selflessness, service, sacrifice, and our weapons of faith, love, and the like.

The Transfiguration (9:2–13)

We come to the third instruction to the disciples.

> **Discipleship Instruction Three:** *The disciples must never forget, however, that while he will suffer and die, Jesus's real identity is glorious divinity and glory; we must remember just who we are dealing with.*

Jesus has just been revealed as Messiah. He has laid down the terms by which a person can join him in his mission to redeem the world. Now, his glory is revealed. The transfiguration is a glimpse of the pre-existent *Logos* of God (John 1:1), a foretaste of the resurrected, ascended, and exalted Jesus John will meet years later on Patmos (Rev 1:12–16).

Mark 9:2 is one of the few times that Mark gives readers some chronological data. It is hard to see anything symbolic in the six days.[28] While tradition places the transfiguration on Mount Tabor around twelve km east of Nazareth, the mountain is more likely to be Mount Hermon, the highest mountain in Israel. It towers 2815 m (9235 ft) above sea level.

As at Jairus's house, Jesus takes his inner circle of Peter, Jacob (James), and John with him (cf. 5:37). While there, Jesus's being is transformed.[29] The Greek is *metamorphoō*, meaning here that his outward form is changed.[30] He and his clothes become brilliantly radiant. The term *stilbō* is used of the bright sun (1 Macc 6:39), lightning (Ezek 21:33), and an angel (Ezek 40:3). Hence, he is shining like the sun! His clothing becomes more dazzlingly white than anything the very best cloth refiner could have produced.

---

28. One thinks of creation in six days (Gen 1:1; Exod 20:11), the six days of not eating unleavened bread at Passover (Deut 16:9), and marching around Jericho in six days (Josh 6:3). However, none seem particularly relevant.

29. The Greek is *metamorphoō* (cf. Eng. metamorphosis) meaning "transformed" into a new "form."

30. BDAG, 639.

Dazzling white indicates that this experience has a supernatural dimension. It recalls OT passages where glorious whiteness is seen on the face of Moses (Exod 34:30) and God (Dan 7:9), the latter connected to the glory of the Son of Man in Dan 13–14.[31] It is a glimpse into Jesus's pre-incarnate heavenly glory. Moreover, it is a foretaste of Christ's exalted ascended glory, seen in the Revelation accounts (cf. Rev 1:13–14). We see here Jesus in the fullness of his deity. It is Jesus "in the form of God" (Phil 2:6), the fullness of God dwelling in Jesus (Col 1:19; 2:9), and Jesus as "the radiance of the glory of God and the exact imprint of his nature" (Heb 1:3).

Then, as if the experience to this point is not enough, Elijah and Moses miraculously appear. Relatively speaking, the presence of Elijah is not a surprise, as his earthly life ended with his being taken to heaven in a whirlwind (2 Kgs 2:11). Moses, however, died on Mount Nebo (Deut 34:1–5). Hence, this event supports that death is not the end of life, for Moses is again alive some years after his death.

The presence of the two figures could represent the coming together of the law (Moses) and the prophets (Elijah) with Jesus, declared by God to be God's final word: "Listen to him" (v. 7). However, Moses was also understood as the first prophet in Israel's prophetic tradition (Deut 18:15–19; 34:10). Another angle is that both Elijah and Moses are redemptive figures. Moses liberated Israel from Egypt (Exod 4—15) and Elijah from the Ba'al prophets (1 Kgs 18). Jesus then is Israel's ultimate redeemer. While this works for Moses, it is not as clear for Elijah. Another possibility is that in Israel's eschatological hopes, this fulfills the belief that Moses also did not die and that the two figures would come at the consummation.[32] Overall, it is likely that Jesus here is the zenith of both Israel's prophetic and redemptive hopes.

Peter's response to Jesus's metamorphosis and the appearance of two of Israel's greats is fascinating. In v. 5, he calls Jesus *rabbi*, the first time Jesus is addressed with the Aramaic term for "teacher" in Mark. He will do so again in 11:21 (see also 10:51; 14:45). This could reflect his ongoing incomprehension of Jesus's messiahship; he should be addressing him as "Anointed One," King, or something similar.

---

31. See Evans, *Mark 8:27—16:20*, 36, for other examples from Judaism and Greco-Roman literature.

32. Evans, *Mark 8:27—16:20*, 36, tells us that some think the two witnesses of Rev 11:3–12 are Moses and Elijah. In rabbinic tradition (Pesiq. Rab. 4.2), Moses and Elijah are seen as similar, especially concerning their redemption of Israel. Also, both Moses and Elijah had revelatory experiences on mountain tops (Exod 20—34; 1 Kgs 19:8). In tradition, both translated to heaven and both had visions of God.

Peter then suggests the building of a booth for each of them (9:5–6). Suggesting booths could be some garbled reference to the tabernacle, from the wilderness experience, perhaps in the sense that Peter thought the kingdom had come (cf. 9:1) and believed that similar events as those that surrounded the Exodus may now occur.[33] It may merely be illustrative of his confusion, as v. 6 suggests.

In *Jesus in a World of Colliding Empires*, I posit the idea that here Peter was thinking militarily.[34] The Greek *skēnē* is often used of military tents in Greek writings. Ancient armies invariably camped in tents arranged around symbols of their particular deities. Closest to the divine symbols were the tents of the military commanders. Israel was no exception. As the people camped in the wilderness, the tabernacle was placed at the center of the camp. The tribes were carefully positioned around it in tents. Moses, Aaron, and the Levites were guarding it (Numb 3:5–39).

Peter may have seen the coming of Moses and Elijah with Jesus as the genesis of the military takeover of the land. The building of tents for the three luminaries would be military in intent. He would probably then have built three more for himself and the sons of Zebedee. They would then perhaps have called the disciples and Israel's men to them to gather around and prepare for war. Then, the new Joshua, radiating God's power with the two great redeemers, would have led the armies of the Lord with Peter, Jacob (James), and John.

Interestingly, in Joshua's conquest, the defeat of King Og in Deut 3 happened at Mount Hermon, the first victory in the conquest. As such, Peter likely thought that with Moses and Elijah, the supernaturally empowered Jesus with the disciples would storm through the land.

However, this second Joshua had other ideas. The two greats from Israel's tradition would remain only briefly. Next, momentously, God would speak in the cloud of his glory. They would not head into battle, but to Jerusalem, where Joshua was to die. Only then would the kingdom come in glory as Christ was raised, ascended, exalted to God's right hand, and the Spirit fell on the disciples. The war is not a military takeover, but spiritual, as the kingdom grows through men and women from all the kingdoms of the world responding to God's love and forgiveness and joining the great Servant King in winning the world through humble service.

In v. 7, a cloud appears. The cloud recalls the *shekinah* glory of God that led Israel through the wilderness and filled the tabernacle and temple

---

33. Evans, *Mark 8:27—16:20*, 37.
34. Keown, *Jesus in a World*, 2:27–29.

(Exod 40:35; 1 Kgs 8:10–11). It hints at God tabernacling in Jesus, as in John 1:14.

Then God speaks. The saying is very like the baptism of Christ. Whereas in 1:11, God addressed Jesus—"*You are* my beloved Son; with whom I am well pleased" (italics added)—this time, God says to the three disciples, "*This is* my beloved Son. Listen to him!" (9:7, italics added). God's love for Jesus is affirmed. The disciples are told that Jesus is the Son of God. Jesus then is not merely as a human king, but the Son of God. Or better, God the Son!

God vindicates the authority of Jesus as his spokesman to the world. All the prophets are now subordinate to the King of kings and Prophet of prophets. Believers forever are to listen to *him*. The verb *akouō* is used in OT passages calling Israel to listen to God's laws (e.g., Deut 4:1; 5:1). It also features in the Shema, the central confession of Israel, recited at least once daily (Deut 6:4).[35] God's declaration means that "the time of Moses and Elijah is over."[36] Later, the writer of Hebrews would capture what is meant here: "Long ago, at many times and in many ways, God spoke to our fathers by the prophets [like Moses and Elijah], but in these last days he has spoken to us by his Son." As such, we are to listen *to him*. Listening to Jesus speak is the essence of Christianity. He is the Word of God. He speaks by his Spirit, primarily through the Scriptures.

In v. 8, the glory of God disappears, as do the two redemptive figures. Theologically, this disappearance and vindication of the Son in the presence of these two OT icons indicates the end of an era, the word of God now constituted around Christ who fulfills (not replaces) the voice of Israel's prophets in the OT.

In v. 9, as they descend Mount Hermon, the disciples are commanded not to tell anyone what they have seen until the Son of Man is raised from the dead. We have another example of the messianic secret (9:9). After Jesus's resurrection, his full glory as God the Son will be declared. Israel is not yet ready. He must die and rise first. Unlike others who had not been able to keep Jesus's identity secret, the disciples obey. Their submission is appropriate, as God has just told them to listen to Jesus.

However, because of their lack of comprehension of a crucified Messiah, they debate what he means by rising from the dead (9:10). With their political and militaristic expectations of a Messiah who would liberate Israel from the gentiles and ultimately rule the world, concepts like his suffering and death

---

35. "Listen" is the present imperative of *akouō*, implying ongoing listening, i.e., "keep listening."

36. Evans, *Mark 8:27—16:20*, 38.

were beyond them, let alone the Messiah rising from the dead. The resurrection of the righteous was expected, but at the end of the age.

The disciples, no doubt pondering the ever so brief arrival of Elijah *after* Jesus's coming, then ask why the teachers of the law expected Elijah to come first. As discussed on 6:15, there were eschatological expectations associated with Elijah. Mal 4:5–6 speaks of God sending "Elijah the prophet before the great and awesome day of the Lord comes." He would "turn the hearts of fathers to their children and the hearts of children to their fathers" lest God would himself come and "strike the land with a decree of utter destruction."[37]

In v. 12, Jesus confirms the idea of Elijah coming to restore all things. Then, in v. 13, he states that Elijah *has come,* with the people doing what they pleased to him. Jesus's words link John the Baptist to Elijah. John is not the literal Elijah, but Elijah was a prototype of John. Malachi's prophecy is fulfilled in him. "As it is written about him" is not easy to explain, as no OT passage refers to the eschatological Elijah suffering. However, it is best understood against the backdrop of 1 Kgs 19:2 and 10, where Elijah suffered at the hands of Jezebel, and so John experiences similar mishandling at the hands of Herod and others.[38]

Verse 12b is cryptic. The Son of Man could here mean "a human," referring to John. If so, the suffering in view is that of Jesus and not John.[39] However, consistent with Mark's use of Son of Man for Jesus throughout the Gospel, the title should be read in the same way here. Jesus, then, is asking why the Son of Man should suffer and be so despised if Elijah is coming. He leaves this unanswered.

This final section is significant for our understanding of John the Baptist in regards to OT prophecy. He is the fulfillment of the expectation of a messenger preparing the way for the Messiah (cf. Mal 3:1; Isa 40) and Elijah, who will come and restore the nation (cf. Mal 4:6). He did this by preaching a baptism of repentance and forgiveness of sin. Baptism prepared people for the coming of Jesus. Sadly, Israel rejected Jesus, and the devastation predicted in Mal 4:6 came to pass with the destruction of the nation at the hands of the Romans in AD 70. John is also the final of the

---

37. Evans, *Mark 8:27—16:20*, 43, notes that the hope of Elijah coming is widely referenced in Jewish sources, including Sir 48:10, 4Q558, and a range of other rabbinic materials (e.g., *m. ʿEd.* 8:7). In some texts, Elijah will have some role in the resurrection of the dead (*Sib. Or.* 2:187–188; *m. Soṭah* 9:15; *b. Sanh.* 113a).

38. Brooks, *Mark*, 144.

39. Evans, *Mark 8:27—16:20*, 44, regards it as John's suffering. Yet, he also concedes that first hearers would not have heard it this way. Surely then, it refers to Jesus's suffering.

OT prophets pointing Israel to Jesus. Now that Jesus has come, the apostles will carry the message to the world.

The Exorcism of a Boy with an Evil Spirit (9:14–29)

The disciples' education here has two interconnected aspects.

Discipleship Instruction Four: *Disciples must have a strong faith and be prayerful.*

a) Disciples are to be people of faith and confidence in God's power given to them.

b) Prayer is required to release that power, and focused prayer is sometimes essential to overcome the enemy in a given situation.

Faith and prayer are hallmarks of true disciples. Jesus, Peter, Jacob (James), and John come down from what is likely Mount Hermon and find that a great crowd is with the disciples and that the disciples are arguing with the scribes. There is no further mention of the scribes in the narrative. It is not completely clear what caused the argument. It may be the disciples' failure to cast out the demon, causing the scribes to ridicule them. Another possibility is that the scribes were attributing Christ's power to Satan, as the Beelzebub controversy in 3:20–30.

The response shows Jesus's celebrity status as the people come to him with great adulation. Jesus naturally asks them about what they are disputing. The Greek term for arguing is *syzēteō*, used in 9:14 and 16 a moment or so earlier of Peter, Jacob (James), and John debating what rising from the dead meant (9:10). At other points in the Gospel, it is used of debates involving the Jewish leaders (8:11; 12:28; see also 1:27).

The disciples do not answer. Instead, a man from the crowd cries out. The shouter is clearly the father of the child brought to be exorcised of a demon. His boy had a demon, which made him mute. Later, we are told it also made him deaf (9:25). We saw this in 7:32–37, where Jesus had cast out a similar spirit. These accounts show that a demon within a person can affect the person's health, including hearing and speech. When we come across a person with such issues, we pray for him or her, knowing the cause might be demonic. However, we should not assume this but should ask for God's guidance, as it could simply be a medical issue. We should cast a demon out only if the Spirit instructs us to do so. Alternatively, we should consider this option if medical assistance fails.

We learn through the account that the demonized boy has had this issue since he was a child (v. 21). The language implies he is no longer a child; hence, we have another example of someone under Satan's snare through most of his life (cf. 5:25). Not only does the spirit render him speechless and deaf, but it takes hold of him and throws him down, often seeking to kill him in fire or water (v. 22). It also causes him to foam at the mouth and makes him rigid, paralyzing him. The spirit tortures him and causes him great pain.

Further, it destroys his father and others as they watch their boy gripped in such a cruel way. We see the destructive intent and power of demons; they roam like roaring lions seeking someone to devour, to "steal, kill, and destroy" (1 Pet 5:8; John 10:10). Their victims are not just the demonized, but those who love the one they seek to destroy. They wreak havoc in a person's life and in the lives of the family and friends.

We find then that the disciples, other than Peter, Jacob (James), and John, who were with Jesus, were not "strong enough" to cast out the demon. The term for strong enough ("able" in some translations) is *ischyō*. It takes us back to 1:7, where Jesus is described with a related word as *ho ischyroteros*, "the stronger one." Mark also uses *ischyō* of the demoniac who is so strong that he cannot be chained (5:4). Here, the demon is extremely powerful, as evidenced by its ability to resist the commands of the disciples. Remembering that the disciples have been given authority to cast out demons and over unclean spirits (3:15; 6:7), their spiritual weakness implies that something is missing here.

Jesus does not immediately cast the demon out. Instead, he cries out, bemoaning the people of Israel—a kind of concise State of the Nation speech—and it is not flattering. He describes Israel at the time ("this generation") as faithless. Their unbelief implies part of the reason for their failure to drive out the demon may be a lack of faith. However, later in the passage, the problem is equally a lack of prayer (v. 29). As such, Jesus is not targeting the disciples per se, but the whole people who lack trust and confidence in God (despite being very religious).

Jesus's words here open up the possibility that the reason the boy and others in Israel are demonized is because of their corporate lack of faith. If this is so, this may have significant repercussions for us in places like my nation, New Zealand. Here, we do not see many demonic manifestations, although we see some. The lack of these may be due to the effect of Christianity over time, the faith of the many Christians in the past protecting the nation. However, in New Zealand, Christianity is declining, and so if this logic here is correct, we may see more demonic activity. The rising problems with mental health—increasing suicide, self-harm, alcohol and drug abuse, violence, and the like—could be indicators that this is going on.

Jesus then asks two questions, querying how long he will be with this generation and how long he must put up with the people of Israel. We see another hint at Jesus's looming death, of which he is well aware. We sense again the frustration of the creator of the universe looking around at what his world had become. They simply do not believe in him enough. They are not what they could and should be—people of confidence in their God. We are challenged to be so.

In vv. 20–27, the deliverance occurs. It is overflowing with lessons for us. When brought to Jesus, as with the other demons in Mark's Gospel, this demon undoubtedly recognizes Jesus as the Son of God and knows he is about to be expelled. Such is his power that the demon instantly attacks the boy—one last attempt to destroy him. Jesus finds out that the boy has been assaulted in this way since childhood, with the demon trying to burn him to death and drown him. We sense the great love of the father for his son, as clearly, he and other family members have repeatedly plucked him from fire and sea in the past. His problem is not a lack of love for his son. We see here an example of the struggle of people who have to care for the demonized, the disabled, and/or the extremely ill. It is a harrowing and exhausting challenge. As such, the exorcism is as much for the family as the child.

The father asks that if Jesus can, would he have compassion on them and help them. Compassion is again that lovely Greek word *splanchnizomai* connoting a well of mercy for a person flowing from the depths of one's being for the plight of others (see on 6:34; see also 8:2).

Jesus's response, "if you can," has a hint of humor, irony, cynicism, sarcasm, or something similar. As if the Messiah healing people throughout the nation could not! Has he not by this time shown his power to do such things? He then states a promise that all believers should hold to with all their hearts: "Everything is possible for the one who believes." These words are a lesson to the faithless generation and for us. We should take careful note that Jesus does not here say that everything will come to pass for the one who believes. It is a trust that God can do anything if he so desires—according to *his* will. God knows what is best.

Sometimes, we can have all the faith in the world, but God chooses to do something otherwise. That does not mean God *could* not do what we ask; it means that he *did* not do it. Later in Mark, Jesus will have God refuse his three prayers for release from his forthcoming suffering (14:35–41). That is because God had to save the world through Jesus's death. God could have taken away the suffering, but he did not. That is his choice. We trust in him, he decides how to respond, and we continue to trust him.

The father of the child then answers with one of the most profound prayers in the Bible, and one we should probably all pray regularly: "I believe! Take away my unbelief!" In v. 22, the father had asked Jesus to help him, using the term *boētheō*. In v. 25, he uses the term again, "*Help* my unbelief!" We see that two healings are going on. First, the boy will be set free from a demon and his hearing and speech restored. Second, his father will be healed from his lack of faith. Both are important, although, since we are justified by faith, whatever our physical condition, one can argue that the healing of the faith deficiencies was more critical than the physical restoration (although both were awesome).

Many of us are like this man. We name Jesus as Lord, and we believe. We know that by our faith, we are justified (Rom 5:1). Nevertheless, we all need more faith, more trust, and more confidence. This man's great prayer should be our cry: "Take away" or "help" our unbelief! Imagine what the church could do if we all had more faith!

Then Jesus commanded the demon to leave the boy and never return. On this occasion, he names the spirit, but in the most general terms, naming it after what it does to the boy. The naming of the spirit leads some Christians to think we must *always* name the spirit in question. However, this is not necessary, for a quick look through the Gospels shows that Jesus did not always name spirits. If the Spirit leads, we should. Otherwise, we should not.

The term translated "command" is *epitassō*, a term of authority used by monarchs and in military situations.[40] Jesus has such absolute authority over demons. At his command, the demon convulses and leaves the boy, leaving him seemingly dead. However, he is not dead. Jesus takes his hand, and he stands up. Later, the disciples ask why they were unable to cast the demon out. Jesus responds that this type requires prayer. Although some texts have "prayer and fasting," the shorter reading is likely the right one.[41]

Hence, we have here a valuable lesson: sometimes healing or deliverance will not be simple but will require more focused prayer. The nature of the prayer is unspecified. It could be personal, prayerful preparation on the disciples' part or prayer as they engage in deliverance (9:27–28). Whichever it is, those of us who wish to engage in effective ministry must be people of prayer. When something is resistant to healing, we pray again. However, we also remember that while God can do anything, it does not mean he will. He does things according to his will. This passage confirms that Jesus was a

---

40. See 1 Esd 4:57; Esth 1:8; Josephus, *Ant.* 1:172, 6:243.

41. Metzger, *Textual Commentary*, 85, notes that this was added in because of "the increasing emphasis in the early church on the necessity of fasting." While "and fasting" is found in most witnesses, the important Alexandrian and the Western types of text do not include it. Hence, it is most likely not original.

man of prayer.[42] His prayerfulness is reflected in his ability to cast out this demon. One might say, Jesus was always "preprayered."

The Second Passion Prediction (9:30–32)

In this passage, Mark backtracks and repeats the first instruction. He will do so a third time in 10:32–33, ensuring that they understand what he is saying. Of course, they fail to grasp his meaning until he rises from death.

> **Discipleship Instruction One** (restated): *Jesus is the Messiah and Son of Man, who must die and rise from the dead.*

The repetition of Instruction One in between Instructions Four and Five tells us how important it is. We have to understand that the death of Jesus is the center of the Christian story.

If it is correct that the previous events occurred around Caesarea Philippi and Mount Hermon in the north of Galilee, Jesus and his group then head south through Galilee. This time, he does not want people to know about his presence, whether to give him time away from the crowds or to teach the disciples. The reason is his desire to continue to instruct the disciples. The content of his teaching is that he (the Son of Man) will be handed over to the hands of people. These people will kill him. Three days later (measured inclusively), he will rise.

Earlier, in 8:31, he had made much the same prediction. The differences are twofold. First, in 8:31, this *must* happen; here, it *will* happen. Second, in 8:31, he will suffer many things and be rejected by the Jewish leadership. Here, he is simply handed over. Otherwise, the details are the same. Mark again uses "Son of Man." This title was discussed earlier with Jesus identifying with Daniel and Enoch's transcendent figure and blending it with the Servant of Isa 53 and the Messiah of Ps 22. He is the glorious transcendent Son of Man, as seen on the Mount of Transfiguration, but he is the Servant as well, and it is servanthood that clothes his glory until his resurrection. As earlier, he will be killed. No details are given. For those with ears to hear, "take up your cross and follow me" implies his crucifixion. Jesus knew he would be crucified but did not state it unambiguously. Also, in both texts, he will rise after three days.

In the previous episode, Peter's response is to rebuke Jesus, only for Jesus to rebuke Satan through him. Here, the disciples simply have no idea what Jesus means by the saying. As discussed on the first passion prediction, this is because they simply have never connected Ps 22 and Isa 53 with the

---

42. See Mark 1:35; 6:46; 14:32–39, especially Luke 5:16.

hopes of a Messiah. They had not considered that the Messiah would not be a triumphant new Moses, Joshua, or David type of figure who would rampage through the country, liberating it from Rome. He would reign as King. God's reign would be imposed through glorious might. He would establish Israel as the world's leading nation, Jerusalem would be the world's capital, and the Torah would be her law. They had no idea of a kingdom established through the King's death and without the use of force other than the power of the word, love, and the Spirit of God.

The three parallel predictions indicate that Jesus's death is the heart of the Christian faith. It is where salvation is found. It is where the Lord reveals what it means to be God's people: humility, service, sacrifice, suffering, selflessness, and love for others. This is our call.

Questions

- Against what yeast of false teaching do we need to be warned today?
- Do you think it significant that Jesus healed the blind man of Bethsaida in two stages, and if so, why? Why not?
- Do you think the placement of the healings of the blind man in Bethsaida and Bartimaeus in Mark 10 is significant? If so, why? Why not?
- What is noteworthy about the place where Peter confesses Jesus is Messiah? What does that tell us about Jesus?
- What does it mean that Jesus is the Christ? How did the disciples understand it at the time? How are we to understand it?
- Why did the disciples fail to understand Jesus's predictions of his death and resurrection?
- Read 8:34–39. What does it teach us about being a follower of Jesus?
- What does the transfiguration tell us about Jesus?
- Why did Peter want to build three tents?
- When we fail to deliver a person from a demon, what should we do?

Lesson Seven: Jesus's Discipleship Training Program Continues (9:33—10:16)

Greatness Is Found in Service (9:33–35)

INSTRUCTION ONE HAS BEEN emphasized, and Jesus begins his tutelage of the disciples to whom he would pass the kingdom over in just a short while. This passage includes an instruction that will be repeated in 10:35–45.

Discipleship Instruction Five: *The path to greatness is service.*

Their movement through Galilee from Caesarea Philippi brings them to Capernaum for the first time since 3:20 (see also 1:21; 2:1). They enter their home, which may be the home of Peter and Andrew, where Jesus had healed Peter's mother-in-law. Jesus had observed that the disciples were arguing as they traveled on the way. Jesus could well have already known what they had been talking about through his divine prescience (2:8) but chooses to ask them concerning their debate.

Their response is silence, possibly because they are embarrassed at the reason for their debate. It could be because they know that the greatest among them is, of course, Jesus, and their argument is pathetic.

The thing they were arguing about was simple: who was the greatest among them. The debate anticipates 10:35–37, where Jacob (James) and John ask Jesus to give them the seats of highest honor on either side of him. Here, we can only speculate who was claiming what. Likely, Jacob (James), John, and Peter had high opinions of themselves, having been chosen first and singled out as Jesus's inner circle. They likely believed too that if they had been present when the disciples sought to cast out the demon from the boy, they would have succeeded. They no doubt felt that they were the kingpins. Others may have been making claims such as Judas or Simon the Zealot; we do not know.

What we do know is that they had yet to grasp the reason that Jesus had twice referred to his death and had urged genuine believers to deny themselves and take up crosses to follow him. He was teaching them that the path to glory is humble service. They wanted the converse: to be viewed as the greatest. Put plainly, this is the danger of pride (a personal vice, of which we are often ignorant).

Wanting to be the greatest is typical of all cultures. In the Roman culture, self-promotion and boasting were an art form, and what mattered was one's status and reputation above all things. It was appropriate to promote oneself and to put others down to gain prestige for oneself and one's family. Every culture has such problems. In New Zealand culture, while humility is highly valued, greatness is achieved through such things as being a great sportsperson, especially a rugby player.

The problem of seeking greatness lies in the Corinthian letters as members of the church vied for honor by favoring one apostle over another: "I follow Paul . . . Apollos . . . Cephas" (1 Cor 1:12). The Philippians were also struggling with selfish ambition and vain conceit (Phil 2:3). Paul points them both to the example of Jesus.

Here, Jesus sits down, the Jewish position of a teacher. He calls the Twelve, who were the leaders among the disciples, chosen by Jesus and sent into mission (3:13–19; 6:7–13). He instructs them on greatness. If a person wants first place in the kingdom of God, he or she must be last. In the ancient world, first meant rulers, aristocrats, ruling priests, and other persons of authority and influence.[1] It meant being like the leading men of Galilee who ate with Herod Antipas in 6:21. Jesus tells them that those who wish to have the highest rank are not to seek self-promotion as the greatest but to do as it says in Phil 2:4: "But in humility count others more significant than yourselves." The first place goes to the one who raises up others.

They must also be "servant of all." Being a servant was a demeaning position in the ancient world. One wanted to be the person served. In the kingdom, greatness is attributed to those who serve others. Indeed, the Christian seeking greatness delights in serving others.

This moment will not be the last time Jesus teaches them about greatness through service. He will do so again in 10:35–45. We see here and throughout Mark that Jesus wants us to connect the way he lived and died with the way we go about our lives. He came as God's Servant and did not seek honor; he sought only to serve those in need. Jesus never used his power to enhance his reputation and did not seek to lead Israel, but used his

---

1. Evans, *Mark 8:27—16:20*, 61. Examples include Luke 19:47; Acts 25:2; 28:17; Josephus, *Ant.* 11:140–41; 18:63–64, 121.

power to help others. When he had completed his service, God would exalt him (Phil 2:9–10).

We are to do the same. We are to accept what God has given us with joy and use what we have to serve others in the hope that they will flourish. Jesus is the Messiah, but he came only to serve. For us, the path of discipleship and greatness in the kingdom is servanthood. Whereas being a slave or servant is to be of no rank in the world, it is the path to kingdom greatness.

The Importance of Children (9:36–37)

Linked to the summons to service, Jesus draws attention to a group of people particularly precious to God.

Discipleship Instruction Six: *Children are the most important people in the kingdom of God and are to be warmly welcomed.*

In the ancient world, in terms of honor, status, and rank, aside from slaves, children were at the bottom of the pecking order. So what Jesus does here provides an illustration of the previous command to seek greatness in taking the lowest rank and being a servant, as well as teaching the disciples of the importance of children.

The child Jesus takes up is a *paidion*, which is a little child under seven years old.[2] By picking up a *paidion*, he takes a person of the lowest rank. He places the child in the center of the Twelve. Such a moment would potentially be terrifying for the child. However, by doing this, Jesus focuses the disciples' attention on this symbol of weakness, humility, and dependence. He thus challenges their values that are focused on gaining rank and honor.

Jesus does not leave the little child there. The Greek *enankalizomai* indicates that he takes the child from the center of the group and hugs it.[3] By holding the young boy or girl with such love and warmth, he instructs the disciples concerning how to treat children. Such is the way they are to be welcomed.

Jesus then tells the disciples that whoever welcomes a child in his name welcomes Jesus himself. As such, Jesus identifies with the children of the world. To love a child is to love God's Son. Furthermore, to welcome the child is not only to welcome Jesus but to welcome God. God himself delights in children, and to receive them with warmth is to welcome God into our midst.

2. BDAG, 749.
3. BDAG, 330.

There is so much that matters here. First, what a glorious thing to see: the creator of the universe taking a child into his arms and pouring out his love on it! This affection shows us how God loves us; we are his beloved children. Second, this moment reminds the disciples of what it means to seek greatness. Greatness is found in caring for the smallest and most vulnerable of people. Third, this verse points to the priority of place that children have in the kingdom. Such a status was culturally shocking, for caring for children was a lowly function. As Evans puts it, "Children were held in little regard in late antiquity. Listening to 'children's talk' was thought to be a waste of time (*m. 'Abot* 3:11)."[4]

This moment implies that children's ministry is the most critical in the church. Caring for children has been demeaned as "women's work." However, we are told here that it is not a lower status ministry or a means to get rid of kids, so parents can get down to the real thing. Neither should children be seen merely as a means to an evangelistic end, as if by having a great children's program, we can successfully grow a church (because the children's parents will like it). Instead, children in their own right are to be welcomed, loved, protected, cherished, and nurtured. They are to be placed at the center of the church and taken up in arms of love and nurtured. True servanthood begins with caring for children. The theme of children and their importance will recur again in 10:13–16.

A Permissive Attitude (9:38–41)

Unusually for Mark, who commonly uses *kai* (and) and *de* (but, and, now) to link sentences, here there is no connective, but rather an asyndeton.[5] The absence suggests a new thread. This lesson is the seventh.

Disciple Instruction Seven: *Disciples should have a permissive attitude to others who wish to serve Christ.*

In other words, if someone is engaging in missional activity on God's behalf, even if that person is not from within our part of the Christian church or community, we are not to prevent his or her service, for we are all on the same side. As will be discussed below, this has implications for new denominations or new churches that emerge, for women in ministry,

---

4. Evans, *Mark 8:27—16:20*, 61.

5. Asyndeton ("not bound together") refers to sentences that have no conjunctive word or phrase that links to a previous part of the sentence (see Wallace, *Grammar*, 658).

and for people who step out into ministry for Jesus but who do not seem to have the right authorization.

Usually, it is Peter who is the spokesman for the disciples. This passage begins with John, the brother of Jacob (James), reporting to Jesus that they have discovered a man who is casting out demons in Jesus's name. It may be that the man had earlier received healing through Jesus or had observed the disciples casting out demons in Jesus's name. The man is not merely attempting to cast demons out, he is actually doing so. There may be a subtle dig at the nine apostles who could not cast out the demon earlier; this man has no such problems. There may even be a hint of jealousy on John's part, although he was up the mountain with Jesus at the time. Anyway, we have to assume the man is a believer in Jesus, and Jesus's power is working through him. As will be amplified below, Jewish exorcists were not uncommon at the time.

John reports to Jesus that the disciples have tried to prevent this man from doing so. The disciples saw his work as illegitimate compared with their own authorized work. In particular, they are concerned that he is "not following *us*" (italics added). This last clause gives an important clue to John's motivation. He is concerned that this person is not following them. As such, we have a classic case of a leader wanting to control his movement. Doing so is not his place: Jesus is Lord of the harvest, and the Spirit leads the mission. The real question is not whether the man is following the disciples, but whether he is following Jesus (not necessarily physically, but in the heart). John's attitude distorts the ideals of Jesus. The disciples should not be threatened by this man. He is working for Jesus and not against him. He and the disciples are allies against a common enemy.

There is an interesting comparative passage in Num 11:26–30. In this passage, the Spirit comes upon the seventy elders who prophesy. Two other men, Eldad and Medad, are also in the camp, and the Spirit comes on them as well. The young Joshua runs to Moses with concern: "Eldad and Medad are prophesying in the camp." He goes on, "My Lord Moses, stop them." Moses's response challenges him: "Are you jealous for my sake? Would that all the Lord's people were prophets, that the Lord would put his spirit on them!"

Here, it is the new Joshua who responds. His answer is permissive rather than restrictive. He emphatically tells the disciples not to stop the man. His reason (*gar*, "for") is that no one can do miracles in his name unless they are supportive of him. The key here is "in my name." "In my name" does not just mean using the formula "in the name of Jesus." It implies doing something by Jesus's power and as per his will. It implies that he does so by the Spirit, who is in Jesus operating where there are faith and the invocation of Jesus's name. While they are not going as far as the Jewish leaders who interpret Jesus's power as demonic (3:22–30), the disciples are doing the same kind of thing. This man ministers in line with Christ's character, and other followers must not speak against him. The Greek for "say bad things about me" is *kakologeō*, "speak evil."

In v. 40, Jesus reinforces this with the statement that "whoever is not against us is for us." Such a saying was a maxim used elsewhere at the time. A similar adage is attributed to the Roman statesman Marcus Tullius Cicero (106–43 BC). He says to Julius Caesar: "We have often heard you say that, while we considered all who were not with us as our enemies, you considered all who were not against you as your friends."[6]

The situation also points to the polarization that the ministry of Jesus brings. People are either for him or against him. This person is clearly for Jesus and the kingdom and should not be stopped. Instead, he should be endorsed if he ministers in the name of Jesus Christ.

The verse also recalls Josh 5:13, where Joshua asks the commander of the Lord's army: "Are you for us, or for our adversaries?" Here, the second Joshua is instructing John using ideas drawn from the first Joshua, in challenging John not to oppose those who are in the same "army."

This passage indicates that the ministry in Christ was spreading spontaneously and not merely through his specific sending of people into mission. We saw this at other points in Mark's Gospel, where people could not be stopped from sharing the good news of his powerful ministry (1:28, 45). Here we see another layer as some people sought to emulate his ministry of deliverance, invoking his power.

People were responding to Jesus in some cases by taking up a ministry. There were Jewish exorcists at the time. In the NT, there were the seven sons of Sceva, a Jewish priest, who tried to cast out demons in the name of Jesus and Paul, only to be beaten up (Acts 19:13–17). Josephus records that Solomon was able to exorcise demons (which is unlikely historically). Josephus describes Solomon's skill in casting out demons as both a science and a method of healing. To do so, Solomon used incantations to drive out the demons permanently.

Josephus goes on to give an account of a Jewish exorcist, Eleazar, who cast out demons in the presence of the emperor Vespasian and his sons and military personnel. He describes his healing method. Eleazar put a ring in the demoniac's nose and pulled the demon out through the person's nostrils. The man fell, and Eleazar commanded him never to return, using the name of Solomon and his incantations. He supposedly commanded the demon to overturn a nearby cup or basin of water as evidence. For Josephus, this

---

6. *Lig.* 11; Evans, *Mark 8:27—16:20*, 65.

showed the power of Solomon.[7] It is little wonder that people observing Jesus sought to use his name to drive out demons.

God spontaneously sending workers by the power of the Spirit is seen through Acts. People like Apollos come to Christ (Acts 18:24—19:1), and often without specific commissioning or sending, simply respond to God by sharing what they have received. We see here evidence of the kingdom as a seed that grows in an unstoppable way.

Verse 41, at first glance, seems disconnected to the previous material. However, it is joined by *gar*, "for." Jesus imagines a person giving a cup of water to one of the disciples. They do so "in my name because [they] belong to Christ." Hence, this is not some random giving of a drink to a disciple. This person is someone invoking Christ's name and gives in line with Christ's will and character. Hence, this is another person in Jesus's team.

The giving of a cup of water seems insignificant. However, in the Middle East, where temperatures can soar, this can be lifesaving. The doing of miracles in Christ's name is one end of the spectrum, the giving of a glass of water, the other. Nevertheless, Jesus assures the disciples that even such an insignificant act is worthy of reward. Furthermore, the disciples would never stop a person from giving them a cup of water. Why stop them from doing miracles?

Both acts are effectively the same, lifesaving activities. Who on earth would stop them? Such generosity illustrates ideas like "freely you have received, freely give" (Matt 10:8). Alternatively, Acts 20:35, "it is more blessed to give than to receive." It corresponds to the sheep and the goats, where people are judged on the way they have treated God's people, even "the least of these my brothers" (Matt 25:31–46). It also takes us to the Samaritan woman of whom Jesus asked for a drink, ending with him giving her and her town the eternal water of life (John 4:7–43).

We must grasp and apply Jesus's attitude. He endorses this man in a permissive way, instructing not that he be stopped but that he be permitted to continue. Such permission giving has significant implications for the church. When women are inspired to serve Jesus in ministry, we should not stop them. If young people or new Christians emerge on the scene, full of desire to share Christ and pray for those in need, woe to us if we get in the way. When we are in a denomination obsessed with process and things like ordination, while ordination has its place, when someone comes along with gifts yearning to use them, we should allow them. Moses looked to a day when all of God's people were priests (Exod 19:6). Christ and Peter tell us that this day has come (1 Pet 2:5, 9; Rev 1:6). Joel predicted that when the

---

7. Josephus, *Ant.* 8:45–49.

Spirit comes, all God's people will prophesy (Joel 2:28–29; Acts 2:17–18). So, we should adopt a permissive attitude, as did Jesus.

However, this should not be mindless; we should support such people. We who are mature in Christ should get alongside them, mentor them, and guide them, without crushing their enthusiasm and nature. We see this magnificently as Priscilla and Aquila in Ephesus took the firebrand Apollos under their wing and taught him "the way" more adequately, that he would be an even more effective minister of the gospel (cf. Acts 18:24–28). Too many Christians are obsessed with process and rules. They inadvertently become Pharisees. Some denominations are so overcome with litigiousness that they crush those who appear, like this man. They often fail to see God has sent them, and so we should allow them to minister in his name.

We also see that God rewards even the smallest acts of mercy from his people. We tend to rate some in the church as bigwigs because they preach, lead worship, cast out demons, heal, or go on overseas mission. Rightfully, we should praise God for them. However, equally, we should honor those who do small things like cleaning toilets, making morning tea, taking a food parcel to a hungry person, welcoming a stranger, and so on. The kingdom is not just about those with the seeming super-gifts that grab the limelight; it is about the small acts of giving that bring life and change the world. God will reward us for those. Such an attitude is not prosperity teaching; the reward is treasure in heaven stored up as people serve the Lord. The disciples may do miracles, but they must also give water and food to those in need.

Avoid Sinning and Causing Others to Sin (9:42–48)

The next discipleship lesson is conveyed graphically and powerfully.

Discipleship Instruction Eight: *Avoid sinning and causing others to sin, or face the consequences.*

There is another clear shift here, despite the connective *kai* (and). Jesus speaks absolutely and inclusively: "Anyone who . . ." He gives a solemn warning to anyone who places an obstacle that causes the least of people (a little one) who believe in him to sin. His words recall 9:36, where Jesus placed a child among the believers and hugged it. Hence, the "little ones" may refer to children.[8] If so, Jesus's words would remind the disciples of the

---

8. Evans, *Mark 8:27—16:20*, 70.

injunction to welcome children to Christ with the added dimension that, in so doing, the disciples must not lead them into sin.

Alternatively, Jesus is not speaking only of children but is thinking more broadly of those among his faithful who are little in the sense of vulnerable or seemingly insignificant. If the term is general, then it refers to anything that causes a believer to fall away. This brings to mind passages in Paul where he urges stronger believers to adapt their behavior and even renounce their rights to ensure that they do not cause a weaker Christian to stumble (1 Cor 8–10; Rom 14–15). Further, in Christ, believers are to treat those who face struggles with greater honor than those who do not (1 Cor 12:24–25). Potentially, this then would include people who are impaired in a range of ways.

The term for "stumbling block, obstacle" is *skandalizō*, from which we get the English term "scandal." It means here something scandalous: "to cause someone to fall away from faith" or "to stumble," i.e., trip up in their faith.[9] The term was used in 4:17 of those who hear the word of God, believe briefly, and then fall away. In 6:3, it is used of those in the Nazareth synagogue who are offended at Jesus. It will be used in 14:27 as Jesus warns them that they will all fall away when he is taken, which Peter denies, but which comes to pass (14:27, 29). It is used four times in this passage, making it the critical term for understanding the text (vv. 42, 43, 45, 47).

In the first use in v. 42, it is where a person causes another to stumble in his or her faith. Such faltering could come in a myriad of ways, whether through enticing a person into sin; failing to warn him or her away from sin; mistreating a person, which causes him or her to sin; or our sinful tendencies influencing a person to sin. In particular, it is where there are vulnerable Christians and when, through our sins of commission or omission, we cause them to stumble. Some Jewish texts have a similar thread. This passage is a warning to Christians not to cause others to stumble and fall in their faith.[10]

The consequence is indirect but harsh. It would be better for the offender to have a giant millstone (*mylos onikos*) hung around the neck and be thrown into the sea. Such a giant millstone or "donkey millstone" would weigh around 739 kg (1,629 lbs or 0.81 ton), around the weight of a good-sized cow. With that around a person's neck, he or she would plummet to the seafloor very quickly and drown. Jesus does not name the fate of that

---

9. See Giesen, "σκανδαλίζω," 3:248.

10. Evans, *Mark 8:27—16:20*, 70, notes other Jewish texts that utilize the notion in a similar way (Sir 9:5; 23:9; Pss. Sol. 16:7). He also comments on the Jewishness of the use of chopping off the hands and feet from 2 Macc 7:4, where Antiochus IV had the hands and feet of a Jewish woman's eldest son chopped off.

person here. However, in what follows, he will speak of the unquenchable fire of Gehenna. Likely, this is what is implied.

Jesus then moves from a person causing others to sin to a person's own propensity to transgress. With three horrific images, he makes the overall point that sin is to be avoided because the fate of sinners is horrific. The pattern for the first two is identical. If your hands cause you to sin, cut them off. Amputating one of our hands is an appalling image of self-mutilation to stop oneself sinning. Cutting off the hand is, of course, not to be taken literally. It is merely a rhetorical device to state the extreme seriousness of sin. The image is also militaristic. In the ancient world, warfare involved attacking with swords and cutting people up. Here, we declare war on our sins. The reason is that it is better to enter life mutilated, missing a hand, foot, or eye, than to end up in the unquenchable fire of Gehenna.

Life (*zōē*) is mentioned here twice (vv. 44, 45) and then replaced with the "kingdom of God" in v. 47. Their interchangeability shows that the two ideas are parallel. Life then has the sense of the abundant life experienced by believers when they enter the kingdom and live in this world (see 10:30). However, more profoundly, it speaks of the reward of eternal life. Notably, "eternal life" and "the kingdom of God" are also used interchangeably in 10:17, 24–25, and 30. The term "saved" is also used in 10:26, and so salvation is another parallel idea. As such, Mark's Jesus is warning readers that to enter life, they must resist sin.

The alternative is to enter Gehenna with a whole body but having engaged in sinful activity. We are not sure whether the Greek *geenna* was in use before the NT, with references like Sib. Or. 4.186 from the end of the first century AD. *Geenna* transliterates the Aramaic term *gêhinnām*, which comes from the Hebrew for the valley of Hinnom. The valley is south and west of Jerusalem (Wadi er-Rababi) and is mentioned in the OT.[11] At this place, King Manasseh and others offered children in child sacrifices.[12] As a result, it was a place associated with horror. Consequently, King Josiah defiled it (2 Kgs 23:10). Jeremiah predicts it will be a place of judgment and burial.[13]

In Jewish apocalyptic literature, references to "a valley, deep and burning with fire" refer to this tradition (e.g., 1 En. 54:1; 56:3). In such contexts, the idea is fused with the Greek idea of Hades.[14] In the NT, *geenna* is a metaphor of eternal punishment that contrasts with eternal life. One of the references to *geenna* is Isa 66:24, cited in this passage (further below). It is found

---

11. See also Josh 15:8; 18:16; Isa 31:9.
12. See 2 Kgs 21:6; 2 Chron 33:6; Jer 32:35.
13. See Jer 7:32; 19:66, see also Isa 30:33.
14. Silva, "γέεννα," *NIDNTTE*, 1:548.

in the NT twelve times, only once outside the Synoptic Gospels (Jas 3:6). Otherwise, as here, Jesus warns people of its fires.[15]

Here *geenna* is mentioned thrice (vv. 43, 45, 47). Notably, this is parabolic, and just as we do not take the amputation of body parts literally, we do not need to take the notion of fiery destruction plainly. Moreover, fire is found throughout the NT as a symbol of judgment.[16] Still, it would be a mistake to disregard Jesus's words as meaningless or as not pointing to something real. As such, it is rightly debated as to whether this refers to an actual fire that annihilates one so that one ceases to exist (annihilation), a fire of eternal punishment and suffering (the traditional view), a figurative way of describing a person dying under God's wrath and not rising to life (conditional immortality), or a metaphor for the desolation of the experience of eternal separation from God. Whatever it is, and one can only be sure by going there, it indicates a horrific eternal fate that contrasts with eternal life. There is no escape once one is there, whether one is eternally dead or experiencing some kind of eternal torment (cf. *Hades* in Luke 16:26).

Jesus then is warning his disciples in no uncertain terms that they must resist sin or face the consequences. Of course, in the fullness of time, Jesus will die for the sins of the disciples, and those who believe can have the confidence of eternal life. However, this warning reminds us that we are still to resist sin. Self-discipline and perseverance will confirm one's reward as a person justified by faith to "enter life." Life here refers to eternal life in the future, renewed heaven and earth.

It is noticeable to the observant that vv. 44 and 46 are missing from most translations, other than the KJV and NKJV. These verses are identical to v. 48, reading "where their worm does not die, and the fire is not quenched." The omission is because these verses are absent from the better manuscripts. It is considered by most, including Metzger, that these words were added by copyists from v. 48.[17]

Finally, in v. 48, Mark's Jesus quotes Isa 66:24, the final verse in Isaiah, in which Jesus gives an additional clarification note concerning *Gehenna*. The full context is as follows, vv.22–24:

> And they shall go out and look on the dead bodies of the men who have rebelled against me. For their worm shall not die, their fire shall not be quenched, and they shall be an abhorrence to all flesh.

---

15. See Matt 5:22, 29, 30; 10:28; 18:9; 23:15, 23; Luke 12:3.

16. See Matt 3:10, 12; 5:22; 7:19; 13:40; 18:8, 9; 25:41; Mark 9:43; Luke 3:17; 16:24; 1 Cor 3:13; Heb 10:27; Jude 7, 23; Rev 18:8; 20:14–15.

17. Metzger, *Textual Commentary*, 86.

In subsequent Jewish writings, this passage sometimes speaks of eternal conscious torment (Jdth 16:17; Sir 7:17). However, worms are also associated with rotting and death. Hence, this could speak of people's eternal suffering or being eternally dead, with worms all that remains. Either way, the image is horrific, with two fates offered those hearing. People will have eternal life in the kingdom of God, or they will face eternal destruction.

We are warned that God takes sin very seriously—indeed, so seriously, that he gave up his one and only Son to die for our sins to save us from the fate that awaits all unredeemed sinners. As those who believe in the Son, we are summoned to use our freedom in Christ to serve, not as a pretext for sin (cf. Gal 5:13). Instead, we are empowered to want to renounce sin and please our God.

We must also realize that this passage is not here to terrify us into believing. Instead, it is to excite us in the hope of eternal life in the kingdom of God. The hope of eternal reward should inspire us to want to resist sin. Sin brings pleasure for a short time, but it leaves a sour aftertaste and leads to destruction. Eternal life will be glorious, and it is worth leaving behind sin and living to please God, knowing that we will have an eternity of joy with him if we are faithful to the end.

Be Salty (9:49–50)

Mark 9 ends with a final lesson concerning spiritual fervor.

> **Discipleship Instruction Nine:** *Keep your spiritual passion salted and live at peace with one another.*

Jesus teaches the disciples that "everyone will be salted with fire."[18] This statement should probably be treated as a separate saying. However, it may refer to the previous verses in which Jesus refers to hell. So, "everyone" would name those who will enter hell and be tested with fire. Alternatively, it may reference everyone being tested severely in this life (1 Pet 4:12).[19] Another option is that it corresponds to the judgment that all will face at the second coming, when each will be judged for his or her work for God (cf. 1 Cor 3:13–15; 4:5–6). Then again, it might be the process of purging or purification that believers must go through to enter the kingdom of God (1 Pet 1:7).[20]

---

18. Some see here an allusion to Lev 2:13 (cf. Ezek 43:24; Ezra 6:9) where Israel is urged to season their cereal offerings. However this has a different sense, i.e., everyone will be salted with fire, not seasoned with salt.

19. France, *Gospel of Mark*, 384.

20. Evans, *Mark 8:27—16:20*, 73; Brooks, *Mark*, 153.

Deciding between these is difficult, but perhaps the latter idea is best as the passage considers the dual outcomes of life: eternal life or Gehenna.

In v. 50, Mark's Jesus continues using the metaphor of salt, explaining the connectedness of these verses. The first use tells us that salt is good.[21] This is true. In our world, salt primarily flavors our food, and such seasoning is good (as countless chefs know). Jews knew all about it because the Dead Sea is the saltiest body of water in the world, 25 percent saline.[22]

In the ancient world, salt was seen as useful for the same reason and a lot more. It was known as "'white gold,' one of the most significant substances in history, along with iron, gold, and wheat. In ancient societies it was a valuable social and economic commodity."[23] It was a symbol of luxury in Egypt, where it was used to mummify the dead. It was used for the preservation of food. It functioned as a symbol of hospitality and intimate friendship. A meal of bread and salt ended ancient conflicts. It was also symbolic of provision, and to eat someone's bread and salt was to be reciprocated in some way. It was used to purify, as a fertilizer, and for burning dung. Salt was added to sacrifices (e.g., Lev 2:13; Ezek 43:24) and tabernacle incense. It symbolized purity (Exod 30:35). It was seen as a divine gift and was also covenantal (Num 18:19; 2 Chr 13:5). Jesus uses the metaphor elsewhere, calling disciples "the salt of the earth" (Matt 5:13; 9:49–50; Luke 14:34–35). Paul calls on the Colossians to season their gospel speech with salt (Col 4:6). By saying salt is good, what follows may imply that salty Christians do good (they do not sin, as per the previous passage).

After stating the goodness of salt, Jesus next asks a rhetorical question expecting the answer "it cannot." Unsalty salt is useless and cannot be resalted. We can get waylaid here by the question of whether salt can lose its saltiness. Stein notes, however, that the disciples' salt came mostly from the Dead Sea, and if processed carelessly, was liable to become insipid or poor tasting and of little use for seasoning.[24] Once it is in this state, it is unusable. In context, it refers to disciples who lose their edge, lapse into sin, are choked by the weeds of life, and are fruitless (as in the parable of the sower, 4:1–20).

Jesus then appeals to them to "have salt in yourselves." The intent is different from being the "salt of the earth" (Matt 5:13). Here, it speaks of disciples keeping their spiritual edge. Others take it as referring to not

---

21. Salt could also be used destructively: to render land barren after war (Judg 9:45; Zeph 2:9), as a symbol of judgment (e.g., Deut 29:16–28), a symbol of barrenness (Job 39:6; Jer 17:6), and a symbol of cursing (Jas 3:9–12, cf. Ezek 47:7–9).

22. Rayburn, "Salt." (I have drawn from this essay through this section).

23. Rayburn, "Salt."

24. Stein, *Luke*, 398. This is because of the carnallite or gypsum in it.

stumbling and so being thrown out, which is how Luke and Matthew apply it.[25] Some suggest it means keeping pure, as salt was used for purification (cf. 2 Kgs 2:19–23). Another view is that it speaks of gracious conduct and speech seasoned with salt (cf. Col 4:6). Another suggestion is that it could be in parallel to "be at peace with one another," referring to excellent relationships in the Christian community. Most likely, it speaks generally to the principle of keeping one's spiritual edge as a believer, rejecting sin, and not causing others to stumble (cf. vv. 42–47).

The final clause urges the disciples to keep at peace with one another. Paul uses the same verb (*eirēneuō*) of relationships with each other and the world in Rom 12:18: "If possible, as far as it depends on you, live at peace with all people." In 2 Cor 13:11, to a church rife with disunity, he appeals to them to "live at peace." Similarly, in 1 Thess 5:13, the Thessalonians are to have "peace among yourselves." Here then, it is a summons to unity. The disciples are to lay aside petty disagreements and contention over who is the greatest, over whether this minister or that should be included, and live by the Christian summons to love one another.

Divorce, Marriage, and Adultery (10:1–12)

The tenth and eleventh precepts relate to family.

> **Discipleship Instruction Ten:** *For a disciple, marriage is for keeps; and where there is divorce, there should be no remarriage, for this is adultery.*

In the background is the situation with Herod: his divorce of King Aretas's daughter and his marriage to Herodias, his brother Philip's former wife (see on 6:14–29). Also in Mark's readers' minds would have been Nero who, as recently as AD 62, on his future wife's orders, had his first wife Octavia killed. He had then married Poppaea Sabina, who had been previously married to Nero's companion Ortho. Poppaea was also supposedly a God-fearer;[26] her conduct suggests otherwise. Around the time of the writing of Mark (AD 65), Nero kicked her to death in a fit of rage while she was pregnant. He then married a third wife, Statilia Messalina, after putting her husband the consul to death.[27] As Israel knew from the propensities of David (2 Sam 11—12), this is the standard stuff of empires, as emperors take women at will. However, the

---

25. Matt 5:13; Luke 14:35, cf. vv. 42–47.
26. Josephus, *Ant.* 20:189–96.
27. Suetonius, *Nero.* 35; Myers, "Nero"; Angus and Renwick, "Nero."

kingdom is not that kind of empire. Such behavior is simply not acceptable and most often has devastating consequences.

Also in the milieu was the ongoing debate between factions of Pharisees at the time. Deut 24:1 was considered the core text concerning divorce in Jewish law. The verse states that a man can divorce his wife if he finds "some indecency in her and he writes her a certificate of divorce and puts it in her hand and sends her out of his house." The Hebrew *'erwat dābār* is the contentious phrase. According to the stricter Pharisaic school of Shammai, this refers only to sexual immorality as grounds for divorce. However, the school of Hillel took it more liberally, interpreting it as permitting divorce even for trivialities, such as a wife messing up the dinner or when the husband found a more attractive woman.[28] The Essenes, however, forbade divorce altogether.[29] As we see in this passage, Jesus agrees with the Essenes. However, to complicate matters, in Matt 19, Jesus sides with the Shammai school.

Coming to the text, Jesus is now beginning his journey to Jerusalem and the cross. He travels from Capernaum (9:33) to Judea across the Jordan, a route that devout Jews took to avoid traveling through Samaria. When in Judea, in an unspecified location, great crowds come to him again. The hordes again show that Jesus's fame is widespread; he can go nowhere in the nation, whether in Galilee or Judea, without being mobbed. He then teaches the crowd, "as was his custom," indicating how central teaching was to his ministry.

In v. 2, some Pharisees come to him. They are more than likely from Jerusalem, although that is not specified. They ask him about the legality of divorce: "Is it legal for a man to divorce his wife?" (10:2). With the story of Herod and Herodias in their ears, Jesus's answer is politically hazardous. John's critique of Herod and his wife had ended his life. The Pharisees may have been trying to trap Jesus so that Herodias would pressure Herod Antipas to have Jesus killed as well.[30]

As he often does, in typical rabbinic style, Jesus answers the question with his own question. He asks them what Moses taught (10:3). As would be expected from legal experts, they respond from Deut 24:1 (see above). Jesus's response is not to enter into the debate but to explain why Moses

---

28. See Stein, *Mark*, 455, who notes the Jewish rabbinic texts *m. Giṭ.* 9.10; *b. Giṭ.* 90a–b.

29. "He shall not take another wife in addition to her, for she alone shall be with him all the time of her life. But if she dies, he may marry another from his father's house, from his family" (11Q 19:57). See also CD 4–5, where Gen 1:27 is cited as Jesus does here; see also Deut 17:17.

30. Evans, *Mark 8:27—16:20*, 82.

gave this command. It was given as a concession to human weakness, more specifically, due to "your hardness of heart" (v. 5). This accusation of hard hearts is found in Deut 10:16 and the prophets (Jer 4:4; Ezek 3:7). What Jesus is saying is that while it is permitted because of human weakness, it is not God's ideal. It is a concession due to Israel's failure. So then, the purpose of the divorce law was not to allow for divorce but to limit it. The use of "your" here is challenging and refers to the people of Israel rather than the Pharisees specifically. However, undoubtedly, they would have taken that very personally as an attack on their commitment.

Jesus then gives them a lesson in a biblical theology of marriage. He reaches back before Moses and even the fall of Adam and Eve to the very origins of humankind. Jesus does so by referring to the two key texts in Gen 1 and 2 that form the foundation of a Christian understanding of gender and marriage. First, he cites Gen 1:27. This text forms part of the "image of God" passage in 1:26–28. Both men and women are made in the image and likeness of God. Gender then is central to our anthropology. The first command given to these image-bearers is that they are to fill the earth (Gen 1:28). This injunction implicitly places heterosexual relationships producing children at the center of the human calling. By doing this, people will spread throughout the world.

He also cites Gen 2:24, where a man leaves his family and is joined to a woman, and they become one flesh, a new family unit. Hence, heterosexual, monogamous, faithful marriages that are characterized by love for God and each other (cf. 12:29–31) are at the center of a Christian understanding of human existence. As such, as Evans says, "Divorce is tantamount to undoing the created order."[31]

Jesus applies these texts, stating that the married couple are no longer two, but one flesh. This oneness has a literal sexual aspect, whereby as they come together, they form one physically entwined entity. More profoundly, it speaks of their collective, spiritual, and emotional oneness. While married people retain their physical and psychological individuality before God, they become one spiritual union.

Jesus then applies this truth, stating emphatically and absolutely that what God has joined together in marriage, let no one, whether husband, wife, or any third party, separate them (10:6–9). So, in marrying, people are living out the created ordinance and intention of God.[32] This also indicates

---

31. Evans, *Mark 8:27—16:20*, 84.

32. Evans, *Mark 8:27—16:20*, 84, notes that the same thing is found concerning the goddess Isis, who says: "I have brought woman and man together" (*SIG* 2:1267).

that faithful, monogamous, heterosexual marriage unions lie at the heart of God's intention for humankind.

We can note here that Jesus's position is not quite in line with the views of the various rabbinic schools; it aligns more closely with the Essenes. As such, both groups were no doubt disappointed. We can also see that Jesus did not say anything directly against Herod, Nero, or any other person. He avoided falling into the trap and saying the sorts of things John had said (6:18). Especially in Mark 11–12, we see Jesus avoiding rhetorical snares with equal aplomb.

His teaching leads to the disciples questioning him further in private (10:10). Jesus builds on this earlier prohibition on divorce, stating that where a divorcee remarries another person, that person commits adultery against the one divorced (10:10–12). They thus break the seventh commandment, "Do not commit adultery" (Exod 20:14; Deut 5:18). According to Mark, adultery is committed whenever a person forms another sexual relationship after having been married, unless the former spouse has died (cf. Luke 16:18; Rom 7:1–3).

We can see here that Mark does not give the permissive clause of Matt 19:9, where divorce is acceptable where there is unfaithfulness (*porneia*). Matthew's recollection of Jesus sees him side more with the Shammai group. Still, there remains ambiguity in Jesus's teaching. The term *porneia* is used in the OT of sexual immorality; however, it is also used of idolatry, especially in Hosea (e.g., Hos 2:6). Hence, while Mark's Jesus may be using *porneia* here only of sexual unfaithfulness, it may have a broader scope. If so, it could indicate the unfaithfulness demonstrated in worshiping false gods, marital abuse or rape, and other gross acts of marital betrayal.

Paul also appears to introduce a permissive clause in 1 Cor 7:12–15 whereby when a non-Christian spouse deserts his or her Christian spouse, the Christian is no longer enslaved. Scholars debate whether this represents permission to remarry or not (albeit to a Christian, cf. 1 Cor 7:39). With all this data, we are left a little uncertain of God's view of marriage, divorce, remarriage, and the question of adultery. What we are confident of is that, ideally speaking, a man and a woman will get married and "until death do they part." Such a lifelong union is the ideal of God.

However, even God's people, at times, have hard hearts, and the permissive clauses may be included in the NT anticipating this. We also are not under law but grace. God is a God of second chances. It seems that, at times, faithful Christians remarry. Perhaps that is not God's ideal, yet God gives them another opportunity. Such people who do remarry are challenged with the same ideal. They are called to be faithful to each other in every way until parted by death.

What we do not see here or at any point in Jesus's teaching is any space for same-sex marriage. That is simply not a category the Bible endorses; it is opposed to same-sex sexual relations from Genesis to Revelation. In 7:21, Jesus condemned sexual immorality as evil, so Mark is no exception. We are also uncertain of the status of a committed de facto relationship. When two people live together, they become one flesh. One could argue that they are married. If so, they should commit to that relationship and seek to be faithful to the end. If they are God's people, they should formalize their relationship before God and his people in a marriage ceremony.

Mark's teaching here is strong and endorses God's ideal that the married do not separate and remarry. Such fidelity is a challenge in places like Malaysia, where about one in four marriages fail. It is even more challenging in New Zealand, where the divorce rate is around 42 percent.[33] Nevertheless, the Christian ideal still stands. Alongside this ideal, though, we have to place grace and God's forgiveness. Being under grace, we should not be legalists and apply the law as has been done to repudiate those who marry a second time or even those in a de facto relationship. Instead, in grace, we challenge them to be utterly faithful and make it a relationship that pleases God. We remain faithful to the gospel and do not compromise marriage as a heterosexual, monogamous, faithful, and loving relationship.

We can also observe that this command applies to both men and women, unlike Deut 24, which allows male divorce but provides no concession for female divorce.[34] Hence, Jesus tightens the Jewish stance to no divorce for either party. In the Greco-Roman world, both men and women could divorce. All in all, we see a radical heightening of the expectation of Christian marriages.

How do we do it? Well, let me pass on a couple of pieces of great advice given to me as a young married Christian man. First, it is not about finding the right wife or placing expectations on one's wife or husband; it is up to us to be the best spouses we can be for the marriage partner. We are summoned to serve one another (Eph 5:21–33).[35] Second, we should never look twice at an attractive person or place ourselves in a potentially compromising situation.

---

33. "Divorce Demography." In New Zealand, one can form a legal union seen as a marriage by the government through a civil union, a traditional marriage, or cohabitation in a defacto relationship for more three years. The overall rate of broken marital relationships in New Zealand is likely much higher than 42 percent.

34. Evans, *Mark 8:27—16:20*, 85, notes that a Jewish woman could not divorce her husband (Josephus, *Ant.* 15:259–60; 18:353–62; *m. Yebam.* 14:1). However, in Greco-Roman society, female divorce was permitted in some circumstances.

35. On Eph 5:21—6:9, see Keown, "Paul's Vision of a New Masculinity."

The Blessing of the Children (10:13–16)

The sixth teaching taught in 9:36–37 is repeated here; the repetition showing its significance (disciples, take note!).

> **Discipleship Instruction Six** (restated): *Children are the most important people in the kingdom of God and are to be warmly welcomed.*

The disciples had not grasped the importance of children, despite Jesus earlier holding a child lovingly in his arms and telling them clearly and unambiguously that they are to welcome children, and to do so is to welcome Jesus and God the Father (9:33–37). Nor had they fully grasped the meaning of Discipleship Instruction Eight that included warnings not to cause one of Christ's little ones to sin (9:42). If they had grasped these two lessons from their teacher, they would never have behaved as they did here. In light of these earlier injunctions, their behavior here is reprehensible.

Jesus is still in Judea, moving closer to Jerusalem and the cross. The narrative goes on, linked with "and" (*kai*). The theme of family continues. In the previous pericope, marriage was considered. Now, it is children. All Christians, especially those who are parents, grandparents, Sunday School teachers, schoolteachers, and children's sports coaches—indeed, anyone who has anything to do with children—must listen carefully to Jesus to ensure we do not make the same mistake as the disciples.

No doubt hearing about Jesus's power and perhaps his particular fondness for children, people were bringing children to Jesus so that he could touch them. A man touching children can sound a bit dubious in some contemporary cultures because to touch a child has negative connotations. However, the thought of Jesus abusing children is vile. Child abuse, in any sense, is repugnant to Jesus and should be equally vile to us. It was through Christ's tender touch that the blessing of God was transmitted to the child. No one who names Jesus as Lord would do anything but act to nurture and protect the most vulnerable from the womb to adulthood (and beyond!).

The purpose of the touch could have been healing[36] or, as the context suggests, blessing (cf. 10:16). It was likely, in some instances, that people asked for healing for their child. At others, the child was simply blessed.

Showing that they had not grasped God's perspective on children, but consistent with the view of children as the lowest-ranked people other than slaves in Roman homes, the disciples rebuke those bringing the children. The term for "rebuke" here is that same term used in the exchange of rebukes in

---

36. Cf. Mark 1:41; 3:10; 6:56; 7:33; 8:22.

8:30–33 (*epitimaō*).³⁷ It is also used of Jesus rebuking demons (1:25; 3:12; 9:25) and the weather (4:39). It will be used again as equally naively by the crowd who rebuke Bartimaeus to be silent as he seeks healing from Jesus (10:48). The forceful term of rebuke indicates that the disciples have the intention of stopping them from approaching Jesus with the children.³⁸ He has better things to do than spend time with kids.

We see again how passionate Jesus is for children; he responds with anger. The term *aganakteō* is used elsewhere in Mark of the disciples being furious with Jacob (James) and John for seeking the favored seats from Jesus (10:41; see also Matt 20:24). The other use is their anger at the seeming waste of money when Jesus is anointed in Bethany (14:5; see also Matt 26:8).³⁹

Here, there are two reasons for his anger. First, he is angry that the disciples are hindering children from coming for God's blessing from Jesus. Second, he is angry that they are directly violating what he has twice taught them. They are not welcoming the children, Jesus, and God, and are putting stumbling blocks in their way.

This passage also tells us how important it is for us to understand and internalize Jesus's teaching. We are to "listen to him" (9:7). We are also to grasp that children are to be cherished in God's kingdom. We are also shown that not all anger is sin. Righteous anger is appropriate when people are hindering the vulnerable from coming to Jesus. Such is the kind of indignation we should have at people who endorse abortion and abuse children and the vulnerable. Crucially, this anger does not lead Jesus to sin (Eph 4:26). He does not act in violence, even though he had the power to do so, had he wished.

Jesus then declares, "Let the little children come to me, do not hinder them." This statement reaffirms the command to welcome them in 9:36; for to welcome children is to welcome Jesus and God, who identifies with them.

He then gives the reason using *gar* (for), "for the kingdom of God belongs to such as these." The kingdom then is not something just for the rich, influential, mature, and esteemed; it belongs to the marginalized and the lowly, such as children.

Mark 10:15 shifts away from allowing children to come to Jesus unhindered to children as role models of what is required to enter the kingdom. To enter the kingdom, all people must receive it like a child. Jesus here is probably

---

37. See also Mark 1:25; 3:12; 4:39; 9:25; 10:48.

38. One pagan reference states: "If you bear a child: if it is a boy, keep it; if it is a girl, throw it out" (P. Oxy. 744.8–10). Who would be a girl in such a context?

39. It is also used of the Jewish leaders' fury when the children sing hosanna at Jesus's entrance into Jerusalem (Matt 21:15) and when Jesus heals on the Sabbath (Luke 13:14).

referring to the tendency of children to receive things with unbridled joy, freedom, and an almost naïve, innocent acceptance.[40] A good example is Christmas when a child gets a present he or she wants. We see utter joy. As the parables of the pearl of great price and treasure hidden in a field tell us (Matt 13:44–46), the kingdom is the most beautiful and valuable thing in the universe. We are to receive it with joy and openness. Such is the attitude an adult must have if he or she seeks to enter the kingdom.

Receiving the kingdom as a child also balances what is said about entry to the kingdom in the rich young man passage that follows. The man must sell everything he has and give to the poor to gain entry. As such, Mark may consider another that aspect of children is their utter dependence on the wealth of others. Children have nothing. The rich ruler has everything he needs. He must become like a child with nothing in order to enter.

Finally, in v. 16, Jesus again takes the children in his arms. The Greek for this is the same as 9:36 (*enankalizomai*). We see in Jesus taking up the children his tenderness that vividly contrasts with the anger he showed a moment ago. He lays his hands on them and blesses them. Christ is not ashamed to show physical intimacy with children. In a politically correct world, this can be problematic. Instead, we should see in it the beauty and power of the creator of the universe, gently taking the most vulnerable of God's image-bearers up in his arms to bless them.

There are a few other things that should be said. All of us who are men need to take note that what Jesus is doing was what was expected of women. Care of children is not merely women's work; we too are to show tender love to children. In fact, in Eph 6:4, men are told to bring them up! Not that we often hear such an idea in a sermon. Also, here, we see the limits of anger. Jesus's anger is directed toward instructing hearers of what is right, not any form of violence. It is redirected as affection to the children. We see here the importance of churches welcoming children. While denominations disagree on infant baptism, we should all agree that we should welcome children warmly, bless them, and make them feel at home and a part of the church from the cradle to the grave. We should also never stop a child coming into the world by aborting him or her. We should never place a barrier to children's faith. For Christians, such things are anathema.

---

40. Evans, *Mark 8:27—16:20*, 94, takes it as imitating the way children obey their parents, "without presumptions of self-importance and self-empowerment."

Questions

- How can we be great in the kingdom of God?
- If we want to be esteemed in the kingdom, how should we treat children?
- What does 9:38–39 teach us concerning our attitudes to others who want to serve Jesus? E.g., women.
- We are not to take Jesus literally in 9:42–48; so, what lessons does he want us to learn concerning sin in the passage?
- What does it mean for Christians to be salty?
- What is a Christian view of marriage and appropriate sexual relationships?
- Is children's ministry not the most important in the church?
- How should we welcome children in the church?

Lesson Eight: Discipleship Training Continues, and Jesus Enters Jerusalem (10:17—11:11)

The Rich Young Man (10:17–31)

The eleventh instruction is about the universal problem of the love of money, a root of all manner of hideous evils (1 Tim 6:10).

> **Discipleship Instruction Eleven:** *If we are to follow Jesus, everything we own is to be invested for him, his kingdom, and those in need.*

As will be demonstrated below, there is more than a hint at family relationships in this passage as well, so the family theme in Instructions Nine and Ten is continued. As if to demonstrate the message of 10:13–16 that one must receive the kingdom like a little child who is without any power and privilege, Mark includes next a story about one of the rich and powerful approaching Jesus. Again, the theme is entry to the kingdom. The man who is among the "first" must be among the "last," like children, who have little. Then, he can enter.

Background to this passage is the Jewish understanding that material wealth is a sign of divine blessing and acceptability to God. This idea came from a misunderstanding of the covenantal blessings and curses (Deut 28; Lev 26). Prosperity, progeny, peace, and physical wellness are consequences of being faithful to the covenant. Hence, it was assumed by many that the absence thereof showed that the person was a sinner.

However, the OT has other material challenging the axiomatic link of prosperity and blessing. A good example is Job, who was a righteous wealthy man who became destitute. Hence, we cannot just say that a person who is disabled, impoverished, unable to have children, or needy is not blessed by God or is being punished by him. Jesus challenges this throughout his teaching. Indeed, we have seen this throughout Mark's Gospel as

Jesus does not treat those suffering as sinners, but as oppressed people requiring liberation (see also Luke 13:1–5; John 9:1–5). The simultaneous forgiveness and healing of the paralyzed man in 2:1–12 also strike at the heart of such poor theology. What happens in this passage continues Jesus's countercultural and radical challenge to false theology.

In Mark and Matthew, the man who approaches Jesus is wealthy (Matt 19:16). Matthew tells readers that he is young (Matt 19:22). Luke adds the detail that he is a leader (*archōn*). He is a Jew, as seen by his fidelity to the law. Hence, he is a rich, young Jewish ruler. He is possibly a figure in the Herodian group, one of the Sanhedrin, a scribe, Sadducee, priest, or Essene.

He appears genuine, kneeling before Jesus (a mark of respect) and addressing him as "good teacher." His approach could mean that he believes Jesus is fundamentally good or that he genuinely accepts him as a good teacher. Whatever his motivation, he likely sees Jesus as a rabbi worthy of hearing. He may have been impressed by Jesus's teaching on marriage and children.

His question is "What must I do to inherit eternal life?" (10:17). In Mark, this question is asked once. In Luke, it is posed twice, in the parallel passage and in the good Samaritan encounter (Luke 10:25–28). The question is another way of finding out how Jesus reads the Torah, for such questions were asked in Jewish circles. "Do" indicates he is enquiring as to what laws he has to obey. "To inherit eternal life" indicates his desire to live forever with God, one of the hopes of second-century Judaism (Dan 12:1–3).

Jesus's response is typical of a rabbi; he answers his inquiry with a question. The question asks why he calls Jesus good when only God is good. This question can be read as a statement of Christ's divinity: "If I am good, and only God is good, then I must be God." However, it can be read conversely as Jesus distancing himself from God: "Why call me good when God alone is good?" It may also be a challenge from Jesus to the man, asking him whether he is saying that Jesus is from God (10:17): "If God is good, and I am a good teacher, then I must be from God." It may be that Jesus is merely trying to point away from himself to God, who has given the law and so defines salvation.

Whatever Jesus means, he lists a series of mainly Decalogue instructions relating to interpersonal relationships (Exod 20:13–17; Deut 5:16–21). These include the command not to murder (sixth commandment), commit adultery (seventh commandment), steal (eighth commandment), and give false testimony (ninth commandment). He adds in the command not to commit fraud (Lev 19:13; Exod 21:10). The final command is to honor one's father and mother (fifth commandment).

Jesus leaves out the first four of the Ten Commandments concerning Israel's relationship with God. He focuses on the other six commandments that concentrate on relationships within the community of God's people. He excludes the final commandment, "do not covet." He rearranges the order, transposing the fifth commandment to last. He inserts "do not defraud" from elsewhere.

The switching of the fifth command to the last place and the insertion of the command not to defraud may be important clues to where the problem lies with the young man. His problem may be connected to being part of a wealthy family through whom he inherited wealth and attitudes to money and others. This young man had grown up as part of the elite who oppress the poor, even if such people do not always know it. He honors his parents and family, yet like them, he defrauds others through his retention of wealth. We have already seen the abuse of this commandment in the Corban passage (cf. 7:8). Jesus may also here target this man's relationship with his family as a point of weakness. If one comes to Christ to enter the kingdom, this may cause them to have to break from their family as the values of the kingdom clash with them (cf. Luke 12:49–56).

The mention of the law also indicates that there is continuity between the ethics of the old covenant and new. The true Jew with a circumcised heart was faithful to such laws. So is the Christian who has received the Spirit. The essence of law continues in the new covenant. The law is inscribed on hearts living to please God, empowered from within by the Spirit. Even if a lot of its legalistic minutiae does not continue, Jesus came to fulfill the law rather than replace it (Matt 5:17–20).[1]

The man assures Jesus that he has kept these commandments since his youth (10:20). This assertion recalls Paul's claim to advance in the Jewish way of life beyond his contemporaries (Acts 26:4, cf. Gal 1:13). Thus, we do not have a non-religious man or a sinner; we have a law-abiding young Jew. However, in the ruler's unhesitant and confidently assured answer, we see another aspect of his problem. He does not see his failure to live up the law. He is overly confident in his righteousness (Phil 3:9). He does not understand that he, like everyone else, falls short of the glory of God (Rom 3:23). For as Paul says, no one can be justified by observing the works of the law (Gal 2:16; 3:11). This man represents the problem the gospel confronts. Everyone, Jew and gentile, is a sinner. Everyone needs a savior, and it is Jesus who came to seek and save the lost (Luke 19:10).

---

1. Similarly, Evans, *Mark 8:27—16:20*, 95, who notes "obedience to the law if it includes love for one's neighbour, will result in eternal life." I would add "with faith and living in relationship with God."

The ruler also points to a challenge for Christians. As people who seek to be faithful, we can easily become over-confident in our righteousness before God and in comparison to others. We must retain a posture of humility before God and other people.

We now have another of the gems in Mark's gospel: "Jesus looked at him and loved him." The Greek for looked is *emblepō*, which has the sense of gazing intently at someone.[2] The second verb is *agapaō*, used for the first time in the Gospel. Later, using this verb, Jesus will tell another Jewish leader that to love God and to love other people are the two greatest commandments (12:31). Here, we have a beautiful and moving statement of how Jesus looks upon the sinner. His attitude recalls the compassion he has on the crowds elsewhere (1:41; 6:34).

Jesus then answers his question concerning what he must do to inherit eternal life. He does not debate the ins and outs of whether he has kept those commandments. Instead, Jesus zeroes in on where his central failure lies. He lacks one thing. Jesus tells him what to do about it. First, he is to "go," a command he gave healed people.[3] He will soon say this to healed Bartimaeus (10:52). Here, the man is not yet set free from his greed and materialism. To go is the first step in his process of being set free from the love of money (Matt 6:24; Luke 16:13–15).

He is to "sell everything," all he owns. Selling everything could be complicated because, in the ancient Middle East, property was often corporately owned, and selling it was not quite the same as a person selling up in individualistic Western contexts. Still, if one is married with children and is asked to do this, then that requires the agreement of one's spouse. Here, to fulfill Jesus's command, he may have to do something like the prodigal son and seek his inheritance so that he can sell it (Luke 15:11–32).

He is then to give to the poor.[4] Notably, Jesus does not tell him to "give *it*," "give *everything*," or "give it *all*" to the poor. Instead, he is to give to the poor. As such, while this could mean the man is to give all the proceeds to the poor and divest himself of everything, it could equally mean that he could

---

2. BDAG, 321. Some think this means Jesus hugged him, but *emblepō* does not mean this.

3. See Mark 1:44; 2:11; 5:19, 34; 7:29; see also 6:31, 33, 38; 8:33; 11:2; 14:13, 21; 16:7.

4. Evans, *Mark 8:27—16:20*, 98, notes that giving all one's assets over is found in some of the Dead Sea Scrolls, especially the community rule scrolls (1QS and 4QS). Josephus, *War* 2:122, states that the Essenes "despise riches" and "surrender their property to the order." There are some similarities with Acts 2:44–45. However, the fundamental difference is that the giving in Acts is *voluntary* and not coerced, unlike the Essene tradition, which is more akin to communism.

keep some of the proceeds for his family's needs. What he must do is cultivate an attitude of giving to the poor generously as he sees a need.

Selling and giving is effectively repentance—a turning away from a love of money and possessions to a love of God that is expressed materially to those in need. In Luke, this is seen in Zacchaeus, who does not give away all he has, but generously gives to the poor and repays those he has defrauded (Luke 19:1–10). Barnabas and others in the early Jerusalem church are other great examples (Acts 4:34–36). Such a repentant attitude and consequential actions are essential for anyone who is rich and wants to follow Jesus.

Jesus assures him that if he does, he will have treasure in heaven. The idea of heavenly treasure is found in Judaism[5] and elsewhere in Jesus's teaching (Matt 13:44; Luke 12:33). It is equivalent to "reward in heaven" (Matt 5:12; 6:1, 23). Notably, this reward or treasure is in heaven, moving the idea away from prosperity thinking whereby one has it on earth now. So, Peter (the man behind Mark's Gospel) speaks of God storing up "an inheritance that is imperishable, undefiled, and unfading, kept in heaven for you" (1 Pet 1:4).

Jesus next gives the man the next step in his path to salvation: "Then come, follow me" (10:21). Eternal life is not gained by selling possessions and giving to the poor, but by following Jesus. As we have seen, following Jesus is the central way Mark describes the right response to Christ, as we see in v. 28.[6] For Mark, this is what it means to repent and believe (1:15). Noticeably, the command to follow is in the present imperative, implying a continuous following. So, he is to follow and keep following, all the way to his death. In the Greco-Roman and Jewish worlds, "following entailed more than mere theological instruction; it involved imitating the teacher's very way of life."[7]

This command is culturally shocking, as wealth was seen as a sign of divine blessing, and all faithful Jews expected to be wealthy in the kingdom. Quite understandably, the response of the man is graphically moving. The Greek *stygnazō* can mean he was shocked, appalled, or became gloomy and dark at Jesus's words.[8] Instead of responding like Zacchaeus in Luke 19:8 or Barnabas in Acts 4:36–37, he goes away irritated, offended, insulted, or sad,

---

5. See Tob 4:8–9; Pss. Sol. 9:5; 2 Bar. 24:1; Sir 29:10–12.

6. See Mark 1:17–20; 2:14; 8:34; 10:52; 15:41.

7. Evans, *Mark 8:27–16*, 99, records examples from Greek literature. The Cynic Diogenes of Sinope says to a prospective disciple: "He commanded him to follow [*ekeleusen akolouthein*]" (Diogenes Laertius 6.36). Socrates summons Xenophon in this way: "Follow me [*epou*] and learn [*manthane*]" (Diogenes Laertius 2.48). He also lists some examples from rabbinic literature. *Manthane* is cognate with *mathētēs*, "disciple."

8. BDAG, 949.

sorrowful, distressed, or grieved (*lypeō*).[9] He goes in such sorrow because (*gar*) he had many possessions (10:22).

He was devastated at Jesus's message because of the cost involved to himself and his family. His response graphically contrasts to that of the fishermen and Levi, who gave up everything to follow Christ (1:16–20; 2:13). This man was not prepared to deny himself and take up his cross and follow Jesus (8:34). He chose to hold onto the world and so will lose his life, rather than give it all up for Jesus and have his life saved (8:35). He answers, "What can a person give in exchange for his life?"—the answer in this case, "his wealth" (8:36). There is an irony here, of course; if he had given up his wealth and followed Jesus, with all of God's people, he would stand ultimately to inherit the world (Matt 5:5; Rom 4:13; 8:17).

Of course, we do not know what happened next. Being shocked and going away sad does not rule out that the man later changed his mind and obeyed Jesus. It does not mean that when Jesus died and rose again, the man did then not join the disciples and do what Jesus had commanded. Nevertheless, at that moment, he was shocked at the thought of doing this.

It is up to us to apply this story to our own lives. For us all, there are things we are called to give up to follow Jesus. For some, it is wealth. In my case, it was my obsession with sports and achieving fame through it. What is Jesus saying to you? Is there one thing you lack? Ask him to reveal it. Then, we should respond obediently to whatever he asks us to do.

We also need to apply this to our ministries of evangelism and discipleship. The call to follow Jesus is not a yes at an altar call to a diminished message of present-day prosperity, as if Jesus says, "Come after me, and I will make your life better, take away your health issues, and fill your bank account!" No, that is the reverse of the call here. The summons of Jesus is a challenge to give up everything and follow Jesus in a lifelong way. However, there is a prosperity teaching here that Jesus will explain in 10:30 below, but it looks very different and is far better because it is eternal.

There is a shift in v. 23 from the rich young man to the disciples. The man's departure gives Jesus a launch pad for him to teach his disciples about wealth. The verb *periblepō*[10] is related to *emblepō* in v. 21 and suggests Jesus looks around at his disciples. He then tells them a terrible truth, that it is difficult for a rich person to enter the kingdom of God. We can note that Jesus does not say it is impossible, but it is difficult. In what follows, it is almost impossible. However, there is hope for the rich, even if it is a difficult challenge that Jesus gives.

---

9. Options given in BDAG, 604.
10. A compound verb made up of *peri* (around) and *blepō* (look, see, watch).

Perhaps because they were stuck in the Jewish mindset that great wealth means God's blessing, they are amazed at his words. However, wealth does not necessarily indicate God's blessing. First, it depends on how a person gained such wealth. Was it gotten by oppressing others? Was it inherited from people who gained wealth through injustice? Was the wealth gotten ethically? Second, is the person retaining the enormous wealth for more than personal needs, with little regard for others in need? Third, are we living simply, or are we living lavishly?

Jesus responds to their amazement by restating the truth (when Jesus restates something, he means it): "Children, how difficult it is to enter the kingdom of God!" The term "children" (*teknon*) stands out here as a term of affection or possibly a statement challenging their maturity.

Jesus gives a parable to explain this. In the story, it is easier to get a camel through a needle's eye than for a rich man to enter the kingdom. On the face of it, this is a joke, and it could perhaps have sparked great laughter from the crowds. Dromedary camels (which are in view here) are enormous animals.[11] Contrastingly, a needle's eye is tiny, millimeters in size. Hence, we have an utterly ludicrous, implausible, and laughable notion.

As a result, understandably, attempts have been made to water down this comparison by arguing that this is a gate called "needle" or that the Greek for "camel" (*kamēlon*) should read "rope" (*kamilon*). However, these arguments lack credence as no such gate existed at the time,[12] and no textual variants support *kamilon* as the correct reading. Hence, this is one of Jesus's parables that is extreme to make the point. It is impossible to get a camel through a needle's eye. Little wonder the disciples are amazed and ask him who can be saved (10:26)!

Jesus then gives them hope for the rich: "With people it is impossible, but not with God. For all things are possible with God" (10:27). Yes, there is hope for the rich. The hope is God. God alone can save people, including the rich. Those who are greedy with the love of money must respond to Jesus's call with radical generosity to the needs of others and follow Jesus without hesitation and with determined obedience. They must be prepared, if called by Jesus to do so, to liquidate their assets and give generously to the needy. Of course, only God can save anyone. We could similarly ask, what hope is there for a killer? A liar? A rapist? A sexual sinner? A violent person? Me? And so on. God is our only hope.

Evans notes here:

11. See "Dromedary." Dromedaries are between 1.7 and 2 m tall (5.6 to 6.6 ft), weigh between 300 and 600 kg (660 to 1,320 lbs), while the hump is around 20 cm (7.9 in) tall.

12. Evans, *Mark 8:27—16:20*, 101, rightly tells us that the so-called Needle Gate dates no earlier than the Middle Ages.

From a Jewish point of view there is great irony in seeing wealth as an obstacle to entering the kingdom of God. Part of the hope for the kingdom centered on the abolition of poverty, sickness, and hunger. In the kingdom of God, all will be wealthy, healthy, and well fed. But too much health and wealth in the present age acts as a distraction and deterrent from preparation for the kingdom. When it comes, many who are wealthy will not be able to enter.[13]

In v. 28, Peter acts again as spokesman, speaking out, "Behold, we left everything, and we have followed you." Jesus assures them solemnly (*amēn*, "truly") that they and any others who leave behind homes, family members, or property, and follow Jesus for his sake and that of the gospel, will receive back a hundred times as much in this age.

What does Jesus mean here? The hundred times back is not literal but symbolic of God's lavish provision for his servants. Likely, this multiplication is received through God's people, who share their resources. Such a hundredfold blessing also implicitly challenges Christians to share our resources with other Christians.

However, this is not a promise of necessary, present, personal prosperity, because their reward also includes persecutions for the sake of Christ and the gospel. Persecution and suffering were Jesus's experience. Between the time of Jesus and Mark's Gospel, the likes of Stephen and Jacob (James) had been killed (Acts 7; 12:1–2). Proximate to the time of this Gospel, Christians had been blamed for the fire of Rome, and Nero had unleashed horrific persecution on the Roman church.

However, not only do disciples have the people of God and all that they own as their blessing along with persecutions, but there is future hope: eternal life in the age to come. Their inheritance is laid up for life in the age to come.

Notably, the passage begins (v. 18) and ends with "eternal life" (v. 30). Eternal life is gained through repentance and faith, through giving up all notions of self-glory, advancement, hoarding wealth and possessions, and following Jesus. Eternal life is both quantitative (forever and ever) and qualitative (without suffering and pain).

The final statement in v. 31 indicates the reversal that the kingdom of God brings. Those who are first in the sense of rank, status, and worldly honor, such as the rich man, will be last, i.e., they will not inherit the kingdom. Those who are last in rank, status, and honor will be first. Such people include the bleeding woman (5:24–34), the demoniac (5:1–20), the children

---

13. Evans, *Mark 8:27—16:20*, 100.

(9:36; 10:13), and the poor (10:46). It is such people who will inherit eternal life with God. Those who follow Jesus will often find their present situation improved as they enter the people of God and experience the blessings of being among God's people as we care for each other.

Those of us in the wealthy West, our prosperity forged on the injustices of colonialism, must be supremely challenged by this. Jesus says elsewhere that we cannot serve both God and money (Matt 6:19–24). We must choose who our master is. The problem for us is that our consumerism, consumption, and materialism are second nature, and we are blind to them. We spend money without regard for what we are doing. Luxuries are treated as necessities. We blindly join the rat race of attaining material possessions along with the rest of this money-obsessed world. However, even in our own countries and in the wider world, poverty, suffering, famine, and material oppression abound. It is our challenge to listen to these words, refuse to water them down, and seek to live as faithful disciples, whatever the cost. Will we take up the challenge? Will we encourage others to do the same, teaching our people what we have been summoned to do by Jesus?

One more comment must be made. All of us fall short of the standard of this passage. The good news is that Jesus died for our sins. Hence, it is by faith in Christ that we receive eternal life, not by a perfect attitude to money. With that said, we should still seek to live up to the ideals of this passage, for this pleases God and can bring other people out of poverty and into salvation.

The Third Passion Prediction (10:32–34)

The first teaching in this section is given again for the third time, showing how important it is for Mark's readers to grasp its significance for their Christian lives.

> **Discipleship Instruction One** (restated for the third time): *Jesus is the Messiah and Son of Man, who must die and rise from the dead.*

Jesus continues his journey to Jerusalem and the cross. Mark records that those with him were astonished and yet afraid (10:32). This verse can seem strange. How can they be both amazed and fearful? One idea is that some were amazed while others were fearful. However, this is not clear. More likely, they were amazed and afraid at the same time. Why would this be? We have to remember that up to this point, the disciples expected that Jesus was a new Joshua about to launch an assault on the Romans to drive them from the land. Hence, they were probably amazed at Jesus's courage, fearlessness, and drive to get to Jerusalem. Nonetheless, despite knowing that Jesus is powerful enough to control the weather (4:39), raise the dead (5:41–42), walk on water (6:48–50), and transfigure before them in the presence of Moses and Elijah (9:2–6), they were also terrified. The two emotions are not mutually exclusive.

Jesus, however, does not plan to annihilate the Romans. For a third time, he explains to the Twelve six things that are about to happen. First, they will go to Jerusalem. Second, he will be handed over the high priests and scribes. Third, these leaders will condemn him to death. Fourth, they will hand him over the gentiles. Fifth, they will spit on him, whip him, and kill him. Finally, he will rise after three days.

Comparing this with the other two predictions (8:31; 9:31), 10:32 adds specificity. The suffering will happen in Jerusalem. His betrayal is mentioned. In 8:31, it is the elders, priests, and scribes who will reject him. Here, the priests and scribes will condemn him to death and hand him over to the gentiles. Jesus makes the first mention of gentiles, anticipating the involvement of Pilate and the Romans. Their spitting, whipping, and killing predict his maltreatment and crucifixion. Finally, as in all three predictions, after three days, he will rise.

While the response in each prediction is different, all three forecasts show that the disciples have no real idea of what Jesus is saying. They likely take it as some kind of parable or do not recognize that he is the Son of Man. In 8:32, Peter rebukes him. In 9:32, they do not understand and are afraid to ask. Here, in vv. 35–45, the only response is Jacob (James) and John seeking the seats of honor beside him. They are not grasping that Jesus is a crucified Messiah and that his service, sacrifice, and death is their life-example.

The reference to gentiles here would not have been easily understood. The Messiah was not expected to suffer at the hands of the gentiles, but rather, he would quash the gentiles. As such, one can understand why the disciples were blind to what Jesus meant.

Christian Leadership Is Service (10:35–45)

We come to a restatement and amplification of Discipleship Instruction Five, "The path to greatness is service." Jesus expands on this here, giving what is arguably the most important teaching on leadership in God's word and in the world. Every Christian who leads must hear this loud and clear.

Discipleship Instruction Twelve: *Christian leadership is not autocratic domination but servant leadership.*

As with the previous prophecy, which was followed by the "who is the greatest" debate,[14] straight after this passion prediction is another story in which the disciples demonstrate selfish ambition and arrogance rather than humble servanthood. Thus, it heightens the clash between the still very worldly values of the disciples and those of God's Servant Messiah.

Jacob (James) and John come to Jesus. Their question is bold and arrogant. First, they address Jesus as teacher rather than Lord or Messiah. They have not fully grasped who Jesus is. Such a question is preposterous when we consider that *they* were demanding that the Son of God do *their* bidding! However, I am aware of Christians who believe that we are given sufficient authority in Christ to tell God what to do. Such Christians are deceived and completely misunderstand the gospel: God is God. Jesus is his Son. God, Father, Son, and Spirit tell us what to do, not the other way around. Jacob (James), John, and those I have encountered have yet to learn this.

The brothers' question is also utterly selfish: "*We* want . . ." (italics added). It is all about what they want, not what is better for others. The content of their demand is also breathtakingly presumptuous: "that you will do for us *anything* we ask" (italics added). Here, Jesus is merely a tool in their quest to be at the head of the pack. While this is typical human behavior and highly consistent with the Roman hunger for status and rank, this is completely opposed to the kingdom of God. With John and Jacob (James) being in the same inner group as Simon Peter, this could indicate their desire to trump him.[15]

Undoubtedly, Jesus recognized the game they were playing. However, he goes along with their request and asks what it is they specifically want of him. He asks them, "What do you want me to do for you?" (v. 36). In 10:51, almost the identical question is asked of Bartimaeus seeking healing for his blindness.[16] Jesus will not grant what the brothers Zebedee are seeking. He

---

14. We can note that this passage falls in the same place in Matthew (Matt 20:28), but at the Last Supper in Luke (Luke 22:24–30). In Matthew, Jesus's mother instigates the request.

15. Wenham, *Easter Enigma*, 34–35, has argued that Jacob (James) and John are Jesus's cousins and that familial loyalties may be tied up in this. This is without warrant from the text.

16. Mark 10:36: *ti thelete [me] poieō hymin*
Mark 10:52: *ti soi theleis poiēsō*
For non-Greek readers, it is important to know that: 1) *thelete* is the same verb as *theleis*, "to want, desire, will"; 2) *hymin* and *soi* are the same term for "you" (*hymin* is plural, *soi* is singular), and they are both dative; 3) *poieō* and *poiēsō* are the same verb, "to do, to make." *Me* is bracketed because it is uncertain. As such, these two questions are pretty much identical.

will accede to Bartimaeus. The different responses show how Jesus searches motives as he responds to our requests.

Jacob (James) and John respond by requesting that one of them sit at his right hand and the other at his left hand in his glory. They seem happy to let Jesus decide who gets the more favored right side. So, there is some degree of humility, at least between them.

Their demand must be considered in terms of their expectations. They are en route to Jerusalem, and as far as they are aware, war is imminent. They expect Jesus to lead them to a glorious victory. They obviously believe they will deserve these seats through their valor in battle. As such, they want to be his prime minister and deputy prime minister, vice president and secretary of state, or something similar, in the kingdom to come. They want the places of the highest rank at the eschatological feast, seated on either side of Jesus (remembering ancient meals had strict seating protocols). This desire is natural in their culture, where places of honor are of great importance in terms of rank and status. We see this lust for status in 12:39, where Jesus severely critiques the scribes for their love of the best seats in the synagogues and places of honor at feasts (cf. Matt 23:6; Luke 14:9–11).

In v. 38, Jesus exposes their ignorance: "You don't know what you are asking." As they have not grasped that Jesus is to go to Jerusalem and be crucified, they have no awareness that they are asking to be killed on either side of him. Later, they will fail to follow Jesus and defend him when he is arrested. Jesus will be killed on the cross reserved for Barabbas. Two of Barabbas's rebel colleagues[17] will be crucified to the right and left of Jesus. Jacob (James) and John will be nowhere to be seen.

The question concerning their capacity to drink the cup from which Jesus will drink uses the idea of a cup metaphorically.[18] It speaks of the cross—Jesus's "cup of suffering." Across the OT prophets and in Revelation, the cup is frequently used figuratively about God's wrath (e.g., Rev 14:10; 16:19).[19] Later, Jesus will take up the cup of wine at the Last Supper, the wine symbolizing his blood that will flow on the cross (14:23 and

---

17. See Keown, *Jesus in a World*, 2:75–76, 115.

18. See also the literal uses of *potērion* in Mark 7:4; 9:41.

19. Specifically, "the cup of his wrath" (Isa 51:17), "the cup of the wine of wrath" (Jer 25:15, cf. Jer 25:17, 28), Babylon as "a golden cup in the Lord's hand" (Jer 51:7), "the cup of staggering" (Isa 51:17; Zech 12:2), a "cup of horror and desolation" and "the cup of your sister Sodom" (Ezek 23:32–33), and "the cup in the Lord's right hand" (Hab 2:16). It is used of comfort: "the cup of consolation" (Jer 16:7). In Matt 23:25 and Luke 11:39, people are likened to a cup. In Rev 17:4, the cup of the harlot is full of abominations and sin (cf. Rev 18:6).

parr.).²⁰ Immediately afterward, he will plead with God to take away this cup in the garden (14:36 and parr.; John 18:11). As such, the cup speaks of Christ's suffering and death.

He also asks whether they can participate in his baptism. Three of the four LXX uses of *baptizō* are of washing (4 Kgdms [2 Kgs] 5:14; Jdth 12:7; Sir 34:25).²¹ The other is of immersion in lawlessness (Isa 21:4). Here, the baptism is used of Jesus's death. Jesus is asking whether they can join him in death. They likely interpreted this as a summons to participate with Jesus in the war with the Romans.

Their response in v. 39 is bold, based on their ignorance of what Jesus is about and their capabilities. Their egos are inflated beyond their realities. They may be the sons of thunder, but their bold exteriors at this stage are not consistent with their terrified hearts. Still, in Greek, their answer is a one-word emphatic statement, *dynametha*: "We can!" or "We are able!"

What follows in v. 39 no doubt filled them with hope. Jesus affirms they will drink from his cup and experience his baptism in suffering. They likely thought Jesus was going to answer in the affirmative after they said this. What they did not know is that Jesus was not interested in war with the gentiles or even in their courage to stand with him in his forthcoming death. Instead, he was looking ahead to the day when the brothers Zebedee would drink from his cup and be baptized in suffering.

Jacob (James), in particular, would experience suffering and death at the hands of Herod Agrippa I (Acts 12:1-2). Although tradition has it that John died an old man in Ephesus, he too was no stranger to suffering. Later, he would be interrogated, flogged, and imprisoned by the Sanhedrin (Acts 4—5). In his later years, he would be exiled on Patmos by Domitian (cf. Rev 1:9).

There is also an irony here. Later, Jacob (James) and John drink from the cup of the Last Supper before Jesus's arrest (14:17-25). Interestingly, Luke places their argument for the seats of prominence at that very supper (Luke 22:24-30). They will be there when Jesus prays for the removal of this cup in the garden (14:32-42). They will experience the baptism in the Spirit at Pentecost (Acts 2:1-4).

However, Jesus then bursts their balloon and tells them that it is not for him to decide who sits at his right and left hand; these places have already been assigned. Here we see limitations of Jesus's authority due to his

---

20. See also 1 Cor 10:16, 21; 11:25-28.

21. In the Pseudepigrapha, one use of *baptizō* is to a generation plunged into the ocean (Sib. Or. 5.478) and the other of Christian baptism (Apoc. Sedr. 14.6). *Baptisma* (baptism) is not in the LXX and uses in the Pseudepigrapha refer to Christian baptism (Sib. Or. 7.84; Apoc. Sedr. 14.5-6).

voluntary self-sacrifice in becoming human. This limitation is seen again concerning the date of his return (13:32). As noted above, there is also the irony of Jesus's crucifixion between two thieves (15:27). Where were John and Jacob (James)? Indeed, where were Peter and the others? Their bravado is not yet matched by their character and actions.

Later on, after Jesus ascended, emboldened by his resurrection and the Spirit, they would grow into different men, ready to share in Jesus's sufferings to bring God's redemption to the world (cf. Phil 3:10; Col 1:24). In their stories, we see how God can take people like us, with our arrogance and egotism, and grow us into mature people who, with great courage, walk in the pattern of Christ.

In v. 41, the other disciples hear about this interaction and are understandably angry. The Greek *aganakteō* is the same word used as 10:14 of Jesus's ire at the disciples for hindering the children from coming to him. Here, the disciples are angry with Jacob (James) and John. At one level, who can blame them? In their demand, the men were implying that they were superior to the others. We see here competitiveness among the disciples in terms of status and personal glory. They want to outdo each other to gain power and status.

Such competition for honor is repugnant and violates the essential Christian virtue of humility. Jesus's teaching challenges Christian pastors who arrogate themselves over others, declare themselves bishops, or seek supposedly higher roles in the church. God calls people into these roles as he wills. Our job is to be faithful in what he has asked us to do and let God raise those whom he wants. Indeed, if we are faithful in small things, God will give us more responsibility as he wills (Matt 25:29; Luke 16:10; 19:17). Christian ministries and churches are not competing with other organizations and churches, nor should leaders vie with each other for status, honor, position, and rank. While we are to have a realistic view of ourselves (Rom 12:3), we are to consider others above ourselves (Phil 2:3).

Jesus takes the opportunity to give the disciples a lesson on leadership. He teaches them the very nature of Christian ministry. They are not to lead like the gentile rulers and officials who rule in an autocratic dominant authoritarian manner. The Roman emperors spring to mind first here. At the time of Jesus, Tiberius Caesar was in office (AD 14–37; cf. Luke 3:1). Indeed, the Sea of Galilee was renamed the Sea of Tiberias in his honor. He was a man of horrendous character. He expelled all Jews from Rome in AD 19.[22] He spent the last eleven years of his office retired on Capri. He "was known

---

22. Josephus, *Ant.* 18:81–84.

for his indulgent lifestyle in his later years—Suetonius accuses him of great lust and cruelty."[23]

After Tiberius came Caligula, who deposed Antipas and Philip Herod and appointed Herod Agrippa I tetrarch over their territories. Caligula demanded that a god with his image be placed in worship places across the empire. He nearly did the same in Israel's temple. He became paranoid and executed many rivals, only to be assassinated himself.[24] At the time of Mark, Nero was descending into lunacy. There were also the Herodians who functioned as mini-despots, as seen in the killing of John (6:14–29). Beyond Israel, many others ruled with force in a world where the more power one had, the greater one was.[25]

Jesus sums up this type of leadership as typical of the gentile world. It is run by those who seem to be rulers[26] when, in fact, God rules. The Greek *katakyrieuō* means "to lord over." It is used of human dominion at creation (Gen 1:28; 9:1) but also of taking possession of a land with force[27] or oppressing the poor (Ps 9:31 LXX). It is used of Jesus in Ps 110:1 (Ps 109:2 LXX). The phrase *hoi megaloi* literally denotes "their great ones." Noticeably they are not God's great ones. For God, greatness comes in the service of others. These people are considered great and exercise forceful authority over those under their dominion.

Jesus tells them such leadership is abhorrent to his kingdom. Christian leaders who aspire to greatness in the kingdom do not gain it through the use of coercive power, political machinations (like Jacob [James] and John), wealth (like the rich young man), violence (like the Romans), charisma, duplicity, deceit (as with the Jewish leaders in Jesus's arrest and trial), and the like.

The next clause, beginning in v. 43, is emphatic: "but not this way among you." The contrast is signaled by *alla*, "but." Jesus states emphatically that followers of Jesus are not to lead in the ways of the world. Christian leadership is not to be expressed through the force of power, personality, wealth, status, office, or rank, inherited or otherwise. Greatness in the kingdom is found in servanthood and voluntary enslavement in the service of the other.

---

23. Pingenot, "Tiberius, Emperor." See also Jefford, "Tiberius," 4.848.

24. Miselbrook, "Caligula, Emperor."

25. Evans, *Mark 8:27—16:20*, 118. See also Keown, *Jesus in a World*, 1:20–45.

26. The Greek is the verb *archō*, a general term for lead. We can note also that the Greek verb *dokeō* is used, which speaks of a subjective evaluation, i.e., "those who seem to rule." In fact, God rules!

27. See Num 21:24; 32:22, 29; 1 Macc 15:30; Ps 9:26 LXX.

"Your servant" (*diakonos*) indicates being servants to one another. The role of servant is a lowly one (not as low as a slave), usually associated with waiting on tables and menial labor and was seen as the opposite of happiness.[28] Contrastingly, being a servant in the kingdom is the greatest of all vocations. Jesus's words here do not mean the renunciation of leadership, but of particular modes of autocratic governance. Those called into Christian ministry over others are still to lead, but as servants and through service.

In v. 44, Jesus speaks again in the language of rank and status. Those who want to be first are not to play the games of the world, such as selfish ambition, seeking personal glory, or promoting oneself. Instead, those who want to be in the first place must be a slave of all. Such a demand was shocking in the first-century Roman world. Being a slave was the lowest of the low. One was owned, had no rights, and lived at the whim of the master. Nonetheless, to be first in the kingdom, one must be a slave of all. "All" here is broad in scope, including, of course, God, other Christians, and the people of the world.

While to be a slave was horrific for a Roman who valued freedom above almost anything (like many people today), it is incredible to see how often the NT writers identify themselves as slaves of Christ. Paul does this in Romans (Rom 1:1), Galatians (Gal 1:10), Titus (Tit 1:1), and Philippians (Phil 1:1, also Timothy).[29] Jacob (James) and Jude, the brothers of Jesus, also describe themselves in this way (Jas 1:1; Jude 1). The man behind Mark's Gospel, Simon Peter, assumes the title in 2 Pet 1:1 and urges all Christians to "live as slaves of God" (1 Pet 2:16). John, one of those seeking God's glory here, also later describes himself as a slave of Christ (Rev 1:1; 22:9).

In 10:45, Jesus gives the christological basis for this from the example of Christ.[30] He (the Son of Man) did not come to be served (the mark of being one of status and high rank), but *to* serve. The juxtaposition of "Son of Man" and "not to be served but to serve" is astonishing in terms of Israel's eschatological expectations. Dan 7:13–14 speaks of the absolute global dominion of the one like a son of man.[31] Hence, all humankind is subjugated to him, at his service as he deems fit as our cosmic ruler. However, the posture of the Son of Man is voluntary service to save others. Christians are to

---

28. Evans, *Mark 8:27—16:20*, 119: "Plato says: 'How can one be happy when he has to serve [*diakonein*] someone?' (Plato, *Gorg.* 491e)"

29. See also 2 Cor 4:5; Col 1:7; 4:7, 12; 2 Tim 2:24.

30. This is a hugely disputed verse among skeptical non-evangelicals who believe it to be a later addition to the text because it appears to have a post-Easter theology. There is no need for us to adopt this position as it is authentic to every manuscript.

31. See also 1 En. 46:4–8; 48:8; 62:5–9; 63:11–12.

respond by giving up all quests for personal glory and taking up the stance of servants, even slaves, to God and all people.

One dimension of this is that Jesus himself did not have slaves or servants. The only people who served Jesus and the disciples were women who did so voluntarily, not by coercion (Luke 8:1–3). Although he was Messiah, his disciples did not serve him. Instead, Jesus served *them* by feeding them (6:30–44; 8:1–10; John 20:12) and washing their feet (John 13).[32]

Somewhere between 15 and 33 percent of the people in the Roman Empire were slaves.[33] They ran the empire for the elite. The Christian "empire" is not to have slaves, something it took God's followers way too long to realize (Gal 3:28; Eph 6:9; Phlm 16). By way of contrast, the high priest had slaves and servants who play roles in the narrative (14:47, 66, 69). We see in Mark two ways of living contrasted: God's kingdom, which serves, and the kingdoms of the world, which demand that the elite be served. We are summoned by Christ to do the former.

Specifically, Jesus came to serve, die the death of a slave, and to give his life as a ransom for many. A ransom is paid to liberate someone from kidnapping or bondage. Jesus's life is the ransom paid to liberate all humankind from enslavement to sin. Of course, we should not push the metaphor as if God paid Satan off to save people. Instead, it is figurative, a metaphor describing the exchange of Jesus's life for our own. It speaks of substitutionary atonement. The term *lytron* is one of the redemption words of the NT.[34] So, Paul writes of Jesus as "a ransom (*apolytron*) for all, which is a testimony given at the proper time" (1 Tim 2:6).

As has been mentioned repeatedly, in taking the position of a servant, Jesus fuses the Son of Man motif with that of the Servant of the Lord in Isa 53. This Servant is "a ransom for many" (Isa 53:10, 12). As such, Mark's Jesus gives a theological interpretation of the cross before it happened and indicates that Jesus not only knew his fate but why he had to die. He had to die as a vicarious sacrifice on behalf of humanity to save them from sin and its consequences. He died to set them free from enslavement to sin and all its consequences into eternal life.

With 8:34 in mind, we see again that true Christian discipleship and leadership is walking in the path of the cross and giving of ourselves for others. Through us, as we live as servants and slaves of all, the ransom

---

32. Washing feet was something that often a slave or servant would do. See Keener, *John*, 901–4.

33. Harrill, "Slavery," 1125.

34. See e.g., Rom 3:24; 1 Cor 1:30; Gal 3:13; 4:5; Eph 1:7; Col 1:14; Heb 9:12; 1 Pet 2:18.

Jesus paid through his life of service and death will spread to more and more people.

At this time, we should question our motivations. Why do we want to be Christians and pursue the things of God? Is it to serve or to gain the esteem of others, those in our church, or among those we know? Is it to enhance our name or that of our families? Is it to attain to higher office in God's church? Is it to earn salvation? While such a desire for honor might be common in many cultures, under God's reign, it is all spurious. Our sole motivation for being leaders must be a desire to serve God and others. We are called to lay down our lives for Christ, for the kingdom, and for the many.

As we scan the NT, we see the writers of the NT repeatedly trying to make this point. They sought to be servants and slaves of others. Two of Paul's letters, in particular, seek to bring this home. The letter to the Philippians, at its theological center, has a hymnic piece proclaiming how Jesus, the one in the form of God with equality of status with God, took the form of a slave to win the world (Phil 2:6–7). Through the letter, Paul urges readers to follow in this pattern and end their disunity (especially Phil 3:17; 4:2–3). The first four chapters of 1 Corinthians call readers to stop their quests for honor and live as Christ has shown them, being slaves of all. Crucially, the apostle whose testimony formed the basis for this Gospel, Peter, urges his Asian readers to follow the example of Jesus's non-retaliatory suffering (1 Pet 2:21–25). We are to do the same wherever we are.

The Healing of Blind Bartimaeus (10:46–52)

The last lesson taught in this section comes as they approach Jerusalem at Jericho.

> **Discipleship Instruction Thirteen:** *Jesus, Son of David, is not here to destroy but to heal, and will use his power only where there is genuine need.*

The path to Jerusalem takes Jesus, his disciples, and a great crowd to Jericho, just over twenty-five km (sixteen mi) to the northeast of the capital.[35] Jericho is an important biblical place. The "city of the palm trees" lay across the Jordan as Israel camped, readying to conquer the land.[36] When the spies checked out the land, they took a particular interest in Jericho (Josh 2:1). In

---

35. The road is mentioned in the Good Samaritan story. Jerusalem is about 752 meters (822 yds) above sea level and Jericho 258 m (282 yds) below sea level.

36. Num 22:1; 26:3, 63; Num 31:12; 33:48, 50; 35:1; 36:13; Deut 34:3.

the city, Rahab, Jesus's ancestor (Matt 1:5), saved them from the local king (Josh 2:2–3). The people of Israel entered the land opposite Jericho (Josh 3:16). They camped on its plains (Josh 4:13, 19; 5:10). There, the first Joshua had his encounter with the commander of the Lord's army.[37] And, of course, Josh 6 is the account of God bringing down its walls and Israel plundering the city completely (other than Rahab). Coming to Jericho especially invoked memories of the conquest of the first Joshua.

Additionally, at Jericho, Elisha refused to leave Elijah, and Elijah's spirit rested on him. He then healed the water of the city (2 Kgs 2:1–18).

Interestingly, in the city was a substantial Hasmonean palace, rebuilt and extended to three palaces by Herod the Great, father of Herod Antipas (6:14–29). One of its palaces was gifted by Herod to Egypt's Queen Cleopatra. The place was magnificent, with Roman bathhouses, swimming pools, gardens, halls, hippodrome, stadium for athletics and boxing, and theater. It was an opulent winter resort for the elite.[38]

What would the second Joshua do in this city? Would he launch an attack on the Herodians? Would he then prepare to bring down the Romans as the first Joshua brought down the Canaanites?

In Mark's account, Jesus initially does nothing but marches on toward Jerusalem with the disciples and crowds. However, as he is leaving Jericho, his journey is interrupted by a man yelling from the side of the road. He is described as a blind beggar and the son of Timaeus, hence, his name Bartimaeus (Aram *bar ṭimay*; Gk *Bartimaios*). The description and naming suggest he became a part of the Christian community from this time on and may have been an eyewitness to this and other events in Mark's account.

As a blind beggar, he is destitute and the very lowest of the low in ancient Israel. Unlike a place like New Zealand, where there is substantial government and social support for a severely disabled person, in Israel, his blindness meant that he was marginalized as accursed and sinful. He is as poor as it gets. Hence, he begs, hoping to scrape together enough to survive. His life expectancy would be incredibly short. His condition is probably similar to the state of Lazarus in Luke 16:20–21. "Covered in sores," licked by local dogs, we can imagine Bartimaeus yearning to eat the scraps from the table of the wealthy who feast at Herod's palaces. Like the blind man of John 9:1–3, his blindness has nothing to do with his own sin. God's glory will be revealed through his healing.

---

37. This may represent an appearance of Christ in the OT, although that is speculative (cf. 1 Cor 10:4; Jude 5).

38. Netzer and Holland, "Jericho (Place)."

As we consider this passage, we can recall the strategic placement of the healing of the blind man before Peter's confession in 8:22–26. The confession immediately precedes the moment where the disciples become spiritually sighted, recognizing that Jesus is Messiah. Their spiritual sight is only partial, however; they do not yet see Jesus fully as *Servant* Messiah. The story of Bartimaeus is positioned immediately before Jerusalem and the disciples ultimately being healed of their partial spiritual sightedness. Nonetheless, it will take Jesus's death, resurrection, and future appearances to complete their healing.

Bartimaeus is physically blind but is as spiritually sighted as the disciples. Probably from hearing the crowds, he realizes that Jesus is present. Notably, Mark here describes Jesus as a Nazarene, referring to his town of origin, not his membership in the Nazarites (Num 6).

Realizing his opportunity for healing, Bartimaeus begins to yell. Identifying Jesus as Son of David shows his spiritual discernment, as the term was used of the Messiah (cf. 2 Sam 7:14; Ps 2:7).[39] This does not mean he fully understood the term or Jesus's full identity. Like all first-century Jews, he likely thought Jesus was a conquering king who would liberate the nation. Still, his confession matches Peter's (8:29). It is even more remarkable coming from a blind man, stuck on the side of a road in Jericho, begging for food, who (unlike Peter) had never physically seen Jesus or his works.

He cries out to Joshua (Jesus), "Have mercy on me!" The cry is found fourteen times in the OT, mostly in Davidic psalms, where the psalmist cries out of deep suffering for help and, ofttimes, healing. So, for example, in Ps 6:3 LXX (6:2 Eng), David cries out, "Have pity on me, O Lord, because I am weak. Heal me, because my bones were troubled" (LES). Again, in Ps 30:10 (31:9 Eng), again David sings, "Have mercy upon me, O Lord, because I am afflicted. My eye was troubled in anger, my soul also, and my belly" (LES).

Here, Bartimaeus, in line with the psalms written *by* David,[40] cries *to* the Son of David using his ancestor's words, pleading for mercy. The crowds will implicitly declare Jesus as Son of David in 11:10 as they sing of the blessedness of David's kingdom they believe is here in Jesus. The idea of Jesus as the Son of David recurs in 12:35–37, where, employing Ps 110:1 and not denying his

---

39. Stein, *Mark*, 495, considers that this does not have any messianic overtones, but gives no adequate reason. Evans, *Mark 8:27—16:20*, 132, is closer when he sees this as akin to a Solomonic identity (Pss. Sol. 17:21), "for David's great son was famous for his healing powers and formulas for exorcism." He rightly says that his request "may also suggest that the blind man sensed the approach of the kingdom of God (after all, this was the essence of Jesus' proclamation)."

40. Of the fourteen, these are in psalms of David with the brackets indicating the Heb/Eng references: Pss 9:14 (9:13); 24:16 (25:16); 25:11 (26:11); 26:7 (27:7); 40:5, 11 (41:4, 10); 56:2 (57:1); 85:3, 16 (86:2, 16). The other three are in Ps 118 (119).

Davidic descent, Jesus challenges his hearers that he is Lord, and so is the divine Son (see also 2:25). Aside from parallel passages to the Markan ones, the concept is also found in other places in the NT.[41]

The response of the crowd is to rebuke him. The term is again *epitimaō*, used in Mark a number of times, especially in the rebuke exchange at Peter's confession.[42] Perhaps echoing the many times Jesus had shut down people who recognized his messianic credentials, the messianic secret, the crowd seeks to silence him. The Greek for "silence" (*siōpaō*) was used by Jesus when he silenced the wind and sea (4:39). However, as is not unusual even today from a beggar who has suffered many indignities,[43] Bartimaeus will not be silenced but even more fervently repeats his cry.

Jesus's response is to stop (the Greek is "stand") and to tell those with him to call him. They are not to stop the least of these coming to Jesus or hinder those as vulnerable as children (cf. 9:42; 10:14). They go and encourage the blind man, giving him two commands and an assurance. The first command is *tharseō*, the word Jesus gave the disciples as he approached them on the boat walking on the sea. As discussed on 6:50, it speaks of being courageous. Bartimaeus is told to get up and is assured that Jesus is calling him.

His enthusiasm and eagerness are demonstrated as he throws away what is probably his most expensive and essential possession, the cloak that keeps him warm in the winter. He springs up and approaches Jesus, guided by someone, led by God, or headed in the direction of his voice. His enthusiasm to come to Jesus speaks of the joy of a new convert. I know that well, vaulting pews to get to the front of the church to give my life to Jesus at around 8 p.m., Sunday, Feb. 24, 1985.

Things get very interesting here in Mark's narrative because Jesus asks him the same question he asked Jacob (James) and John in the previous passage: "What do you want me to do for you?" (10:36). Jesus's response will be very different. In the previous passage, Jacob (James) and John were motivated by personal ambition. They did not need anything. They wanted to manipulate Jesus, to use his power for their own goals of attaining rank and status. They are implicitly refused as Jesus defers to God the Father for such a decision. Unlike the Zebedee brothers, Bartimaeus is a genuine seeker who is in deep trouble as a blind and poor man. He is homeless and has nothing. Jesus is happy to use his power for this pure desire for restored sight. He will use his power only for the genuine needs of others.

---

41. Matt 1:1, 6, 17, 20; 9:27; 12:23; 15:22; Luke 1:27, 32, 69; 2:4, 11; 3:31; 15:16; Rom 1:3; 2 Tim 2:8; Rev 5:5; 22:16, cf. Acts 13:34; Rev 3:7.

42. See Mark 1:25; 3:12; 4:39; 8:30, 32, 33; 9:25; 10:13.

43. Evans, *Mark 8:27—16:20*, 133.

Bartimaeus addresses Jesus as rabbi, rather than Son of David. In this case, calling him teacher rather than Son of David is not a change of heart but is profoundly respectful and hopeful; he recognizes Jesus is both. Jesus declares him saved: "Go, your faith has saved you!" (my translation).

For the third time in Mark's Gospel, faith is specified as a means by which God's healing power is released (2:5; 5:34). As discussed, faith is not always mentioned, but it certainly is a factor on occasions. Here, as with the bleeding woman, it is Bartimaeus's faith, whereas in 2:5, it is the faith of those who brought the man. Elsewhere, faith is also important (5:36; 9:23–24). Later, Jesus will urge the disciples to have faith in God, and the impossible will become possible (11:22–25).

Again, *sōzō* is used of Bartimaeus's healing, which has the double sense of his being healed of his blindness, and, more notably, saved for all eternity. He is now a citizen of the kingdom of God. Having been told to go, Bartimaeus has complete freedom to go where he wills and do what he likes. However, he chooses what is best, immediately following Jesus along the road. His response mirrors the fishermen in 1:16–20 and is an excellent description of becoming a Christian. Once we have come to Jesus and believed, this is what we are to do. His healing would see him welcomed into the wider community, showing again that Jesus's healings are not just individualistic; they see people reintegrated into society. It would also remove any shame for his father, Timaeus.

As noted, the placement of this story is critical. For Mark, this is a true story. Still, the placement before entering Jerusalem allows it to function as a precursor to the next stage in the healing of the spiritual blindness of the disciples. Through the cross and the empty tomb, they are about to learn that not only is Jesus Messiah, but he is also the Servant.

The Entry to Jerusalem (11:1–11)

The entry to Jerusalem marks the end of the section where Jesus teaches the disciples much of what they need to know about discipleship in God's kingdom. However, this whole section will build on Discipleship Lesson One—*Jesus is the Messiah and Son of Man, who must die and rise from the dead*—and narrates the story of his death. It is when he has died, been buried, and risen, that the real meaning of all he has taught them will come into focus. They will also learn more about discipleship in his debates with the Jewish leaders on, most importantly, the priority of love. After he is raised, they will no longer see Jesus as if seeing a tree; they will see him as the Jesus of the transfiguration. They will know that his death is their salvation. Equally, they will understand that his life and death is their life pattern. They will then set out to live it (as should we).

The path to Jerusalem continues. Jesus and his disciples arrive at the towns of Bethphage (location unknown)[44] and Bethany.[45] The latter town is about three km (two mi) from Jerusalem on the road from Jericho on the slopes of the Mount of Olives.[46] In this town and on this trip, Jesus is anointed at the home of Simon the leper (14:3). In Luke, he blesses the disciples at Bethany before ascending to heaven from the Mount of Olives (Luke 24:50; Acts 1:9–11). In Mark, Jesus will go back and forth from the town in his final week (11:11–12). It is also where Mary, Martha, and Lazarus live (John 11:1; 12:1). It is unclear whether he stayed at the home of Simon or of Martha's family.

The towns are located at the Mount of Olives, a hill crucial to Israel's eschatological expectations (cf. Zech 14:4).[47] From one of these towns on the mount, Jesus sends two unnamed disciples to "go to the village ahead of you." Scholars are unsure if this is Bethphage or Bethany.[48] There, they are to find a donkey colt that has not been ridden, untie it, and bring it to him. He prepares them for anyone who might question this, telling them to say that "the Lord needs it and will send it back here shortly." It is unclear whether this has been prearranged or represents prophetic insight.[49] The term Lord (*kyrios*) could mean God or Jesus as master. It could point to an elevated view of Jesus as Lord, even if not in the full christological sense after his resurrection. The former may be intended.[50]

Getting a donkey foal appears to be an intentional fulfillment of the prophecy of Zech 9:9:

---

44. Earle, "Bethphage," notes that its existence near Jerusalem is confirmed in the Talmud. As it is mentioned before Bethany, many scholars surmise it is east of Bethany, on the lower slopes of the Mount of Olives.

45. This is not to be confused with Bethany across the Jordan in John 1:28.

46. The home of Mary, Martha, and Lazarus (John 11:1).

47. The mention of Mount of Olives is hardly coincidence, as Jesus intentionally fulfills Zechariah's prophecy (Zech 14:4): "On that day his feet shall stand on the Mount of Olives, which lies before Jerusalem on the east; and the Mount of Olives shall be split in two from east to west by a very wide valley; so that one half of the Mount shall withdraw northward, and the other half southward."

48. Scholars debate the identity of the town without conclusion.

49. Evans, *Mark 8:27—16:20*, 143, takes it as prearrangement. France, *Gospel of Mark*, 431, sees it as a prearrangement that Mark interpreted supernaturally.

50. Some take it as the master of the donkey, but that makes little sense in the flow. As Evans, *Mark 8:27—16:20*, 143, notes, it is probably not Jesus, as Mark never calls him Lord in this way; rather, it is probably God.

> Rejoice greatly, O daughter Zion! Shout aloud, O daughter Jerusalem! Lo, your king comes to you; triumphant and victorious is he, humble and riding on a donkey, on a colt, the foal of a donkey.

If so, Jesus is fully aware of what his entry entails and how it is the fulfillment of Israel's prophetic hope. He comes on a donkey, a symbol of peace, rather than astride a white horse with military force. In 11:4–6, the two disciples do as asked, find a colt as expected, untie it, answer the questions of those nearby, and return to Jesus with the colt.

Mark 11:7–10 describes the entry of Jesus on a donkey. Cloaks are placed on the colt, and Jesus sits on it. Jesus riding a donkey into the city recalls Israel's King Solomon entering Gihon with great fanfare on David's mule (1 Kgs 1:38). The placing of clothing upon the donkey as a saddle is reminiscent of the coronation of King Jehu (2 Kgs 9:13).[51] Such symbolism speaks of Jesus, the Davidic King, entering Jerusalem.

A great crowd ("many people") also spread their cloaks on the road while others spread branches ("tall grass or reeds") from the fields, and there is a great chorus of song. The use of palms and other vegetation calls to mind the Feast of Tabernacles (2 Macc 10:7).[52]

The snippet of the song sung is Ps 118:25–26. They were perhaps singing the whole psalm, one of the Hallel Passover songs (Pss 113—118). This psalm was sung at Passover, Pentecost, Tabernacles, and Dedication.[53]

The content of the song is highly christological and soteriological. It is chiastic in structure, beginning and ending with hosanna, with two parallel blessings in its center. *Hosanna* is an acclamation of praise, meaning "save," and so crying out for the salvation of God. In such a setting, this would involve deliverance from Rome. However, Jesus has come to save all humankind, Romans included, from sin and its consequences. "Blessed is he who comes in the name of the Lord" refers to the Messiah. The second half is highly messianic, "Blessed is the coming kingdom of our father David" again focused on the hopes of a Davidic Messiah. It finishes with "Hosanna in the highest."

The adoring crowd believe that Jesus is the Messiah entering the city. No doubt their song was accompanied by huge expectations that the hopes of Israel will be met, the gentiles vanquished, Jesus established as the Davidic messianic king, and God's reign inaugurated. Ultimately, the world would be

---

51. Evans, *Mark 8:27—16:20*, 143.
52. France, *Gospel of Mark*, 433.
53. Brooks, *Mark*, 179.

subjugated to God, not with violent force, but with people wielding the sword of the Spirit, the word of God (13:10; Eph 6:17).

Having entered the city, Jesus then goes to the temple (11:11). It would be the venue for much of the pre-crucifixion action leading to his death. This day he took a look around and then returned to Bethany, no doubt to ready himself for what was to follow.[54] No doubt, at this time, he noticed the moneychangers and traders.

Questions

- How can the wealthy be saved?
- What is the right Christian attitude to riches?
- Why does Jesus tell us three times about his death in Mark 8—9?
- What were Jacob (James) and John truly seeking (10:37)? How did they fail? How did they turn that around?
- How can we be great in the kingdom of God?
- Read Mark 10:43–45. In what ways should Christian leadership be distinct from the leadership patterns of the world?
- Compare the answers of Jesus to the same questions he asks of Jacob (James) and John (10:36) and Bartimaeus (10:51): why does Jesus grant Bartimaeus his request but rejects that of Jacob and John?
- Why is Bartimaeus such a great example to us all?
- What did the crowds imagine Jesus would do when he entered Jerusalem as their Messiah?
- Why did they sing from Ps 118?

---

54. Evans, *Mark 8:27—16:20*, 146, suggests that this awkward end to the day indicates that Jesus was rejected at the temple. This is not necessary.

Lesson Nine: Jesus Curses a Tree and Clears the Temple, and Controversies Intensify (11:12—12:40)

The Cursing of the Fig Tree (11:12–14)

THE PASSAGE 11:12-25 IS another Markan sandwich.[1] The emphasis falls on the central account, the temple clearing. The fig tree accounts which frame the temple clearing enhance the probability that the fig tree is symbolic of Israel.

Mark 11:12–25

A¹ Cursing of the fig tree (11:12–14)

B   Clearing of the temple (11:15–19)

A² Cursing of the fig tree (11:20–25)

The next day, Jesus and his group leave Bethany for Jerusalem. Jesus is hungry, showing his genuine humanity.[2] He sees a fig tree in leaf and goes to see if it has fruit. Fig trees were noteworthy fruit trees to Israel. In the OT, they symbolize peace and security (cf. Mic 4:4; Zech 3:10). Leaves often emerged on the fig tree after it fruited, which explains Jesus's approach. When he reaches the tree, he finds nothing on it except leaves, as it was not the season for figs. Fig trees fruit twice: in late May into June, with the later and more abundant harvest that ripens from the end of August into October.[3]

---

1. See Mark 3:20–35; 5:21–43; 6:16b–31; 14:1–11; 14:53–72; 15:40–16:1.

2. Some scholars get excited about Jesus's hunger, asking why he has not had breakfast with his disciples. I prefer to take the text as reading that he was hungry, rather than to seek an ingenious and unnecessary solution.

3. Evans, *Mark 8:27—16:20*, 154.

This event happens just before Passover, so it is mid-March,[4] coming into spring. As such, fig trees would not have had fruit at this time.

The seasonal absence of fruit raises the question of what Jesus was doing. He may have been looking for winter figs left on the tree or early figs, which may appear in early spring before the leaves.[5] Otherwise, the whole point of what happens is not to find anything genuine on the tree, but to perform another miracle with the fig tree representing Israel (cf. Hos 9:10; Joel 1:7).[6] Whatever his motivation, Jesus then curses the fig tree, commanding that no one will never eat its fruit again.[7] Mark also notes that his disciples heard him say it, which is important for interpretation.

Scholars dispute whether this should be taken as a symbolic story referring to Israel and the temple. However, the way that Mark uses it as a frame around the temple clearing makes it patently clear that it should. The barrenness of the tree would then refer to the absence of righteousness and faith in Israel and its rejection of God's Son, the Messiah. Its cursing correlates with the end of the age of Judaism in rejection of Christ and its temple system. There is an intertextual link between Jer 7:11 mentioned in 11:17 and Jer 8:13, where Jeremiah states of Israel, "There will be no figs on the tree, and their leaves will wither," further pointing to a symbolic intention in Mark's arrangement.

Still, it is also a miracle in its own right. As in the calming of the storm (4:35–41) and walking on water (6:45–52), it shows Jesus's absolute power over the created order. For those with eyes to see, it points to his power as a prophet, or more accurately, his divine sonship. It also becomes a valuable story for teaching on the power of faithful prayer.

The Clearing of the Temple (11:15–19)

After the cursing of the fig tree, "and then they came to Jerusalem" is not just a geographical and chronological note, but has a sense of foreboding and tension as to what will now happen. The disciples and his adoring crowds who believed he was the Davidic Messiah likely expected him to begin to

---

4. We are unsure whether Jesus died in AD 30 or AD 33. Passover was Friday, March 22, in 30, and Sunday, March 22, in 33. Hence, this must be in mid-March in our calendar.

5. Evans, *Mark 8:27—16:20*, 154.

6. Figs are used figuratively of Israel in Jer 24, where those who go into Babylonian exile are good figs God whom will build up, and those who go to Egypt are bad and will be punished (see also Jer 29:17).

7. Addressing nature is common in the biblical narrative (Num 20:8; Josh 10:12; 24:26–28; Matt 4:3; Luke 4:3).

seize control of the nation, call the leaders to him, and assault the Roman pagan filth (as they saw them).

Jesus has other ideas. The Greek *hieron* suggests he enters again into temple courts. These courts were area outside the temple proper, in the Court of the Gentiles, something confirmed in the OT passages upon which Jesus draws (see the image below).[8]

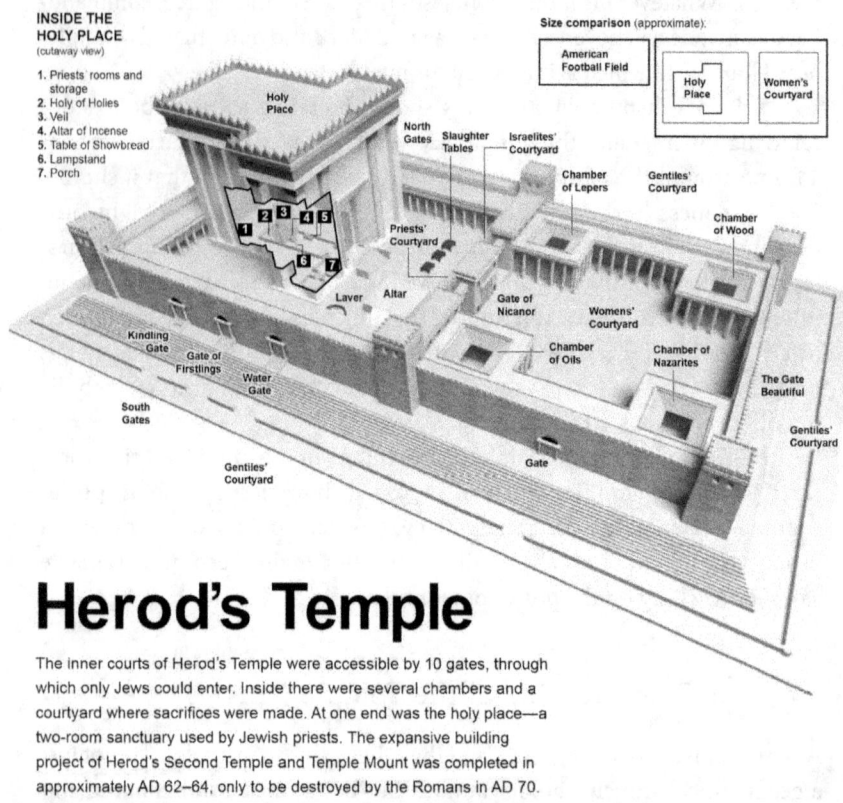

Figure 7: Herod's Temple [9]

8. Josephus, *Ag. Ap.* 2:103–104 (Thackeray), writes, "The outer court was open to all, foreigners included; women during their impurity were alone refused admission. To the second court all Jews were admitted and, when uncontaminated by any defilement, their wives; to the third male Jews, if clean and purified; to the fourth the priests robed in their priestly vestments. The sanctuary was entered only by the high-priests, clad in the raiment peculiar to themselves."

9. Karbel Multimedia, "Herod's Temple." Used by permission.

Having observed it the day before, he was aware that the area was full of traders, moneychangers, and those who sold doves (or pigeons). It was logical that there was a thriving business around the temple with its elaborate sacrificial system. Authorized by the high priest Caiaphas, the money changers exchanged the pilgrim's money from the nations into supposedly pure Tyrian shekels so that they could buy animals to sacrifice. Exchanging the money ensured that the coins were changed into coins of equal weight and value, and the idolatrous images were removed.[10]

It was Passover, so the population of Jerusalem would have swollen by many tens of thousands, with all pilgrims and locals wanting to purchase an unblemished lamb to sacrifice to God. Reinhardt estimates that during Passover, around 85,000 to 300,000 pilgrims came into the city, swelling its population from the usual 60,000 to 120,000 to anything from 200,000 to half a million.[11] Josephus records that about 255,600 lambs were sacrificed at Passover in AD 66.[12] A similar number was likely sacrificed this particular year. The doves or pigeons (*peristera*) were purchased by the poor, who could not afford the more significant and expensive sacrifices (1:44).[13]

Amid the chaos, smell, and noise, Jesus begins driving out sellers and buyers, overturning the moneychangers and dove sellers' tables, and refusing entry to those carrying goods in or out. By doing this, Jesus was taking a substantial risk. With so many devout Jews at Passover, the Jewish priests and leaders overseeing the temple processes, and the Romans observing things from the Fort of Antonia,[14] this was a dangerous, subversive, and disruptive act. One thinks of images of contemporary pilgrimages in places like Mecca, such as the Hajj. Imagine what it would be like for a Muslim to disrupt their worship!

In v. 17, Jesus draws from two OT texts, Isa 56:7 and Jer 7:11. Isa 56 is a prophecy where God will gather to himself faithful foreigners and eunuchs who are welcomed to worship Yahweh, are included in God's covenant people, and minister in his name. They will worship at God's house of

---

10. See Nylund, "Court of the Gentiles."
11. Reinhardt, "Population Size of Jerusalem."
12. Josephus, *War* 6:424; Nylund, "Court of the Gentiles."
13. See also Lev 5:7; 12:6–8; 14:22; Luke 2:24. Evans, *Mark 8:27—16:20*, 172, notes that the Mishnah tells of one occasion where pigeons were being sold within the temple precincts at exorbitant prices, causing Simeon ben Gamaliel to teach "that women could offer a pair of pigeons for as many as five live births or miscarriages and then be eligible to take part fully in the feasts." This had the effect of seeing the price drop dramatically (*m. Ker.* 1:7).
14. Bridges, "Antonia, Tower of," 78.

prayer and make sacrifices and offerings. As such, the temple will be called a "house of prayer for all peoples."

In Jeremiah 7, the prophet is sent to stand at the temple and proclaim repentance to Israel. Israel is warned not to trust the words "this is the temple of the Lord, the temple of the Lord, the temple of the Lord" (Jer 7:4). Israel is summoned to execute justice and stop oppressing immigrants and others. Jeremiah condemns their propensity to sin while going to the temple, declaring their forgiveness and salvation. Jeremiah asks, "Has this house, which is called by my name, become a den of robbers in your eyes?" The clear answer is yes, and so the Babylonian exile is coming.

Jesus here stands in the tradition of two of Israel's great prophets, challenging their system that is stopping people, including the gentiles, from coming unhindered to worship God at his temple. Israel's leaders are failing and must repent. Similarly, in the mid-60s, an uneducated peasant, Jesus Ben Ananias, was flogged severely for entering the temple, crying out a message of doom. He encountered the same adverse reaction from Jews and Romans alike.[15] Both of these Jesus's were right. Another exile was coming. It came.

This act probably stimulated further messianic anticipation among the supporters of Jesus, with them anticipating an imminent assault on the Roman authorities. Some scholars believe Jesus was a revolutionary seeking a violent takeover at the temple mount.[16] However, as Hengel has pointed out, this is not likely, for such radical action would have brought Roman intervention. Instead, we have a prophetic symbolic attack on the temple system.[17] Sanders takes it as a symbolic event, arguing that Jesus's actions were a prophetic statement that the time of the temple system was over because it was now becoming obsolete, with the Jerusalem temple replaced by the heaven-made eschatological temple.[18] Mark 14:58, which reads "We heard him say, 'I will destroy this man-made temple and in three days will build another, not made by man'" fits this, with Jesus's actions interpreted by this false accusation.

Others, like Chilton, believe Jesus was acting in the tradition of other Jewish religious teachers whose actions led to a violent response from the authorities, e.g., the pelting of the king with lemons as he was about to

---

15. See Josephus, *War* 6:300–309. See Evans, *Mark 8:27–16:20*, 177, for a number of parallels.

16. E.g., Brandon, *Jesus and the Zealots*; Aslan, *Zealot*.

17. Hengel, *Was Jesus a Revolutionist?*, 17–18.

18. Sanders, *Jesus and Judaism*, 61–76.

offer sacrifice or the cutting down of the golden eagle affixed to the gate of the temple.[19]

All in all, we should take the temple action as a prophetic and messianic appeal to Israel to repent of her sins of injustice, exclusion, oppression of the poor, extortion, and the exclusion of gentiles from worship and prayer. We should also see here the limits of the use of force for a Christian. Jesus does not attack people or animals, but prophetically and symbolically disrupts their corrupt worship.

Not unsurprisingly, the recipients of his wrath, the chief priests and teachers of the law who were overlooking the temple system and endorsing the trade practices, were highly offended and again looked for a way to kill him. However, they were held back because they were afraid of him, while the crowd continued to be impressed by his teaching (11:18). The nature of their fear at this point is unclear. They may have been afraid of his power or concerned with what would happen if they made moves to kill him.

The Withered Fig Tree and the Importance of Faith and Prayer (11:20–25)

After the clearing of the temple, Jesus and the disciples return from Jerusalem to Bethany. As they pass the fig tree, Peter acting as spokesman for the disciples[20] draws Jesus's attention to the dead tree. Its withering is a fulfillment of Jesus's imprecation against the tree (11:20–21). Again, we see his divine power and prophetic ability.

There is no attempt to liken the fig tree to Judaism, although the implication is evident when one considers how it frames the story of the temple clearing. Instead, Mark uses the opportunity to teach about the power of faith, which will lead to answered prayer.

Jesus summons the disciples to "have faith in God." He goes on to tell them that if they do not doubt but believe, they can tell a mountain to be taken up and thrown into the sea.[21] Indeed, whatever they ask for in prayer, if they have belief, they will receive it. These are the sharpest statements on the power of faith in Mark's Gospel. The right response to the kingdom's nearness is faith (1:15). Such trust is the response of children in 9:42. In 2:5, 5:34, and 10:52, faith is the basis for the healing of the disabled man, the bleeding woman, and Bartimaeus. In 4:40, Jesus bemoaned the disciples'

---

19. Chilton, *Temple of Jesus*, 73, 100–103, 183. See Josephus, *War* 1:648–55; *Ant.* 13.372–73; 17:149–67.

20. See Mark 8:29, 32; 9:5; 10:28; 14:29.

21. See also Matt 17:20; Luke 17:6; 1 Cor 13:2.

lack of faith. Jairus is told not to fear but believe (5:36). Earlier, Jesus told the father of the demonized boy that everything is possible for the person who believes (9:23), leading him to declare his faith and to ask for Jesus to remove his doubt (9:24). Jesus then told the disciples that prayer is required for the deliverance of some demons (9:29).

Here, Jesus's words are inclusive of all people ("anyone"). Such faith can move "this mountain." The hill in mind could be the Mount of Olives, which would have been in view (cf. Zech 14:4). Alternatively, it is the Temple Mount itself. There are other Jewish references to moving mountains, such as *T. Sol.* 23:1, where a demon says to Solomon, "I am able to move mountains," or *b. B. Bat.* 3b, "I will uproot mountains." However, the idea of faith moving mountains is unique.[22]

In context, the point is not necessarily that they could actually move that mountain, but rather, by faith, immense obstacles can be removed. Indeed, the whole image is outrageous and utterly impossible; hence, it is a metaphorical saying telling the believer that with faith, the impossible in God becomes possible (cf. 10:27; see also 9:29).

Interestingly, in the wider NT, there is a figurative fulfillment of this story. As Paul most clearly articulates in Galatians and Romans, Jesus inaugurated the era of faith and not law observance as a means to justification (Gal 3:23). In so doing, the Temple Mount (cf. Gal 4:25) was, in a sense, removed and thrown into the sea. Its system was fulfilled in Jesus, the Messiah. The recognition that it has always been faith that justifies, along with the coming of Christ as God's atoning sacrifice for sin, caused Mount Zion to lose its religious significance. Now, God is forming a people in Jesus, the dwelling place of God of earth. In him is established the temple of the Holy Spirit. The temple has, in a figurative sense, been thrown into the sea by faith.

It is noticeable that the object of faith is God, not a believer's determination to believe or the explicit content of what is prayed. Hence, the power of faith does not lie with us, but with God. Similarly, "it will be done for him" means that it is God who does the impossible, not the believer. The withering of the fig tree is an example of the power of faith.

Jesus then applies this to prayer, telling the disciples comprehensively that "whatever you ask for in prayer, believe that you have received it, and it will be yours" (11:24). Parallel and similar sayings are found elsewhere in the Gospels.[23] One thinks of Jesus's prayer ministry,[24] his appeals for dis-

---

22. See Evans, *Mark 8:27—16:20*, 189, for further detail.
23. See Matt 21:22; John 14:13–14; 15:7, 16; 16:23–24.
24. See Mark 1:35; 6:46; 14:32, 35, 39.

ciples to pray (13:33; 14:38), and the use of Jer 7:11 here. As Marshall notes, "Mark sees prayer as faith verbalized."[25]

Jesus builds on this theme of prayer and tells them that when they come to prayer,[26] they must forgive anything that they have against others. The result/purpose of this (*hina* clause) is that God in heaven ("Father") will also forgive the sins of the one praying (11:25).[27] Forgiveness of others is not given as a condition of answered prayer but is simply something people should do. The line in the Lord's Prayer "forgive us our trespasses as we forgive those who trespass against us" (Matt 6:12) shows that this is something Jesus emphasized.

This passage raises questions about prayer that are not answered. If we isolate it as the only word on prayer in the NT, we could easily believe that prayer that is not answered is due to lack of faith, wavering in doubt, or a failure to forgive. However, in 14:36, the man who calmed a storm, walked on water, healed many, raised the dead, cast out demons, and cursed a fig tree, did not have his prayer answered. Jesus prayed for release from the suffering of the cross thrice, but he did not receive a positive response from God.

Hence, faith is essential for answered prayer but does not guarantee a positive outcome. God answers in regards to our relationship with him and his will ("yet not what I will, but what you will," 14:36). Jesus then died despite his prayers. Did Jesus lack faith, waver in doubt, or not pray enough? No is clearly the answer to all three questions. Hence, the point Jesus is making here is not that if we have enough faith, every prayer we pray will be answered affirmatively; it is that we should pray with faith in God and not doubt him. He decides the answer, and it may be that a mountain is moved. At other points, God may have another plan. What do we do then? We trust in God.

Jesus's Authority is Challenged (11:27–33)

From 11:27 to the end of chapter 12, we have a series of controversy narratives that record clashes between Jesus and the Jewish authorities.[28] The

---

25. Marshall, *Faith as a Theme*, 171.

26. "Stand praying" is typical of the Jewish mode of prayer. The eighteen benedictions or Amidah of the Synagogue were called the "Standing" prayer. See Eisenberg, *JPS Guide*, 421.

27. Compare Matt 5:21–26; 6:12; Luke 6:37.

28. Some question how the writer Mark knew of these deliberations through these chapters. However, as established, Peter is the source of his Gospel, and he was there

section is replete with provocative teaching in the temple courts that further strengthens their desire to kill him. Jesus's antagonizing of the Jewish leaders would probably have confounded the disciples who, at some point, expected him to ally with them to overcome the Romans. Jesus does nothing of the sort. Instead, he seals his fate as a crucified Messiah.

Here, in the first narrative, Mark records that Jesus and the disciples have returned to the temple from Bethany. Three groups of leaders from the Jewish Sanhedrin come to Jesus: chief priests (see on 8:31), scribes (see on 1:22), and elders (see on 8:31). No doubt utterly stunned by Jesus's entry and clearing of the temple, they approach Jesus in the temple courts (v. 27). Their approach recalls the first and third passion predictions where the chief priests, elders, and scribes will reject Jesus and hand him over to be killed, and so this moment creates an ominous tone (8:31; 10:33).[29]

Their questions concerning Christ's authority were reasonable when we consider who they were. It was their job to protect Israel's religion from corruption. Furthermore, being under Rome, they needed to ensure there would be no revolutionary impulses, especially at Passover, when the place was teeming with people. At another level, their questions were a joke. Before the scribes, Jesus healed the disabled man lowered through the roof in Capernaum (2:6) and cast out a demon from a boy (9:14). They had earlier known that he casts out demons; however, they had explained that away by the outrageous idea that Jesus himself was demonized (3:22).

Each group had reason to be concerned about Jesus. The crowds loved Jesus's authoritative teaching when compared to the scribes (1:22). The chief priests, including the high priest, ran the Sanhedrin and had charge over the religion of the nation. Jesus had come from nowhere and had healed on the Sabbath. The elders were likely annoyed by Jesus's disregard for their teaching on ritual purity (7:3).

They ask the same question in two ways: by what authority and by whose authority is he doing "these things"? The things in view could refer to his whole ministry,[30] but, in particular, the clearing of the temple and its challenge to their authority over temple worship, especially at a crucial time like Passover (11:27–28). Their goal was likely to trick Jesus into admitting his ministry was self-authorized or that he stood above the priests; either

---

(see Mark 11:27, "they"). Moreover, Joseph of Arimathea (named in the Gospel and so possibly one of Mark's sources) may have been one of those who was in the group challenging Jesus (Mark 15:43). We also know there were priests among the early Christians (Acts 6:7). As such, Mark had plenty of opportunity to know of this discussion.

29. Evans, *Mark 8:27—16:20*, 199.

30. Evans, *Mark 8:27—16:20*, 202, notes "Jesus' teaching (1:21–22, 27), exorcisms (1:23–27; cf. 3:22–30), and forgiving of sins and healing (2:1–12)."

way, he was in trouble. They probably believed the "what" authority was his own. The "who" they believed to be Satan.

Jesus answers their questions with a question of his own. Such a strategy of answering a question with a question was well established in Greek rhetoric and Jewish wisdom and rabbinic tradition. Answering a question with questions is found all over Jesus's teaching in Mark.[31] Furthermore, by answering with a question, Jesus refuses to respond to theirs, showing that he has little respect for their authority.

He tells them that he will reply to their inquiry if they answer his question. Notably, Jesus demands they answer him twice in vv. 29–30. Jesus subtly exerts his authority over them. His question concerning John the Baptist's authority challenges them to give their theological interpretation of John. For the leaders, doing so is problematic, because John had baptized Jesus, anointed him, and saw Jesus as the Messiah (1:7–11). Furthermore, the crowds from Jerusalem and Judea that were present at Passover had thronged to John (1:5). The content and manner of his question then are full of irony and challenge.

Jesus's question leads them to debate their best answer. Even Israel's best minds are struggling against this wannabe from Nazareth. Not that they were stupid. They reason rightly that to recognize John's ministry as being from heaven, they would authorize him and Jesus, and then killing him would be out of the question. If they answer it was from humankind, they would upset the crowds who had gone to John for baptism.

They opt then to say, "I don't know." Feigned ignorance was the best option they could come up with. However, in so doing, they display their ignorance before the crowds and tacitly allow Jesus to dominate them. As such, this situation is highly ironic and reinforces the authority of Christ. Furthermore, they should know where John's authority came from; that is their job.

True to his word, Jesus then refuses to respond to their inquiries, based on their failure to answer his question (11:33). By refusing to answer, he challenges their authority. Through this narrative full of irony, Jesus is portrayed as inciting further anger from the Jewish leadership, baffling them with his brilliance, and making them look stupid. He is thus full of God's wisdom, calling to mind God's wisdom from Prov 8.

---

31. See Mark 2:19, 25; 10:2, 18; 12:15–16, 24; cf. 2:8; 3:23; 3:33; 8:12; 10:38; 14:48.

The Parable of the Tenants (12:1–12)

There is no shift of context, so Jesus is still in the temple precincts. He begins to teach in parables. Earlier, he had responded with parables to the claim by the Jerusalem scribes that he was demonized (3:23). Mark 4:1–34 includes four parables and states their centrality to his teaching to the crowds. Aside from a parable concerning bodily waste to the disciples in the house (7:17), this is the first mention of parables since Mark 4. The use of a parable shows that Jesus does not consider these leaders to be people of the kingdom. As with Israel's leaders at the time of exile, they see and hear but do not understand and thus do not seek God's forgiveness (4:11–12). Parables here is plural; hence, it is likely Mark has selected only this one because of its relevance to the context.

The story is simple and based on the standard practice of building a vineyard in the first century. "A man" is the central character. From the story, we can see he is wealthy, as he has a plot of land and many slaves. He plants a vineyard, fences it, digs a pit for a winepress, builds a watchtower, and rents it to tenant farmers.[32] He then leaves on a journey. When the appropriate time comes,[33] he sends a slave to collect fruit from the harvest of his vineyard. However, rather than giving the owner the fruit, the tenant farmers beat the slave and send him back with nothing.[34] The second comes, but they kill him. A third is sent but is struck on the head and disgraced. A fourth is killed. Then many others are sent, some beaten, some killed.

The implication of v. 6 is that the man has no more slaves to send, only his beloved son. Expecting that the tenants will respect his son, he sends him, only for them to kill him and throw him out of the vineyard in the hope of claiming the inheritance, the vineyard. In v. 9, the parable concludes with Jesus asking what the lord of the vineyard will do. He answers himself: he will come and destroy the tenant farmers and give the vineyard to others who will care for it better.

The parable is then reinforced with a quote from Ps 118:22–23. The citation is from the same psalm sung as Jesus entered Jerusalem. Here, Jesus is alluding to himself as the repudiated and killed son. He is the rejected stone that becomes the cornerstone. However, this stone is the work of the Lord and beautiful to those with eyes to see.

---

32. Evans, *Mark 8:27—16:20*, 232, notes that the farmers are wealthy commercial farmers and not peasants.

33. Usually, after a three- to five-year period, the owner would collect a portion of money from the sale of fruit and/or wine.

34. Evans, *Mark 8:27—16:20*, 233, notes that this is not totally uncommon and gives examples; hence, it has a ring of realism.

The parable fits nicely into the flow of Jesus's teaching in the temple; it is a story designed to challenge the Jewish leadership in terms of their rejection of Jesus. It is highly allegorical, calling into question the penchant of many scholars in the twentieth century to reject any allegorical interpretations of Jesus's parables. Unequivocally, some parables are allegorical.[35]

The farmer is quite obviously intended to be God. The image of Israel as God's vineyard is a regular OT feature, especially the song of the vineyard in Isa 5:1–7.[36] The wording is highly influenced by Isa 5 and especially 5:2.[37] The fence, wine press, pit, and watchtower should not be over-allegorized but probably indicate the care God took to establish and protect Israel and ensure it was fruitful.[38]

The tenant farmers represent Jesus's antagonists, the leadership of the Jewish nation. The failure of Israel's leadership to care for the vineyard is a strong OT prophetic motif carried on here (Isa 3:14; 5:1–7; Jer 12:10). They are tenants, given stewardship of God's land and people.

The servants represent the prophets who have been sent repeatedly from God, calling for the leadership and people of Israel to repent, only to be rejected, beaten, and killed. Examples of the killing of the prophets are found in the OT.[39] Tradition has it that Isaiah was sawn in two (Heb 11:37). Jeremiah was purportedly stoned to death. Micah was supposedly killed by Joram. Amos was killed by a blow to the temple. Zechariah, son of Jehoida, was killed at the temple altar.[40] Jesus elsewhere bemoans Israel's killing of the prophets.[41] The specifics of beating over the head should probably not be over-allegorized; they point to the dishonorable maltreatment of the prophets (cf. 2 Sam 10:2–5).[42]

The "beloved son" clearly refers to Jesus. This parable shows again that Jesus was fully aware of his divine sonship. Of course, in Mark's narrative, this had been declared by God at his baptism (1:11) and his transfiguration (9:7). It is thus provocative and christological.[43]

---

35. Keown, *Discovering the New Testament*, 1:522–26.
36. See also Isa 1:8; 3:14; 27:1–6; Jer 12:10; Ezek 19:10–14.
37. See Evans, *Mark 8:27—16:20*, 232, gives details.
38. Some take the tower as the temple.
39. See 1 Kgs 19:10, 14; Neh 9:26; Jer 2:30; 26:20–24; 2 Chron 36:15–16.
40. *Liv. Pro.* 2:1; 6:1–2; 7:2; 23:1.
41. See Matt 23:37; 11:47, 49; 13:34; cf. Acts 7:52; 1 Thess 2:15.
42. See Evans, *Mark 8:27—16:20*, 232, gives details.
43. Contra Evans, *Mark 8:27—16:20*, 233, who rejects the christological notion. In light of the baptism/transfiguration, it is evidence of Jesus's christological self-awareness.

The theft of the vineyard recalls one of the worst moments in Israel's history, when Ahab stole Naboth's vineyard (cf. 1 Kgs 21:2–3, 16). The desire to kill the son recalls Joseph's brothers (cf. Gen 37:20); however, here, there is no stay of execution.

The killing of the son recalls the three passion predictions (8:31; 9:31; 10:33). The throwing of the body outside the vineyard refers to non-burial, which was disrespectful in the ancient world. The question as to what the owner of the vineyard will do recalls Isa 5:5: "And now I will tell you what I will do to my vineyard."

Verse 9 suggests judgment on Israel (cf. Matt 21:43) and refers to the fall of Jerusalem and its sacking in AD 70 by the Romans. The giving of the vineyard could refer to the land of Israel being given over to be trampled by the gentiles (Luke 21:24). More likely, it refers to the extension of Israel through Jesus and his people throughout the world.

The quotation of Ps 118:23–24 reinforces this from the Jewish Scriptures (cf. 12:24) by stating that the stone (Jesus) that the builders (leaders of Israel) rejected has become the cornerstone. The stone in view is "the capstone" or the "head of the corner" rather than the foundation stone. The use of Ps 118 (cf. 11:9–10) again suggests that Jesus is calling for the Jewish leaders to recall the entry to the city and recognize who he is (the Messiah). It also shows the importance of Ps 118 for Christian thought. In Isa 28:16, as Paul and Peter write, Jesus is the Messiah who was to come, who is Isaiah's tested, precious stone laid as the foundation and cornerstone in Zion (Rom 9:33; 1 Pet 2:6; Acts 4:11).

Here, Jesus is using temple language. In Jesus, God is laying a new temple. Jesus is the cornerstone holding together its walls at the head of the corner (Acts 4:11; Eph 2:20) and also its foundation (1 Cor 3:10). Later, Jesus would be tried and convicted, in part due to his supposed warning that he would destroy the temple. We know from John's Gospel that this refers to something said at the temple clearing and that Jesus meant his death and resurrection (15:29; John 2:19–21). At Jesus's death, the curtain in the inner sanctuary of the temple would be rent. Its tearing symbolizes the opening of access into God's inner sanctum in the heavens for all people of faith, and not merely the high priest on the Day of Atonement (15:38). People will be added onto this foundation, and so God's people are now God's temple, and the temple continues to be developed as people are added.[44]

The story continues to build the hostility between the Jewish leadership and Jesus. It is political in orientation, and as with the previous story, Jesus challenges the Jewish leaders' perception of reality, their authority, and their

---

44. See 1 Cor 3:10–17; 16:19; Eph 2:19–22.

attitude to the prophets, John the Baptist, and to Jesus himself. The tension is building and the ground prepared for the fulfillment of the three passion predictions of the suffering of the Son of Man, the Servant King.

In v. 12, the leaders rightly recognize that this parable is a deliberate attack on them. However, rather than yielding to their king in repentance and faith, they look for an opportunity to arrest him. They are deterred for fear that the crowd would revolt. His time has not yet come. Soon, it would, and Jesus would go without violent resistance to them, enabling them to destroy him as they wished.

Paying Taxes to Caesar (12:13–17)

Some Pharisees and Herodians are sent from the Jewish leadership ("they sent") to again test Jesus (12:13).[45] The reference to different groups of Jewish leaders strengthens the sense that Jesus was up against all the leaders of Israel, and the tension continues to build. The combination is unusual in that whereas the Herodians accepted the paying of taxes to Rome, the Pharisees rejected it.[46] These disparate groups were united in their opposition to Jesus and used their differing views in their attempts to bring him down.

They flatter him, calling him teacher, a "man of integrity" who is not "swayed by people's opinions" and who is unconcerned about "who they are." Additionally, he teaches "the way of God in accordance with the truth." Flattery is a common tactic and a new strategy to draw Jesus into an error through apparently endorsing him. However, it contradicts their refusal to accept his authority and respect his viewpoint (see 11:27–33).

They ask him whether they should pay taxes to the Romans ("to Caesar") (12:14–15). Again, this is a trick question. If Jesus says no, he will be guilty of refusing to pay taxes and give honor to the rule of Rome. As such, the Jewish leaders would have grounds to have him charged with sedition. If he says yes, he could be seen as a traitor to the nation and a Roman collaborator and so lose popular support. The Jewish leaders could then take him to Pilate without crowd reprisals. Most in the crowd would expect him to oppose paying taxes, as it was anticipated that the Messiah would rid Israel of Roman and gentile oppression.

However, either through prophetic or intuitive insight, Jesus recognizes their duplicity (hypocrisy) and challenges them: "Why are you trying to trap me?" One can sense his frustration at this point. He then

---

45. "They" are probably the priests, elders, and scribes or the Sanhedrin.

46. Some think the Herodians are Essenes, but this is far-fetched; better, that they were members of the Herodian administration.

asks his antagonists to bring him a denarius, equivalent to one day's basic wage. By doing so, Jesus commands them. He also exposes that they have a denarius, suggesting that they support the Romans and their coinage. Their doing so could upset those with zealot tendencies. He asks them whose portrait and inscription is engraved on it (12:15–16). His opponents correctly note that it is Caesar's. The coin probably carried an image of Tiberius, who reigned at the time.[47]

Jesus then takes this as an admission that the money belongs to Caesar and states, "Give to Caesar what is Caesar's." As such, Jesus endorses the payment of taxes to Rome. However, he does so in an almost flippant manner and with a good deal of ambiguity. We see that he also supports the payment of the temple tax in Matt 17:25–27. Paul, similarly, encourages the Roman Christians to pay taxes to Rome—likely at a time when some Romans were resisting doing so (Rom 13:1, 7).

Mark's Jesus then adds, "And give to God what is God's" (12:17). The final statement suggests that what one gives to God is more important, and here involves total allegiance, worship, and praise. Furthermore, the imperial cult demanded that people worship the emperor. Jesus is pointing out implicitly that this is not acceptable. Justin Martyr, in the mid-second century, understood "Jesus' pronouncement to mean that tax was to be paid to Caesar, but worship was to be given to God alone, and not Caesar (*1 Apol.* 17.2)."[48]

"And they were amazed at him" again demonstrates Jesus's authority and wisdom that completely baffled his opponents and reinforced their antagonism. He had cleverly avoided their snare, and in so doing, had challenged them to honor God and to faithfully continue to pay taxes.

Marriage at the Resurrection (12:18–27)

Now it is the turn of the Sadducees to come to test Jesus. Their intrusion is the only appearance in Mark's Gospel, although some Sadducees would have been a part of the Sanhedrin and priests.[49] The Sadducees were one of the leading groups in Israel, alongside the Pharisees and Essenes.[50] Their name perhaps derives from Zadok, a high priest during the reigns of David and

---

47. Evans, *Mark 8:27—16:20*, 247, notes, "its legend probably read: TI CAESAR DIVI AVG F AVGVSTVS, 'Tiberius Caesar Augustus, Son of Divine Augustus.'"
48. Evans, *Mark 8:27—16:20*, 247.
49. See Mark 11:18, 27; 14:1, 10, 43, 47, 53–55, 61, 63, 66; 15:1, 3, 10–11, 31.
50. Josephus, *Ant.* 18:11.

Solomon.⁵¹ They may have emerged in the Hasmonean period, were mainly priestly and elite, and were favorable toward Rome. Sadly, we have none of their writings. From what we can glean from secondary sources, they rejected fate for free will⁵² and did not believe in angels or spirits (Acts 23:8). Most of the Sadducees were based in Jerusalem. Their interest in Jesus may have been piqued by Jesus's dramatic entry into the city, his attack on the temple (which priests supervised), his ministry, and his debates with the other leaders.

Two other aspects of their belief system are essential for understanding this passage. First, they denied a bodily resurrection.⁵³ Second, they accepted only the Torah as authoritative and rejected the oral laws of the Pharisees.⁵⁴ The mention of the Sadducees after the other Jewish groupings reinforces how Jesus is totally up against it. None of the Jewish leadership acknowledges who he is. His presence forces severely divided groups of Jewish leaders to conspire together to bring down what they consider a pseudo-messiah.

They come to challenge his view of resurrection. Mark agrees with other sources that they reject the bodily resurrection. According to Josephus, they are annihilationists,⁵⁵ and they reject rewards and punishments in the afterlife.⁵⁶

To do so, they come to Jesus with a parable, perhaps mimicking and parodying his use of parables. The story is long and convoluted, involving seven brothers who successively marry the same woman, only to die and leave her widowed. Such a sequence of marriages and deaths is, of course, a ridiculous occurrence,⁵⁷ yet it is a suitable vehicle to test Jesus's view on the resurrection and to make him look stupid. The real test is the climax where they ask Jesus whose wife will she be at the resurrection, i.e., will she not be

---

51. E.g., 2 Sam 15:24–37; 20:25; 1 Kgs 1:8, 32–45. Das, "Sadducees," notes that their name could also come from the Hebrew adjective "just" or "righteous" (צַדִּיק, *tsaddiq*), or, "the name was originally an ambiguous, allusive designation like the Dead Sea Scrolls' 'Wicked Priest' or 'Seekers of Smooth Things.'" Evans, *Mark 8:27—16:20*, 252, favors that their name came from Zadok (2 Sam 8:17). He notes that a small number believe that the Qumran founders were Sadducean, as they are sometimes called sons of Zadok. He also mentions that they tended to work with the Sanhedrin (Acts 4:1–4; 15:17–18). However, not all the priests were Sadducees.

52. Josephus, *Ant.* 13:171–73; *War* 2:164–65.

53. See also Acts 4:2; 23:6–7; Josephus, *Ant.* 18:16; *War* 2:165.

54. Josephus, *Ant.* 13:297–98; 18:16. See Das, "Sadducees."

55. "The Sadducees hold that souls perish along with bodies," i.e., they are annihilationists (Josephus, *Ant.* 18:16).

56. "As for the persistence of the soul [ψυχῆς] after death, penalties in Hades, and rewards, they will have none of them" (Josephus, *War* 2:165).

57. See 2 Macc 7 (cf. 4 Macc 8—13); Tob 3:7–15 as possible background stories.

married to all men for eternity? Their poser tests Jesus to see whether he believed in the resurrection (12:18–23).

Behind this is the Jewish idea of Levirate marriage. In this arrangement, a brother would marry his deceased brother's childless wife to give her descendants (Gen 38; Deut 25:5–10).[58] In ancient societies, it was essential for a woman to have children. A woman had two places in life: in her father's home as an unmarried virgin or married with children in her husband's home.[59]

The use of Moses here reinforces that the Sadducees accepted only the first five books of the Bible as authoritative. It was commonly held by Jews at the time that the Torah would be perfectly lived in the age to come.[60] They may also have been testing Jesus concerning his teaching on the insolubility of monogamous marriage, the marriage union being unbreakable (cf. 10:9).

Jesus's reply is direct and brutal. He tells some of the greatest minds and priests in Israel very bluntly that they are wrong (cf. 12:10). They have two interconnected problems that give the reasons for their failure: they "do not know the Scriptures" nor "the power of God." The first of these would have cut deeply. It would be like having told the NT lecturer of Laidlaw College that he did not know the Scriptures. Of course, none of us knows everything about all the Scriptures, so people like NT scholars are not always right!

The first of these statements challenges their ability to read and interpret Scripture. They recognize the importance of Levirate marriage but fail to see in the same OT the clear teaching on the resurrection. There is also no hint in the Scriptures that there will be marriage in the age to come. They have read this conclusion *into* the text (eisegesis).

The second problem is that they fail to recognize the power of God to raise the dead, for which the OT hopes. They should know better. Earlier in Mark, Jesus had raised Jairus's daughter (5:21–43). We know of two other similar events with the widow of Nain's son and Lazarus (Luke 7:11–17; John 11:1–44). Elijah and Elisha raised the dead (1 Kgs 17:17–24; 2 Kgs 4:18–37). Daniel foresaw the resurrection of the righteous and wicked to judgment (Dan 12:1–3). They simply did not know God's power. They are like people who claim to be Christian but then reject spiritual gifts, miracles, and resurrection. They simply do not understand the power of God who can do anything if he so desires.

---

58. "Then Judah said to Onan, 'Lie with your brother's wife and fulfill your duty to her as a brother-in-law to produce offspring for your brother.'"

59. Evans, *Mark 8:27—16:20*, 253.

60. Evans, *Mark 8:27—16:20*, 253.

In v. 25, Jesus teaches on the nature of the resurrection. He tells them that at the resurrection, risen humanity will be like angels in that they will no longer marry nor be given in marriage. The belief that humans in heaven will be angel-like is well attested in the literature of the period.[61] However, there is nothing here that indicates that people *do* become angels. These words of Jesus seem to rule out marriage in the age to come.

In v. 26, Jesus explains that the hope of the resurrection is implied in their limited canon, the books of Moses. To do so, he creatively cites one of the pivotal moments in the OT, the appearance of God to Moses at the burning bush at which he revealed his divine name (Exod 3:6). The key to this lies in the Greek "I am" (*egō eimi*), which in the LXX is in the present tense. Although Mark drops the verb *eimi*, the present tense is implied, and the original Greek includes it.

The same thing applies to 12:29, where "is" is implied (see the next section). Here, God says to Moses that "I am (present tense) the God of Abraham, Isaac, and Jacob." As he *is* God of the patriarchs many years after their deaths, they are living at the time.[62] As such, the patriarchs are alive, raised—and God is the God of the living and not the dead.[63] The transfiguration confirms the resurrection from the dead with Moses and Elijah, long since gone, appearing with Jesus. Their ongoing existence could imply some kind of intermediate state. Alternatively, when we die, we might move out of the space-time continuum of planet Earth and are raised and can, at God's behest, translate back into history. Either way, the resurrection of the dead is confirmed. Demonstrating that resurrection is found in the Torah is noteworthy, as it shows that the hope of the resurrection is found in the earliest books of the Bible.

The Great Commandments (12:28–34)

A teacher of the law was listening to the previous debate between Jesus and the Sadducees. He observes the quality of Jesus's answer to their question on the resurrection. His affirmation of Jesus's view suggests that he is from the Pharisees, as they accepted the resurrection from the dead.[64] He then

---

61. Evans, *Mark 8:27—16:20*, 255. See 1 En. 104:4, 6: "You are about to be making a great rejoicing like the angels of heaven . . . for you are to be partners with the goodhearted people of heaven"; 2 Bar. 51:5, 10: "And they shall be made like angels."

62. Gen 25:8; 35:29; 49:33.

63. Brooks, *Mark*, 196.

64. Acts 23:6–8; Josephus, *War* 2:162–166.

approaches Jesus to ask him which is the most important commandment in the OT (literally, "Which commandment is first of all?") (12:28).⁶⁵

The scribes identified 613 separate commandments in the Scriptures, of which 365 were negative, and 248 were positive. They then divided them into heavy or light, depending on their importance. Jesus is being asked to assess the heaviest of the commandments. We find a similar question asked by a gentile of Hillel in rabbinic sources: "What is hateful to you, do not to your neighbor: that is the whole Torah, while the rest is the commentary thereof."⁶⁶ The answer Jesus will give is consistent with a range of Jewish texts that endorse the importance of the love of God and other people.⁶⁷

It is difficult to gauge the motives of this scribe. He may have been genuinely impressed with Jesus's answer and have come with good intent and genuineness. Alternatively, he may have been trying another angle of attack on Jesus, trying to trap him into saying something that would reduce his popularity or enable them to arrest him. Because there is no indication of his negative attitude and because Jesus tells him he is close to the kingdom, he is perhaps well-motivated, impressed by Jesus's previous answer, and wanting to hear his genuine view on this issue.⁶⁸

Jesus responds by endorsing the Jewish delight in Deut 6:4–5. This passage forms the basis of the *Shema,* which was an essential part of the Jewish faith, quoted at worship and daily.⁶⁹ Its name is derived from the first Hebrew word in it: *šᵉmǎʿ*, "hear." It includes a statement of God's oneness and then the command to love him with everything we are and have.

The passage reinforces Jewish monotheism, and while Christians believe in a Triune God, this is one Triune God, not three gods. This command defines worship in the fullest sense as love for God. Such worship and service is the priority of Christian life. Such love is not merely our pouring our souls out in worship on a Sunday, but a whole life motivated to reciprocate the love God has for us.

The command is comprehensive, involving the whole being, as is evidenced by the recurring "all" and the anthropological terms heart (whole heart), soul (whole soul or life), and mind (whole thought). For Mark's

---

65. Brooks, *Mark*, 197.

66. B. *Šabb.* 31a.

67. See T. Iss. 5:2; T. Iss. 7:6; T. Dan 5:3; Philo, *Spec.* 2:63; Evans, *Mark 8:27–16:20*, 265.

68. Some scholars like Gundry, *Mark*, 710, take him as hostile. However, Evans, *Mark 8:27–16:20*, 263; France, *Gospel of Mark*, 478; and Brook, *Mark*, 197, see him positively.

69. The full Shema included three passages (Deut 6:4–9; 11:13–21; Num 15:37–41) and was to be recited every morning and evening.

Greco-Roman situation in Rome, mind was added to ensure that readers recognized that they were to love God through their minds as well as through the passions of the heart. For Jews, the heart included the mind and passions. By including heart and mind, Mark ensured that his Roman and Greek readers recognized they were to love God from heart and mind. In other words, we love God with everything. We think deeply about him and love him cognitively. We pour out our hearts to him in adoration. We love him from the depths of our being. We adore God!

"From all your strength" speaks of the total focus of our energies on loving God. We love him with our bodies, devoting them to his service in ethical righteousness, work, and effort. We love him with all our power until our last breath. While we will do much else on earth, every aspect of our lives is devoted to him, motivated to return love to the God who is love and loves us.

This law is, in essence, a summary of the first four commands of the Decalogue, including pure devotion to the one God, retaining space in our lives for prayer and worship, and refusing to blaspheme God in our words, attitudes, and behaviors. We see here that, understood correctly, Christianity stands in continuity with Judaism as it was intended. It is interesting to connect this law to the generous act of the widow in 12:41–44, who, in her devotion, gives her last two coins to the temple treasury, a demonstration of loving God with all she has.

Jesus goes on to tell the scribe that the second most important law is Lev 19:18b: "Love your neighbor as yourself" (12:31). The importance of this command is consistent with other Jewish teachings. For example, Rabbi Aqiba says of "but you shall love your neighbor as yourself" that "this is the encompassing principle of the Law."[70] Hillel states that the whole law is summarized in a single principle: "What is hateful to you, do not do to your neighbor; that is the whole Law."[71]

One critique of Israel by the prophets was that Israel loved God but failed to love one another. A great example is Isa 1:10–17, where Isaiah rebukes Israel's failed worship; they make all the right sacrifices but have no concern for the poor and needy. As such, God repudiates Israel's worship. Similarly, in the story of the good Samaritan, the priest and Levite are focused on their work, maintaining Israel's religion; however, they fail to love their neighbor in the ditch. The good Samaritan does so (Luke 10:25–37). The point is, true faith involves love in both sentiment and action for the needy (cf. 1 Cor 13:1–8).

70. Sipra Lev. 200 on Lev 19:15–20.
71. *b. Šabb.* 31a.

In this command, the command is based on the assumption that one will love oneself. The contemporary idea of self-hate is a product of Western radical and narcissistic individualism. As such, recognizing the real problem of self-loathing, the command can be read as "love your neighbor as you yearn to be loved."

Luke 10:25–37 deals with the question of "Who is my neighbor?" The neighbor is all humankind, even an enemy. When our neighbor is in need—and for Jesus, this means anyone in need—we are to respond with love and mercy. Loving all people fits with Lev 19:34, where Israel is summoned to love the immigrant in their land as well. Christians are to love indiscriminately.

Elsewhere in the NT, this command is stressed again and again, and we as Christians cannot grasp it enough or do it sufficiently. For Paul, the entire law is summed up in the command, and to love fulfills the law (Rom 13:9, 10; Gal 5:14). Christians are obligated to love others (Rom 13:8). Every spiritual gift is made meaningful when exercised in love (1 Cor 13:1–3). Love is outworked in a range of other attitudes and actions toward others (1 Cor 13:4–7; Gal 5:22–24). Love transcends all other attitudes and ethics because it will go on for eternity (1 Cor 13:13).

Hence, we are to pursue love and do all things in love (1 Cor 14:1; 16:14). Love compels our mission (2 Cor 5:14; Phil 1:16; 1 Thess 1:3), service of the other (Gal 5:13, cf. Eph 4:2), and speech (Eph 4:15). Husbands are to love their wives as Christ loves us (Eph 5:2, 25). Love is our very clothing (Col 3:14; 1 Thess 5:8). We are to abound in it (1 Thess 3:12) and be shaped by it (1 John 3:18). Our love is the basis on which the people of the world should discern whether we are Christ's disciples (John 13:34–35).

Addressing Jesus honorifically as teacher,[72] the scribe is very warm to Jesus's answer ("well said"). He confirms the importance of the two commands, adding that the love of one's neighbor "is more important than all burnt offerings and sacrifices." Seeing love as more important than sacrifice is a recurring idea stated explicitly or implicitly throughout the OT. The sacrificial system of the people of God can be motivated by love or be empty and vacuous (12:32–33).[73] Jesus's words here warn us as Christians. We can do all the right things like giving money to the church, supporting mission, going to church, raising our hands in worship, and the like. However, without love, this is empty and gains us nothing (1 Cor 13:1–3).

---

72. This could be ironic but appears genuine.

73. See 1 Sam 15:22; Hos 6:6; Isa 1:11; Jer 6:20; Amos 5:22; Mic 6:6–8; Pss 39:7 (40:6 Eng); 50:18 (51:16 Eng); 1 QS 9:4; 4Q266.

Hearing the scribe's positive response, Jesus declares that he is not far from the kingdom of God. That is, he is on the cusp of "getting it" and entering the kingdom through repentance and faith. However, soon the Jewish leaders will conspire to show a lack of love toward Jesus and condemn him to an illegal and torturous death. Jesus knows they will do it, and yet does not attack them or rebuke them. He loves them to the last—in Luke, asking God to forgive them (Luke 23:34).[74] This man just needs to realize who Jesus is, that he is not merely the teacher but is the Messiah and Son of God in whom he should believe and whom he should follow to gain entry into the kingdom.

This encounter informs our understanding of the status of very good and loving unbelievers who share many Christian values with genuine believers. Such people are "close to the kingdom of God," but must come to the point of repentance and faith to enter God's reign.

This encounter ends the period of direct questions seeking to trap Jesus. Jesus has defeated Israel's leaders publicly, powerfully refuting their challenges to his authority and theology. Hence, they do not ask him any more questions in this way. Instead, having failed to understand the Shema and Lev 19:18, they will conspire to have him killed.

Jesus Is *Adonai* (12:35–37)

Mark's temple court narrative continues. Jesus is continuing to teach in the temple courts. Now that the questions of the Jewish leaders have dried up, he goes on the offensive and begins with a question.

Likely with Jewish leaders in his hearing, he asks why the scribes consider that the long-awaited Messiah is to be a descendant of David (12:35). This passage highlights the prevailing view that the Messiah would be a king from the line of David. Such an expectation is reasonable considering the plethora of texts that point in this direction.[75] Indeed, in what follows, Jesus is not rejecting that idea. The NT endorses that Jesus is a descendant of David and that this is a legitimate aspect of his coming. Jesus's Davidic descent has already been affirmed in Mark's Gospel when Bartimaeus identifies Jesus as "Son of David" (10:47, 48), something Jesus does not refute. Similarly, as Jesus entered the city, the crowds implicitly declared him to be a descendent

---

74. While this verse is not included in some important ancient witnesses, it is likely an authentic saying of Jesus. See Omanson and Metzger, *Textual Guide*, 152.

75. E.g., 2 Sam 7:14; Isa 9:6; 11:1; Jer 23:5; 33:15; Zech 3:8; 6:12; T. Sol. 1:7. Evans, *Mark 8:27—16:20*, 272, also notes a range of rabbinic examples.

of David as they sang of the coming kingdom of David (11:10).[76] Here, what Jesus is asking is why the scribes say the Messiah is *just* the son of David.

Jesus quotes Psalm 110:1, the most cited OT passage in the NT.[77] Mark draws on the LXX. However, initially, Jesus likely drew on the Hebrew, and this is important if we are to understand this passage. In Ps 110:1, David sings,[78] "The Lord (*kyrios*; Heb. *Yahweh*) said to my Lord (*kyrios*; Heb: *Adonai*): 'Sit at my right hand until I put your enemies under your feet.'"

The key to understanding this is to note the Hebrew words here. The first *kyrios*, "Lord," is Yahweh. The second *kyrios*, "Lord," is Adonai, another OT term for God. As such, Jesus is saying, "Yahweh said to Adonai . . ."

As such, Jesus is pointing out that David is here calling the second figure, who is known in Jewish expectations to be the Messiah, Lord in the sense of Adonai. As he is Adonai, it means that whether or not he is a descendant of David, the Messiah is much more—he is God! (12:37).[79] Jesus here cleverly implies his divinity and his dominion. He will be seated at God's right hand until God has put all his enemies under his feet.

Evans suggests that this shows that Jesus's understanding of messiahship was not based on Davidic descent but on the Son of Man in Dan 7:13–14.[80] However, Jesus does not deny his Davidic descent; he states that his messiahship is *more* than Davidic descent. As Brooks says,

> Jesus is more than Son of David; he is Son of Man, i.e., the representative of all humanity and not just the Jews, who had to suffer and then be exalted at God's right hand. Still more important he is Son of God![81]

We can also note here that the quote of the Psalm is preceded by "David said *in the Holy Spirit*" (italics added). These words show that for Mark and Jesus, the OT Scriptures are not merely documents written by people;

---

76. See Matt 1:1, 6, 17, 20; 9:2, 27; 12:23; 15:22; 20:30, 31; 21:9, 15; 22:42, 43, 45; Luke 1:27, 32, 69; 2:4, 11; 3:31; 18:38–39; 20:41–44; Acts 13:34; 15:16; Rom 1:3; 2 Tim 2:8; Rev 3:7; 5:5; 22:16; see also John 7:42.

77. A psalm highly quoted in the NT; cf. Matt 22:44 = Mark 12:36 = Luke 20:43; Acts 2:35; 1 Cor 15:25; Heb 1:13; 10:13.

78. Much contemporary scholarship rejects the Davidic authorship of this psalm. I see absolutely no reason to reject Davidic authorship; clearly, Mark's Jesus accepted it.

79. Some soften all this, taking *Adonai* as "lord" in the sense of an important person. I think Jesus is taking it the other way here.

80. Evans, *Mark 8:27—16:20*, 274.

81. Brooks, *Mark*, 201.

they are inspired by the Spirit. We thus have a great example of texts that undergird a theology of the inspiration and authority of the Scriptures.[82]

In this passage, Jesus does not develop further the notion of "seated at the right hand" in terms of his own person, but it is implied. He will state it more directly to the high priest at his trial (14:62). Neither does he develop the idea of ruling until God puts all enemies under his feet. However, after the resurrection and ascension, both ideas are fully applied by the NT writers, who interpret this as Jesus's exaltation to the right hand of God as his regent and sharer in his reign.[83]

Who are these enemies? They no doubt include spiritual forces like Satan and his demons. They also includes any humans who reject God and his Son, who has now come to earth, sent by God the Father, to exercise the reign at God's right hand. They include anyone who claims to be his follower but grossly corrupts his gospel.

What does this entail? As the NT plays out, it is clear that the consequences for these enemies are death and then destruction. This destruction is eternal. Earlier in Mark, Gehenna was alluded to; people will be destroyed in Gehenna (9:42–48, see on that passage for options on interpretation).

When will this be? This universal rule at God's right hand begins the moment Jesus rises from the dead, ascends, and is exalted to God's right hand to rule. The Spirit will be poured out. The good news of the kingdom will spread out, and people will willingly yield to his reign, confessing his lordship and bowing at Christ's feet (cf. Phil 2:9–10). Ultimately, however, every human and spiritual being, whether they accept Christ's lordship or not, will bend the knee before Jesus when he returns. Those who have yielded willingly in this life will live with this Messiah forever in the age to come. Those who do so reluctantly at the judgment will be banished to Gehenna.

The response of the crowd again is delight, reinforcing Jesus's popular appeal. However, this popularity will soon come to a screeching halt. The upshot of all this is that Jesus is Adonai, God's Son, Messiah, and the only response is to bow in worship and love him with everything we have.

Beware the Teachers of the Law (12:38–40)

Jesus continues going on the offensive now, openly and provocatively denouncing the scribes who have been questioning him. We can assume some of them are still listening, yet Jesus is unafraid to challenge their attitudes

---

82. See also, e.g., 2 Sam 23:2; Acts 28:25; 2 Tim 3:16; 2 Pet 1:21; Heb 3:7; 10:15.
83. See Acts 2:33–34; 5:31; 7:55, 56; Rom 8:34; 1 Cor 15:24–28; Eph 1:20; Col 3:1; Heb 1:3, 13; 8:1; 10:12–13; 12:2; 1 Pet 3:22.

and practices. He warns his hearers to watch out for them. Earlier, Jesus had used the same Greek word *blepō* in the imperative, warning believers to "pay attention (*blepete*) to what you hear" (4:24) and more relatedly, "watch out (*blepete*) for the yeast of the Pharisees and the yeast of Herod" (8:15). He has just critiqued the Sadducees as ignorant of the Scriptures and the power of God. Now it is the scribes' turn. His critique is their desire for honor and exercising their faith not out of genuine love for God (as he has just endorsed), but to gain status. They are vain, self-absorbed, and arrogant.

Their first issue is that they loved to be noticed. Such leaders made a big thing of being seen in public with long robes. The *stolē* here refers to the long white *tallith*, "a shawl worn during formal prayer and other religious acts in the synagogues."[84] These scribes liked wearing them around in public, drawing attention to themselves, and inflating their already arrogant egos. Such attitudes can be a problem where clergy still wear clerical clothing. While wearing clerical clothing is arguably appropriate at times, and despite many clergy people being humble and faithful Christian leaders, at times, it can be nauseating and extremely counter-cultural observing them in their regalia.

Second, they liked to be "greeted in the marketplaces." The *agora* was the central commercial area of the ancient towns. These scribes wanted people to acknowledge them as they walked around. In the ancient world, it was common practice for those of lower rank to attribute public honor to those of higher rank, and in particular, those who had a better knowledge of the Torah (cf. *y. Ber.* 2.1). The first and second are probably linked. They wore their temple clothing in public to ensure the general populace knew who they were and paid the appropriate respect. The kingdom of God is bringing a new world order where there are no such notions of rank and status, and everyone greets and acknowledges the other with respect.

Third, they delighted in taking the seats of status at gatherings. The best seats were at the front of the box in which the Torah was stored.[85] These scribes loved being in those seats, which were reserved for dignitaries, honored guests, and, in particular, the scholars and scribes.[86] Banquets at the time also had careful rules for seating the highest ranked above the lowest ranked. The most honored were seated beside the host.[87]

Jesus's comments here recall Jacob (James) and John seeking the best seats at the right and left of Jesus earlier (10:37). Jesus perhaps had an eye

---

84. Brooks, *Mark*, 202.
85. Witherington, *Gospel of Mark*, 334.
86. Evans, *Mark 8:27—16:20*, 278.
87. Witherington, *Gospel of Mark*, 334.

on them as he gave this warning. Mention of eating also calls to mind the two feeding encounters of Jesus in Mark's Gospel (6:30–44; 8:1–10). There were no groups seated in the best seats. Indeed, the disciples were not even seated at the feeding of the five thousand; they were waiting on the crowds of poor and hungry.

Further, if anyone should have been in the best seat, it was Jesus. However, in the feeding of the five thousand, the Servant King took the roles of host and waiter as he broke and distributed the food. The disciples collected baskets to eat later. Then, during the feeding of four thousand, it was Jesus who broke the food and distributed himself: he was host and waiter. In the kingdom, there are no such seats of honor. Notably, at the Last Supper, there is no mention of anyone in seats of honor (14:17–25). When we are put in a position to sit in them, we should consider Jesus's teaching in Luke 14 of preferring the "lowly seats" (Luke 14:7–11).

Fourth, Jesus critiques the scribes for their oppression of widows ("they devour the houses of widows"). Scholars debate a range of settings for this. Perhaps they took payment for legal services, which was forbidden. As lawyers, they may have cheated widows out of their estates. It could indicate their abuse of the hospitality of widows. They may have taken money for their prayers. Perhaps they were securing debts against widow's houses and then claiming them when the debts were unpaid.[88] None of these are provable; suffice it to say, they were ripping off widows of their estates.

This critique leads into the story of the widow in 12:41–44. She may have been a recipient of their injustice so that she gave her last mite to the temple treasury. Indeed, it could that it was through the temple treasury that the scribes were fleecing widows, by demanding their giving and forcing the likes of the poor widow to feel a need to give everything to the work of the temple, putting themselves deeper into poverty. This criticism also warns us of pressuring or enticing people to give to the church (as if they will be wealthy if they do or warning them of judgment). Some people are poor and should not have that pressure put on them. Each should give without compulsion, as they are able, willingly, and according to their means (1 Cor 16:2; 2 Cor 9:7).

Fifth, they prayed long prayers to impress and gain prestige ("for the sake of appearance say long prayers") (vv. 38–40). Jesus's words here do not necessarily preclude long prayers, but they challenge believers never to be motivated by impressing others with the quality of one's prayers. However, Jesus elsewhere endorses short private prayers based on our awareness that God already knows what we need before we pray (Matt

---

88. See Evans, *Mark 8:27—16:20*, 278.

6:1–4). The Lord's Prayer itself, a short to-the-point prayer, is the paradigm of prayer (Matt 6:9–13).

Finally, Jesus warns that the scribes will be severely punished for such indiscretions; they will "receive greater condemnation." Such a warning is hardly surprising, as they are violating the second great commandment just stressed above. We are also here reminded of Jesus's warning to the Jewish leaders that "whoever exalts himself will be humbled, and whoever humbles himself will be exalted" (Matt 23:12). Jesus's warning may hint at the possibility that there are degrees of punishment in eternity.

Jesus's critique has implications for all Christians and especially for leaders. We are to be humble, not working to make an impression on others, to gain power, status, rank, and privilege, or to increase our wealth. Instead, we serve God and others to please our Father, who delights in us, his children. As Paul says in Gal 1:10: "Am I trying to please people? If I were still trying to please people, I would not be a slave of Christ" (my translation).

Questions

- What are the main lessons from the cursing of the fig tree?
- Read Isa 56 and Jer 7 and consider the relationship of these passages to the temple clearing.
- How do we interpret Mark 11:22–24?
- How was the parable of the tenants fulfilled?
- Should Christians pay taxes?
- Why is there no marriage in the resurrection?
- Consider Jesus's use of Exod 3:6 in 12:26 and explain his argument.
- What does the saying "Give to Caesar what is Caesar's, and give to God what is God's" imply for Christian attitudes to the state and taxes? What is the limit on our allegiance to the state?
- Consider the two great commandments. Where are our blind spots? What needs to change?
- Knowing that the first "Lord" in 12:36 is Yahweh and the second is Adonai in the citation of Ps 110:1, explain what Jesus is saying about his identity in the discussion.
- What does 12:38–40 say to contemporary Christian leaders concerning clerical clothing and seeking honor?

Lesson Ten: The Widow, the Olivet Discourse, and the Lead-Up to Jesus's Death Begins (12:41—14:42)

The Widow's Offering (12:41–44)

THE SCENE SHIFTS TO Jesus seated opposite the place where the offerings were made to the temple treasury, the *gazophylakion*. In the LXX, it speaks of "the storeroom and treasury of the temple."[1] In the Mishnah (*m. Šeqal.* 6:5), there is mention of the point where people made offerings into thirteen receptacles. These were trumpet-like with funnels that were tapered at the top to stop people stealing money from them. One of them was set apart for general, voluntary contributions,[2] and this may have been the one into which the woman put her offering, although we cannot be sure.[3] As this was in the open, she could have been subjected to scorn from priests, while those who gave large gifts could have gained honor.[4] Jesus, however, sees things differently.

Jesus observed the woman put in two *leptons*. The lepton was worth 1/128th of a denarius. In that a denarius was worth a day's wages for the laborer, we can estimate that in New Zealand currency, this was equivalent

---

1. Balz, "γαζοφυλάκιον." He cites 2 Esdr 20:38; 22:44; and 1 Macc 14:49. He also notes that John 8:20 has this more general sense of "magnificent treasury built by Herod in the north part of the women's court" (Josephus, *War* 500; *Ant.* 19:294).

2. This is where the temple tax was paid. The temple tax supposedly involved all Jewish males, other than priests over twenty, paying an annual tax of half a shekel, a day's wage (*m. Šeqal.* 1:3–4; Josephus, *War* 7:281). However, not all paid the tax, and at the time of Jesus, it may have been voluntary. After the fall of Jerusalem, women were forced to pay it. It is likely, then, that this does not refer to the actual tax, but a voluntary offering. On the tax, see Schmidt, "Taxes," 806. Jesus paid it (Matt 17:24–27).

3. Balz, "γαζοφυλάκιον."

4. Balz, "γαζοφυλάκιον."

to a two-cent coin.⁵ Jesus's observation is that the women put in more proportionally, even though the others gave greater sums of money. In fact, she gave all the money she had.

This passage is understood by scholars in two ways. The traditional view is that Jesus was impressed with the offering and that this is a lesson showing that it is not just giving that matters, but the percentage given. So, the woman is commended and given as an example to be emulated. She stands then in contrast to the rich young man and is like the disciples who gave up everything they had for Jesus (10:17–31). Conversely, those who appear generous are not to be emulated because Jesus is critiquing giving that leaves a person with far more than one needs. What matters is the giver and heart.⁶

However, there is a problem with this view. If the woman is an example, she is commended for putting herself into deeper poverty. Still, Jesus might be honoring her for loving God with all she had. Paul similarly commends the Macedonians for giving out of their poverty to the needs of the famine-stricken Jerusalem Christians (cf. 2 Cor 8:1–4). However, later in the same passage, Paul states to the Corinthians that he does not want them to make themselves destitute in their giving to the Jerusalem collection but wants fairness (2 Cor 8:13). So, there are questions in this view.

The alternative idea is that Jesus here is not wanting his disciples to be impressed and emulate the woman. Instead, he is drawing their attention to her oppressed state. In so doing, he is encouraging the disciples not to oppress the likes of this widow. This passage then sits alongside other examples of oppression in Mark. These include the scribes mentioned in the previous passage (12:38–40), the Corban oppressors (7:9–13), and the rich ruler (10:18–31). In context, this view may be preferable. Another possibility is that both ideas have value: she is a role model for others, but the story also carries the warning against injustice.

The Destruction of the Temple and Signs of the End of the Age (13:1–13)

This chapter of Mark is variously called the eschatological discourse, the prophetic discourse, the little apocalypse, or the Olivet discourse as it is given on the Mount of Olives. It is a much-disputed passage. Some consider it is totally focused on the destruction of the temple by the Romans

---

5. At the time of writing, the minimum wage in New Zealand is $17.70. For an eight-hour day, that is $141.60, and so 1/128th of that is about 1.11 cents. The lepton is then equivalent to three Malaysian ringitts or .0068 USD.

6. France, *Gospel of Mark*, 493; Brooks, *Mark*, 202.

in AD 70 (especially scholars). Others consider that it refers to events before the return of Christ (especially in popular Christianity). Another perspective sees 13:1–13 as focussed on the fall of Jerusalem, while 13:14–23 refers to the end of the age.[7] Others take the passage in some way as a blend of both ideas.

My view is that while the sermon is a response to the request of the disciples concerning the fall of the temple, the content cannot be fully explained by contemporary events. It applies equally to the return of Christ that climaxes the narrative.

One of the core reasons I take this perspective is 13:10, which speaks of the gospel being preached to all nations. While the gospel had made good progress from Israel to the northern regions of Africa, through Turkey and Greece to Rome, the gospel had made little impact on the nations by the time of the writing of Mark's Gospel. It had barely penetrated east to China; northeast into the Russian steppes; deeper south beyond the Sahara; and north into Europe, the U.K., and the lands beyond the Danube and Scandinavia. To suggest that the gospel was preached to all nations by AD 70 is nonsense. Instead, the chapter presupposes a substantial period of evangelization before the events in question are fulfilled.

Another key reason is "the end" in 13:13. While it can be taken apocalyptically as the end of the world as we know it when Jerusalem falls, more likely, "the end" refers to the end of this age.[8] The term has the meaning of "the end of the age" in Paul's writings, Hebrews, and Revelation.[9] Matthew interpreted Mark this way, as the references earlier in this paragraph demonstrate.

In addition, OT prophecies are often double-layered. Such double meaning is especially true of the pre-exilic prophets who blended predictions about the return from exile with the eschatological age.[10] As such, this passage functions like those OT prophetic oracles that had dual horizons. While having an immediate focus on the forthcoming fall of Jerusalem, it is also anticipatory of the events leading to the return of Christ.[11] Seeing the end of the age as the focus of the passage is not without problems, mainly because the discussion starts with the Jerusalem temple. However, it seems the best reading of the text.

---

7. France, *Gospel of Mark*, 495. See also Evans, *Mark 8:27—16:20*, 293.
8. See Matt 13:39, 40, 49; 24:4; 28:20.
9. See 1 Cor 1:8; 10:11; 15:24; Heb 3:14; 9:26; Rev 2:26.
10. See, e.g., Isa 10:20–23; 35:1–10, 51–52.
11. See also Brooks, *Mark*, 206.

The temple narrative continues with Jesus leaving the temple with his disciples, probably through the eastern gate by the Court of the Gentiles that faces the Mount of Olives (see above). One of the disciples notes the temple with its massive stones and impressive buildings (13:1).[12] The grandeur of the temple is confirmed by Josephus, who records that the stones were massive, including one that was twenty meters long.[13] Evans notes that excavations have unearthed enormous stones up to fifteen meters long and weighing 420 to 600 tons.[14]

Jesus's reply is surprising and unexpected. He tells them that these impressive buildings will be utterly destroyed, so much so that not one stone will be left on another, but all will be knocked down, building on OT prophecy and allusions (13:2).[15] The beginning of the passage refers to the fall of Jerusalem, which occurred under the Roman emperor Titus in AD 70. Because of this, some date Mark immediately after this point. However, as Evans notes, it is unlikely that the demolition of the temple occurred instantly but probably took years, making this perspective unlikely.[16] A saying like this (and John 2:20) may be behind the accusation at Jesus's trial that Jesus would destroy the temple (14:58).

Later, or so it seems, from the sense of the narrative, Peter, Jacob (James), John, and Andrew are seated with Christ on the Mount of Olives just to the east of the temple, giving them a good view of the Temple Mount.[17] They ask Jesus privately when all this will happen and what signs will be given that these things are about to happen[18]—a reasonable request (13:3-4).

Jesus responds. He warns them to watch out for messianic pretenders and false teachers who might lead them astray (13:5-6). Josephus refers to some prophetic claimants before the fall of Rome.[19] However, none took

---

12. Josephus, *War* 5:222–23, speaks of the outward face of the temple being covered in gold and reflecting so magnificently at the rising of the sun that people had to avert their eyes. From a distance, the brilliant white temple looked like a snow-covered mountain.

13. Josephus, *War* 5:224 (45 cubits). France, *Gospel of Mark*, 495, states that this is hard to believe.

14. Evans, *Mark 8:27—16:20*, 299.

15. See, e.g., 2 Sam 17:13; Hag 2:15; Mic 3:12; Jer 26:17–19; Amos 9:1; Ps 137:7.

16. Evans, *Mark 8:27—16:20*, 298.

17. Evans, *Mark 8:27—16:20*, 298, notes it is a favorite spot for pilgrims to observe the temple.

18. Typical of the Jewish penchant for signs (Mark 8:11; cf. 1 Cor 1:22; Exod 3:12; Isa 7:11).

19. See Josephus, *Ant.* 20:97–99. He tells of a Theudas, who believed he could part the river Jordan and had his head chopped off. He is referenced in Acts 5:36. In *Ant.* 20.102, he tells of the sons of Judas, Jacob (James) and Simon, who led a revolt and were

the name Messiah, although bar Kochba did so in the uprising of AD 132. However, in the time since the fall of Jerusalem, many have claimed to be Jesus Christ, especially in the last three centuries.[20]

Jesus warns them of war, whether actual or merely rumored (13:7; cf. Jer 51:46).[21] For those who take this as the fall of Jerusalem, this was a time of relative peace in the Roman Empire. However, there were wars in Parthia in AD 36 and between the Nabateans and Antipas in AD 36–37 (related to the events of 6:14–29), as well as some local uprisings.[22] The war with Rome in AD 66 could also be in mind, but this has implications for the dating of Mark, which most take at a time preceding this. These first-century conflicts do not account for the detail in the passage as well as for the scope and intensity of global conflicts from the previous two centuries.

Jesus then warns them of earthquakes (13:8). Josephus records that there was an earthquake in Jerusalem in AD 67.[23] There is also mention of an earthquake in Philippi in Acts 16:26 (AD 49–50). There was a significant earthquake in Asia Minor in AD 61, which saw the destruction of Laodicea and Colossae (which was never rebuilt).[24] Pompeii was partially destroyed by an earthquake in AD 62. Others argue that there has been an increase in the intensity of earthquakes in recent history. However, a detailed examination of recent earthquakes calls this into question.[25]

Jesus also warns of famines (13:9). There is evidence of famine in the NT period. One example is that of Acts 11:28, which precipitated the first of Paul's collections for Jerusalem (AD 46).[26] There were also others which led to the second Jerusalem collection (Rom 15:26; 1 Cor 16:1–4; 2 Cor 8—9). Famines have been experienced throughout history, including many in recent times.[27]

---

crucified. In *Ant.* 20.167–168, he mentions the Egyptian, who convinced a number of people that he could make the walls of Jerusalem fall down from the Mount of Olives. Four hundred people were killed, but the Egyptian escaped. Paul is accused of being this Egyptian in Acts 21:38.

20. See "List of People Claimed to Be Jesus."

21. For those who take this as referring to the fall, there was a time of relative peace in the Roman Empire. However, there were wars in Parthia in AD 36, between the Nabataeans and Antipas in AD 36–37, and local uprisings.

22. Evans, *Mark 8:27—16:20*, 511.

23. Josephus, *War* 4:286–87.

24. France, *Gospel of Mark*, 512.

25. See Austin and Strauss, "Earthquakes and End Times."

26. See Josephus, *Ant.* 3:320, 20:101, during the reign of Claudius, prompting the first gift to Jerusalem.

27. "List of Famines."

These events Jesus describes as the beginning of birth pangs, suggesting that they are the first sign of the events to which history is heading.[28] This idea draws on the rabbinic notion of the birth pangs of the Messiah (cf. John 16:21; Rom 8:22).[29] Some extend the analogy to increasing intensity, but that is not necessarily the case; their existence could merely signal the beginning of the birth pangs.

Jesus then warns them of great persecution from sanhedrins. The plural may speak of different iterations of the Jewish Sanhedrin, or it could mean local councils. They will also be persecuted in synagogues, speaking of Jewish persecution. Such Jewish persecution is found throughout Acts.[30] The phrase "governors and kings" refers to gentile rulers and the likes of the Herods. Paul appears before such people throughout Acts.[31]

Then Jesus tells them that the gospel must first be preached to all nations (13:10). This verse is interpreted in Matt 24:14 as the end of the age ("and then the end will come"). As noted above, the Christians at the time knew the gospel needed to reach all nations. They realized there was much work to do. As such, this presupposes a substantial time after the writing of Mark to the end of the age. I have also argued elsewhere that the NT writers were not expecting the imminent return of Christ, as they knew the mission to the nations had a long way to go.[32] Jesus then encourages them that in such times of persecution, the Spirit will give them the words that they need. Consequently, they do not need to worry about what they will say (13:11).

Jesus warns that households will be torn apart, with family members betraying their siblings, children, and parents (13:12). These could relate to events that occurred in the Neronian persecution. It is undoubtedly the experience of the church ever since that families have been torn apart as a result of one coming to faith. A version of this happened for a period in my family when I became a Christian; thankfully, my family softened over time. That is not always the case. Jesus warns that all humanity will hate Christians (13:13). He tells them that it is those who persevere ("stand firm") to the end who will be saved (13:13). To avoid an eschatological interpretation of "the end," some take *telos* here as "finally" or "completely." I think it more

---

28. See Exod 15:14; Deut 2:25; Isa 13:8; 21:3; 26:17; Jer 4:31; 6:24; Hos 13:13; Mic 4:9; Nah 2:11 (LXX 10); 1 Thess 5:3 for the imagery in the OT.

29. Evans, *Mark 8:27—16:20*, 309, notes that rabbinic literature mentions the birth pain of the Messiah, along with the retribution of Gehenna and the wars of Gog and Magog (Mek. on Exod 16:28–36).

30. See Acts 4:5–22; 5:27–41; 6:12; 22:30; 23:1; 24:20, see also Josephus, *Ant.* 20:200.

31. See Acts 24:10–27; 25:1–12; 25:23—26:32.

32. Keown, "Imminent Parousia," 242–63.

naturally should be interpreted eschatologically, i.e., the end referring to the return of Christ. On another level, it refers to the end of a particular person's life if the person dies before that day.

The Tribulation and the Return of Christ (13:14–37)

Some commentators see a break in the passage in v. 14. At this verse, Mark's Jesus shifts from speaking of the fall of Jerusalem to the end of the age, or the "great tribulation." Alternatively, this continues to speak about the fall of Jerusalem. Another alternative is that both the fall of Jerusalem and the ends of the age are in view. In my thinking, there is a shift here, although in vv. 14–23, we may have a double-layered prophecy with the things that will happen in Jerusalem as a foreshadowing of the eschaton.

Jesus warns readers that when they see "the abomination that causes desolation standing where he ought not to be," then those in Judea should flee without turning back for their essential clothing (13:14–16). In other words, they need to get away with what they have as fast as possible. The details connote a terrifying and destructive event. The abomination that causes desolation is found in Dan 9:27; 11:31; and 12:11, and similar language is found in 1 Macc 1:54. These passages, in initial context, refer to the statue of Zeus Olympus and the pagan altar that Antiochus IV Epiphanes of Seleucid Syria erected in the temple in 167 BC.

Different possibilities are given for this event. Some can be ruled out because they predate Mark's Gospel. In 63 BC, the Roman general Pompey conquered Jerusalem and profaned the temple by entering the holy of holies. In AD 26–27, Pilate set up idolatrous standards with embossed figures of the emperor in Jerusalem. He brought them down only from fear of revolution.[33] More provocatively, after Jesus's death, in AD 40, Caligula unsuccessfully attempted to erect his statue in the temple. Roman soldiers also carried their standards into the Jerusalem temple.

If the passage is purely about the fall of Jerusalem in AD 70, Titus profaned the temple during the war of AD 66–70.[34] In AD 67–68, Zealots under John of Gischala took over the temple as a base and appointed a mock high priest to carry out temple ritual.[35] However, none of these satisfactorily explain the reference to an abomination that causes desolation "standing" where it should not be, i.e., in the temple. Alternatively, this is

---

33. Josephus, *Ant.* 18:55–59; *War* 2:169–74; Hoehner, "Pontius Pilate," 615.
34. Brooks, *Mark*, 212.
35. Josephus, *War* 4:150–157.

more general, and "where he ought not to be" could simply be Jerusalem, and so this refers to the Roman invasion. In favor of this is the reference to Judea. If so, then the apocalyptic language is the end of the world as we know it, rather than the end of this phase of history. Then again, this could be figurative, another way of expressing the sentiment of 2 Thess 2:4, where the man of lawlessness seats himself in the "temple of God," i.e., as every religion and religious figure in the world.

However, across the NT, we find the concept of an antichrist, a vile figure arising to challenge God and his people before the return of Christ. Such a person is found in this passage and parallels (13:14; Matt 24:15).[36] Other ways this figure is described are as a "man of lawlessness" who is a "son of destruction" (2 Thess 2:1–12), the antichrist (1 John 2:18), and the beast (Rev 13). It seems there is a tradition that at the culmination of this age, before Christ's return, a figure will arise who will oppose God and his people. The likes of Antiochus Epiphanes and the Roman Caesars prefigure this adversary. He is like all despots who seek to take over the world with rapacious force. He is the antithesis of Jesus.

Specific mention of Judea could indicate the final events of history will center on Jerusalem and Judea, or the events of the fall of Jerusalem prefigure what will happen all over the world, with Judea being representative of all places.

There are different views on the role of the nation and the land of Israel in the end times. Some take the nation as central. Others dispense with it altogether, believing that the church is now Israel renewed, and all promises relating to the land are void. The answer may lie in a middle position: salvation is in Christ, and the religious system of Israel has culminated and continues in Christ. However, some texts could indicate that the culmination of history will be focused in and around the physical land of Israel (cf. Zech 14; Luke 21:20–24).

Whether this speaks only of the fall Jerusalem or the end of the age, Jesus warns the people of Judea that they must flee without returning for their possessions.[37] He bemoans the experience of those who are pregnant and nursing infants; such people cannot drop everything and run. He then

---

36. Luke rewrites this: "When you see Jerusalem surrounded by armies, then know that its desolation is near" (Luke 21:20).

37. Evans, *Mark 8:27—16:20*, 321, asks "why would anyone be on the rooftop of his house?" He notes that "it was the custom in Jewish Palestine of late antiquity to use the flat roof of one's house for prayer or worship (Jer 19:13; Zeph 1:5; Acts 10:9), sleep (1 Sam 9:25), storing or drying fruit (Josh 2:6), proclaiming news (Isa 15:3; 22:1; Matt 10:27), or celebrating festivals (Neh 8:16)."

encourages his hearers to pray that it will not occur in winter (another indication that Jesus does not know when this will occur).

Winter is a difficult time to travel; suffering would be severely increased (13:17–18). Jesus tells them that it will be a time of suffering unrivaled since creation or in the future (13:19, cf. Dan 12:1). Again, this statement transcends the fall of Jerusalem, unless it is outrageous hyperbole.[38] Evans notes that when one considers the horrible events of biblical history such as Sodom and Gomorrah, Noah's flood, and Israel's exile, "this is quite a claim."[39] Such a description suggests a tribulation of incomparable suffering. Some (e.g., Evans) take this as the situation in Judea at the time of the fall of Jerusalem.[40] However, these details transcend the events of AD 70 and point instead to the end of the age.

Jesus encourages the disciples that God will cut short those days for the sake of his elect people (13:20). Reference to the elect and the scope of the evil suggest a global phenomenon with the whole of humanity facing extinction. One thinks of contemporary nuclear, biological, chemical warfare; the development of AI; new weapons; digital technologies; pandemics; and global warming. He warns them not to listen to those who declare that the Messiah is coming or has come. He cautions that false deceptive Christs and prophets will arise who do signs and wonders, even leading some of God's people astray (13:21–22). He tells them to be on their guard, because he has warned them (13:22).

In vv. 23–24, Jesus then speaks of a time after the suffering[41] (a tribulation, cf. vv. 14–23) where there will be signs in the sky: the sun and moon darkened, with stars falling from the sky and the heavens shaken by cataclysmic events. Such astral events can all be taken literally, as depicting asteroids, meteorites, or a nuclear holocaust. However, the language is also found in the OT of the events of the Babylonian exile, and so could be apocalyptic imagery to portray the end of the world as Israel knows it, e.g., the fall of Jerusalem (cf. Isa 13:10; 34:4). Some see here a theophany.[42] Evans, Wright, and others see

---

38. The siege of Jerusalem lasted five months, hardly suitable for the description here.

39. Evans, *Mark 8:27—16:20*, 322.

40. France, *Mark*, 524, notes that there are a number of correlations with Josephus's account of the war.

41. Some take this to be about the fall of Jerusalem, e.g., Evans, *Mark 8:27—16:20*, 533.

42. See Judg 5:5; Amos 9:5; Mic 1:4; Hab 3:6; Nah 1:5; Pss 18:7; 114:7; Job 9:6; T. Mos. 10:1; Sib. Or. 3:796–803; T. Levi 4:1; 1 En. 57:2.

here apocalyptic language to describe the shaking of world events in the fall of Jerusalem and international affairs.[43]

That Mark is here looking toward the return of Christ becomes clearer in v. 26. Then the Son of Man (Jesus) will come in the clouds with power and glory (13:26). This vision is taken from the prophecy of Dan 7:13–14. While some take this as a metaphorical statement concerning the enthroning of Christ after his resurrection,[44] it seems better to take it as the return of Christ. The early church certainly took it this way.

The term *angelos* can refer to human emissaries as with John the Baptist in 1:2.[45] As such, the gathering in v. 27 can be read missionally as the ingathering of God's elect from the nations through the proclamation of the gospel.

However, in Mark and the NT, angels are most often God's heavenly servants.[46] Besides, this verse parallels Mark 8:38, where the Son of Man coming with his angels is the second coming. Consequently, the OT hope of the Messiah plays out in two stages: first, he comes as the Servant Messiah, to die for the world (cf. Isa 53). Later, he will return in full glory, as anticipated in Dan 7. Luke adds an interim stage between the two: God pours out his Spirit out to empower his servants to bring God's people into the kingdom. Finally, God will send out his angels to the ends of the earth to gather his elect (13:27; cf. 8:38; Matt 13:41; 2 Thess 1:7). This collecting of God's elect points to the completion of the mission mentioned in 13:10: "The gospel is preached to all nations." Then, when the mission is complete, Jesus returns with his angels and gathers his elect.

In vv. 28–29, we have a parable to exhort readers to be ready for that day. Stein notes that the branches of a fig tree begin to swell and sprout leaves in March and April, indicating that summer is near.[47] Likewise, when the signs outlined in this passage are complete, then readers will know that Christ is imminent ("at the very gates") (13:28–29).

In v. 30, Jesus tells them that this generation (*genea*) will not pass away until these things have happened (13:30). The nature of the generation is disputed depending on one's perspective of the above events. We can take *genea* in its literal sense of those living at the time and listening. Mark's use of *genea* in 8:12 has this sense, as do 8:38 and 9:19. If so, this

---

43. Evans, *Mark 8:27—16:20*, 533.
44. Evans, *Mark 8:27—16:20*, 534.
45. See Matt 11:10; Luke 7:24, 27; 9:52.
46. See 1:13; 8:38; 12:25; 13:32.
47. Stein, *Mark*, 618.

could refer to the fall of Jerusalem.[48] Some consider here that Jesus is stating that he will return within this generation, an imminent parousia. If so, we have a failed messianic prophecy. However, as discussed earlier, it is unlikely that Mark believed Jesus would return quickly, for the whole world had to hear the gospel before this event.[49]

There are other possibilities for *genea,* such as Israel as a people or all humanity. Another possibility is that "this generation" points to those alive at the time of the events of vv. 14–25. If so, this statement becomes a note of assurance that the events will not see the world and humanity utterly destroyed before God intervenes to shorten the days, save the elect, and return his Son to earth. If the return of Christ is in view, this is perhaps the best interpretation.

Jesus tells them that heaven and earth will pass away, but his words will not (cf. Isa 40:6–8; Bar 4:1; Matt 5:18), adding a note of assurance. Some limit "my words" only to the previous verse 30;[50] however, the statement seems to speak of all Jesus's teaching, and so is a strong claim to authority. Jesus is placing his words on a par with those of God in creation and through the OT. Jesus's words here could suggest that the age's end will see the dissolution of the cosmos (cf. 1 Pet 3:10). Others argue for a renewed earth. The latter is to be preferred.[51]

Jesus then answers the question of when this will occur (cf. 13:4). He tells them that no one knows when Jesus will return, not the angels nor himself. Only God knows when (13:32). We see here Jesus's voluntary renunciation of his divine omniscience during his incarnation on earth.[52] It does not suggest that he cannot know or that he does not know presently in his heavenly exaltation. He warns them to be ready for that day whenever it is (13:33).

He tells them that his disciples are like servants (literally, "slaves") put in charge of his house while the owner has gone away: always be ready for the return of the owner, i.e., Jesus (13:34–36). The return here makes it unlikely that v.26 refers to anything other than the parousia of Christ. Again, we have a comparison of ministry with servanthood. He warns them to "be awake" for that day (13:36–37). Unlike the tenants who

---

48. France, *Gospel of Mark*, 539, and Brooks, *Mark*, 217, who both claim this is the most natural sense of *genea*. True, but it is not the most natural sense of "all these things," so the problem is not solved.

49. Keown, "Imminent Parousia," 242–63.

50. Evans, *Mark 8:27—16:20*, 336.

51. Matt 19:28; Acts 3:21; Rom 8:19–23; 1 Cor 15:24–28; Rev 21—22.

52. A number of writers, particularly from the early church, have found this embarrassing and sought ways to soften it.

abused God's vineyard (12:1–12), they are to watch over God's house with diligence. The reference to sleeping ironically calls to mind 14:32–39, where the disciples fall asleep in the garden.

Anointing at Bethany (14:1–9)

This section of Mark is beautiful and haunting. It begins the lead-up to Christ's passion. It is set two days before the Passover (Gk *pascha*; Heb *pesach*) and the feast of the unleavened bread (*chag hammatstsoth*). The Passover celebrated the deliverance of Israel from Egypt (Exod 12). The Feast of the Unleavened Bread recalls Israel eating unleavened bread in their Passover meal and feast that followed.[53] The two events remind Israel of her deliverance from Egypt. The event "helped sustain the Israelite community by prompting them to remember their common history and the foundations of their common beliefs."[54] It was celebrated on 14 or 15 Nissan (the first month of the Jewish year) and the feast from 15 to 21 Nissan (April/May). In AD 30, that would be around April 4–11, and AD 33 April 1–7, depending on when Jesus died. Evans notes that the Romans were always edgy at this time, as it was a popular time for an uprising.[55]

We can note too that after the events of this particular Passover and feast, these celebrations will forever be transcended by Jesus, the Passover Lamb of God. Hence, Christians celebrate Easter, not Passover, and for those who believe in Jesus as Messiah and Son of God, that is most definitely right.

The chief priests and teachers of the law were again looking for a way to arrest Jesus and kill him by stealth, representing a development in their desire to get Jesus throughout the narrative. They were concerned at doing it publicly because it could excite a popular uprising (14:1–2), as seen at other times.[56]

Jesus has returned from Jerusalem to Bethany, three km (two mi) east of Jerusalem (11:1, 11). He is at the home of Simon the leper (cf. John 12:2) for a meal which Martha prepared (cf. John 12:2). There is a possibility that there were quarters for lepers there, and if so, he may be in one (cf. 11Q19 46:16–18). This and Matthew's parallel account are the only mention of Simon in the NT. While he may still be a leper, it is most likely in light of Mark's record of Jesus's comprehensive healing ministry that he had earlier

---

53. See Exod 12:1–20; 13:6–7; 23:15; 34:18; Lev 23:5–8; Num 28:16–25; Deut 16:1–8.
54. Nyberg, "Unleavened Bread, Feast of."
55. Evans, *Mark 8:27—16:20*, 354.
56. See Josephus, *Ant.* 17:213–15; 20:105; *War* 2:224.

been healed by Jesus.⁵⁷ If not, Jesus's presence in his home is remarkable because to be in his home, eating with him, was again breaking rules of ritual purity (see on 1:40–45; Lev 13). According to John, Martha is doing the serving, which may indicate that Simon is single (John 12:2).

More sensation occurs as a woman anoints Jesus's head with an alabaster jar of costly perfume (nard) that she breaks over his head (14:3). Although some claim differently, this event is not the same as in Luke 7, where the details and setting are significantly different.⁵⁸ This woman is identified as Mary of Bethany by John (John 12:3). While the Greek says it was shattered, this likely refers to the breaking of the neck of the bottle. The language suggests that all the nard was poured over Jesus's head. The NT adjective *pistikos* translated "genuine" can also mean "pure," affirming its quality.

Nard or "spike-nard" is one of the most expensive of ancient perfumes.⁵⁹ It usually came from India, drawn from plants shaped like spikes. It was opened only on special occasions and was very expensive. Pliny the Elder, writing in Italy (AD 23–79), describes it as the supreme perfume oil that was highly expensive, worth "one hundred denarii per pound."⁶⁰ John estimates that there is a *litra* of oil⁶¹ (less than a pound), while Mark, Matthew, and John all assess its value as three hundred denarii, affirming its great value in Israel at the time.

Anointing in the OT was associated with a coronation. Josephus uses the term in Mark of the pouring (*katēcheō*) of oil at the anointings of Saul and Jehu.⁶² Anointing oil was poured on the head of priests (Exod 29:7; Lev 8:12) and kings.⁶³ The woman may have seen her actions as anointing Jesus as the Messiah, Christ—the Lord's anointed one (1 Sam 16:13; Ps 18:50).⁶⁴ If so, this is a daring, scandalous act. Her anointing recalls Luke

---

57. Evans, *Mark 8:27—16:20*, 359, believes it is improbable that he is still a leper, or the disciples and the woman would not have been in his home. Yet, Jesus's attitude to sinners and the sick means their presence in the home cannot be ruled out.

58. For example, Luke 7 is set in the home of a Pharisee (not a leper); the woman is a sinner; she anoints his feet, not his head; she weeps on him; and the conversation is utterly different. The two events cannot be plausibly harmonized.

59. Evans, *Mark 8:27—16:20*, 359.

60. Pliny the Elder, *Nat.* 12.26.

61. 11.5 ounces or 327 grams.

62. Josephus, *Ant.* 6:54; 9:108.

63. See 1 Sam 10:1; 16:11, 13; 2 Sam 2:4; 5:3; 1 Kgs 1:39; 2 Kgs 9:6; 11:12; 23:30; 1 Chron 11:3; Ps 89:20; 133:2.

64. Evans, *Mark 8:27—16:20*, 360. See also 1 Sam 2:10, 35; 12:3; 15:17; 24:6, 10; 26:9, 11, 16, 23; 2 Sam 1:14, 16; 2:7; 3:39; 5:17; 12:7; 19:21; 22:51; 23:1; 1 Kgs 1:45; 5:1; 1 Chron 14:8; 29:22; 2 Chron 6:42; 23:11; Pss 45:7; 105:15; 132:10; Isa 45:1; Lam 4:20;

4:18, where Jesus cites Isa 61:1 and declares himself the anointed one whom Isaiah predicts will come (cf. Dan 9:25–26). Later in the passage, Jesus sees this as his anointing for burial. After this, his full anointed messiahship will be revealed in his resurrection. However, her anointing still functions messianically; it is just that he has to die and rise first.

The response of those present can be described as oafish and insensitive.[65] Still, in light of Jesus's concern for the poor, it is a natural response to her generous act (10:21; 12:42–44). In Mark, it is unclear who among those present responded in such a way; but they were likely disciples, something that Matthew confirms (Matt 26:8). John records that it was Judas (John 12:4). Their response is described by the same word used in 10:14 and 41 (*aganakteō*)—anger. They question the waste of such an amount of perfume. John records that Judas's concern was because of his theft (John 12:6). They value the nard at three hundred denarii, which in New Zealand in 2019 would be about $42,500.[66] Such a large amount of money could feed a worker and his family for nearly a year. This detail emphasizes the radical extravagance of the act.

The term used for "censured her" is *embrimaomai*, that was used of Jesus strongly demanding that the healed leper present himself to the priest (1:43). It is used in John 11:38 of Jesus being moved by Lazarus's death, so it carries emotional force and indicates that they admonished her sternly. We see here again the arrogance of the disciples who cannot understand the notion of servant leadership. It is also another example of their incomprehension at Jesus's identity as Messiah.[67] It further carries more than a hint of sexism from the men who saw themselves at the center of God's kingdom purposes. If a woman can anoint Jesus for his redemptive death, women can serve Jesus, too.

One might have expected the socially minded Jesus to join the chorus of rebuke; after all, the woman was using resources that could have been sold to feed the poor. However, surprisingly, rather than rebuking her, Jesus comes to her defense. He tells them starkly, "Leave her alone!" He confirms that what she has done for him is a beautiful thing (14:5).[68] He then addresses the issue of the poor raised by the protestors, alluding

---

Zech 4:14.

65. Evans, *Mark 8:27—16:20*, 360, sees their action as oafish and insensitive; however, their response to me is quite understandable.

66. With a minimum wage of $17.70 per hour for a 40-hour week (114,621 ringitt; $26,365 USD).

67. Brooks, *Mark*, 221.

68. A "beautiful thing" is a technical term for charity, cf. Evans, *Mark 8:27—16:20*, 361, who attributes this idea to Daube.

to Deut 15:11a: "The poor you will always have with you, and you can help them anytime you want." In v. 4 of the same passage in Deuteronomy, we read, "There will be no poor among you," calling God's people to seek to remove poverty from the people of God. However, Deut 15:11 and this verse indicate that poverty will never be eradicated.

His words that follow indicate that disciples in the future should have concern for the poor, as they will always be there. However, they will not have Jesus physically with them. As such, the woman's act of lavish grace is to be honored. In a way, this reminds readers of 2:20 where Jesus implies that the disciples should not mourn and fast while Jesus is present; there will be plenty of time for that when he is gone. Similarly, there will be plenty of time to care for the poor; now, Jesus is to be prepared for burial. We have here then another passion prediction pointing to his imminent death (14:7).

In v. 8, Jesus vindicates the woman and interprets her actions as an anointing for his burial rather than for his coronation. Later, three other women would go to the tomb (Mary Magdalene, Mary the mother of Jacob [James], and Salome), to anoint his body. They would find that he has risen. He did not need to be anointed; this woman had done so for him.

In v. 9, Jesus declares that what she has done will be preached throughout the world in memory of her. This statement is remarkable for a range of reasons. It shows that the proclamation of the gospel will include stories such as this—seemingly insignificant moments in the life of Jesus. A myriad of other accounts of such people will be told as well. Indeed, the Gospels are full of such great tales that must all be told to proclaim the gospel fully. Jesus's statement also tells us that this woman's particular story should be told as we preach the story of Jesus's death throughout the world. It reinforces the necessity for the gospel to be preached to all the nations; here, it is the whole world (cf. 13:10). When the mission is completed, Jesus will send angels to every part of the world to gather his people (13:27). This verse also confirms that Jesus and Mark foresaw a period of mission to the world between Jesus's death and resurrection and the end of the age. Again, this pushes against the prevailing flawed consensus that Jesus and Mark believed in an imminent parousia. They did not think this, because they stated that the whole world needed to hear the gospel.[69]

This passage is also instructive when we consider how we should use the money God gives his people. Some Christians tend to be almost communistic in their zeal that every cent *has* to be used for social justice. They are right to emphasize care for the poor and needy. Nevertheless, there is a place for lavish and seemingly wasteful spending when it is motivated by a heart

---

69. Cranfield, *Gospel*, 417.

of love and worship, as it was for this woman. An example is when money is spent on church buildings. While it can seem a waste of resources, spending money to enhance the mission of God by having facilities that are welcoming, warm, and sustainable, in which people can worship God and enjoy rich Christian fellowship, and that serve as a hub for mission, is not a waste of money in every instance. Giving lavishly to the work of God involves all sorts of acts of sacrifice like this one. We need to take care we are not on the side of the disciples criticizing the likes of this woman.

Judas Betrays Jesus (14:10–11)

At this point, the narrative takes a sinister turn. Judas is mentioned for the first time since 3:19, where he is described as one of the twelve "who betrayed him." We can assume that since then, he has fully participated with the others in the life and ministry of Jesus. As such, his betrayal is horrific. He is a traitor and a turncoat. He goes to the chief priests. These were important priestly members of the group of seventy-one-member Sanhedrin that governed Israel's religion and many aspects of her political life.

Earlier, in 8:31 and 10:33, Jesus had predicted that he would be rejected and handed over by them, condemned to death. We also read in 11:18 that after Jesus cleared the temple, they were seeking to destroy him. They had questioned Jesus's authority in 11:27–33 and heard him tell the parable of the tenants, further cementing this desire (12:1–12). Earlier in the chapter, their move to sneakily arrest him and kill him was anticipated (14:1). Now, with Judas's treachery, this begins to play out. With their fervent yearning to get rid of Jesus, they are understandably delighted that their chance has come, and they promise Judas silver. He thus goes away to find an opportunity to betray Jesus (14:11–12).

Some people try to redeem Judas, but there is nothing positive in this account; he is Jesus's betrayer. His reasons for his betrayal are not clear. He was, to some extent, motivated by material greed. Luke and John tell us that he did so under the influence of Satan (Luke 12:3; John 13:2). John confirms that he was a thief and motivated by a desire for wealth (John 12:4). John also describes him as a traitor (John 18:2). In Acts 1:25, Luke tells us that he went to "to his own place," which likely means eternal condemnation.[70]

In 14:21, Jesus pronounces a woe oracle over his betrayer and tells the other disciples that "it would have been better for that man if he had not been born," confirming a terrible destiny for Judas. We noted earlier that

---

70. Peterson, *Acts of the Apostles*, 128, writes that this is "a euphemism for his final destiny, most likely death and the judgment of God beyond that."

the name Iscariot could indicate that he is one of the Sicarii, the assassins. If so, he may have become disillusioned with Jesus for continuously speaking of death and dashing his messianic aspirations. Who knows? From his day on, to be a Judas is to be a traitor. So, his memory lives on in infamy, for all the wrong reasons.

The Last Supper (14:12–25)

There is no shift of scene from the last episode, so we should assume Jesus remains in Bethany, perhaps at the home of Simon or Mary, still smelling sweetly from the nard. It is now the first day of the Feast of Unleavened Bread, the night of the Passover meal at which the lamb is sacrificed. The language may indicate that Jesus himself killed the lamb; if so, he would have slit its throat, drained the blood, and the priest would have sprinkled the blood at the base of the altar (*Tg. Onq.* Exod 24:8). If so, the scene has shifted to the temple courts. This lamb is the last sacrifice Jesus would make. Soon, he would become the final and ultimate sacrifice for the sins of the world.

Jesus's disciples ask Jesus where he wants to prepare the Passover meal, i.e., take the slaughtered lamb and eat it (14:12). Jesus, as with the quest for the donkey (11:1–6), promptly sends two unnamed disciples with clear instructions to go into the city. We have no idea who the two were except that we can rule out Judas, at least if Jesus already knows that he is his betrayer (cf. John 6:70). This likely means leaving the temple precincts and going into the city. There they would be greeted by a man carrying a jar of water whom they are to follow (14:13).

The organization indicates that Jesus has set this up, likely because he was concerned for secrecy, especially now that he knows the leaders are after him and that Judas has betrayed him. It was also imperative that Jesus celebrates his final Passover, so forever linking his death to the great feast, inaugurating a new exodus, and establishing the covenantal and sacramental meal of God's renewed people.

They are to go to the house he enters and address the owner, telling him that "the teacher asks, 'Where is my guest room where I may eat the Passover with my disciples?'" (14:14). This question may be a password to allow entry.[71] This person will show them a large upper room furnished and ready for the meal, again indicating that things are set up. They are then to make preparations there (14:15).

They follow Jesus's instructions (14:16). Some surmise that there were women involved, possibly from the family of the house owner or perhaps the

---

71. Evans, *Mark 8:27—16:20*, 374.

women traveling with Jesus. The young man who later flees naked may be from the household (14:52). If this is Mark, the writer, it may be his mother Mary's home in Jerusalem, which became the base for the Jerusalem church (Acts 12:12). There were likely women there, as it was women who traditionally tended to food preparation and cooking. If so, Mark's mother Mary may have been central to this, along with those who later went to the tomb (Mary Magdalene, Mary the mother of Jacob [James], and Salome) and perhaps Jesus's mother. Others, like Joanna and Susanna, may also have been involved (Luke 8:3). Rather than stemming from prophetic insight, this appears all well organized, under the veil of secrecy to avoid the authorities.

The details indicate that for Mark and the other Synoptic writers who follow Mark's chronology, the Last Supper is a Passover meal, and Jesus died a day later. There is a chronological problem with John, who seems to imply that the meal took place the day *before* the Passover and that Jesus died on the Passover (John 18:28; cf. John 19:14, 31, 42). Paul's reference to Jesus as the Passover lamb seemingly supports John (1 Cor 5:7). Some see John as presenting a theological perspective and accept the Synoptic chronology. Others suggest that in the year Christ was crucified, Jews of Palestine celebrated Passover on the Saturday and Diaspora Jews on Friday. Another option is that the Passover was celebrated on two days because of a dispute between Pharisees and Sadducees or because of the large crowds.[72] Some contend that the lambs were slaughtered on 13–14 Nissan and eaten on 14–15 Nissan, so on different days. Some aver that Jesus kept the Passover according to the Essene calendar. However, none of these views can be proven.[73] Overall, it was most likely the Passover meal, and France may be correct that it was held a day early at Jesus's behest because he knew that he would be killed the next day.[74] Furthermore, Jesus can still be the Passover lamb for Paul, as this is figurative rather than literal.

On the day of the sacrifice, at least for Mark, the Twelve come together with Jesus to eat the supper (14:18). There were probably also women there (cf. Luke 10:38–42) and even children who were permitted to ask questions.[75] As they share the supper in the classic ANE reclining position, no doubt according to traditional Jewish Passover custom (unless it was not the Passover meal, cf. John), Jesus announces that one of those eating with him would betray him (14:18, cf. Ps 41:9). Such betrayal by a close ally is

---

72. See Brooks, *Mark*, 225.

73. See Evans, *Mark 8:27—16:20*, 371, for detail. He hesitatingly accepts John's view and believes that the Markan perspective is confused and edited; over time, early Christians associated the final meal with the Passover.

74. France, *Gospel of Mark*, 559.

75. Evans, *Mark 8:27—16:20*, 374.

scandalous and traitorous in any culture. In ANE cultures, it is reprehensible to eat with someone and then betray that person. This revelation naturally brings great distress (literally, "grief") and shock so that, one by one, each of them denies their involvement: "Surely not me" (v. 19).

All bar one of them, of course, is speaking the truth, something readers know, but those present at the time, aside from Judas and Jesus, do not. Matthew 26:25 and John 13:25–26, in different ways, have Jesus indicate that it is Judas. In Mark, Jesus only specifies that it is one of the twelve who is eating with him (14:20). To this point in the narrative, this could indicate any of them. Jesus again notes his death to come and, as at other points, indicates it is the fulfillment of Scripture.[76] In his saying concerning the Son of Man going as is written, Jesus draws on the suffering Messiah of Ps 22 and fuses the Son of Man of Daniel with the suffering of the Messiah and the Servant.

He states how terrible it will be for his betrayer with a "woe" imprecation ("Woe to that one ... " cf. 13:17). This statement confirms that the destiny of Judas is eternal destruction (14:21 cf. Acts 1:25). This horrendous fate is reinforced with "it would have been better for him if he had not been born."

Mark then records the institution of the Lord's Supper, which for Christians transcends Passover, now fulfilled in the final Passover Lamb (1 Cor 5:7, cf. John 1:29). However, unlike Passover, which is celebrated once a year, the Lord's Supper should be remembered each time believers gather together in worship. It is a covenantal celebration reminding believers of the pivotal moment in the Christian story. While they are eating, Jesus takes a loaf of the unleavened bread that was eaten at the festival, blesses it,[77] and breaks it, saying, "Take it; this is my body" (14:22).

How did the disciples who were expecting war and lacked any notion of a dead Messiah understand Jesus's words? It is likely that the words "my body" would not have been understood as Jesus's corpse. It could be have been a collective singular referring to the bodies that he and the disciples would kill and leave lying in the open as he demolished the gentiles opposing God—"my bodies killed."[78] Alternatively, it could even have been seen as a symbol of their unity as one body. "Broken" did not have to be

---

76. Especially Isa 53; Ps 22; Zech 13:7; Dan 7:21, 25; 9:26.

77. One blessing from *m. Ber.* 6:1 reads: "Blessed are You, O Lord our God, King of the universe, who brings forth bread from the earth."

78. See LXX where *sōma* is used of corpses, often after war: Gen 15:11; Josh 8:29; 1 Kgdms (1 Sam) 31:10, 12; 3 Kgdms (1 Kgs) 13:24, 28, 29; 4 Kgdms (2 Kgs) 19:35; 1 Chron 10:12; 28:1; 1 Esdr 3:4; 2 Esdr 19:26 (Neh 9:26); Esth 9:14; Jdt 13:9; Tob 1:18; 1 Macc 11:4; 2 Macc 9:7, 9, 29; 12:26, 39.

his death but could have referred to wounds experienced as he gave his all to defeat the enemies of God. Of course, none of this is true. The breaking of bread was a symbolic act pointing to his violent death.[79] The *estin* "is" here does not mean that the bread *is* his body as in transubstantiation but "signifies" or "represents."

He then takes up a goblet of wine. In the Mishnah, during the Passover meal, four goblets of wine were drunk. As the second cup was drunk, the Passover story was recited after a child's question (*m. Pesaḥ.* 10:4). France reasons it may have been then that Jesus spoke of the redemption taking place through him. Alternatively, Jesus said it over the cup of blessing, the third cup after the main course.[80]

He then gives thanks[81] and offers it to all of them (including his betrayer), and they all drink from it. They appear to have shared the same cup, including Judas and the others. Sharing the meal with Judas is an astonishing act of grace, considering what he is about to do. The sharing of the cup calls to mind 10:38–39, where Jacob (James) and John boldly believe they can drink of the cup of the suffering. They can drink of the cup of the Last Supper that represents his death, but yet they lack the courage to join him in his suffering. Their day will come when Jacob (James) is beheaded at the behest of Agrippa I ten to thirteen years later (Acts 12:1–2) and two to three decades later when John is imprisoned in Patmos.

Jesus then says, "This is my blood of the covenant, which is poured out for many." For initial hearers, "my blood" did not have to have been Jesus's blood. It could have represented the blood he would shed as he destroyed the enemies of God—"blood shed by me." However, Jesus does not have this in mind; it is his own blood.

This meal is a cataclysmic moment in history. It recalls Exod 24:1–8 when the covenant was established with the throwing of blood against the altar. In v. 8, we read, "And Moses took the blood and threw it on the people, and said, 'Behold the blood of the covenant.'" Hence it looks back to this event. It also looks forward to the long-awaited new covenant dreamed of by the prophets.[82] Jesus announces the inauguration of this covenant through his blood ("my blood"), which is about to be shed. The

---

79. Evans, *Mark 8:27—16:20*, 374, notes other prophetic symbolic acts (cf. Isa 20:2; Jer 19:10; Jer 28:10; Acts 21:11).

80. France, *Gospel of Mark*, 569.

81. The blessing above *m. Ber.* 6:1 includes: "Blessed are You, O Lord our God, King of the universe, who creates the fruit of the vine."

82. Isa 42:6; 49:8; 55:3; 59:21; 61:8; Jer 31:31–34; 32:40; 50:5; Ezek 16:60; 34:25; 37:26; Zech 9:11; Mal 3:1.

writer of Hebrews recognizes this aspect of the covenant; Jesus's blood ratifies the new covenant.[83]

Mark does not record it as the *new* covenant, as do Luke and Paul (Luke 22:20; 1 Cor 11:25). Still, it is arguably implied. "Which is poured out for many" recalls the Servant covenantal references. In Isa 42:6, God gives the Servant "as a covenant for the people, a light for the nations" (cf. 49:8). This Servant will die, bearing his people's iniquities, pouring his soul out for them (Isa 53:10–12). He gives his life as a ransom for many (10:45). He is the Servant Messiah through whom the covenant is established. Even more than with the bread, there is no hint of transubstantiation.

Jesus then finishes the supper scene by telling the disciples solemnly that "I will not drink again of the fruit of the vine until that day when I drink it anew in the kingdom of God" (14:23–25). This statement speaks of his departure from the world of vineyards and again is foreboding. However, it is also encouraging as it speaks of the day in the future when the kingdom is consummated, and Jesus will again drink from the earth's vineyards at the eschatological feast.[84] Jesus drinking again from the vines of the world suggests the restoration of the cosmos (Rev 21—22).

Jesus Predicts Peter's Denial (14:26–31)

Mark records that they sing a song and go to the Mount of Olives (14:26). The mention of singing is the only explicit reference to Jesus or the disciples doing so, although it can be assumed that like all Jews who attended synagogues, they sang regularly. Some read into the lack of singing in the Gospels that we sing too much in the contemporary church. While it can be argued on other grounds that music is overly dominant in our worship,[85] this is a weak argument, given the many commands to sing in the biblical narrative (Eph 5:16; Col 3:16). The actual song is probably one of the Hallel Psalms associated with the Passover (Pss 113—118). It may again be Ps 118, which was already featured twice in the Jerusalem narrative (11:10; 12:10–11).[86] The events of the supper point to Jesus's death. As

---

83. Heb 9:14, 18–22, 25; 10:4, 19; 12:24.

84. See Isa 25:6; Luke 13:28–29; 14:15–24; 22:30.

85. Keown, "How Much Should We Sing?," 4–13.

86. Citing Ps 118:22–23, 25. While any of these psalms would be appropriate, another possibility that stands out is Ps 116, where the psalmist sings of being encompassed in "the snares of death" and "the pangs of Sheol" and cries out for deliverance (vv. 3–4). This deliverance is experienced (vv. 8–9). The psalm also refers to the blessedness of the deaths of God's holy people (v. 15) and names Jerusalem (v. 19).

throughout Mark, there is little evidence that the disciples realize that his passion is imminent.

On the Mount of Olives, Jesus predicts that they will all fall away (*skandalizō*). Jesus's prediction is another example of his prophetic insight seen at points in Mark's Gospel (see on 2:8). *Skandalizō* is the same term used in 4:17, where hearers of the word fall away due to persecution and where little ones are caused to fall away.[87] Their falling away fulfills 4:17, while Peter's restoration shows that people can be restored to a saving relationship with Christ.

Here, Jesus is quoting Zech 13:7: "I will strike the shepherd, and the sheep will be scattered" (14:27). The shepherd is Christ (cf. Ezek 34:23–24), a common metaphor applied to his ministry (6:34).[88] He describes his disciples as his sheep, who will be scattered when the shepherd is struck (killed; another passion prediction). Such predictions are found across the OT and Jewish tradition.[89] Importantly, this occurs on the Mount of Olives for it is from this mountain that Jesus will ascend, and to this mountain he will return and bring an end to death and suffering (Acts 1:9–12; Zech 14:4).

He then tells them that when he arises (resurrection), he will go before them to Galilee (14:28). There is no evidence that the disciples understood what this meant. This prediction anticipates the resurrection, where the young man will instruct the women to tell the men to go to meet him in Galilee (16:7). His words anticipate not only the resurrection but also the appearances to come in Galilee, even if Mark does not record them. We need to read Matt 28 for this.

Peter again functions as spokesman with great boldness, declaring, "Even if all fall away, I will not!" (14:29). Jesus responds by stating that on this very night, before the rooster crows twice (the early morning), Peter will deny him three times (14:30). Stubbornly and seemingly courageously, Peter reasserts his determination, telling Jesus that he will not deny him and, if necessary, that he is prepared to die with him (14:31).[90] The others echo his rebuttals. As they heard Jesus speak in this way, they likely understood it militarily: the battle was coming, and Jesus thinks our hearts will melt and our courage fail us. They likely saw it as Jesus firing them up for battle, rather than an actual prediction. Their response was "No way!" Their

---

87. See Mark 9:42, 43, 45, 47; see also 6:3.

88. See also Matt 9:36; 18:12; 25:32; Luke 15:3–7; John 10:1–17.

89. See Num 27:17; 1 Kgs 22:17; 2 Chr 18:16; Ezek 34:8, 12, 15; Zech 10:2; Bar 4:26; Pss. Sol. 17:4, 21, 26–28; Tg. Isa 6:13; 8:18; 35:6; 53:8.

90. See also the accounts of the Maccabean martyrs in 2 Macc 6–7.

reality was "Yes way!" However, there was a way to come back. Judas did not take it. Peter and the others did.

Anguish in Gethsemane (14:32–42)

After the supper, Jesus goes with his disciples to the garden of Gethsemane on the Mount of Olives. The mount was traditionally a place of prayer (cf. Exod 11:23; 2 Sam 15:32).[91] Gethsemane means "oil press," and its location is now uncertain.[92] It was a favorite place for Jesus, who went there often with his disciples (cf. John 18:2). Their frequent visits possibly explain how Judas could find him.

While there, Jesus instructs eight of the Twelve (minus the three and Judas) and any others there (e.g., the naked man, 14:51) to sit and wait while he goes to pray with his inner circle of Peter, Jacob (James), and John (14:32–33).[93]

Jesus is full of deep distress and anguish. He tells the disciples, "My soul is greatly grieved to the point of death."[94] Here, *psychē* (soul) speaks of his whole inner being, which was in deep travail. This powerful expression of grief indicates the reality of his suffering and pain and his genuinely frail humanity (cf. Heb 4:15). Jesus knows what he will face and is profoundly challenged by it.

He then leaves the three disciples and commands them to remain there and watch from nearby (14:34). What comes in v. 38 suggests they were expected to pray. He goes further into the garden to cry out to God. In Luke 22:41, this is "a stone's throw," i.e., less than a hundred meters.[95] The Greek *piptō* suggests he does not throw a stone but throws himself on the ground. Likely he was prostrating himself before God in a position of worship and humility.[96]

---

91. Evans, *Mark 8:27—16:20*, 409.

92. See Nease, "Gethsemane," who notes possible locations. First, it could be across the Kidron Valley on the western slopes of the Mount. Second, the garden area with a number of old olive trees preserved by the Franciscans, including the Church of All Nations (this is the area tourists visit), is possible. Otherwise, it may be near the former site at other sites maintained by different denominations.

93. See also Mark 5:37–43; 9:2–8; 13:37.

94. This is the language of lament from the OT: Pss 42:4–5, 11 (LXX 41:5, 6, 12; MT 42:5–6, 12); 43:5 (LXX 42:5); Jonah 4:9; Sir 37:2.

95. Having been a cricketer, I know that a really good arm can throw a cricket ball one hundred m plus, and so this must be less. Depending on the stone, perhaps one might think about fifty m (54 yds), give or take?

96. See Gen 17:1–3; Num 14:5; 16:4, 22, 45; 20:6.

His prayer is a lesson on how to pray in moments of crisis. It shows us that sometimes God will not save us from suffering, as it is an essential part of his plans. It tells us, however, that we should still pray for deliverance in such instances. God will strengthen us and grow our character through such times of crisis (Rom 5:2–5; Jas 1:2–4). When we pray, like Jesus here, we should trust God for the outcome. We should not despair in unanswered prayer; there is no such thing. God may not answer as *we* want, but as *he* wills, even if it is just with comfort, strength, and character refinement. Here, God's purpose is to save the world. Hence, Jesus *has* to die. God will not deliver him from the pain, but he will cause him to remain faithful until "it is finished" (John 19:30).

He begins, "If it is possible." Jesus is not questioning God's ability to do anything, as v. 36 indicates. However, he is conceding that it may not be possible, because it is through his death that God will inaugurate the new covenant and bring forgiveness to many. He prays that the hour may pass from him, asking for deliverance from the horrors he knows he is about to face—as evidenced by his earlier predictions. Here we see Jesus's preparedness to walk the path to the cross, but his desire to find another way, if there is one.

What he prays is further explained in v. 36. In ANE custom, prayer was usually spoken aloud and not silently.[97] Jesus begins by addressing God as "Abba, Father." *Abba* is the Aramaic for "father," and so we have another example of Aramaic retained in the text with Mark translating it for Greek and Roman readers.[98] The term has been understood to be baby language akin to *dada* or *daddy*, but this evidence is now questioned.[99] However, it was rarely used in prayer outside of the NT and carried some sense of familial intimacy.[100] Paul also uses this language of God (Rom 8:15–16; Gal 4:6). Both his and Jesus's uses indicate a deep relational connection with God.

Jesus then declares his absolute faith in God for anything with the words, "Everything is possible for you." Such statements of God's omnipotence are found in 9:23 and 10:27. Knowing that God can do anything, and yet fully aware that he must die for the world, he pleads with God "to take this cup from me." As in 10:39, the cup is that of his suffering in which he drinks God's wrath on sin. It also alludes to the cup at the Last Supper,

---

97. Evans, *Mark 8:27—16:20*, 412.

98. See also 5:41; 7:1, 34; 14:36; 15:34.

99. Barr, "'*Abbā* Isn't 'Daddy,'" 28–47.

100. See Silva, *NIDNTTE*, 1:85–87, drawing on the evidence of Joachim Jeremias, *Prayers of Jesus*, 11–65. R. Nehemiah spoke "the will of Abba in heaven" (Lev. Rab. 32:1 [on Lev 20:4]). R. Ḥanan ha-Neḥba, urged people to pray "Abba, Abba, give us rain" and distinguishes between the Abba who provides rain and one that does not (*b. Taʻan.* 23b).

which symbolizes his shed blood (14:23–24). The cup refers to the terrible humiliation, pain, and death he is about to endure, of which he seems fully aware. He is asking God to take it away.

Jesus then adds the caveat, "Yet not what I will, but what you will" (14:35–36). Even though he has absolute faith in God, his Father, and knows that he can do all things, Jesus allows for God's will to rule over his preferences. Sometimes, zealous faith-motivated Christians urge us never to concede to God's will in this way. Clearly, they are wrong, for Jesus is our model. His words also remind us of the Lord's Prayer, where we pray, "Your will be done" (Matt 6:10). Such verses indicate that true faith in God allows for his will to rule over our desires and perspectives. Recognizing that God's will is what matters is essential for balancing extreme statements on the power of faith, such as 11:22–24. Faith can move mountains; sometimes God does not want the mountain to move. His will reigns.

Here Jesus's prayer is not answered with a yes but is rejected, with God effectively saying, "No!" However, the effect of the prayer is that Jesus is empowered with sufficient courage to accept God's answer and face God's will for his life, to suffer and die to save the world. Praise God!

Jesus then returns and arouses and rebukes his disciples, who failed to obey his command to stay awake. He warns them to watch and pray lest they fall into temptation (here the temptation was to fall away and deny Jesus). Jesus states one of the great truisms: the spirit (our desire) is willing, but our flesh is weak (14:37–38, cf. Rom 7—8). Our weakness is why prayer is so critical. Through prayer, our body is strengthened to yield to God's desires by the Spirit.

Jesus then returns and prays a third time for God to spare him from the ignominy and agony of the cross. The threefold prayer of Jesus calls to mind the threefold prayer of Paul for the removal of his thorn in the flesh. As with Jesus, Paul asked God to deliver him. Three times God said, "No!" Nevertheless, Paul learned through this that his thorn was a gift for him to guard him against arrogance and for God's strength to be seen in his weakness (2 Cor 12:7–9). It is sometimes the same with us in our trials; through them, God refines us and causes us to be more dependent on his power than on our own strength.

Again, Jesus returns to find the disciples asleep (14:39–40). He rebukes them for their failure and tells them that his hour has come and his betrayer is approaching. Obviously, this is Judas with a mob to arrest him (14:41–42).

The repeated warnings not to sleep but to pray are essential for discipleship. There is a time to plead with God, to arise in the night, to resist sleep, and to be watchful and pray. This is one of them. An implied lesson here is that of Peter, who failed to pray and then failed to persevere and so denied Christ; if he had prayed, he might have successfully stood for Christ. We must learn this lesson and be prayerful!

Questions

- Considering the question of whether we should read the widow's offering as a positive example or negative (condemning the scribes), what do we learn from it?
- Is Mark 13 about the fall of Jerusalem, the end of the age, or both?
- From Mark 13, on what signs can we rely to help us get a sense of the return of Christ (knowing we can never know the actual date)?
- How should we live as we await the second coming?
- What do we learn about money and worship from the anointing of Jesus at Bethany by Mary?
- Is Mary's story being told throughout the world as much as it should be?
- Why did Judas betray Jesus?
- What did the disciples think Jesus meant when he spoke of the Passover bread and wine as his body broken and blood poured out?
- What do we learn about prayer from God refusing Jesus's Gethsemane prayer?
- What do the respective stories of Judas and Peter tell us about the Christian life?
- Was there a way back for Judas if he had chosen it?

Lesson Eleven: Jesus's Arrest, Trial, Crucifixion, Burial, and Resurrection (14:43—16:8, 20)

Betrayal and Arrest (14:43–52)

As Jesus spoke of his approaching betrayer, "one of the twelve" arrives. Notably, his name is dropped from the narrative; however, observant readers recognize Judas. One can only imagine the horror and anger felt by the other eleven as Jesus's prediction of betrayal is confirmed. He had with him an armed mob with swords and clubs sent by the Jewish priests, scribes, and elders to arrest Jesus (v. 43). Jewish leaders sending a mob to arrest Jesus sounds crazy from our point of view from "men of the cloth"; however, it is well attested that the ruling priests of the first century were unscrupulous and capable of endorsing thuggery.[1] Furthermore, Christian history is littered with church leaders who have been prepared to kill in the name of their so-called faith. Reference to the three groups recalls Jesus's first prediction of his rejection and death (8:31).

Judas had likely set up a signal by which Jesus could be identified, a kiss. The *philēma* was a touch on the lips. The kiss was practiced widely and spoke of a close familial bond. It also indicated equality of status, as only people of equal standing kissed one another on the lips. Those of

---

1. See Josephus, *Ant.* 20:181, notes that "they actually were so brazen as to send slaves to the threshing floors to receive the tithes that were due to the priests, with the result that *the poorer priests starved to death*"; 20.206–207: "But Ananias had servants who were utter rascals and who, *combining operations with the most reckless men*, would go to the threshing floors and *take by force* the tithes of the priests; nor did they refrain from *beating those who refused to give*. The ruling priests were guilty of the same practices as his slaves, and no one could stop them" (Loeb, italics added). Cf. *J.W.* 6.300–309. There are a number of rabbinic texts that bemoan their attitude; cf. Evans, *Mark 8:27—16:20*, 423, for detail.

lower status would kiss their superior on the cheek or feet.[2] We see this in the holy kiss practiced in the NT churches.[3] Here, we have a decidedly unholy kiss, a traitorous kiss whereby a "brother" betrays another by the most intimate of relational acts.

He addresses him as rabbi, possibly to further aid identification. The epithet is dripping with irony, since for Judas, Jesus is no longer his teacher (let alone Messiah), but a traitor to the nation to be handed over to be killed. Realizing that Judas has led them to their victim, the leaders seize Jesus (vv. 45–46). Interestingly, this is Judas's last word in this Gospel, and it is false.

Perhaps inspired to believe that this was the moment of a messianic uprising, one of the disciples strikes the servant of the high priest with his sword, severing his ear (v. 47). John identifies him as Simon Peter and the servant as Malchus (John 18:10). Peter here partially lives up to his determination to remain with Jesus to the end and not deny him. Mark gives no details of Jesus healing the slave or his rebuke of Peter.[4] Ideally, this should have been the first and last act of retributive aggression by one of Jesus's disciples. We are not to respond to violence with violence.

It is interesting to note here that the high priest has a slave (*doulos*). Slaves were prevalent among wealthy Romans. However, while there are OT Jews who had slaves (Gen 21:10–13; Eccl 2:7), Israel's people were not to have slaves from among their people. They could have slaves from other nations (Lev 25:44–46).[5] Their abhorrence of slavery was based on God's delivering them from bondage as slaves in Egypt.[6] Jewish slaves were to be set free after six years unless voluntarily choosing to remain in bondage (Exod 21:2–10; Deut 15:17). If a person was poor and sold him- or herself into slavery, that person was to be treated as a hired worker or sojourner and was to be set free in the year of Jubilee (Lev 25:39). If the high priest was observing the law, this slave was a foreigner. If not, the high priest was violating the law. More importantly, we see a glaring contrast between the high priest and the Messiah, who had no slaves but came to serve others (10:45).

In Mark's account, Jesus speaks to his antagonists, asking whether they have come in this way to arrest him with swords and clubs as if he is a *lēstēs*. The term can mean a thief, bandit, or an insurrectionist. The latter is likely correct.[7] He queries their seizing him with a mob when they could have taken

---

2. Herodotus, *Hist.* 1.134.
3. Rom 16:16; 1 Cor 16:20; 2 Cor 13:12; 1 Thess 5:26. See further Ehorn, "Kiss."
4. See Matt 26:52–55; Luke 22:51; John 18:11, who fill out these details.
5. See also 1 Sam 4:9; 1 Kgs 9:21–22; Jer 34:9–16.
6. See Exod 1:13–14; 6:5; Lev 25:42; 26:13; Deut 15:15; 16:12; 24:18, 22; Ezra 9:9.
7. Evans, *Mark 8:27—16:20*, 425, supports "insurrectionist" and sees Jesus referring

him at any time while teaching in the temple courts every day. We know that they did not do so because of Jesus's popularity and their consequential fear of a rebellion, opting to take him by stealth (12:12; 14:1-2). Jesus then states, "But let the Scriptures be fulfilled" (12:48-49). What Scriptures are in view is unclear, but perhaps the most apparent link is Isa 53:12: "He was numbered among the transgressors" (Luke 22:37). Alternatively, it speaks more broadly of the whole Scriptures that point to a suffering Messiah.

In v. 50, this causes the courage of Peter and the other disciples to fail them. They *all* flee, and Jesus is left alone with his antagonists. His earlier predictions that the sheep would be scattered and that they would all fall away is fulfilled (14:27-29; cf. Zech 13:7).

The scene concludes with one of the most puzzling and amusing moments in Scripture. It features a young man (*neaniskos*), someone between twenty-one and twenty-eight years of age.[8] Initially, this young man alone dared to follow Jesus. However, he is grabbed, causing him to leave his garment and flee naked (12:52). We learn in the next passage that Peter follows at a distance. If this is a reference to the author, then the two bravest of the disciples worked together to write this Gospel. Still, the courage of both men failed. While a range of options has been given for this man,[9] it seems best to see it as an autobiographical note of Mark, the author.[10]

Before the Sanhedrin (14:53-65)

The section from Mark 14:53-72 is another of Mark's sandwiches, Jesus's trial and condemnation framed by Peter's denial.

---

to the huge number of people who sought to take over kingships at the time.

8. Philo, *Opif.* 105. In *The Secret Gospel of Mark*, he comes and asks Jesus the secrets of the kingdom; however, this is a later Gnostic development.

9. Evans, *Mark 8:27—16:20*, 428, notes John the son of Zebedee (hardly likely, as he is one of the Twelve); Jacob (James), the brother of Jesus; or the rich ruler. Some find background to this in Joseph fleeing Potiphar's wife (Gen 39:12-13); others in Amos 2:16 or Isa 40:30-31. But there is nothing really to link these to this. People are fascinated by this account and look for symbolic meaning.

10. See Gundry, *Mark*, 882. He entertains the idea that Judas and the arrestors went to Mark's house, where the disciples had eaten the Last Supper, looking for Jesus. Then, not finding Jesus there, Judas went to the garden to look for him. John Mark, having been wakened by the betrayer coming to his house and without having had time to get fully dressed, trailed Judas there.

Mark 14:53–72

A[1] Peter's denial (14:53–54)

B *Jesus's trial and condemnation (14:55–65)*

A[2] Peter's denial (14:66–72)

Jesus is led away by the group to the high priest. At the time, Joseph Caiaphas was in the role. He was son-in-law to Annas, high priest before him (AD 6–15) and still influential in Jewish politics.[11] The Romans appointed the high priest at this time. In John's Gospel, he speaks of the profitability of Jesus dying rather than the whole nation, which John interpreted as a prophecy (John 11:49–52; 18:14). Josephus also mentions his installation and removal from office in the period AD 18 to 36.[12] A grave has been found in Jerusalem with the family "Caiaphas" on two ossuaries, including one with the name "Joseph, son of Caiaphas," which may refer to him and his family's tomb.[13]

The assembly of the various leaders recalls Jesus's prediction that they would reject him in 8:31. The gathering of the Sanhedrin shows meticulous planning. This get-together was no impromptu meeting.[14]

Mark includes details concerning Peter, which become important in his denial. Showing superior courage to the rest of the disciples, he has followed Jesus and is with the servants in the courtyard by the fire (14:54). Being among the servants put Peter in considerable danger as he had earlier sliced the ear off the priest's slave, and he was also sitting among Sanhedrin officials.[15]

As Mark's readers already knew, the leaders had been unsuccessful debating Jesus publicly to find a reason to condemn him (11:27—12:34). Now, they had devised a plan to take him by stealth (14:1). Having seized him, they needed evidence to condemn him to death (14:55). The Sanhedrin had significant authority, but under Roman rule, they were not permitted to sentence someone to death (John 18:13).[16] Their approach was to give a reason to hand him over the Romans to have him killed.

---

11. See Matt 26:3, 57; Luke 3:2; John 11:49; 18:13–14, 24, 28; Acts 4:6.

12. Josephus, *Ant.* 18:34–35, 95.

13. Kennedy, "Caiaphas." Evans, *Mark 8:27—16:20*, 441.

14. Contra Evans, *Mark 8:27—16:20*, 441. Although hastily organized, the ability of all to attend quickly suggests something for which the council was ready at any time.

15. See earlier in the translation note on *hyperetēs*.

16. Incidentally, this shows how the killing of Stephen was completely illegal (Acts 7).

Two to three eyewitnesses were required under Jewish law to have him condemned and handed over to die.[17]

Many came and gave false witness to Jesus's illegal activity; however, they could not agree (14:56). Out of these inconsistent testimonies, the only specific charge referred to a supposed threat from Christ to destroy the temple and in three days, to build another without human hands. There is little in Mark's narrative to help us comprehend this apart from the temple clearing episode. However, Mark's account includes no such reference and prediction. A possibility is Jesus's prediction in 13:2 that the temple will be destroyed. Still, this was spoken to only one of his disciples (13:1). His mention of the "abomination that causes desolation" in 13:14 was spoken to only four of the disciples. It hardly accounts for this testimony.

John's version of the temple clearing includes a saying that may lie behind the testimony. John then interprets the saying as a reference to Jesus's death and resurrection (John 2:18–22). It could be that this saying caused the rumor mentioned here in Mark.

The charge itself is intriguing and has the ring of authenticity. As implied in John, in the saying, Jesus was speaking of the destruction of the Jerusalem temple and God building a temple comprised of people.[18] This saying fits with Jesus as the cornerstone (12:10) and the rending of the temple curtain, opening up access to the holy of holies for all humankind (15:29). Nonetheless, it is hardly surprising that hearers understood such a saying as a threat against the temple. However, the testimonies lacked consistency. If there had been consistent testimony, Jesus would assuredly have been condemned to death on this charge alone. Some thirty years later, another Jesus, Jesus ben Ananias, was put to death for making this very threat.[19]

In the interrogation by the high priest, Jesus is challenged to answer the charge. Jesus says nothing. Jesus's near silence here and before Pilate (15:2–5) fulfill Isaiah's prediction of a lamb led to slaughter without opening his mouth (Isa 53:7).

One of the critical moments in Mark comes in 14:61, as the high priest directly questions Jesus's identity. He asks if he is the Messiah and the Son of the Blessed One. The two ideas are linked in the priest's thought (see on 1:1). As a pious Jew, the priest chooses not to use God's name as an act of reverence toward Yahweh.

Jesus's response is stunning and provocative. First, he says *egō eimi*. This simple phrase can be translated, "I am he." Alternatively, Jesus is

---

17. Num 35:30; Deut 17:6; 19:15; Matt 18:16; 2 Cor 13:1; 1 Tim 5:19; Heb 10:28.
18. See also 1 Cor 3:10–17; 6:19; Eph 2:18–22.
19. Josephus, *War* 6:300–309.

taking things a step further and answering affirmatively, while using the name of Yahweh. If so, he is identifying himself with God the Father. Scholarship is torn on this, with many playing down such a thought.[20] Still, in 12:35–37, using Ps 110:1, Jesus had already identified himself as Adonai reigning at God's right hand. Furthermore, in 6:50, the same *egō eimi* formula is used as he walked on the sea. As discussed on that passage, this likely implies Jesus's divine identity. In John's Gospel, the many "I am" sayings more certainly point in this direction.[21] At the very least, here, his statement may have been provocative.

Jesus's next statement that those present will see the Son of Man seated at the right hand of the Power and coming with the clouds of heaven draws directly on two important OT predictions of the one to come: the Son of Man in Dan 7:13–14 and the Messiah who will sit at God's hand until his enemies are under his feet in Ps 110:1. Here, Jesus is associating himself with both of these two figures. As noted above, Jesus had already drawn on Ps 110:1 in 12:35–37. We should note here another name for God: the Power. Such a name for God speaks both of God's omnipotence and also of Jesus choosing not to use God's name directly (like the high priest).

Like the theologian he must be in order to have been high priest, he understands but repudiates Jesus's claims; and as a religious politician desperate to protect his nation and religion, his response is predictable and direct (vv. 63–64). The tearing of the clothes as an expression of rage, horror, or grief is not uncommon in the biblical narrative.[22] Such a response shows he is utterly appalled at Jesus's claims. He decries the need for more witnesses, for to him, Jesus has condemned himself with his words.

His cry concerning Jesus's blasphemy indicates that he considers Jesus's words a violation of the third commandment (Exod 20:7), a contravention of God's supreme honor and deity. His reaction could be due to Jesus's assumption of the divine name "I am," something which would easily justify his death (cf. John 8:58). His claim to be Messiah would not in and of itself deserve the death penalty. However, his acceptance of the title "Son of the Blessed One" may have been seen as identification with God in being (cf. John 5:18).

Assuming the name "Son of Man" would not likely have provoked his death, as this was used of people and prophets. However, his assertion that

---

20. See Evans, *Mark 8:27—16:20*, 450.

21. The Greek *egō eimi* translates God's name when Moses meets God at the burning bush (Exod 3:14). Similar to the view I have expressed here is Brooks, *Mark*, 243.

22. E.g., Gen 37:29; 44:13; Num 14:6; Josh 7:6; Judg 11:35; 2 Sam 1:11; 13:19; 1 Kgs 21:27; 2 Kgs 2:12; 5:7; 6:30; 11:14; 18:37; 19:1; 22:11; 2 Chron 12:13; 34:19; Esth 4:1; Job 1:20; Isa 37:1; 1 Macc 4:39; 11:71.

he would be seen "seated at the right hand of the Power" suggests a very close identification with God and his appointment as God's regent. Similarly, the claim that he would be "coming with the clouds of heaven" suggests him coming as the agent of God to destroy God's enemies.

These words seem a direct challenge to the leaders' authority and a warning of their destruction. In reality, they are the combined effect of Jesus drawing together in himself these threads of Israel's hope that causes the reaction.

Considering Jesus's bitter opposition to the leaders and their radical monotheism (which is not unlike that of zealous Muslims today), it is not surprising that the high priest and the whole of the Sanhedrin condemned Jesus to death. It is unclear whether "all" should be seen as hyperbole or not. In Mark, later, one of its members, Joseph of Arimathea, will come and take his body for burial (15:43–46; cf. Luke 23:50–51). John's Gospel speaks of Nicodemus, who was also a member of the council, being active in this as well (John 19:38–39; see also John 3:1–15; 7:50). Either they were also part of this but later changed their minds, or Mark is speaking hyperbolically. Either way, they are complicit in their silence.

Their response is vile and violent. As in many cultures, spitting is a mark of contempt and shames the recipient.[23] In their spitting on Jesus, they fulfill the disgracing of God's Servant expected by Isaiah (Isa 50:6). They also fulfill the prediction of the maltreatment of the Son of Man in 10:34. The Roman soldiers would spit on Jesus as they mocked him later (15:19; Matt 27:30). There is some irony here, as Jesus has twice in Mark's narrative healed with spittle (7:33; 8:23). These antagonists spit to destroy.

They also blindfold him and strike him with their fists (cf. Isa 50:6). They mock him, again fulfilling 10:34. Their command to "Prophesy!" is also ironic, as their treatment of him was itself a fulfillment of the prophecies concerning Isaiah's Servant and the Davidic Messiah of Ps 22. Their demand that he prophesy shows their spiritual blindness to the many prophecies that ironically they were fulfilling in their maltreatment of Jesus. He is then taken away by guards, who beat him again. So, Jesus's physical suffering begins (14:65). What a terrifying and horrific experience, especially for the creator of the cosmos. Horror! Nonetheless, his appalling maltreatment was for us, as he took upon himself the consequences of our sin.

---

23. E.g., Num 12:14; Deut 25:9; Job 17:6; 30:10.

Peter Denies Jesus (14:66–72)

The narrative now returns to Peter by the fire in the courtyard. The homes of the wealthy and powerful had large and impressive courtyards and housed many servants. As noted on 14:47, the high priest's ownership of slaves contrasts him with the one who came to be a slave, not to be served by them. The girl now mentioned is likely a foreigner, as Jews should not have Israelite slaves. That she recognizes Peter as one of Jesus's followers suggests she had heard him speak with a Galilean accent or had seen him at some point. Her accusation puts Peter in a dangerous position, with Jesus on trial in the house. As Peter had cut off the ear of a slave of the high priest, the threat is extreme (14:47).

Peter's courage fails him. He denies the charge, the first of his three denials Jesus had predicted (14:30). Claiming incomprehension, Peter lies (v. 68). His fear is seen as he moves away to the gate. However, the girl is persistent and follows him, beginning to say to those milling about, perhaps awaiting the outcome of the trial, that Peter is "one of them" (14:69). Again, Peter denies this accusation.

Then, perhaps after some of the bystanders had discussed this possibility, one speaks up and emphatically states that "certainly, you are one of them." He confirms this by observing that he is a Galilean, probably because he recognized his accent (v. 70).

At this point, Peter's courage completely evaporates, and he reacts strongly. We see his propensity to anger and swearing (making his coming transformation even more remarkable). He begins to curse and invokes an oath as he swears to them that he does not know the man they were talking about (v. 71). Peter's courage has evaporated into anger and lies.

A rooster crows the second time, causing Peter to recall Jesus's prophecy. The Greek suggests that Peter throws himself down onto the ground forcefully. He then weeps, showing his pain and remorse. Peter's bold assertions and then his failure are the tragic story of a man who loses courage and like a cornered rat, lies, denies, and is exposed as a weakling who cannot follow through on his words.

However, we must take care not to be too hard on Peter. It was indeed a dangerous situation, and if he had acknowledged his connection to Jesus, he might have ended up on the cross beside Jesus. We all fall short of the glory of God in many ways. Peter came back from this and became a great leader who never again denied Jesus. Later, according to tradition, Peter had the courage to die by crucifixion upside down in Nero's circus.[24]

---

24. Eusebius, *Hist. eccl.* 2.25.5–8.

So, while this time Peter failed, we are given hope in his story—hope that we in our weakness can come back and become great. Sadly, the same cannot be said of Judas.

Before Pilate (15:1–15)

Very early the next day (Friday), the leaders of Israel, having decided Jesus must die (14:64), bind him and deliver him to Pilate (v. 1). Pontius Pilate was the Roman prefect of Judea in the period AD 26 to 37.[25] He usually resided in Caesarea Maritima, but during important times like Passover, stayed in Jerusalem, either at Fortress Antonia or Herod's palace. Evidence from Philo, Josephus, and Luke indicates that he was a despicable man. Philo describes him as a "man of an inflexible, stubborn, and cruel disposition," adding that "briberies, insults, robberies, outrages, wanton injuries, executions without trial, and endless and supremely grievous cruelty" marked his administration.[26] Josephus also relays several examples of his brutality and says he was ultimately removed from office for his brutality against the Samaritans. In Luke 13:1, the prefect's brutality is also mentioned when Jesus is told about "the Galileans whose blood Pilate had mingled with their sacrifices."[27]

In Mark, Jesus appears before him. Mark makes no mention of Pilate sending him to Herod Antipas (cf. Luke 23:6–16). However, if Pilate was domiciled in Herod's palace, as is likely, then leaving out that detail makes sense, with the other Gospel writers conflating the account. What is agreed is that in all accounts, Jesus is interrogated by Pilate, and no basis to sentence him to death is found. Yet, under pressure from Israel's leaders, Pilate sentences Jesus to death.

Mark records some of Pilate's interrogation of Jesus, raising the question of the source of the material. It could be a reconstruction or a reminiscence from the risen Christ passed onto the disciples, or perhaps one of those present became a Christian and relayed the information to Mark (or Peter).

Pilate asks him first if he is the "king of the Jews." The term is a Roman designation, and the question probably arose from the messianic

---

25. Evans, *Mark 8:27—16:20*, 477, notes that calling him "procurator" is anachronistic, and inscriptions and biblical texts support us seeing him as "prefect." The prefect was a military governor, whereas the procurator had broader civil authority and was concerned to protect the emperor's financial interests.

26. From Evans, *Mark 8:27—16:20*, 477, quoting Philo, *Legat.* 38:301–302.

27. For detail, see Evans, *Mark 8:27—16:20*, 477.

claims of Christ that would have been known to Pilate through general knowledge or the Sanhedrin. It also corresponds with Pilate's incredulity at Jesus's refusal to answer in v. 5.

Jesus's response is ambiguous, as evidenced by the NRSV and NIV translations. The NRSV takes it as "You say so,"[28] Jesus not agreeing but stating that this is Pilate's viewpoint. The NIV takes it as "Yes, it is as you say," indicating Jesus's acceptance of his messianic status but with a degree of reluctance (15:2).[29] The former is to be preferred, for if Jesus had been directly positive, he would have been convicted instantly for usurping Caesar.[30] Ambiguity on the part of Jesus was the hallmark of the earlier narratives, and so it is here. He may even be asking a question: "Do you say so?"

The chief priests then speak for the prosecution, accusing Jesus of many things. The emphasis would have been on actions and words of Jesus that threatened Roman rule and peace. His purported threat on the temple, supposed claims to be king over Caesar, their assessment as one demon-possessed or mad, and his insurrection, among other "many charges," would no doubt have been passed on in an attempt to convince Pilate (15:3).

In v. 4, Pilate seeks to get him to answer the charges (15:4). Jesus, however, refuses to answer, and Pilate is amazed.[31] His amazement probably refers to Jesus's lack of interest in defending himself (15:5). John gives more details of the discussion, including an interaction over the nature of Jesus's kingship and the epistemological question, "What is truth?" (John 18:28–38). For John, and no doubt Mark, the answer is Jesus himself (John 14:6).

Other accounts tell us that Pilate was skeptical about the charges against Jesus (Matt 27:19; Luke 23:14; John 18:38). While Mark does not say this directly, Pilate's preparedness to release Jesus, Mark's assessment that Pilate recognized that the Jewish leaders were motivated to have Jesus punished out of envy (v. 10), and Pilate's question of the crowd, "What crime has he committed?" (v. 14), all imply that Pilate was unconvinced by the charges.

Mark records that at the time of the Passover and Tabernacles Feast, it was customary for the governor ("he") to grant clemency to a prisoner as requested by the people—the so-called *privilegium paschale*, "special Passover law" (v. 6). Knowing the custom, interested parties (the crowd) come to Pilate, seeking that he carry this out (15:8). Pilate's response is to offer to release to them Jesus ("the king of the Jews"). Pilate was convinced

---

28. Evans, *Mark 8:27—16:20*, 478.

29. See also Mark 8:30; 14:62. France, *Gospel of Mark*, 628, sees it as a recent consensus; I am surprised, as the Greek does not demand this.

30. Brooks, *Mark*, 248.

31. A fulfillment of Isa 53:7: "Yet he did not open his mouth."

that the Jewish leaders were motivated out of envy in bringing Jesus to him. It is not surprising that they were envious: Jesus had repeatedly embarrassed them with his wisdom in public debate, had performed many miracles, taught with authority, and was hugely popular among the people (*hoi polloi*).

The chief priests, however, exert influence over the crowds and encourage them to release a certain Barabbas. A widely attested textual variant on Matt 27:17 reads "*Jesus* Barabbas," which leads to the possibility that this was his full name. Barabbas means "son of Abba." We know from 14:36 that Abba means "Father" in Aramaic. As such, in the playing out of this scene, there is immense irony. Jesus, the true Son of God, is being put to death in place of someone who, by name, is also "Jesus, son of God." Mark tells us little about him. Elsewhere, the NT confirms that Barabbas was a notorious prisoner (Matt 27:16).

Luke tells us that Barabbas was a man imprisoned for an insurrection in Jerusalem and murder (Luke 23:18). John records that he was a *lēstēs*, which could mean a bandit or, as is more likely here, a revolutionary (John 18:40).[32] So, for Mark, the true Son of God and King of the Jews committed to love and non-violence is condemned to death, while another who sought to claim Israel's throne by force is released. We can surmise that Jesus dies on the cross reserved for Barabbas, while the rebel goes free. Those crucified beside him are undoubtedly his comrades in the rebellion.

There is also more than a hint of penal substitution here. Jesus will die in the place of a terrible sinner, bearing his sentence, and dying for him, while the sinner is pardoned and goes free. His death in place of Barabbas subtly anticipates the penal and substitutionary effect of the cross for repentant sinners.

Pilate's response is to ask the crowd what they want him to do with Jesus ("the king of the Jews") (15:12). The crowd's response is to shout with great brutality, "Crucify him!" Pilate' questions the reason for this. All that he gets back is another demand for him to be crucified. We see here the stunning reversal of Jesus's fortunes from his triumphal entry to the city (11:1–11).

Pilate was a classic Roman politician. He sought to uphold Roman justice; but there were times to act with political expediency, and this was one of them. Sensing the possibility of a riot like the one Barabbas had instigated and wanting to satisfy the crowd at a time of year that was worrisome to the Romans (Passover), he relents and releases Barabbas. He has Jesus flogged and hands him over to be crucified (15:15). The sentence

---

32. BDAG, 594.

shows that Jesus was not a citizen; instead, he is sentenced to be punished as a criminal or slave. For Pilate, Jesus's innocence is neither here nor there; what matters is the *Pax Romana*.

Flogging or scourging was done with a whip of several leather straps laced with sharp items such as nails, glass, or rocks. As a result, the recipient was severely cut up and the back muscles devastated.[33] The devastating effects of flogging can be understood by watching the flogging scene in the film *The Passion of the Christ*. The irony of Pilate's release of a known violent offender and threat to Roman rule instead of an innocent man who healed the sick, raised the dead, and renounced violence is graphic. It reveals the poverty of humanity in its political intrigue. Jesus's death was not only salvific for human sin; it was a demonstration of the fullness of human sin and disgrace. Ironically, by the time Mark writes, he is in the heart of the Roman world, and the story of Jesus is penetrating deeply into it. Eventually, because of the condemnation of Jesus, Jesus would become the God of the Roman world. There is so much irony in this passage, it is stunning.

There is a tragic total absence of dissenting voices in Mark's narrative. Peter is nowhere to be seen, nor are the other disciples. The scene is one of drama, raging crowds, injustice, political expediency, the release of a known murderer and insurrectionist, and the punishment of an innocent man. It is a tragedy of the highest order, even when compared with Shakespeare at his best.

Mocked and Beaten by the Soldiers (15:16–20)

Following Pilate's order, Jesus is taken away by the soldiers to the Praetorium, the official residence of the governor.[34] A cohort is gathered to deliver him for crucifixion. The soldiers were probably recruited from around Palestine and other parts of the Roman Empire and were under Pilate's command.[35] The cohort may have been a literal Roman group of about six hundred soldiers or is used here in a loose fashion of a band of soldiers. If it is the former, the large number could indicate Pilate's concern at an uprising.

33. Evans, *Mark 8:27—16:20*, 483. For example, Josephus, *War* 6:304 (Whiston): "Where he was whipped till his bones were laid bare; yet did he not make any supplication for himself, nor shed any tears, but turning his voice to the most lamentable tone possible, at every stroke of the whip his answer was, 'Woe, woe to Jerusalem!'"

34. We are unsure of its location. Less favored today is an old favorite, the fortress of Antonia; some think it was in Herod's upper palace; and others think in the Tyropoeon Valley.

35. Evans, *Mark 8:27—16:20*, 489.

The soldiers dress him in purple. Purple was the color of royalty. Hence, they were mocking the notion that he was king of the Jews.[36] The soldiers crown him with a crown of thorns crudely twisted together, again mocking his supposed royalty. By this stage, Jesus had been up all night praying. He had also been tried and beaten by the Sanhedrin. Thorns had been pressed down into his skull, and he had endured a terrible flogging. The pain must already have been unbearable, and he was considerably weakened.

They mock him, hailing his royalty ("Hail, king of the Jews"). The salute is quite like the Latin imperial greeting *Ave, Caesar, victor, imperator,* meaning "Hail, Caesar, victor, emperor."[37] They repeatedly beat him his head with a reed. The reed may have symbolized a scepter. Again, he is spat on (14:65). They kneel before him, pretending to worship him (15:16–19). Later, one of these soldiers will recognize him as God's Son (15:39). Some years later, another soldier, Cornelius, will convert (Acts 10—11). Roman soldiers will be converted through Paul's Roman imprisonment (Phil 1:12–13; 4:22). Again, ironies are everywhere.

One cannot see what was done to Jesus in purely secular terms. There was no doubt spiritual mockery going on as these Romans, who believed in the Roman and Greek gods and the kingship and deity of Caesar, mocked the weakness of Jesus's God in the face of their own. They bowed before Caesar as the "son of God," and so their mockery has an irony for Mark and his Roman readers. After the completion of the mockery, they place his cloak back on him and then lead him away to crucify him (15:20).

Crucified (15:21–32)

There is a sudden shift in the narrative to a seemingly insignificant passerby who is drawn into the narrative. He is named as Simon of Cyrene, from a North African city on the Mediterranean near modern Shahhat, Libya, where at the time, many Jews lived. Later, Jews from Cyrene would be at Pentecost (Acts 2:10), and some would oppose Stephen (Acts 6:9). It was through Cyrenians that the gospel spread to gentiles in Antioch (Acts 11:20). A key Cyrenian figure in Antioch was the prophet and teacher Lucian (Acts 13:1). It is possible that Simon was in the city for the feast. He is named, as are his sons Alexander and Rufus. The naming of all three suggests they became part of the Christian church and may have been involved in some of

---

36. See Suetonius, *Tib.* 17.2, who says of Caesar that he was "clad in the purple-bordered toga and crowned with laurel."

37. Evans, *Mark 8:27—16:20*, 490.

those things credited to Cyrenians in Acts.[38] Someone with the name Rufus is mentioned in Rom 16:13, and this could be Simon's son. Here, Simon is simply conscripted to carry Jesus's cross. The language suggests Simon may have been unwilling, and so coercion was employed.

The account suggests that Jesus was carrying his cross (crossbar) initially, but due to his immense suffering thus far, he was unable to bear it. It is unclear whether Jesus was carrying the crossbar or the whole cross, although most assume the former. The practice of the one to be crucified carrying the cross was standard.[39]

Albeit involuntarily, Jesus and Simon are living examples of the appeal of 8:34. Ironically, Jesus is unable to carry his cross. Sometimes, to succeed in bearing our particular crosses, we need the support of others (cf. Gal 6:2). This episode illustrates for the disciples the meaning of that verse. They are also to walk their own Via Delarosa in the cause of Christ as they follow him. It is likely at the time of writing that many in Rome had recently carried their crosses due to Nero's persecution. Peter will do so, too, as will Paul (not literally, as he died by beheading). Our challenge is to emulate their examples and sustain our cross-bearing until our deaths, while assisting others to do the same.

They arrive at the place of crucifixion. It is Golgotha, which Mark explains means "place of the skull" (also *Kranion*, Luke 23:33). The name could be due to its function for killing. More likely, it is named this way due to its skull-like shape.[40] It was outside the city (cf. Heb 13:12–13). Its location is likely inside the Church of the Holy Sepulchre.[41]

The soldiers offer Jesus wine mixed with myrrh. The concoction could be a crude anesthetic or another aspect of their mockery of Jesus as supposed king, as wine mixed with myrrh was a delicacy (cf. Luke 23:36–37).[42] Jesus declines it (15:23). His refusal is not an act of abstinence or a Nazarite vow, for we know Jesus drank wine (Matt 11:19; John 2:1–12). It could be so that he is not dulled, so that he can fully drink the cup of suffering before him. Possibly, it is due to his earlier comment that he will never drink wine again until the consummation (14:25).

---

38. On Cyrene, see Shirokov, "Cyrene."

39. Evans, *Mark 8:27—16:20*, 499, notes that Plautus and Plutarch record that the condemned man carried his own cross (the *patibulum*) through the city to the place of crucifixion. Josephus, *War* 5:449–51, records examples of crucifixions.

40. Franklin, "Golgotha."

41. See further Franklin, "Golgotha," for a discussion on the possible sites, including the less likely garden tomb.

42. See Pliny the Elder, *Nat.* 14.15.92: "The finest wine in early days was that spiced with the scent of myrrh."

Verse 24 is abrupt: "And they crucified him." Crucifixion was barbaric and was used frequently by Persians, Indians, Assyrians, and later the Greeks and Romans, to deal with troublemakers, slaves, and criminals. It involved being hung on a cross, a tree, or a wall, and having nails driven into the hands and feet. Death came through shock or asphyxiation as the victims tired of attempting to breathe while forcing themselves up against the nails. It involved public humiliation, with the victims crucified naked in a public place, attached to a stake, cross, or tree. Their bodies were often left to rot. Crucifixion is one of the more horrible, painful, and demeaning ways a person can die.[43]

Because of its barbarity, there are few descriptions of crucifixion in ancient literature. The brevity of this verse supports this. Roman crucifixion followed this pattern with variation:

> It included a flogging beforehand, and victims often carried the crossbeam to the place of crucifixion, where they were nailed or bound to the cross with arms extended, raised up, and perhaps seated on a sedicula, or small wooden peg.[44]

Crucifixion was for slaves, criminals, and non-citizens. Hence, Jesus died in the most humiliating way possible. He died as a slave.

Mark includes that they divided his clothes and gambled for them with the use of lots. The casting of lots for his clothes fulfills the prophecy of Ps 22:18. With Jesus's words in 15:34, it shows that the first Christians made the connection between Ps 22 and the crucifixion. The psalm is an astonishingly accurate depiction of crucifixion. The practice of dividing up the crucified victim's possessions was common. The casting of lots was not throwing dice as we might imagine but a crude game, perhaps like guessing the number of fingers behind the back.[45]

In vv. 25–29, more details are given. Jesus was crucified at the third hour in the Jewish day (9 a.m.).[46] Above him was the charge "the king of the Jews." The title suggests that Jesus was killed for treason against the Roman emperor, treated as a traitor, insurrectionist, and pretender

---

43. However, there are many others equally horrific. See, "List of Methods of Capital Punishment."

44. Hengel, *Crucifixion*, 22–32. See also Green, "Death of Jesus."

45. Evans, *Mark 8:27—16:20*, 502.

46. We have a slight chronological problem with John 19:14, which times things later. This could be due to confusion of Greek letters, could be a theological reordering so that Jesus died at the same time as the slaughter of the Passover lamb, or could indicate different reminiscences. It shows that the early Christians were not concerned to collude to dot their i's and cross their t's and points to authenticity.

to Caesar's throne. John tells us that this was written in three languages, Aramaic, Latin, and Greek (which was likely to ensure all could read the reason for his death).[47] The practice of placing titles on the cross is well attested.[48] Ironically, while this was intended as mockery, for Mark and other believers, it is true.

Two rebels are crucified, one to his right, the other to his left.[49] They were probably Barabbas's fellow rebels. Sadly, Jacob (James) and John are nowhere to be seen, despite claiming that they wanted the seats on either side of him (10:37). Their day would come. The early church linked this to Isa 53:12 ("he was numbered with the transgressors"), as seen in the textual variant to that effect (cf. Luke 22:37). Mark tells us that both rebels abuse him from the cross, insulting, mocking, and challenging him. Luke tells us that one of them recognizes Jesus's sovereignty and divine nature and seeks salvation from him (Luke 23:39–43). It may be that initially he abused Jesus (cf. 15:32) and then repented when he saw Jesus's behavior on the cross. Alternatively, we may simply have different eyewitness recollections of the same event.

In v. 29, others from the crowd also mock him and especially his supposed claim to destroy and rebuild the temple. We see here the public nature of his crucifixion and allusion again to Ps 22, this time v. 7: "All who see me mock me, they hurl insults, shaking their heads." The Greek for "mocked" is "blasphemed" and points to Mark's Christology: in abusing Jesus, they were mocking the Son of God (cf. 14:64). The charge of temple destruction probably indicates that this was circulated as a reason for his death.

In vv. 31–32, Mark tells readers that those who had instigated his demise from the Jewish leadership (chief priests and scribes) also mock him among themselves, challenging Jesus to save himself and prove he is the Christ, their king. At one level, this mockery is savage and spiteful, with Jesus where they want him. However, it is also a final appeal for Jesus to perform a sign proving he is truly is their Messiah (cf. 8:11–12). They are still stuck in ideas of a military Messiah and cannot conceive that one hung on a tree is their king.

What they do not know is that in his death, in his accursedness on the cross, he is taking on himself the curse of sin for all humankind (Gal

---

47. Evans, *Mark 8:27–16:20*, 503, tells us that the Latin would read like this: *IESUS NAZARENUS REX IUDAEORUM*; the Hebrew: *yēšûa' hannoṣrî melek hayyĕhûdîm*). In Greek, *HO BASILEUS TŌN BASILEUS TŌN IOUDAIŌN*.

48. Evans, *Mark 8:27–16:20*, 504, notes other examples of placards placed for crucified men.

49. Some speculate that they were associates of Barabbas, which is possible but in fact entirely speculative.

3:13; cf. Deut 21:23). He is dying for the sins of the world and will rise again to be a different kind of ruler than anything they could imagine, a crucified and raised Messiah who conquers a world with love, humility, and service. In effect, Jesus does do what they ask, but even more dramatically. He dies and is buried. He *then* rises and presents himself over forty days, giving conclusive proofs of his resurrection (Acts 1:3). Despite all this, the Jewish leaders will still not believe in him. Even the sign of Jonah is unconvincing because of their presuppositions.[50] They need more signs and wonders (1 Cor 1:22–24).

The failure of Jesus to respond to their mockery amplifies the rejection of Jesus by Israel's leaders. How can he be the Messiah and Savior of the world if he cannot save himself? However, they simply had no idea who they were dealing with, or that in their killing of Jesus, they were ensuring that the Servant Messiah would die to save the world. He will not come down from the cross, but he will rise from the dead, ascend, and come in the clouds of glory at his return as King. In v. 32, Mark adds that the soldiers also insult him heavily. One of them would be converted within minutes.

The Death of Jesus (15:33–41)

Mark records that darkness fell over the region ("the whole land") from noon ("the sixth hour") to 3 p.m. ("the ninth hour"). The event is unexplained and could be a miraculous event (cf. Josh 10:12–13). Alternatively, it could refer to a solar eclipse or another astronomical incident. Such events were interpreted as portents of world events by Greeks and Romans. Darkness was also associated with judgment, and this could imply as much (cf. Exod 10:22; Jer 15:9; Joel 2:10).

Jesus cries out loudly at 3 p.m. ("the ninth hour") from Ps 22:1: "*Eloi, Eloi, lama sabachthani?*"—"My God, my God, why have you forsaken me?" (15:33–34). These words are interpreted theologically by many Christians who consider that Jesus, at this moment, literally took upon himself the sins of humankind. As he took on the actual sins of people, now sinful, he was abandoned by God.

However, this is unlikely for a couple of reasons. It assumes Jesus had human sins on him in a literal sense. Sin is not a quantity in this sense. Second, it assumes that if he did so, he would be sinful himself. It seems to treat sin as a contagion. Third, in Ps 22, David does question God's abandonment. However, David does so knowing God has not abandoned him completely, but because he is in a terrible plight and feels abandoned.

---

50. Matt 12:39; 16:4; Luke 11:29–30.

No faithful Jew, David or Jesus, would ever believe God had completely abandoned him or her, even when sinful. Finally, such thinking also leads to the horrible idea that when we sin, God abandons us. If so, we are perpetually abandoned, because we all sin.

Rather than Jesus taking on the sins of the world and actually being abandoned by God, this is Jesus giving Israel its final chance to recognize him. Ps 22 was featured through the narrative in a range of ways (above). Here, Jesus directly cites its first words. In doing so, he declares to the crowds that he is the figure toward which Ps 22 is pointing. As noted, Ps 22 describes the scene of the cross amazingly well. Jesus then is calling for Israel to recognize him and yield to him. He is feeling forsaken, even though he knows he is not abandoned by God.

The crowd does not comprehend this final appeal to recognize that Jesus is their Messiah. Instead, they interpret his words as a summons to Elijah that reveals their hope that Elijah would come in the end times.[51] We see again that their eschatological expectations blinded them to their Messiah. As discussed in the transfiguration passage (9:2–13), John is the predicted Elijah figure. He has come, and now he is gone. Elijah himself did come to meet Jesus in the same episode.

Someone offers Jesus sour wine, which fulfills Ps 69:21 (68:22 LXX). The person giving it to him urges people to leave him alone to see if Elijah will come. Their promptings could be irony or an act of mercy. Either way, Elijah does not come.

In 15:37, Mark abruptly records, "With a loud cry, Jesus breathed his last." The idea of death as breathing one's last breath is common in the Scriptures.[52] Mark records that simultaneously, the curtain in the temple was ripped in two ("from top to bottom") (15:38). The curtain could have been the outer curtain (Exod 27:16), but it was most likely the one that hid the holy of holies (cf. Exod 26:31–37). Its rending is highly symbolic. Jesus has died for threatening to destroy the temple, yet at his death, it is only the temple curtain that is torn. The sundering of the curtain points to the now inevitable destruction of the whole temple, which will occur in forty or so years.

It also links to the tearing of heaven and the coming of the Spirit at his baptism (1:11). Now, the temple curtain is torn, and the same Spirit will soon come from the throne room upon all believers and not just Jesus.[53] It also speaks of the enthronement of Jesus in the holy of holies as the Messiah, God's Son, and High Priest after the order of Melchizedek (Ps 110:1, 4). For

---

51. See Mark 15:35; cf. 6:15; 8:28; 9:12; Mal 3:6; 4:1; Sir 48:10.
52. Gen 25:8, 17; 35:29; 49:33; Acts 5:5, 10; 12:23.
53. Evans, *Mark 8:27—16:20*, 509.

the writer of Hebrews, Jesus becomes the curtain that is split at that moment (Heb 6:10; 9:3; 10:20). The split of the curtain has an even deeper meaning. It signifies the end of the role of the temple in terms of defining the people of God. For Christians, it also ends the temple system that is now and forever constituted in the one crucified for our sins. The tearing speaks of the opening of access to the inner sanctum of God's presence through the one who is now both the temple of God and the temple curtain, Jesus Christ.[54]

At this point, the centurion confesses, "Surely this man was the Son of God" (15:38). This admission could simply be the man recognizing Jesus's greatness, for "son of God" can refer to someone of divine esteem. Nevertheless, for Mark writing in Rome years later, surely, he sees more here. The whole Gospel is about Jesus as the Messiah and God's Son (1:1). It is the same confession made by demons (3:11; 5:7), by God at Jesus's baptism and transfiguration (1:11; 9:7), and from Jesus's own lips (12:6, 37; 13:32; 14:61–62).

For Mark, this is no mere recognition of Jesus's greatness by the centurion. Instead, it is a massive statement for a Roman. This significant military leader confesses that the one Caesar crucified is *divi filius* ("the Son of God"). Although the Roman gods have triumphed over this fake "son of god," he recognizes, with extraordinary insight, that somehow, this is a Son of God over the Roman pantheon.

Furthermore, the one who oversaw Jesus's death turns to Christ, recognizing who he is. This reminiscence is vital for Mark's Roman readers who are reading about the brutal killing of the Messiah and Son of God by their own people. Interestingly, in Mark's Gospel, the first person in the world who accepts a crucified Messiah is a Roman soldier. It shows there is hope for sinners, even the centurion responsible for Jesus's death. His transformation mirrors that of the Sanhedrin figure, Joseph (see below). The transformations of this soldier, Joseph, and Peter show that Judas could have found forgiveness had he sought it.

Mark 15:40 to 16:1 form the final of Mark's sandwich framing devices. Jesus's burial and the women's presence as witnesses to it are highlighted. This section throws the spotlight on the importance of Jesus's burial and is significant for authenticating the empty tomb encounter.

Mark 15:40–16:1

A^1 Women (15:40–41)

B Burial of Jesus (15:42–46)

A^2 Women (15:47–16:1)

---

54. See Rom 5:1–2; Eph 2:14; Heb 9:3; 10:20.

It is somewhat surprising to be told that some of his followers were present at Jesus's death, with the women watching from a reasonable distance. We have here the first mention of these women in the Gospel, but it is significant. They were with Jesus in Galilee and served him. Their presence at the cross marks them as more courageous than the men, who are nowhere to be seen. Their commitment to serving him shows they are on the path to kingdom greatness, something the men must learn (9:35; 10:43–44).

The first mentioned is Mary Magdalene, meaning she is from Magdala, a town presently being excavated on the west coast of the Sea of Galilee between Capernaum and Tiberias. She will go to the tomb in the next chapter, and according to Matthew and John, is the first to meet the risen Jesus (Matt 28:9–10; John 21:1–18). Luke tells us that Jesus cast out seven demons from her, suggesting she had a complicated past (Luke 8:2).

The others are another Mary, the mother of Jacob (James) "the younger" and Joses. Salome may be the wife of Zebedee and mother of Jacob (James) and John (Matt 27:56); and if so, for Matthew, she was the instigator of Jacob (James) and John's desire to be Jesus's right- and left-hand men.[55] Mention of these women observing Jesus's burial is essential for the account of the burial and empty tomb to come.

The reference to "Jacob (James) the younger and Joses" leads some to believe this to be Jesus's mother (cf. 6:3). However, most see the wording as pointing to another Mary. John 19:25 confirms that this is Mary, wife of Clopas. Jacob (James) the younger and Joses were probably known to the Romans. Jacob (James) is called "the younger" to distinguish him from Jacob (James), the brother of Jesus.[56] The reference to these women's origin in Galilee and their support for Jesus coincides with Luke 8:1–2, where Mary Magdalene, Joanna, and Susanna are mentioned. The "many others" in Luke then probably includes Salome and Mary the wife of Clopas. These women are contrasted with Peter and the others, who are nowhere to be seen.

Jesus Is Buried by Joseph of Arimathea (15:42–47)

The scene now shifts to the end of the day, probably between 4 and 5 p.m. on the pre-Sabbath day. Remembering that Jews begin the day at 6 p.m.,

---

55. Similarly, see Witherington, "Salome (Person)." This also raises the possibility that more than a few of the woman traveling with Jesus were family members of the disciples.

56. See Brooks, *Mark*, 264, for more.

the Sabbath began at this time on the Friday evening. It was almost time for the evening meal.

Here we have another great surprise in the narrative. There has been no indication that any in the Sanhedrin were supporters of Jesus. On the contrary, the whole council had rejected Jesus and sentenced him to death (14:55; 15:1). The group included Joseph, as v. 43 makes clear. However, Luke tells us that he did not agree with the council's decision concerning Jesus (Luke 23:51). If that is so, Mark does not indicate that he resisted the decision of the group.

Stunningly, Joseph of Arimathea[57] boldly goes to Pilate and asks for Jesus's body. In John, he does so "secretly for fear of the Jews" (John 19:38).[58] Mark describes him as a man "who was himself waiting for the kingdom of God" (cf. Luke 23:51), suggesting that Joseph was a God-seeker. Matthew tells us he was wealthy (Matt 27:57) and that he placed Jesus in his own tomb (Matt 27:58). For Mark, he acts generously, buying linen to wrap Jesus. All that is said of him suggests that he was a secret supporter of Jesus who did not speak; or that he spoke up, but Mark did not report it; or that he supported Jesus's death sentence, but came to believe in him as he watched him die.

Some question his motivation. It is proposed that he was taking Jesus's body to ensure it was not stolen. Alternatively, he may have done it to ensure the land was not defiled by Jesus remaining on the cross overnight into the Passover Sabbath (cf. Deut 21:22–23). Another possibility is his concern for observing the Jewish practice of burying the dead. Some limit his motivation to seeing Jesus as a prophet, and as such, Joseph believed he deserved an appropriate burial.[59]

However, his actions indicate that whatever his view of Jesus earlier, he is now a supporter of Jesus. As such, we have another example of conversion in the Gospel of Mark. He is the first politician of significance to come to Jesus.[60] With the Roman centurion's confession, Mark anticipates the many surprising converts to come in the future.

---

57. Meiklejohn and Bruce, "Arimathea," note that Eusebius and Jerome identified Arimathea with Ramah or Ramathaim-zophim (the birthplace of Samuel; cf. 1 Sam 1:19). It is possibly the modern Rentis, about 15 km northeast of Lydda and 30 km northwest of Jerusalem.

58. This could be seen as a contradiction, Mark stating he went "boldly" and John that he went "secretly" because of 'fear of the Jews." However, boldness may be found within fear, and he did not let fear overcome him. He is an unsung hero of the NT.

59. See Evans, *Mark 8:27—16:20*, 520, on these views.

60. Later the Corinthian city treasurer, Erastus, will join the Christian movement (Rom 16:23; 2 Tim 4:20, cf. Acts 19:22).

In 15:44–45, we read of Pilate's surprise that Jesus is dead, and so the prefect seeks confirmation, receiving it from the centurion. The soldier is the same man who has just confessed Jesus's divine sonship. Pilate's surprise is due to the speed of death, as crucified victims often took two to three days to die.[61] However, for readers, this is not a surprise due to the great suffering Christ had endured.

Joseph wraps him in linen cloth as was the custom and places him in the tomb hewn out of rock. Matthew tells us that it is Joseph's own tomb. If so, it is a remarkable act of grace, as Jewish custom forbade the burial of an executed criminal in the family tomb until one year after that person's death, at which time the person's bones were gathered into an ossuary and could then be buried in the family tomb.[62] Scholars debate whether Joseph buried the two criminals as well, which is worthless because they are simply not mentioned. In Jewish culture, Jesus's family should have done this. As he was a rabbi with followers, his disciples could also have gone to get his body and bury him, as did John's disciples earlier (6:29). Instead, it is a leader of the Jewish judiciary responsible for sentencing Jesus to death who does it.

He wraps Jesus in a linen cloth (*sindona*, "shroud"),[63] which he has himself purchased (again pointing to his generous sacrifice). He rolls a stone over the door (15:46). The moving of the stone indicates that he had others with him, which is logical as he also had to bear the body to the tomb and dress it in linen. As discussed in the next chapter, the stone was large (16:4). That Joseph had help is supported by the Pharisee Nicodemus's presence in Mark's narrative (John 19:27, cf. John 3:1).

Mark is careful to note that Mary Magdalene and the other Mary see where Jesus is laid (15:47). This detail is significant both for the next part of the narrative and for apologetically dismissing the "wrong tomb" theory. The wrong tomb view hypothesizes that the disciples wrongly identified Jesus's tomb, leading to the false conclusion that Jesus rose from the dead. There is no mention of the soldiers (cf. Matt 27:62–66).

The burial of Jesus is vital theologically. It shows that the same Jesus who lived and died is the person who rose from the grave. Baptism replays his burial, as we symbolically participate in the burial of Christ, buried with him to rise to new life (Rom 6:1–4). There is no indication in Mark

---

61. See Evans, *Mark 8:27—16:20*, 520, who notes the description of Seneca, *Dial.* 3.2.2 as "long-drawn-out agony." He adds other examples.

62. Evans, *Mark 8:27—16:20*, 520. As a result, some question Matthew's remark and believe it was a criminal's tomb and a place of shame.

63. Is this the Shroud of Turin? John 19:40 somewhat confuses this with the plural "linen cloths"; it is not clear in what Jesus was buried. On the Shroud, see Geisler, "Shroud of Turin," *Baker Encyclopedia*, 705–6.

that Jesus went to hell after his death, which has very little biblical support. The tearing of the temple curtain suggests, instead, that he went to open the way to God.

Jesus Is Risen (16:1–8)

After the Sabbath (cf. Luke 23:56b) indicates after 6 p.m. on the Saturday evening. Mary Magdalene, Mary the mother of Jacob (James), and Salome had purchased spices for the anointing of the body. Early the next morning (Sunday), they come to the tomb to anoint Jesus's body, carrying the spices (16:1). The proper preparation of the body for burial was necessary for Jewish culture. Their urgency was due to the speed of decay in the ANE heat. Their inability to anoint him may be, in some spiritual way, because he had already been anointed in Bethany earlier in preparation for his death (14:3–11).

Understandably, they are worried about who would roll the stone away (16:3). The concern is unsurprising because such stones were 1.5 to 2 meters in diameter and of varying thicknesses. They could weigh several hundred pounds.[64] Mark describes this stone as "very large." When the women come to the tomb, however, the problem is resolved as the stone has been rolled away (16:4).

No doubt full of a blend of grief, uncertainty, and fear, they enter the tomb. Rather than finding the deceased Jesus wrapped in the linen cloth and laid in it, they find a young man dressed in white. Other Gospels describe him as dazzling like lightning (Matt 28:3) and gleaming (Luke 24:4). It recalls Jesus on the Mount of Transfiguration (9:3).[65] He is seated at the right-hand side of the tomb (16:5). The right side does not seem significant. Neither is there a clear link to the young man who flees from the garden losing his linen robe (although some see such connections as significant). Although not clearly stated by Mark, Matt 28:2 clarifies that this is an angel and that there were two angels present (similarly to Luke 24:4). Matthew also states that there was an earthquake that rolled the stone away (Matt 28:2). As one might imagine, when faced with the empty tomb and an angel (or two), the women are considerably perplexed (*ekthambeō*).[66]

The man (or angel) tells them not to be so alarmed (again *ekthambeō*). He states the purpose of the women: they are seeking Jesus the Nazarene, who was crucified. This man has divine prescience; he somehow knows their mission. He then tells him the astonishing news that Jesus is risen;

---

64. Evans, *Mark 8:27—16:20*, 535.
65. See too 2 Macc 5:2; Rev 7:9, 13; 10:1.
66. BDAG, 303.

the first to proclaim the gospel is an angel sent from God. The passive tense indicates that God raised him. The angel then shows them the place where he was laid as evidence. There is no mention of a shroud.

The angel then commissions the women to go and tell the disciples and Peter that Jesus has gone ahead of them to Galilee and that they will see him there as foretold by Jesus (14:28). Reference to Peter is the last mention of a disciple by name and forms an inclusio with 1:16, suggesting that Peter is the primary eyewitness for the Gospel.

The shorter ending of Mark records that the women flee in terror and amazement due to their great fear. Initially, they tell no one what had happened (16:8). If this is the original end to Mark's Gospel, it is written to accentuate the lack of understanding experienced by the disciples that the women's situation exemplifies. It leaves the reader hanging.

The passion and resurrection predictions throughout the Gospel indicate that Mark believes that Jesus rose from the dead.[67] However, the shorter ending has no appearance of Jesus to support this; all that is left is the incomprehension of the disciples. Finishing with such perplexity fits with the whole narrative as the disciples struggle to understand that Jesus is the Messiah (cf. 1:1—8:27) and then that he is Servant Messiah who must suffer and die for the nation and world. The account ends with the women in disarray and fear. The men know nothing of the empty tomb. All in all, there is confusion.

Some scholars believe that the original longer ending of Mark has been lost and that this included the appearance narratives (e.g., Gundry).[68] However, it could end this way as a rhetorical device. With such an open ending, readers have to join the dots. The women must have gone to the disciples, and they must have met up with Jesus. We can be sure the women overcame their trepidation because the Gospel of Mark itself exists. Thankfully, also, we have the other Gospels, which tell the story of Jesus's appearances. Then, reader have to answer the question "Who is this man?" (cf. 4:41). More importantly, the ending challenges readers to consider their response. Mark's answer: "Repent and believe the good news" (1:15).

Aside from the incarnation and the return of Christ that will supersede any event in history, the resurrection is undoubtedly the most glorious day in history. Our Lord Jesus was raised to be the Ruler and Savior of the world. All that is left is to worship him forever. Amen.

---

67. See 8:31; 9:10, 31; 10:34; 14:28; 16:6.

68. See Gundry, *Mark*, 1009–1012, who gives a strong twelvefold argument that it was lost.

Jesus Appears and Commissions the Disciples (16:9–20, disputed)[69]

In the main, the details of these verses line up with Luke's account in Luke-Acts, indicating that it is probably a later interpolation, based mainly on Luke's writings. However, the reference to the first appearance to Mary Magdalene may indicate a knowledge of Matthew or John's accounts (Matt 28:9; John 20:11–18). Just because these are a later addition does not render them of no value. These verses are still very early and found in many manuscripts as early as the second century.[70] Hence, they are an early recollection of the apostolic period and give insight and confirmation to the other accounts.

Drawing perhaps on John 20:11–18, Jesus appears first to Mary Magdalene. She is described as the one from whom seven demons were cast out, which is found in Luke 8:2. She then goes and tells the others, who were in deep grief; however, they do not believe her story (16:9–11).

Clearly referencing Luke 24:13–43, Jesus then appears to two on the road to Emmaus (16:12). These two go and tell the others, who again do not believe it (16:13). "In another form," points not to Jesus's being non-human but transformed (cf. 1 Cor 15:35–49).

His appearance to the eleven while eating is from Luke 24:36–43. Jesus rebukes them for their lack of faith and refusal to accept the testimony of Mary and the two travelers (16:14).

Jesus then sends out the disciples in mission and ascends. The sending has links to Luke's two versions of the Great Commission (Luke 24:44–49; Acts 1.6–8). They are told to go and preach the gospel (cf. 1:1) to all the world. Those who believe and are baptized will be saved, while those who do not believe will be condemned. Notably, while baptism is a requirement for salvation, failure to be baptized is not linked to condemnation. Hence, it is not entirely clear that baptism is a requirement for salvation.

He promises them that miraculous signs will accompany those who believe (16:17). They will heal the sick and handle deadly snakes. Acts includes many instances of healing. The reference to snakes calls to mind Paul in Malta (Acts 28:3–6). The mention of drinking deadly poison without harm may draw on another early church event that is not recorded in the NT.

---

69. The NRSV notes another short ending: "And all that had been commanded them they told briefly to those around Peter. And afterward Jesus himself sent out through them, from east to west, the sacred and imperishable proclamation of eternal salvation." Evans, *Mark 8:27—16:20*, 550, rightly observes that the language of Matthew's commission and Acts is presupposed. Metzger, *Textual Commentary*, 103, informs us that this ending is found in only a few later manuscripts.

70. See Metzger, *Textual Commentary*, 102–105.

Jesus's ascension and his being seated at the right hand of God is Lukan (16:19).[71] The disciples going out and preaching "everywhere" and performing signs as Jesus commanded summarizes Acts (16:19–20).

Questions

- Why did Mark tell the story of the young man who fled naked in the garden?
- Why did the high priest condemn Jesus to death?
- Why did Pilate condemn Jesus to death?
- What is so ironic about the way the soldiers dressed Jesus and the title on the cross?
- What would it be like to be crucified? Consider what God our Creator and his Son have done for us. Worship him!
- Why did Jesus have to die?
- What might have caused Joseph of Arimathea to move from one who condemned Jesus to one who gives him a burial?
- Does Mark end his Gospel at 16:8? If so, why? If not, why not?
- Why did later writers add the endings?
- What does the longer ending tell us about Christians in the second century?

How Then Are We to Live?

So, what do we learn from Mark's Gospel about how to live? Of course, that is for you to decide. Indeed, Mark leaves the end of his Gospel hanging for that very reason: to challenge readers to consider what they will do with his gospel of Christ. Here, I will share a few of my own thoughts.

Some write off Mark as a construct made up by someone who wanted people to believe in Jesus. However, why would Mark write such fiction? What could be gained? The early Christians were persecuted horrifically, especially in Rome, where all evidence suggests he wrote. Peter, the source for the Gospel, was martyred. It was not as if Mark and the early Christians could gain wealth and power through their message. In actual fact, his

---

71. See also Luke 24:50–51; Acts 1:9–11; 2:33; 5:31.

Gospel put them in great danger, as Rome would seek to stop this message as it spread through the empire.

In my view, the reason Mark ends his Gospel as he does is to invite readers to consider who Jesus was and is. For Mark and his source, the Apostle Peter, he is definitely a man. Yet, he is more: he is the Messiah, Son of God, and Son of Man, raised from the dead to be Lord of the universe. He challenges us to come to the same conclusion as we read his Gospel. Mark lays out the evidence. Jesus fulfilled a multiplicity of OT passages. He healed the sick, cast out demons, fed massive crowds with a little food, walked on water, calmed the storm, and raised the dead. Jesus also predicted the future, and it came to pass, such as the fall of Jerusalem only a few years after Mark's writing. He cursed a fig tree to its destruction. He rose from the dead. Who else could do that except someone who is sent from God?

For me, Jesus is the Messiah, God the Son, and Daniel's Son of Man. He is the key to unlocking the mysteries of the universe: How did it come to be here? Why are we here? Why do we exist? The universal law of cause and effect demands a cause. Now that Jesus has come, we know that it is his God that created the cosmos. Jesus is God's Gospel to us; the Word made flesh, who has come to us to reveal God to us. The right response to this is to join the Roman centurion and say, "Surely this man is the Son of God" (15:39). We are to move beyond fear and bewilderment, and as we know the women did at the tomb, run to the world and tell them about this Jesus. He is our salvation. Further, he is *their* salvation, and we have to tell them, as Mark has told us.

Mark's Gospel tells us how to live. Like Jesus, we are to renounce seeking worldly power, adulation, status, glory, and wealth, and use what we have in his service. We live to serve our King. As "slaves of all," we live to serve others, believers or not. We are to emulate his relentless life of self-denial, self-giving, sacrifice, suffering, humility, and love, and go to the sick, the poor, the weak, the frail, the discouraged, the lonely, the dying, the demonized, and all those who are marginalized in our world and use all we have for their salvation and growth as people made in the image of God. We are to turn the values of the world upside down by being a family of God that embraces diversity and welcomes sinners into its midst.

We are to live the lives of disciples: believing, worshiping, praying, loving, comforting, giving, and pouring ourselves out for the church, its mission, and the lost sheep of the world. Like Jesus filled with God's *splanchnizomai*, we are to be moved in our guts by compassion to do this. We are to turn away from seeking worldly glory and prosperity to see the kingdom of God grow. It begins with us repenting and believing. We continue to do this, turning from sins as we recognize them in ourselves. It means trusting God every day up to the moment of our final breath or when Jesus returns.

Mark also gives us hope that Jesus is returning. There will be a terrible time leading into this. An abomination that causes desolation will come. He will deceive many. Nevertheless, that should not faze us, for it signals that Jesus is near. He will come and slay the abomination with his breath (2 Thess 2:8). In the meantime, we are to take the gospel of Jesus to every nation, telling the story so that people in every corner of God's world can know the truth that Mark tells us. Then, when that day comes, of which the Father alone knows, Jesus will come in the clouds of glory, with his angels, and will gather his people to him. Mark tells us little of what comes next. We have to read the rest of the NT for that. However, we know it will include our being saved and inheriting eternal life as promised to the disciples in the account of the rich young man. So, we have a considerable incentive to live faithfully for Jesus and endure to the end.

In the meantime, I encourage and implore you, love God! Love each other! Serve one another! Love the lost! Deny yourselves. Take up your cross and proudly and boldly carry it through your life, never ashamed of Jesus and his words, living to please our King, God the Father, Jesus his Son, by the power of the Spirit. Amen.

Final Questions

What has Mark's Gospel taught concerning:

- God?
- His kingdom, his reign?
- Jesus?
- How to live?
- How the church should worship, be community together, and do mission?
- Mission?
- Money?
- The world to come?

Bibliography

Algie, Brian. "Caesarea Philippi." In *LBD*, n.p.
Angus, S. and A. M. Renwick. "Nero." In *ISBE*, 3:521–23.
Arndt, William F., and F. Wilbur Gingrich. *A Greek-English Lexicon of the New Testament and Other Early Christian Literature: A Translation and Adaption of the Fourth Revised and Augmented Edition of Walter Bauer's Griechisch-Deutsches Worterbuch zu den Schriften des Neuen Testaments und der ubrigen urchristlichen Literatur*. 2nd ed., revised and augmented by F. Wilbur Gingrich and Frederick W. Danker from Walter Bauer's 5th ed., 1958. Chicago: University of Chicago Press, 1979.
Aslan, Reza. *Zealot: The Life and Times of Jesus of Nazareth*. New York: Random House, 2013.
Austin, Steven A., and Mark L. Strauss. "Earthquakes and the End Times: A Geological and Biblical Perspective." Institute for Christian Research (website). Jan. 14, 1999. http://www.icr.org/research/index/researchp_sa_r06/.
Barr, James. "'*Abbā* Isn't 'Daddy.'" *JTS* 39 (1988): 28–47.
Barry, John D. "Servant Songs." In *LBD*, n.p.
Barry, John B., David Bomar, Derek R. Brown, Rachel Klippenstein, Douglas Mangum, Carrie Sinclair-Wolcott, and Lazarus Wentz, eds. *Lexham Bible Dictionary*. Bellingham, WA: Lexham, 2016.
Balz, Horst Robert. "γαζοφυλάκιον." In *EDNT*, 1:232.
Balz, Horst, and Gerhard Schneider, eds. *Exegetical Dictionary of the New Testament*. 3 vols. Grand Rapids.: Eerdmans, 1990.
———. "μόδιος." In *EDNT*, 2:436.
Barry, John D., David Bomar, Derek R. Brown, Rachel Klippenstein, Douglas Mangum, Carrie Sinclair Wolcott, Lazarus Wentz, Elliot Ritzema, and Wendy Widder, eds. "Leaven." In *LBD*, n.p.
———."Wineskin." In *LBD*, n.p.
Bauckham, Richard. *Jesus and the Eyewitnesses: The Gospels as Eyewitness Testimony*. Grand Rapids: Eerdmans, 2006.
Baum, A. D. "Synoptic Problem." In *DJG2*, 911–19.
Black, David Alan. "New Testament Semitisms." *Bible Translator* 39, no. 2 (Apr. 1988) 215–23.
Bowden, Andrew M. "New Testament Semitisms." In *LBD*, n.p.
Brand, Chad, Eric Mitchell, and Holman Reference Editorial Staff, eds. *Holman Illustrated Bible Dictionary*. Nashville: Holman Bible Publishers, 2003.

Brandon, Samuel George Frederick. *Jesus and the Zealots: A Study of the Political Factor in Primitive Christianity.* Manchester, UK: Manchester University Press, 1967.

Bratcher, Robert G., and Eugene Albert Nida. *A Handbook on the Gospel of Mark.* UBSHS. New York: United Bible Societies, 1993.

Bridges, Linda McKinnish. "Antonia, Tower of." In *HIBD*, 77–78.

Bromiley, Geoffrey W., ed. *The International Standard Bible Encyclopedia.* Rev. ed. 4 vols. Grand Rapids: Eerdmans, 1979–1988.

Brooks, James A. *Mark.* NAC 23. Nashville: Broadman & Holman, 1991.

Campbell, William Sanger. "'Why Did you Abandon Me?': Abandonment Christology in Mark's Gospel." In *The Trial and Death of Jesus: Essays on the Passion Narrative in Mark*, edited by Geert Van Oyen and Tom Shepherd, 99–117. Paris: Peeters, 2006.

Charlesworth, James H., ed. *Apocalyptic Literature and Testaments.* Vol. 1 of *The Old Testament Pseudepigrapha.* New York: Yale University Press, 1983.

Chilton, Bruce. *The Temple of Jesus. His Sacrificial Program Within a Cultural History of Sacrifice.* University Park, PA: Pennsylvania State University Press, 1992.

Ciampa, Roy E. "Decapolis." In *DNTB*, 266–68.

Cranfield, C. E. B., ed. *The Gospel According to St. Mark: An Introduction and Commentary.* Cambridge Greek Testament Commentaries. Cambridge, UK: Cambridge University Press, 1966.

Danker, Frederick William, ed. *A Greek-English Lexicon of the New Testament and Other Early Christian Literature.* 6th ed., based on Walter Bauer's *Griechisch-Deutsches Wörterbuch zu den Schriften des Neuen Testaments*, edited by Kurt Aland and Barbara Aland, with Viktor Reichman, and on previous English editions by W. F. Arndt, F. W. Gingrich, and F. W. Danker. Chicago: University of Chicago Press, 2000.

Das, Andrew A. "Sadducees." In *LBD*, n.p.

DeHoog, J. W. "Corban." In *ISBE*, 1:772.

DeMoss, Matthew S. *Pocket Dictionary for the Study of New Testament Greek.* Downers Grove, IL: InterVarsity, 2001.

Derrett, Duncan J. "Why and How Jesus Walked on the Sea." *Novum Testamentum* 23, fasc. 4 (Oct. 1981) 330–48.

Dicken, Frank. "Herod Antipas." In *LBD*, n.p.

Dittenberger, Wilhelm, ed. *Sylloge Inscriptionum Graecarum.* 4 vols. 3rd ed. Leipzig, Germ.: Hirzel, 1915–1924.

"Divorce Demography." Wikimedia Foundation. Last edited April 8, 2021. https://en.wikipedia.org/wiki/Divorce_demography.

Dockery, D. S. "Baptism." In *DJG*, 55–58.

Dodd, C. H. "The Framework of the Gospel Narrative." *Expository Times* 43 (Oct. 1931–Sept. 1932) 396–400.

Donfried, Karl P. "Chronology." In *ABD*, 1:1002–22.

"Dromedary." Wikimedia Foundation. Last edited April 26, 2021. https://en.wikipedia.org/wiki/Dromedary.

Earle, R. "Bethphage." In *ISBE*, 1:474.

Ebeling, Jennie R. "Roof." In *EDB*, 1142.

Edwards, James R. *The Gospel According to Mark.* PNTC. Grand Rapids: Eerdmans, 2002.

Ehorn, Seth M. "Kiss." In *LBD*, n.p.

Eisenberg, Ronald L. *The JPS Guide to Jewish Traditions*. 1st ed. Philadelphia: Jewish Publication Society, 2004.

Evans, Craig A. *Mark 8:27—16:20*. WBC 34B. Dallas: Word, 2002.

Evans, Craig A., and Stanley E. Porter, Jr., eds. *Dictionary of New Testament Background: A Compendium of Contemporary Biblical Scholarship*. IVP Bible Dictionary Series. Downers Grove, IL: InterVarsity, 2000.

Fairhurst, Libby. "Jesus Walked on Ice, Study Says." Phys.Org. Apr. 4, 2006. http://www.physorg.com/news63367761.html.

Ferry, Sara. "Tyre." In *LBD*, n.p.

France, R. T. *The Gospel of Mark: A Commentary on the Greek Text*. NIGTC. Grand Rapids: Eerdmans, 2002.

Franklin, J. Chase. "Golgotha." In *LBD*, n.p.

Freedman, David Noel, ed. *The Anchor Bible Dictionary*. 6 vols. New York: Doubleday, 1992.

———, ed. *Eerdmans Dictionary of the Bible*. Grand Rapids: Eerdmans, 2000.

Fruchtenbaum, Arnold G. *The Messianic Jewish Epistles: Hebrews, James, First Peter, Second Peter, Jude*. 1st ed. Tustin, CA: Ariel Ministries, 2005.

Garland, David E. *Mark*. NIVAC. Grand Rapids: Zondervan, 1996.

Geisler, Norman L. *Baker Encyclopedia of Christian Apologetics*. Baker Reference Library. Grand Rapids: Baker Books, 1999.

Giesen, H. "σκανδαλίζω." In *EDNT*, 3:248.

Green, Joel B. "Death of Jesus." In *DJG*, 147–63.

Green, Joel B., Jeannine K. Brown, and Nicholas Perrin, eds. *Dictionary of Jesus and the Gospels*. 2nd ed. IVP Bible Dictionary Series. Downers Grove, IL: IVP Academic, 2013.

Green, Joel B., Scot McKnight, and I. Howard Marshall, eds. *Dictionary of Jesus and the Gospels*. IVP Bible Dictionary Series. Downers Grove, IL: IVP Academic, 1992.

Guelich, Robert A. *Mark 1—8:26*. WBC 34A. Dallas: Word, 1989.

Gundry, Robert H. *Mark: A Commentary on His Apology for the Cross*. Grand Rapids: Eerdmans, 2000.

Hackett, Conrad and David McClendon. "Christians Remain World's Largest Religious Group, but They Are Declining in Europe." Pew Research Center. Apr. 5, 2017. https://www.pewresearch.org/fact-tank/2017/04/05/christians-remain-worlds-largest-religious-group-but-they-are-declining-in-europe/.

Harrill, J. Albert. "Slavery." In *DNTB*, 1124–27.

Hengel, Martin. *Crucifixion in the Ancient World and the Folly of the Message of the Cross*. London: SCM, 1977.

———. "Literary, Theological and Historical Problems in the Gospel of Mark." In *The Gospel and the Gospels*, edited by Peter Stuhlmacher, 209–51. Grand Rapids: Eerdmans, 1991.

———. *Studies in the Gospel of Mark*. Philadelphia: Fortress, 1985.

———. *Was Jesus a Revolutionist?* Philadelphia: Fortress, 1971.

Hilgert, E. "Ships; Boats." In *ISBE*, 4:482–8.

Hixon, Elijah. "Diatessaron." In *LBD*, n.p.

Hoehner, H. W. "Chronology." In *DJG*, 118–22.

———. "Pontius Pilate." In *DJG*, 615–16.

Hooker, Morna D. *The Gospel According to Saint Mark*. Black's New Testament Commentary. London: Continuum, 1991.

"How Do Seeds Sprout?" Wonderopolis (website). https://www.wonderopolis.org/wonder/how-do-seeds-sprout.
Howard W. Hoehner, "Chronology." In *DJG*, 118–22.
———. "Pontius Pilate." In *DJG*, 615–16.
Hurst, Lincoln D., and Joel B. Green. "Priest, Priesthood." In *DJG*, 634–36.
Hurtado, Larry W. *Mark*. Grand Rapids: Baker, 2011.
———. *Studies in the Gospel of Mark*. Philadelphia: Fortress, 1985.
Irvin, D. "Sew." In *ISBE*, 4:428–29.
Jackson, Jeffrey Glenn, ed. *New Testament Use of the Old Testament*. Bellingham, WA: Faithlife, 2015. Logos.
Jefford, C. N. "Tiberius." In *ISBE*, 4:847–48.
Jeremias, Joachim. *New Testament Theology: The Proclamation of Jesus*. New York: Scribner's, 1971.
———. *The Prayers of Jesus*. Translated by J. Bowden, C. Burchard, and J. Reumann. SBT, 2nd ser., 6. Naperville, IL: Allenson, 1967.
Josephus. *The Life. Against Apion*. Translated by H. St. J. Thackeray. Loeb Classical Library 186. Cambridge, MA: Harvard University Press, 1966.
———. *The Works of Josephus: Complete and Unabridged*. Translated by William Whiston. Peabody, MA: Hendrickson, 1987.
Kähler, M. *The So-Called Historical Jesus and the Historic Biblical Christ*. Translated by C. E. Braaten. Philadelphia: Fortress, 1964.
Karbel Multimedia. "Herod's Temple." In *Logos Bible Software Infographics*. Bellingham, WA: Lexham, 2009.
Kee, Howard Clark. "Medicine and Healing." In *ABD*, 4:659–64.
Keener, Craig S. *The Gospel of John: A Commentary*. Grand Rapids: Baker Academic, 2012. Logos.
Kelly, Joseph. "Wine," In *LBD*, n.p.
Kennedy, T. Michael. "Caiaphas." In *LBD*, n.p.
Keown, Mark J. "An Imminent Parousia and Christian Mission: Did the New Testament Writers Expect Jesus's Imminent Return?" In *Christian Origins and the Establishment of the Early Jesus Movement*, edited by Stanley E. Porter and Andrew W. Pitts, 242–63. Texts and Editions for New Testament Studies 12; Early Christianity in its Hellenistic Context 4. Leiden, Neth.: Brill, 2017.
———. *Discovering the New Testament: An Introduction to Its Background, Theology, and Themes: The Gospels and Acts*. Vol. 1. Bellingham, WA: Lexham, 2018.
———. "How Much Should We Sing?" *Stimulus* 19, no. 3 (Nov. 2012) 5–13.
———. *Jesus in a World of Colliding Empires: Mark's Jesus from the Perspective of Power and Expectations*. 2 vols. Eugene, OR: Wipf & Stock, 2018.
———. "Paul's Vision of a New Masculinity (Eph 5:21—6:9)." *Colloquium* 48, no. 1 (May 2016) 47–60.
Liddell, Henry George, Robert Scott, Henry Stuart Jones, and Roderick McKenzie. *Greek-English Lexicon with a Revised Supplement*. 9th ed. Oxford: Clarendon, 1996.
"List of Famines." Wikimedia Foundation. Last edited Apr. 12, 2021. https://en.wikipedia.org/wiki/List_of_famines.
"List of Methods of Capital Punishment." Wikimedia Foundation. Last edited Mar. 13, 2021. https://en.wikipedia.org/wiki/List_of_methods_of_capital_punishment.

"List of People Claimed to Be Jesus." Wikimedia Foundation. Last edited Apr. 25, 2021. https://en.wikipedia.org/wiki/List_of_people_claimed_to_be_Jesus.

Long, Phillip J. "Gennesaret." In *LBD*, n.p.

Louw, Johannes P., and Eugene Albert Nida. *Greek-English Lexicon of the New Testament: Based on Semantic Domains*. 2 vols. New York: United Bible Societies, 1996.

Marshall, Christopher D. *Faith as a Theme in Mark's Narrative*. SNTSMS 64. New York: Cambridge University Press, 1989.

McDonald, Lee Martin. "Anti-Marcionite (Gospel) Prologues." In *ABD*, 1:262–63.

Meiklejohn, J. W., and F. F. Bruce, "Arimathea." In *NBD*, 80.

Metzger, Bruce Manning. *A Textual Commentary on the Greek New Testament*. 2nd ed. Companion to United Bible Societies' Greek New Testament, 4th ed. New York: United Bible Societies, 1994.

Miller, Jeffrey E. "Tax Collector." In *LBD*, n.p.

Miselbrook, Jeremy S. "Caligula, Emperor." In *LBD*, n.p.

Myers, Allen C., ed. *The Eerdmans Bible Dictionary*. Grand Rapids: Eerdmans, 1987.

———. "Nero." In *EBD*, 758.

Nease, Owen. "Gethsemane." In *LBD*, n.p.

Netzer, Ehud, and T. A. Holland. "Jericho (Place)." In *ABD*, 3:723–40.

Nyberg, Meredith Faubel. "Unleavened Bread, Feast of." In *LBD*, n.p.

Nylund, Jan H. "Court of the Gentiles." In *LBD*, n.p.

Omanson, Roger L., and Bruce Manning Metzger. *A Textual Guide to the Greek New Testament: An Adaptation of Bruce M. Metzger's Textual Commentary for the Needs of Translators*. Stuttgart, Germ.: Deutsche Bibelgesellschaft, 2006.

Osborne, Grant R. "Elder." In *DJG*, 201–3.

Patzia, Arthur G., and Anthony J. Petrotta. *Pocket Dictionary of Biblical Studies*. Downers Grove, IL: InterVarsity, 2002.

Peterson, David G. *The Acts of the Apostles*. PNTC. Grand Rapids: Eerdmans, 2009.

Pingenot, Jesse. "Tiberius, Emperor." In *LBD*, n.p.

Plummer, A., ed. *The Gospel According to St Mark*. Cambridge Greek Testament for Schools and Colleges. Cambridge, UK: Cambridge University Press, 1914.

Rayburn, Robert G., II. "Salt." In *LBD*, n.p.

Reinhardt, Wolfgang. "The Population Size of Jerusalem and the Numerical Growth of the Jerusalem Church." In *Palestinian Setting*, edited by Richard Bauckham, 237–65. Vol. 4 of *The Book of Acts in Its First Century Setting*. Grand Rapids: Eerdmans, 1995.

Sanders, E. P. *Jesus and Judaism*. London: SCM Press, 1985.

Sarlo, Daniel. "Sea." In *LBD*, n.p.

Schmidt, T. E. "Taxes." In *DJG*, 804–6.

Shirokov, Peter. "Cyrene." In *LBD*, n.p.

Silva, Moisés, ed. *New International Dictionary of New Testament Theology and Exegesis*. Grand Rapids: Zondervan, 2014.

Stein, Robert H. *Luke*. NAC 24. Nashville: Broadman & Holman, 1992.

———. *Mark*. Baker Exegetical Commentary on the New Testament. Grand Rapids: Baker Academic, 2008.

———. "Synoptic Problem." In *DJG*, 784–92.

Stoops, R. F., Jr. "Peter and Paul, Passion of." In *ABD*, 5:264.

Strack, H.L., and P. Billerbeck. *Kommentar zum Neuen Testament aus Talmud und Midrasch*. 6 vols. Munich: 1922–1961.

Strange, James F. "Dalmanutha." In *ABD*, 2:4.
Swanson, James. *Dictionary of Biblical Languages with Semantic Domains: Greek (New Testament)*. Oak Harbor, WA: Logos Research Systems, 1997.
Tan-Gatue, Peter. "Scribe." In *LBD*, n.p.
Torrey, C. C. *The Four Gospels: A New Translation*. London: Hodder & Stoughton, 1933.
Udd, Kris J., and Melton B. Winstead. "Bethsaida." In *LBD*, n.p.
Wenham, J. W. "Did Peter Go to Rome in A.D. 42?" *Tyndale Bulletin* 23 (1972) 97–102.
———. *Easter Enigma*. Grand Rapids: Zondervan, 1984.
Wenkel, David H. "Sicarii." *LBD*, n.p.
Winstead, Melton B. "Galilee, Sea of." In *LBD*.
Witherington, Ben, III. *The Gospel of Mark: A Socio-Rhetorical Commentary*. Grand Rapids: Eerdmans, 2001.
———. "Salome (Person)." In *ABD*, 5:906–7.
Witte, Brendon R. "Messianic Secret." In *LBD*, n.p.
Wood, D. R. W., and I. Howard Marshall, eds. *New Bible Dictionary*. 3rd ed. Downers Grove, IL: InterVarsity, 1996.
Wright, N. T. *Jesus and the Victory of God*. COQG. London: Society for Promoting Christian Knowledge, 1996.

Subject Index

Aaron, 143n15, 154
abandon(s), abandoned, abandonment, 76, 102n30, 111, 279–80, 292
Abba, *Abbā*, 18, 100, 260, 260n99, 260n100, 273, 291
Abel, 25
abhorrence, abhorrent, 173, 199, 264
abiding, 68n23, 187
ability, 38, 98, 105, 158, 161, 215, 226, 260, 266
abolition, 192
abomination that causes Desolation, 10, 243, 267, 290
abominations, 196n19
aborting, abortion, 124, 182, 183
Abraham, Abram 36, 98, 99, 102, 129, 150, 227
abstinence, 276
Adam, 36, 38, 54, 145, 178
Adonai, viii, 231, 232, 232n79, 233, 236, 268
adult, adulthood, 44, 181, 183
adulterous, adultery, vii, 109, 125, 176, 179, 186
adversaries, adversary, 37, 147, 168, 244
advocate (the Spirit), 37
Africa, African, 31, 151, 239, 275
afterlife, 225
age, ages, 13n40, 31–32, 38, 48, 61n4, 97, 102, 104, 107, 122, 156, 191, 192, 211, 226–27, 233, 238, 239, 242–45, 247, 251, 262, 265
agora, 234
agrarian, 81, 83, 113
Agrippa, I, 197, 199, 256
Ahab, 109, 222

alabaster, 249
alcohol, 125, 158
Alexander (the Great), 11, 17, 128, 142
Alexander (son of Simon), 275
Alexandria, 7, 10
Alexandrian text, 160n41
allegorical, 221
alluded, alludes, alluding, allusion(s), 98, 138, 174, 220, 233, 240, 250, 260, 278
Alphaeus, 56, 69
ambassador, 68
ambiguity, ambiguous, ambiguity, 54, 145, 179, 224, 225n51, 272
ambition, 69, 107, 164, 195, 200, 205
Amen, *amēn*, 78, 192, 286, 290
Americas, 84
Amidah, 217n26
Ammonites, 37
Amos, 23n64, 143n15, 221, 230n73, 240n15, 245n42, 265n9
Amputating, amputation, 172, 173
Ananias, (Jesus Ben), 214, 267
Ananias (High Priest), 263n1
anathema, 183
Andrew, (disciple), 43, 47, 56, 141, 163, 240
ANE, xiii, 254–55, 260, 285
anesthetic, 276
angel(s), *angelion, angelos*, 17, 30, 31, 33, 36–38, 45–46, 91, 99, 117, 148, 150–52, 225, 227, 246–47, 251, 285–86, 290
anger, angered, angry, 50n22, 65, 131, 182–83, 198, 204, 219, 250, 263, 270

297

SUBJECT INDEX

anguish, ix, 259
animals, 11, 37–38, 61, 63, 87, 92–93, 129, 191, 213, 215
Anna, 60
Annas, 266
annihilate, annihilation, annihilationists, 173, 194, 225n55
anointed, anointing(s), anoints, v, viii, 1, 17, 24n66, 27, 33–37, 39–41, 43, 45, 47, 49, 51, 53, 55, 57, 106, 143, 143n15, 144, 153, 182, 207, 219, 248–51, 285
anonymity, anonymous, 6n7, 18
antagonism, antagonists, antagonizing, 218, 221, 224, 264–65, 269
anthropological, anthropology, 178, 228
Antichrist, 244
Antioch, (Syria), 8, 11n31, 123, 275
Antioch (Pisidian), 106
Antiochian Missions, 8–9, 12, 60
Antiochus Epiphanes IV, 171n10, 243–44
Antipas, 20, 64, 107, 109n42, 138, 141, 143, 149, 164, 177, 199, 203, 241n21, 271, 292
Anti-Marcionite Prologue, 10, 10n27,
Antonia (Fortress), 213n14, 271, 274n34, 292
apocalypse, 238
apocalyptic, apocalyptically, 45, 135, 145n18, 172, 239, 244–46, 292
apodosis, 136
Apollos, 78n39, 164, 169–70
Apologetics, apologetically, 82, 284, 293
Apostle(s), xi, 8, 22, 34, 67–69, 72, 75, 78, 85, 98, 104, 105n37, 107, 111–12, 115, 143–44, 164, 157, 167, 202, 252n70, 289, 295
apostolic, 104, 287
Aqiba, 229
Aquila, 12, 170
Arabia, 109
Aramaic, 2, 7, 11, 100, 122, 131, 134, 153, 172, 203, 260, 273, 278
Aretas IV Philopatris, 109

Antipas (Herod), 20, 64, 107, 109, 109n42, 138, 141, 143, 164, 177, 199, 241n21, 271, 292
Antipas (Rev 2:13), 149
Arimathea, ix, 28, 95, 218n28, 269, 282, 283n57, 288, 295
Aristarchus, 75n35
Aristobulus II, 71
Ark of the covenant, 44
army, armies, 24, 148, 154, 168, 203, 244n36
Aron Kodesh, 44
arrest(s), arrested, arrestors, ix, 8, 21–22, 76, 135, 196–97, 199, 223, 228, 248, 252, 261, 263–64, 265n10, 267, 263, 265, 269, 271, 273, 275, 277, 279, 281, 283, 285, 287, 289
arrogance, arrogant, arrogate, 127, 195, 250, 234, 261
art, 164
ascend(s), ascended, ascending, ascension, ascending, 26, 67, 99, 152–54, 198, 207, 233, 258, 279, 287, 288
Asia Minor, 6, 241
Asia(n), 84, 149, 202, 241
assassinated, 110, 199
assassins (Sicarii), 69, 253
Assyrians, 71, 99, 277
asteroids, 245
astral, 245
asyndeton, 166, 166n5
atheistic, 103
athletics, 203
Atonement, atoning, 29, 51n24, 59–60, 201, 216, 222
Auckland, 83
August, 210
Augustine, Augustinian, x, 2–3
Augustus, 11, 107, 141–42, 224n47
Australasia, 84
Authorship, v, 6, 232n78

Baal-Zebub, 71
Babylon, Babylonian(s), 7, 33, 34n3, 40–41, 71, 99, 121, 139, 196n19, 211n6, 214, 245

SUBJECT INDEX

banquet(s), 111, 114–15, 129, 134, 234
baptism, baptize(d), v, 1, 7, 17, 34n3, 35–37, 57, 89, 102, 155–56, 183, 197, 197n21, 219, 221n43, 280–81, 284, 287, 292
Baptist (John), v–vi, 17–20, 27, 30, 33–36, 45, 57, 59, 104, 107–9, 111, 140, 143, 156, 219, 223, 246
Barabbas, 21, 24, 29, 196, 273, 278
Bar Kochba, 241
Barnabas, 8, 9n22, 60, 106, 123, 189
Bartimaeus, viii, 19, 25, 28, 93, 103, 118, 140–42, 162, 182, 188, 195–96, 202–6, 209, 215, 231
bathhouses, 203
Bathsheba, 74
beasts (Daniel), 145
beast (Revelation), 244
beasts (wild), 93
Beatitudes, 66
Beelzebub, Beelzebul, 71, 157
beggar, begged, begging, 105, 203–4, 205
beheaded, 109, 111, 149, 256, 276
belief(s), 41, 97, 153, 215, 225, 227, 248
believe(d), believes, believing, 1, 3, 11, 13n37, 20, 24–25, 30–31, 33, 35–36, 39, 41–43, 45, 49, 53, 57, 75, 79, 92–93, 99, 103, 107, 117, 130, 135–36, 148, 151, 159–60, 163, 170–71, 173–74, 186, 189, 195–96, 200n30, 204, 206, 208, 211, 214–17, 225n51, 226, 228, 231, 240n13, 240n19, 244, 247–48, 249n57, 251, 254n73, 256, 264, 275, 279–80, 282–83, 284n62, 286–89
believer(s), 9, 20, 31, 48, 57, 72, 77–78, 80, 82–83, 109, 125, 131, 145, 155, 159, 164, 167, 170–72, 174, 176, 216, 231, 234–35, 255, 278, 280, 289
benedictions (Eighteen), 217, 26
benevolence, 51
Bernice, 128
Bethany, viii, 27, 182, 207n44, 207n45, 209–210, 215, 218, 248–49, 253, 262, 285

Bethphage, 207, 207n44, 292
Bethsaida, 47, 66, 112, 116, 141n5, 142, 162, 296
betray(s), betrayal, betrayed, betrayer, betraying, vii, ix, 20, 29, 69, 76, 150, 179, 194, 242, 252–56, 261–64, 265n10
Bible(s), xiii–xv, 7, 13, 13n37, 20n47, 41, 159, 180, 226–27, 291–96
biblical, xiii–xv, 14n41, 65, 114, 121, 138, 178, 202, 211n7, 245, 257, 268, 271n25, 285, 291, 293–96
biological, 245
bird(s), 36, 51n24, 75, 83, 84n48
bishop(s), 6, 198
blaspheme, blasphemed, blasphemer, blaspheming, blasphemous, blasphemy, 53, 55, 64, 127, 229, 268, 278
bleed, bleeding, blood, bloody, vi, 17, 23, 28, 51, 94, 96, 98, 100–101, 103, 111–12, 120, 134, 192, 196, 206, 215, 253, 256–57, 261–62, 271
blessed, blessedness, blesses, blessing, blessing(s), vii, 2, 27, 37–38, 61, 73, 81, 99, 115, 133, 169, 181–83, 185, 189, 191–93, 204, 207, 208, 255, 256, n86, 267–68
blind, blindness, blinded, blindly, vii–viii, 50n21, 67, 75, 97, 119–21, 131, 133, 139–41, 144, 162, 193–95, 202–6, 236, 269, 280
blindfold, 269
Boanerges, 68
boat(s), 67, 74, 86–87, 89, 112, 116, 117n7, 118, 134, 205, 293
bodies, bodily, body, 51, 19, 22, 29, 42, 45, 92, 100, 106, 111, 133, 150, 172–73, 175, 220, 222, 225n55, 229, 251, 255–56, 261–62, 269, 277, 283–85
bold, boldly, boldness, 96, 147, 150, 152, 195, 197, 256, 258, 270, 283n58, 290
booth, tax, 55
booth (tent), 55, 78, 154
Booth, Catherine, 78

bread, 29, 63, 105, 113, 115, 118, 129, 132–33, 135, 138, 139n3, 140, 152n28, 175, 248n54, 253, 255n77, 256–57, 262, 295
bride, 60
bridegroom, 60, 66
Britain, 151
bronze Age, 61n4
brother(s), 69, 108, 109, 141, 167, 176, 226, 226n58, 264, 265n9, 282,
brother-in-law, 226n58
build(s), builders, building, buildings, built, 44, 53n26, 81, 83, 89, 95, 108, 142, 154, 162, 179, 206, 211n6, 214, 217, 220, 222–23, 237n1, 240, 252, 267
burial, buried, buries, bury, burying, ix, 19, 27–29, 73, 109, 111, 146, 172, 206, 222, 250–51, 263, 265, 267, 269, 271, 273, 275, 277, 279, 281–85, 287–89
burn, burning, burnt, 51n24, 70, 112, 159, 172, 175, 227, 230, 268n21

Caesar(s), viii, 11, 17, 18, 19, 24, 109, 142, 143, 223, 224n47, 236, 244, 272, 275n36, 278, 281
Caesar, Augustus, 11, 141, 142, 224
Caesar, Jesus, 33
Caesar, Julius, 168
Caesar, Tiberius, 107, 142, 198, 224
Caesarea, Maritima, 142, 271, 291
Caesarea, Philippi, 17, 39, 130, 142, 142n7, 161, 163, 271
Caiaphas, 213, 266, 266n13, 294
Caligula, 10, 107, 199, 243, 295
camel, 35, 61, 191
Canaanite(s), 34, 129, 203
Cantha, 93n16
Capernaum, 26, 44, 47–48, 52, 55, 64, 66, 70n26, 95, 101, 119, 128, 134, 163, 177, 218, 282
Capri, 198
capstone, 222
care, cares, cared, caring, 25, 31, 48, 51, 67, 70–71, 77, 87, 97, 102n30, 112–13, 116, 122, 132, 144, 149, 159, 166, 183, 193, 220–21, 251–52, 270
carnallite, 175n175
carpenter, 102
Catholic, 47, 98, 102
celebrate(s), celebrated, celebrating, celebration(s), 60, 110, 244n37, 248, 253–55
celebrity, 110, 157
celibate, 47, 125
census, 11n30
centurion, 10, 28, 128, 130, 281, 283–84, 289
Cephas, 56, 164
cessationists, 72
chag hammatstsoth, 248
chained, 83, 158
chariot, 108
charisma, charismatic, 62, 73, 199
charity, 250n68
chi (Greek letter), 26n73
chiasm, chiastic, 26, 26n73, 28, 94, 118, 123, 208
child, children, vii, 2, 22, 25, 27n75, 34n3, 41, 74, 94, 96–97, 98n22, 100, 101–2, 116, 122, 124, 129, 133, 145, 150, 156–59, 165–66, 170–72, 178, 181, 182, 182n38, 182n39, 183, 183n40, 184–86, 188, 191–92, 198, 205, 215, 226, 236, 242, 254, 256
childbirth, 96
childhood, 159
childless, 109, 226
childlikeness, 22n59
China, 31, 151, 239
chose, chosen
Chrestus, 12
Christ, viii, 1, 12, 14n40, 17, 22, 29–31, 33–37, 39, 41–43, 50, 56, 60, 65, 68n23, 69, 71, 75–77, 81, 81n43, 82, 89, 93, 95–98, 106–8, 115–16, 119, 122–23, 128, 136, 141, 143–46, 148–51, 153–55, 157, 162, 166, 168–71, 174, 181, 183, 186–87, 189–90, 192–93, 195, 197–98, 200–203, 203n37, 211, 216, 218–19, 230, 233, 236,

239–44, 246–49, 254, 258, 262, 267, 271–72, 274, 276, 278, 281, 284, 286, 288, 294
Christian(s), viii, xiii, 5–7, 10–12, 29, 34, 36, 44, 47–49, 51–52, 59–60, 62, 64, 68–69, 72–73, 75–79, 81–82, 84n49, 85, 91–92, 95, 104, 109, 111–16, 123–27, 131, 134–35, 136, 142, 144, 148, 149, 158, 160–62, 164, 166, 169–71, 175–76, 178–81, 183–84, 187–88, 192–95, 197, 197n21, 198–203, 206, 209, 215, 218n28, 222, 224, 226, 228, 230–31, 234, 236, 238, 242, 248, 251–52, 254n73, 255, 261–63, 271, 275, 277, 277n46, 279, 281, 283n60, 288, 291–94, 296
Christianity, 9, 11–12, 44, 84, 114, 155, 158, 229, 239, 292, 294
Christlike, 77
Christmas, 110, 183
christological, Christology, 129, 200, 207–8, 221, 221n43, 278, 292
Christs, false, 27n75, 245
chronological, chronology, 9, 9n23, 25, 52, 152, 211, 254, 277n46, 292–94
church(es), 6n7, 7, 7n10, 8–10, 12–13, 20, 28n76, 34, 42–44, 46, 48–49, 57–58, 60, 62, 66, 68–69, 75, 77–78, 81, 83–84, 100, 105, 106, 114–15, 123, 125, 128, 136–38, 160, 160n41, 164, 166, 169–70, 176, 183–84, 189, 192, 198, 202, 205, 230, 235, 242, 244, 246, 247n52, 252, 254, 257, 259n92, 263–64, 275–76, 278, 287, 289–90, 295
Cicero, 168
circumcised, circumcision, 12, 187
cistern, 63
cities, city, 10, 17, 46, 83–84, 89, 92, 93n16, 112, 121, 128, 141–42, 202–3, 208–9, 213, 222, 225, 231, 253, 273, 275, 276n39, 283n60
citizen (s), 206, 274, 277

civic, civil, 146, 180n33, 271n25
Claudius, 8, 10, 12, 241n26
clean, cleanness, cleansed, cleansing, 45, 50, 51n24, 96–97, 112, 120, 134, 212n8
Clement of Alexandria, 7n10, 10
Cleopatra, 203
clergy, clerical, 234, 236
Clopas, 282
Cloth(s), vi, 60, 61, 61n4, 63, 98, 152, 263, 284n63, 285
clothed, clothes, clothing, 24, 51, 61, 96–97, 120, 133, 152, 161, 208, 230, 234, 236, 243, 268, 277
cloud (s), 24, 38, 154, 246, 268–69, 279, 290
Codex Sinaiticus, 14
Codex Washingtonianus 13n40
Codex Vaticanus, 14
codices, 13n36
coerced, coercion, coercive, 188n4, 199, 201, 276
cognate, 88, 189n7
cohort, 274
coin(s), coinage, 11n30, 213, 224, 229, 238
collection, Jerusalem (first), 241,
collection, Jerusalem (second), 8, 238, 241,
collector(s), Tax/Toll, 25, 56, 56n33, 58, 60, 69, 85, 295
colonialism, 193
Colossae, 241
colt, 207–8
comforter (Paraclete), 27
comfort, comfortable, comforted, comforting, 22n56, 38, 64, 83, 87, 90, 92, 196n19, 260, 289
coming, Jesus (first), 35, 156, 216, 231
coming, Jesus (second), 22n56, 36, 174, 246, 262
coming, of Elijah, 154, 156n37
coming, of Moses, 154
coming, of the Kingdom, 40, 42, 61, 62, 72n32, 151, 208, 232
coming, of the Messiah, 34, 35, 40, 108, 135, 143n15, 245

coming, on the clouds of heaven, 24, 268–69
coming, Son of Man, 246
coming, of the Spirit, 36, 280
commander(s), 105, 110, 122, 127, 154, 168, 179, 186, 203
Commandment(s), Ten, 38, 63, 124–25, 187, 268
Commandment(s), Great, viii, 121–22, 188, 227–31, 236
commandments, 121, 149n24, 189n7, 287n69
commands, 21, 41, 46, 51, 64, 67, 93, 131, 144, 147, 158, 205, 224, 229–30, 257, 259
commission, Great, 30, 75, 287n69
communism, communistic, 188n4, 251
community, communities, 6, 12, 42–44, 47, 50, 90, 94–96, 99, 107, 114, 166, 176, 187, 188n4, 203, 206, 248, 290
compassion, compassionate, compassionately, 50, 50n22, 51–52, 94, 98, 110, 112–13, 116, 132, 135, 159, 188, 289
competing, competition, competitiveness, 198
compromise, 180
compulsion, 37, 235
conceit, 164
condemn(s), condemned, condemnation, 24, 28, 79, 108, 118, 136, 141, 180, 194, 214, 231, 236, 252, 262, 265–69, 273–74, 276n39, 287–88
conditional (sentence), 136
conditional immortality, 173
confess, confessed, confesses, confessing, confession, vii, 1, 17, 28, 34, 39, 86, 88, 107–8, 138–43, 145, 147, 149, 151, 153, 157, 159, 161–62, 204–5, 233, 281, 283–84
confidence, confident, confidently, 25, 99, 127, 134, 157–60, 173, 179, 187–88
conflict, 45, 59–60, 62, 146, 152, 175, 241

confused, confusion, 19, 19n46, 142n7, 154, 207n45, 254n73, 277n46, 284n63, 286
congregation, 65
conjunction, 7n10, 60
conjunctive, 166n5
conquer(s), conquered, conquering, conqueror, 18, 128, 202, 204, 243, 279
conquest(s), 88, 147, 154, 203
consolation, 118, 196n19
consumerism, 125, 193
consummated, consummation of the kingdom, 31, 40, 153, 257, 276
consumption, 193
contagion, contagious, contagiousness, 50, 50n20, 279
contaminated, contamination, 51, 56
controversy, controversies, controversial, v–viii, 33, 59, 53, 56, 59, 63–64, 71, 112, 117, 120, 123, 149, 157, 210, 217, 229
conversation, converse, 63, 87, 98, 101, 150, 164, 249n58
conversion, convert, converted, converts, 57, 71, 73, 77–78, 82, 130, 144, 205, 275, 279, 283
cooking, 120, 254
Corban, 27n75, 100, 122n24, 187, 238, 292
Corinth, 10
Corinthian(s), 10, 164, 202, 238, 283n60
corn, 63
Cornelius, 123, 275
cornerstone, 220, 222, 267
coronation, 36, 208, 249, 251
corpse(s), 100, 255, 255n78
corrupt(s), corrupted, corrupting, corruption, 19, 45, 56, 91, 123, 127, 138, 140, 148, 150, 215, 218, 233
cosmic, cosmos, 31, 135, 200, 247, 257, 269, 289
council, Jerusalem, 12, 123
council (Sanhedrin), 42, 266n14, 269, 283
councils (local), 242
counselor (Spirit), 37

countercultural, 186
countryside, 35, 120
courage, courageously, 20, 43, 54, 88, 98, 109, 118, 150, 193, 197–98, 205, 256, 258, 261, 265–66, 270, 282
court, Herod, 64
Court, of the Gentiles, 212, 212n8, 213n10, 240, 295
courts, royal, 45
court(s), Temple, 212, 218, 231, 253, 265
Court, women's, 237n1
courtyard(s), 266, 270
cousin(s), 8n20, 36, 195n15
covenant community/people, 99, 213
covenant, new, 17, 23, 29, 143n15, 187, 256–57, 260
covenant, old, 187, 256
covenantal, 175, 185, 253, 255, 257
covet, covetousness, 125, 187
cow, 171
cowardly, 88
coworkers, 9
cradle, 183
craft, 126
craftsman, 102
creation, 35–36, 38, 40, 51, 63–64, 87, 88, 93, 115, 129, 131, 136, 152n28, 183, 199, 211, 245, 247, 256, 289
creative, creativity, creatively, 28, 54, 88, 141, 277
Creator, 38, 129, 159, 166, 183, 269, 288
creatures, 43, 87
Cretan, 34n3
cricket, cricketer, 259n95
crime, 272
criminal(s), 24, 274, 277, 284n62
crop(s), 77, 74
cross, crosses, vii, 11–12, 19, 22, 22n59, 24–25, 31, 37, 49, 76–77, 86, 88, 103, 105, 108, 110, 145–47, 149–52, 161, 164, 177, 181, 190, 193, 196, 201, 206, 217, 260–61, 270, 273, 276, 276n39, 277, 277n46, 278–80, 282–83, 288, 290, 293
crossbar, crossbeam, 276, 277
cross-bearing, 22n59, 276

crowd(s), crowded, vi, 21, 21n51, 39, 46, 50, 52–53, 55, 66–67, 69–70, 74, 84, 86, 95–97, 98, 110, 112, 114–16, 119, 123, 132–33, 137, 139, 148, 157, 161, 177, 182, 188, 191, 202–5, 208–9, 211, 215, 218–20, 223, 231, 233, 235, 254, 272–74, 278, 280, 289
crowing, crows, 117, 258, 270
crown, crowned, 24, 66, 275, 275n36
crucified, crucifixion, crucified, crucify, ix, 7, 11–12, 17, 21, 23–24, 29–30, 135, 145–46, 148–49, 151, 155, 161, 194, 196, 198, 209, 218, 241n19, 254, 263, 265, 267, 269–71, 273–75, 276n39, 277, 277n44, 278, 278n48, 279, 281, 283–85, 287–89, 293
cruciform, 144
cubits, 240n13
cult(s), 34n3, 59, 224
cultural, culturally, culture(s), 43, 47, 54, 80, 106, 110, 114, 122, 126, 137, 164, 166, 181, 189, 196, 202, 234, 255, 269, 284–85, 292
cunning, 126
cup(s), 40, 168–69, 196, 196n19, 197, 256, 260–61, 276
currency, 237
curse, cursed, curses, cursing, viii, 27, 91, 126, 175n21, 185, 210, 211, 213, 215, 217, 219, 221, 223, 225, 227, 229, 231, 233, 235, 236, 270, 278, 289
curtain, 29, 36, 222, 267, 280–81, 285
cushion(s), 87, 87n5, 88
custom(s), 56, 62, 101, 120, 177, 244n37, 254, 260, 272, 284
cut, cutting, 90, 147, 172, 215, 226, 245, 270, 274
Cynic(s), cynicism, 105, 159, 189n7
Cyprus, 9
Cyrene, Cyrenian, Cyrenians, 275–76, 276n38, 295
Cyrus, 113

Daddy, 260, 260n99, 291
Dalmanutha, 134, 134n46, 138, 296

SUBJECT INDEX

Damascus, 93n16
dance, danced, dancing, 108–110
danger(s), dangerous, 54, 65, 67, 81, 86, 88, 93, 97, 103, 127, 138, 140, 164, 213, 266, 270, 289
Daniel, 18, 40, 55, 99, 119, 145, 161, 226, 255, 289, 295
Danube, 239
dark, darkened, darkness, 23, 48, 72, 79, 93, 116, 189, 245, 279
daughter, vi–vii, 27, 94–96, 98, 98n22, 99, 108–9, 111, 128–29, 141, 176, 208, 226
David, 17–18, 34, 37, 40, 63, 74, 109, 113, 128, 143n15, 162, 176, 202, 204, 204n39–40, 206, 208, 224, 231–32, 279–80, 291, 293, 295–96
Davidic, 11, 17, 30, 34, 36, 39, 113–14, 143n15, 144, 146, 204–5, 208, 211, 231–32, 232n78, 269
day, eighth, 51n24
Day, first of the unleavened bread, 253
Days, Ancient of, 145
Day, Lord's, 64
Day, of Atonement, 29, 59–60, 222
Day of the Lord, 156
days, forty (Wilderness), 38
days, forty (Sinai), 38
days, forty (Purity), 96
days, forty (Christ's appearances), 279
days, six (creation), 152, 152n28
days, six (Passover), 152, 152n28
days, six (Jericho), 152, 152n28
day, the (Consummation), 24, 60, 243, 246, 247, 257
days, three (resurrection), 132, 145, 146, 147, 161, 161, 194, 214, 267, 290
days, tribulation, 245, 247
dead, death(s), deceased, die(s), died, dying, vi, viii–ix, 1, 7–8, 9, 9n22, 9n23, 10–12, 14n40, 17–20, 23–24, 27–30, 34, 34n3, 35–36, 39–41, 46, 50n20, 51n24, 52, 55, 60, 62, 66–68, 71, 75, 78–79, 86–87, 89–97, 92, 95, 97, 99–105, 107–113, 120, 122, 135–36, 141–42, 143n15, 144–45, 146n20 147—156, 156n37, 157, 159, 160–62, 164, 173–76, 177, 177n29, 179, 188n40, 189–90, 193–94, 197, 201–2, 204, 206–7, 209, 211n4, 215, 217, 221–22, 225, 225n51, 225n56, 226–27, 231, 233, 237, 248, 252n70, 254, 255, 257n86, 274, 239, 241, 243, 245–47, 249–53, 255–61, 263, 263n1, 266–71, 273–74, 276, 277, 277n44, 277n46, 278–85, 286, 288–89, 292–93
Dead Sea, 111, 175
Dead Sea Scrolls, 188n4, 225n51
deaf, deafness, vii, 121, 130–31, 133, 139, 140–41, 157–58
debate(s), debated, debating, 3, 26, 29, 35n6, 46, 54, 90, 123, 134, 155, 157, 163, 173, 177, 179, 188, 195, 206, 207n48 219, 225, 227, 235, 266, 273, 284
debauchery, 126
Decalogue, 186, 229
Decapolis, 66, 66n22, 89, 93, 93n16, 130–32, 134, 292
decay, 285
deceit, deceive(d), deceiving, deception, deceptive, 74–75, 126, 147, 195, 199, 245, 290
decree, 156
Dedication, Feast of, 208
deeds, 106, 144
De facto relationship, 180n33
defile, defiles, defiled, defilement, 97, 123, 172, 212n8, 283
defraud(s), defrauded, 187, 189
deities, 154
deity, 64, 153, 268, 275
deliverance(s), delivered, deliverer, delivering, 17, 22–23, 25, 33, 41, 46–49, 52, 67–68, 70, 72, 74, 89–90, 94, 96, 103, 104n33, 107, 119, 143n15, 159–60, 168, 208, 216, 248, 257n86, 260, 264
Demas, 76–77
demography, 180n33, 292
demon(s), 19–21, 23, 30, 37, 45–49, 49, 52, 67–72, 74, 87, 89–91, 90–95,

101, 105–6, 108, 114, 119, 128–29, 144–45, 157–63, 167–70, 182, 216–18, 233, 281–82, 287, 289
demoniac, vi, 25, 28, 46, 72, 89, 90–92, 94, 106, 111, 130, 157–58, 167–68, 192
demonized, demon-possessed, vi, 29, 48, 50, 70–71, 90, 94, 103, 117, 158–59, 216, 218, 220, 289
demonology, 92
denarii, denarius, 11, 114, 224, 237, 249–50
denial(s), denied, denies, deny, denying, ix, 20, 25, 28–29, 70, 76–77, 108, 144–51, 164, 171, 190, 204, 225, 232, 255, 257–58, 261–62, 264–66, 270, 289, 290
denomination(s), 62, 166, 169–70, 183, 259n92
depraved, depravity, 29, 80
desert(s), 19, 20, 37, 132, 179
desolation, 10, 173, 196n19, 243, 244n36, 267, 290
despots, 199, 244
destitute, 135, 185, 203, 238
destruction, viii, 10, 27n75, 66, 87–88, 90–93, 120, 122, 124, 139, 150, 156, 173–74, 233, 238, 241, 244, 255, 267, 269, 278, 280, 289
devil, 46, 126, 147
Diaspora, 254
Diatessaron, 13, 13n39, 293
Diogenes of Sinope, 189n7
disabled, 64–65, 95, 103, 110, 132, 159, 185, 203, 215, 218
disciple(s), v, ix, 1, 12, 17–18, 19, 19n46, 20–22, 24–25, 28–31, 33–35, 37, 39, 41–47, 49, 51, 53, 55–57, 59–60, 63, 66–68, 70, 73, 75–76, 78, 81n43, 83–84, 86–88, 91, 93–94, 97–99, 101, 104–6, 108–111, 113–20, 124, 128–29, 132–36, 138–45, 147–49, 149n24, 151–52, 154–58, 160–71, 173–76, 179, 181–82, 189, 189n7, 190–95, 198, 201–9, 210n2, 211, 215–18, 220, 230, 235, 238–40, 245, 247–48, 249n57, 250–53, 255, 257–59, 261–62, 264, 265, 265n10, 266–67, 271, 274, 276, 282n55, 284, 286–90
discipleship, vii–viii, 10, 24–25, 44, 47, 56, 93, 138–39, 141, 143, 145, 147–49, 151–53, 155, 157, 159, 161, 163, 165, 167, 169–71, 173–77, 179, 181, 183, 185, 187, 189–91, 193–95, 197, 199, 201–3, 205–7, 209, 261
discipline, 173
discouraged, 79, 289
discourse, eschatological, 238
Discourse, Olivet, viii, 237, 238
discourse, prophetic, 238
disease(s), 46, 49–50, 96
disgrace(d), 220, 269, 274
dish, 110
dishonorable, 221
disobeys, 52
dispute, disputed, disputing, ix, 9, 141, 151, 157, 200n30, 134, 211, 238, 246, 254, 287
diverse, diversity, 19, 20, 66, 69, 289
Divi Filius, 281
divine, 19, 34, 45, 50n20, 53n27, 88, 101, 117–18, 130, 145, 145n17, 154, 163, 175, 185, 189, 205, 211, 215, 221, 224n47, 227, 247, 268, 278, 281, 284–85
divinity, 54, 87–88, 118, 152, 186, 232
divorce, divorced, divorces, divorcee, vii, 22n59, 27n75, 29, 45, 109, 125, 176–80, 180n33, 180n34, 292
doctor(s), 57, 97, 97n21
doctrine, 64
dog(s), 129–30, 203
Domitian, 197
donkey, 171, 207, 207n50, 208, 253
dough, 138
doulos, 264
dove(s), 36, 213
dragon, 88
dream, dreamed, dreams, 18, 39, 46, 121, 256
dress, dressed, 11, 265n10, 275, 284, 285, 288

drink, 62, 123, 169, 196–97, 256–57, 260, 276, 287
dromedary(ies), 191, 191n11, 292
drug(s), 135, 126, 158
drunk, drunkenness, 61, 109, 126, 256
dulled, dullness, 65, 276
dumb, 113
dung, 175
duplicity, 121, 135, 199, 223

eagle, 215
ear, 51n24, 264, 266, 270
earth, 31, 35–36, 42, 46, 47, 54–55, 84, 124, 128, 132, 143n15, 144, 150, 169, 173, 175, 178, 189, 216, 227, 229, 233, 246–47, 255n77, 257
earthenware, 51n24
earthly, 67, 153
earthquake(s), 121, 241, 241n25, 285, 291
east, eastern, xiii, 13, 31, 66, 84, 87, 96, 100, 111, 129–30, 132, 151–52, 169, 188, 207n44, 207n47, 239–40, 248, 287n69
Easter, 195n15, 200n30, 248, 296
eat(s), eaten, eating, 30, 35, 55–57, 63, 70, 75, 97, 112, 114–16, 120, 123, 129–30, 132, 137, 152n28, 175, 203, 211, 235, 248–49, 253–55, 265n10, 287
eclipse, 279
ecological, 92–93
economic, economies, 92–93, 125, 141, 175
Eden, 84, 115
edification, 57
education, 157
eggshells, 120n22
Egypt, 11n31, 29, 102, 153, 175, 203, 211n6, 248, 264
Egyptian, 34n3, 241n19
eisegesis, 226
Ekron, 71
El-Araj, 141
Eldad, 167
elder(s), 45, 60, 93n16, 120, 146, 146n21, 167, 194, 218, 223n45, 249, 249n60, 263, 276n42, 295

Eleazar, 168
elect, elected, 55, 95, 145–46, 245–47
Eleusinian Mystery Religions, 34n3
Elijah, 20, 23–24, 24n66, 35, 35n5, 38, 59, 90, 101, 108–9, 117, 143, 153, 153n32, 154–56, 156n37, 194, 203, 226–27, 280, 293
Elisha, 24, 34–36, 59, 101, 116, 203, 226
Eloi, Eloi, lema sabachthani, 100, 279
emissaries, emissary, 19, 68, 70, 135, 246
Emmaus, 287
emotion(s), emotional, 65, 100, 118, 178, 194, 250
emperor(s), 11, 33, 107, 142n7, 143n15, 168, 176, 198, 199n23, 199n24, 224, 240, 243, 271n25, 275, 277, 295
empire(s), xv, 12, 24, 41, 43, 68, 111, 119, 145, 148, 154, 176, 177, 199, 201, 241, 241n21, 274, 289, 294
empower(s), empowered, empowerment, 45, 94n17, 106, 116, 154, 174, 183n40, 187, 246, 261
encourage(s), encouraged, encouragement, 11–12, 58, 74, 79–81, 112, 118, 125, 131, 152, 193, 205, 224, 238, 242, 245, 257, 273, 290
end of the age, viii, 32, 156, 211, 238–39, 242–45, 251, 262
end times, 241n25, 244, 280, 291
end, the, 1, 174, 239, 242–43
ends of the earth, 31, 246
end of the world, 244–45
endure, endured, 12, 38, 149, 261, 275, 284, 290
enemies, enemy, 19, 33, 37, 40, 84, 88, 110, 143n15, 157, 167–68, 230, 232–33, 256, 268–69
Enki, 34
Enoch, 18, 146, 161
enthroned, enthronement, enthroning, 40, 246, 280
entry, Jerusalem, viii, 141, 206–9, 218, 222, 225, 273
entry, Kingdom, 183, 185, 206, 231
envy, 126, 272–73

Epaphras, 75n35
Ephesus, 170, 197
Epiphanes, 243–44
epistemological, 272
epistles, 20n47, 293
equality, 202, 263
Erastus, 283n60
escape(s)(d), escaping, 10, 38, 173, 241n19
eschatological, eschatologically, eschatology, 35n6, 40, 61, 81, 115, 129, 134, 146, 153, 156, 196, 200, 207, 214, 238–39, 242–43, 257, 280
eschaton, 38, 81, 131, 144, 151, 243
Essene(s), 63, 120, 177, 179, 186, 188n4, 223n46, 224, 254
eternal, 72, 190
eternal Davidic king/shepherd, 36, 113
eternal destruction, 66
eternal judgment/punishment/ destruction/loss/separation/ fate/torment/death/suffering/ condemnation, 65, 66, 80, 87, 91, 124, 149–50, 172–74, 233, 252, 255
eternal life/reward/salvation, 13, 37, 79, 84, 150, 169, 172–75, 186, 187n1, 188–89, 192–93, 201, 287n69, 290
eternity, xi, 34, 47, 81, 113, 122, 144, 150, 174, 206, 226, 230, 236
ethic(s), ethical, ethically, 3, 22n59, 25–26, 29, 52, 74, 109, 187, 191, 229–30
ethnicity, 137
Euodia, 78
euphemism, 252n70
Europe, 31, 84, 151, 239, 293
euthanasia, 124
evangelicals, 200n30
evangelism, evangelistic, evangelization, evangelize, evangelizing, 9, 25, 42–44, 46, 52, 67, 74, 79, 94, 104–5, 114, 166, 190, 239
evangelist(s), 28, 39, 67, 79, 106
Eve, 36, 178

evil(s), vii, 40–41, 45–46, 48, 50n20, 65, 72, 72n32, 89–90, 92, 105, 109, 123, 126–27, 145–46, 123, 157, 168, 180, 185,245
exalt(s), exaltation, exalted, 152–54, 165, 232–33, 236, 247
execute, executed, execution(s), executioner, 11n30, 199, 214, 222, 271, 284
exegesis, exegetical, xiv, 103, 291, 295
exhausted, exhausting 115, 159
exile(d), 12, 40–41, 71, 76, 102, 121, 197, 211n6, 214, 220, 239, 245
existence, 4, 20, 178, 207n44, 227, 242
exodus, the, 88, 154,
exorcise, exorcised, exorcism(s), exorcist(s), exorcized, vi–vii, 46–47, 52, 67–68, 72n32, 85, 89, 94, 106, 128, 157, 159, 167–68, 204n39, 218n30
expectation(s), 21, 34, 40, 47, 56, 108, 136, 143, 143n15, 146, 151, 155–56, 180, 196, 200, 207–8, 231, 232, 280, 294
eye(s), 12, 37, 61, 65–66, 74, 89, 97, 121, 126, 129, 137, 139, 139n3, 141, 172, 191, 204, 211, 214, 220, 234, 240
eyewitness(es), 8, 8n16, 8n17, 116, 203, 267, 278, 286, 291
Ezekiel, 55, 113, 145
Ezra, 145n18, 174n18, 264n6

face(s), faced, 38, 54, 99, 103, 124n26, 149–50, 153, 170–71, 173–74, 191, 240, 240n12, 259–61, 275, 285
factions, 177
fairness, 238
faith, viii, xv, 12, 14, 18, 20, 25, 27–28, 37, 49–51, 53, 58, 65, 75–80, 88, 94, 96, 98–99, 101, 103, 118, 130, 140, 149–50, 152, 157–60, 162, 167, 171, 173, 183, 187n1, 192–93, 206, 211, 215–17, 217n25, 222–23, 228–29, 231, 234, 242, 260–61, 263, 287, 295

faithful, faithfully, 12, 13n39, 38, 64, 75, 78–79, 101, 105, 109, 116, 125, 171, 174, 178–80, 185, 187–89, 193, 198, 211, 213, 224, 234, 260, 280, 290
faithless, 158–59
fall, of Jerusalem/temple, 10, 31, 45, 222, 237n2, 239–41, 243–45, 245n41, 247, 262, 289
fall, of Rome, 240
Fall, the, 42, 54, 84, 178, 241n21
false Christs, 27n75, 245
false gods, 150, 179
false teachers/teaching/theology, 76, 138, 162, 186, 240
false testimony/accusation/witness, 186, 214, 267
fame, famous, 46–47, 54, 66, 109, 119, 126, 177, 190, 204n39
familial, families, family, 9, 9n22, 25–27, 42–43, 70–71, 73, 85, 93–94, 99–100, 100n22, 101–2, 104, 106, 111–12, 122–23, 158–59, 164, 176, 177n29, 178, 181, 185, 187, 189–90, 192, 195n15, 202, 207, 242, 250, 253, 260, 263, 266, 282n55, 284, 289
famine(s), 8, 193, 238, 241, 241n27, 294
farm, farmer(s), 81, 81n43, 82, 102n28, 220n32, 221
Farrer-Goulder Hypothesis, 5
fast, fasting, vi, 57, 59–60, 84, 140, 160, 160n41, 251
fate(s), 29, 171–74, 201, 218, 225, 255
Father, God, xi, 18, 93, 100, 103, 116, 131, 151, 181, 195, 205, 217, 233, 236, 260–61, 268, 273, 290
father(s), 17, 43, 51, 56, 73, 122, 155–60, 177n29, 186, 203, 206, 208, 216, 226, 260
fear, fearful, 1, 14, 51, 87–89, 98–99, 108, 117–18, 121, 123, 193, 215–16, 223, 243, 265, 270, 283n58, 285–86, 289
fearless, fearlessness, 88, 193
Feast(s), festivals, 108, 110, 196, 203, 213n13, 244n37

Feast, eschatological, 61, 115, 129, 196, 257
Feast, tabernacles, 208
Feast, festival, unleavened bread/Passover, 138, 248n54, 253, 253, 255, 272, 275, 295
feed(s), feeding, vii, 110, 112, 116, 129, 134, 139–40, 201, 235, 250
feeding 4,000, vii, 132–34, 137, 140, 201, 235
feeding 5,000, vii, 30, 110, 112–16, 118–19, 134, 137, 140, 201, 235
feel, feeling(s), 65–66, 98, 125, 183, 235, 279–80
feet, 31, 42, 95, 101, 105, 128, 171n10, 201, 201n32, 207n47, 232–33, 249n58, 264, 268, 277
fellowship, 57, 252
female(s), 94, 97, 180, 180n34
fence(s), 121, 220, 221
fermented, 61, 138
fever, 47
fidelity, 25, 180, 186
field(s), 63, 74, 83, 183, 208
fight, 152
finances, financial, 80, 97, 105, 271n25
fire(s), flame, 11, 37–38, 69, 75, 121, 149, 158–59, 172–74, 174n18, 192, 266, 270
firebrand, 170
firstborn, 117
fish, fisherman, fishermen, fishers, fishing, 25, 42–44, 47, 55, 58–59, 68, 85, 114–16, 119, 133, 139, 141, 190, 206
fists, 269
flagellum, 11n30
flatter, flattering, flattery, 158, 223
flesh, 38, 173, 178, 180, 261, 289
flock(s), 113–14, 142
flog, flogged, flogging, 11n30, 197, 214, 273, 274–75, 277
flood(s), 87, 141n5, 245
floor, 65n16, 263n1
flour, 138
flower, 115
flute, 100n25
foal, 207–8

folklore, folktale, 83, 92
follow(s), followed, follower(s), following, vii, 8, 10–12, 13n40, 19–21, 25–26, 29, 43–44, 47, 51, 54, 56–57, 59, 62–63, 66, 71, 73–74, 80, 82, 90, 95, 96, 110, 105, 107, 112, 128, 139–40, 142, 145, 148–51, 161–62, 164, 167–68, 172–73, 175, 183, 185, 189, 189n7, 190–93, 195–97, 199, 201–2, 206, 209, 231, 233, 248, 251, 253–54, 265–66, 270, 274, 276, 277, 282, 284
folly, 293
food(s), 18, 29, 63, 72, 82, 92, 101, 105, 110, 113–16, 120, 123, 129, 133, 170, 175, 204, 235, 254, 289
fool, foolish, foolishness, 100, 110, 127, 139, 142, 172
forbearance, 132
force(s), forced, forceful, forcefully, forcing, 11, 24, 27n75, 48, 70, 72, 82–83, 88–91, 93, 105, 116, 130, 133, 162, 182, 199, 208–9, 215, 225, 233, 235, 237n2, 244, 250, 263n1, 270, 273, 277
foreign, foreigner(s), 23, 35, 40, 144, 212n8, 213, 264, 270
forests, 142
forever, 62, 123, 145–46, 151, 155, 186, 192, 233, 248, 253, 281, 286
forgive(s), forgiven, forgiveness, forgiving, 18, 20, 27n75, 29, 30, 34, 41, 49, 52, 52n25, 53, 53n27, 54–58, 63, 72, 95, 118, 154, 156, 180, 186, 214, 217, 218n30, 220, 231, 260, 281
forsaken, 100, 279–80
Franciscans, 259n92
fraud, 186
free, freed, freedom, freely, 24–25, 35, 38, 40, 44, 46–47, 62, 66, 88, 92–93, 100, 104, 115, 129, 144, 152, 160, 169, 174, 183, 188, 200, 201, 206, 225, 264, 273
friend(s), friends, friendship, xi, 22, 56–58, 60, 63, 106, 158, 168, 175

fruit, fruited, fruitful, 73, 77, 79, 83, 112, 116, 210–11, 220, 220n33, 221, 244n37, 256n81, 257
fruitless, 133, 175
fulfill, fulfilled, fulfilling, fulfillment, 14n40, 18, 23, 29–30, 34–35, 38–40, 42, 51–52, 62, 69n25, 82, 84, 101, 108, 113, 131, 147, 153, 155–56, 187–88, 207–8, 215–16, 223, 226n58, 230, 236, 239, 255, 258, 265, 267, 269, 272, 277n31, 280, 289
fullness, 44, 46, 99, 133–34, 151, 153, 173, 274
fury, 29, 182n39

Gabriel, 99
Gadara, 89, 93n16
Gadarenes, 89
Galasa, 93n16
Galatians, 76, 200, 216
Galilean(s), 26, 135, 270, 271
Galilee, vii, x, 6n7, 11n31, 14–15, 26, 30, 36, 39–40, 46, 49, 52, 55, 64, 66, 68, 74, 86, 87n4, 101, 104–5, 107, 110, 116, 116n6, 117, 119, 130–31, 134, 141–42, 161, 163–64, 177, 198, 258, 282, 286,
Gamaliel, 45, 213n13
Ganges River, 34n3
garden, 8, 11, 29, 36, 38, 49, 78, 83–84, 103, 114–15, 115n5, 197, 203, 248, 259, 259n52, 265n10, 276n41, 285, 288
garment(s), 35n5, 61n4, 90, 265
gate(s), 61n4, 83, 191n12, 215, 240, 246, 270
Gaul, 107
Gehenna, 172–73, 175, 233, 242n29
gems, 188
gender, 178
genealogy, 34, 129
generation, 38, 80, 121, 136, 158–59, 197n21, 246–47
Genesis (book), 106,
Genesis, 142, 154, 180
Gennesaret, 97, 119, 119n19, 119n20

gentile(s), 11–12, 18, 22, 28–29, 42, 67, 69, 89, 91, 93–94, 106, 120, 123, 128–30, 132–33, 137, 143n15, 148, 150–51, 155, 187, 194, 197–99, 208, 212–13, 213n10, 213n12, 214–15, 222–23, 228, 240, 242, 255, 275
gentleness, gently, 79, 183
geographical, geographically, 6n7, 93n16, 130n39, 211
Gerasa, 89, 93n16
Gerasenes, 89, 95
Gergesa, 89
Gergesenes, 89
Germination, 82
Gethsemane, ix, 20, 29, 49, 100, 103, 259, 259n92, 262
ghost, 117–18
gifts, gifted, giftings, 37, 67, 72–73, 80, 106, 122, 127, 150, 169–70, 175, 203, 226, 230, 237, 241n26, 261
Gihon, 208
Ginosar, 119
girl, 90, 95–97, 100–101, 129, 165, 182n38, 270
Gischala, 243
giving, 22, 26, 40, 63, 65, 76, 81, 133, 150, 169–70, 188n4, 189, 192, 194, 201, 205, 220, 222, 230, 235, 238, 240, 252, 279–80, 289
Global warming, 245
glorious, gloriously, 29, 33, 42, 67, 144–46, 152–53, 161–62, 166, 174, 196, 286
glory, xv, 14n40, 18, 24, 75, 81, 135, 146, 150–55, 161, 164, 187, 192, 196, 198, 200–201, 203, 246, 270, 279, 289–90
gluttony, 110
Gnostic, 34n3, 265n8
goats, 3, 113, 169
goblet(s), 256
God, vi, xi, xiii, xv, 1n1, 11, 13, 13n40, 14, 17–22, 22n59, 24, 24n65, 28–31, 31n80, 32–33, 33n1, 34–35, 35n6, 36–44, 44n16, 45–53, 53n27, 54–57, 59–69, 69n25, 70–81, 81n43, 82–84, 84n48, 85, 87–91, 91n11, 92–97, 97n21, 98–110, 113–27, 129–37, 139–40, 143, 143n15, 144–45, 145n17, 146–53, 153n32, 154–60, 162, 164–66, 169–74, 176, 178, 178n32, 179–87, 187n1, 188–99, 199n26, 200–204, 204n39, 205–7, 207n50, 208–9, 211, 211n6, 213–17, 219–24, 226–36, 238, 244–48, 250–53, 253n70, 255, 255n77, 256, 256n81, 257, 257n86, 259–62, 264, 267–68, 268n21, 269–70, 273–75, 278–81, 283, 285–86, 288–90, 296
god, Ba'al, 90
god of Ekron, 71
god of this world, 75
god, Pan, 142
god(s), Roman, 275, 281
God-fearer, 176
goddess (Isis), 178n32
gods, Caesars, 18
gods, false, 150, 179
gods, Greek, 275
gods, tritheism, 228
Gog, 242n29
Golan, 86, 117
gold, golden, 175, 196n19, 215, 240n12
Golgotha, 276, 276n40
Goliath, 37
Gomorrah, 245
good, goodness, iv, 1, 3, 11, 19, 24, 30, 33, 36, 39–42, 45, 48–50, 50n22, 63–65, 68, 71–72, 74, 76–79, 89–90, 92, 113, 127, 134–36, 168, 175, 183, 185–86, 193, 202n35, 211n6, 224, 227n61, 228–29, 231, 233, 239–40, 259n95, 286
Gospel(s), i, iii–v, xi, xiii, xv, 1–3, 5–6, 6n7, 7, 7n11, 8, 8n18, 9–10, 10n24, 11–12, 12n35, 13n39, 14, 17–21, 24, 28, 28n76, 29–35, 39, 41–42, 44, 48–49, 53–54, 54n29, 75, 78, 89, 91, 91n14, 93–95, 97, 99, 102, 107–8, 110, 114, 116, 118–19, 128, 128n37, 141–43, 143n13, 144–45, 156–57,

SUBJECT INDEX

159–60, 168, 173–74, 174n19, 185, 188–89, 192, 200, 202, 206–7, 207n49, 208, 208n52, 215–17, 217n28, 218n29, 222, 224, 228n68, 231, 234, 234n85, 235, 238n6, 239, 239n7, 240n13, 241n24, 243, 247n48, 251n69, 254n74, 256n80, 257–58, 264, 265n8, 266, 268–69, 271–72, 272n29, 281–83, 285–86, 288–90

gospel, 1–9, 9n22, 10–34, 36, 38, 40–42, 44, 46, 48–50, 52, 54, 56, 58, 60, 62, 64, 66, 68–72, 74–80, 82–84, 88–90, 92, 94, 96, 98, 100, 102, 104, 106, 108, 110, 114, 116, 118, 120, 122, 124, 126, 128–30, 132, 134, 136, 140, 142–43, 143n15, 144, 146, 148–52, 154, 156, 158, 160, 162, 164, 166, 168, 170, 172, 174–76, 178, 180, 182, 184, 186–88, 190, 192, 194–96, 198, 200, 202, 204, 206, 208, 212, 214, 216, 218, 220, 222, 224, 226, 228, 230, 232–34, 236, 238–40, 242, 244, 246–48, 250–52, 254, 256, 258, 260, 262, 264, 266, 268, 270, 272, 274–76, 278, 280, 282, 284, 286–88, 290

gossiping, 46
govern(ed), governance, 107, 64, 102, 200, 252
government, 55, 180n33, 203
governor(s), 11n30, 242, 271, 271n25, 272, 274
grace, 12, 24, 64–65, 79, 96, 109, 125, 179–80, 251, 256, 284
grain, 51n24, 61, 63, 79, 82, 116, 138
grapes, 61
grass, 114–15, 208
gratitude, xi, 81, 124
grave(s), 78, 146, 183, 266, 284
Great Sea, 142n7
greatness, vii, 47, 163–66, 194, 199, 281–82
Greco-Roman, 41, 122, 126, 130, 153n31, 180n34, 189, 229
Greece, 31, 239

greed, greediness, greedy, 56, 125–26, 140, 188, 191, 252
Greek(s), xiii–xiv, 1–2, 5, 7, 9–14, 20, 26, 34, 36–37, 40–41, 50, 54, 56, 59–60, 65, 70–71, 73, 76, 80, 82, 87–89, 91, 97–100, 102, 104–5, 112–15, 117–18, 122, 124, 127–29, 131, 133–34, 136, 142, 144, 145n17, 147, 149, 152, 152n29, 154, 157, 159, 165, 168, 172, 183, 188–89, 189n7, 191, 195n16, 197–99, 199n26, 205, 212, 219, 227, 229, 234, 249, 259–60, 268n21, 270, 272n29, 275, 277, 277n46, 278, 278n47, 279
grief, grieved, 65, 190, 255, 259, 268, 285, 287
groom, 60
grow(s), growing, grown, growth, vi, 12, 20, 31, 40, 43, 68, 74, 77–79, 81–84, 85, 88, 101–2, 106, 141, 154, 166, 169, 187, 198, 260, 289, 295
grumble, 131
guard(s), guarding, 154, 245, 261, 269
guidance, guide, 130, 157, 170, 205, 217n26, 231n74, 293, 295
guilt, guilty, 51n24, 223, 263n1
gypsum, 175n24

Hades, 83, 172–73, 225n56
hair(s), 35, 35n5, 51n24, 87
Hajj, 213
Hallel Psalms/Passover Songs, 208, 257
hand(s), handed, 8, 14n40, 27n75, 29, 36, 39, 44, 47, 48, 51, 56, 64, 66, 68, 71–72, 95, 100, 100n25, 107, 110, 120, 120n21, 120n22, 123, 131, 134, 141–42, 154, 156, 160–61, 171n10, 172, 177, 183, 194, 196, 196n19, 197, 218, 230, 232–33, 252, 264, 266–69, 282, 273, 277, 285, 288
handwriting, 13n36
happiness, happy, 196, 200n28, 205

hard, hardened, hardness—hearts, 62, 65–66, 76, 118, 120, 139n3, 140, 178–79
harlot, 196n29
harm, 126, 158, 287
harvest(s), 63, 78–79, 81–83, 106, 167, 210, 220
Hasmonean, 203, 225
hate(d), hateful, hatred, 56, 69, 73, 126, 228–30, 242
heal(s), healed, healing(s), vi–viii, 11, 17, 22, 24–25, 27, 27n75, 30, 42, 46–50, 50n20, 50n21, 51, 51n7, 52, 52n25, 53, 53n27, 54–55, 57–58, 64–67, 70, 74, 84–85, 92–97, 97n21, 98, 98n22, 99–101, 103–4, 104n33, 105–7, 111, 114, 119–21, 128–31, 137, 140–43, 143n15, 159–60, 162–63, 167–68, 170, 181–82, 186, 188, 195, 202–4, 204n39, 205–6, 215, 217–18, 218n30, 248–50, 264, 269, 274, 287, 289, 294
healer, 47–48, 52, 98
health, healthy, 48, 57, 70, 157–58, 190, 192
hear(s), heard, hearing, hearers, 6, 18, 36, 39, 41, 43, 53–54, 70, 74–80, 96, 107, 121, 131, 139n3, 143, 148–49, 150–51, 156, 156n39, 157, 160–61, 168, 171, 174, 181, 183, 186, 194, 198, 204–5, 211, 214, 220, 228, 231, 234, 245, 247, 251, 252, 256, 258, 267, 270
heart(s), 19, 25, 26n73, 29, 36, 39, 44–47, 57, 53, 62, 65–66, 75–76, 92, 99, 114, 118, 120–21, 123, 127, 133, 139, 139n3, 156, 159, 162, 167, 178–79, 186–87, 197, 206, 227n61, 228–29, 238, 251, 258, 274
heaven(s), 14n40, 24, 26, 31, 35–36, 46, 69, 81, 84, 108, 115, 131, 134–35, 143n15, 151, 153, 153n32, 170, 173, 189, 207, 214, 217, 219, 222, 227, 227n61, 245, 247, 260n100, 268–69, 280
heavenly, 45, 153, 189, 246–47

Hebrew, 7, 11, 20n47, 24n65, 35n7, 36, 65n17, 74, 102, 118, 120, 122, 147, 172, 177, 225n51, 228, 232, 278n47
heels, 94
hegemony, 43
Heger, 45
Hell, 90, 127, 174, 285
help(s), helped, helper, helpful, helping, xi, 6, 8, 9n21, 18, 25, 37–38, 48, 51–52, 57, 61, 63, 65, 93, 95, 97, 115, 132, 159–60, 165, 204, 248, 251, 262, 267, 284
hemorrhaging, 27, 94
herald, heralded, 47, 49, 84, 108
herd, 91–92
heretic, 13n39
hero, 283n58
Herod Agrippa I, 197, 199
Herod Antipas, 20, 39, 64, 107–9, 109n42, 110, 116, 137–38, 140–43, 156, 164, 176–77, 179, 199, 203, 234, 241, 241n21, 271, 292
Herod Philip, 17, 142, 142n7, 199
Herod the Great, x, 64, 71, 107, 141–42, 203, 212, 237n1, 274, 294
Herodians, Herods, vii, 24, 42, 64, 66, 107, 109, 138, 142–43, 199, 186, 203, 223, 242
Herodias, 107–9, 176–77
Herodotus, 264n2
heterosexual, 124, 124n26, 178–80
Hierapolis, 6
hill(s), 86, 89, 116, 207, 216
Hillel, 177, 228–29
Hindu, 34n3
Hippo, Hippos, 93n16
Hippodrome, 203
historian, historic, historical, historically, 6, 7, 7n13, 7n14, 10, 28n76, 129, 168, 293–94
historicity, 7, 110–11
history, 9, 38, 40, 71, 82, 110, 113, 116, 136, 175, 222, 227, 241–42, 244–45, 248, 256, 263, 286, 292
Holy of holies, 243, 267, 280
holiness, 45, 120
Holocaust, 245

SUBJECT INDEX

holy, iv, 44–45, 51, 56–57, 60, 72, 96–98, 109, 120, 144, 151, 216, 232, 243, 257n86, 264, 267, 276, 280
home(s), 8, 20, 26, 41, 44, 47, 56, 70n26, 73, 93, 95–96, 99, 106, 113–15, 122–23, 128–29, 132, 141–42, 163, 181, 183, 192, 202, 207, 207n46, 226, 248–49, 249n57, 249n58, 253–54, 270
homeless, 205
hometown, 102, 102n30
homosexuality, 124n26
honest, 124, 126, 147
honey, 35
honor(s), honored, honoring, xi, xv, 43, 68, 93, 101–2, 121–22, 142n7, 150, 163–65, 170–71, 186–87, 192, 194, 196, 198, 202, 223–24, 234–38, 251, 268
hope(s), hoped, hopeful, hoping, xv, 1, 14, 18, 21–23, 29, 33–35, 38–40, 46, 48, 76, 78, 97, 99, 104, 107–8, 112–13, 121, 131, 139, 143, 146, 150, 153, 156, 156n37, 162, 165, 174, 186, 190–92, 197, 203, 206, 208, 220, 226–27, 246, 269, 271, 280–81, 290
hopeless, 94
horror(s), 12, 172, 196n19, 260, 263, 268, 269
horse, 208
hosanna, 182n39, 208
Hosea, 179
hospitable, hospitality, 8, 114, 129, 134, 175, 235
hospitals, 122
host(s), hosting, 8, 114, 121, 133, 135, 234–35
hosts, Lord of, 121
hostile, hostility, 122, 222, 228n68
hour, 48, 61n4, 114, 117, 238n5, 250n66, 260–61, 277, 279
house(s), 44, 49, 70–72, 96–97, 100, 102, 128, 141, 152, 177n29, 213–14, 220, 235, 244n37, 247–48, 253, 265n10, 270
household(s), 129, 242, 254
housekeeping, 47

hovered, 36
hugs, hugged, 165, 170, 188n2
human(s), humanity, humankind, 19, 29, 36–38, 40–41, 51, 53–54, 63, 66, 69, 70, 72, 91–93, 113, 117, 121, 136, 138, 147, 155–56, 178–79, 195, 198–99, 200–201, 208, 210, 219, 227, 230, 232–33, 242, 245–47, 259, 267, 274, 278–79, 287
humble, humbled, humbles, humility, 11, 22n59, 24, 36, 42, 133, 144, 148–49, 152, 154, 162, 164–65, 188, 195–96, 198, 208, 234, 236, 259, 279, 289
humiliating, humiliation, 261, 277
humor, humorous, 74, 159
hunger, hungry, 37, 39, 63, 67, 115, 129, 132, 135, 170, 192, 195, 210, 210n2, 235
hunting, 48–49
hurricane, 86
husband(s), 125, 176–78, 180, 180n34, 226, 230
hyperbole, hyperbolic, hyperbolically, 35, 48, 245, 269
hypocrisy, 121, 223
hyssop, 51n24

ice, 118, 118n14
idea(s), 2, 7, 10, 26, 33, 41, 54, 59–60, 64, 67, 74, 82, 84, 88, 91, 102, 107–110, 114–15, 132–33, 136, 138, 140, 145, 147, 150–51, 154, 156, 161–62, 168–69, 172, 175, 183, 185, 189, 193–94, 196, 204, 212, 216, 218, 226, 230–31, 233, 238–39, 242, 250n68, 253, 265n10, 267, 278–80
ideal(s), ideally, 25, 43, 56, 61, 93, 125, 167, 178–80, 193, 264
identity, vi, 18–19, 19n46, 21, 28, 32, 36–37, 45–46, 48, 88–89, 95, 99, 101, 107, 119, 132, 134–37, 140, 142–44, 146–47, 152, 155, 204, 204n39, 207n48, 236, 250, 267–68
ideologies, ideology, 31, 40, 84

idolatrous, idolatry, 150, 179, 213, 243
Idumea, 66
ignominy, 261
ignorance, ignorant, 121, 164, 196–97, 219, 234
illegal, 231, 266n16, 267
illegitimate, illegitimately, 135, 167
illness, illnesses, 45, 119
imitate, imitating, 148, 183n40, 189
Immanuel, 89
immature, 147
immersion, 197
immigrant, immigrants, 214, 230
immigration, 83
imminent Parousia/return, 31n79, 151n27, 242, 242n32, 246–47, 247n49, 251
immorality, 109, 124–26, 177, 179–80
imperative(s), 30, 41, 145n16, 15535, 189, 234, 253
imperator, 275
imperial, 108, 110, 224, 275
imperishable, 13, 189, 287n69
implicitly, implied, imply, implying, 35, 47–48, 60n3, 71, 90, 97, 106, 122, 145, 150, 155, 158, 161, 166–67, 172, 175, 178, 189, 192, 198, 204–5, 224, 227, 230–33, 236, 251, 254, 257, 261, 267–68, 272, 279
impossible, 88, 190–91, 206, 216
impoverishment, 48, 114, 132, 185
imprecation, 215, 255
imprisoned, imprisonment, imprisons, 10, 75, 108, 149, 197, 256, 273, 275
impurity, 109, 123, 212n8
inaugurate(s), inaugurated, inaugurating, inauguration, 17, 24, 40, 208, 216, 253, 256, 260
inbreaking, 46
incantation(s), 47, 168
incarnate, incarnation, 18, 45, 89, 116, 146, 153, 247, 286
incense, 175
incest, 124
inclusio, 74, 286

inclusive, inclusively, inclusively, 147, 161, 170, 216
incoming, 61–62
incomprehension, 71, 82, 134, 153, 250, 270, 286
inconsistency, inconsistent, 103, 267
incorruptible, 14n40
incredulity, 82, 272
indecency, 177
India, 249
Indians, 277
indignation, 182
indiscretions, 236
individualism, individualistic, 114, 188, 206, 230
individuality, 178
infamous, infamy, 86, 253
infancy, infant(s), 18, 34, 183, 244
infinite, 150
influence(d), influencing, influential, 9, 83, 97n21, 123, 146–47, 164, 171, 182, 221, 252, 266, 273
inherit, inheritance, inherited, inheriting, 14n40, 38, 150, 186–93, 199, 220, 290
iniquities, 139, 257
initiate, initiative, 25, 48, 59, 101, 132–33
injunction(s), 121, 145, 171, 178, 181
injured, injuries, 51, 271
injustice(s), 29, 65, 191, 193, 215, 235, 238, 274
innocence, innocent, 183, 274
innovation, 59, 146
insane, insanity, 90, 108
insatiable, insatiableness, 125
inscribed, inscription(s), 187, 224, 271n25
insight, 46, 53–54, 93, 97, 116, 207, 223, 254, 258, 281, 287
insolence, 127
inspiration, inspire(d), 81, 169, 174, 233, 264
institution(s), 44, 91, 255
instruct(s), instructed, instructing, instruction(s), instructive, 17, 19, 21, 60, 105, 105n37, 128, 132, 145, 148, 152, 157, 161,

163–66, 168–69, 170, 174, 176, 181, 183, 185–86, 189, 193–94, 202, 251, 253, 258, 259
instruments, 100n25, 102n28
insult(s), insulted, insulting, 189, 271, 278–79
insurrection, insurrectionist, 264, 264n7, 272–74, 277
integrity, 92, 223
intellectual, intelligence, 127
Intermediate State, 227
interpolation, 14, 14n41, 287
interpretation(s), interpretative, interpreted, interpreter, interpreting, interpret(s), xi, 6, 21, 23, 28, 50n20, 60, 63, 65, 71, 108, 119, 177, 197, 201, 207n49, 211, 214, 219, 221, 233, 239, 242–43, 247, 251, 266–67, 279
interrogated, interrogation, 197, 267, 271
intertextual, 211
intervene(s), intervening, intervention, 35–36, 101, 214, 247
intimacy, intimate, 42, 174, 183, 260, 264
intrigue, intrigued, intriguing, 102, 109, 114, 128, 148, 267, 274
invaded, invasion, 24, 68, 71, 154, 244
invested, 185
invitation, invite(s), invited, inviting, xi, 18, 74, 92, 110, 115, 129, 133, 289
invocation, invoke(s), invoked, invoking, 55, 90–91, 99, 115–16, 122, 167–69, 203, 270
IRD, 55
Irenaeus, 6–7, 10, 13
iron, 175
ironic, ironical, ironically, ironies, irony, 24, 26, 28, 57, 66, 147, 150, 159, 190, 192, 197–98, 219, 230n72, 248, 264, 269, 273–76, 278, 280, 288
irritated, irritation, 136, 189
Isaac, 36, 129, 227

Isaiah, 23, 30, 33, 41, 61, 75, 78–79, 99, 120–21, 143, 146, 173, 221–22, 229, 250, 267, 269
Isaianic, 121
Isis, 178n32
island, 128
isolate(d), 49, 217
Israel, 17–18, 21, 23–24, 24n66, 29–30, 35, 37–43, 48–50, 52–54, 59, 61–62, 64, 66–69, 69n25, 71–72, 75, 78–79, 83, 88–89, 93, 99, 102, 107, 113, 117, 120–23, 128–30, 132–34, 139, 142–43, 143n15, 144, 146–48, 150–53, 153n32, 154–59, 162, 164, 174n18, 176, 178, 187, 199–200, 202–3, 207–8, 210–11, 211n6, 214–15, 218–24, 226, 229–31, 239, 244–45, 247–49, 252, 264, 269, 271, 273, 279–80
Israelite(s), 74, 122, 129, 151, 248, 270
Italy, 10, 249
itinerant, itinerated, itinerates, 49, 86, 108

Jacob (OT), 69, 102, 121, 129, 227
Jacob (James), *Jacobus, Jacomaus*, 20, 20n47, 43–44, 47, 56, 68–69, 74, 100–102, 149, 152, 154, 157–58, 163, 167, 182, 192, 194–95, 195n15, 200, 205, 209, 234, 240, 240n19, 251, 254, 256, 259, 265n9, 278, 282, 285
Jairus, vi, 27, 94–97, 98n22, 99–101, 103, 111–12, 118, 135, 152, 216, 226
jar, 249, 253
jealous, jealousy, 167
Jehoida, 221
Jehu, 24n66, 34, 208, 249
Jeremiah, 108, 139, 143, 172, 211, 214, 221
Jericho, 152n28, 202n35, 203, 203n38, 204, 207
Jerome, 13–14, 283n57

SUBJECT INDEX

Jerusalem, viii, xi, 6–10, 12, 21, 26, 27n75, 29, 31, 35, 42, 45, 50n20, 66, 71, 90, 120–21, 123, 139–142n7, 146, 154, 162, 172, 177, 181, 182n39, 185, 189, 193–94, 196, 202, 202n35, 203–4, 206–7, 207n44, 207n47, 208–211, 213, 213n11, 214–15, 219–20, 222, 225, 237n2, 238–41, 241n19, 241n26, 243–44, 244n36, 245, 245n38, 245n41, 246–48, 254, 257, 257n86, 262, 266–67, 271, 273, 274n33, 283n57, 289

Jesus, v–x, xiii, xv, 1, 5–9, 11–125, 127–65, 167–75, 177–296

Jew(s), Jewish, Jewishness, 7, 12, 17–20, 20n47, 22–24, 27–29, 31, 34–35, 39, 41–43, 43n15, 44–45, 47, 51, 53–57, 59, 61, 64, 66–67, 69–73, 74–75, 83, 88, 91, 93, 95–96, 98, 101, 104, 106, 109, 120, 122–23, 128–30, 134–37, 140, 143, 145, 147–49, 156n37, 157, 161, 164, 167–68, 171, 171n10, 172, 174–75, 177, 177n28, 180, 180n34, 182n39, 185–89, 191–92, 198–99, 204, 206, 212n8, 213–14, 216–17, 217n26, 218–19, 221–23, 225–26, 228–29, 231–32, 236, 237n2, 240n18, 242, 244n37, 248, 254, 257–58, 263–64, 266–67, 270–73, 275, 277–80, 282–83, 283n58, 285,

Jezebel, 156

Joanna, 254, 282

John Mark, v, xi, 6, 6n7, 7, 8, 8n19, 9, 32, 265n10

John the Baptist, 1, 17, 18–19, 19n46, 20, 23, 27, 30, 33–36, 39, 45, 57, 59, 62, 89, 104, 107–9, 111, 140, 143, 156, 177, 179, 199, 219, 223, 242, 246, 280, 284

John the Apostle, 6, 20, 43–44, 47, 56, 68–69, 100–101, 152, 154, 157–58, 163, 167–68, 182, 194–95, 195n15, 196–200, 205, 209, 234, 240, 256, 265n9, 278, 282

John of Gishala, 243

Jonah, 86–87, 136, 259, 279

Joram, 221

Jordan River, 36, 88, 117, 130, 177, 202, 207n45, 240n19

Joseph Caiaphas, 266

Joseph (Jesus's father), 20, 102

Joseph of Arimathea, ix, 28, 95, 111, 218n28, 269, 281–84, 288,

Joseph (Patriarch), 222, 265n9,

Joses, 102, 282

Joshua, 1, 18, 59, 88, 102, 136, 154, 162, 167–68, 203–4

Joshua (new), 1, 11, 24, 24n65, 34, 68, 88, 91, 136, 150, 152, 154, 167–68, 193, 203–4

Josiah, 172

journey, 8–9, 20, 111, 119, 132, 177, 193, 203, 220

joy, joyfully, joyfulness, rejoice(d), rejoicing, 40, 61, 76, 78, 93, 121, 165, 174, 183, 205, 208, 227n61

Jubilee, 264

Judah, 71, 102, 226n58

Judaism, 11, 25, 42, 44, 59–62, 76, 90, 97n21, 108, 111, 153n31, 186, 189, 211, 214n18, 215, 229, 295

Judaize, Judaizers, 76, 130

Judas Iscariot, viii, 20, 20n48, 21, 69, 76–77, 102, 141, 163, 250, 252–53, 255–56, 259, 261–64, 265n10, 265, 271, 281

Judas (revolutionary), 240n19

Jude, 76, 200

Judea, 6n7, 49, 66, 104–5, 131, 177, 181, 219, 243–45, 271

Judean(s), 35, 61n4

judge(s), judged, 45, 113, 150, 169, 174

judgment, 3, 55, 65, 86, 106, 113, 127, 145, 150, 172–74, 175n21, 222, 226, 233, 235, 252n70, 279

judiciary, 284

Julia, 141

Julias, 141

Julius Caesar, 168

June, 114, 210

Junia, 78n38

justice, 81, 114, 214, 251, 273

justification, justified, justifies, justify(ing), 45, 130, 160, 173, 187, 216, 268
Justin Martyr, 7n10, 102n28, 224
juxtaposition, 99, 200

Kerioth, 69
Kersa, 89
kerygma, 8
kidnapping, 201
Kidron Valley, 259n92
kids, 166, 182
kill(s), killed, killer(s), killing, 11–12, 21, 27, 29, 43, 51, 62, 65–66, 75, 78–79, 87, 95, 101, 108–9, 111, 124, 143, 145–47, 149, 158, 161, 176–77, 191–92, 194, 196, 199, 215, 218–22, 231, 241n19, 248, 252–55, 258, 263–64, 266, 266n16, 276–77, 279, 281
kin, 43
kind, 17, 19, 36, 61, 83, 116, 124n26, 136, 140, 144–45, 147–48, 158, 168, 173, 177, 182, 194, 227, 279
king(s), 1, 17–18, 24, 24n66, 30, 34, 35n5, 36–37, 39–43, 62, 74, 77, 80, 90, 92, 107, 109–110, 113, 129, 133, 142–44, 146–48, 153–55, 162, 172, 176, 203–4, 208, 214, 223, 231, 235, 242, 249, 255n77, 256n81, 271–73, 275–79, 289–90
kingdom, vi, 1, 11, 17–21, 24–25, 30–32, 39–44, 46–47, 49, 52, 54, 56–57, 61–62, 67–69, 71–72, 72n32, 73–74, 77–81, 81n43, 84, 84n48, 92, 94, 105–110, 119, 133, 137–38, 143–44, 149, 151, 154, 162–66, 168–70, 172, 174, 177, 181–85, 187, 189–92, 195–96, 199–202, 204, 204n39, 206, 208–9, 215, 220, 228, 231–35, 246, 250, 257, 265n8, 282–83, 289–90
kingdoms, xv, 84, 110, 145, 154, 201
kingship(s), 24, 265n7, 272, 275
Kinnereth, 119
kiss, kissed, 263–64, 264n3

knapsack, 105
kneading, 138
knee(s), 50, 66, 89, 233
kneel, kneeling, 186, 275
knifing, 69
know(s), knowing, knowledge, known, 1, 7, 9, 13n38, 18–21, 29–30, 35, 37–40, 47, 50–52, 56, 61, 67–69, 71, 74–75, 82–83, 86–87, 90–91, 95, 98, 102, 104, 107–8, 112–13, 116, 119–20, 124, 127–30, 132, 134, 136, 141–46, 149, 151–52, 157, 159–61, 163–64, 174–75, 187, 190, 194, 195n16, 196–98, 202, 205–6, 218, 218n28, 219, 222, 226, 231–32, 234–36, 239, 244, 244n36, 245–47, 253, 255, 259, 259n95, 260–62, 265, 270, 272–74, 276, 278–80, 282, 285–87, 289–90
Kuala Lumpur, xi

labor, laborer, 114, 200, 237
Laidlaw College, xi, xv, 226
Lake (Galilee), 86–87, 89, 112, 116–17, 119, 134, 136, 141
lake of fire, 37
lamb(s), 29, 51n24, 213, 248, 253–55, 267, 277n46
lament, 100, 259n94
lamentable, 274n33
lamp(s), vi, 31, 79–80, 85
land(s), landed, 1, 12, 38, 52, 56, 68, 88, 112, 117, 119, 130, 143, 154, 156, 175n25, 193, 199, 202–3, 220–22, 230, 239, 244, 279, 283
language, languages, xiii, 11, 41, 70, 73, 88, 100, 103, 129–30, 158, 200, 222, 243–46, 249, 253, 259n94, 260, 276, 278, 287n69
Laodicea, 241
last days, 36, 123, 155
Last Supper, viii, 8, 61, 195n14, 196–97, 235, 253–57, 259–60, 265n10
Latin, 10, 12–13, 13n36, 20n47, 55n31, 91n12, 104, 275, 278n47
Latinisms, 10
laugh, laughter, 100, 191

laurel, 275n36
law(s), viii, 12, 21, 29, 44, 51–57, 63–65,
    91, 97, 109, 120–22, 124–25,
    130, 153, 155–56, 162, 177–80,
    186–87, 187n1, 215–16, 225,
    227, 229–30, 233, 248, 264,
    266–67, 272, 289
lawbreaker(s), 63, 65
lawful, 65
lawgiver, 18
lawlessness, 13n40, 197, 244
lawn, 115
lawyers, 235
Lazarus, 3, 203, 207n46, 226, 250
lead(s), leading, led, viii, xv, 1, 22,
    37–38, 43, 46, 68–69, 79, 84, 90,
    100n25, 103–4, 108–9, 110, 123,
    127, 130, 132, 139, 141, 147,
    149, 151, 154, 160, 162, 164,
    167, 170–71, 174, 179, 182, 194,
    196, 198–99, 199n26, 200, 205,
    209, 214–16, 219, 224, 235, 237,
    239–40, 240n19, 241, 243, 245,
    247–49, 251, 253, 255, 257, 259,
    261, 264, 266–67, 273, 275, 280,
    282, 284, 290
leaders, 9, 12, 17–20, 23–24, 27–29,
    39, 42, 45, 51, 55, 57, 59–62,
    64, 66–72, 75, 91, 95–97, 100,
    105–7, 110, 112–13, 115–16,
    121–23, 131, 134–35, 137, 140,
    145–48, 157, 164, 167, 182n39,
    186, 188, 194, 198–99, 202, 206,
    212–14, 218–20, 222–23, 225,
    231, 234, 236, 253, 263–64, 266,
    269, 270–73, 279, 281, 284
leadership, viii, 22n59, 24, 29, 44, 64,
    68–69, 95, 100, 111, 139, 146,
    161, 194, 198–201, 209, 219,
    221–23, 225, 250, 278
leaf, leaves, 210–11, 246
learn, learned, learner(s), learning, xv,
    35, 59, 64, 68–69, 91, 99, 102,
    110–11, 144, 158, 184, 189n7,
    195, 206, 261–62, 265, 282, 288
least, 27, 65, 104, 107, 128, 146, 155,
    169–70, 196, 205, 253–54, 268
leather, 35, 35n5, 274
leaven(s), leavening, 138, 138n1

Lebanon, 14, 31, 128
lecturer, xv, 226
leftovers, 110, 115, 133
legal, 51, 65, 96, 104, 177, 180, 180n33,
    235
legalism, legalistic, legalists, legality,
    legalizing, 63–65, 180, 177, 187
legend, 224n47
legion(s), 11, 90–91, 91n12, 94–95, 101,
    129
legitimate, legitimized, 34, 69, 125, 231
leisure, 93
lemons, 214
lenders, 65
leper(s), leprosy, leprous, 22, 26, 49–50,
    50n20, 51–52, 56, 134, 207, 248,
    249n57, 249n58, 250
lepton(s), 237, 238n5
lesson(s), v–ix, xv, 1, 33, 59, 86, 112,
    116, 132, 138, 148, 159–60, 163,
    166, 170, 174, 178, 181, 184,
    185, 198, 202, 206, 210, 236–38,
    260–63
letter(s), 7, 9–10, 12, 13n36, 26n73, 76,
    78n39, 122, 164, 202, 277n46
Levi, 25, 55–57, 59, 69, 190
Leviathan, 88
Levirate marriage, 226
Levite(s), Levitical, 45, 51, 53, 98, 147,
    154, 229
liar, lie(s), 13, 67, 191, 216, 270
liberate(d), liberating, liberation,
    liberator, 18, 23, 29, 35, 40, 43,
    56, 68, 72, 88, 90, 94, 153, 155,
    162, 186, 201, 204
Libya, 275
licentiousness, 126
life, live, lived, lives, living, ix, xi, xv, 1,
    6, 8–9, 12, 14, 17, 20, 25, 29, 31,
    36–37, 39–41, 43–45, 48, 50,
    50n20, 51, 51n24, 54, 57, 58,
    60–61, 63, 65, 67–69, 73–74, 77,
    79, 80, 82–84, 87–88, 90, 92–93,
    95, 97, 99, 100–101, 106, 109,
    111, 113–14, 116, 119, 124–26,
    132, 134, 136–37, 140–41, 144,
    147–49, 149n25, 150, 150n25,
    150n26, 151, 153, 158, 164,
    169–70, 172–77, 177n29, 178,

SUBJECT INDEX

180, 186–87, 187n1, 188–94, 200–203, 205, 207, 213, 213n13, 226–29, 233, 243, 246, 251–53, 257, 261–62, 264, 275–76, 284, 288–89.
lifelong, 68, 179, 190
lifesaving, 169
lifestyle, 144, 199
light(s), 11, 31, 56, 72–73, 75, 79–80, 82, 92, 135, 181, 221, 221n43, 228, 248, 250, 257
lightning, 152, 285
limelight, 170
linen, 283–84, 284n63, 285
lintels, 53n26
lions, 158
lips, 45, 121, 263, 281
liquid(s), 51n24, 62
liquidate, 191
listen, listened, listening, 18, 37–38, 72, 74–75, 80, 84, 148, 153, 155, 155n35, 166, 181–82, 193, 227, 233, 245, 246
literal, literary, literalize, 7, 14, 26, 44, 73, 91, 105, 113, 117, 126, 156, 172–73, 178, 184, 192, 196n18, 199, 228, 245, 246–47, 254–55, 274, 276, 279
litigiousness, 170
litra, 249
loaf, loaves, 63, 114–16, 119, 133, 138–39, 139n3, 255
loan, 91n12
loathing, 230
locusts, 35
logic, logical, 158, 213, 284
Logos (Divine), 34, 145, 152
lonely, 289
long, longing, 40, 67, 143, 284n61
longer Ending, 13n39, 32, 288
look(s), looked, looking, 6, 26, 39, 48, 57, 73–74, 82, 107, 115, 126, 131, 135, 143, 151–52, 159–60, 169, 173, 180, 188, 190, 190n10, 197, 209, 211, 215, 219, 223, 225, 240n12, 246, 248, 265n9, 265n10
Lord, vi, 6, 18, 25, 41, 61, 63–64, 71, 83, 93, 100, 106, 113, 121, 129, 134, 146–47, 150–51, 154, 156, 160, 162, 167–68, 170, 181, 195–96, 199, 201, 203–5, 207, 270n50, 208, 214, 217, 220, 232, 232n79, 236, 249, 255n77, 256n81, 261, 286, 289
lordship, 29, 91, 118, 233
Lord's Supper, 61, 255
lost, xi, 2–3, 14, 17, 26, 29, 51, 76, 79, 92, 109, 113, 150–51, 187, 286n68, 289–90
lots (cast), 277
love, loving, loved, loves, loving, lovingly, xi, 11, 21, 22n59, 24–25, 36–38, 40, 50, 64–65, 69, 72, 76–77, 79, 93, 98, 101, 109, 122, 125, 136, 144, 147–48, 152, 154–55, 158–59, 162, 165–66, 176, 178, 180–81, 183, 185, 187n1, 188–89, 191, 196, 206, 218, 228–31, 233–34, 238, 252, 273, 279, 289–90
lovely, 42, 159
lowest, 165, 181, 200, 203, 234
lowly, 166, 182, 200, 235
Lukan, 288
Luke, 2–7, 9–10, 10n27, 13n39, 14, 14n42, 19n46, 26, 30n78, 34–36, 38, 40, 42, 42n14, 44–45, 48–50, 50n21, 50n23, 51–54, 56n34, 59n1, 60–61, 61n7n 61n10, 61n11, 63n13, 69, 71n30, 72–74, 78–79, 81n41, 81n42, 87n6, 89, 90n10, 93, 97, 97n21, 99, 101–2, 102n29, 102n31, 104n34, 106, 108, 110, 112–13, 115–16, 117n8, 128–30, 133n44, 135–36, 139, 141, 143n15, 150–51, 161n42, 164n1, 173, 173n15, 173n16, 175, 175n24, 176, 176n25, 179, 182n39, 186–89, 195, 195n14, 195–96, 196n19, 197–98, 201, 203, 203n41, 205, 207, 211n7, 213n13, 215n21, 217n27, 222, 226, 229–31, 232n76, 232n77, 235, 244, 244n36, 246, 246n45, 249, 249n58, 252, 254, 257, 257n84, 258n88, 259, 264n4, 265,

Luke *(continued)*, 266n11, 269, 271–73, 276, 278, 279n50, 282–83, 285, 287, 288n71
Luke-Acts, 10, 78, 287
luminaries, 78, 154
lunacy, 199
lust, 196, 199
Luther, 13n37
luxuries, luxury, 175, 193
LXX, 98, 120, 197, 197n21, 199, 199n27, 204, 227, 232, 237, 242n28, 255n78, 259n94, 280
Lydda, 283n57
Lydia, 78

Maccabean, 258n90
Macedonians, 238
Machaerus, 111
machinations, 29, 140, 199
mad, madly, madman, madness, vi, 70–71, 92, 101, 272
Magdala, 66, 119, 134, 282
magic, magical, 47–48, 97
magnet, 95
Magog, 242n29
mainline denominations, 62
mainstream society, 50
Malachi, 35, 108, 156
maladies, 131
Malaysia, Malaysian, xv, 40, 180, 238n5
Malchus, 264
male(s), 43–44, 51n24, 180, 212n8, 237n2
malevolence, 126
malice, 126
malicious, 95
malign, maligned, 127, 149
Malta, 287
Malthace, 107
maltreatment, 71, 149, 194, 221, 269
mammon, 100
man, men, vii–viii, 1, 3, 8, 14, 18, 22n56, 23–24, 26, 29–30, 35, 35n5, 35n6, 38, 40, 42–43, 45–47, 49–50, 50n21, 51–57, 60, 64–65, 68–69, 72–73, 78, 85, 89–97, 103, 105–7, 109, 115–17, 119, 130–31, 133, 135, 140–42, 145–46, 148–49, 150n26, 153–57, 160–62, 164, 167–70, 173, 177–78, 178n32, 179–81, 183, 185–94, 197–201, 203–4, 205n39, 206, 214–15, 217–18, 220, 223, 226, 231–32, 238, 244, 246, 250, 252–55, 258–59, 263, 263n1, 265, 268–69, 270–71, 273–74, 276n39, 278n48, 281–86, 288–90
Manasseh, 172
manifestations, 36, 158
manipulate, manipulating, 124, 126–27, 205
Manna, 38, 116, 132, 134
manuscript(s), 13, 13n36, 13n38, 13n39, 13n40, 33n1, 50n22, 173, 200n30, 287n69
March (month), 114, 211, 211n4, 246
March, marching, 152n28, 203
Marcion, 10n27
Marcus Tulllius Cicero, 168
marginalization, marginalized, 17, 22, 45, 48, 50, 50n20, 67, 71, 96, 182, 203, 289
margins, 144
Mark, i, iii–v, xi, xv, 1–14, 17–37, 39–45, 47–48, 50, 52–61, 63, 65–66, 69–78, 81–95, 97, 99–123, 125, 130–35, 139–45, 149–56, 158–59, 161–62, 164, 166, 168, 170–83, 185–89, 191–93, 195–96, 199–201, 203–211, 213–21, 224–29, 231–36, 238–51, 253–60, 262–69, 271–96
Markan, 7, 7n10, 26, 52, 52n25, 70, 87, 94–95, 98–99, 103, 136, 205, 210, 254n73
marketplace(s), 120, 234
marital, marriage(s), marry, marrying, married, vii–viii, 25, 47, 108–9, 124, 124n26, 125, 176–77, 177n29, 180, 180n33, 184, 186, 188, 224–27, 236
Martha, 207, 207n46, 248–49
martyrs, martyred, 258n90, 288
Mary Magdalene, 78, 78n38, 251, 254, 282, 284–85, 287

SUBJECT INDEX 321

Mary, mother of Jesus, 99, 102,
Mary, mother of Jacob (James), 251, 254, 282, 284–85
Mary, mother of Mark, 8, 254
Mary, of Bethany, 207, 207n46, 249, 253, 262
masculinity, 180n35
master, 24, 35n7, 59, 91, 129, 193, 200, 207n50
materialism, materialistic, 77, 188, 193
Matthew, 2–7, 9, 19, 19n46, 25–26, 30, 34, 38, 56, 69, 81, 100, 103, 110, 113, 125, 129, 151, 176, 179, 186, 195n14, 239, 248–50, 255, 282–84, 284n62, 285, 287n69
mature, maturity, 79, 106, 170, 182, 191, 198
maxim(s), 74, 80, 102, 168
May, 210, 248
meal(s), 29, 110, 114, 116, 133, 175, 196, 248, 253–54, 254n73, 256, 283
measure(s), 11n30, 79–81, 85
Mecca, 213
Medad, 167
medical, medicine, 48, 67, 97n21, 104, 157
Mediterranean, 75, 275
mega-afraid, 88
mega-calm, 86
mega-wind, 88
mega-storm, 86
Megiddo, 119n19
Meholah, Abel, 25n66
Melchizedek, 90, 280
memory, memories, 203, 251, 253
Menander, 150n26
menial labor, 200
menstrual, menstruation, 96
mental, 41
mental health/illness, 158, 45
mentor, 170
mercy, 93, 159, 170, 204, 230, 280
Mesopotamia, 119n19
message(s), xi, 18, 31, 33, 35, 39, 41–42, 44, 52–53, 57, 75, 79–80, 82, 85, 89, 93, 111, 121, 141, 157, 185, 190, 214, 288–89
messenger, 156

Messiah(s), 1, 11–12, 14, 17–21, 23–24, 28, 33–35, 35n6, 36, 38–41, 43, 54–55, 61, 75, 87–88, 90, 99, 101–2, 108–9, 119, 121, 132, 135–36, 140–43, 143n15, 144–52, 155–56, 159, 161–62, 165, 193–95, 201, 204, 206, 208–9, 211, 216, 218–19, 222–23, 225, 231–33, 241–42, 242n29, 245–46, 248–50, 255, 257, 264–65, 267–69, 278–81, 286, 289
messiahship, 18, 21, 39, 46, 66, 86, 88, 107, 119, 140–41, 143, 147, 153, 232, 250
messianic, messianically, 20n47, 21–22, 22n55, 22n56, 38, 69, 128, 131, 144, 155, 204–5, 205n39, 208, 214–15, 240, 247, 250, 253, 264, 271–72
messianic Secret, 21–22, 22n55, 22n56, 46, 48, 55, 93, 101, 128, 141, 144, 155, 205
metal, 102n28
metaphor, metaphorical, metaphorically, 43, 81, 88, 138, 172–73, 175, 196, 201, 216, 246, 258
meteorites, 245
Micah, 221
Midian, 134
might, mighty, 101, 115–16, 150–51, 162
milieu, 177
militarily, militaristic, military, military, 1, 11, 19n46, 68, 91, 105, 110, 117, 136, 142, 143n15, 151, 154–55, 160, 168, 172, 208, 258, 271n25, 278, 281
milling, 270
millstone, 171
mimicking, 225
mind(s), minded, 6, 19, 34, 39, 41, 45, 54–55, 60, 64, 71–72, 74–75, 81, 83, 87, 89–90, 92, 97, 117–19, 127, 129, 133, 136, 138–39, 171, 176, 190, 198, 201, 208, 216, 219, 226, 228–29, 235, 241, 248, 250, 256, 261, 269, 287
mindless, 170

mindset, 191
minister(s), ministered, ministering, 14, 24n65, 26, 37–38, 49, 52, 62, 69, 72–73, 86, 92–94, 104, 107, 110, 114, 129–30, 168, 170, 176, 190, 196, 198, 213, 293
ministry, iv–vi, x, 1, 9, 14–18, 22, 26n69, 29, 33–35, 37, 39, 41–53, 55, 57, 61, 66–75, 82–83, 86, 93–95, 97, 102, 104, 104n33, 112, 114–16, 120, 129–31, 136, 143, 160, 166–69, 177, 184, 198, 200, 216, 218–19, 225, 247–48, 252, 258
miracle(s), vi–vii, 19–20, 22, 24, 26, 39, 47, 52, 64, 86–87, 89, 91, 93–95, 97, 99, 101, 103–5, 107–9, 111–13, 115–19, 121, 123, 125, 127, 129, 131–33, 135–37, 139–40, 142, 167, 169–70, 211, 226, 273
miraculous, miraculously, 78, 136, 153, 279, 287
mirror(s), 126, 140, 140, 206, 281
miscarriages, 213n13
Mishnah, Mishnaic, 45, 65, 91, 120n21, 213n13, 237, 256
mission, missional, missionally, 9, 12, 19, 22n56, 29–31, 45, 49, 55, 57–58, 60, 67, 69, 73, 76, 78–79, 81n43, 104–7, 110–15, 129, 132–34, 137, 142, 151–52, 164, 166–68, 170, 230, 242, 246, 251–52, 285, 287, 289–90, 294
missionaries, missionary, 8–9, 26, 43, 69, 106
misunderstand, misunderstanding, misunderstands, misunderstood, 136, 139, 185, 195
mite, 235
Moabitess, 129
mob, mobbed, 96, 177, 261, 263–64
mock, mocked, mockery, mocking, ix, 24, 29, 114, 149, 243, 269, 274–75, 278–79
model(s), 52, 182, 238, 261
modern, 105, 116, 275, 283n57
moment(s), 35–37, 50, 53–55, 74–75, 94, 109, 114, 129, 132, 142–43, 157, 164–66, 183, 190, 204, 218, 222, 227, 233, 251, 255–56, 260, 264–65, 267, 279, 281, 290
monarchical, 142
monarchs, 160
monetary, money, 8, 56, 77, 81, 92, 97, 100, 105, 114, 125, 182, 185, 187–89, 191, 193, 213, 220n33, 224, 230, 235, 237–38, 250–52, 262, 290
moneychangers, 209, 213
monogamous, 124n26, 178–80, 226
monotheism, 228, 269
month(s), 245n38, 248
moon, 245
moral(s), morality, 92, 109, 127
morning, 48, 117, 170, 228n69, 258, 285
Mosaic, Moses, 18, 24n65, 38, 59, 66, 117, 122, 134, 136, 153, 153n32, 155, 162, 167, 169, 177–78, 194, 226–27, 256, 268n21
mother, 8–9, 43, 47, 102, 107, 122, 186, 195n14, 251, 254, 282, 285
mother-in-law, 47, 52, 163
motivated, motivation(s), motives, 81, 113, 135, 147, 167, 186, 196, 202, 205, 211, 228–30, 235, 251–52, 261, 272–73, 283
mountain(s), mount, 24n65, 26, 49, 67, 83, 86, 141–42, 152, 153n32, 167, 215–17, 240n12, 258, 261
Mount Arbel, 86, 116
Mount Hermon, 142, 152, 154–55, 157, 161
Mount of Olives, 207, 207n44, 207n47, 216, 238, 240, 241n19, 257–59, 259n92
Mount of Transfiguration, 18, 38, 100, 108, 161, 285
Mount Nebo, 153
Mount Sinai, 38
Mount Tabor, 152
Mount (temple), 214, 216, 240
Mount Zion, 216
mourn, mourned, mourners, mourning, 59, 60, 100, 100n25, 151, 251
mouth, 113, 123, 158, 267, 272n31
mouthpiece, 20, 38
mud, 53, 53n26, 117

SUBJECT INDEX

mule, 208
multiplication, multiplicity, multiply, 44, 96, 133–34, 192, 289
multitude, 125
mummify, 175
Muratorian Canon, 7, 7n10
murder, murderer, 124, 124, 186, 273, 274
muscles, 274
music, 257
Muslim(s), 213, 269
mustard, vi, 31, 78, 82–83, 85
mute, vii, 130, 131, 141, 157
mutilated, mutilation, 90, 172
mutual, mutually, 105, 194
muzzling, 87
myrrh, 276, 276n42
mysteries, mystery, 79, 101, 289
mystery Religions/cults, 34n3, 59, 101

Nabateans, Nabatea, 109, 241
Naboth's vineyard, 222
nailed, nails, 274, 277
Nain, 135, 226
naïve, naively, 182–83
naked, nakedness, 8, 109, 254, 259, 265, 277, 288
name(s), named, naming, 1, 2, 4, 6n7, 8, 13n39, 17, 19, 20n47, 24, 44–45, 54, 56, 68–69, 71, 74, 78, 89–91, 91n11, 95–96, 98, 102, 107, 113, 118, 127, 132, 142, 142n7, 143, 146, 149, 160, 165, 167–71, 174, 181, 202–3, 208, 213–14, 218n28, 224, 225n51, 227–28, 241, 253, 257n86, 263, 266–67, 268n21, 273, 275–76, 286
Naphtali, 119
narcissistic, 230
nard, 249–50, 253
narrated, narrates, 14, 107, 206
narrative(s), 8n18, 18, 24, 28, 30, 34, 53, 55, 59, 64–65, 70, 86, 96, 98, 109, 120, 131–32, 134, 157, 181, 201, 205, 211n7, 217–19, 221, 231, 239–40, 248, 252, 255, 257, 263, 267–70, 272, 274–75, 280, 283–84, 286, 292, 295

Nathan, 34, 36, 74, 109
nation(s), 14, 21, 31, 35, 40, 43, 46, 49, 56, 71, 74, 82–84, 93, 121, 130, 132, 139, 146, 148, 151, 156, 158–59, 162, 177, 204, 212–13, 218, 221, 223, 239, 242, 244, 246, 251, 257, 259n92, 264, 266, 268, 286, 290
national, nationalism, nationalists, 12, 59, 85
native, 6n7, 12
natural, naturally, 48, 85, 87–88, 92, 114, 118, 157, 196, 243, 247n48, 250, 255
nature, 22, 89, 98, 107, 141, 153, 160, 170, 193, 198, 211n7, 215, 227, 246, 272, 278
Nazarene, 35, 204, 278, 285
Nazareth, 20, 44, 70n26, 101, 103–4, 152, 171, 219
Nazarite(s), 204, 276
necessities, necessity, 160n41, 193, 251
neck, 171, 249
need(s), 4, 6, 18–19, 30–31, 37–38, 42, 44, 48–49, 50–51, 57, 61n4, 63–64, 67–68, 70, 72–74, 78, 82, 87, 93, 95–97, 97n21, 98, 101, 104, 109–110, 112, 114–16, 122, 125, 132, 135–37, 139–40, 149, 151, 160, 162, 164, 169–70, 173, 183, 185, 187, 189–91, 200, 202, 205–7, 230–31, 235–36, 238, 242–43, 251–52, 258, 268, 276, 279
needle, 61, 191, 191n12
needy, 25, 110, 140, 185, 191, 229, 251
negative, negatively, 97n21, 129, 181, 228, 262
neglect, 73
Nehemiah (Rabbi), 260n100
neighbor, 63, 187, 228–30
Nero, 7, 11, 14, 75–76, 150, 176, 176n27, 179, 192, 199, 270, 276, 291, 295
Neronian, 149, 242
nest, 83, 84n48
nets, 43
New Zealand(ers), xv, 40, 55, 83, 114, 158, 164, 180n33, 203, 237, 238n5, 250

Nicodemus, 95, 269, 284
night, 11, 60, 82, 82n44, 90, 117, 253, 258, 261, 275
Nile, 134
Nimshi, 24n66
Nineveh, 61n4
Nissan, 248, 254
Noah, 245
Nob, 63
nobility, noble, 83, 146
noise, 121, 213
nominal, 77
noon, 279
normal, 71
north, northern, northward, 14, 31, 71, 119, 128, 130, 134, 141, 142n7, 151, 161, 207n47, 237n1, 239, 275
northeast, northeastern, 31, 89, 93, 202, 239, 283n57
northwest, northwestern, 66, 128, 134, 142, 151, 283
nose, nostrils, 168
notorious, 273
noun, 41, 88, 96n19
nuclear, 245
Nun, 102
nursing, 244
nurture, nurtured, 106, 166, 181
Nympha, 78, 78n38

oath(s), 91, 270
obedience, obediently, obey (s), obeyed, obeying, 57, 59, 74, 80, 88, 93–94, 131, 143, 155, 183, 186, 187n1, 190–91, 261
obligated, 230
observance, observant, observation, observe(s), observed, observers, observes, observing, 12, 53, 64, 66n22, 68, 69n25, 105, 107, 120, 135–36, 163, 167, 169, 173, 180, 187, 213, 216, 227, 234, 237–38, 240n17, 263, 264, 270, 282–83, 287n69
obsessed, obsession, 120, 136, 140, 169–70, 190, 193
obsolete, 214
obstacle (s), 82, 170–71, 192, 216

obstinacy, 65
ocean, 197n21
Oceania, 84
Octavia, 176
October, 210
offended, offender, offense, offensive, 92, 102, 141, 171, 189, 215, 231, 233, 274
offer, offered, offering(s) (sacrifice), 51n24, 96, 138, 172, 174, 174n18, 213n13, 214–15, 230, 237, 237n2, 238, 262
office, 107, 198–99, 202, 266, 271
official(s), 11, 11n30, 130, 198, 266, 274
offspring, 226n58
Og, 154
oil, 36, 51n24, 61, 98, 106, 249, 259
ointments, 97
olive trees, 259n92
Olivet Discourse, viii, 237–38
omission(s), 13, 171, 173
omnipotence, 260, 268
omniscience, 247
Onan, 226n58
oneness, 178, 228
Onesimus, 78
openness, 183
opinions, 163, 223
opponent(s), oppose(d), opposing, opposition, 20, 26, 64–65, 76, 105, 107, 168, 180, 195, 223, 224, 244, 255, 269, 275
oppress(ed), oppressing, oppression, oppressors, 35, 40, 56, 186–87, 191, 193, 199, 214–15, 223, 235, 238
opulent, 110, 203
oracle(s), 239, 252
oral gospel, 2
oral law(s), 57, 63, 121, 225
oral presentation, 33
oral tradition, 3,
order, 5–6, 14n40, 87–88, 118, 147, 165, 178, 183, 187, 188n4, 211, 234, 268, 274, 280
orders, 105n37, 114, 144, 176
ordinance, 178
ordination, 69, 169
organic, 53, 53n26, 83

SUBJECT INDEX

organization(s), 105, 198, 253
oriental, 82n44
orientation, 25, 222
Origen, 7n10, 89
origin(s), 47, 66, 90, 101, 121, 178, 204, 282
original, 1, 6n7, 13, 13n37, 14, 14n41, 18, 26, 30, 32, 42, 73, 89, 120, 125n28, 126n30, 141, 160n41, 227, 286
originator, 5
Ortho, 176
ossuaries, ossuary, 266, 284
OT, 2, 23, 23n64. 34-35, 40, 44, 46, 57, 59, 61, 63, 90, 97n21, 104, 108-9, 118-19, 131, 143, 153, 155-57, 172, 179, 185, 196, 203n37, 204, 210, 212-13, 221, 226-28, 230, 232, 239-40, 242n28, 245-47, 249, 258, 259n94, 264, 268, 289
otherness, 45
overabundance, 78
overcame, overcome(s), overcome, 25, 38, 72, 83, 157, 170, 218, 283n58, 286
oversaw, overseeing, oversight, 95, 147, 213, 281

pacifist, 124
pagan, 90, 182n38, 212, 243
pain, painful, painfully, 29, 100, 110, 158, 192, 242n29, 259-61, 270, 275
palace(s), 203, 271, 274n34
Palestine, x, 16, 52, 61, 93, 128, 244n37, 254, 274
pallet, 53, 55
palm Trees, 202, 208
Pan, 142
pandemics, 245
Paneas, 142
Panias, 142
Panium, 142
Pantheon, 281
Papias, 2n3, 6n7, 7
papyrus, papyri, xiv, 102
parable(s), vi, viii, 3, 22, 24, 29, 31, 52, 54, 59-63, 65, 69, 73-75, 77-81, 81n43, 86, 119, 147, 175, 183, 191, 194, 220-21, 223, 225, 236, 246, 252
parabolic, 173
Paraclete, 37
paradigm, 236
parallelism, 65n17
paralytic(s), paralyzed, paralyzing, 27n75, 52n25, 53-54, 56, 64, 158, 186
paranoid, 199
parchment, 13n36
pardoned, 273
parents, 8, 100-101, 122, 124, 166, 181, 183n40, 187, 242
Parousia, 31n79, 151n27, 242n32, 247n49, 251, 294
Parthia, 241, 241n21
party, 60, 110, 115, 129, 137, 178, 180
passion, vii-viii, 24, 28-29, 48, 145-46, 148, 161, 174, 193, 195, 218, 222-23, 248, 251, 258, 274, 286
passionate, passionately, passions, xv, 52, 57, 62, 83, 127, 182, 229
Passover, 29, 114, 152n28, 208, 211n4, 213, 218-19, 248, 253, 254, 254n73, 255-57, 262, 271-73, 277n46, 283
pastor(s), 49, 113, 198
paterfamilias, 43
patibulum, 276n39
patience, patiently, 39, 65, 132
patient, 65, 133
Patmos, 152, 197, 256
patriarchal, 42-43, 47
Patriarchs, 227
Paul, xi, 7, 7n15, 8-9, 9n22, 10-12, 30, 36, 38, 42, 60, 75, 75n35, 76, 78, 78n39, 79, 83, 90-91, 95, 99, 102, 105-6, 123, 125-26, 130, 136, 138, 149-51, 164, 168, 171, 175-76, 179, 180n35, 187, 200-202, 216, 222, 224, 230, 236, 238-39, 241, 241n19, 242, 254, 257, 260-61, 275-76, 287, 294-95
pax, 11, 274

peace, peaceful, 11, 18, 38, 40, 67, 87, 99, 147, 174, 176, 185, 208, 210, 241, 241n21, 272
pearl, 183
peasant(s), 214, 220n32
peck, 11n30
peg, 277
Pella, 93n16
penal, 273
penalties, penalties, 122, 225n56, 122, 268
peninsular, 128
Pentecost, 8, 12, 36, 40, 151, 197, 208, 275
Pentecostalism, 62
people(s), xv, 9, 11, 18–22, 22n59, 24–25, 28–31, 34–36, 39, 41–52, 52n25, 53–59, 62–69, 69n25, 70, 72–79, 81–82, 84–85, 87–88, 90–95, 98–100, 102, 102n30, 103, 105–6, 109, 112–16, 118–24, 126–37, 139, 141, 143, 145–46, 148, 150–52, 154, 156–62, 165–74, 176, 178–82, 186–88, 190–93, 196n19, 198–203, 205–6, 208–9, 213–18, 220–24, 226–27, 227n61, 228, 230–37, 240n12, 241n19, 241n20, 242, 244–47, 251–53, 256–57, 257n86, 258, 260n100, 263–64, 265n7, 265n9, 267–68, 272–73, 279–81, 288–90, 295
perceive(s), perceived, perceives, perceiving, perception, 28, 89, 50, 97, 99, 120, 129, 132, 139, 141–42, 222
percussion, 100n25
Perea, 66, 107
perfect, perfectly, 40, 89, 99, 116, 193, 226
perfume(s), 249–50
pericope, 60, 142, 181
perish, perishing, 87, 225n55
permission(s), permissive, permits, permitted, permitting, 63, 65, 125, 166–67, 169–70, 177–79, 180n34, 212n9, 254, 266
perpetrator, 98

perpetual, perpetually, 102, 280
perplexed, perplexity, 88, 285–86
persecute(ed), persecuting, persecution(s), 11–12, 14, 75–76, 96n19, 149, 192, 242, 258, 276, 288
perseverance, persevere, 79, 173, 242, 261
Persians, 277
persistence, persistent, 225n56, 270
personalities, personality, 68, 199
Peter, vii, ix, xi, 1, 6-7, 7n10, 8—10, 10n25, 11—13, 17–20, 28–31, 38, 42–44, 45n17, 47, 49, 52, 56, 68, 75–76, 78, 88–89, 95, 98–101, 107–8, 116, 123, 138, 141–44, 147–49, 152–54, 157–58, 161–63, 167, 169, 171, 189, 192, 194–95, 198, 200, 202, 204–5, 215, 217n28, 222, 240, 257–59, 261–62, 264–66, 270–71, 274, 276, 281–82, 286, 287n69, 288–89, 293, 295–96
pews, 205
phantasm, 117
Pharisaic, Pharisee(s), vii, 42, 45, 53, 57, 59, 60, 63–64, 66, 90, 95, 120–22, 124, 134–36, 138, 140, 146–47, 170, 177–78, 223–25, 227, 234, 249n58, 254, 284
Philadelphia, 93n16, 293–94
Philemon, 76
Philip, 17, 69, 78, 78n39, 106, 108–9, 141–42, 142n7, 176, 199
Philippi, 17, 39, 90, 130, 142, 142n7, 142n11, 161, 163, 241, 291
Philo, 43n15, 228n67, 265n8, 271n26
Philopatris, 109
Philosopher(s), 59, 105
Phoebe, 78
Phoenicia, Phoenician, 128
photosynthesis, 82
physical, physically, 43, 47, 50, 94, 99, 114, 116, 127, 142, 149, 160, 167, 178, 183, 185, 204, 244, 251, 269
physician(s), 57, 97, 97n21
picture, 26, 74, 84, 89, 146n20

SUBJECT INDEX

pierced, 151
pigeons, 213, 213n13
pigs, 91–93
Pilate, ix, 24, 194, 223, 243, 243n33, 267, 271–74, 283–84, 288, 293–94
pilgrim(s), pilgrimages, 12, 119, 213, 240n17
pious, 120, 267
Pisidian Antioch, 106
pit, 63, 127, 220–21
pitcher, 11n30
pity, 204
placards, 278
place(s), placed, placement, 6–8, 11, 11n31, 14, 21, 29, 36, 40–41, 45, 46, 49, 50, 50n21, 53, 53n26, 60, 64, 66–67, 69–70, 82–83, 88, 90, 92, 103–4, 106–7, 112, 114, 116, 123, 132–33, 134, 142–43, 147, 149, 152, 154, 158, 162, 164–67, 169, 170, 172, 178, 180, 183, 187, 195n14, 196–97, 199, 200, 202—203, 203n38, 204–5, 206, 208, 213, 216, 218, 226, 237, 244, 251–52, 254, 256, 259, 273, 275–76, 276n39, 277, 278n48, 283, 283n57, 284, 284n62, 286
plains, 203
plan(s), planning, 1, 49, 103, 105, 194, 217, 260, 266
planet Earth, 47, 93, 227
plant(s), planted, planting, 9, 24, 76, 79, 81, 81n43, 82–84, 220, 249
Plato, 200n28
platter, 109
plausibly, 249n58
Plautus, 276n39
play(s), player, players, playing, 34, 74, 100n25, 131, 140, 164, 195, 200–201, 233, 246, 252, 195, 268, 273
plead(s), pleading, 91, 197, 204, 260–61
please(s), pleased, 36–37, 81, 124, 155–56, 174, 180, 187, 193, 236, 290
pleasure, 36, 81, 93, 174
pledge, 41
plenty, plentiful, 78, 218n28, 251
plight, 110, 113, 132, 159, 279

Pliny, 93n16, 131n40, 249, 249n60, 276n42
plot, plotted, 27, 66, 107, 114–15, 115n5, 220
plow(ed), plowing, 74, 102
plunder(ed), plundering, 24, 72, 152, 203
Plutarch, 102, 102n30, 276n39
poison, 287
polarization, 168
poles, wooden, 53n26
policeman, 124
political, politically, politician, politics, 22n56, 24, 29, 33, 45, 53–54, 68, 108, 140, 142, 147, 155, 177, 183, 199, 222, 252, 266, 268, 273–74, 283
poll tax, 11n30, 56
Polybius, 142n8
Pompeii, 241
Pompey, 243
pools, 203
poor, poorer, poverty, 8, 22, 25, 48, 51n24, 67, 97, 100n25, 110, 115, 132, 134, 140, 143n15, 149, 175, 183, 186–89, 192–93, 199, 203, 205, 213, 215, 229, 238, 235, 250–51, 263n1, 264, 274, 289
Pope(s), 47
Poppaea (Sabina), 176
populace, 108, 144, 234
popular, popularity, 21, 66, 223, 228, 233, 239, 248, 265, 273
population, 213, 213n11, 295
portending, portends, portents, 69, 139, 279
portrait, 143n15, 224
positive, positively, 53, 97n21, 102, 129, 217, 228, 228n68, 231, 252, 262, 272
possessed, possession (demonic), 47, 71, 89, 90, 147, 199, 205
possessions (material), 25, 72, 97, 124, 189–90, 192–93, 244, 277
possibility, possibilities, 2, 4, 5, 8n19, 11, 11n31, 27n75, 65, 100, 107–8, 128, 134, 141, 153, 157–58, 236, 238, 243, 247–48, 257n86, 267, 270, 273, 282n55, 283

possible, possibly, 2, 6, 8, 13, 21, 23n64, 33n1, 74, 76, 92, 89, 125, 127, 132, 143n15, 146n20, 163, 159, 176, 186, 191, 206, 216, 218n28, 225n57, 243, 253, 259n92, 260, 264, 274n33, 275, 276n41, 277, 278n49, 283n57

posture, 188, 200

potency, potent, 51

potential, potentially, 46, 51, 56, 69, 124, 140, 145, 148, 165, 171, 180

Potiphar, 265n9

pound(s) (money), 249, 285

pour(s), poured, pouring, 29, 40, 62, 151, 166, 228–29, 233, 246, 249, 256–57, 262, 289

power, v–vi, 11, 13n40, 14n40, 17–21, 29, 31, 33, 35–41, 43, 45–47, 49–55, 57, 59, 61, 63, 65–67, 69, 71–73, 75, 77–79, 81–83, 85, 87–90, 92, 94–104, 106–7, 109–111, 117, 120, 125, 130–31, 133, 135–36, 139–40, 143, 147–49, 151, 154, 157–59, 162, 164–65, 167–69, 181–83, 185, 198–99, 202, 205–6, 211, 215–16, 226, 229, 234, 236, 246, 261, 268–69, 288–90

powerful, powerfully, 40, 68, 71–74, 86–87, 89, 96, 151, 158, 168, 170, 185, 194, 231, 259, 270

powerless, 17

powers, 23, 204n39

practice(s), practiced, 34n3, 60, 61n4, 62, 74, 105, 122, 215, 220, 234, 263n1, 264, 276–78, 283

praetorium, 11n30, 274

praise, 127, 170, 208, 224, 261

pray, prayed, prayer(s), prayerful, prayerfulness, praying, prays, viii, 6, 22, 25, 25n68, 29, 38, 48–49, 58–60, 68, 72, 75–76, 90, 103, 106, 112, 116, 132, 137, 141, 157–61, 169, 197, 211, 214–17, 217n26, 229, 234–36, 244n37, 245, 259–60, 260n100, 261—262, 275, 289

preach(es), preached, preacher, preaching, 8, 12, 19, 22, 26, 30–31, 34–35, 39–43, 44, 49, 52, 54, 68, 70, 74–75, 78–79, 90, 94n17, 104n33, 105–8, 114, 129, 131, 156, 170, 239, 242, 246, 251, 287–88

predict(s), predictable, predictably, predicted, predicting, prediction(s), vii–ix, 19, 29, 31, 60, 76, 113, 117, 120–21, 145–48, 156, 161–62, 169, 172, 193–95, 218, 222–23, 239, 250–52, 257–58, 260, 263, 265–67, 268–69, 270, 280, 286, 289

Prefect, 271, 271n25, 284

prefer(s), preferable, preferred, 10n23, 20n47, 21, 25, 35n6, 41, 50n22, 64, 93, 210n2, 235, 238, 247, 261, 272

prefigure(s), 31, 151, 244

pregnant, 176, 244

preparation(s), preparatory, prepare(s), prepared, preparedness, preparing, 9, 19, 20, 31–32, 34, 38, 43, 67, 76, 93, 96–97, 105, 109, 147–51, 154, 156, 160, 190–92, 203, 207, 248, 251, 253–54, 258, 260, 263, 272, 285

preprayered, 161

prescience, 53, 163, 285

presence, present, presentation, presented, presenting, presently, presents, 9, 11, 18, 33, 36, 40, 53, 57, 61–62, 64–66, 81, 83, 88–89, 91, 97, 99, 101–2, 110, 115–16, 122, 128, 131–32, 141, 145, 148, 153, 155, 155n35, 161, 163, 168, 183, 189–90, 192–94, 204, 219, 225, 227, 247, 249, 249n57, 250–51, 254–55, 268, 271, 279, 281–82, 284, 285

preservation, preserve(s), preserved, 64, 92, 149n25, 150n25, 175, 259n92

president (synagogue), 95

president (vice), 196

press (grape, oil), 221, 259

pressed, pressing, 61, 96, 96n19, 275
pressure, pressuring, 12, 177, 235, 271
pretender(s), pretending, pretentious, 49, 240, 275, 277
preternatural, 116
pretext, 174
prey, 127
pride, proudly, 127, 164, 290
priest(s), priesthood, priestly, 42, 45, 47, 51, 51n24, 52–53, 63, 90, 95, 102, 118, 144, 146–47, 147n22, 164, 168–69, 186, 194, 201, 212n8, 213, 215, 218n28, 222, 223n45, 224–25, 225n51, 226, 229, 233, 237, 237n2, 243, 248–50, 252–53, 263, 263n1, 264, 266–70, 272–73, 278, 280, 288
primitive, 292
primordial, 87
principal, 59
principle(s), 59, 64, 80–81, 176, 229
priority(s), prioritize(d), prioritizing, priority, 25, 43, 58, 70, 73, 85, 166, 206, 228
Priscilla, 12, 78, 78n38, 170
prison, prisoner, 39, 75n35, 111, 272–73
private(ly), 84, 112, 128, 130, 179, 235, 240
privilege, xi, 185, 236, 272
problem(s), problematic, 2n2, 7n13, 7n14, 31, 51, 51n24, 89, 91, 95, 98, 120–21, 137, 139, 158–59, 164, 167, 183, 185, 187, 193, 219, 226, 230, 234, 238–39, 247n48, 254, 277n46, 285
proceeds (financial), 188–89
proclaim, proclaiming, proclamation, 13, 17, 19, 34, 42, 75, 77, 79, 89, 106, 117n13, 129, 139, 143n15, 202, 204n39, 214, 244n37, 246, 251, 286, 287n69
procurator, 271n25
Prodigal Son, 188
produce, 20n47, 61n4, 77–79, 83, 226n58
product, 61, 230
profaned, 243
profession, 56
professional (mourners)
professionally, xi, 100
Professor Dr Paul Cheng, xi
profit, profitability, 150, 266
profligate, 126
progeny, 185
progress, progressive(ly), 49, 119, 142, 239
prohibited, prohibiting, prohibition, 91, 142, 179
project, 39
prologue(s), 10n27, 295
prominence, prominent, prominently, 8, 40, 50, 110, 132, 134, 197
promise(s), promised, 18, 38–40, 43, 91n11, 117, 139, 159, 192, 244, 252, 287, 290
promotion, 164
prompting(s), promptly, 241n26, 248, 253, 280
pronouncement, 99, 224
proofs, proves, 54, 279
propensity, propensities, 172, 176, 214, 270
property, 124, 188, 188n4, 192
prophecies, prophecy, prophesies, prophesy, prophesying, 83–84, 156, 167, 170, 195, 207, 207n47, 213, 239–40, 243, 246–47, 266, 269, 270, 277
prophet(s), vi, 17–18, 20–21, 23, 25n66, 27, 34, 35n6, 36, 39, 55, 59, 66, 79, 82, 101, 102, 104, 108–9, 113, 116, 119, 121, 129, 139–40, 143, 143n13, 145–46, 153, 155–57, 167, 178, 196, 211, 214, 221, 223, 229, 239, 245, 256, 268, 275, 283
prophetic, prophetically, 1, 23, 34–35, 53, 82, 104, 153, 207–8, 214–15, 221, 223, 238–40, 254, 256n79, 258
proposition, propositional, 17, 30
prosecution, 272
prosperity, prosperous, 37, 80–81, 128, 170, 185, 189–90, 192–93, 289
protect, protecting, 75, 92, 158, 166, 181, 218, 221, 268, 271n25

protestants, 98
protestations, protestors, 76, 250
prototype, prototypical, 43, 156
provable, prove, proven, 54, 101, 134–36, 235, 254, 278
provenance, v, 10
proverb, 102
provide(s), provided, provider, providing, 18, 38, 55, 64, 73, 82, 101, 105, 110, 116, 132, 134, 139, 165, 180, 260n100
province, 128
provision(s), 30, 51n24, 105, 111, 116, 132–34, 142, 175, 192
provocative, provocatively, provoked, provoking, 120, 136, 218, 221, 233, 243, 267–68
prudence, 127
Pseudepigrapha, 197n21, 292
pseudo-Christians, 77
pseudo-Messiah, 225
psychological, 178
public, publicly, 29, 48, 55n31, 60, 84, 96, 101, 135, 147, 231, 234, 248, 266, 273, 277–78
publicans, 55
punished, punishment(s), 50n20, 53, 80, 172–73, 185, 211n6, 225, 236, 272, 274, 277n43, 294
puppet, 107
puppy, 129
purchase(d), 213, 284–85
pure, purification, purify, purified, purifying, purification, purity, vii, 25, 29, 34n3, 45, 57, 96, 98, 100, 120–21, 123, 125, 143n15, 174–76, 205, 212n8, 213, 218, 229, 249
purple, 24, 275, 275n36
purpose(s), xv, 6, 14, 27n75, 37–38, 42, 45, 57, 63, 65, 76, 78, 92, 103, 106, 117, 132, 144, 145n17, 178, 181, 217, 250, 260, 285
pursue, pursuing, 49, 202, 230
puzzle(s), puzzling, 54, 77, 265

quadrans, 11
quart, 11

Queen Cleopatra, 203
Quelle, xiv, 3
quest(s), 195, 201–2, 253
question(s), questioned, questioning, v–ix, xv, 1, 6n7, 14, 19n46, 30, 32, 35, 53–54, 57, 60n3, 69, 71, 75, 77, 79, 84, 80, 87–88, 101–4, 111, 114, 117, 125, 133, 137, 139, 143, 148, 150, 159–60, 162, 167, 175, 177, 179, 184, 186, 188, 195, 195n16, 196, 202, 205, 207–9, 211, 217, 217n28, 219, 221–23, 227–28, 230–31, 233, 236, 238–39, 241, 247, 250, 252–54, 256, 260, 262, 267, 271–73, 279, 283–84, 284n62, 286, 288, 290
Qumran, 42, 43n15, 63, 225n51
quotation(s), quote(s), quoted, quoting, 2, 7n10, 10, 23, 45, 102, 121, 173, 220, 222, 228, 232n77, 258, 271n26

Rabban (Rabbi) Gamaliel, 45
Rabbi Aqiba, 229
Rabbi Hanan ha-Nehba 260n100
Rabbi(s), 24, 45, 59, 63, 153, 186, 206, 229, 264, 284
Rabbinic, 35n7, 45n18, 59, 122, 143, 149n24, 149n25, 153n32, 156n37, 177n28, 179, 189n7, 219, 228, 231n75, 242, 242n29, 263n1
race (ethnic), 137
radiance, radiant(ed), radiating, 67, 152–54
radical, 22n59, 31, 35, 42–43, 73, 180, 186, 191, 214, 230, 250, 269
rage, raging, 176, 268, 274
Rahab, 129, 203
raiment, 212n8
rain, 260n100
raise(s), raised, raising, rise(s), risen, rising, (the dead), arise, rose (from death), vi, ix, 1, 18, 20, 30, 40–41, 94–95, 100–101, 108, 111, 135, 138, 144–45, 146n20, 151, 154–55, 161, 190, 193–94,

206, 217, 226–27, 233, 237, 250–
    51, 258, 271, 274, 279, 282n55,
    284–86, 289
raka, 100
Ramah, 283n57
Ramathaim, 283n57
rampage, 162
ran, run(s), running, 39, 72, 90, 92, 120,
    129, 135, 167, 199, 201, 218,
    244, 289
random, 291
rank(s), ranked, 96, 143, 164–65, 181,
    192, 195–96, 198–200, 205, 234,
    236
ransom, 11, 17, 29, 201, 257
rapacious, 244
Rapana, 93n16
rape, rapist, 179, 191
rascals, 263n1
rat race, 193,
rat, 270
rationalistic, rationality, 118
realism, 220n34
realm, 71–72
reap(s), 150
reasoning, 89
rebel(s), rebelled, rebellion, rebellious,
    46, 139, 173, 196, 265, 273, 278
rebuild, rebuilding, rebuilt, 84, 203, 241,
    278
rebuke(s), rebuked, rebuking, 20, 28,
    46, 87, 93, 114, 123, 132, 139,
    144–45, 147–48, 161, 181–82,
    194, 205, 229, 231, 250, 261,
    264, 287
receptacles, 237
reciprocal, reciprocate(d), reciprocity,
    37, 74, 80–81, 155, 175, 228, 256
reckless, 263n1
recline(d), reclining, 56, 87, 114, 254
recollection(s), 179, 278, 287
reconciled, reconciling, 9, 69
recreate, recreation, 36, 63–64, 87, 112
recuperation, 112, 115
Red Sea, 117
redeem, redeemer(s), redemption,
    redemptive, 18, 30, 42, 55, 69,
    72, 81, 131, 152, 153n32, 154—
    155, 198, 201, 250, 252, 256
reed(s), 208, 275
refinement, refiner, refines, 152, 260,
    261
reformation, 62
regent, 233, 269
regulations, 64, 121
reign(s), reigned, reigning, 1, 8, 10–11,
    18, 24, 34, 37, 40–42, 79, 87,
    140, 144, 146, 162, 202, 208,
    224, 231, 233, 241n26, 261, 268,
    290
reject(s), rejected, rejecting, rejection, 2,
    10n27, 13n39, 20–21, 28, 35, 39,
    60, 72, 75–76, 78–79, 90, 94–95,
    102–3, 106, 121, 123, 125–26,
    130, 138, 145–47, 149, 156, 161,
    176, 194, 209n54, 211, 218, 220,
    221n43, 222–23, 225–26, 231,
    232n78, 233, 252, 261, 263, 266,
    279, 283
relational, relationship(s), v, 1–2, 7, 24,
    32, 42, 59, 68, 92, 103, 124–25,
    176, 178–79, 180n33, 184–86,
    187n1, 217, 236, 258, 260, 264
relative (family), 9n22, 102, 241n21
release(s), released, 29, 51n24, 97,
    98n22, 131, 157, 159, 206, 217,
    272–74
reliability (Papias), 6n7
religion(s), 34n3, 53, 59, 84, 218, 229,
    244, 252, 268
religious, 43, 51, 59–60, 62, 67, 71–72,
    84n49, 97, 99, 121, 140, 146–47,
    158, 187, 214, 216, 234, 244,
    268, 293
relovution, 101
remarriage, remarry, remarries, 109,
    125, 176, 179–80
remedies, 48
remember(ed), remembering, 6, 8, 38,
    43, 67, 125, 139n3, 152, 158,
    160, 193, 196, 248, 255, 282
remind(s), reminded, reminder,
    reminding, 35–36, 66, 73–74,
    81, 83, 90, 115–16, 134, 166,
    170, 173, 236, 248, 251, 255, 261

reminiscence(s), reminiscent, 7n10, 208, 271, 277n46, 281
remorse, 20n48, 270
renamed, renaming, 56, 68, 102, 141–42, 198
renegade, 134
renew(ed), renewal, renewing, 17, 20, 42, 56, 62, 69, 73, 84, 107, 115, 136, 143n15, 173, 244, 247, 253
renounce(d), renouncing, renunciation, 22n59, 106, 171, 174, 200, 247, 274, 289
renowned, 69
Rentis, 283n57
rents (land), 220
repent(ed), repentance, repentant, repenting, 11, 18, 24–25, 30, 34–37, 39, 41, 42–43, 49, 51, 59, 65, 75, 79, 80, 105–6, 122, 136, 139, 156, 189, 192, 214–15, 221, 223, 231, 273, 278, 286
repercussions, 158
repetition, 161, 181
replace(s), replaced, replacement, 5, 62, 69n25, 155, 172, 187, 214
report(s), reporting, 100, 112, 167, 283
represent, 48, 60, 62, 74, 81n43, 84, 92, 153, 203n37, 221
repudiate(s), repudiated, repudiation, 25, 98, 109, 180, 220, 229, 268
reputation, 164
Reqem, 45
request(s), requested, requesting, 49, 92, 134–35, 195, 195n14, 196, 204n39, 209, 239–40, 272
requirement(s), requirements, 51, 96, 287
resalted, 175
resentment, 126
residence, resided, 11n30, 142, 271, 274
resist(ed), resistance, resistant, 12, 19, 38, 62, 90, 109, 124–27, 158, 160, 172–74, 223–24, 261, 283
respect, respectful, 50, 68, 79, 147, 186, 206, 219–20, 223, 234
respond(ed), respondent, responding, response(s), vi, 17–19, 21, 25, 30–31, 39, 41, 43, 50, 51, 53–54, 56–57, 63, 65, 67, 70–71, 73–75, 80, 87–88, 90–94, 96, 98, 100–102, 112, 118, 129, 131, 136–37, 147, 153–54, 157, 159–61, 163, 167–69, 177, 182, 186, 189–91, 194, 196–97, 201, 205–6, 214–15, 217, 219–20, 228, 230–31, 233, 239, 240, 250, 250n65, 258, 264, 267–69, 272–73, 279, 286, 289
responsibilities, responsibility, responsible, 95, 101, 198, 281, 284
rest, 63–64, 110, 112, 115–16, 128, 228, 266
rest home, 122
restoration, restorative, restore(s), restored, restoring, 20, 24, 39, 42, 46–47, 49–50, 63–64, 66–67, 69n25, 76, 92, 94, 99, 107–8, 121, 129, 135, 140–42, 156, 160, 205, 257–58
restrain, 90
result, 22, 50, 54, 76, 79, 110, 113, 172, 187n1, 191, 217, 242, 263n1, 274, 284n62
resurrected, resurrection(s), resurrects, viii–ix, 1, 7, 9, 17–18, 21–22, 29–30, 40, 42, 46, 50n20, 62, 69, 93, 95, 97, 101, 107–8, 136, 140, 142, 143, 143n13, 143n15, 144, 147, 151, 152, 155–56, 156n37, 161–62, 198, 204, 207, 222, 224–27, 233, 236, 246, 250–51, 258, 263, 265, 267, 269, 271, 273, 275, 277, 279, 281, 283, 285–87, 289
retaliatory, 202
reticence, 132
retire, retired, retirement, 114, 122, 198
retribution, retributive, 242n29, 264
return of Christ, viii, 24, 31, 40, 37, 115, 151, 198, 233, 239, 242–44, 246–47, 258, 262, 279, 286, 290, 294
return of Elijah, 108, 143
reveal(s), revealed, revelation, revelatory, 1, 13n40, 17–19, 21, 38–39, 71, 80, 142–43, 151–53,

153n32, 162, 190, 203, 227, 250, 255, 274, 280, 289
revenue, 55
reverence, 267
reversal, 82n44, 192, 273
reviles, reviling, 126, 127n32
revived, revivication, 34n3, 143
revolt, revolution, revolutionaries, revolutionary, revolutionist, 22, 24, 29, 34, 39, 46, 69, 93, 101, 131, 141, 144, 214n17, 218, 223, 240n19, 243, 273, 293
reward(s), 81, 169–70, 172–74, 189, 192, 225, 225n56
rhetoric, rhetorical, 26n73, 71, 148, 150, 172, 175, 179, 219, 296, 286,
rich(es), richer, viii, 3, 22, 25, 43, 59, 75, 96–97, 110, 113, 115, 150, 149–50, 182–83, 185–86, 188n4, 189–92, 199, 209, 238, 252, 265, 290
riddle(s), 54
ridicule(d), 24, 71, 98, 100, 157
right, rightfully, rightly, 6, 7n10, 11, 25, 39, 51n24, 64–65, 68, 77–78, 92, 97, 101, 106, 124n26, 129, 139, 154, 160, 166–67, 170, 173, 180, 183, 189, 191n12, 196, 196n19, 197, 204n39, 209, 211, 214–15, 219, 223, 226, 229–30, 232–34, 248, 251, 268–69, 278, 282, 285, 287n69, 288–89
righteous, righteouss, righteousness, 14n40, 43, 57, 65, 109, 143n15, 145, 150, 156, 182, 185, 187–88, 211, 225n51, 226, 229
rights, iv, 171, 200
rigid, 32, 158
ringitt(s), 238n5, 250n66
riot, 273
risk, 213
rites, ritual(s), ritually, 34n3, 45, 57, 98, 100, 120n22, 121, 123, 130, 140, 218, 243, 249
rivalry, rivals, 71, 199
River, Ganges, 34n3
River, Jordan, 117, 130, 240n19
River, Leontes, 240

road(s), roadways, 51, 55, 105, 110, 119n19, 202n35, 203–4, 206–8, 287
robberies, robbers, 214, 271
robe(s), robed, 61n4, 212n8, 234, 285
rock(s), 68, 118, 274, 284
role(s), 9, 34, 47, 44, 52–53, 57–58, 100, 131, 156n37, 182, 198, 200–201, 235, 238, 244, 266, 281
roll(s), rolled, rolled, 30, 119, 284–85
Roman, 1, 3, 10, 11, 11n30, 12, 20–22, 24, 29, 33–34, 41, 43, 47, 55–56, 68, 75, 91n12, 102, 107, 110, 117, 122, 126, 128, 130–31, 136, 140, 143, 143n15, 148–49, 151–52, 156, 164, 168, 180–81, 189, 192–95, 197–201, 203, 208, 212–14, 216, 218, 222–24, 229, 238, 240–41, 241n21, 243–44, 248, 260, 264, 266, 269, 271–75, 277, 279, 281–83, 289
Rome, 7, 9, 10, 10n25, 11—12, 18, 31–32, 39, 66, 69, 71, 75, 75n35, 76, 109, 121–22, 128, 130, 136, 142, 162, 192, 198, 208, 218, 223–25, 229, 239–41, 276, 281, 288–89, 296
roof(s), rooftops, 53, 53n26, 218, 244n37, 292
room, 29, 65, 100, 253, 280
rooster, 117, 258, 270
root(s), 63, 82, 126, 185
rope, 191
rot, rotting, 174, 277
rowing, 87
royal, royalty, 17, 34, 45, 109, 130, 275
Rufus, 11, 275–76
rugby, 40, 164
rule(s), ruled, ruler, ruling, 2, 11–12, 18, 20, 22–25, 40, 42–43, 50, 59n1, 64, 67, 71, 75, 84, 95–97, 102, 105n37, 107–9, 120, 124, 135, 142, 144–45, 147–48, 150, 155, 164, 170, 183, 186–88, 188n4, 190, 198, 199, 199n26, 200, 223, 227, 233–34, 238, 243, 242, 249, 249n57, 253, 261, 263, 263n1, 265n9, 266, 272, 274, 279, 286

rumor, rumored, 241, 267
rupture, 62
Russia, Russian, 31, 151, 239
Ruth, 129

Sabbath, vi, 18, 26, 27n75, 29, 44, 57, 63–65, 85, 95, 101, 118, 120–21, 123, 140, 182n39, 218, 282–83, 285
sacking, 222
sacramental, sacraments, 115, 253
sacred, 5, 13, 63, 287n69
sacrifice(s), sacrificed, sacrifices, sacrificial, 36, 52, 70, 96, 99, 110, 148, 152, 162, 172, 175, 194, 198, 201, 213–16, 229–30, 252–54, 271, 284, 289, 292
sacrilegious, 63
sad, sadly, sadness, 38, 75–77, 96, 102, 107–9, 111, 131, 139, 150, 156, 189–90, 225, 271, 278
saddle, 208
Sadducean, Sadducee, 42, 45, 53, 146–47, 186, 224, 225, 225n51, 225n54, 225n55, 227, 234, 254, 292
safely, safety, 44, 105
Sahara Desert, 239
sailing, 117
saint, 293
salem, 90
sales, sell, sellers, selling, sold, 25, 37, 56, 97, 183, 188–89, 213, 213n13, 250, 264
saline, 175
saliva, 131
Salome, 251, 254, 282, 282n55, 285, 296
salt(y), salted, saltiest, saltiness, 72, 79, 174, 174n18, 175, 175n21, 175n22, 175n23, 176, 184, 295
salute, 275
salvation, salvific, 13, 33, 35, 37–38, 42, 49, 76, 90, 99, 140, 162, 172, 186, 189, 193, 202, 207–8, 214, 244, 274, 278, 287, 287n69, 289
Samaria, 6n7, 66, 66n22, 177
Samaritan(s), 51, 69, 107, 169, 186, 202n35, 229, 271
Samuel, 17, 34, 36, 109, 283n57, 292

sanctuary, 96, 212n8, 222
sanctum, 29, 222, 281
sandals, 35n7, 105
sandwich, Markan, 26–27, 52n25, 70, 94, 99, 104, 210, 265, 281
sane, 150
sang, 232, 257
Sanhedrin(s), ix, 42, 45, 111, 146–47, 186, 197, 218, 223n45, 224, 225n51, 242, 252, 265–66, 269, 272, 275, 281, 283
sarcasm, 159
Satan, Satanic, 13n40, 14n40, 19, 24, 35, 37, 49, 57, 67, 70–72, 72n32, 73, 75, 91, 119, 135, 144, 147–48, 152, 157–58, 161, 201, 219, 233, 252
satisfied, satisfy(ing), 13, 110, 115, 133, 136, 140, 273
Saturday, 64, 254, 285
Saul, 8, 34, 37, 109, 249
savage, 120, 278
save, saved, saving, 24–25, 36, 42, 65, 78–79, 91, 99, 103, 125, 135, 149n25, 150, 159, 172, 174, 187, 190–91, 200–201, 203, 208, 206, 209, 242, 247, 258, 260–61, 278–79, 287, 290
Savior, 134, 141, 187, 279, 286
sawn, 221
sayings, 54, 118, 216, 268
scale, 50n20
scandal, scandalous, 102, 171, 249, 255
Scandinavia, 151, 239
scarlet, 51n24
scattered, scattering, 22, 29, 81, 113, 258, 265
scent, 276n42
scepter, 275
scholar(s), scholarship 2–3, 5–6, 8, 13, 35n6, 40, 56, 77, 78, 103, 130n39, 146, 151, 179, 207, 207n44, 207n48, 210n2, 211, 214, 221, 226, 228n68, 232n78, 234–35, 238–39, 268, 284, 286, 293
school(s), 106, 177, 179, 181, 295
schoolteachers, 181
science, scientific, 45, 82, 104, 168

SUBJECT INDEX

scope, 179, 200, 241, 245
scorn, 237
scourging, 274
scraps, 129–30, 203
screeching, 233
scribe(s), xi, 26, 44, 45, 53, 55, 57, 59,
    70–72, 74, 108, 115, 147, 157,
    186, 194, 196, 218, 220, 223n45,
    228–31, 231–36, 238, 262–63,
    278,
script, 13n36
Scripture(s), iv, xi, 49, 54, 57, 63, 90,
    102, 155, 222, 226, 228, 232–34,
    255, 265, 280
scroll(s), 14, 30, 44, 143n15, 188n4,
    225n51
Scythopolis, 93n16
sea, vii, 26, 43, 55, 66, 68, 74, 86–87,
    87n4, 88–89, 101, 111, 116n6,
    117–19, 130, 134, 141–42,
    142n7, 152, 159, 171, 175,
    188n4, 198, 202n35, 205,
    215–16, 225n51, 268, 282, 292,
    295–96
seafloor, 171
seals (spirit), 37
season, seasonal, 79, 174n18, 175,
    210–11
seasoned, seasoning, 79, 174–76
seat(s), seated, seating, 69, 96, 115, 118,
    133, 163, 182, 194, 196–97,
    232–35, 237, 240, 244, 268–69,
    277–78, 285, 288
secondary, 225
secrecy, secret(s), secretly, 21, 22n55,
    22n56, 31–32, 46, 48, 55, 66–67,
    80, 93, 101, 128, 128, 131, 141,
    144, 155, 205, 253–54, 265n8,
    283n58, 296
secretary, 196
sect, 11
secular, 275
security, 210
sedicula, 277
sediment, 141n5
sedition, 223
seed(s), vi, 31, 73–75, 78, 81, 81n43, 82,
    82n45, 83–85, 119, 169

seek(s), seeker(s), seeking, 6, 19–20, 38,
    43, 55, 66–67, 69, 79, 81, 91–92,
    97, 101, 112–13, 116, 125–27,
    129, 134–35 158, 164–66, 180,
    182–83, 187–88, 193–95, 198,
    200, 202, 205, 209, 210n2, 214,
    220, 225n51, 231, 234, 236, 244,
    251–52, 272, 278, 284–85, 289
seize(d), seized, seizing, 66, 70, 212,
    264, 266
Seleucid, 128, 243
self-abandonment, 126
selfish, 69, 164, 195, 200
selflessness, 152, 162
semantic, xiii, 88, 295–96
seminaries, seminary, xi, xv, 105
Semitic, 99
Semitisms, 7, 7n13, 11, 291
send(s), sending, sent, vi, 12–13, 19n46,
    22, 27–28, 30–31, 38, 47, 60, 68,
    75–76, 80, 82, 84, 86–87, 89,
    91–93, 94n17, 95, 97, 99, 100–
    101, 103, 104–9, 110–11, 114,
    134, 142, 150, 156, 164, 168–69,
    170, 177, 207, 214, 220–21, 223,
    233, 246, 251, 253, 263, 263n1,
    271, 286–87, 289
Seneca, 284n61
sensation, 249
sense(s), sensed, sensing, 26, 37, 40, 45,
    50, 52, 54, 57, 65–69, 71, 87, 89,
    96–98, 100, 102, 104, 107, 109,
    118, 123, 127, 127n32, 134–35,
    143–44, 145n17, 147, 150, 154,
    159, 171–72, 174n18, 181, 188,
    192, 204n39, 206–7, 207n50,
    211, 216, 223, 228, 232, 232n79,
    237n1, 240, 246, 247n48, 260,
    262, 271, 273, 279
senseless, 139
sensible, 102n30, 135
sensitivities, 92
sensuality, 110
sentence (law), sentencing, 29, 266, 271,
    273–74, 283, 284
sentence(s) (syntax), 26, 40, 136, 132,
    166, 166n5
sentiment, 229, 244

separate(s), separated, separation, 13n36, 57, 73, 173–74, 178, 180, 228
Sepulchre, 276
sequence, 26, 130n39, 225
seriously, seriousness, 2, 172, 174
sermon, 52, 55, 101, 183, 239
serpent, 88
servant(s), servanthood, serve(s), served, service, serving, vii–viii, xi, 1, 11, 17, 19, 22n59, 23–24, 24n65, 25, 29–30, 32, 36–38, 47–48, 51, 69, 70, 77–78, 81, 106–7, 110, 115, 130, 132–33, 141–42, 144, 146, 146n20, 147–50, 152, 154, 161, 162–66, 169–70, 174, 180, 184, 193–95, 199, 200n28, 201, 201n32, 202, 204, 206, 221, 223, 228–30, 235–36, 246–47, 249, 250, 252, 255, 257, 263n1, 264, 266, 269–70, 279, 282, 286, 289, 290–91
services, 48, 95, 235
setting(s), v, 11, 18, 48, 55, 70, 75–76, 83–84, 91, 104–5, 120, 129–30, 133, 135, 152, 208, 235, 249, 295
seventy elders, 167
Seventy-one (Sanhedrin), 42,
Seventy-two (Luke 10:1), 104n34, 106
severing, 264
sew, sewing, sewn, 61n4, 62, 294
sex, sexual(ly), sexuality, 109, 124, 124n26, 125–26, 177–80, 184, 191
sexism, 250
sextarius, 11n30
shade, 83–84
shadow, 98
Shahhat, 275
Shakespeare, 274
Shalom, 42, 67, 94, 99
shame, shamed, shames, 43, 73, 135, 206, 269, 284n62
Shammai, 177, 179
Shaphat, 25n66
share(s), shared, sharer, sharing, 7, 24, 42–43, 52, 72, 75–79, 84, 89, 106, 111, 144, 150, 168–69, 192, 198, 231, 233, 254, 256, 288

sharp, sharpest, sharply, 9, 51, 86, 144, 215, 274
shatter, shattered, 42, 62, 84, 109, 249
shawl, 234
shed, 17, 256, 261, 274n33
sheep, 3, 29, 76, 110, 113, 116, 169, 258, 265, 289
shekel(s), 213, 237n2
Shekinah, 154
Shema, 74, 155, 228, 228n69, 231
Sheol, 257n86
shepherd(s), shepherding, 29, 110, 113–14, 116, 142, 258
shine(s), shining, 79, 80, 152
ships, 117n7, 293
shirt, 105
shock, shocked, shocking(ly), 1, 25, 109, 166, 189–90, 200, 255, 277
shore(s), shoreline, 55, 86, 112, 119, 134, 141
shout, shouter, 67, 157, 208, 273
shrine, 142
shrink, 61
siblings, 242
Sicarii, 69, 69n24, 253, 296
sick, sickbed, sickness(es), 30, 47–48, 50–51, 53–55, 57, 67, 93, 97, 97n21, 99, 106, 120, 131, 192, 249n57, 274, 287, 289
sickle, 63
Sidon, 66, 128, 130
siege, 245n38
sigh(s), 131, 136
sight(ed), sightedness, 64, 141, 140–42, 204–5
sign(s), vii, viii, 24, 39, 66, 72, 96, 106, 119, 128, 134–38, 140, 142, 185, 189, 238, 240, 240n18, 242, 245–46, 262, 278–79, 287–88
signal(s), signaled, signaling, 79, 39, 131, 199, 242, 263, 290
significance, significant, significantly, 4, 9, 13–14, 40, 52, 57, 73, 84, 89, 100–102, 115, 142, 156, 158, 162, 164, 169, 175, 181, 193, 213, 216, 241, 266, 281–85
significantly, 59, 66, 68, 249
signified, signifies, 61, 256, 281
Silas, 9, 78, 78n39, 90, 149

SUBJECT INDEX

silence(s), silenced, silencing, silent(ly), 21, 23, 46–48, 53, 87, 93, 101, 111, 131, 144, 147, 163, 182, 205, 260, 267, 269
Silvanus, 78n39
silver, 252
Simeon, 102, 213n13
similitudes, 145n18, 146
Simon (Peter), 44, 47–49, 68, 99, 195, 200, 264
Simon of Cyrene, 149, 275–76
Simon the leper, 207, 248–49, 253
Simon the revolutionary, 240n19
Simon the Zealot, 69, 163,
sin(s), sinful(ness), sinned, sinner(s), sinning, vii, 11, 14n40, 18–20, 22n59, 23, 25, 27n75, 29, 34–35, 38–39, 41–42, 44, 50, 50n20, 51, 51n24, 52, 52n25, 53–58, 63, 68, 72–74, 76, 78, 85, 91, 106, 118, 120, 123, 124n26, 125, 127, 137–38, 140, 144, 146n20, 150, 152, 156, 170–76, 181–82, 184–88, 191, 193, 196n19, 201, 203, 208, 214–17, 218n30, 249n57, 249n58, 253, 260, 269, 273–74, 278–81, 289, 290
Sinai, 38
sing(s), singing, song(s), sung, 61, 100n25, 120, 146, 182n39, 204, 208–9, 220–21, 232, 257, 257n85, 257n86, 291, 294
single(s), singleness, 47, 125, 229, 249
singular, 195n16, 255
sinister, 252
sink(ing), 86–87
Sirach, 97n21
sister(s), 8, 71, 100, 102, 196n19
skeptical, skeptics, 4, 6, 28n76, 200n30, 272
skill, 168
skin(s), 11, 50, 61, 105
skull, 275–76
sky, 245
slander(ing), slanderously, 127n32
slaughter(ed), 253–54, 267, 277n46
slave(s), slavery, 24, 90, 165, 181, 200–201, 201n32, 201n33, 202, 220, 236, 247, 263n1, 264, 266, 270, 274, 277, 289, 293
slay, slaying, 143n15, 290
sleep(s), sleeping, 82, 82n44, 100, 244n37, 248, 261
sliced, 266
slope(s), 92, 207n44, 259n92
small, smallest, smallness, 12, 47, 83, 89, 108, 133–34, 166, 170, 198, 225n51, 277
smell, smelling, 213, 253
snake(s), 134, 287
snare(s), 158, 179, 224, 257n86
snow, 240
social, socially, 50, 81, 97–99, 106, 114, 122, 126, 175, 203, 240–51
societies, society, xiv, 44, 47–48, 50, 107, 109, 175, 180n34, 206, 226, 292–93
Socrates, 189n7
Sodom, 196n19, 245
soften(s), softened, softer, 75, 103, 232n79, 242, 247n52
soil, vi, 73, 75–76, 106
sojourner, 264
soldier(s), ix, 3, 24, 151, 243, 269, 274–76, 279, 281, 284, 288
solemn, solemnity, solemnly, 72, 91, 144, 170, 192, 257
solitude, 116
Solomon(ic), 34, 71, 128, 143n15, 168–69, 204n39, 208, 216, 225
Son of Abba (Barabbas), 273
Son of Alphaeus, 56, 69
Son of David, 203–4, 204n39, 206, 231–32
Son of God, Son of the Blessed One, God the Son, the Son, my [beloved] Son, Son of the Most High God, his Son, only Son, divine Son, xi, 1, 1n1, 7, 11, 14, 17–18, 20–24, 28, 29, 33, 33n1, 34, 35n6, 37, 39–41, 43, 55, 61, 67, 75, 84, 87–89, 91n11, 95, 99, 101–2, 108, 118–20, 132, 135–36, 146, 155, 159, 165, 174, 195, 205, 211, 220–22, 231–33, 247–48, 267–68, 273, 275, 278, 280–81, 284, 288–90

son of Herod, 64, 142,
son(s) of Jacob, 69, 102
Son of Man, 22n56, 35n6, 156, 161, 193–94, 200–201, 206, 223, 232, 246, 255, 268–69, 289
son of Nun, 102
Son, Prodigal/lost, 51, 188
Sons of Sceva, 168
son of Timaeus, 203,
son-in-law, 266
son(s) (other), 9, 20, 24n66, 29, 33, 36, 54, 60, 107, 130, 135, 141, 145, 159, 168, 171n10, 221–22, 224n47, 225n51, 226, 275–76, 281
son(s) of Zebedee, 20n47, 68, 154, 265n9
son(s) of Simon of Cyrene, 275–76
sons of Judas (revolutionary), 240n19
Sons of thunder, 197
song(s), 61, 120, 146n20, 208, 221, 257, 291
sonship, 211, 221, 284
sophistry, 122
sores, 203
sorrow, sorrowful, 190
soteriological, 208
soul(s), 19, 36, 204, 225n55, 225n56, 228, 257, 259
sound(s), 6, 20n47, 103, 128, 151, 181, 263
sour, 174, 280
source(s), x, 3, 4, 5, 7–8, 18–19, 44, 55, 83, 87–89, 95–96, 102, 106, 123, 156n37, 217n28, 218n28, 225, 228, 271, 288–89
south, southern, southward, 31, 36, 66, 71, 89, 93, 128, 161, 172, 207n47, 239
southeast, 66, 130
sovereign, 89
sovereignty, 278
sow(s), sower, sowing, vi, 7, 31, 54, 73–75, 81, 83, 85, 175
space, 7, 116, 130, 180, 227, 229
Spain, 151
sparrow, 87, 93, 97

spat, spit(s), spitting, spittle, 130–31, 141, 194, 269, 275,
specter, 118
speculate, speculating, speculative, speculator, 11n30, 115, 133, 163, 203n37, 278n49
speed, 284–85
spell, 47
spend, spending, spent, 38, 90, 97, 141–42, 149–50, 182, 193, 198, 251–52
sphere, 24
spiced, spices, 276n42, 285
spies, 202
spike-nard, 249
Spirit, vii, xi, 8, 30, 35–38, 40, 45, 57, 65, 72–73, 75, 83, 85, 98, 106, 130, 149, 151, 154–55, 157, 160, 162, 167, 169–70, 187, 195, 197–98, 209, 216, 232–33, 242, 246, 261, 280, 290
spirit(s), 13n40, 38, 45, 72, 90–92, 117, 104–5, 122, 136, 157–58, 160, 167, 203, 225, 261
spiritual(ly), 14n40, 24, 42, 60, 68, 72–73, 91, 94, 97, 99, 113–14, 116, 119, 121, 129, 136, 139, 140–42, 144, 152, 154, 158, 174–76, 178, 204, 206, 226, 230, 233, 269, 275, 285
spiteful, 278
split, 9, 88, 207n47, 281
spontaneous, spontaneously, 46, 168–69
sport(s), sportsperson, 40, 105, 164, 181, 190
spouse(s), 125, 179, 180, 188
spread(s), spreading, 11, 29, 31, 40, 46–47, 66, 71, 78, 80, 82, 84, 114, 119–21, 131, 168, 178, 202, 208, 233, 275, 289
sprig, 83
Spring, 82, 114, 133, 198, 211
springs, 205
sprinkle(d), 51n24, 253
sprout(s), 82, 82n45, 246, 294
squalls, 86
stadium, 203
staff (stick), 134

staggering, 196n19
stagnate, 106
stake, 277
stalk, 82
stance, 180, 201
stand(s), standing, 35, 47, 58, 62, 65, 67, 69–70, 80, 88, 145, 147, 151–52, 160, 180, 190–91, 197, 205, 207n47, 214, 217n26, 229, 238, 242–43, 257n86, 263
stars, 245
starved, 263n1
state, 158, 292
statesman, 168
Statilia Messalina, 176
statue(s), 98, 243
status, 22, 37, 105, 121, 144, 157, 164–66, 180, 192, 195–96, 198–200, 202, 205, 231, 234, 236, 263–64, 272, 289
steal(s), stealing, stole, stolen, 19, 72, 75, 119, 124, 158, 186, 222, 237, 222, 283
stealth, 248, 265–66
stepdad, 102
Stephen, 78, 78n39, 106, 149, 192, 266n16, 275
Steppes, Russian, 239
stewardship, 221
stick, 74
stitch, 61
stomachs, 123
stone(s), stoned, 30, 53n26, 65n16, 102n28, 117, 135, 149, 220–22, 240, 259, 259n95, 284–85
storeroom (Temple), 237
stories, story, 1, 11, 20, 29–30, 32–33, 35, 38, 41, 54, 61–64, 71, 73–74, 81–82, 84, 88–89, 92, 94–97, 102, 108–112, 118, 133, 138, 141, 161, 177, 185, 190–91, 195, 198, 202n35, 204, 206, 211, 215–16, 220–22, 225n57, 229, 235, 238, 251, 255–56, 262, 270–71, 274, 286–88, 290
storm(s), vi, 18, 86–87, 90, 94, 99, 111, 116, 118, 135, 154, 211, 217, 289
Strabo, 119n19

strange, 14, 47, 193, 296
stranger(s), 115, 170, 197
straps, 274
strategic, strategy, 142, 106, 204, 219, 223
street, 96
strength, strengthen(s), strengthen(ed), strengthening, 9, 38, 45, 49, 68, 90, 218, 223, 229, 260–61
stressed, 230, 236
strike(s), striking, struck, 29, 94, 117, 156, 186, 220, 258, 264, 269
stroke, 274n33
strong(ly), stronger, 10, 24, 35, 37, 45, 57, 62, 70, 72, 86, 90, 114, 116, 123, 157–58, 171, 180, 221, 247, 250, 270, 286n68
structures (Judaism), 62
structures, family, 122
structure(s), structurally (of and in Mark), 17–18, 28, 118, 123, 140, 208
struggle(s), struggling, 1, 19, 38–39, 102, 116–17, 135, 159, 164, 171, 219, 286
stubborn, stubbornly, 139, 258, 271
stumble, stumbling, 20, 102, 171, 176, 182
stunned, stunning(ly), 46, 53, 66, 84, 93, 115, 135, 218, 267, 273–74, 283
stupid, 71, 100, 219, 225
style, 7, 13n36, 136, 177
subject(s), subjected, subjection, subjugated, subjugating, 24, 42–43, 140, 148, 200, 209, 237
subjective, 199n26
submission, submit(s), submitting, 36, 59, 91, 128, 148, 155
subordinate, 9n21, 155
subsistence, 67
substitution, substitutionary, 201, 273
subtle, subtlety, subtly, 72, 127, 135, 167, 219, 273
subversive, 213
succeed(s), succeeded, succeeded, success(ful), successfully, 21, 25n66, 38, 66–67, 90, 103, 163, 166, 262, 276

succession, 64
Suetonius, 12n34, 131n40, 176n27, 199, 275n36
suffer(s), suffered, suffering(s), 10–12, 25, 38, 46, 61, 81, 94, 98n22, 131, 145–46, 146n20, 148–49, 152, 155–56, 156n39, 159, 161–62, 173–74, 186, 192–94, 196–98, 202, 204–5, 217, 223, 232, 245, 255–56, 258–61, 265, 269, 276, 284, 286, 289
sufficiency, sufficient(ly), 49, 110, 133, 136, 195, 230, 261
suicide, 158
summer, 246
sun, solar, 88, 152, 240n12, 245, 279
sunday, 64, 147, 181, 205, 211n4, 228, 285
sundown, 64, 82n44
superhuman, 90
supernatural(ly), 36, 153–54, 207n49
superscription, 7
supersede(d), superseding, 29, 63, 83, 286
supplication, 274n33
support(s), supported, supporter(s), supporting, supportive, xi, 3, 7, 9, 9n22, 10, 53n26, 60, 80–81, 105, 121–22, 135, 153, 167, 170, 191, 203, 214, 223–24, 230, 254, 264n7, 271n25, 276–77, 282–86
supremacy, supreme(ly), 69, 78, 90, 118, 130, 193, 249, 268, 271
surrender, 188n4
survive, 139, 203
Susanna, 254, 282
suspicion, 63
sustain, sustainable, 71, 93, 248, 252, 276
sustenance, 112
swearing, swears, 270
swimming, 203
sword(s), 143n15, 172, 209, 263–64
symbol(s), symbolic(ally), symbolism, symbolize(s), symbolized, symbolizing, 20, 29, 34, 34n3, 36, 106, 133, 152, 154, 165, 173, 175n21, 192, 196, 208, 210–11, 214, 215, 222, 255–56, 256n79, 261, 265n9, 275, 280, 284
sympathetic, 9n22
symposia, 114
synagogue(s), 26, 44–47, 52–53, 64, 65n16, 66, 95–96, 101, 107, 115, 135, 146, 171, 196, 217n26, 234, 242, 257
synopsis, 2
Synoptic Gospels, Synoptics, v, 1, 2n2, 3–6, 24, 32, 94, 173, 254
Syntyche, 78, 78n38
Syria, Syrian, 8, 11n31, 31, 93, 119n19, 123, 128, 243
Syrophoenicia(n), vii, 22, 28, 103, 128, 133

Tabernacle(s), tabernacling, 51n24, 63, 154–55, 175, 208, 272
Tabgha, 66
table(s), 56, 65, 114, 116, 129–30, 200, 203, 213
Tabor, 152
Tacitus, 11n32, 75n36, 131n40
tactic(s), 126, 223
takeover, 154, 214
talented, 106
talitha koum, 100
tall, 86, 191n11, 208
Talmud, xiv, 207n44, 295
taste, 105, 151, 175
Tatian, 13n39
taught, teach(es), teacher(s), teaching(s), taught, viii, 1, 6–7, 17–18, 21–22, 22n59, 25–26, 35n7, 37, 39, 44, 45, 45n18, 46–47, 52–53, 55, 58–59, 67–68, 70, 73–74, 76, 79–81, 83–86, 87, 95, 99, 101, 104, 104n33, 106, 110, 113, 120–21, 123–24, 138, 143n15, 144–45, 148, 153, 156, 161–62, 164–65, 170, 174, 177, 179–82, 184–86, 189–90, 193–95, 198, 202, 206, 211, 213n13, 214–15, 218, 218n30, 219–21, 223, 226–27, 229–31, 233, 235, 240, 247–48, 253, 264–65, 273, 275, 290

SUBJECT INDEX

tax(es)/toll(s), viii, 11n30, 22n59, 55n31, 56, 223–24, 236, 237n2, 295
tax/toll collector(s), 25, 56, 56n33, 58, 60, 69, 85
team(s), xi, 42, 47, 56, 63, 69, 105–6, 110, 169
tear(ing), 36–38, 61n4, 90, 222, 268, 280–81, 285
tears, 274n33
tectonic, 141n5
telos, 242
temperatures, 169
tempest, 86, 121
temple, viii, x, 10, 27, 27n75, 29, 36–37, 45, 60, 62, 65, 112, 121, 142, 147, 154, 199, 209, 209n54, 210–12, 212n9, 213, 213n13, 214—215, 215n19, 216—221, 221n38, 222—225, 237, 237n2, 227, 229, 231, 233–40, 240n12, 240n17, 243–44, 252–53, 265, 267, 272, 278, 280–81, 285, 292, 294
tempted, temptation, tempting, v, 17, 26, 37–38, 46, 49, 60, 72, 109, 129, 135, 261
tenant(s), viii, 29, 54, 220–21, 236, 247, 252
tender, tenderness, 83, 181, 183
tension(s), 12, 108, 134, 211, 223
tent(s), 51n24, 154, 162
terrified, terrify, terrifying, 19, 51, 88, 165, 174, 194, 197, 243, 269
territorial, territories, 91, 89, 106, 128, 130, 133, 137, 199
terror, terrorize, 88, 90, 93, 98–99, 118, 286
Tertullian, 7n10
tested, testing, tests, 38, 57, 135, 174, 222, 226
tests, 226
testifies, testimony, testimonies, 7, 52, 93, 267, 106, 116, 130, 150, 186, 201–2, 287, 291
tetrarch, tetrarchy, 64, 107, 141, 199
Textual critics, criticism, variant(s), issues 12–13, 13n37, 14, 33n1, 50n22, 89, 130n38, 160n41, 173n17, 191, 231n74, 273, 278, 287n69, 287n70, 295
Textus Receptus, 12–13
Thaddeus, 69
thankfully, thanking, thanks, 116, 133, 242, 256, 286
theater, 203
theft, thief, thieves, 56, 72, 77, 124, 198, 222, 250, 252, 264
theme(s), theme, 1, 24, 39, 43–44, 55, 74, 79, 89, 98–99, 102, 107, 140, 166, 181, 185, 217n25
Theo (The Expected One), 119
theologian, theological(ly), theology, xiv, 7n13, 7n14, 26–27, 30, 36, 50n21, 68n23, 81, 98, 102–3, 119–20, 134, 155, 178, 186, 189, 200n30, 201–2, 219, 231, 233, 254, 268, 277n46, 279, 284, 294–95
theophany, theophanies, 117, 245
therapeutic, 106, 131
Thessalonians, 176
Theudas, 240n19
think(s), thinking, thought(s), 7, 27n75, 30–32, 33n1, 40–41, 43, 49, 57, 68n23, 69, 74, 91, 117–18, 121, 127, 129–30, 136, 139, 143n13, 147, 150, 152n28, 153n32, 154, 160, 162, 166, 171, 181, 188n2, 189, 197, 204, 213, 216, 222, 223n46, 228–29, 232n79, 242–43, 245, 251, 258, 259n95, 262, 267–68, 274n34, 280, 288
Thomas, 69, 102
thorn(s), 24, 78, 261, 275
Thracian, 34n3
threat(s), threatened, threatening, 63–66, 88, 106, 149, 151, 167, 267, 270, 272, 274, 280
Three-source Hypothesis, 2n3
threshing, 263n1
threw, throw(s), throwing, thrown, 37, 43, 54, 129, 158, 171, 176, 182n38, 205, 215–16, 220, 222, 256, 259, 259n95, 270, 277, 281
throat, 253
throne, 29, 145, 273, 278, 280

thuggery, 263
thumb, 51n24, 72
thunder, thunderous, 68, 121, 197
Tiberias (city), 282
Tiberias (Sea), 198
Tiberius, 107, 142, 198–99, 199n23, 224, 224n47, 294–95
time(s), xv, 6n7, 7–10, 12, 13n38, 14, 18–19, 20n47, 21, 25–26, 26n69, 28–29, 31–32, 38–40, 42, 46, 48–49, 51n24, 52—53, 55, 57, 59–60, 61n4, 62—63, 65–68, 70, 72–73, 75–81, 84, 91n12, 92–93, 95–96, 100–101, 103, 107, 109, 111–13, 122–23, 128, 130–34, 139, 141–42, 143n15, 144—146, 148–52, 153, 155, 158–59, 161–64, 166–68, 171, 173–74, 176–77, 177n29, 179–80, 182, 188, 191–94, 198–99, 201–6, 209, 211, 214, 218, 220, 223–24, 226–27, 234, 237n2, 238n5, 239, 241, 241n21, 241n25, 242, 244–49, 251–52, 254n73, 255, 258, 260–61, 265n7, 265n10, 266n14, 270–76, 277n46, 278, 280, 283–84, 290, 291–92
timeless, 74
timetable, 32
Timothy, 78, 78n39, 79, 200
tired, tiredness, 110, 115, 277
Tishbite, 35n5
tithes, 263n1
Titus, 78, 78n39, 200, 240, 243
Tobit, 97
today, 1–2, 10, 14, 42, 48–49, 58, 68, 76, 82, 84–85, 89, 96, 102, 106, 113–14, 119, 128, 136, 137, 147, 149, 162, 200, 205, 269, 274n34
toe, 51
toga, 275n36
toilet(s), 123, 170
tomb(s), 17, 30, 89–91, 111, 147, 206, 251, 254, 266, 276n41, 281–84, 284n62, 285—286, 289
tongue, 12, 131
tool, 195

Torah, 44, 63, 101, 120, 122, 149n24, 150n25, 162, 186, 225–28, 234
torment, 91, 173–74
torn, 11, 26, 242, 268, 280
tortures, torturous, 158, 231
touch(es), touched, touching, 47, 51, 56, 67, 95–100, 120, 130–31, 181, 263
tourists, 259n92
tower(s), 142, 152, 213n14, 221n38, 292
town(s), 21, 44, 47–48, 52, 69, 89, 94, 106, 119, 120, 128, 141–42, 169, 204, 207n48, 234, 282
townsfolk, 92
tract, tractates, 9, 120n21
trade, traders, 56, 65, 209, 213, 215
tradition(s), traditional(ly), 3, 6, 7n10, 10, 20, 24, 34–35, 59, 64, 104, 120–22, 128, 143, 152, 153, 153n32, 154, 172–73, 180n33, 188n4, 197, 214, 219, 221, 238, 244, 254, 258–59, 270, 293
tragedy, tragic(ally), 20, 29, 76, 270, 274
train(ed), training, vii–viii, 43, 105–6, 138–39, 141, 143, 145, 147, 149, 151, 153, 155, 157, 159, 161, 163, 165, 167, 169, 171, 173, 175, 177, 179, 181, 183, 185, 187, 189, 191, 193, 195, 197, 199, 201, 203, 205, 207, 209
traitor(s), traitorous, 223, 252–53, 255, 264, 277
Trajan, 13n39
trampled, tramples, 117, 222
transcend(s), transcended, transcendent, 18, 55, 99, 145–46, 161, 230, 245, 248, 255
transfiguration, transfigure(ed), vii, 18, 21, 37–38, 46, 100, 108, 151–52, 152n29, 161–62, 194, 206, 221, 221n43, 227, 280–81, 285
transformation(s), transform(s), transformed, 37, 44, 47, 72, 101, 107, 152, 270, 281, 287
transgress, transgressors, 172, 265, 278
Transjordan, 66, 86
translate(s), translated, translation(s), translator, xiii, 7, 11, 13n37, 34,

SUBJECT INDEX

50, 65, 67, 74, 80, 83, 86, 108, 113, 115n5, 118, 122, 126–27, 130–31, 135, 144, 153n32, 158, 160, 173, 206, 227, 236, 249, 260, 266n15, 267, 268n21, 272, 291

transliterated, transliterates, transliteration, transliterations, 20n47, 100, 122, 172

transparent, 126

transport, 56

transubstantiation, 256–57

trap(ped), 19, 63–64, 177, 179, 223, 228, 231

travail, 259

travel(s), traveled, traveler(s), traveling, 42–43, 52, 56, 68, 86, 105–6, 134–35, 143, 163, 177, 245, 254, 282n55, 287

treachery, 29, 252

treason, 277

treasure, 81, 141, 170, 183, 189

treasurer, 283n60

treasury, 229, 235, 237n1

treat(ed), treatment, 50, 97, 165, 169, 171, 174, 184, 186, 193, 264, 269, 277, 279

tree(s), viii, 27, 78, 83–84, 84n48, 112, 115, 142, 144, 202, 206, 210–11, 213, 215–17, 219, 221, 223, 225, 227, 229, 231, 233, 235–36, 246, 259n92, 277–78, 289

trembling, 98

trepidation, 286

trespass(es), 217

trial(s), tried, Jesus, ix, 21, 28, 87, 135, 199, 222, 233, 240, 263, 265–67, 269–71, 273, 275, 277, 279, 281, 283, 285, 287, 289, 292

trials (suffering), 261

tribes, 68–69, 148, 154

tribulation, viii, 76, 243, 245

trick(y), trickery, 117, 126, 218, 223

trip, 9–10, 109, 112, 138, 171, 207

triumph(s), triumphal, triumphant, triumphed, 38, 146, 162, 208, 273, 281

Triune God, 41, 228

trodden, 61

trouble(d), 48, 204–5, 219

troublemakers, 277

trough, 138

true, 14, 18, 25, 71, 82, 88, 102, 109–110, 136, 150, 157, 166, 175, 187, 201, 206, 219, 229, 239, 247n48, 256, 261, 273, 278

truism(s), 62, 71, 261

trumpet, 237

trust(s), trusting, trustworthy, 7, 25, 41, 88, 99, 103–5, 111, 134, 158–60, 214–15, 217, 260, 290

truth, 13n40, 14n40, 72, 82, 178, 190–91, 223, 255, 272, 290

tuned, 140

tunic, 105

Turin, Shroud of, 284n63

Turkey, 6, 31, 239

turn(s), turned, turning, 39, 41, 57, 61–62, 72, 76, 78, 94, 106, 116, 134–35, 139, 147, 156, 189, 209, 224, 234, 243, 252, 274n33, 281, 289

turncoat, 252

tutelage, 163

twelve, the, vi, 1, 27–28, 30, 67–68, 84–86, 94n17, 104–7, 111–12, 115, 164–65, 252, 254–55, 259, 263, 265n9

twigs, 83

type(s), 11, 57, 160, 160n41, 162, 199

tyrant, 11

Tyre, 66, 128, 128n35, 130–31, 293

Tyrian, 213

Tyropoeon, 274n34

unafraid, 51, 65, 233

unambiguously, 161, 181

unanswered, 156, 260

unashamed, 151

unbearable, 275

unbelief, unbeliever(s), unbelieving, 13, 20, 25, 51, 73, 75, 82, 101, 103–4, 125, 136, 140, 158, 160, 231

unblemished, 51–52, 213

unbridled, 183

SUBJECT INDEX

uncertain, uncertainty, 10, 61, 64, 70, 89, 108, 115, 133, 173, 179–80, 195, 259, 285
uncial(s), 13–14
unclean, uncleanness, 13, 45–46, 50–51, 56, 90, 92, 96–99, 104, 120, 123, 134, 158
uncontaminated, 212
unconverted, 148
unconvinced, unconvincing, 272, 279
uncreation, 87
undefiled, 189
understand(s), understandable, understanding(s), understandably, understood, xv, 1, 2, 4, 6, 8, 10–14, 16, 18–20, 22, 24, 26, 28–30, 32, 34, 36–40, 42, 44, 46, 48, 50, 52, 54–56, 58, 60, 62, 64–66, 68, 70, 72, 74, 76, 78–80, 82, 84–85, 87–88, 90, 92, 94, 96–98, 100, 102, 104, 106, 108–110, 113–14, 116, 118–20, 122–24, 126, 128, 130–34, 136, 139–42, 144, 146, 148, 150–54, 156, 158, 160–62, 164, 166, 168, 170–72, 174, 176, 178, 180, 182, 184–92, 194, 196, 198, 200, 202, 204, 206–8, 212, 214, 216, 218, 220, 222, 224–26, 228–32, 234, 236, 238, 240, 242, 244, 246, 248, 250, 252, 254–56, 258, 260, 262, 264, 266–68, 270, 272, 274, 276, 278, 280, 282, 284–86, 288, 290
undrinkable, 61
uneducated, 214
unexpected(ed), unexpectedly, 28, 36, 151, 240
unfaithfulness, 179
ungodly, 122
unholy, 120, 264
Union, Civil, 180
unity, 176, 255
universal, universally, 95, 105, 138, 185, 233, 289
universe, 159, 166, 183, 255–56, 289
university, 78
unlawful, 63, 108, 124
unleavened, 138, 152, 248, 255, 253, 295

unmarried, 226
unpaid, 235
unproductive, 78
unquenchable fire, 172
unredeemed, 174
unreliable, 97
unrighteousness, 65
unrivaled, 245
unsalty, 175
unscrupulous, 263
unsophisticated, 7
unsuccessful(ly), 101, 104, 112, 243, 266
unsurprised, unsurprising(ly), 7719, 48, 56, 108, 215, 285
untie, untying, 35, 207–8
untouchable, 51
unusual(ly), 48, 60, 93, 130–31, 166, 205, 223
unwashed, 120
unwilling, 108, 276
upheld, uphold, 36, 64, 125, 273
Upper Room, 253
uprising(s), 22, 241, 248, 264, 274
uproot, 216
Urevangelium, 2
urgency, 285
Uriah, 74
useful, 9, 78, 175
useless, 78, 175
usurping, 272
utensils, 120

vacuous, 230
vain, 121, 164, 234
Valley, Hinnom, 172
Valley, Kidron, 259
Valley, Tyropoeon, 274
valor, 196
valuable, value(d), 32, 43, 92–93, 150, 160, 164, 175, 183, 200, 211, 213, 238, 249–50, 287
values, 92, 165, 187, 195, 231, 289
vanquished, 208
vegetation, 208
vehicle, 225
veil, 254
veneration, 67
vengeance, 44
veracity, 135

SUBJECT INDEX 345

verb, verbal, 5, 17, 28, 41, 48, 52, 79, 88, 96, 104, 124–25, 132, 155, 176, 188, 190, 195, 199, 227
verbalized, 217
Vespasian, 168
vessel, 51, 61, 117
vestments, 212
Via Delarosa, 276
Via Maris, 119
vicarious, 201
vice, 127, 150, 164, 196
victim(s), 29, 158, 264, 277, 284
victor, victorious, victory, 31, 33, 152, 154, 196, 208, 275
view(s), viewed, viewpoint, 2–3, 5–6, 8, 10, 14, 20, 37, 50, 53, 62, 72, 77, 79, 92, 102–3, 107–9, 116, 124–25, 127, 134, 143, 150–51, 156, 164, 173, 176, 179, 181, 184, 191–92, 198, 207, 216, 218, 222–23, 225, 227–28, 231, 238–40, 243–44, 247, 254, 263, 265, 268, 272, 283–84, 289
vigilant, 135
vile, 181, 244, 269
village(s), 52, 89, 104, 120, 122, 141–42, 207
vindicated, vindicates, vindicating, vindication, 30, 136, 146, 155, 251
vine(s), vineyard(s), 37, 61, 220–22, 248, 256–57
violate(s), violated, violating, violation, 63, 98, 100, 120, 122, 126, 182, 198, 236, 264, 268
violence, violent(ly), 11, 24, 29, 34, 86, 144, 158, 182–83, 191, 199, 209, 214, 223, 256, 264, 269, 273–74
virgin, virginity, 102, 226
virtue(s), 125, 198
viscera, 50
vision(s), 84, 97, 99, 121, 123, 141, 145, 153,180, 246, 294
vocation(s), 44, 47, 105, 200
vocative, 91
voice(s), 18, 36–37, 80, 131, 155, 205, 274
void, 122, 244

voluntarily, voluntary, 148, 188, 198–201, 237, 247, 264
vow, 91, 276
vulnerable, 166, 171, 181–83, 205
vultures, 84

Wadi er-Rababi, 172
wage(s), 114, 224, 237–38, 250
wailing, 100
waist, 35n5
wait(s), waiter(s), waiting, xi, 24, 47, 54, 73, 100, 110, 112, 115–16, 133, 200, 235, 259, 283
wakened, woken, awaken, 82, 87, 100, 142, 265n10
walk(s), walked, walking, vii, 7, 18–19, 49, 55, 63, 75, 101, 116–18, 118n14, 118n17, 120, 133, 135, 137, 141, 148–49, 194, 198, 201, 205, 211, 217, 234, 260, 268, 276, 289, 292–93
wall(s), 65n16, 203, 222, 241n19, 277
war(s), warfare, 12, 19, 22n55, 43, 69, 71, 88, 91, 97n21, 109–110, 141n4, 151–52, 154, 172, 175n21, 188n4, 196–97, 213n12, 214n15, 215n19, 225n52, 225n53, 225n56, 227n64, 237n1, 237n2, 240n12, 240n13, 241n23, 242, 243n33, 243n35, 245n40, 255, 248n56, 255n78, 267n19, 274n33, 276n39
warn(s), warned, warning(s), vii, 22, 72, 76, 79–80, 115, 121–22, 124, 131, 138–41, 143–45, 147, 149, 151, 153, 155, 157, 159, 161–62, 170–74, 181, 214, 222, 230, 234–36, 238, 240–45, 247, 261, 269
warrior(s), 11, 42, 140
wash(es), washing, 27n75, 34, 51n24, 96–97, 120n22, 197, 201n32
waste(d), wasteful, 115, 166, 182, 220, 250–52
watch(ed), watching, 19, 38, 64, 72–73, 78, 100–101, 117, 130, 158, 190n10, 234, 240, 248, 259, 261, 274, 282–83
watchtower, 220–21

water(s), 18, 36, 49, 51n24, 61–62, 79, 82, 86–87, 89, 98, 101, 116–17, 118n17, 120n22, 124n26, 133–35, 137–38, 141n5, 158, 168–70, 175, 191, 193–94, 203, 211, 217, 253, 289
wave offering, 51n24
waves, 87, 117
waver, wavering, 217
way(s), xv, 2, 6, 10, 14, 24–25, 28n76, 30, 32, 34, 36, 38, 40, 43–44, 50n22, 54–55, 57, 60, 69–70, 78–79, 82–83, 85, 90, 98, 101–3, 106–7, 109, 113, 116, 119, 122–23, 130, 131, 135, 137, 139–41, 143, 148–50, 152, 155–56, 156n39, 158–59, 163–65, 169–71, 171n10, 173–75, 179, 182, 183n40, 186–87, 189n7, 190, 195, 199–201, 207n50, 209, 211, 215, 218–19, 223, 227, 231, 232n79, 238–39, 242, 244, 246–47, 247n52, 248, 250–51, 255, 258–62, 264, 269–70, 276–77, 280, 285–86, 288
weak(ing), weakened, weaker, weakling, weakness, 20, 38, 62, 83, 109, 123, 158, 165, 171, 178, 187, 204, 257, 261, 270–71, 275, 289
wealth, wealthy, 22n59, 25, 48, 72, 77, 81, 109, 148, 150, 183, 185–87, 189–93, 199, 203, 209, 220n32, 235, 236, 252, 264, 270, 283, 288–89
weapons, 19, 107, 152, 245
weather, 86, 135, 182, 194
wedding, 60, 115
weeds, 175
week, 21, 59, 64, 207, 250n66
weeps, 249n58, 270
weigh(t), weighing, weightier, 121, 171, 191, 213, 240, 285
welcome(s), welcomed, welcoming, 47, 53, 93, 105, 110, 114–15, 165–66, 170–71, 181–84, 206, 213, 252, 289
well, wellness, 2, 6, 9, 21, 29–30, 36–37, 40, 41, 44, 59, 67, 69, 71, 92, 97n21, 99–100, 105, 114–15, 129, 131, 146–47, 150, 155, 159, 161, 163, 165, 167, 177, 180, 185, 192, 205, 219, 227–30, 241, 251, 254, 263, 269, 278, 280, 284
west, western, 13, 76, 83, 86, 101, 116, 119, 129, 134, 142n7, 151, 160n41, 172, 188, 193, 207n47, 230, 259, 282n92, 287n69
westerners, 45, 114
wheat, 74, 175
whip, whipped, whipping, 194, 274, 274n33
whirlwind, 86, 108, 121, 153
white, whiteness, 97, 152–53, 175, 208, 234, 240n12, 285
wholeness, 42, 47, 92–93
wicked, 225n51, 226
widow, widowed, viii, 135, 225–26, 229, 235, 237–39, 241, 243, 245, 247, 249, 251, 253, 255, 257, 259, 261–62
wife, wives, xi, 43, 108–9, 125, 176–77, 177n29, 178, 180, 212, 225–26, 226n58, 230, 265n9, 282
wild, 11, 37–38, 93
wilderness, 18–19, 21, 38, 52, 116, 132, 135, 154
willing, willingly, 38, 50, 233, 235, 261
wind(s), windstorm, 31, 46, 86–88, 116–19, 144, 205
wine, winemaking, winepress, 29, 61, 61n5, 62–63, 135, 196, 196n19, 220n33, 221, 256, 262, 276n42, 280, 294
wineskin(s), vi, 60–62, 62n12, 63, 84, 121, 291
winning, win(s), 17, 40, 43, 88, 136, 148, 154, 202
winter, 203, 205, 211, 245
wisdom, 18, 45, 97n21, 101, 127, 148, 219, 224, 273
wish(es), wished, 31, 73, 104, 160, 164, 166, 182, 223
withdraw(s), withdrawing, withdrew, 58, 66, 110, 123, 207n47
wither(ed), withering, viii, 64, 95, 107, 211, 215–16

SUBJECT INDEX 347

witness(es), witnessed, 1n1, 95–96, 104, 106, 153n32, 160n41, 231n74, 267, 268, 281
woe, 169, 252, 255, 274n33
woman, women, vi–vii, 14, 17, 19, 22, 27–28, 30–31, 42, 47, 61, 69, 78, 89, 94–98, 98n22, 99–100, 100n25, 101, 103, 105, 111–12, 116, 120, 128–29, 133, 148, 154, 166, 169, 171n10, 176–87, 178n32, 179, 180n34, 183–84, 192, 201, 206, 212n8, 213n13, 215, 225–26, 237n1, 237n2, 238, 249, 249n57, 249n58, 250–54, 258, 281–82, 282n55, 285–86, 289
womb, 181
won, 40
wonder(s), 39, 46, 64, 169, 191, 245, 279, 294
wonderful(ly), 50, 113, 121
wood, wooden, 53n26, 102n28, 277
Word of God, God's Word, the Word, xv, 18–19, 24, 31, 33–35, 46, 50, 52, 68, 74–80, 82–84, 110, 113–14, 119, 122, 129, 131, 145, 155, 162, 171, 177, 194, 205, 209, 219, 258, 289
words, 2, 7, 10–11, 14, 30–31, 38, 44, 50, 72–74, 79, 84, 87–88, 99–100, 106, 108, 118, 120–21, 129, 136, 143–44, 147, 150–51, 156, 158–59, 166, 170, 173, 189, 191, 193, 200–201, 204, 214, 216, 227, 229–30, 232, 235, 242–43, 247, 251, 255, 258, 260–61, 268–70, 272, 277, 279–80, 290
work(s), worked, working, xv, 2, 5–9, 13, 19–21, 25, 31, 33, 37, 43–44, 48, 52, 54, 61–62, 64–65, 68, 70, 72–73, 78–81, 91, 93, 95, 102, 104, 106, 115, 130, 135, 147, 153, 166–67, 174, 183, 187, 204, 220, 225, 229, 235–36, 242, 252, 265
worker(s), 9, 78, 102, 108, 169, 250, 264
world(s), xv, 1n1, 9, 11, 14, 18–20, 23–25, 29–31, 33, 35–36, 38–42, 44, 46–49, 51–52, 55, 57, 59, 61–62, 67–69, 72, 72n32, 74–78, 80–82, 84, 84n49, 87, 92–93, 101, 103, 105, 105n37, 106–7, 109–110, 113–16, 119, 119n18, 122, 125–26, 129–30, 132–33, 136–38, 140, 142, 144–45, 147–48, 150–52, 154, 154n34, 155, 157, 159, 162, 164–65, 170, 172, 175–76, 178, 180, 183, 189–90, 193–94, 196n17, 198–99, 199n25, 200–202, 208–9, 222, 230, 234, 239, 244–47, 251, 253, 257, 260–62, 274, 279–81, 286–87, 289–90, 293–94
worldly, 19, 105n37, 109, 192, 195, 289
worldview, 148
worm(s), 173–74
worried, worry, worrisome, 139–40, 242, 273, 285
worship, worshiping, worship, 46, 57, 63–64, 66, 68, 89–90, 98, 112, 121, 127, 130, 145, 170, 179, 199, 213–15, 218, 224, 228–30, 233, 244n37, 252, 255, 257, 259, 262, 275, 286, 288–90
worth, worthy, 93, 150, 169, 174, 186, 237, 249
worthless, 284
wound(s), wounded, 94, 256
woven, 141
wrath, 29, 65, 79, 173, 196, 196n19, 215, 260
wrong tomb theory, 284

Xenophon, 189n7

Yadaim, 120n21
Yahweh, 64, 86, 116, 118, 213, 232, 236, 267–68
year(s), 12, 14n40, 38, 40, 51n24, 57, 59, 76, 81, 84, 94–95, 97, 100, 121, 128, 133, 152–53, 165, 180n33, 197–99, 213, 220n33, 227, 240, 248, 250, 254–56, 264–65, 267, 273, 275, 280–81, 284, 289
yearn(ed), yearning, 30, 52, 131, 169, 203, 230, 252

yeast, 138, 140, 162, 234
yell(ing), 203–4
yield(ed), yielding, 20–21, 37, 41, 74, 77, 92, 131, 223, 233, 261, 280
yoke(s), 102n28, 149n24
young, younger, viii, 8, 30, 43, 59n1, 62, 67, 83, 96, 100, 149, 165, 167, 169, 180, 183, 185–87, 190, 199, 238, 254, 258, 265, 282, 285, 288, 290
youth, 187

Zacchaeus, 56, 189
Zadok, 224, 225n51
zeal, zealous, 53, 56, 64, 69, 85, 251, 261, 269
Zealot(s), 69, 163, 214, 224, 243, 291–92
Zebedee, 20n47, 43–44, 68, 154, 195, 197, 205, 265n9, 282
Zechariah, 99, 207n47, 221
Zeus Olympus, 243
Zion, 208, 216, 222

Author Index

Aland, Barbara, viii, 292
Aland, Kurt, 292
Algie, Brian, 142n11, 291
Angus, S., 176n27, 291
Arndt, William F., xiii, 291, 292
Aslan, Reza., 214n16, 291
Austin, Steven A., 241n25, 291

Barr, James, 260n99
Barry, John D., 62n12, 146n20
Brown, Derek, 138n1, 291
Balz, Horst Robert., 237n1, 237n3, 237n4
Balz, Horst, and Gerard Schneider., 79n40
Bauckham, Richard., 7, 8n16, 8n17, 291, 295
Baum, A.D., 2n2, 291
Bauer, Walter, xiii, 291, 292
Billerbeck, P., xiv, 295
Black, David Alan., 7n13, 291
Bowden, Andrew M., 7n13, 291
Brand, Chad, 291
Brandon, Samuel George Frederick, 214n16, 292
Bratcher, Robert G., 117n9, 126n31, 292
Bridges, Linda McKinnish, 213n14, 292
Bromiley, Geoffrey W., 87n5, 292
Brooks, James A., 8n19, 54n29, 86n3, 89n8, 91n13, 114n4, 156n38, 174n20, 208n53, 227n63, 228n65, 232, 232n81, 234n84, 238n6, 239n11, 243n34, 247n48, 250n67, 254n72, 268n21, 272n30, 282n56, 292
Brown, Jeannine K. 293

Bruce, F. F., 283n57, 295

Campbell, William Sanger, 102n30, 292
Charlesworth, James H., 145n18, 292
Chilton, Bruce., 214, 215n19, 292
Ciampa, Roy E., 93n16, 292
Cranfield C. E. B., 251n69, 292

Danker, Frederick William, xiii, 291–92
Das, Andrew A., 225n51, 225n54, 292
DeHoog, J. W., 122n24, 292
DeMoss, Matthew S., 13n36, 41n14
Derrett, Duncan J., 117n12, 292
Dicken, Frank, 109n42, 292
Dittenberger, Wilhelm, 292
Dockery, D. S., 34n3, 292
Dodd, C. H., 8n18, 292
Donfried, Karl P., 9n23, 292

Earle, R., 207n44, 292
Ebeling, Jennie R., 53n26, 292
Edwards. James R., 12n35, 26, 26n74, 292
Ehorn, Seth M., 264n3, 292
Eisenberg. Ronald L. 217n26, 293
Evans, Craig A., 143, 143n12, 143n15, 144n16, 146, 146n24, 146n25, 150, 150n26, 153n31, 153n32, 154n33, 155n36, 156n37, 156n39, 164n1, 166, 166n4, 168n6, 170n8, 171n10, 174n20, 177n30, 178, 178n31, 178n32, 180n34, 183n40, 187n1, 188n4, 189n7, 191, 191n12, 192n13, 199n25, 200n28, 204n39, 205n43, 207n49, 207n50,

Evans, Craig A. *(continued)*, 208n51, 209n54, 210n3, 211n5, 213n13, 214n15, 216n22, 218n29, 218n30, 220n32, 220n34, 221n37, 221n42, 221n43, 224n47, 224n48, 225n51, 226n59, 226n60, 227n61, 228n67, 231n75, 232, 232n80, 234n86, 235n88, 239n7, 240, 240n14, 240n16, 240n17, 241n22, 242n29, 244n37, 245, 245n39, 245n41, 246n43, 246n44, 247n50, 248, 248n55, 249n57, 249n59, 249n64, 250n65, 250n68, 253n71, 254n73, 254n75, 256n79, 259n91, 260n97, 263n1, 264n7, 265n9, 266n13, 266n14, 268n20, 271n25, 271n27, 271n27, 272n28, 274n33, 274n35, 275n37, 276n39, 277n45, 278n47, 278n48, 280n53, 283n59, 284n61, 284n62, 285n64, 287n69, 293

Fairhurst, Libby, 118n14, 293
Ferry, Sara, 128n35, 293
France, R. T., 54n29, 143n13, 174n19, 207n49, 208n52, 228n68, 238n6, 239n7, 240n13, 241n24, 245n40, 247n48, 254, 254n74, 256, 256n80, 272n29, 293
Franklin. J. Chase, 276n40, 276n41, 293, 293
Freedman, David Noel, 293
Fruchtenbaum, Arnold G., 20n47, 293

Garland, David E., 11n33, 293
Geisler, Norman L., 284n63, 293
Geisen, H., 171n9, 293
Gingrich, Wilbur, xiii, 291, 292
Green, Joel B., 147n22, 277n44, 293–94
Guelich, Robert A., 7n10, 33n1, 34n3, 35n4, 35n6, 35n7, 47n19, 50n20, 50n22, 54n30, 56, 56n32, 59n2, 63, 63n15, 65n16, 66n22, 69n25, 72, 72n32, 72n33, 72n34, 78n37, 81n43, 82n44, 83n46, 90, 90n9, 91n12, 92n15, 95n18, 97n20, 99n23, 100n25, 100n27, 104n33, 105n36, 107n40, 111n44, 120n21, 130n39, 131n40, 134, 134n45, 293
Gundry, Robert H., 228n68, 265n10, 286, 286n68, 293

Hackett, Conrad, 84n49, 293
Harrill, J. Albert., 201n33, 293
Hengel, Martin., 7, 7n11, 7n13, 7n14, 214, 214n17, 277n44, 293
Hilgert, E., 117n7, 293
Hixon, Elijah., 13n39, 293
Hoehner, Howard W., 9n23, 243n33, 293–94
Holland, T. A. 203n38, 295
Hooker, Morna D., 91n14, 100n24, 294
Hurst, Lincoln D., 147n22, 294
Hurtado, Larry, 7n12, 294

Irvin, D., 61n4, 294

Jackson, Jeffrey Glenn, ed. 23n64, 294
Jefford, C. N., 199n23, 294
Jeremias, Joachim., 117n13, 260n100, 294
Jones, Henry Stuart, xiv, 294
Josephus., 22n55, 97n21, 107n39, 109, 109n42, 110, 111n44, 119n19, 122, 141n4, 142n9, 142n10, 160n40, 164n1, 168, 169n7, 176n26, 180n34, 188n4, 198n22, 212n8, 213, 213n12, 214n15, 215n19, 224n50, 225, 225n52, 225n53, 225n54, 225n55, 225n56, 227n64, 237n1, 237n2, 240, 240n12, 240n13, 240n19, 241, 241n23, 241n26, 242n30, 243n33, 243n35, 248n56, 249, 249n62, 263n1, 266, 266n12, 267n19, 271, 274n33, 276n39, 294

Kähler, M. 28n76, 294
Kee, Howard Clark., 97n21, 294
Keener Craig S., 201n32, 294
Kelly, Joseph., 61n5, 294

SUBJECT INDEX

Kennedy, T. Michael., 266n13, 294
Keown, Mark J., 1n1, 2n2, 2n3, 2n4,
   3n5, 5n6, 6n7, 11n31, 14n43,
   22n57, 22n59, 26n72, 31n79,
   31n81, 119n18, 151n27, 154n34,
   180n35, 196n17, 199n25,
   221n35, 242n32, 247n49,
   257n85, 294
Klippenstein, Rachel, 138n1, 291

Liddell, Henry George, xiv, 294
Long, Phillip J., 119n19, 119n20, 295
Louw, Johannes P., 60n3, 295

McClendon, David, 293
McKenzie, Roderick, xiv, 294
Mangum, Douglas, 138n1, 291
Marshall, Christopher D., 217, 217n25, 295
Marshall, I. Howard, 296
McDonald, Lee Martin., 10n27, 295
Meiklejohn, J. W., 283n57, 295
Metzger, Bruce Manning., 14n40,
   33n1, 50n22, 130n38, 160n41,
   173, 173n17, 231n74, 287n69,
   287n70, 295
Miller, Jeffrey E., 56n33, 295
Miselbrook, Jeremy S., 199n24, 295
Mitchell, Eric, 291
Myers, Allen C., ed. 176n27, 295

Nease, Owen., 259n92, 295
Netzer, Ehud, 203n38, 295
Nida, Eugene Albert, 117n9, 126n31, 295
Nyberg, Meredith Faubel., 248n54, 295
Nylund, Jan H., 213n10, 213n12

Omanson, Roger L., 231n74, 295
Osborne, Grant R., 146n21, 295

Perrin, Nicholas, 293
Patzia, Arthur G., 26n73, 295
Peterson, David G., 252n70, 295
Petrotta, Anthony J. 26n73, 295
Pitts, Andrew W. 294
Pingenot, Jesse., 199n23, 205

Plummer A., 128n37, 295
Porter, Stanley E. 293–94

Rayburn, Robert G., II. 175n22, 175n23, 295
Reichman, Viktor, xiii, 292
Reinhardt, Wolfgang., 213, 213n11, 295
Renwick, A. M., 176n27
Ritzema, Elliot, 291

Sanders, E. P., 214, 214n18, 295
Sarlo, Daniel, 295
Schmidt, T. E., 237n2, 295
Scott, Robert, xiv, 294
Shepherd, Tom, 292
Shirokov, Peter, 276n38, 295
Silva, Moisés, 71n29, 96n19, 102n28,
   172n14, 260n100, 295
Sinclair-Wolcott, Carrie, 138n1, 291
Stein, Robert H., 2n2, 71n31, 86n2,
   102n31, 175, 175n24, 177n28,
   204n39, 246, 246n47, 295
Stoops, R. F., Jr., 7n15, 295
Strack, H. L., xiv, 295
Strange, James F., 134n46, 296
Strauss, Mark L., 241n25, 291
Stuhlmacher, Peter, 293
Swanson, James., xiii, 296

Tan-Gatue, Peter., 45n17, 147n23, 296
Torrey, C. C., 10n24, 296

Udd., Kris J. 141n5, 141n6, 296

Van Oyen, Geert, 292

Wenham, J. W., 10n25, 195n15, 296
Wenkel, David H., 69n24, 296
Wentz, Lazarus, 291
Widder, Wendy, 291
Winstead, Melton B., 87n4, 116n6, 296
Witherington, Ben, III., 234n85,
   234n87, 282n55, 296
Witte, Brendon R., 22n55, 22n56, 296
Wood, D. R. W., 296
Wright, N. T., 31n80, 245

Scripture Index

Genesis

1	178
1:1	152n28
1:1–2	36, 87
1:26–28	178
1:27	23n64, 177n29, 178
1:28	178, 199
1:31	131
2	178
2:1–4	64
2:2–3	63, 64
2:24	23n64, 178
3:24	36
5:3	23n64
6:1–4	45, 66
9:1	199
14:18–22	90
15:1	99
15:11	199
17:1–3	259
18:14	23n64
21:10–13	264
22:2	23n64, 36
25:8	227n62, 280n52
25:17	280n52
27:28	61
35:29	227n62, 280n52
37:20	222
37:29	268n22
38	226
38:8	23n64
39:12–13	265
44:13	268
48:15	113n1
49:33	227n62, 280n52
50:1–14	97n21

Exodus

1:13–14	264n6
3:2	23n64
3:6	23n64, 227, 236
3:12	240n18
3:14	118n16, 268n21
3:15	23n64
3:16	23n64
4	134
4—15	153
6:5	264n6
10:22	279
11:23	259
12	248
12:1–3	248n53
12:6	23n64
12:15	23n64, 138n2
12:23	117
13:6–7	248n53
15:14	242n28
16	116
16:28–36	242n29
16:35	38
19:6	169
20—34	153n32
20:7	268
20:8–11	63
20:10	64
20:11	152n28

Exodus (continued)

20:12	23n64, 122
20:12–16	23n64
20:13–17	186
20:14	125, 179
20:17	122
21:2–10	264
21:10	186
23:15	248n53
23:18	138n2
23:20	23
24:1–8	256
24:8	23, 253, 256
24:13	24
24:18	38
26:1–37	280
27:16	280
29:7	249
30:35	175
33:18	117n10
33:22	117n10
34:6	117
34:6–7	53
34:18	248n53
34:30	153
40:35	155

Leviticus

2:11	138
2:13	174n18, 175
5:7	213n13
8:12	249
12:1–8	96
12:7	98
13	249
13–14	50, 50n20
14	51
15:19–30	96
16	29
18:16	23n64, 109
19:13	186
19:18	23n64, 231
19:18b	229
19:15–20	229
19:34	230
20:4	260
20:9	23n64, 122
20:22	109
23:5–8	248n53
24:16	23n64
25:39	264
25:42	264n6
25:44–46	264
26	185
26:13	264n6
27:17	23n64

Deuteronomy

2:25	242
3	154
3:17	119
4:1	155
4:35	23n64
5:12	64
5:16	23n64, 122
5:16–20	23n64
5:16–21	186
5:18	179
6:4–5	23n64, 74, 155, 228
6:4–9	228n69
7:13	61n9
10:16	178
11:13–21	228n69
11:14	61n9
15:4	251
15:11	23n64, 251
15:11a	251
15:15	264n6
15:17	264
16:1–8	248n53
16:9	152n28
16:12	264n6
17:6	104n35, 267n17
17:17	177
18:15	23
18:15–18	66, 82
18:15–19	153
19:15	104n35, 267n17
20:8	88
21:22–23	283
23:25	23n64, 63
24	180
24:1	23n64, 177

24:3			23n64
24:14	23n64	24:18	
			264n6
24:22			264n6
25:5			23n64
25:5–10			226
25:9			269n23
28			185
29:16		28	
			175n21
32:8			90n10
32:14			61n9
33:28			61n9
34:1–5			153
34:3			202n36

Joshua

2:1	202
2:2–3	203
2:6	244n37
3	88
3:16	203
4:13	203
4:23	117
5:13	168
6	203
6:3	152n28
7:6	268n22
8:29	255n78
9:4–13	62
10:12	221n7
10:12–13	279
10:13	88
11:1	119
15:8	172n11
18:16	172n11
19:35	119
22:5	23n64

Judges

5:5	245
7:3	88
7:16	79
9:13	61n6
9:45	175n21
11:35	268n22

1 Sam

1:19	283n57
2:10	249n64
2:35	249n64
4:9	264n5
9:1–27	34
9:25	244n37
10:1	249n63
11	37
12:3	249n64
15	109n43
15:17	249n64
15:22	23n64, 230n73
16:1–13	17, 34
16:11	249n63
16:13	249, 249n63
17	37
21:1–6	23n64, 63
24:6	249n64
24:10	249n64
26:9	249n64
26:11	249n64
26:23	249n64
31:3	59
31:10	255n78
31:12	255n78

1 Kingdoms (LXX)

31:10	255n78
31:12	255n78

2 Samuel

1:11	268n22
1:12	59
1:14	249n64
1:16	249n64
2:4	249n63
2:7	249n64
3:39	249n64
5:2	113
5:17	249n64
7:7	113
7:14	143n15, 204, 231n75
8:17	225n51

2 Samuel (continued)

10:2–5	221
11—12	176
12	109n43
12:7	249n64
13:19	268n22
15:24–37	225n51
15:32	259
17:13	240n15
19:21	249n64
20:25	225n51
22:51	249n64
23:1	249n64
23:22	233n82

1 Kings

1:8	225n51
1:32–45	225n51
1:38	208
1:39	249n63
1:45	249n64
5:1	249n64
8:10–11	155
9:21–22	264n5
13:24	255n78
13:28	255n78
13:29	255n78
17:17–24	101, 226
17:18	23n64
18	109, 153
18:4	116
18:13	116
18:28	90
19:2	156
19:4–8	38
19:8	153n32
19:10	156, 221n39
19:11	117n10
19:14	221n39
19:16	24
21:2–3	222
21:16	222
21:17	268n22
22:17	23n64, 113n2, 258n89

3 Kgdms (LXX)

13:24	255 n78
13:28	255n78
13:29	255n78

2 Kings

1:2	71
1:8	23n64, 35, 35n5
1:28–53	34
2	20
2:1	108
2:1–18	203
2:11	108, 153
2:12	268n22
2:19–23	176
4:18–37	226
4:32–37	101
5:7	50, 268n22
5:14	197
6:30	268n22
9:1–13	34
9:6	249
9:13	208
11:12	249
11:14	268n22
12	74
12:9	23
18:37	268n22
19:1	268n22
19:35	255
21:6	172
22:11	268n22
23:10	172
23:30	249

4 Kingdoms (LXX)

5:14	197
19:35	255n78

1 Chronicles

10:12	255n78
11:3	249n63

14:8	249n64	**Esther**	
17:6	113		
28:1	255n78	1:8	160
29:22	249n64	4:1	268n22
		5:3	23n64
		5:6	23n64
2 Chronicles		9:14	255n78
6:42	249n64		
11:12	113	**Job**	
12:13	268n22		
15:6	23n64	1:20	268n22
16:12	97n21	9:6	245n42
18:16	23n64, 113n2	9:8	117
23:11	249n64	13:4	97n21
24:19	102n31	14:17	61n4
33:6	172n12	16:15	61n4
33:11	43n15	16:21	55
34:19	268n22	17:6	269n23
36:15–16	221n39	30:10	269n23
36:16	102n31	38:1	86n2
		38:37	62
		39:6	175
1 Esdras (LXX)		41:1	34n15
		41:4	88
3:4	255n78	42:2	23n64
4:57	160n40		
		Psalms	
2 Esdras (LXX)			
		2	34
19:26	255n78	2:7	23n62, 36, 204
20:38	237n1	6:2	204
22:44	237n1	8:4	55, 145
		9:14	205n40
		9:26	199n27
Ezra		9:31	199
		12:10–11	23n62
6:9	172n18	15:24	23n62
9:9	264n6	15:29	23n62
		15:34	23n62
		18:50	249
Nehemiah		18:7	245n42
		22	30, 146, 161, 255, 255n76, 269, 277, 278, 279, 280
8:16	244n37		
9:26	221n39, 255n78		
9:26–30	102n31	22:1	23n62, 108, 146, 279

Psalms (continued)

22:7	23n62, 278
22:18	23n62, 277
23	113
23:1	113
24:16	204n40
25:11	204n40
26:7	204n40
28:9	113n1
30:10	204
39:7	230n73
40:5	204n40
40:11	204n40
41:9	23n64, 254
42:4–5	259n94
42:11	259n94
43:5	259n94
45:7	249n64
46:4	90n10
50:14	90n10
56:2	204n40
57:2	90n10, 230n73
69:21	23n64, 280
73:11	90n10
78:35	90n10
78:56	90n10
78:71	113
80:17	55, 145
85:3	204n40
85:16	204n40
87:4	88n7
89:20	249
103:3	23n63
104:15	61n6
105:15	249n64
106:14–15	61n9
107:11	90n10
110:1	23n63, 199, 204, 232, 236, 268, 280
110:4	280
113—118	208, 257
114:7	245n42
116	257n86
116:3–4	257n86
116:8–9	257n86
116:15	257n86
116:19	257n86
118	204n40, 209, 222, 257, 204n40
118:3–3	257n86
118:8–9	257n86
118:15	257n86
118:19	257n86
118:22–23	23n62, 220, 257n86
118:23–24	222
118:25–26	21, 23n62, 208
119:83	62
132:10	249n64
133:2	249n63
137:7	240n15

Proverbs

3:9–10	61n9
8	219
8:22–31	18
20:1	61n8
23:21	61n8
31:6	61n7

Ecclesiastes

2:7	264
3:7	61n4
9:7	61n6
9:7–9	61n9

Isaiah

1:6	106
1:8	221n36
1:10–17	229
1:11	230n73
3:14	221n36, 221
5	221
5:1–2	23n64
5:1–7	61, 221
5:2	221
5:5	222
6:9–10	23n64, 75, 139
7:11	240n18
9:1–7	143n15
9:6	231n75
9:6–7	40
10:20–23	239n10
10:24	90

SUBJECT INDEX

11:1	36	44:22	53
11:6–8	38	44:28	113
13:8	242n28	45:1	249n64
13:10	23n64, 245	45:21	23n64
14:12–20	45	45:22	118n16
14:60–61	23n64	49:1–6	146n20
15:3	244n37	49:4	146n20
19:12	23n64	49:7–12	146n20
20:2	256n79	49:8	256n82, 257
21:3	242n28	50:4–9	146n20
21:4	197	50:6	269
22:1	244n37	50:6–7	146n20
24:11	61n6	50:10–11	146n20
25:6	257n84	51:17	196n19
25:6–8	115	52:7	33n2, 41n13, 42
26:17	242n28	52:13–53:12	146, 146n20
27:1–6	221n36	53	30, 161, 201, 246, 255n76
28:16	222		
29	121	53:7	267, 272n31
29:13	23n64, 120, 121	53:10	102
29:18	131	53:10–12	257
29:18–19	121	53:12	201, 265, 278
29:22	121	55:3	256n82
30:7	88n7	56	213, 236
30:33	172n11	56:7	213
31:9	172n11	56:7	23n64
34:4	245	58:6	44n16
35:5–6	23n64, 131	59:21	256n82
35:1–10	239n10	60:6	41n13
35:51–52	239n10	61:1	33n2, 40, 41n13, 250
37:1	268		
37:29	43n15	61:1–2	44
40	156	61:1–3	146n20
40:3	23, 34, 36	61:8	256n82
40:6–8	247	65–66	46
40:9	33n2, 41n13	65:25	38
40:11	113	66:22–24	173
40:30–31	265n9	66:24	172, 173
41:4	118n16		
41:13	99		
41:27	33n2, 41n13	**Jeremiah**	
42:1	36		
42:1–4	146n20	2:30	221n39
42:4	146n20	4:4	178
42:5–9	146n20	4:31	242n28
42:6	256n82, 257	5:2	23n64
43:1	99	5	139
43:10–11	118n16	5:15	139
43:25	23n64, 53	5:18	139
		5:21	139

Jeremiah (continued)

5:23	139
5:25	139
6:20	230
6:24	242n28
7	214, 236
7:4	214
7:11	23n64, 211, 213, 217
7:32	172n13
8:13	211
8:22–9:6	97n21
12:10	221, 221n36
15:9	279
16:7	196n19
16:16	43n15
17:6	175n21
17:16	113
19:10	256n79
19:13	244n37
19:66	172n13
22:22	113
23:5	143n15, 231n75
24	211n6
25:15	196n19
25:17	196n19
25:28	196n19
26:17–19	240n15
28:10	256n79
29:17	211n6
31:10	113n1
31:31–34	256n82
32:35	172n12
32:40	256n82
33:15	143n15
34:9–16	264n5
35:15	102n31
46:11	97n21
50:5	256m82
51:7	196n19
51:8	97n21
51:34	88n7
51:46	241

Ezekiel

2:5	102n31
2:6	55, 145
3:7	178
12:2	21n64
12:13	43n15
13:18	61n4
16:60	156n82
17:20	43n15
17:22–24	83
19:10–14	221n36
21:33	152
23:32–33	196n19
28:1–19	45
29:3–5	88n7
32:2–8	88n7
32:7–8	23n64
34	113
34:8	258n89
34:12	258n89
34:15	258n89
34:23	113
34:23–24	143n15, 258
34:24–28	143n15
36:25–27	35
37:24	113n3
40:3	152
43:24	174, 175
47:7–9	175n21
47:10	43n15

Daniel

3:26	90n10
4:2	90n10
4:11–12	83n47
4:20–21	83n47
5:18	90n10
5:21	90n10
7	246
7:9	153
7:13	23n63, 40, 55, 145, 146, 200, 242, 246, 268
7:13–14	18, 153
7:15–28	146

7:21	255n76	4:9	259n94
7:21–22	146		
7:25	146, 255n76	\multicolumn{2}{c}{**Micah**}	
8:17	55		
9:26	255n76	1:4	245n42
9:6	102n31	3:12	240n15
9:25–26	250	4:4	210
9:27	23n64, 243	4:9	242n28
10:12	99	5:4	113n3
10:19	99	5:6	113n3
11:31	243	6:6–8	230n73
12:1	23n64, 245	7:6	23n64
12:1–3	108, 186, 226		
12:11	243		

Nahum

1:5	245n42
1:15	41n13
2:11	242n28

Hosea

2:6	179
2:8	61
6:6	23n64, 230n73
9:7	102n31
9:10	211
13:13	242

Habakkuk

1:14–17	43n15
2:16	196n19
3:6	245n42

Joel

1:7	211
2:10	23n64, 279
2:28–39	170
2:31	23n64
3:13	23n64
3:15	23n64

Zephaniah

1:5	244
2:9	175n21

Haggai

1:1	102
2:15	240n15
2:19	61n9

Amos

2:16	265n9
5:22	230n73
8:9	23n64
9:1	240n15
9:11	143n15, 245n42

Zech

2:6	23n64
2:10	23n64
3:1	102
3:8	143n15, 231n75
3:10	210
4:14	250n64

Jonah

1:4	86
1:5	87

Zech (continued)

6:12	231n75
8:6	23n64
9:9	21, 207–8
9:11	256n82
10:2	113n2, 258n89
10:7	61n6
11:4	113
11:7	113
12:2	196n19
12:7	143n15
12:10	151
13:4	23n64
13:7	23n64, 29, 113, 255, 258, 265
14	244
14:4	207, 207n47, 216, 258

Malachi

3:1	23, 34, 108n41, 156, 256n82
3:6	280n51
4:1	280n51
4:5	108n41

Apocrypha

Tobit

1:18	255n78
2:10	97
3:7–15	225
4:8–9	189n5

Judith

11:9	23n64
12:7	197
13:9	255n78
16:17	174

Wisdom of Solomon

5:23	86n2

Sirach

7:17	174
9:5	171n10
23:9	171n10
29:10–12	189n5
34:25	197
37	97n21
37:2	259n94
38	97n21
48:1–14	108n41
48:10	86n2, 156n37, 280n51

Baruch

4:1	247
4:26	258n89

1 Maccabees

1:54	23n64, 243
3:56	88
4:39	268n22
4:46	23
6:39	152
9:27	23
11:4	255n78
11:71	268n22
14:41	23
14:49	237n1
15:30	199

2 Maccabees

5:2	285n65
6—7	258n90
7	225n57
7:4	171n10
9:7	255n78
9:9	255n78

9:29	255n78
10:7	208
12:26	255n78
12:39	255n78

2 Esdras

20:38	237n1
22:44	237n1
19:26	255n78

4 Maccabees

8–13	225n57

Matthew

1—2	34
1:1	232n76
1:5	203
1:6	205n41, 232n76
1:17	205n41, 232n76
1:20	205n41, 232n76
1:23	89
2:6	113
3:10	173n16
4:1–11	26, 38
4:2	60
4:3	113, 211n7
4:3–4	135
4:4	129
5—7	3, 26, 52, 55
5:5	190
5:12	102n31, 189
5:13	175, 176n25
5:13–16	72
5:16	79, 80
5:17–20	187
5:18	247
5:21–26	217n27
5:22	100, 131, 173n15
5:29	173n15
5:30	173n15
5:37–37	91
6:1	189
6:9–13	236
6:10	261
6:12	217n27, 217
6:16	59
6:16–18	60
6:19–24	193
6:23	100, 189
6:24	131, 188
6:24–34	139
6:33	43
8:5–13	128, 130
8:5–15	3
8:9–13	129
8:19	59
8:28	89
9:2	232n76
9:9	56
9:12	97
9:13–15	2
9:17	62
9:27	205n41, 232n76
9:35	104
9:36	50n23, 258n88
9:38	106
9:49–50	175
10:2–4	104n32
10:3	56
10:6	129
10:8	169
10:25	71n30
10:27	244n37
10:29	93
11:2–6	19n46
11:5	143n15
11:10	246n45
11:19	276
11:21	141
11:47	221n41
11:49	221n41
12:11	64n13
12:23	205n41, 232n76
12:24	71n30
12:27	71n30
12:31	72
12:39	136, 279n50
12:39–41	87
13	74
13:24	81n42
13:31	81n42

Matthew (continued)

13:33	81n42, 138
13:34	221n41
13:39	239n8
13:40	239n8
13:41	246
13:43	81n42
13:44	81n42, 189
13:44–46	150, 183
13:45	81n42
13:47	81n42
13:49	239n8
13:52	81n42
13:57	102n29
14:14	50n23
15:5	122
15:22	205n41, 232n76
15:26	129
15:32	50n23
16:4	87, 136
16:14	108
16:18	68, 83
17:20	215n21
17:24–27	237n2
17:25–27	224
18:9	173n15
18:10–14	113
18:12	258n88
18:16	104n35, 267n17
18:23	81n42
19	177
19:9	125, 179
19:16	186
19:21	81n41
19:22	186
19:28	247n51
20:1	81n42
20:24	182
20:28	195n14
20:30	232n76
20:31	232n76
21:9	232n76
21:43	222
22:2	81n42
21:15	232n76, 182n39
21:22	216
22:1–14	115
22:42	232n76
22:43	232n76
22:44	232n77
22:45	232n76
23:6	133, 196
23:12	236
23:15	173n15
23:23	131, 173n15
23:25	196n19
23:29–31	102n31
23:31–46	169
23:34–35	102n31
23:37	221n41
24:4	239n8
24:14	242
24:15	244
25:1	81n41
25:29	198
25:31–46	3
25:32	113, 258n88
25:41	37, 91
26:3	266n11
26:8	182, 250
26:25	255
26:27–28	61n10
26:29	61n11
26:52–55	264
26:53	91
26:57	266n11
27:3	77
27:3–5	20n48
27:16	273
27:17	273
27:19	272
27:30	269
27:34	61n7
27:48	61n7
27:56	282
27:57	283
27:58	283
27:62–66	284
28	258
28:2	285
28:3	285
28:9	287
28:9–10	282
28:18–20	30n78, 106
28:20	239n8

Mark

1	26n69
1:1	17, 18, 33, 35n6, 41, 57, 108, 144, 267, 281, 287
1:1–8	17, 43–35
1:1—2:17	33–58
1:1—8:27	286
1:1—8:29	1, 7, 36
1:2	34, 246
1:2–3	23
1:2–15	30
1:4–6	34
1:4—3:6	39
1:5	35, 219
1:6	23n64
1:7	35, 45, 149, 158
1:7–8	19
1:7–11	219
1:8	90
1:9	26n71, 36, 101
1:9–11	17
1:10	6, 26, 36
1:11	23n62, 23n64, 155, 221, 280, 281
1:12–13	17, 19, 23, 26, 37–38
1:13	93, 129, 135, 246n46
1:14	26, 33, 39
1:14–15	17, 18, 24, 34, 39–42, 44, 47, 52
1:15	25, 30, 40, 45, 99, 189, 215, 286
1:16	8, 19, 26, 286
1:16–20	19, 20, 22n58, 25, 25n67, 42–48, 55, 190, 206
1:16—8:26	17, 42–142
1:17	19n45, 25, 56n35
1:17–20	189n6
1:21	44, 45n18, 163
1:21–22	218n30
1:21–24	26
1:21–28	22n59, 44–46, 47, 95
1:21–34	26, 52, 103n32
1:22	18n44, 21, 29, 45n18, 53, 218
1:23	117
1:23–24	19
1:23–27	218n30
1:24	66, 90, 101
1:25	21n53, 87, 144, 182, 182n37, 205n42
1:26	46
1:27	21, 45n18, 157, 218n30
1:28	29, 165
1:29–34	47–48, 95
1:32	19n45
1:32–33	21
1:32–34	47, 119
1:33	26n70
1:33–34	66
1:34	19n45, 21n52, 21n53, 26n70, 37n10
1:35	26n70, 48–49, 116, 117, 161n42, 216n24
1:35–37	22
1:35–39	26, 49
1:36	26n70, 48, 143
1:36–39	49, 58, 58
1:37	26n70
1:38	26n70
1:38–39	22n59
1:38–40	26
1:39	19n45, 26n70, 37n10
1:40	26, 26n70, 50
1:40–45	46, 49–52, 103n32, 249
1:41	26n70, 113, 181n36, 188
1:42	26n70
1:43	26n70, 250
1:43–44	21n53
1:44	26n70, 188n3, 213
1:45	21, 22, 29, 131, 165
2	26n69, 69

Mark (continued)

Reference	Pages
2:1	26, 163
2:1–2	52–55
2:1–5a	52n25
2:1–12	27n75, 50n21, 52–55, 95, 103, 186, 218n30
2:2	21n51
2:4	21n51
2:5	118, 206, 215
2:5–7	29
2:5–11	18
2:5b–10a	27n75, 52n25
2:6–12	23n60
2:6	20, 53, 71, 147, 218
2:7	23n64
2:8	53, 53n26, 163, 219n31, 258
2:10	145
2:10b–12	52n25
2:11	55, 188n3
2:13	25, 45n18, 21n51, 25, 26, 190
2:13–14	22n58
2:13–16	25
2:13–17	19, 25n67, 55–57, 69
2:14	25, 69, 149, 189n6
2:15	56, 68
2:16	20n49, 29, 71
2:17	97n21
2:18	25, 59
2:18–20	57, 59–60
2:18—3:6	23n60
2:18–4:34	59–87
2:19	219n31
2:20	251
2:20—3:6	57
2:21	61
2:21–22	60–62
2:23	23n64, 26n71
2:23–24	63
2:23–27	63–64
2:23—3:6	120
2:25	205, 219n31
2:25–28	23n64
2:27	63
2:28	18, 118
3	26n69, 120
3:1–6	27n75, 64–66, 95, 103n32, 107
3:3–4	65
3:4	87
3:6	29, 55, 64
3:7	21n52, 66
3:7–12	26, 66–67, 95, 103n32, 119
3:7–35	66
3:8	21n52, 128
3:9	21n51, 74
3:9–11	67
3:10	181n36
3:11	19, 19n45, 46, 90, 281
3:12	21n53, 67, 144, 182, 182n37, 205n42
3:13	6, 26
3:13–19	67–70, 104, 164
3:14	75, 94n17
3:15	19n45, 37n10, 104, 158
3:16	20, 143
3:16–19	22n58
3:19	252
3:20	21n51, 26, 163
3:20–21	27, 70
3:20–24	70–73
3:20–30	23, 157
3:20–35	27, 94n17, 95, 210n1
3:21	26, 101
3:22	20n49, 26, 29, 37n10, 120, 218
3:22–23	71
3:22–27	19
3:22–30	23n60, 27, 70, 167
3:23	37n10, 74, 219n31, 220
3:24	71, 72
3:25	71
3:26–27	35
3:27	72, 90

3:28–30	72	4:35–41	18, 19, 86–89, 103n3, 118, 211
3:29	85		
3:30	72	4:35–6:29	86–111
3:31	26, 101	4:36	21n51
3:31–34	25n67	4:38	18n44, 45n18
3:31–35	27, 70	4:39	26n71, 144, 182, 182n37, 194, 205, 205n42
3:32	21n51		
3:33	219n31		
4	26n69, 52, 74, 220	4:40	25, 90, 215
4:1	21n51, 21n52	4:41	18, 111, 286
4:1–2	45n18	5	26, 112, 120
4:1–9	74	5:1–5	90
4:1–20	22, 31, 54, 73–79, 119, 175	5:1–20	25, 28, 46, 89–94, 103n32, 129, 130, 192
4:1–34	22n59, 220		
4:2	67	5:2	221
4:3	74	5:3	90
4:4	26n71, 75	5:4	158
4:5–6	76	5:5	90
4:7	77	5:6	46
4:10–13	84	5:7	23n64, 90, 91, 281
4:11–12	78, 85, 220	5:9	11, 91
4:12	23n64, 75, 78, 79, 139	5:9–13	92
		5:13–18	19n45
4:13	21n54	5:15	11, 92
4:13–20	74	5:18–20	93
4:14–15	75	5:19	188n3
4:15	19	5:19–20	106
4:16–17	76	5:20	21, 89
4:17	76, 171, 258	5:21	21n51, 21n52, 95
4:18–19	77	5:21–24a	94
4:21	11n30, 80	5:21–24	27
4:21–22	31		
4:21–23	79–80	5:21–43	27, 46, 94–101, 103, 210n1, 226
4:23	80		
4:24	234	5:22–24	95
4:24–25	80–82	5:24	21n51, 21n52, 96
4:25–26	108	5:25	96, 158
4:26	81	5:25–34	27, 53, 94, 192
4:26–29	40, 81–83	5:27–28	67
4:26–34	24	5:29	98
4:27	31	5:29–43	18
4:29	23n64	5:31	21n51, 96
4:30	81	5:34	28, 188n3, 206, 215
4:30–32	31, 40, 83–84		
4:33–34	84–94	5:35	18n44, 96, 99, 100
4:34	21n54	5:35–43	27, 94
		5:36	118, 206, 216

Mark (continued)

5:37	20, 44, 143n14, 152
5:37–43	259n93
5:38	45n18, 100
5:39	53n26
5:41	131, 260n98
5:41–42	194
5:42	21
5:43	21n53, 101
5:45–52	18
5:46	97n21
6	26, 111
6:1	26
6:1–6a	101–4
6:1–6	20
6:2	45n18
6:3	171, 282
6:4	102
6:5	103
6:6	45n18
6:6b–13	27, 104–7
6:7	19, 104, 105, 158
6:7–13	25, 30, 75, 94n17, 164
6:12	156
6:12–13	105, 106
6:13	19, 37n10, 98, 156
6:14	20
6:14–29	27, 107–111, 199
6:15	20, 21, 280n51
6:14–16	143
6:14–29	104, 143, 176, 203, 241
6:15	156
6:16	108
6:16b–31	27, 104, 201n1
6:18	23n64, 179
6:21	164
6:23	23n64
6:27	11n30
6:25–59	132
6:30–31	27, 104
6:30–44	18, 112–16, 103n32, 132, 201, 235
6:30—8:13	112–63
6:31	21n52, 188n3, 115
6:33	188n3
6:34	21n51, 21n52, 23n64, 45n18, 50n23, 113, 159, 188, 258
6:37	11, 25, 30, 97, 132, 137
6:38	133, 188n3
6:40	114
6:41	133
6:42	133
6:43	115
6:45	21n51, 112, 141
6:45–52	116–19, 103n32, 211
6:46	49, 161n42, 216n24
6:48–50	194
6:50	268
	6:50–205
6:50–52	19
6:51	118
6:52	132, 140
6:53–56	97, 119–20, 103n32
6:56	181n36
7	2
7:1–16	29
7:1–21	23n60
7:1–23	20n49, 27n75, 57, 97, 134
7:2	120
7:3	218
7:4	11n30, 196n18
7:5	120
7:6	120
7:6–7	23n64
7:8	121, 187
7:9–13	122, 238
7:10	23n64
7:11	100, 131
7:13	122
7:14	21n51
7:14–15	123
7:16	13
7:17	21n51, 21n54, 220
7:17–23	123

SUBJECT INDEX

7:21	180	8:27–30	142–45
7:21–23	25, 120–27, 137	8:28	20, 21, 107, 280n51
7:22–23	109		
7:23	126	8:29	18, 19, 20, 39, 86, 204, 215n20
7:24–30	46, 103, 128–30		
7:26	37n10	8:29–30	21
7:26–30	19n45	8:29–31	21
7:28	129	8:30	21n53, 46, 144, 205n42, 272n29
7:29	28, 188n3		
7:30	128	8:30–33	28, 182
7:31	132	8:30–16:8	17, 36
7:31–32	109, 130–32	8:31	21n50, 30n77, 45n18, 53n28, 161, 194, 218, 222, 252, 263, 266, 286n67
7:31–37	46, 103n32		
7:32–37	157		
7:33	21n51, 141, 181n36, 269		
7:33–34	131	8:31–32	29
7:34	100, 136	8:31–33	19, 145–48
7:37	23n64, 131	8:32	144, 147, 194, 215n20, 205n42
8	26		
8—9	209	8:32–33	20
8:1	21n51, 21n52	8:33	19, 23, 144, 188n3, 205n42
8:1–9	132–34		
8:1–10	18, 103n32, 201, 235	8:34	21n51, 25, 70, 189n6, 190, 201, 276
8:2	21n51, 50n23, 159		
8:4	132	8:34–36	25
8:6	21n51	8:34–37	25
8:8	133	8:34–38	22n59
8:10–13	134–37	8:34–39	162
8:11	135, 157, 240n18	8:34—9:1	148–52
8:11–12	278	8:35	66, 190
8:11–13	23n60	8:36	190
8:12	219n31, 246	8:38	25, 31, 150, 151, 246
8:13	136		
8:14–21	138–40	9	26
8:14–9:32	138–62	9:1	30n77, 53n28, 152, 154
8:15	138, 234		
8:16	139	9:2	40, 44, 152, 100, 143n14, 151
8:18	23n64, 139		
8:21	19	9:2–6	194
8:22–26	103n32, 140–42	9:2–8	18, 21, 259n93
8:22	141, 181n36	9:2–13	152–57, 280
8:22–26	204	9:3	285
8:23	269	9:4–5	108
8:26	21n53	9:5	153, 215n20
8:27	143	9:5–6	154
8:27–29	17	9:6	154

369

Mark (continued)

9:7	18, 23, 23n62, 26n71, 80, 155, 182, 221, 281
9:8	155
9:9	29, 46, 155
9:10	155, 157, 286n67
9:11	23n61, 108
9:11–12	23n64
9:12	35, 108, 280n51
9:12b	156
9:13	108
9:14	20n49, 21n21, 21n51, 157, 218
9:14–29	46, 103, 157–61
9:15	21n51
9:16	157
9:17	18n44, 21n51, 45n18
9:18	37n10
9:19	246
9:20	19, 46
9:20–27	159
9:21	158
9:22	158, 160
9:23	216, 260
9:23–24	206
9:24	25, 216
9:25	21n51, 142, 157, 160, 182, 182n37, 205n42
9:26	26n71
9:27–28	160
9:28	37n19
9:28–29	21n54
9:29	25, 49, 90, 158, 216
9:30–31	21n54
9:30–32	161–62
9:31	29, 30n77, 45n18, 53n28, 194, 222, 286n67
9:32	19, 69, 194
9:33	177
9:33–35	22, 163–65
9:33–37	181
9:33–10:16	163–84
9:34	87
9:35	25, 47, 282
9:36	170, 182, 183, 193
9:36–37	165–66, 181
9:38	18n44, 19n45, 37n10, 45n18
9:38–39	184
9:38–41	166–70
9:40	168
9:41	196n18
9:42	171, 181, 205, 215
9:42–48	170–74, 184, 233
9:42–50	25, 38, 127
9:43	171, 173n16
9:44	13, 172, 173
9:45	171, 172
9:46	13, 173
9:46–52	103
9:47	37, 171, 172
9:47–50	22
9:48	173
9:49–50	174–76
9:50	175
10	125, 162
10:1	21n51
10:1–12	22n59, 25, 29, 109, 176–80, 125
10:2	219n31, 135, 177
10:3	177
10:4	23n23
10:5	178
10:6–8	23n23
10:6–9	178
10:9	226
10:10	179
10:10–11	21n54
10:10–12	179
10:13	145, 193, 205n42
10:13–16	2, 22n59, 25, 166, 181–83, 185
10:14	198, 205, 250
10:15	182
10:16	181, 183
10:17	18n44, 45n18, 172, 186
10:17–22	25, 59n59, 93, 150
10:17–31	22n59, 25, 185–93, 238

10:17—11:11	185–209	10:45	17, 29, 47, 145, 200, 257, 264
10:18	219n31		
10:18–22	43, 75	10:46	21n51, 193
10:18–31	238	10:46–52	19, 93, 140, 202–6
10:19	23n64, 25n67	10:47	231
10:20	18n44, 45n18, 187	10:48	87, 145, 182, 182n37, 231
10:21	25, 31, 48, 81, 97, 149, 189, 190, 250		
		10:49	118
10:22	190	10:51	153, 195, 209
10:23	190	10:52	25, 95n16, 188, 189n6, 215
10:24–25	172		
10:25	61	11	112
10:26	172, 191	11—12	179
10:27	23n23, 191, 216, 260	11:1	248, 273
		11:1–6	253
10:28	20, 25, 189, 192, 215n20	11:1–11	21, 206–9
		11:2	188n3
10:29–31	25n67	11:2–3	53n28
10:30	172, 190, 192	11:4–6	208
10:31	192	11:7	153, 154
10:32–34	193–94	11:7–10	208
10:32	19, 193, 194	11:8	21n52
10:32–33	161	11:9–10	23n62, 222
10:32–34	193	11:10	204, 232, 257
10:33	21n50, 218, 222, 252	11:11	117, 209, 248
		11:11–12	207
10:33–34	29, 53n28	11:12–14	27, 210–11
10:34	30n77, 269, 286n67	11:12–23	95
		11:12–25	27, 210
10:35	45n18	11:12—12:40	210–36
10:35–37	69, 163	11:14	53n28
10:35–45	22n59, 163, 164, 194–202	11:15–19	27, 37, 65, 210, 211–15
10:35–52	28	11:17	23n23, 211, 213
10:36	195, 195n16, 205, 209	11:18	21n50, 21n51, 29, 45n18, 215, 224n49, 252
10:37	209, 234, 278		
10:38	196, 219n31		
		11:19	117
		11:20–21	215
10:38–39	256	11:20–25	27, 210, 215–17
10:39	197, 260	11:21	8, 20, 153
		11:22–24	25, 236, 261
10:39–40	53n28	11:22–25	206
10:41	182, 198	11:24	49, 216
10:43	47, 199	11:25	49, 217
10:43–44	282	11:26	13
10:43–45	25, 209	11:27	20n49, 218, 218n28, 224n49
10:44	200		

Mark (continued)

11:27–28	218
11:27–33	217–19, 223, 252
11:27—12:34	29, 266
11:27—12:38	23n60
11:29–30	219
11:32	21n51
11:33	219
12:1	23n23
12:1–11	54
12:1–12	29, 220–23, 248, 252
12:6	220, 281
12:8	37, 53n28
12:9	220
12:10	226, 267
12:10–11	257
12:11	243
12:12	21n51, 223, 265
12:13	223
12:13–17	22n59, 223–24
12:14	11n30, 18n44, 20n49, 45n18
12:14–15	223
12:15	11, 135
12:15–16	219n31, 224
12:17	224
12:18–23	226
12:18–27	224–27
12:19	18n44, 20n49, 23n23, 45n18
12:24	219n31, 222
12:25	227, 246
12:26	23n23, 227, 236
12:28	20n49, 157, 228
12:28–34	22n59, 227–31
12:29	227
12:29–31	23n23, 121, 178
12:31	188, 229
12:32	18n44, 23n23
12:32–33	230
12:33	23n23
12:34	20
12:35	45n18, 231
12:35–37	204, 231–33, 268
12:36	23n63, 232n77, 236
12:37	21, 21n51, 21n52, 232, 281
12:38	45n18
12:38–40	233–36
12:39	133, 133n44, 196
12:40	49
12:41	21n51, 23n23
12:41–44	22n59, 31, 229, 235, 237–38
12:41—14:42	237–62
12:42	11n30, 48
12:42–44	250
12:43–44	53n28
12:48–49	265
12:52	265
13	10, 31, 121, 262
13:1	18n44, 45n18, 240, 267
13:1–13	238–43
13:2	240, 267
13:2–4	31
13:2–37	54n28
13:3	20, 21n54, 143n14, 240
13:3–4	240
13:4	247
13:5–6	240
13:5–23	27n75
13:7	241
13:8	23n23, 241
13:9	241
13:10	25, 31, 40, 46, 49, 75, 130, 209, 239, 242, 246, 251
13:11	242
13:12	23n23, 242
13:13	31, 239, 242
13:14	10, 23n23, 243, 244, 267
13:14–16	243
13:14–23	239, 243, 245
13:14–25	247
13:14–37	243–48
13:17	255
13:17–18	245
13:19	23n23, 245
13:20	245
13:21–22	245
13:22	245

13:23–24	245	14:22	115, 133
13:24–25	23n23	14:23	196
13:24–27	31	14:23–24	61, 261
13:26	246, 247	14:23–27	257
13:27	23n23, 31, 246, 251	14:24	17, 23, 29
		14:25	61, 276
13:28–29	246	14:26	257
13:28–30	32	14:26–31	54n28, 257–59
13:30	31, 246	14:27	23n23, 76, 113, 171, 258
13:32	198, 246n46, 247, 281		
		14:27–28	30n77
13:32–34	32	14:27–29	265
13:33	217, 247	14:27–31	29
13:34	117n8, 32	14:28	258, 286, 286n67
13:34–36	247	14:29	20, 76, 219n20, 171, 258
13:35	117		
13:35–37	32	14:30	258, 270
13:36–37	247	14:31	20, 258
13:37	259n93	14:32	216n24
14:1	21n50, 29, 45n18, 224n49, 252, 266	14:32–33	259
		14:32–38	49
14:1–2	27, 248m 265	14:32–39	161n42, 248
14:1–9	29, 248–52	14:32–42	25, 197, 259–62
14:1–11	27, 201n1	14:32–50	103
14:3	207, 249	14:33	20, 43n14, 44, 100
14:3–9	27	14:34	259
14:3–11	285	14:35	216n24
14:5	11, 182, 250	14:35–36	261
14:7	23n23, 48, 251	14:35–41	159
14:8	251	14:36	18, 29, 54n29, 100, 131n43, 197, 217, 260, 260n98, 273
14:9	31, 75, 251		
14:10	224n49		
14:10–11	27, 29, 252–53		
14:11–12	252	14:37	20
14:12	23n23, 253	14:37–38	261
14:12–25	253–57	14:38	38, 49, 217, 259
14:12–26	29	14:39	216n24
14:13	188n3, 253	14:39–40	261
14:14	18n44, 45n18, 253	14:41–42	261
14:15	253	14:43	21n50, 29, 224n49, 263
14:16	253		
14:17–25	197, 235	14:43–45	29
14:18	23n23, 254	14:43–52	263–65
14:18–20	29	14:43	21n51
14:18–21	54n28	14:43—16:8	263–88
14:19	255	14:45	153
14:20	255	14:45–46	264
14:21	188n3, 252, 255		

Mark *(continued)*

14:47	29, 201, 224n49, 264, 270
14:48	219n31
14:48–50	29
14:49	45n18
14:50	265
14:51	259
14:51–52	8
14:52	254
14:53	21n50
14:53–54	28, 266
14:53–55	224n49
14:53–59	29
14:53–65	265–69
14:53–72	28, 265, 210n1, 265, 266
14:54	20, 266
14:55	28, 266, 283
14:55–65	28, 266
14:56	267
14:58	214, 240
14:60–64	29
14:61	18, 224n49, 87, 267
14:61–62	281
14:62	20, 23n63, 118, 144, 233, 272n29
14:63	224n49
14:53–64	268
14:64	271, 278
14:65	23n23, 29, 269, 275
14:66	201, 224n49
14:66–72	20, 28, 29, 266, 270–71
14:68	270
14:69	201, 270
14:70	270
14:71	270
14:72	8
15:1	21n50, 224n49, 271, 283
15:1–15	29, 271–74
15:2	272
15:2–5	267
15:3	224n49, 272
15:4	272
15:5	272
15:6	272
15:6–15	21
15:7	24
15:8	21n51, 272
15:10	272
15:10–11	224n49
15:11	21n51, 24
15:12	24, 272
15:14	272
15:14–16:1	280n51
15:15	11n30, 21n51, 273
15:16	11n30
15:16–19	275
15:16–20	29, 274–75
15:17–20	24
15:20	275
15:19	269
15:21–31	21
15:21–32	275–79
15:23	23n23, 61n7, 276
15:24–27	29
15:25–29	277
15:26	24
15:27	198
15:28	13
15:29	222, 267, 278
15:31	21n50, 224n49
15:31–32	24, 278
15:32	278, 279
15:33	23n23
15:33–34	279
15:33–41	279–82
15:34	100, 131n43, 260n98, 277
15:35	280n51
15:35–36	108
15:36	23n23, 61n7
15:37	280
15:38	29, 36, 222, 280, 281
15:39	11, 24, 28, 275, 289
15:40	19
15:40–41	28, 42n14, 281
15:40—16:1	28, 210n1, 281
15:41	189n6

15:42–46	28, 281	2:37	60
15:42–47	28, 282–85	3:1	198
15:43	95, 218n28, 283	3:2	266n11
15:42–46	269	3:17	173n16
15:44	11	3:21	6
15:44–45	284	3:31	205n41, 232n76
15:45	11	4:1–13	26, 38
15:46	284	4:3	211
15:47	42n14, 284	4:3–4	135
15:47—16:1	28, 281	4:14	45
16:1–5	30	4:16–21	44
16:1–8	42, 285–86	4:16–30	101
16:1	285	4:18–19	40, 33
16:3	285	4:18–20	36
16:4	284, 285	4:22	101
16:5	285	4:24	102n29
16:7	8, 19, 44, 188n3, 258	4:25–26	108
		5:10	99
16:8	1, 14, 30, 32, 286, 288	5:16	161
		5:31	97n21
16:9–11	287	6	3
16:9–20	13, 287–88	6:12	6
16:12	287	6:15	56n34
16:13	287	6:19–49	26
16:14	13n13, 287	6:20–49	52
16:17	287	6:23	102n31
16:19	288	6:37	217n27
16:19–20	288	7	249, 249n58
16:20	263	7:1–10	3, 128, 130
		7:11–17	135, 226
		7:13	50n23
	Luke	7:18–23	19n46
		7:22	143n15
1—3	34	7:24	246n45
1:1	5	7:27	246n45
1:1–4	13n39	7:48	53
1:13	99	8	74
1:15	35	8:1–2	282
1:17	108	8:1–3	42n14, 201
1:27	232n76	8:2	14, 282, 287
1:30	99	8:3	254
1:32	90n10, 205n41, 232n76	8:26	89
		8:28	90n10
1:35	90n10	8:43	97n21
1:69	205n41, 232n76	9:10	112, 116
2:4	205n41, 232n76	9:54	69
2:11	205n41, 232n76	9:57	59n1
2:24	213n13	9:57–60	93

Luke (*continued*)

9:57–62	73
9:61	59n1
9:52	246n45
10:1	104n34, 106
10:13	141
10:25–28	186
10:25–37	229, 230
10:33	51
10:34	61n7, 106
10:38–42	254
11:5	117n8
11:15	71n30
11:18	71n30
11:19	71n30
11:29–30	136, 279
11:29–32	87n6
11:39	196n19
11:47–51	102n31
12:3	173n15, 252
12:6	93
12:6–7	87
12:10	72
12:22–34	139
12:33	81n41, 189
12:49–56	187
12:51–53	71
13:1	271
13:1–5	50, 54, 186
13:14	182n39
13:15	63n13
13:18	81n42
13:28–29	257n84
13:28–30	129
13:33–34	102n31
14	235
14:5	63n13
14:7–11	133n44, 235
14:9–10	196
14:15–24	129
14:15–24	257n84
14:16–18	115
14:26	73
14:34–35	175
14:35	176n25
14:32–37	176n25
15:3–7	158
15:7	114
15:11–32	188
15:16	205n41
15:20	51
16:10	198
16:13–15	188
16:18	179
16:19–31	3, 150
16:20–21	203
16:24	173n16
16:26	173
16:31	136
17:6	215n21
18:12	60
18:15–18	2
18:22	81n41
18:38–39	232n76
19:1–10	189
19:2–10	56
19:8	189
19:10	79, 18
19:17	198
19:47	164n1
20:41–44	232n76
20:43	232n77
21:20	244n36
21:20–24	244
21:24	222
22:20	61n10, 257
22:24–30	195n14, 197
22:28–30	61n10
22:30	257n84
22:37	265, 278
22:41	259
22:51	264n4
23:6–16	271
23:14	272
23:18	273
23:33	276
23:34	231
23:36	61n7
23:36–37	276
23:39–43	278
23:50–51	269
23:51	283
23:56b	285
24:4	285
24:13–32	14n42

SUBJECT INDEX

24:13–43	287
24:36–43	287
24:44–49	287
24:46–49	14n42, 30n78
24:50	207
24:50–51	71
24:50–53	14n42

John

1:1	152
1:1–2	145
1:1–5	13n39
1:1–18	34
1:14	155
1:21	35, 108
1:25	35, 108
1:28	207n45
1:29	29, 255
1:44	47, 141
2	135
2:1–11	61
2:1–12	62, 276
2:18–22	267
2:19–21	222
2:20	240
2:24	54
3:1	369
3:1–9	95
3:1–15	269
3:16–17	79
4:7–43	169
4:22	35
4:26	119n17
4:40	92
4:44	102
4:46–54	130
5:18	268
6:14–15	66
6:15	22
6:20	119n17
6:25–59	132
6:35	119n17
6:41	119n17
6:70	253
7:42	232n76
7:50	95, 269
7:53—8:11	13n39
8:12	119n17
8:17	104n35
8:20	237n1
8:58	268
9	50
9:1–3	2–3
9:1–5	54, 186
9:1–7	131
9:9	119n17
10	113
10:1–17	257n88
10:10	158
10:11	119n17
10:14	119n17
11:1	207, 207n46
11:1–44	226
11:25	119n17
11:38	250
11:49	266
11:49–52	266
12:1	207
12:2	248, 249
12:3	249
12:4	250, 252
12:6	250
12:15	99
13	201
13:2	252
13:25–26	255
13:29	77
13:34–35	230
14:6	119n17, 272
14:13–14	216n23
14:16	37n9
14:26	37n9
15:1	119n17
15:4	68n23
15:6–7	68n23
15:7	216n23
15:16	216n23
15:26	37n9
16:7	37n9
16:21	242
16:23–24	216n23
18:2	252, 259
18:5	119n17
18:6	119n17

John (continued)

18:10	264
18:11	197, 264n4
18:13	266
18:13–14	266n11
18:14	266
18:24	266n11
18:28	254, 266n11
18:28–38	272
18:38	272
18:40	273
19:14	254, 277n46
19:23	61n4
19:25	282
19:27	284
19:29	61n7
19:30	260
19:31	254
19:37	151
19:38	283
19:38–39	269
19:39	95
19:40	284n63
19:42	254
20:1–18	78n38
20:11–18	14n42, 287
20:12	201
20:21	30n78
20:24–29	69
21	20
21:1–18	282
21:25	13n39

Acts

1:3	279
1:6–8	287
1:8	30n78, 106
1:9–11	14n42, 207, 288n71
1:9–12	158
1:13	56n34
1:15–19	20n48
1:25	252, 255
2:1–4	14n42, 36, 106, 197
2:10	275
2:17–18	170
2:33	288n71
2:33–34	233n83
2:35	232n77
2:44–45	188n4
3:1–10	14n42
3:21	247n51
3:22–23	66n21
4—5	197
4:1–4	225
4:2	225n53
4:5–30	242n30
4:6	266n11
4:11	222
4:34–36	189
4:36–27	189
5:5	280n52
5:10	280n52
5:15	98
5:27–41	242n30
5:31	233n83, 288n71
5:36	22, 240n19
6—7	87n39
6:1–8	106
6:7	78, 95, 218
6:9	275
6:12	242n30
7	192, 266n16
7:52	221n41
7:54–60	149
7:55	233n83
7:56	233n83
8	78n39
10—11	275
10:9	244n37
10:17–33	123
11:20	275
11:27–30	8
11:28	241
12:1–2	192, 197, 256
12:1–3	149
12:12	8, 254
12:23	280n52
12:24	78
12:25	8
13:1	275
13:1–3	104n34

13:2–3	60
13:5	8, 9
13:13	8, 9
13:34	205n41, 232n76
13:49	78
13:51	106
14:23	60
15	12, 123
15–17	78n39
15:5	95
15:16	232n76
15:17–18	225n51
15:36–41	9
15:37	8
15:39–40	104n34
16	78n38
16:17	90
16:24	117n8
16:26	241
18	78n39
18:2	12, 78n38
18:9	99
18:18–26	78n38
18:24–28	170
18:24—19:1	169
19:10	78
19:12	98
19:13–17	168
19:20	78
19:22	283n60
20:7	64, 117n8
20:35	169
21	78n39
21:11	256n79
21:38	22, 241n19
22:30	242n30
23:1	242n30
23:6–8	227n64
23:8	225
24:10–27	242n31
24:20	31
25:1–12	242n31
25:2	164n1
25:23—26:32	242n31
26:4	187
27:24	99
28:1–6	13n42
28:3–6	287
28:17	164n1
28:25	233n82

Romans

1:1	200
1:3	205n41, 232n76
1:16	35, 129, 150
1:18	65
2:5	65
2:8	65
3:8	136
3:23	187
3:24	201n34
4:13	150, 190
5:1	160
5:1–2	281n54
5:2–5	260
6:1–4	284
7—8	261
7:1–3	179
8:1–17	37n8
8:15–16	260
8:17	150, 190
8:19–23	246n51
8:22	242
8:23	131
8:34	233n83
9"33	222
11:3	102n31
12:3	198
12:4–8	37n8
12:18	176
13:8	230
13:9	230
13:10	230
14—15	12, 171
14:1—15:3	123n25
15:26	241
16:1–2	78n38
16:7	78n38
16:13	11, 276
16:16	264n3
16:23	283n60

1 Corinthians (continued)

1:8	239n9
1:12	10, 164
1:22	66, 136, 240n18
1:22–24	279
1:30	18, 201n34
9:5	10
10:4	203n37
10:11	239n9
10:13	38
10:16	197n20
11:25	61n10, 257
11:25–28	197n20
11:26	61n11
12—14	37
12:24–25	171
13:1–3	230
13:1–8	229
13:2	215n21
13:4–7	230
13:13	230
14:1	230
15:24	239n9
15:24–28	233n83, 247n51
15:25	232n77
15:35–49	287
16:1–4	241
16:2	64, 235
16:19	78n38
16:20	264n3
16:22	134

2 Corinthians

1:21–22	37
4:1–3	126
4:4	119
4:5	200n29
4:4–6	75
5:2	131
5:4	131
5:14	230
10—13	76
10:3	19
2:13	78n39
7—8	78n39
8—9	241
8:1–4	238
8:13	238
9:7	235
12:7–9	261
13:1	104, 267n17
13:5	77
13:11	176
13:12	264n3

Galatians

1:10	200, 236
1:13	187
1:14	42
2	78n78
2:11–14	123
2:16	187
3:11	187
3:15	201
3:23	216
3:28	201
4:5	201
4:6	260
4:25	216
5:9	138
5:13	174, 230
5:14	230
5:21	61n8
5:22–24	230
6:2	276

Ephesians

1:7	201
1:14	37
1:20	233n83
2:14	281n54
2:18–22	267n18
2:19–22	222n44
2:20	222
4:2	230
4:11	37n8, 113
4:15	230
4:26	182
5:18	61n8
5:2	230
5:16	257
5:21–23	180
5:21—6:9	180n35, 294

5:22–23	60
5:25	230
6:4	183
6:9	201
6:10–18	91
6:17	209

Philippians

1:1	200
1:12–13	275
1:16	230
1:20	150
2:3	164, 198
2:4	164
2:6	153
2:6–7	202
2:9–10	165, 233
2:12–13	37
2:15	80
3	76
3:1–11	12
3:2	130
3:5	102
3:9	187
3:10	198
3:17	202
4:2–3	202, 78n38
4:4	40
4:19	115, 139
4:22	275

Colossians

1:7	200n29
1:14	201n34
1:19	153
1:24	198
2:9	153
3:1	233n83
3:14	230
3:16	257
4:5–6	79
4:6	175, 176
4:7	200n29
4:9	78
4:10	7, 8, 9, 11, 42, 75n35
4:14	42, 76, 78n38

1 Thessalonians

1:1	78n39
1:3	230
1:10	65
1:23	65
2:3–6	126
2:15	102, 221n41
3:12	230
5:3	242n28
5:8	230
5:13	176
5:16	40
5:26	264n3

2 Thessalonians

1:1	78n39
1:7	151, 246

1 Timothy

1:3–7	76
2:6	201
5:8	43, 73
5:18	87
5:19	104, 267n17
5:23	61n7
6	77
6:10	185

2 Timothy

1:6	150
2:8	205n41, 232n76
2:9	83
2:24	200n29
3:1–9	76
3:16	233n82
4:2	79
4:10	76, 78n38
4:11	9
4:20	282n60

Titus

1:1	200

Philemon

16	201
22	78
23	75
24	7, 9, 11, 76

Hebrews

1:3	153, 232n77, 233n83
1:13	233n83
1:14	38
3:7	233n82
3:14	239n9
4:15	38, 259
6:10	281
7:1	90
8:1	233n83
9:3	281, 281n54
9:12	201n34
9:14	257n83
9:18–22	257n83
9:25	257n83
9:26	239n9
10:4	257n83
10:12–13	233n83
10:13	232n77
10:15	233n82
10:19	257n83
10:20	281
10:27	173n16
10:28	267n17
11:37	221
11:32–38	102n31
12:2	233n83
12:24	257n83
13:12–13	276
13:17	131
13:20	113
13:23	78n39

James

1:1	200
1:2–4	260
1:22	74
2:19	45
3:6	173
3:9–12	175n21
5:9	131
5:14–15	106

1 Peter

1:4	189
1:7	174
2:5	169
2:6	222
2:9	169
2:16	200
2:18	201n34
2:21–25	202

2 Peter

1:1	200
1:21	233n82
3:9	65, 122
3:15	56, 122

1 John

1:24	68n23
2:27–28	68n23
2:18	244
3:17	230
4:4	51
4:13	68n23

Jude

1	200
5	203
7	173n16
23	173n16

Revelation

1:1	200
1:6	169
1:7	151
1:9	197
1:10	64
1:12–16	152
1:13–14	153
1:17	99
2:13	149
2:26	239n9
3:7	205n41, 232n76
5:5	205n41, 232n76
7:7	113
7:9	285n65
7:13	285n65
10:1	285n65
11:1–10	102n31
11:3–12	153n32
12:7	45, 45
13	244
14:10	196
16:6	102n31
16:19	196
17:4	196n19
18:3	60
18:6	196n19
18:8	173
18:23	60
18:24	102n31
19:15	65
20:9	91
20:10	37, 46
20:14–15	173n16
21—22	36, 247n51, 257
21:1–4	38
21:2	60
21:4	46
21:8	46, 88
21:27	46
22:9	200
22:16	205n41, 232n76

www.ingramcontent.com/pod-product-compliance
Lightning Source LLC
Chambersburg PA
CBHW071238300426
44116CB00008B/1084